marketing

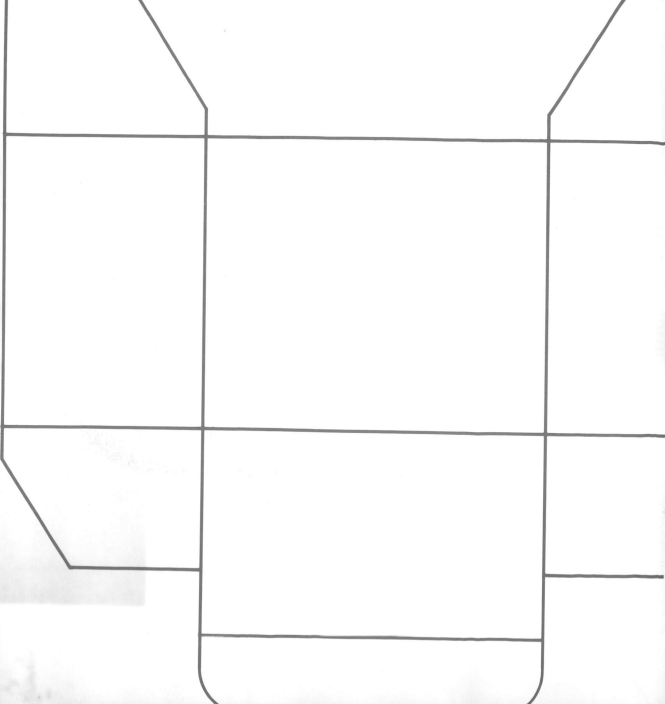

James L. Heskett

1907 PROFESSOR, GRADUATE SCHOOL OF BUSINESS ADMINISTRATION, HARVARD UNIVERSITY

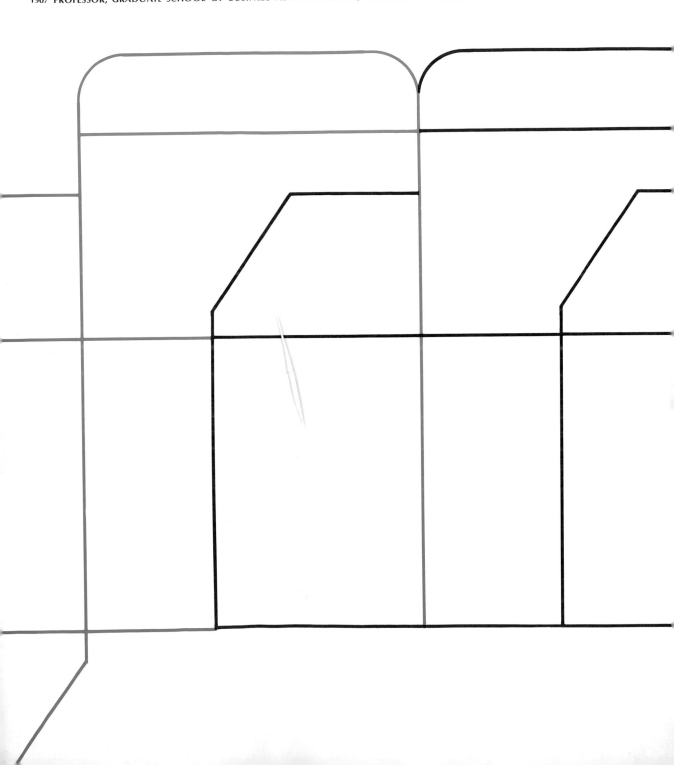

marketing

macmillan publishing co., inc.
NEW YORK

collier macmillan publishers
LONDON

MACMILLAN PUBLISHING CO., INC.
866 Third Avenue, New York, New York 10022

COLLIER MACMILLAN CANADA, LTD.

Library of Congress Cataloging in Publication Data

Heskett, J   L
   Marketing.

   Bibliography: p.
   Includes index.
   1. Marketing.   I. Title.
HF5415.H42   658.8   75-14257
ISBN 0-02-353940-2

Printing: 1 2 3 4 5 6 7 8   Year: 6 7 8 9 0 1 2

To Marilyn, My Heart

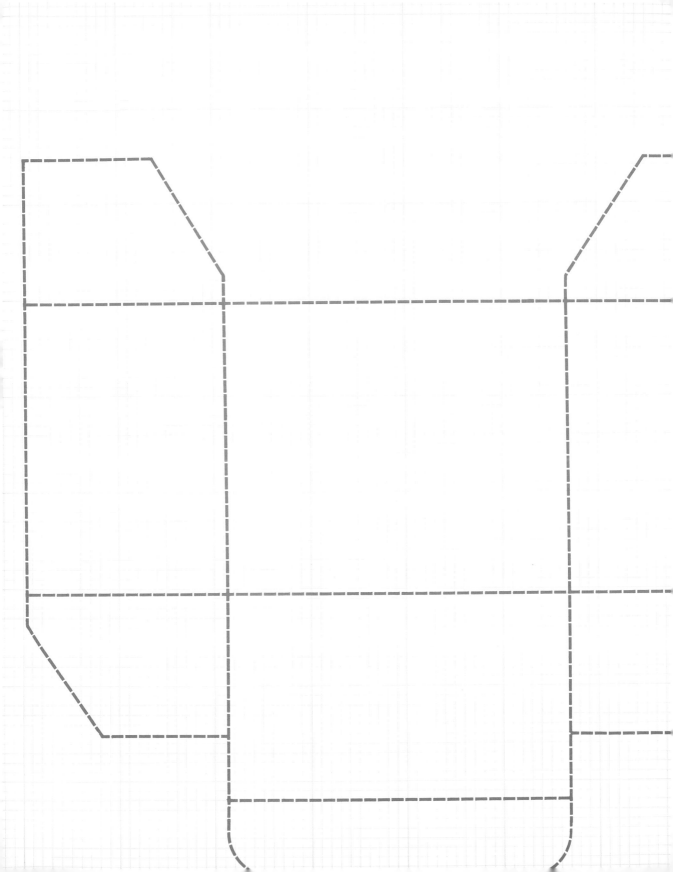

contents

preface
to the student

I wrote this book for you. Not because I have anything uniquely profound to say about marketing, but because I thought it might make a longer-lasting impression on you than other books on the subject you could be reading at this moment.

It represents my conviction that marketing can be as exciting in the classroom as it can be in real life, that what you really need is a vehicle to help you organize knowledge and attitudes that you bring to the subject, whether you've ever formally taken a course in marketing or not.

It reflects my concerns that the marketing of services is now more important, from a dollar and social standpoint, than the marketing of products; that the marketing of complex systems ranging from information to power systems grows in importance each day and may differ from selling soap; that the marketing of political candidates, community services, and religion may have a greater impact on society than all marketing effort expended on behalf of tangible products manufactured by profit-oriented enterprises; that the marketing means used to achieve the objectives of a better way of life, whatever that is, may be as important as the objective itself.

Marketing displays some strong pedagogical biases. For example, the presentation of the subject matter seeks to involve you. The book literally is addressed to you.

From time to time, you'll find me directing questions to you, questions intended partly to rouse you from the numbness that often attends the reading of assigned material from a textbook. They are intended as well to make explicit those questions that may cross your mind as you read, to help you test and document your progress, and to serve as vehicles for in-class or, better yet, outside-class discussions. In some cases, I just thought they were interesting questions to ponder. In any event, if you'll spend a few moments with many of these questions as you encounter them, you'll find yourself anticipating my material to a greater and greater extent as you move through the book. If, eventually, you find yourself thinking, "I could have written this book," or "I would have written it differently," both of us will have achieved an important objective. Numbers in the margin of the text are intended to facilitate reference to the questions.

We are told that the environmental and systems approaches to the teaching of marketing are waxing while the functional, institutional, and managerial approaches are waning. I have sought to borrow from each of these approaches where it seemed desirable.

In keeping with marketing practice, you may ask how this book can be positioned against various market segments and its competitors. It is intended primarily for use in a first course in marketing, to challenge students with varying amounts of experience but essentially to introduce the subject. Because of its format, it may have appeal, as well, for independent study.

The objective of the book is to present in a memorable way a selected set of concepts that scholars, managers, and consumers have found useful. It is not to provide a marketing encyclopedia. Several encyclopedic works are listed in Appendix A.

The heroes of the book are marketing practitioners, not marketing researchers, theorists, or philosophers. Its unifying concept is its decision orientation. But the approach is not intended primarily to develop managerial talent, although it may help.

I have made use of fewer examples presented in somewhat greater length than in comparable books on marketing. The objective in doing this is to present not only enough information to illustrate one or more points, but also to provide the basis for contrast and comparison among the examples. As a result of this effort, it's my hope that you'll be able to formulate patterns or guidelines to explain for yourself various marketing phenomena and suggest appropriate courses of action in response to marketing problems.

I will ask you to make decisions, beginning in the first chapter. The material is designed to enable you to do so without any previous background in marketing. I've elected this approach to (1) get you into the habit of making business-oriented decisions, (2) encourage you to supplement this material with your thinking, and (3) help you remember certain basic concepts until such time as you might make practical use of them. At first, you'll feel uneasy about committing yourself on the basis of limited knowledge. But your decisions will come easier, and the resources from which you can draw will increase, as we go along.

More important, the book is organized around inputs to a manager's decisions regarding marketing problems. I'll introduce elements of the decision-making process early and then introduce pertinent information about marketing in the process of examining each element in greater detail.

Quite often you'll be asked to assume the role of a marketing manager, which you may assume qualifies this book for use only in conjunction with an advanced undergraduate or graduate course in "managerial marketing." My view is that this approach is valid even if you've not been introduced to the subject formally. It is essential to an understanding of *why* marketing is, as well as its practice. It helps as well in enabling us to understand how it affects us (and how you can use it) in one or more of our potential roles as a consumer, an employee, a manager of a function other than marketing in an organization, a venture capitalist, a stockholder, a leader of a direct-action movement, a union executive, a regulator, or others.

Like a parent's view of Cream of Wheat, major concepts of this book are intended to "stick to your ribs," to stay with you, along with those inescapable items of trivia that are imbedded forever in our minds—the result of the work of an expert communicator and a willing recipient. (For example, I'm sure I, as a willing recipient, won't soon forget a fact I read the other day—a McDonald hamburger contains 1.6 ounces of meat.) Achieving this intention requires that you put concepts to some use, that you feel a need to have them, as you are introduced to them. It requires that they not be buried in definitions that are of most use to marketing philosophers and research scholars. Perhaps Cream of Wheat serves again as a pretty good example of the simplicity of presentation that I seek to achieve in order to send home major concepts and their use.

On this matter of definitions, I don't mean to sound like an anarchist. After all, definitions are important both as an effective shorthand in communications with others interested in marketing and as a means of injecting some precision into a formerly imprecise subject. But rather than my formulating the definitions for your nodding approval, I'll ask you to form your own as we come face to face with various topics. To allow you to compare yours with those formulated by the establishment, I've included a glossary of marketing terms in Appendix B.

A selection of typical sources of information useful to you in your temporary (and, I hope, more permanent) role as a marketing decision maker is presented and referenced in Appendix A. I've attempted to limit footnotes only to those required by law or professional courtesy to minimize their intrusion on the discussion.

Each chapter takes up a different topic. As a result, chapter lengths vary a great deal, because of the variability in the amount of material relevant to various topics that suit our purposes. I've left it to you to divide topics into chunks with which you are comfortable for reading, dialogue, and comprehension.

Our first stop in the book is a meeting with Sheldon Dietz, not one of the leading figures in marketing management. Once you've met him, though, he's hard to forget. And he and his business provide us with an opportunity to develop a road map for the remainder of our discussion. That discussion develops along the following lines.

Whether our product is a breakfast cereal, haircut, or presidential candidate, it requires definition. The knowledge about what our product really is enables us to relate it to a specific group of potential customers and to estimate its ultimate market potential. In estimating market potential, it is important to consider environmental forces exerting changing influences on markets—forces with economic, social, and legal dimensions that literally influence the sizes and profiles of potential markets. The results of this approach, arrayed against our perceptions of organizational objectives, strengths, and weaknesses, allow us to determine whether a product is right for our organization. These are the concerns of Chapters 2 through 4.

Given the desirability of the product, we must turn to the task of pricing it. Yes, even a presidential candidate can be thought of as having a price tag attached; whether you want to view the process in this light is a matter we'll want to discuss further. At the same time, we'll need to decide on the type and amount of other ingredients in the marketing recipe: advertising, packaging and branding, personal sales effort, and the means by which marketing messages and the product itself can be delivered to potential and actual customers. This gives us an opportunity to explore marketing opportunities from a variety of viewpoints—those of the manufacturer, wholesaler, retailer, transporter, consumer, and other parties who cooperate in the distribution of goods and services. These topics are covered in Chapters 5 through 10.

At this point, we should understand something about the process of decision making in marketing without knowing much about sources of information important to the decision process. Having established the need for information, we'll consider ways of getting it in Chapter 11.

Getting information is one thing. Putting it to use in the appraisal of the chances for success for a marketing program is another. Both of these topics are matters for discussion in Chapter 12.

Strategic decisions and inspired ideas in marketing a product, service, or person make for heady discussions. But the success or failure of even the most creative marketing program depends largely on the organization and control mechanisms by which it is implemented. Furthermore, this gives us an opportunity to look in on marketing personnel at their jobs and find out what they really do, rather than what sensational movies set in the executive suite, Vance Packard, or advertising achievement might have us believe. My hope is that in this portion of the book, comprising Chapters 13 and 14, we can get a balanced view of the excitement, the satisfactions, and the drudgery of marketing activities. This is important to your decision to begin or continue your career in marketing.

Results of the marketing process, and the way in which different groups in society view these results, offer a vehicle for raising more philosophical issues. Where you come out on these issues, and what each may mean for marketing management, is our major concern in Chapter 15. This, too, should be important to you in your career decision. And it should set the stage for a look into the future of marketing effort in the concluding Chapter 16.

At no point along the way will we get into the age-old argument about whether marketing is an art or science. Rather, I like to think of marketing as a craft. A craft that, if it is to be practiced, requires not only a good intuitive sense but also conceptual knowledge, a sense of direction, and alas, a common language of the sort that definitions provide.

Material is arranged so that questions about marketing as a craft are raised first and often. But we can't leave it at that. Marketing, as a craft to be practiced indiscriminately, may be a bit like expertise in the use of explosives. As the discussion proceeds, questions about the proper application of the craft will be brought to your attention. In discussing them, you may learn something about yourself.

In fact, if you learn something about yourself while learning something about marketing as a craft, my efforts will have been rewarded threefold.

acknowledgments

This book has put me in debt to six groups of people outside my family. Former and current colleagues at The Ohio State University and Harvard University, respectively, have, I'm sure, contributed many conceptual ideas to the material. They include professors Theodore N. Beckman, Robert D. Buzzell, Richard N. Cardozo, E. Raymond Corey, W. Arthur Cullman, Scott M. Cunningham, William R. Davidson, Alton F. Doody, James F. Engle, Stephen A. Gneyser, Theodore Levitt, John B. Mathews, Robert B. Miner, William M. Morgenroth, Derek A. Newton, Robert F. M. Nourse, Walter J. Salmon, Benson P. Shapiro, Ralph J. Sorenson, Steven H. Star, Louis W. Stern, and Ralph G. M. Sultan. In particular, I am indebted to a colleague, Ms. Lorna Daniells, whose work on her book, *Business Information Sources* (University of California Press, 1976), coincided with mine in preparing Appendix A. Her vast knowledge of a wide variety of information sources found in many libraries made my task easier. A group of practicing marketers were willing to allow their experiences to be used as illustrative examples of those ideas. Two perceptive secretaries—Linda Brown and Karen Peters—helped me get the ideas down on paper in legible form. Approximately sixty student reviewers from fifteen colleges and universities both kept me on target and provided encouragement through their responses to manuscript draft materials. When they were finished, several anonymous colleagues on other campuses took up the task of review. One who was not anonymous to me, and who offered many helpful suggestions, was Professor

Jeffrey A. Barach. And four Macmillan editors—Alexander H. McLeod, John C. Neifert, Franklin I. Khedouri, and Sandra J. Schwede—were willing to go along with the idea of a textbook written for, and reviewed by, students, in spite of the commonly held view among publishers that textbooks are bought by teachers, not students.

JAMES L. HESKETT

CAMBRIDGE, MASSACHUSETTS

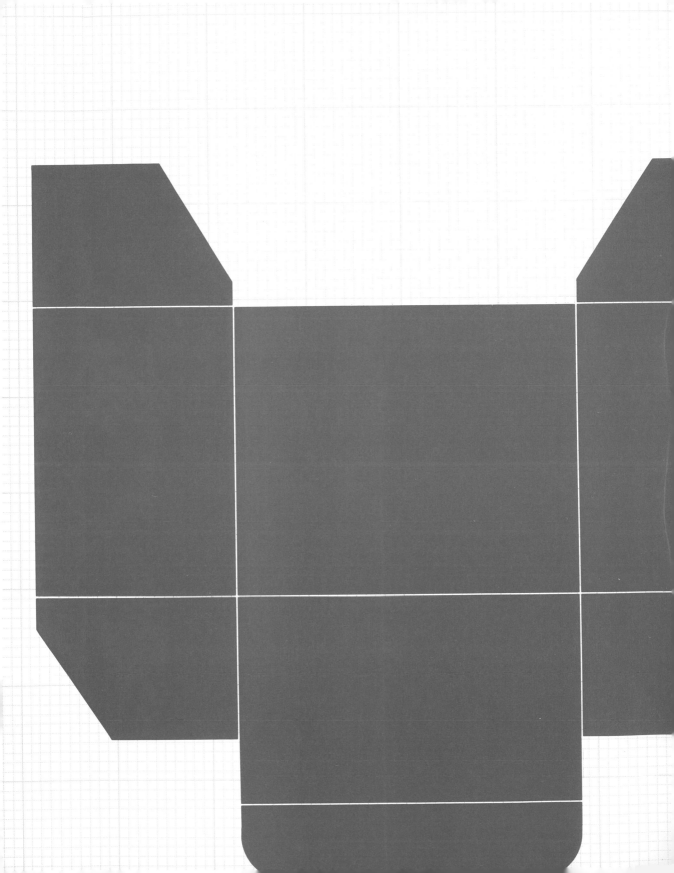

a six-foot trip 1

Upon meeting Sheldon Dietz, you're confronted with a big, toothy grin as your hand disappears into his hammy grip. Later, you'll be hailed on the street in a voice that can be heard for a city block. He likes to talk about a wide range of subjects, only one of which is his business. As he tells you about nearly twenty years in the history of The Six-Footer Company, ask yourself what you would do if you owned his company and how your approaches to marketing would differ from his. Ponder and respond to the numerous questions posed from time to time in the chapter before moving ahead. In the process of getting to know Dietz and his business, you should get a quick introduction to marketing and some feel for the plan of this book. And you may learn something about yourself.

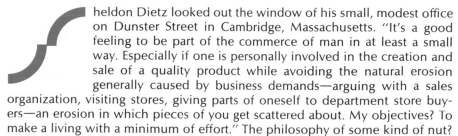

heldon Dietz looked out the window of his small, modest office on Dunster Street in Cambridge, Massachusetts. "It's a good feeling to be part of the commerce of man in at least a small way. Especially if one is personally involved in the creation and sale of a quality product while avoiding the natural erosion generally caused by business demands—arguing with a sales organization, visiting stores, giving parts of oneself to department store buyers—an erosion in which pieces of you get scattered about. My objectives? To make a living with a minimum of effort." The philosophy of some kind of nut? A poor example for potential managers? Or a shrewd person and businessman?

The owner of The Six-Footer Company, a small company that manufactures and sells knitted wool scarves and related cold weather apparel in college and fashion colors, told how his company grew as an offshoot of "The Tie That Binds." It was part of a business life that included several real estate ventures and a swordfishing business.

"After college, graduate business school, and three years in the Navy during World War II, I wanted to be an actor. But I couldn't afford it. Graduate school had made a businessman out of me, but I like people with more personality than one usually can afford in business. Nevertheless, after six months with a school chum in his ladies' hosiery business, another friend and I formed G. S. Harvale & Co., Ltd. A college tailor gave us an idea there was a market for school ties. We had found a mill in New Jersey that could produce ties with woven emblems. Our first product was the Old School Tie, a line of ties with university colors and emblems for use by fraternities, alumni, and others. Eventually, we found a good market, largely by means of direct mailings of promotional material among corporate and other organizations such as the Mobil Oil Corporation, Wadawanuck Yacht Club, Bankers Trust Company, and the Myopia Hunt Club. We used direct mail because we couldn't stomach going to stores or calling on other people ourselves. The nature of selling activity didn't appeal to us.

"Very quickly our sales reached $100,000 per year, enough to enable each of us to pull $15,000 per year out of the business, not a bad salary in the late forties. Neither of us were married. We lived in the same loft in New York City where we did all of our packing, mailing, and marketing work. We had two employees, but no formal partnership agreement other than mutual trust. Not even a handshake.

"We were not afraid to work, though, and on occasion we would put in long hours for several days in a row. But we attempted to enjoy each other's company as we went along. For example, we both would take a trip out to see our friend at the mill in New Jersey because it was more pleasant than going alone.

"After six years our life-styles had diverged. I was married, living in Norwalk, Connecticut, and becoming more and more anxious about things like the commute to work and the ability of the business to support my family. My anxiety provoked my partner to make me an offer: go on together and not be so anxious, buy him out, or be bought out. After we set the price at about $33,000 for a half, I offered to sell my share to him.

"We had considered the idea of producing and selling scarves similar to English school scarves imported from that country. He suggested I take the scarf idea to see if I couldn't do something with it. That was really the beginning of

THE SIX-FOOTER COMPANY

We had noticed the signs of a burgeoning fashion trend, and I really thought I could easily pick up a bundle, but to some extent I was caught by my own greed."

The first year, 1953, had its ups and downs. Dietz had bought a used knitting machine for $100, found a source for yarn, and located someone to operate the machine. After being knitted, the scarves had to be tied at the color change points, turned inside out, sewn up, and fringed with tied yarn. In total, finishing operations could be completed at the rate of about four dozen scarves in an eight-hour day. The machine produced knitted material at the rate of about a dozen scarves per hour.

Early in the season, Dietz convinced *Seventeen* magazine to run a several-page spread featuring Six-Footer scarves in various school colors. The feature listed some one hundred leading department stores where the scarves could be purchased. About half the stores sent in fall orders for a total of about 100 dozen scarves. "At that point, we thought we were going to be able to sit back and pick our customers. We shipped the scarves. Winter came. Then nothing happened. Not one reorder. Nothing. It was a very warm fall and winter.

"Clearly, The Six-Footer Company could not survive on this basis. I knew we had an attractive, high-quality product, priced to sell in stores for $5. Our competition ranged from lightweight scarves made from cotton and increasingly from synthetic yarns and selling for $2.95 and $3.95 at retail up to the English imports, a little heavier than ours and selling in the stores for $8." (A typical Six-Footer scarf is shown in Figure 1-1.)

To conserve on capital and minimize risk, Dietz bought minimum quantities of yarn and had scarves manufactured to order, carrying almost no inventory of finished product. Costs of materials and manufacturing for a Six-Footer scarf, not including time contributed by Dietz and his wife, were $1.95, or about 65 per cent of the $3 price for which the scarf was sold to retail stores.[1] Thus, on a $5 scarf sold to the retailer for $3 (with a $2 divided by $5, or 40 per cent gross margin to the retailer), The Six-Footer Company's gross margin before marketing and administrative expenses was about $1.05 (the $3 selling price to retailers less $1.95 in material and manufacturing costs), or about 35 per cent of the company's selling price.

Typically, about 15 per cent of winter scarf sales occurred during the early fall, 70 per cent between Thanksgiving and Christmas, and 15 per cent later in the winter. "It was nearly Thanksgiving that first year, with no reorders from the department stores. I had to reassess the situation quickly."

(1)
(2)

If you were Dietz, how would you assess the potential for The Six-Footer Company? Where would you start? With its prices? Selling plans? Advertising? Locations in which its products were sold? With the product itself? Jot down some of your thoughts before continuing.

---

[1] These and other cost figures in this paragraph have been disguised.

Figure 1-1. A page from
a sales catalog
showing a typical scarf
manufactured and sold
by The Six-Footer
Company.

THE SIX-FOOTER* This is a photograph of a genuine Six-Footer. It
is knit of fine virgin worsted
wool yarn. It is hand knotted at
every color change. It is hand
fringed. All Six-Footer colors
are custom dyed.

The Six-Footer is available in
color combinations of all American
schools and colleges in both the
broad striped pattern as shown and
in regimental patterns available
on request. It is priced at $42 a
dozen.

*Registered Trademark.
The Six-Footer Company

beginnings

A logical basis on which we could initiate a marketing appraisal for The Six-
Footer Company is provided by the product itself, ways of describing it, and
the implications these descriptions might have for marketing strategy.

the product

We could describe a basic Six-Footer scarf literally as six feet long, eight inches wide, containing about one-half pound of wool, with a six-inch knotted fringe at either end, and coming in thirty-six colors and a large number of color combinations. Our description might include its box. In fact, this is the way that a production-oriented or engineering-oriented person might approach the task of describing the product. But such descriptions don't provide us with much to go on for the subsequent development of a marketing strategy.

(3) To provide us with marketing clues, we might describe a product in terms of the needs it fulfills. What are these needs in the case of the Six-Footer, a scarf produced in university and college color combinations? Needs for warmth, fashion, status, a sense of belonging, economy? Needs created by nostalgia? Other needs?

markets

An identification of needs fulfilled by the product could lead us to conclusions about why potential customers would actually buy Six-Footer scarves. Reasons for purchase might be directly related to potential groups of customers, as
(4) suggested by the matrix in Figure 1-2. Are the needs of current single students the same as those of alumni, student "couples," nonalumni athletics fans,
(5) parents of students, or other members of a university community? How would
(6) you match needs and potential customer groups shown in Figure 1-2? Are there both customer and need categories that you would add to those shown in the figure?

Figure 1-2. A market matrix for Six-Footer college scarves.

Potential Customer Groups

Possible Needs Fulfilled by the Product	Single Students	Alumni	Student "Couples"	Athletics Fans	Parents of Students	Other Members of University Community		
Warmth								
Fashion								
Status								
A Sense of Belonging								
Economy								
Needs Associated with Nostalgia								

(7)

Upon defining potential user groups and needs satisfied for each, we might begin to ask ourselves questions about the size of each potential user group and the strength of possible selling appeals based on needs we might associate with each. To this information, we might want to add data about how various groups of potential users go about buying scarves. For example, when do they buy? Where do they buy? How often do they buy? And on the basis of what types of information?

Armed with this type of information, either from definitive sources or the best estimates we might prepare, we would be able to estimate potential sales. Or would we? Up to this point, we have assumed that all customers for Six-Footer products would be users. What about those buying the product to give it as a gift? How important is this group compared to the buyer-user group?

competition

Before estimating short-term sales possibilities, we might want to consider also the nature of competing products, their qualities (actual or perceived), prices, brand characteristics, and possible affiliations with more complete lines of products.

the company itself

(8)
(9)

(10)

Could you foresee the Six-Footer scarf as just one of an eventual line of products? What kind of product line? Would our knowledge of knitting and relationships with current production sources apply to other items in the line? Could they be sold through similar outlets? To similar customer groups? In a manner similar to Six-Footer scarves? In short, would the product fit with current operations or proposed programs?

other elements of a marketing strategy

(11)

Having identified customer groups and needs, we should be able to form some opinions about appeals that might be used in promoting our product. How might we communicate these appeals best? By means of television? Newspaper? Forms of advertising in which The Six-Footer Company might pay part of the cost and a retail outlet the rest? Displays on retail store sales floors?

(12)
(13)

What part should direct sales effort play in communicating this message? Over all, what part of our promotional budget and time should be devoted to indirect (advertising, publicity) forms of communication rather than more personal, direct forms?

(14)

Should we attempt to communicate our message all the way to the ultimate customers or merely to our immediate customers, wholesale or retail establishments? To what extent would our choice of media depend on this decision?

In fact, through what type of sales outlet should we sell our product? For example, based on what you know about Six-Footer scarves at this point, would you have selected department stores as your first outlets for the product? Why? What other types of outlets might you have preferred, or would you also want to consider? How might we reach these outlets? Through direct sales effort? Through wholesalers with the knowledge and capability to reach retail outlets? What types of wholesalers? Or would we be well-advised to think in terms of selling to customers by means of direct-mail advertising and sales solicitation effort of our own?

economic analysis

Dietz limited his initial out-of-pocket dollar investment in The Six-Footer Company to a $100 used knitting machine and perhaps $500 for promotional materials, legal expenses, office supplies, and travel. Far more important was his commitment of a year of his time to the initial organizational, product-development, and promotional activities. Once committed to the project, this represented an investment of time on his part that, based on his recent level of compensation, might be valued at $15,000.

With an average gross margin of $1.05 per scarf (35 per cent of the $3 price to retailers), it would take sales of about 14,300 units ($15,000 divided by $1.05) during the first year to pay Dietz for his time. And this assumes no provision for his wife's time or expenses other than those for yarns and manufacturing. Based on the same assumptions, what would be the first-level sales level necessary to support the Dietzes in the manner to which they were accustomed if, instead of selling Six-Footer scarves to retail outlets for $3 per unit, they were to sell them directly to individual customers for $5 per unit? If the latter course of action required a first-year expenditure of $5,000 for direct mailings of advertising materials?

Do the numbers of units of sales you calculated here appear reasonable or feasible when compared with the size of the potential customer groups that you identified earlier?

Over the longer-term future, how would your appraisal of matters external to The Six-Footer Company affect prospects of company growth, personal compensation, and profit? For longer-term sales forecasting, our concerns might shift to such matters as the likelihood of competitors' reactions to the introduction of our product. What form might these reactions take? Price, promotional, or product-development retaliations? A change in the nature and location of outlets for the sale of competing products? Assuming no patent protection for Six-Footer scarves (although Dietz did immediately begin the registration necessary for trademark protection), what might be competitors' capabilities, their resources, for reacting? How fast might we expect them to do so?

How would fashion trends affect this product? Is it fashion sensitive? If so, how often and for how long might we expect it to be in fashion? Would its

(27)   sales be affected by economic cycles? And what would you expect long-term
            trends to be in the size and make-up of various customer groups?
(28)   How would these potential market conditions compare with sales needs
(29)   for The Six-Footer Company? What types of investments might be required?
(30) (31)   What kind of income stream might be possible over the long run? What level
            of income and return on investment might this indicate for Dietz?

research

Given the number of questions we have raised, if you were Dietz you might
be inclined to say, "To hell with the venture. If I have to approach it like a
General Motors making a $100 million investment, forget it." On the other hand,
before investing any more of your time, you might want to engage in some
modest research effort to shed some light on the possible chances for your
success.

(32)   Is there any type of modest research effort, costing perhaps $1,000, that we
            could suggest to Dietz to help him reduce uncertainties surrounding this
(33)   business venture? Or should he continue his marketing efforts and learn by
            experience?
(34)   If you were in Dietz's place, having experienced his high hope and initial
            disappointment, what would you do? Look for a new venture? A new product?
(35)   Someone to blame? New customers? Your old partner? New outlets? Would
(36)   your responses be the same as you might expect his to be? How would they
            differ? Give this some thought before continuing with the Six-Footer saga. This
            will allow you to compare your thinking with his.

□ □ □

onward, upward, and . . .

"Quickly, but reluctantly, I hit the road to call on college bookstores, beginning
close to home at New Haven. In college towns, I also called on specialty stores,
such as those selling sporting goods, or men's and women's clothing. In addition to New England, I traveled to college towns as far south as North Carolina
and as far west as Wisconsin."

In all, Dietz generated an additional fifty customers among these stores. At
as many as twenty of them, he was forced to offer to place a dozen scarves
at each store on consignment, an arrangement under which he agreed to expect
payment from the store only as the scarves were sold to the store's customers.
In addition, he essentially absorbed inventory risks by agreeing to take back
any items left unsold at March 31.

Heavy sales in major bookstores near the Yale and Harvard University
campuses balanced off small consignment accounts, and over all Six-Footer sales
to all types of retail stores for the first season, 1953–1954, were approximately

(37)
(38)

$18,000.[2] According to your previous calculations, would this have been sufficient to compensate Dietz for his time? With time to plan for the following year, what new marketing strategies would you suggest for the 1954–1955 season?

□□□

the 1954–1955 season

As his major new marketing effort for the 1954–1955 season, Dietz made arrangements to exhibit Six-Footer products at the National Association of College Bookstores' Trade Show, held in Chicago in July 1954. "I remember two things about that experience," he recalled. "The show got us a lot of attention, and it was so hot in the exhibit hall that I never went to another of those shows."

In the spring of 1954, Dietz had established a store-visitation schedule that he followed from there on, varying it only when it appeared that the company's sales were particularly slow. "If the year was going poorly, I got out and worked." Otherwise, his annual sales routine involved spending a week visiting five to ten of the largest Six-Footer accounts, representing approximately 50 per cent of the company's sales. In late February or early March Dietz left home to call on accounts in New Haven, Connecticut; Princeton, New Jersey; West Point, New York; and Annapolis, Maryland. In addition, approximately two hundred old and potential accounts were sent short letters in early April reminding store managers of Six-Footer, requesting an order by April 30 to facilitate spring and summer production scheduling, and indicating the amount of Six-Footer merchandise bought during the previous year, where appropriate.

"Finishing, not knitting, represented the bottleneck in the production operation. In order to cope with a sales peak during the Thanksgiving-Christmas period and keep two people busy at the plant all year, I figured we needed to obtain orders for about 1,000 dozen scarves during the spring. Although we didn't achieve this in 1954–1955, we did later. There was no incentive for early purchases; our customers paid us on a net cash (on receipt of merchandise) basis. On the other hand, there wasn't any incentive from the factory for me to obtain those early orders to keep my supplier's people busy. But I knew it would cost him more if we didn't get the early sales, and, just as important, it gave us a jump on the market in order to meet customers' needs during the peak season as well."

Another innovation was instituted in 1954. Dietz' wife drew a cartoon box cover that could be produced in different colors to match the school names placed on the cover. For example, all Six-Footers shipped to stores near the Princeton University campus were sent in boxes on which covers of the type shown in Figure 1-3 were pasted. "This gave us a personal touch that our larger competitors couldn't afford to match. It is typical of the way we used our small size to compete."

[2]Actual sales and income figures for this and other years have been disguised, but relationships have been preserved to facilitate analysis.

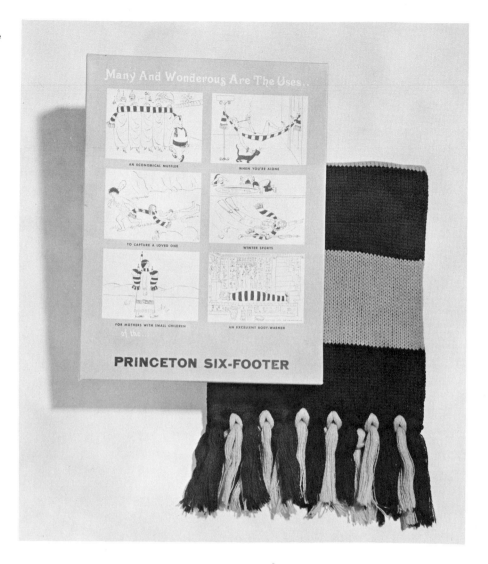

Sales during the second year of operation, 1954, grew to $55,000. By the following year, the Six-Footer line had been expanded to include items shown in Figure 1-4. However, because items were manufactured to order, and merchandise was placed on consignment with new customers only as a means to induce purchases during the first year, the company carried almost no inventory of finished product. Sales during 1955 were $85,000, and income before Dietz' salary and taxes reached $16,500.

"Our sales were beginning to take off. We were beginning to get a feel for our markets. Although sales were increasing in our most important stores, they varied from campus to campus each year, depending on such factors as fashion, the weather, and even the success of the local football team."

Figure 1-4. A page from a catalog prepared by the Harvard Cooperative Society, showing products of The Six-Footer Company. (The Harvard Cooperative Society is an organization that operates three retail stores on or near the campuses of Harvard University and the Massachusetts Institute of Technology.)

THE HARVARD SIX-FOOTER is the college classic. Maroon and white 100% virgin wool. In our amusing cartoon gift box. **5.00** #106

THE FOUR-FOOTER and matching mitten for children 4-10. Mittens in small, medium and large sizes. Four-footer and mitten set **5.00** #107

THE HARVARD TOQUE will keep any head warm. Extra heavy knit in maroon and white virgin wool. **1.95** #109

They are in the bag! **HARVARD MITTENS** Maroon and white striped virgin wool in small, medium and large ladies' sizes. Each pair in its own muslin Harvard Mitten gift bag. **1.95** #108

We're crazy for the **HARVARD STOCKING CAP** and the **HARVARD BRAIN-WARMER** Both maroon and white 100% virgin wool Stocking cap **2.50** #110 Brain warmer **1.95** #111

The above are also available in Tech colors

12

fashion to the front

"Coming into the 1956–1957 season, we knew that six-foot scarves and related items were going to be fashionable, and not just in the college communities. We knew, too, that we had neither the marketing capabilities to capitalize on the fashion interest nor the manufacturing capability to meet sales demands resulting from an extensive marketing effort." By this time, Dietz had acquired five knitting machines to help ease the peak burden on the mill supplier.

"We were faced with a real decision, whether to expand the business beyond the size we had originally intended or suffer the frustrations of seeing a good market opportunity pass us by. We were beginning to think seriously about some aspects of the business for the first time."

The fashion potential for knitted scarves and related items raised questions regarding product design and color combinations, appropriate outlets for fashion- as opposed to college-oriented products, the need for increased selling effort, and the nature of competition in the fashion business.

Product Design. "Production in fashion colors presented no problem. Naturally, if we were to introduce new designs, our people at the mill would have to get used to making them. And if we were to shoot for sales of, say, $300,000 per year we would have to build inventories of perhaps $75,000 prior to the retail buying season for these items."

Outlets. Fashion-oriented merchandise was sold in outlets other than those with which Six-Footer had been dealing, such as women's apparel shops and department stores. In any one of the company's current market areas, they were much more numerous than college bookstores, student men's and women's clothing stores, and sports shops. For example, in Cambridge, Massachusetts, there were three college bookstores, about twenty potential men's and women's clothing stores serving students, and two sport shops suitable for the sale of Six-Footer items. However, in the metropolitan Boston area alone there were over three hundred women's apparel shops as well as more than one hundred different department store organizations of various types. Within a large department store, there might be separate buyers purchasing for two or more departments handling children's wear, teen fashions, and apparel for other groupings of older customers.

Selling Effort. Dietz considered several possible ways of increasing Six-Footer's selling effort. He could hire full-time salesmen to cover perhaps two hundred stores each. He was familiar with at least one man who could be hired for about $125 per week in salary and perhaps $5,000 per year in expenses. Full-time salesmen could be assigned either to marginal sales regions or to the most populous areas, some of them already good markets for Six-Footer college items. They could be assigned only to "fashion" as opposed to "college" accounts, or perhaps on some other basis.

Secondly, Dietz could align his company with one or more women's accessory wholesalers. These organizations, employing their own salesmen, sold complete lines of women's handbags, belts, hats, gloves, and other accessories to both specialty shops (specializing in women's apparel or accessories) and

13

women's departments in department stores. They could, if they gave his product any attention, produce substantial sales. However, they would require a margin of 25 per cent of the retailer's purchase price (or $9 of the $36 currently charged a retailer for a dozen Six-Footer scarves, for example) for their services. To use wholesalers, Dietz would have to raise the prices of his products, accept a lower margin per unit for Six-Footer, or perhaps both.

"As other alternatives, I could hire part-time salesmen and pay them a straight commission of 10 per cent of sales with no expense allowance. However, I could expect them to stay with me only during the peak sales season.

"Of course, the hiring of personnel would begin to complicate the business. Up to this time, the only person we had employed was a part-time office employee. The product was shipped directly from the mill to our customers. Our office was at our home in Connecticut.

"Manufacturers' representatives, selling related products from several major and many smaller manufacturers, could be contracted for at the same 10 per cent commission rate. With manufacturers' representatives, the problems associated with sales peaks would be lessened, but if a product of a smaller manufacturer didn't sell well, a manufacturers' rep wouldn't hesitate to drop it.

"Finally, I could do what I swore I wouldn't do; hit the road and call on new potential retail accounts, including department store buyers, again."

Competition. As Six-Footer might expand, competition would become more important. "Up to 1956, we weren't big enough to bother any competitors. I'm sure our product came to their attention, but they made no effort to react. The major competition for the volume end of the market offered items made from synthetic yarns, with scarves priced at $3.95 and even $2.95. However, the potential for fashion sales induced them to improve their styles and colors without increasing their prices, making them a bit more competitive to us. After all, to buy a Six-Footer at $5, a customer would have to sense the differences in weight, the quality of construction, and the richer color of dyed woolen yarns. He or she would have to want the more comfortable feel of the product and the features that wool provides."

(39)
Let's stop and think for a moment about where we stand. For example, how compatible would a new Six-Footer fashion line be with the existing college line? From a manufacturing point of view? From a marketing point of view?

(40)
(41)
Is it time for an analysis of the business and its marketing opportunities similar to the one we prepared in the fall of 1953? Where do we start?

(42)
(43)
Given the experience of several years on which to base sales projections for this company, what do you think of its business potential? If you were the owner of the company, would you do anything to capitalize on the sales

(44)
(45)
potential you foresee for it? Would you advise Sheldon Dietz to do this? Assuming Dietz were willing to sell the company, its $1,000 worth of knitting machinery, its modest inventory, its Six-Footer trademark, and its customer list and sign an agreement not to compete with Six-Footer on similar types of

(46)
merchandise in the future, would you buy it? If so, how much would you pay for it? Jot down some notes to yourself regarding these questions before proceeding.

□ □ □

the year of the scarf

"We couldn't sit around and watch the world go by. As a result of my spring rounds of the ten largest college markets and the write-ups in fashion magazines, we knew there would be a fashion boom in large, ample scarves. Even the number of infringements on the Six-Footer trademark increased. A clipping service and friends as well clipped and sent us ads for competing products that appeared to be trading on the Six-Footer name. We followed up on every apparent violation with a letter threatening possible legal action. Among stores we so threatened were several department stores.

"We designed some 'fashion' color and striping combinations, but we didn't change the basic styles or construction of the items we were offering. We did, however, obtain a second trademark, 'Joseph's Coat,' for a subsequently popular, multicolored line of scarves."

Several of the company's college bookstore accounts were planning to feature the Six-Footer in their local advertising. To capitalize further on sales potential, Dietz hired a full-time salesman, Dan Manzon. For a salary of $125 per week, a leased car, and expenses, Manzon was to develop new accounts, beginning with department stores. In addition, Six-Footer entered into an agreement with a manufacturers' representative to sell on behalf of the company largely in college bookstores. As the selling season approached, Dietz also hired a part-time salesman to call on accounts in the Boston metropolitan area. Both of the latter sales agreements called for a straight 10 per cent commission on sales to be paid to the salesmen.

"I still had visions of our cracking into the big department store market, with orders of one hundred dozen units. But Manzon found that it was too tough for departmental buyers at the stores to buy only one item from a new resource. After all, they were besieged by salesmen and had to allocate their time carefully. They'd say, 'Your product is the same as . . . ,' and name some competitor putting out junk. They couldn't or wouldn't take the time to check out the quality that they were getting along with the higher price."

Both the manufacturers' rep and the part-time salesman devoted effort to Six-Footer products only during the fall of 1956. By mutual agreement, neither continued their relationship with Six-Footer after the season.

In spite of marketing problems, Six-Footer sales in calendar 1956 rose to about $120,000, with profits before salaries and taxes of about $28,000. For the 1956–1957 season, sales were estimated to have been about $130,000. Comparative operating statements for 1953 and 1956 are shown in Table 1-1.

□□□

year of the scarf plus one

"Just as we knew that the fashion cycle was coming on in the spring of 1956, we could sense that it had passed by the following spring. A variety of other events probably contributed to the sales pattern that developed at that time. Our full-time, salaried salesmen decided not to stay with us. We decided

Table 1-1 **Comparative operating statements for 1953 and 1956, The Six-Footer Company**[a]

| | Calendar Year | | | |
| | 1953 | | 1956 | |
Item	In Dollars	As % Of Sales	In Dollars	As % Of Sales
Sales	15,990	100.0	120,040	100.0
Cost of goods sold	9,740	61.0	73,230	60.8
Gross margin	6,250	39.0	46,810	39.2
Expenses				
Salaries and commissions				
Administrative	—	—	2,400	2.0
Sales	—	—	8,370	7.0
Other selling expenses	2,350	14.7	3,720	3.1
Advertising	—	—	—	—
Postage	170	1.1	640	.5
Utilities	360	2.3	700	.6
Telephone	420	2.6	830	.7
Insurance	370	2.3	1,020	.9
Taxes, other than on income	120	.8	470	.4
Other	220	1.4	1,010	.9
Total expenses	4,010	25.2	19,160	16.1
Profit before income tax and owner's compensation	2,240	13.8	27,650	23.1

[a]Actual sales and net income figures have been disguised.

to move our home from Connecticut to Martha's Vineyard off the coast of Massachusetts, but to leave the office responsibilities for Six-Footer with a friend of ours in Mamaroneck, New York. Up to this time, we had had a part-time office employee, but she agreed to take over on a full-time basis working out of her home. I continued to do my spring selling." (Sales and net income before taxes or withdrawals by Dietz for The Six-Footer Company for the years 1953 through 1969 are shown in Figure 1-5.)

other interests

After the 1956–1957 peak in Six-Footer sales, Dietz became more and more interested in real estate. Work as a laborer for the contractor who was building his summer home led to an interest in construction and real estate. In 1961, he acquired an old office building and some residential property in Cambridge, Massachusetts. In each case, the property was acquired, great care was exercised in its renovation, and it was rented out. These buildings later won several awards for architectural design. "One of my goals is to improve things, to exert

Figure 1-5. Sales and net income for The Six-Footer Company, 1953–1969.

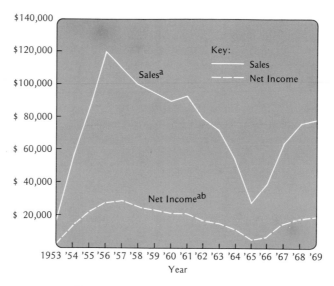

[a]Actual sales and income figures have been disguised.
[b]Before owner's salary or income tax.

some pressure for good taste, and in some small way to contribute to an improved quality of life."

On occasion, these goals presented potential conflicts with business interests. For example, in 1964, the Harvard Cooperative Society (Coop), operators of the store that was by far the largest outlet for Six-Footer products, announced the construction of an annex bookstore on a block-long street on which Dietz and a partner had purchased an old warehouse that they had renovated into a handsome store and office building. The Coop's architectural plan and its provision for traffic flow were so objectionable to Dietz that he (1) began a series of arguments before the Cambridge City Council, the Cambridge Board of Zoning Appeals, Governor Endicott Peabody, and a Massachusetts Superior Court, (2) collected hundreds of signatures for a petition to save an old carpenter shop on the annex site, (3) sent copies of the book *God's Own Junkyard,* which contained photographs of urban and rural blight, to every director of the Coop, and (4) announced that he would nominate nine Harvard and MIT professors to oppose the official nominees for the Coop's board of directors. As a result, the Coop quietly negotiated an agreement (1) to repave the block-long street with cobblestones and red brick at an estimated cost of about $40,000, (2) to defray half ($5,000) of Dietz's court costs, and (3) to alter its plans to provide an off-street truck-loading dock.

This was just one of Dietz's local efforts on behalf of improved city planning. Others included a battle to save trees intended for removal to facilitate the widening of a main thoroughfare. At one point, in fact, Dietz formed a Society for the Preservation of the United States for Human Beings.

His objectives were further reflected in a swordfishing venture that he formed in 1964, Chilmark Fleet Company, Inc. "After we moved up to Martha's Vineyard in 1958, I became interested in the fishing business generally, and specifically in the operation of fishing boats to seek out and make available high-quality fresh swordfish to the eastern markets. Up to this time, American consumers had to be content with the vastly inferior frozen product shipped in from Japan and Canada. By designing and having built two long-line fishing boats, our aim was to make really fresh swordfish available to the consumer at reasonable prices the year around. In order to do this, our ships had to fish the entire eastern coast, seeking out the swordfish or tuna on each trip. Although we brought in record catches, the costs of finding the fish and encountering miserable weather to and from the fishing grounds during the winter months made it uneconomical." The venture, formed in 1964, was ended in 1968 with the leasing of the boats for use in oceanographic work.

a holding action at six-footer

Meanwhile, back at The Six-Footer Company, Dietz handled marketing affairs according to his previous routine after the departure of his part-time and full-time sales representatives. During this period, it had been necessary for him to devote more time to manufacturing matters than to marketing.

"Our first contract manufacturer was not producing the quality we desired in the product. Our scarves, for example, were coming in with weaknesses near the point where the yarn ends were tied together to produce the striping effect. The knitter complained that the problems were with low-quality yarn. I even went to the Wool Bureau in New York, where they told me that there was 'little basic research on the matter.' That was good for a laugh.

"I wanted to switch resources, but I was afraid that a new manufacturer might steal our ideas, or in some way be confronted with a conflict of interest. Finally, my wife prevailed, and from a trade directory we got the name of a glove and scarf manufacturer in upstate New York who agreed to manufacture for us on the same basis as our previous supplier. I merely moved my machinery from the New Jersey plant to his plant, and things went well until he went out of business. For a time after this, we obtained our product from another upstate New York mill and finished the individual items ourselves in Boston.

"I learned several things from this experience. First of all, my only bargaining weapons with a supplier, given our small size, were highly personal ones like kindness and appeals to his indulgence. However, the fact that we owned our own equipment gave us the ability to switch sources with a minimum of effect on quality.

"Finally, in 1966, when the second of our New York suppliers went out of business, we moved the production to our current supplier in North Carolina, a business operated by a man who I had gotten to know from the old Harvale business. He was a contract manufacturer of hosiery, and when he wants to retire, he probably feels that The Six-Footer production may give him just enough to do and sufficient income to retire on."

During this period, costs for raw materials and manufacturing were relatively constant, and the prices for Six-Footer products were changed very little.

the second coming

"After hitting the bottom in 1965, sales began to increase again with no notice-able increase in sales effort on our part. In 1967, they doubled over the previous year, and we began to regain our enthusiasm.

"The next year, we recorded another sizeable increase, thanks in part to a part-time salesman, a Harvard College student who I took on somewhat reluctantly because of our previous aborted experience with a hired salesman. I paid him $3.50 per hour for the time he put in and a 5 per cent commission on sales. Mainly because he was able to sell a big order to a large department store in Boston, Filene's, he sold more than $10,000 worth of merchandise just prior to the holiday season. Three other part-time salesmen who we engaged that year together didn't sell as much as this one man.

"I began to think more seriously about recruiting college students as com-mission salesmen, but was somewhat discouraged by the amount of effort required to recruit them and the slim chance that they would stay with us more than one year."

the Father Jeffcoat promotion

Encouraged by the increasing sales, Dietz began the first of a series of new promotional ideas to attempt to build greater stability into The Six-Footer Company's sales record. Following up on an order for 14 dozen scarves from the Don Bosco Preparatory High School in Ramsay, New Jersey, The Six-Footer Company launched what Dietz referred to, with tongue in cheek, as "The Father Jeffcoat Promotion." This involved mailing about one thousand letters of the type shown in Figure 1-6 to the principals of high schools in New England and the Middle-Atlantic regions. As a result of this promotion, which Dietz esti-mated may have cost about $600 for the mailing and free samples, the Company received twenty nine replies and orders for 12 and $7/12$ dozen scarves. "Needless to say, we didn't repeat the program. But it got us to thinking about similar kinds of efforts that we might begin."

By this time, Dietz and his wife had moved to Cambridge, where Dietz relocated The Six-Footer Company's offices at the Dunster Street location. He maintained a simple business operation. "An important element in my strategy was to work with responsible people and delegate the jobs to them. Our supplier in North Carolina makes the complete product. I visit him about every other year. I never see the person who reviews our books at the end of the year. When we kept an office in New York, we visited the woman who ran it for us only twice. Now that I'm running the office here in Cambridge, it has further simplified the business."

With a return to popularity of full, long scarves, sales of the Six-Footer products were approaching the 1957 peak. "Visions of 1957–1958 came back. In that year, for example, we sold 180 dozen, or more than 2,300 scarves near the Harvard University campus, whose student population of about ten thou-sand was only 40 per cent undergraduates. At Yale that year we sold 125 dozen."

Figure 1-6. The "Father Jeffcoat" promotion letter.

THE SIX-FOOTER COMPANY

BOX 179, HARVARD SQUARE, CAMBRIDGE, MASSACHUSETTS 02138 • TELEPHONE: 617/491-2229

1 January 1969

Dear Principal:

If you would like to see a Six-Footer in your school colors we will be happy to send you one. The Six-Footer is a school muffler which our company has been making for the past sixteen years for over 250 schools and colleges.

Recently we received an order for fourteen dozen Six-Footers from Father James Jeffcoat, faculty advisor to the Student Council at Don Bosco Preparatory High School, Ramsey, New Jersey. After he received his scarves, Father Jeffcoat wrote, "The Six-Footers are the talk of the campus." We were happy with this report but not surprised. College and high school students do enjoy identifying themselves with their schools. When they wear the Six-Footer in school colors the means of identity is handsome and useful.

The Six-Footer is usually sold through the school book store or athletic store. It is also a profitable item for fund raising by student and parent groups because of the ample margin between the wholesale and usual retail selling price.

We write you because we feel Father Jeffcoat's experience can be duplicated at your school. We hope you will write us for a sample and your school will have its own Six-Footer this winter.

Sincerely,

THE SIX-FOOTER COMPANY

Sheldon Dietz

SD:jld

"We didn't make a special effort to capitalize on this fashion cycle, we just rode with it." In fact, the Dietzes spent most of the 1970–1971 season in London, hiring a sales manager to maintain contacts with customers and the plant. Without special effort in 1970, sales once again reached $120,000 and produced profits before taxes and the owner's salary of $19,700, reduced somewhat by the salary paid to the sales manager, who had filled in temporarily for Dietz.

Having returned from London to reestablish residence in Cambridge and Martha's Vineyard, Dietz began exploring ways of maintaining some portion of the style market for Six-Footer products beyond the 1970–1971 season. "In 1969, 20 per cent of our sales were in noncollege color combinations. This rose

Table 1-2 An Analysis of The Six-Footer Company's Sales, by Type of Merchandise and Type and Location of Sales Outlet, 1970

Type of Merchandise	10 Largest Customers (All College Bookstores) (in %)	145 Other College Bookstores (in %)	20 College Men's Clothing Stores (in %)	15 College Women's Clothing Stores (in %)	10 Noncollege-Oriented Stores (in %)	Totals (in %)
	Proportion of Total Sales Volume (by Type and Location of Outlet)					
Six-foot scarves, college colors	25.1	19.3	6.7	3.5		54.6
Six-foot scarves, fashion colors	12.3	7.8	2.2	3.4	2.6	28.3
Four-foot scarves, with matching children's mittens	.8	.5			—	1.3
Ladies' mittens	.8	.4	—	—	—	1.2
Children's mittens	.9	.2	—	—	—	1.1
Toque caps, college colors	4.7	1.7	—	.4	.5	7.3
Ladies' Brain-Warmer, college colors	1.7	.6	—	.4	.5	3.2
Stocking caps, college colors	2.0	.5	—	—	—	2.5
Other, including the Six-Footer doll	.5	—	—	—	—	.5
Totals	48.8	31.0	8.9	7.7	3.6	100.0[a]

[a]Total equals approximately $120,000.

to 30 per cent in 1970, in spite of the fact that we continued to sell primarily through college-oriented stores." (An analysis of the company's sales, by type and location of sales outlet as well as product-line item, is shown in Table 1-2.)

the Many-Color Collection

As a result of this exploration, the Many-Color Collection was developed. It consisted of a handsome, nicely-finished display rack crafted out of white oak, capable of holding ten dozen Six-Footer scarves in noncollege color combinations. A picture of the collection on display is shown in Figure 1-7.

Tested during the 1970–1971 season, the Many-Color Collection was offered to some two hundred outlets, including approximately thirty men's and women's clothing stores, by means of the letter shown in Figure 1-8. As indicated in the letter, ten racks placed in college-oriented stores during the 1970–1971 season had produced an average of about 30 dozen sales per rack, with a range of from 8 to 90 dozen per rack. Included among the ten Many-Color Collection displays were one each placed in the men's and women's clothing departments at the Harvard Coop's main store. Roughly 90 dozen were sold from the rack in the men's department and about 55 dozen from the rack

Figure 1-7. Six-Footer's
Many-Color Collection,
displayed on the
company's specially
constructed display rack.

Figure 1-7. Six-Footer's Many-Color Collection, displayed on the company's specially constructed display rack.

in the women's department. However, the latter rack was displayed in a lower-traffic location in the store.

"This program represented at least a small investment for us. For example, the racks cost us about $56 each. In addition, because of the quantities involved and the typically conservative nature of college bookstore managers, we guaranteed to take back any merchandise left unsold on March 31."

In response to the letter shown in Figure 1-8, twenty two stores agreed to display the Many-Color Collection during the 1971–1972 season. In addition, two manufacturers' representatives who handled a variety of items stocked in college bookstores, with whom 10 per cent commission agreements had been reached, placed another eighteen display racks, eleven in Colorado and Idaho and seven in the East. In was estimated that these fifty displays (including ten from the previous year) produced sales of about 500 dozen fashion-color scarves during the season.

planning for the future

increasing replenishment capability

"Here in Cambridge, where we sell a substantial portion of our total sales through one outlet, I have been making an effort to determine the sales rate of our product just prior to, and during, the season in order to be able to anticipate the rate of fill-in orders as we go into the season. The necessity for this has increased as it becomes more and more difficult for us to respond quickly to retailer needs during a peak season that lasts for only about thirty days. Few store managers have the time or have established the procedures to be able to check on the rate of sale of our products. They rely on us to be able to respond to their needs. However, I have to order yarn four weeks in advance of the production in North Carolina. The plant requires a lead time, from order to delivery, of three weeks. This makes it hard for us to be able to respond to retailers when we operate without ongoing retail sales information and almost no finished product inventory."

product-line planning

At this point, Dietz began to consider once again a further expansion of the company's product line. He was cautious about any further development that did not fit into the current pattern of products offered by the company, or that did not meet the standards of quality for current Six-Footer products. He had had samples of an inexpensive elastic sweatband made up at the mill and was thinking of selling it for use by joggers or those engaged in other forms of strenuous work or play. This item could be sold in bags of a dozen for perhaps $2.00 per bag, a price at which users might throw them away rather than launder them after their use.

a new promotional program

In spite of the experience with the 1969 high school promotion, Dietz was intrigued with the possibility of creating some type of award program in which a school might, instead of awarding other articles of apparel for outstanding achievements in athletics or other activities, award individually designed scarves with emblems or various types of attached insignia. This idea, Dietz thought, might be marketed to the athletic departments of high schools.

THE SIX-FOOTER COMPANY

BOX 179, HARVARD SQUARE, CAMBRIDGE, MASSACHUSETTS 02138 ● TELEPHONE 617/491-2229

9 April 1971

Charles E. Vayne, Manager
University Book Center
Johns Hopkins University
Charles & 34th Streets
Baltimore, Maryland 21218

Dear Mr. Vayne:

Each year at this time we write to ask if you would be kind enough to review your Six-Footer needs for the coming fall and winter. If we could have your order by April 30 it would be a great help in ordering our yarns and scheduling production to keep our experienced help busy during spring and summer.

Last year you ordered 6 dozen Six-Footers.

This year, in addition to our traditional Six-Footers, you may want to try our Many-Color Collection which we tested in a group of college bookstores last season.

It is a striking assortment of 120 combinations of colors and stripings ranging from bold to conservative. The enclosed photograph taken in the Harvard Coop shows a portion of the collection on our especially designed and very handsome white oak display rack. The rack is 54″ long by 18″ wide. It sets up with just four screws and displays 10 dozen Six-Footers at one time.

Bookstore managers in the nine college bookstores* where the Many-Color Collection was tested were highly pleased with the sales results which equalled or surpassed sales of the traditional Six-Footer. They found that the entire display enlivened their stores, provided effortless self-service selection and required little attention of their sales help. All of these stores are re-ordering for this coming year.

It will be simple for you to try the Many-Colors in your store. You do not have to be concerned with any inventory problem since any merchandise in this Collection left unsold as of 31 March 1972 is returnable for full credit. The display rack is loaned to you at no charge. We recommend that you try our assortment of

competition and market appraisal

"I was pretty sure we didn't want to become another Champion," Dietz remarked in referring to Champion Products, Inc., perhaps the leading company in the manufacture and sale of college-oriented apparel, including T shirts, sweatshirts, jackets, scarves, caps, and novelty items such as beach towels. "Champion does about $20 million in sales per year and employs a captive sales force of about eighty people with assigned geographic territories covering the country. Their merchandise is monogrammed with college colors and insignia and is lower in quality than what we would want to get involved in. For example, Champion scarves comparable in size and design to ours, but made

THE SIX-FOOTER COMPANY

BOX 179, HARVARD SQUARE, CAMBRIDGE, MASSACHUSETTS 02138   ●   TELEPHONE: 617/491-2229

– 2 –

Charles E. Vayne   9 April 1971

ten dozen for a complete display, or at least eight dozen if you should prefer. We will price-ticket for you if you include the information on the enclosed order form.

      If you have any questions concerning this Collection or your regular Six-Footer order, do not hesitate to call us collect and we will give you an immediate answer.

Sincerely,

THE SIX-FOOTER COMPANY

Joseph L. Dobrovolski
Sales Manager

JLD:lt
Encls. (2)

*Test stores for the Many-Color Collection:

	Dozen	
Harvard	145	(2 Racks, Men's & Ladies' Depts.)
Yale	54	
Princeton	33	
Pennsylvania	16	
Oberlin	12	
Cleveland State	10	
Brandeis	9	
Bucknell	8	
Williams	8	

Please note that the above is in addition to their traditional Six-Footers.

of 100 per cent acrylic fiber, sell to retail stores for $23.10 per dozen in quantities up to 12 dozen, and for $22.50 per dozen in larger quantities. This contrasts with our prices of $39.50 to $45 per dozen, depending on the particular style."

    Champion was only one of a number of manufacturers specializing in products designed for purchase primarily by college students. The over-all market for wearing apparel and related items sold in or near college campuses was estimated to approximate $5 billion. Of the total enrollment of about six million college students, it was estimated that about 60 per cent was located in areas of the country experiencing some weather cold enough to require heavy outer garments.

In 1971, the company's sales declined once again to $95,000, producing an income before salaries or taxes of $21,500. Approximately 35 per cent of the sales were of items in noncollege colors.

Dietz once again divided his time between his local real estate interests and The Six-Footer Company. "I have no schedule. My only daily commitment is with myself to go swimming in the university pool."

(47) (48)

If you were in Dietz's place, what would you do with this business? As a personal friend, would you advise Dietz to follow a similar course of action? Do you think he would take your advice?

(49)

(50)

Assuming that it is time for another appraisal of the business and its potential, how do you now assess the company's products? Its markets? Its competition? Its marketing strategy, including its selling, advertising, and other promotion effort; its channels of distribution, including the nature of its retail outlets; and its prices?

Looking at this situation from another viewpoint, assume you were the manager of the largest bookstore on or near a campus with which you are familiar, a bookstore stocking the usual wide line of nonbook items sold to college students. Would you be interested in taking on the Many-Color Collection under the conditions stated in the letter in Figure 1-8? What considerations would govern your decision?

(51)

(52)

Let's assume for the moment that Dietz has decided to follow one possible proposal designed to help him develop his markets systematically: the designation of college representatives, students on individual campuses. How would you suggest to him that he design his program?

(53)

Now, assume that the proposed program is just as you have designed it. As a potential representative of The Six-Footer Company in your college community, would you be interested in the company's program? Why? What do you have to know to respond to this question? How would you go about getting the information? Based on assumptions about what this information might be (before actually collecting it), under what terms, if any, would you be interested in becoming a Six-Footer college sales representative?

(54)

(55)

(56)

(57)

In order to help you organize in your mind some of the possible confusion created by the questions posed in this chapter, a flow diagram of the approach to marketing strategy formulation that we will be following is presented in Figure 1-9. You may want to refer to it from time to time. It provides the organizational structure for much of this book, as suggested by pieces of the diagram to which various chapters refer, which will be found reproduced on their respective opening pages.

summary

A road map can give us some idea of where we have been on our trip, where we can go, and how we can get there. Make no mistake about it, we've covered a great deal of ground in this chapter, not only developing an outline of the marketing strategy formulation process but also suggesting the general nature of the outline that will be followed through much of the book.

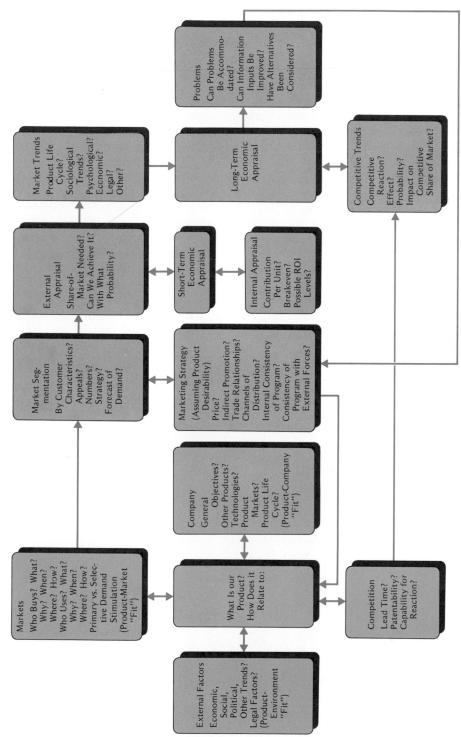

Figure 1-9. Flow diagram of an approach to marketing strategy formulation.

In reviewing the marketing efforts of The Six-Footer Company, a manufacturer of scarves and other articles of outerwear, we first examined the product and the needs it could fulfill for various groups or segments of potential customers. A more complete examination of the context in which the product would be marketed included an appraisal of potential competition and other environmental trends as well as the plans, policies, and capabilities of The Six-Footer Company.

Next we turned to various means by which the product might be sold: elements of a marketing strategy. These included the amount and type of advertising and personal selling effort, the types of retail outlets through which it might be sold, the possible use of wholesalers, prices at which it might be offered to ultimate buyers, and margins with which it would be sold to wholesalers or retailers. The economic implications of each possible combination of elements was reviewed, suggesting the volume of sales required to meet a particular goal for company profits or, in this case, the owner's income. This was compared with the potential size of the market for the product among the most attractive market segments, resulting in an estimate of the likelihood of success for a particular combination of product and marketing strategy. Finally, we had to be willing to recycle the entire process upon encountering low probabilities of success for certain strategies.

If marketing, as portrayed in this Six-Foot trip, seems disjointed and somewhat confusing, don't panic. We'll try to sort out the confusion as we go along. But marketing, alternately exciting and dull, beautiful and crass, scientific and creative, is a crazy field of study and practice. Whether we are the sender or recipient of a "standard of living" through marketing, now is the time to find out something about the subject. As our first step, we'll take a closer look at the relationship between products and their potential markets.

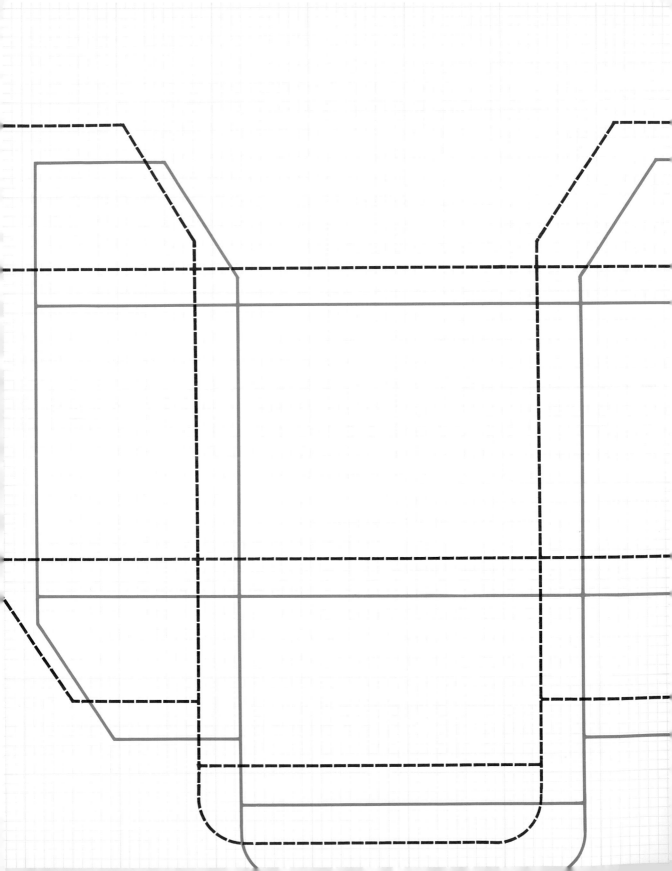

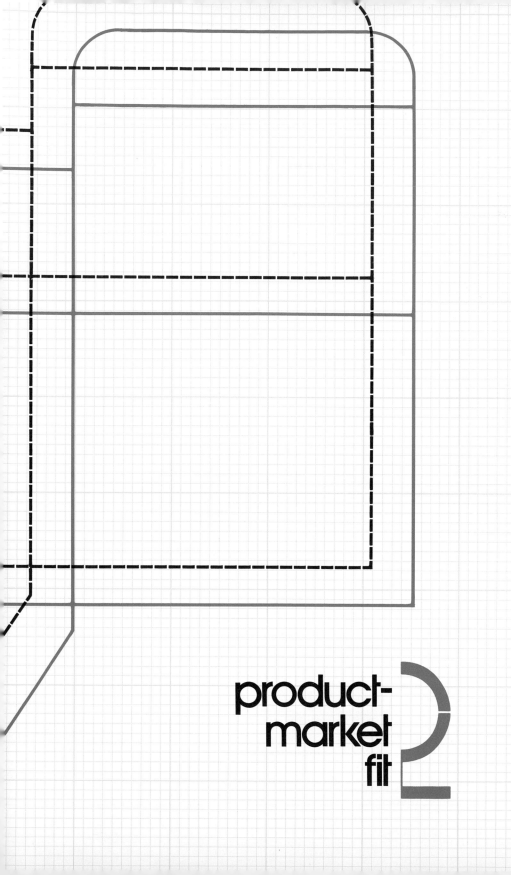

product-market fit 2

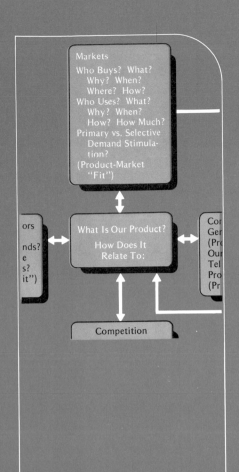

Markets

Who Buys? What?
Why? When?
Where? How?
Who Uses? What?
Why? When?
How? How Much?
Primary vs. Selective
Demand Stimula-
tion?
(Product-Market
"Fit")

ors
nds?
e
s?
it")

What Is Our Product?

How Does It
Relate To:

Co
Ge
(Pr
Ou
Tel
Pro
(Pr

Competition

Foreign shoe manufacturers opened up the United States market when they discovered the old adage, "If the shoe fits, wear it." For they had enjoyed labor-cost advantages over their United States counterparts for years. It wasn't until they began the mass production of styles desired by Americans for feet that were narrower and longer than most others in the world that European shoe manufacturers in particular spelled the death knell for many of their American competitors.

The fit between products and prospective markets is the focus of our thoughts here. Without it, little can be done through other marketing efforts to rescue a failing product. With it, even poorly designed promotional efforts may appear to be successful. Here, we must begin to develop ways of looking at markets and products so that you will never regard products and people in their roles as prospective buyers in the same manner again. In addition, we'll review recent trends in thinking about ways of bringing markets and products together. This is the kind of thinking that can lead to the production of perfectly fitting footwear rather than the kind that has to be forced onto the foot with a shoe horn.

First, however, it's important that we develop a mutual understanding of the buying process and the possible roles that marketing effort can play in it. To do this, we'll first shift the scene from Sheldon Dietz's office in Massachusetts to North Carolina, a "far piece" on foot even in perfectly fitting shoes.

identifying customer needs

In the depths of the Great Depression of the early 1930s, two entrepreneurs from the tobacco country of North Carolina explored ways to expand the market for a soft drink that was popular locally. They noted that the custom of the industry was to charge consumers a two-cent deposit on all bottles removed from the retailers' premises. (Remember, this was before the day of the throw-away container.) Retailers in turn paid two-cent per bottle deposits on beverages at the time the product was delivered to their premises by bottlers. In fact, these deposits far exceeded the cost of the contents of the bottles.

The two entrepreneurs noted that retailers and bottlers alike suffered from an acute shortage of working capital. They decided that if they could find a low-cost source of bottles, they could help finance their business with the two-cent deposit. They could also help their retailer-customers finance their businesses as well on the working capital supplied by individual consumers through their bottle deposits. And what better source of low-cost bottles than the junkyard?

Searching near and far for an adequate source of used bottles, they could locate only one suitable type of clear glass bottle in sufficient quantities and at a low enough price. Because it was a used beer bottle and twelve ounces in size, a question was raised as to its suitability for an industry that traditionally had adhered to the smaller bottle popularized by Coca-Cola. But it could be bought for one-half cent per bottle.

With a one-half cent bottle, the local soft drink could be offered to retailers for a one-cent per bottle deposit. Retailers in turn would be encouraged to push the new brand to consumers in order to realize the one-cent per bottle difference between the deposit paid to the bottlers and that received from consumers. The one-cent per bottle deposit paid by retailers could help supply working capital for the bottling operation. The attractiveness of the economics outweighed the desire to adhere to industry custom. As a result, the two marketing-oriented entrepreneurs decided to capitalize on what they regarded initially as a potential disadvantage by promoting their product with this radio jingle:

> Pepsi Cola hits the spot.
> Twelve full ounces, that's a lot.
> Twice as much for a nickel too.
> Pepsi Cola is the drink for you.

(1) (2)　　Why was this strategy successful? However apocryphal the story might be, what does it tell us about the process of relating products or services and markets? The first step in this process, and a basic task of marketing, is the identification of customer needs.

The identification of customer needs is important because such needs contribute directly to buying motives. The behaviorist Abraham H. Maslow's "hierarchy of needs" provides us with a classic listing of basic human needs.[1] According to Maslow, man's first need is to survive. His need for water, food, and shelter sufficient for survival transcends all others. He will forego other needs, including that of safety, to seek survival. Other levels of need, shown in the left-hand portion of Figure 2-1, are, in order: safety, belongingness and love (acceptance by one's closest relatives and friends), esteem and status (standing relative to others), and self-actualization (understanding of self and self-satisfaction). An important element of Maslow's theory is that we cannot strive to fulfill a higher-level need unless we have met those below it in the hierarchy.

Figure 2-1. The process of a customer's translation of needs into buying decisions.

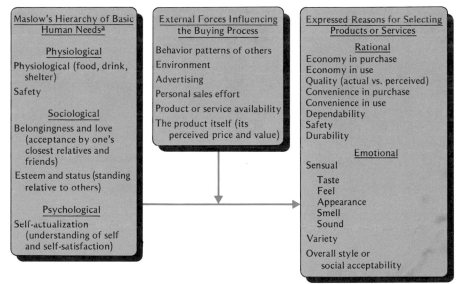

Forces Contributing to the Translation of Needs Into Buying Decisions

aAdapted from Abraham H. Maslow, "A Theory of Human Motivation," *Psychological Review*, **50**: 370–396 (July, 1943).

[1] Abraham H. Maslow, *Motivation and Personality* (New York: Harper, 1954).

translation of needs into buying decisions

Ask a student why he or she selected a particular college or university, and they are likely to give answers such as:

> It was close to home.
> Many of my friends decided to go there.
> Its academic reputation was very high.
> People there seemed to care about me when I visited the campus.
> They gave me a football scholarship.
> Friends of mine who had gone there told me that it was a great party school.

These reasons are surface expressions of more basic needs. They provide the basis for a good deal of the efforts expended in the design and marketing of university educational programs. They help explain why an individual may have selected one school over another.

But why did the individual decide that he or she needed a college education in the first place?

The response to this question should be different for different individuals. One might have sought the security that a better job would give by means higher education might provide. Another might be concerned primarily about the fact that going to college is "the thing to do." How are each of these motivations related to Maslow's basic needs? For example, what characteristics would you expect each of these persons to have? How would you analyze your own process of selecting a college or university in these terms? In order to further explore your ideas regarding causes for buying decisions, you might want to relate each of the expressed reasons for selecting products or services, shown at the right side of Figure 2-1, to the list of basic needs shown at the left.

Factors other than the degree to which basic needs have been satisfied play a major role in the product- or service-selection process. For example, which of the reasons for buying a product, listed in Figure 2-1, do you think would be uppermost in the minds of the following individuals in the purchase of a typewriter: (1) the office manager of the company for which the typewriter is being purchased, (2) the purchasing manager of the company for which the typewriter is being purchased, (3) the individual buying a typewriter for his or her own use, and (4) the individual buying a typewriter as a high school graduation gift for a close relative? Why do your answers differ for each of these?

For many years, it was assumed that the level of basic need that an individual sought to fulfill was correlated directly with his or her wealth, income, or social class in society. The availability of data regarding income, home ownership, and place of residence, among others, provided a convenient means of relating the design of products and marketing strategies to this so-called demographic data. More recently, the size, diversity, and—perhaps most important of all—the universally high level of affluence in the United States have brought into question the future usefulness of concepts about the basic needs of humans for marketers in a post-industrial economy.

(3)
(4)
(5)
(6)

(7)

(8)

35

Clearly, the focus must shift to a detailed exploration of Maslow's highest levels of need. For example, one well-known social researcher identified several years ago a number of then-current (ever-changing) social trends that alter consumption. This list of social trends, summarized in Table 2-1, reflects the growing sophistication of individual needs in a postindustrial society. Review the list in Table 2-1. Do you identify yourself with any of these trends?

Yankelovich has suggested, by means of illustration, that:

The United States automobile market has moved steadily away from cars as symbols of material success to cars as expressions of personalization.[2]

Table 2-1 The 31 Social Trends That Alter Consumption*

Group 1: Psychology of Affluence

1. Toward *physical self-enhancement*—the things people do to enhance their looks
2. Toward *personalization*—the need to be "a little different" from other people
3. Toward *physical health and well-being*—what people do to take better care of themselves
4. Toward *new forms of materialism*—the new status symbols and the extent of deemphasis on money and material possessions
5. Toward *social and cultural self-expression*—the "culture explosion"
6. Toward *personal creativity*—the growing conviction that being "creative" is not confined to the artist
7. Toward *meaningful work*—work that is challenging and meaningful over and above how well it pays

Group 2: Quest for Excitement, Sensation, Stimulation, and Meaning to Counteract the Practical and Mundane Routines of Life

8. Toward the *"new romanticism"*—the desire to restore romance, mystery, and adventure to modern life
9. Toward *novelty and change*—reaction against sameness and habit
10. Toward *adding beauty to one's daily surroundings*—the stress on beauty in the home
11. Toward *sensuousness*—greater emphasis on touching, feeling, smelling, and psychedelic phenomena
12. Toward *mysticism*—the search for new modes of spiritual experience and beliefs
13. Toward *introspection*—an enhanced need for self-understanding and life experiences

Group 3: Reaction Against the Complexity of Modern Life

14. Toward *life simplification*—the turning away from complicated products, services, and ways of life
15. Toward *return to nature*—the adoption of more "natural" ways of dressing, eating, and living
16. Toward *increased ethnicity*—finding new satisfactions and identifications in foods, dress, customs, and life-styles of various ethnic groups
17. Toward *increased community involvement*—greater involvement in local groups
18. Toward *greater reliance on technology versus tradition*—greater confidence in science and technology
19. *Away from bigness*—the departure from the belief that "big" necessarily means "good"

[2] Daniel Yankelovich, "What New Life Styles Mean to Market Planners," *Marketing/Communications*, (June 1971), pp. 38–45. The quote appears on p. 39.

Table 2-1 (Continued)

Group 4: Penetration of Certain New Values at the Expense of
Traditional Puritanical Values

---

20. Toward *pleasure for its own sake*—putting pleasure before duty
21. Toward *blurring of the sexes*—moving away from traditional distinctions between men and women and their roles
22. Toward *living in the present*—straying from traditional beliefs in planning, saving, and living for the future
23. Toward *more liberal sexual attitudes*—the relaxation of sexual prohibitions
24. Toward *acceptance of stimulants and drugs*—greater acceptance of artificial agents for mood change, stimulation, and relaxation
25. Toward *relaxation of self-improvement standards*—the inclination to stop working as hard at self-improvement
26. Toward *individual religions*—rejection of institutionalized religions and the substitution of more personalized forms of religious experience

---

Group 5: Trends Which Have a Direct Impact on Marketing As Well
As on Other Facets of Modern Life

---

27. Toward *greater tolerance of chaos and disorder*—less need for schedules, routines, plans, regular shopping and purchasing, and order and cleanliness in the home
28. Toward *challenge to authority*—less automatic acceptance of the authority and "correctness" of public figures, institutions, and established brands
29. Toward *rejection of hypocrisy*—less acceptance of sham, exaggeration, indirection, and misleading language
30. Toward *female careerism*—belief that more challenging and productive work for a woman is needed
31. Toward *familism*—renewed faith in the belief that the essential life satisfactions stem from activities centering on the immediate family unit

---

*Source: Based on Daniel Yankelovich, "What New Life Styles Mean to Market Planners," *Marketing-Communications*, (June 1971), pp. 38–45. See pp. 40 and 41. Note that these trends were identified at one point in time, early 1971.

(10) (11)
(12)
(13)
(14)

What does he mean? Which of the social trends identified in Table 2-1 might explain this? What implications have they had for various categories of products, such as foods, women's clothing, and education? Which of them do you think have peaked out and are already obsolete? Which of Maslow's needs is reflected in each of these trends?

buying as a problem-solving process

Whatever their basic needs, individuals translate those needs into specific buying decisions. The means by which they do so has come to be regarded by many as the process of solving problems created from within or without, problems whose solution may create the need for a product or service. For example, it can be argued that some persons buying television sets are not purchasing entertainment for themselves, but are seeking a means to make home life with children bearable. The process by which the problem is solved is, however, not as simple as the act of purchasing a television set.

The process may begin by identifying alternative solutions to the problem, possibly including hiring a baby-sitter, sending the children to nursery school, getting a dog, or sticking it out by encouraging the children to develop interests that may keep them out of each others' and their parents' way. Based on an intuitive assessment of the economics, convenience, and over-all feasibility of various alternatives, it may be concluded that the purchase of a television set is the best answer. During this process, it is likely that a substantial amount of consultation with friends and relatives (often referred to as "reference groups" for someone facing a buying decision), an observation of their family behavior patterns, and exposure to advertising may hasten the narrowing of alternatives.

As the decision to purchase a television set is reached, information collection on which to base a purchase decision will already have begun. Sources again include word-of-mouth advice (again, from "reference groups"), consumer reports and other published sources, advertising, personal selling, and past experience, among others. If the television set is to be placed in a public area of the home, such as the living room, primary attention may be given to the style of cabinet in which it is housed. If it is to be used by several members of the family for several purposes, its portability may be important. This may lead to the selection of a specific type or size of television set. At this same stage, the price may be decided on, followed by stages in which the brand to be bought and the outlet at which the set is to be purchased are decided on. In the process, a certain amount of recycling of decision steps may take place. All of this is shown for a hypothetical buyer in Figure 2-2. And each individual may follow slightly different methods for solving problems involving the purchase of goods or services. For example, how would you describe individuals purchasing television sets in the following order of decision-narrowing steps, as opposed to the individual whose buying behavior is outlined in Figure 2-2:

(15)
1. An individual deciding on television, brand, the store outlet, the type and size of set, and the price, in that order?

(16)
2. An individual deciding on television, store outlet, price, brand, and type and size of set, in that order?

Nor does the problem solving process end with the purchase of a product or service. In the case of television, this process certainly includes considerable evidence that customers "replay" their purchase decisions. How else can we explain the high rate of interest in advertisements for television sets by individuals who have just purchased them? Or the exchange of information about automobile performance by individuals who have just purchased automobiles? Psychologists have identified this stage as the one in which a buyer experiences doubts about the "rightness' of his or her decision (formally referred to as "postpurchase dissonance"). At this point, it is thought that many buyers need reassurance that they have made a good decision. The nature of the reassurance may influence the buyer's repurchase decision, particularly in cases where the decision is made sufficiently frequently that postpurchase dissonance is not forgotten.

We can imagine the purchase process in much greater detail than any company could afford to measure it for any sizeable number of individuals.

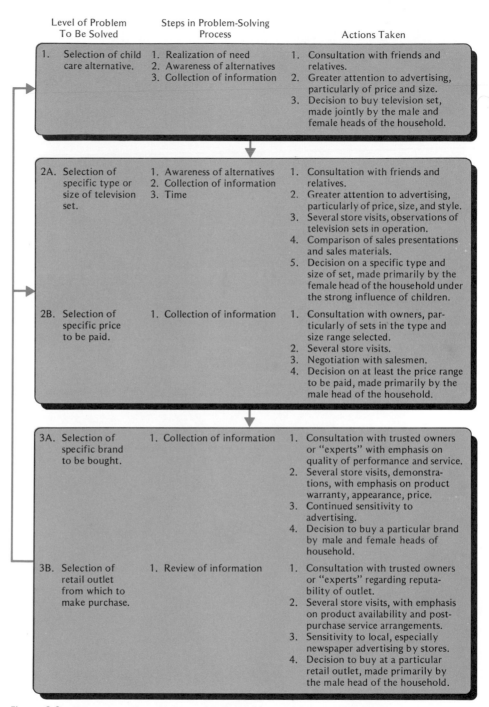

Level of Problem To Be Solved	Steps in Problem-Solving Process	Actions Taken
1. Selection of child care alternative.	1. Realization of need 2. Awareness of alternatives 3. Collection of information	1. Consultation with friends and relatives. 2. Greater attention to advertising, particularly of price and size. 3. Decision to buy television set, made jointly by the male and female heads of the household.
2A. Selection of specific type or size of television set.	1. Awareness of alternatives 2. Collection of information 3. Time	1. Consultation with friends and relatives. 2. Greater attention to advertising, particularly of price, size, and style. 3. Several store visits, observations of television sets in operation. 4. Comparison of sales presentations and sales materials. 5. Decision on a specific type and size of set, made primarily by the female head of the household under the strong influence of children.
2B. Selection of specific price to be paid.	1. Collection of information	1. Consultation with owners, particularly of sets in the type and size range selected. 2. Several store visits. 3. Negotiation with salesmen. 4. Decision on at least the price range to be paid, made primarily by the male head of the household.
3A. Selection of specific brand to be bought.	1. Collection of information	1. Consultation with trusted owners or "experts" with emphasis on quality of performance and service. 2. Several store visits, demonstrations, with emphasis on product warranty, appearance, price. 3. Continued sensitivity to advertising. 4. Decision to buy a particular brand by male and female heads of household.
3B. Selection of retail outlet from which to make purchase.	1. Review of information	1. Consultation with trusted owners or "experts" regarding reputability of outlet. 2. Several store visits, with emphasis on product availability and post-purchase service arrangements. 3. Sensitivity to local, especially newspaper advertising by stores. 4. Decision to buy at a particular retail outlet, made primarily by the male head of the household.

Figure 2-2. The process by which one family might acquire a new television set.

And our imaginations may lead us to impart greater emphasis than is deserved for various stages in the process. But, clearly, the process is a complex one and provides a rationale for marketing research and scientifically designed marketing effort.

the role of marketing in the buying process

All of the many views of the role of marketing in the buying process concern the means by which marketing effectively influences the demand for goods and services. Four of these many points of view are of particular interest to us here. These include the two extremes of the spectrum of views on marketing and society as well as two views of the basic methods by which marketers achieve their goals.

The extremes of thinking regarding marketing and society range from those who regard marketing as part of the problems of society to those who see it as an aid in the problem-solving process. Both interpretations are based generally on different views of the relationships shown in Figure 2-3. This simple

Figure 2-3. Two views of influence relationships between culture, individual customers, and marketing effort.

Situation A[a]
"Marketing as Part of the Problem"

Culture   Marketing Effort

Individual Customers

Situation B[a]
"Marketing as Part of the Solution"

Culture   Marketing Effort

Individual Customers

[a]Arrows are intended to suggest both the direction and strength of influence.

diagram, comparable to an abstract painting with much of the detail omitted, pictures the buying decision resulting from a complex set of interrelationships among the individual, the culture of which he or she may be a part, and marketing effort.

marketing effort as part of the problem

Those who picture marketing as part of the problem maintain, among other things, that the strength of the influence of marketing effort on the culture and, both directly and indirectly, on the individual is comparatively strong, as suggested by the size of the arrows shown in situation A in Figure 2-3. This view would maintain, for example, that when an advertisement for Carter Hall pipe tobacco emphasizes the female-attracting power of the product with such phrases as "pass the word–the chicks are back" (to the user of the product), it not only influences the pipe tobacco smoker to buy the product, but reinforces undesirable cultural attitudes that males hold toward females in our society. In a more general sense, it would picture advertising generally as presenting an unreal way of life, one that few people can attain (assuming that it is worth attaining); of raising expectations that cannot be fulfilled in the short-term future; and, as a result, of fostering unrest in our society.

Although most of marketing's critics concentrate their attacks on advertising, others claim that marketing effort leads to the creation of products that are not essential, products often designed to be differentiated from competition in some unimportant aspect. Thus, marketing is said not only to be wasteful, but to engage productive capacity in nonessential ways. Similarly, marketing is alleged to support an unnecessary number of wholesalers and retailers, "middlemen" intermediate to manufacturers and final consumers. Because each of these receives a return for its effort, such middlemen are said to contribute to high prices. In fact, most advertising, product-development effort, and distributive activities are thought by marketing's detractors to add to costs and prices rather than reduce them.

Much of marketing effort, according to this point of view, creates demands by creating needs, in a sense by creating problems to be solved by subsequent purchases. At what stage of the buying process pictured in Figure 2-2 would this view insert marketing effort as a major influence on buyer behavior?

(17)

marketing effort as part of the problem-solving process

At the opposite extreme are those who picture marketing as a product of the culture, as merely reflecting the values of a society, and as appealing to values already held by customers in order to sell a product, service, or point of view. Thus, although the amount of influence of marketing effort on customer decisions may be great, it can only be effective if it responds to changes in cultural and individual values rather than attempts to influence them. This view holds that if actual or would-be pipe smokers didn't harbor predatory views toward females already, Carter Hall's campaign would not be successful, and it would have to seek out a campaign theme that more closely conformed to the views of pipe smokers.

Similarly, this view holds (1) that poorly designed products or services with little utility cannot be marketed successfully, regardless of the magnitude or the quality of the marketing effort; (2) that middlemen either contribute to the more efficient distribution of products or services or they are driven out of business by the forces of more efficient distributive arrangements; and (3) that marketing effort leads to efficiencies that actually reduce the costs and prices at which products and services are sold.

Its supporters maintain that marketing effort basically is designed to respond to customer needs and values, regardless of whether one approves of them. As such, much effort helps customers solve problems. At what stage of the buying process shown in Figure 2-2 would you inject marketing effort as a major influence to reflect these views?

At this point in our discussion, your views regarding marketing and society may not be formulated fully. They may be based largely on advertising you have seen, the helpfulness of salespeople you have dealt with, the usefulness of products and services you have bought on the basis of marketing claims, articles you have read in various news publications, perhaps personal business experiences, and in all cases the views and influences of others. Nevertheless, it might be interesting to attempt to position yourself, in terms of the views you hold toward marketing, on the scale relating those who view marketing as a part of the problem to those who view it as part of the problem-solving process. Why did you position yourself where you did?

marketing effort as an influence on primary demand

Marketing effort can be pictured as assisting at different stages in the customer's problem-solving process. Returning to our previous example of the family faced with the basic alternatives of turning to greater parental effort, day-care services, baby-sitters, or television to solve its problem of child supervision, information supplied by the marketing efforts of day-care center franchisers, television set manufacturers, or an association of child psychologists may provide assistance in the decision. To the extent that such efforts stimulate a potential customer for a type of service or a type of product rather than an individual brand of product, we say that they influence the *primary demand* for day-care services or television sets. They stimulate a customer for an industry as opposed to a particular company in that industry. In a sense, they can be pictured as expanding the total market, shown as a pie-shaped entity in example A in Figure 2-4, for a generic type of product, service, or idea. At what point in Figure 2-2 would marketing effort intended to influence primary demand be expected to exert the greatest influence?

(18)

(19)

(20)

Figure 2-4. The expansion of primary and selective demand for a product or service, in this case day-care services.

Example A[a]

Expansion of Primary Demand for Day-Care Services by Day-Care Service C

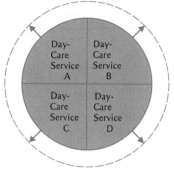

Example B[a]

Expansion of Selective Demand for Day-Care Services by Day-Care Service C

[a]The area within each circle denotes the total size of the market; portions of the area defined by lines interior to the circles denote the shares of the market held by various competitors.

marketing effort as an influence on selective demand

Marketing effort continues to assist and influence potential customers after a basic decision has been made to contract for a type of service, buy a type of product, or adopt a political view. At this point, the decision of which service, which product, or which political candidate might best solve the problem has to be made. The quantity of information about available day-care services or television sets may be great, the sources varied, and the objectivity of various sources questioned. But marketing effort provides information as well as influential arguments on which the selection of individual services or products can be made. At this stage of the process, which you might also want to identify in Figure 2-2, marketing effort can be said to influence *selective demand,* the demand for one competing service or product as opposed to another. The objective of this effort is to influence the size of the piece of the total pie that might be obtained for one competing service or product, as pictured in example B in Figure 2-4. Notice here that the size of the total pie doesn't change, only the way in which it is divided.

The concept of marketing effort as an influence on primary or selective demand is an important one in the definition of a marketing strategy for a product, service, or company. But it is more perfect in theory than in practice, because it requires a careful definition of a product in order to have meaning in a specific situation. For example, if the product is narrowly defined as portable television sets, then any effort made to convince potential customers to buy portable as opposed to console television sets could be considered as an effort to influence the primary demand for portable sets. If, instead, the product was defined as all types of television sets, what would constitute the expansion of primary demand? What would your answer be if the product were defined as all home entertainment devices? Or all home furnishings?

In establishing the usefulness of this concept, consider the following situations in which companies might place more emphasis on primary or selective demand stimulation as a basic objective of marketing effort. For example, IBM has manufactured about 70 per cent of the world's central processing units (computers), which are the heart of computerized data-processing systems. "The other computer company," Honeywell Information Systems, has manufactured about 10 per cent. Which of these companies would be more interested in increasing the primary demand for central processing units? What other factors do you think might influence a company's decision to influence primary demand for its products or services?

Turning back to the story about the development of Pepsi-Cola with which we opened this chapter, in what way did marketing effort influence demand for that product? It suggests that marketing plays a broader role in commercial activity than that of influencing potential customers to buy products, services, or ideas.

For marketing to play an effective role in the development and sale of products or services that meet the needs and help solve the problems of potential customers, appropriate targets for marketing effort, so-called target markets, must be defined.

the market—a sum of many parts

Many regard "the market" as an amorphous entity. The implications of this are dangerous. They include assumptions that potential customers share more or less the same problems, have more or less the same needs, and behave more or less the same way in solving their problems. Consider the situation confronted by the Department of Defense in the recent development and marketing of its new product, the Volunteer Army.[3]

An act of Congress signed by the president in 1972 brought an end to a 32-year period during which the United States government had the power to

[3]Much of the information in this example is drawn from William Leavitt, "Selling the Military Life," *Boston Globe Sunday Magazine,* (March 25, 1973), pp. 14 ff.

draft individuals into military service. It placed a burden on the Department of Defense to manage a transition to a 2.3-million member all-volunteer force, requiring, for example, the recruitment of 381,000 recruits for the active-duty force during the year beginning July 1, 1973. Its available resources included an advertising budget of $67.5 million for fiscal 1973, of which the largest share, $26.7 million, was allocated to the Army. To assist it in its efforts, the department contracted for the services of a marketing research organization.

customer needs

Field investigations disclosed that the most likely candidate for the Volunteer Army expressed a number of needs: (1) the desire to strike out on his or her own, (2) the need for structure, typically to assist an individual not quite ready to chart his or her own course, (3) the desire for travel, and (4) the need for a reduction of uncertainty about, and fear of, what Army life was all about—the need for a "deal."

the nature of the market—segmentation

Potential customers for the Volunteer Army could be described at least on three dimensions, including age, nature of current residence, and family economic status, as shown in Figure 2-5. Each cubicle in this three-dimensional market matrix (called a marketing grid in its two-dimensional form by some) represents a set of characteristics by which potential recruits might be identified. In marketing terms, each cubicle represents a segment of the total market. The process by which such a matrix is developed is called market segmentation.

Figure 2-5. A market matrix showing potential groups of customers for the Volunteer Army.

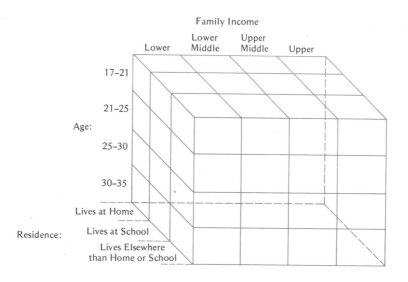

45

Why segment a market? Among other reasons, the Army, like many commercial firms, had only $26.7 million to promote its product to some 31 million males between the ages of seventeen and thirty five. That figures out to just 86 cents to spend on each eligible male candidate, less than the price of one decent mailing. And it includes nothing for eligible females, potential candidates younger than seventeen, and parents over thirty-five who, in many cases, help their children decide to enter the Volunteer Army. With a current total cost of recruitment averaging close to $1,000 per recruit, the Army had to make every advertising dollar count.

Marketing research allowed the Army to identify the market segment with which it potentially could obtain the greatest number of recruits per dollar of advertising and personal sales. Which one of those shown in Figure 2-5 do you think it was?

□ □ □

The research suggested that the market segment for which recruiting advertising ought to be designed was the male between seventeen and twenty-one, living at home, and a member of a lower middle-class family.

The dimensions of age, living arrangements, and family income represented handy means by which the most receptive segments of the market for the Volunteer Army could be identified. Of greater importance for the subsequent design of a "product" and marketing efforts on its behalf are explorations of needs that a product can fulfill and potential uses perceived for it by various audiences of potential "buyers."

market segmentation by needs and uses

A knowledge of the potential needs that a product fulfills and the uses to which it can be put help explain why certain segments of a prospective market will be most receptive to a product. For example, among the needs that potential candidates for the Volunteer Army might have are those for excitement, escape, education, income, independence, travel, maturity, skills, a job, an outlet for patriotism, public service, inclusion in a group, or discipline. The degree to which each of these needs might be perceived could vary among segments of potential "buyers" and those who influence the buying process. In Figure 2-6, for example, what relative emphasis on needs suggested here would likely be perceived by two potential recruits, one of seventeen years of age living at home in a lower-income family and another of thirty years of age, married with one child, and unemployed? What relative uses for the Volunteer Army might be envisioned by the seventeen-year-old described here and his or her parents?

Interviews with potential volunteers and their families disclosed that they placed high values on a good place to work, learn, and enjoy themselves. In contrast, they were not concerned about having a way of venting a patriotic spirit difficult to arouse in peacetime.

46

When was the last time you got promoted?

It's tough to get ahead when you have to start so far behind. No skills. No experience. No jobs to look forward to, except the ones anyone can do.

You can change all that right now. Today's Army has over 300 jobs that demand skill and experience.

And we'll give you the skill and experience to perform them. Training in construction, computers, whatever you want to become skilled at, is yours for the asking.

Unlike most job training courses, you are paid for attending ours. Starting at a good salary. Plus free meals, free housing, free medical and dental care, and 30 days paid vacation each year.

The promotions will come fast, too. Whether you stay in the Army, or go on to a job in civilian life. And after your enlistment's up you can still receive up to 36 months financial assistance at the college of your choice.

To start promoting yourself, send the coupon or see your Army Representative.

Today's Army wants to join you.

Figure 2-6.   An example of an advertisement used to promote the Volunteer Army in 1973. Source: N. W. Ayer ABH International, New York.

Whatever your reaction to these efforts might be, they provide evidence that the Pentagon, the biggest business in the world, is seeking more of a marketing orientation to overcome periodic sales resistance.

the product—the sum of many views

Efforts to identify customer problems, needs resulting from those problems, and the most promising market segment in which to market a problem-solving product or service can provide guidance in designing a marketing program for an existing product. Or they can provide the basis for a new product design. Putting it another way, they can assist both products in search of markets and markets in search of products. The development of freeze-dried coffee in 1963 by General Foods provides an excellent illustration of the latter type of situation.[4] It was a particularly significant decision in view of the fact that the company at the time possessed the largest share of the market, through its Maxwell House and other brands, for both regular and soluble (instant) coffee.

[4] Much of the information included in this example is based on General Foods Corporation, case no. 1-571-023 (Boston, Mass.: Intercollegiate Clearing House, copyright © 1967, Columbia University, and copyright © 1968 by the Board of Trustees of the Leland Stanford Junior University).

coffee drinkers' problems

Traditionally, coffee drinkers had established freshly brewed coffee as the standard for a "good cup of coffee." Surveys showed that characteristics of a good cup of coffee, ranked in order, were (1) flavor and taste, (2) freshness, (3) good aroma, (4) ability to give the drinker a lift, (5) ability to relax the drinker, and (6) strength without bitterness. A major concern with regard to regular coffee was that it was a bother to prepare, particularly important because coffee played so many roles so often throughout the consumer's day. Soluble coffee, developed in 1950, dealt with this problem and led directly to a doubling of between-meal coffee drinking between 1950 and 1963, whereas very little change occurred for mealtime coffee drinking.

However, soluble coffee was perceived as being inferior in taste to regular coffee. With both, consumers expressed an inability to achieve a consistently good cup of coffee.

As a result of development work supported by the largest investment in the company's history for a period of some thirteen years, the freeze-drying process for making coffee was perfected. It produced a coffee superior in flavor to other instants. And it retained the solubility, and hence the convenience, of its instant coffee predecessor.

product-oriented product description

The research group's description of the freeze-dried coffee product at that time might have included the following elements:

> Freeze-dried coffee is produced by blending, roasting, grinding, and brewing a strong coffee solution at a temperature and pressure somewhat higher than those used in normal home preparation, but roughly similar to the process for soluble coffee. At this point, the solution is flash-frozen, subjected to a vacuum, and warmed to cause "sublimation" of the frozen solution's liquid content, leaving spongelike dehydrated coffee solids that can be ground and packaged for sale as soluble (instant) coffee. The density or concentration (weight per unit of volume) of the resulting product is 25 per cent greater than that of previous soluble coffees. Compared to spray-dried coffee (its predecessor), it produces a flavor with less astringency or "mouth feel," has more aroma in the cup (comparable to regular), appears as an irregular crystal as opposed to a powdery consistency for spray-dried, and is more soluble in cold water and produces less foam in the cup than spray-dried. It can now be produced at a cost per unit of 35 per cent more than existing soluble coffee.

At this point, a product-marketing group was assigned to the freeze-dried product and given the responsibility for carrying out consumer research and developing and implementing the most effective marketing strategy for the new product.

customer-oriented product description

The view of the product-marketing group toward the product was influenced by phrases that consumers typically had used to describe coffee. These included (1) a force to provide energy or stimulation, (2) a tension reliever with an implicit reward and, consequently, an aid to mental health, (3) a convenience food and a "snack," (4) an appetite depressant, (5) a medication (with apparent emetic qualities), (6) a "friend" in and of itself, and (7) a visible symbol of adulthood. Drinking coffee was universally associated with the sociability of a friendly gathering.

In addition, freeze-dried coffee was seen by the product-marketing group as offering a flavor clearly superior to that of spray-dried and comparable to that of ground; of providing the basis for a consistently successful coffee-making experience; and representing an economic alternative (in that it required only one-half teaspoon as opposed to the conventional rounded, full teaspoon of spray-dried to make a cup of coffee). In fact, one of the product's few shortcomings was that inevitably it might be associated with spray-dried coffee and thus be shunned by consumers who predominantly were regular coffee drinkers.

Blind taste tests showed that (1) 47 per cent of a sample of soluble coffee drinkers preferred the freeze-dried coffee to Instant (spray dried) Maxwell House and (2) 44 per cent of a sample of regular coffee drinkers preferred it to ground Maxwell House coffee.

Regardless of the technical characteristics of the product, it was important for the marketing group to communicate those characteristics perceived to be of greatest importance to that portion of the buying and using public toward which the product might be directed. In the process, a number of decisions had to be made:

1. Pricing the product to represent a small or large premium per production unit over that for spray-dried coffee (which in turn sold for a premium over regular coffee)
2. Giving the product a name that would associate it with Maxwell House ground coffee or Instant Maxwell House, such as Maxwell House Freeze-Dried Coffee; or giving it a name such as Prima, Nova, or Kaaba, entirely new to the company; or creating a compromise between the two types of names, such as Maxim
3. Packaging the product in the same package quantities (two ounce, four ounce, and eight ounce) and shapes as spray-dried coffee, thus resulting in smaller package sizes; or putting it in packages of different sizes and shapes
4. Advertising it by means, among others, of (a) an announcement explaining the freeze-dried process, emphasizing the fact that the product was an entirely new form of coffee, or (b) a "perfect percolator" theme, stressing the case with which consistently good coffee could be made with the product
5. Introducing it to the public by means, among others, of (a) two-ounce samples with 25-cent repurchase coupons delivered door-to-door, (b)

mailed coupons redeemable for free jars of the product, or (c) mailed packets of six individually measured servings with a 25-cent repurchase coupon

6. Providing to retailers the typical below-average margin of 13 per cent of the price to consumers that retailers realized on coffee products; or offering some other, presumably higher, margin as an incentive to them to accept the product and stock it in larger quantities on the shelf

product- and customer-oriented views compared

(30) "People do not rush out and buy new, faster quarter-inch drills. They buy faster quarter-inch holes."[5] Which of these views of a quarter-inch drill is product-oriented as opposed to customer-oriented?

(31) Relationships between product- and customer-oriented views of freeze-
(32) dried coffee are presented in Table 2-2. Which do you think are more important to the customer? Which do you think were of the greatest concern to the
(33) General Foods executives responsible for product design and manufacturing-plant management? Based on what you know at this point about the situation, how would you decide the marketing issues listed here for freeze-dried coffee?

(34) Can the approach suggested in Table 2-2 be used to review the design of
(35) the Volunteer Army? What would the results of this process look like?

The coordination of marketing and product-development activities is critical to a successful market-oriented organization. This coordination requires a flow of information from customers and others through the marketing organization to those responsible for product development. It requires a responsive attitude

Table 2-2 **Contrasts Between Product-oriented and Customer-oriented Views of Freeze-dried Coffee**

A Product-Oriented View of Maxim	Versus	A Customer-Oriented View of Maxim
Emphasis on the process by which the product is created		Emphasis on the *results* of the process by which the product is created
Emphasis on characteristics of the product's aroma, astringency, and appearance		Emphasis on characteristics of the product, *as per-ceived by the customer*
Emphasis on product density and concentration		Emphasis on the manner in which product density and concentration might affect usage and coffee-making results
Emphasis on cost in relation to comparable products made by the company		Emphasis on the perceived cost by the consumer, taking into account the relative cost, convenience, and quality of results produced by alternative products
Emphasis on product density and subsequent package requirements		Emphasis on the role of the package for both display purposes in the store and for purposes of usage by the ultimate consumer

[5]"New Products: The Push Is on Marketing," *Business Week*, (March 4, 1972), pp. 72–77. Quote on p. 72.

Figure 2-7. The product, as viewed by various parties to its development, sale, purchase, and installation.

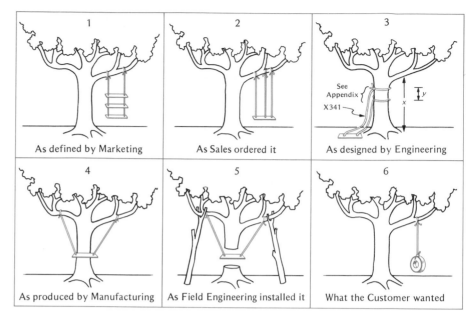

1 — As defined by Marketing	2 — As Sales ordered it	3 — As designed by Engineering
4 — As produced by Manufacturing	5 — As Field Engineering installed it	6 — What the Customer wanted

on the part of the latter. And it suggests the need to overcome product-oriented objections to problems that arise in producing new and more varied products. The failure to coordinate attitudes and product definitions in the process of product design, manufacture, and marketing can result in the outcome pictured in the cartoon in Figure 2-7.

relating product to market segments— product positioning

The market for coffee in 1963 could be segmented along a number of dimensions, including consumption patterns and geographic regions.

For example, General Foods' marketing-research department found that 48 per cent of all coffee-drinking families—representing 54 percent of all coffee volume—drank regular (ground) coffee exclusively. Another 28 per cent—representing 18 per cent of all coffee volume—drank instant coffee exclusively. The remainder consumed both forms.

The amount of coffee consumed per capita ranged from 2.54 cups per person per day in the east to 3.38 cups per person per day in the west. Furthermore, the ratio of soluble to all coffee consumed ranged from about 20 per cent in the west to about 40 per cent in the east. In total, the amount of coffee consumed per capita had been on the decline for several years.

Of equal importance in formulating a marketing strategy for the new freeze-dried coffee was the knowledge that (1) General Foods' existing share of the total market for ground coffee was 36 per cent in the east, but only 13.5

per cent in the west, and (2) its share of the soluble (instant) coffee market was 50.7 per cent in the east and 47.1 per cent in the west. It was believed that there would be no significant competition from other companies' freeze-dried coffee products for a period of at least two years.

The marketing group could elect one of several strategies for relating its new product to the potential market segments. First, it could represent the product as possessing the flavor of regular coffee and the convenience of instant coffee, a strategy to displace sales of regular coffee with those of freeze-dried. Secondly, it could present the product as a superior form of instant coffee, clearly intended primarily to gain a share of the existing soluble coffee market. Or it could introduce the product as an entirely new form of coffee, a strategy that might influence and enlarge the primary demand for coffee in general while diverting some regular and some instant-coffee drinkers to freeze-dried.

(36)
(37)

(38) (39)
(40)

(41)

Toward which segment of the market would you have advised General Foods to direct its new product? Given this additional information and a decision regarding market segments, how would you decide the issues posed on p. 49? Are there more basic questions that you would like to explore further? If so, which? Is there other information, which might be obtained by asking potential buyers or through some other means, that you would like to have on which to base a decision? If so, what?

The process of relating a product to potential markets has been termed *product positioning*. It can be used in the design and introduction of products with significantly different characteristics than competitors, such as freeze-dried coffee, to largely uninformed market segments. The term also has been picked up by advertising managers to denote the means by which products, often of essentially the same composition and capabilities, can be given a character that will appeal primarily to certain segments of a market. It is thought to be particularly effective in aiding a company in gaining a share of a market dominated by a competing product, or in aiding a company with a dominant share in fending off competition by adding new products, each of which captures a dominant share of a particular market segment. For example,

> Jim Jordan, vice-president of the Batten Barton, Durstine & Osborn [advertising] agency, gives [an] . . . explicit account of why he switched Schaefer's advertising campaign from the former, positionless theme of "What do you hear in the best of circles? Schaefer all around" to the current, "Schaefer is the one beer to have when you're having more than one."
>
> "Beer commercials used to be the same as soft-drink commercials," Mr. Jordan says. "There were guys and girls on beaches, swirling around, presenting pilsner glasses to each other." He adds: "We went out and talked to a lot of beer drinkers." And it turned out that "15 per cent of the people of this country drink about 85 per cent of the beer." These 25–49-year-old middle-income men routinely down three or four bottles an evening, but they complained that "the flavor seemed to fade a little" as they sloshed further through a six-pack, Mr. Jordan says.
>
> "We thought, gee, we ought to address ourselves to the problem they were talking about." Although Schaefer didn't change its beer formula, the admen found a couple of quirks in the brewing process that they felt would justify a new claim: Schaefer was uniquely designed to taste the same after you were tight as it did when you were stone sober. The result: Lowly Schaefer quickly

passed Ballantine, then Rheingold, and now—Mr. Jordan says—it is neck-and-neck with Budweiser as the largest selling beer in the East.[6]

In order to position a product, a company must resist the temptation to appeal to all segments of a market, particularly when a competitor has established a firm position for its product.

[An expert on positioning] argues that United Air Lines has monopolized the friendliness position. So rival American Airlines, he says, should abandon the vacationer to United and appeal to the businessman with a speedy, no-nonsense approach. He says American's current advertisements go part-way, but not far enough, toward the man-in-a-hurry position. "American's afraid they'll give up too many trips to Disneyland," he says. "They want to have their cake and eat it too."[7]

Product positioning is a process by which market segments and products are brought together. It can make marketing effort more efficient by bringing products and services, either in terms of their real or perceived features, to the attention of the most receptive market segments. And it can be used to revive existing products and services as well as introduce new ones.

(42)
(43)
(44)
How are the views of marketing as part of a problem-solving process and product positioning in its narrowest sense related? Which is most functional or valuable? To whom? Your responses to these questions may help explain why marketing occupies an ambiguous position in the minds of many.

Marketing skills, tools, and concepts have many uses. The United States market in particular has provided the proving ground for most of these skills, tools, and concepts. Why? A number of hypotheses can be advanced. But to understand the possible reasons why this increased sensitivity to the needs of the market has occurred recently in this country, it is useful to look back at least to some of the basic eras in the commercial history of the country.

pathway to the marketing era

In the earliest era of United States commercial history, families produced individually much of what they consumed and traded or "bartered" with others for much of the remainder of the goods and services they required. From this era we moved quickly into a period in which families increased their ability to barter by establishing so-called cottage industries in which the family produced in an organized fashion much more of a given item than it could consume. Among other characteristics, the combination of relatively good education, greed, ingenuity, and a tradition of English capitalism in our forebearers probably led to the development of a remarkable array of tools and machines to increase the productivity of the individuals in both agriculture and manufac-

[6]Jonathan Kwitny, "Why Is Schaefer Beer the One Beer to Have When Having More . . . ?" *Wall Street Journal,* (Dec. 13, 1972), p. 1.
[7]Ibid., p. 21.

turing. As historian Carl N. Degler has put it, "Capitalism came [to the United States] in the first ships."[8] Those who came in the decades immediately following the American Revolution literally brought England's industrial revolution with them.

The rapid development of agriculture and industry was fostered by a combination of ample fertile land and natural resources; a highly motivated populace; a ready market, especially for agricultural commodities such as cotton in England; and an excellent source of new machines and technology to feed further the productive cycle. The farms and manufacturers of the country needed only the creation and maintenance of an effective system of wholesalers to dispose of all they could produce and in turn supply their needs, often from abroad.[9]

The "land of opportunity" soon began attracting immigrants from Europe in sufficient numbers to form its own domestic markets. Furthermore, the development of an extensive rail system to supplement and replace heretofore important waterways not only provided a vast market for labor and materials, but also made possible (1) a more rapid development of interior markets and (2) larger marketing territories for individual producers. This both created the need for extensive quantities of capital and the opportunity for speculative returns on investments, thereby placing an early emphasis on investment both from domestic and foreign sources, financial management, and wholesalers able to distribute the products of geographically concentrated manufacturers to many small, remotely located markets.

Market growth and the development of an efficient network for distributing products over relatively great distances for that time laid the basis for so-called scientific management, the development of mass production concepts such as the assembly line, and the ascendancy of production as a vital and glamorous factor in the commercial growth of the country.

The financial crash of 1929 may have signaled a temporary disenchantment with the financial community. And as buying power in the market declined, the machines and factories nearly ground to a halt. The eyes of the nation shifted to marketing and to our distributive capacity. But did they do so with the expectation that marketing effort could pull the nation out of the depths of the Great Depression? No. Instead, various marketing institutions found themselves under severe criticism for their alleged contributions to economic instability. The same wholesale organizations that had helped foster efficient production by providing the means whereby manufacturers could market their products in the far corners of the country were charged with the responsibility for having created excessive costs and overly high prices. Cries of "eliminate the middleman" were heard once again.

At the same time, the chain store movement, in which retailers began to create and acquire multiple sales outlets, was seen as a potential threat to competition, reasonable price levels, the small retailer, the consumer, and even the nation's economic well-being. In other respects, the inability of customers to buy because of a lack of money was seen as a failure of marketing efforts to create demand at a time when the nation's industries sorely needed markets

[8] Carl N. Degler, *Out of Our Past* (New York: Harper, 1959), p. 1.
[9] For an extensive study of this functional era, see Glenn Porter and Harold C. Livesay, *Merchants and Manufacturers* (Baltimore: John Hopkins, 1971.)

(45) (46)

for their products and services to provide jobs to make available the resources for customers to buy. What is the logic of this view? Do you agree with it?

In many respects, World War II made up for the continuing gap between excessive productive capacity and insufficient markets in the United States. In a grisly sense, it provided a tremendous new market, a nearly insatiable customer for the nation's factories. Wages increased as workers began working forty, then fifty, and even sixty hours per week—much of it on time and a half (150 per cent of their normal hourly wage), double time, and even triple time. Because of the lack of goods for domestic consumption, much of these wages was saved. By the end of the war, there was a long, loud clamor for all types of goods, a so-called seller's market requiring little marketing expertise.

Thus, it is not surprising that many sellers were not prepared for the competition for limited markets that once again began to reappear in the early 1950s. Again marketing caught the attention of many people. This time not as a scapegoat for economic collapse, but as a potential means of obtaining larger shares of still wealthy markets willing and able to reward effective marketing effort. As a result, the pendulum in the search for top executive talent in many segments of American business swung from those with extensive backgrounds in finance, law, and production to marketing.

(47)

Why do you think that the ascendancy of emphasis on marketing expertise is associated with national economic "maturity"?

the marketing concept—a new corporate way of life

At the General Electric Co. in May of 1955 several executives of the Consumer Products Division were discussing the division's marketing policy when they decided to coin a name for what they observed going on at General Electric and several other companies. GE executive John McKitterick generally is credited with having originated the term:

> Where the pre-1940 period was preoccupied with trying to make the same product cheaper, the postwar period saw a new dimension added to competition, in which the focus was to try and make the old product better, or even more bold, to try and launch a new product. . . . we became so impressed with the results of focusing on what would be better for the customer rather than merely cheaper that we invented a now familiar phrase—"the marketing concept"—to describe this triumph of innovation over productive capacity.[10]

Henceforth, *marketing concept* would be used to designate the primary objective of the business as "the identification and satisfaction of customer needs at a profit."

Consider the case of the Reliance Electric Co., a Cleveland-based manufacturer of industrial motors, drives, and measuring equipment with sales of several

---

[10]John B. McKitterick, "What Is the Marketing Management Concept?" in *The Frontiers of Marketing Thought and Science,* ed. Frank M. Bass (Chicago: American Marketing Association, 1957), pp. 71–81. Quote on p. 75.

hundred million dollars.[11] For the first sixty years of its existence, the company relied solely on the high quality engineered into its products and a direct sales force headed typically by a successful former salesman charged with selling a broad product line to all customers. Over time, this failed to produce a growth rate in sales equal to progressive competitors such as the General Electric Co. In the words of a senior vice-president: "We came out with quality products, but they didn't set the world on fire." In the words of the president: "You always [heard] engineers telling salesmen to sell what they already have." Occasionally, the approach produced much less desirable results:

> In the late 1950s, for instance, Reliance engineers designed what they thought to be an ultra-futuristic drive. It relied on a complex system of vacuum tubes to convert incoming alternating current power to direct current. But customers decided the drive was too complicated for most plant electricians to understand or fool with. It also proved too sensitive to the moisture, dirt, and temperature adversities of a plant environment. So what looked revolutionary in the lab flopped on the market.[12]

In 1965, a new company president encouraged a review of Reliance business philosophy, product line, and marketing approach. Based on conversations with customers, the company's executives found that many Reliance products possessed unneeded features that had been thought desirable by its engineers, features for which customers did not want to pay. Furthermore, many customers were found to regard Reliance as a small producer of electric drives with limited engineering capability. As a result, the company decided to (1) increase its marketing research and advertising effort; (2) reorganize small divisions that had grown up around specific products into larger divisions organized around markets; (3) create an industrial marketing department with twelve specialists to oversee the company's thirty one markets and feed engineers, product managers, and others information about shifting requirements in those industries; and (4) coordinate all of these efforts through a senior marketing executive. According to the president, "Now we tell manufacturing, 'Don't come back and say you can't design a product to fit a new market need. Tell us instead what it takes to build it.'" A special advertising program proclaimed, "The man from Reliance has only one engineered drive for you . . . the one you need."

Within three years, the company's annual growth rate had doubled. In the food industry alone, Reliance doubled its market share of electric motor sales simply by cleaning up the motor it made. Seeing that its motor did not fit the needs of an industry demanding easy-to-clean equipment, its engineers were encouraged to build a new motor, one with smooth contours and without pockets to collect dirt.

(48) In contrasting what happened before and after 1965 at Reliance, how would you describe the important changes that took place?

The changes that took place at Reliance Electric in 1965 indicate the way in which the adoption of the marketing concept in a company can influence its entire organization and method of doing business. In identifying these changes, you already have formulated a practical picture of what happens under the

---

[11]Material for this example is drawn from "Putting Customer Demands First," *Business Week,* (Nov. 28, 1970), pp. 62–63.
[12]Ibid.

(49)
(50)
(51)
marketing concept. Do you think it is a coincidence that Reliance Electric and General Electric are competitors in certain markets? How is product positioning, as described earlier, related to the marketing concept? Does the story, whether fact or fable, describing the development of Pepsi-Cola illustrate early adherence to the marketing concept?

the present status of the marketing concept

The marketing concept has become, in the words of one corporate president, "a way of business life."[13] But just how widely it has been adopted has been examined only recently. One study, for example, explored the extent to which the marketing concept has been adopted and implemented in a sample of 640 companies selected from twenty one manufacturing classifications. In this study, management consultant Carlton P. McNamara concluded that (1) consumer goods companies have tended to adopt and implement the marketing concept to a greater degree than industrial goods companies, and (2) large companies have tended to adopt and implement the marketing concept to a greater degree

(52)
(53)
than small and medium-sized companies.[14] How would you explain the results? Do they make sense to you?

An additional finding of interest to us in this study was that in McNamara's 640 companies, which responded from a randomly selected sample of 1,492, more top executives claimed a business background in marketing than in any other functional area such as finance, manufacturing, law, engineering, or research and development. This augurs well for the continued support of the marketing concept among American companies, and for those who would seek the route to the top of their organizations through marketing.

In recent years, we have seen evidence that the marketing concept is a highly exportable idea. The number of companies in Japan and Western Europe adopting and implementing the concept have grown perhaps proportionately with the extent to which they have developed markets in the United States. An indication of the extent to which the idea has spread is provided by a comment made several years ago in a published article by the president of the national bank of a European country to the effect that his country "can't take the stand that we should sell what we produce. Rather, we must produce what we can sell."[15] The country? Hungary.

The marketing concept is simple and straightforward. Perhaps that is why it is often taken for granted, forgotten, or periodically overlooked, producing disastrous results even in companies that avow its importance.

It implies that we need to (1) determine customer needs, (2) design a product or service to meet those needs, (3) select an appropriate target market segment for it, and (4) determine a method for marketing the product or service

[13] Fred J. Borch, "The Marketing Philosophy As a Way of Business Life," in *The Marketing Concept: Its Meaning to Management* (New York: American Management Association, 1957).

[14] Carlton P. McNamara, "The Present Status of the Marketing Concept," *Journal of Marketing*, **36:**50–57 (Jan. 1972).

[15] "Will Success Spoil . . . Hungary is Prospering, Straining Soviet Ties," *Wall Street Journal*, (Feb. 22, 1973), p. 12.

at a profit. The first of these can be accomplished through marketing research of a formal or informal nature. The second and third depend on an effective coordination of marketing, research and development, and production efforts to define a product and its appropriate target markets. The fourth involves a complex range of efforts to encourage customers to use a product or service and make the product or service available to them.

A customer-oriented philosophy holds that, in a business, marketing and the adherance to the marketing concept make everything else possible.

summary

The identification of customer needs is central to any marketing effort. Customer needs contribute directly to buying motives. Buying motives in turn influence purchasing decisions. The translation of basic needs into specific buying decisions has come to be viewed as a problem-solving process. The process itself is one in which potential buyers realize a need, identify alternative ways of alleviating it, collect information about such alternatives, take action through a purchase, and even seek ways of confirming the "rightness" of a decision after it is made.

There are widely varying views of marketing's role in society. Many hold that marketing efforts play a valuable role in the problem-solving process engaged in by buyers, helping them relieve already existing needs. They maintain that marketing in most cases can lead to increased efficiencies and reduced cost of production and distribution. Marketing's critics, on the other hand, claim that marketing efforts often are part of the problem, because they create needs that did not exist, needs that can be resolved only through the purchase of nonessential goods and services.

To the extent that marketing efforts influence potential customers to purchase a type of product as opposed to a particular brand of product, we say that they stimulate primary demand. Marketing effort designed to influence the selection of competing brands often is referred to as stimulating selective demand.

Marketing effort basically is intended to bring together potential customers and the products and services for which they might have a need. This requires careful market and product definition. The process of bringing markets and products together can be made more efficient through the segmentation of markets into potential buyer and user groups. These groups can be referred to along dimensions such as age, income, and occupation. But most important is the manner in which members of each segment perceive products in terms of the potential uses to which they can be put. Similarly, products must be defined and described in terms of potential uses, not more common physical specifications. The process of relating products to potential markets has been termed product positioning.

Functional eras of business activity through which the United States economy has passed include those most heavily emphasizing the logistics of land development; means of financing the productive capacity needed to serve expanding markets; scientific management and the development of mass production concepts; and, only recently, marketing effort required to make production more relevant to the needs of potential markets. This has led to the relatively recent adoption in many organizations of the marketing concept, essentially one that designates the primary objective of business activity as the identification and satisfaction of customer needs at a profit.

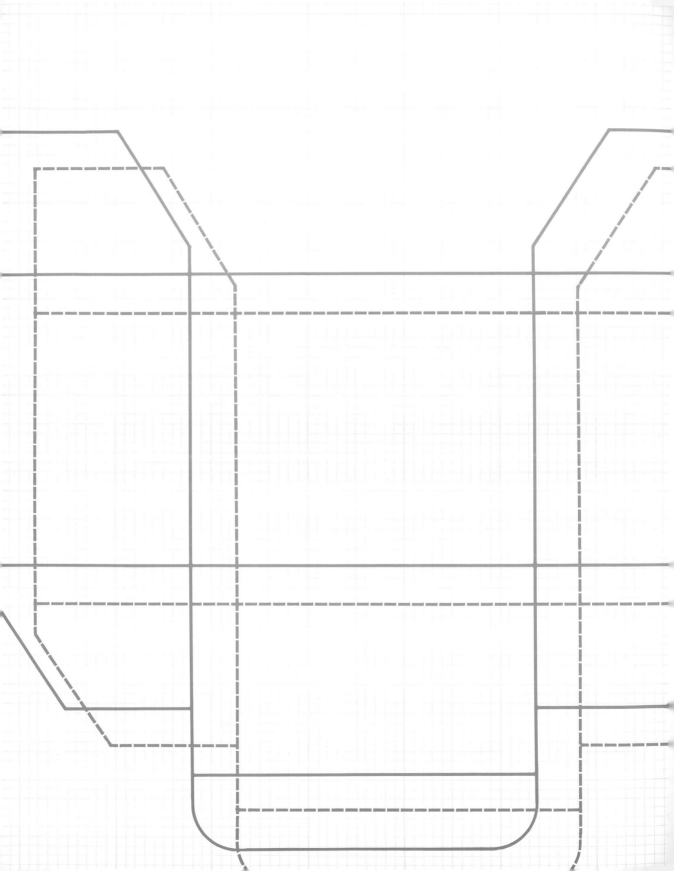

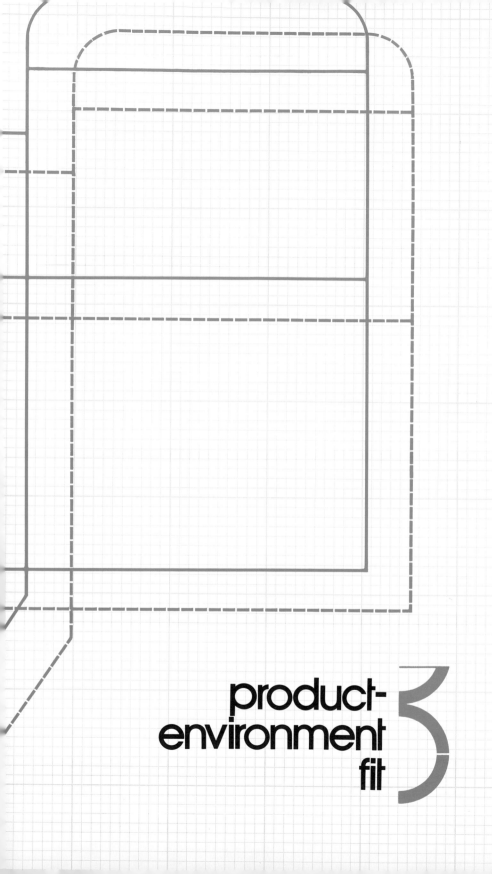

product-
environment
fit

3

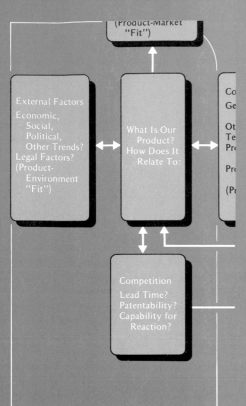

You've probably seen a cartoon similar to one in which a confident, often pompous, individual pronounces, from a raised platform that looks suspiciously like a giant's toe: "What are you all worried about? I don't see any giant."

At times, forces that influence our lives and businesses are so large that we fail to see them coming. How many of your friends anticipated the so-called energy crisis of 1973–1974 even as late as the spring of 1973? Characteristically, I ordered the largest automobile I've ever owned at about that time.

Environmental trends occur over long periods of time, and in many cases are reasonably predictable, providing the basis for even predicting specific events within a range of several years. In fact, many forecasters had been tracking the growing likelihood of an energy shortage. They were surprised merely by its timing, precipitated by a less easily predictable political decision.

When the effects of environmental changes are felt, however, they often register quite an impact. For this reason, an exploration of some of the environmental dimensions affecting marketing decisions and performance in this chapter is intended to (1) sensitize you to the nature and importance of environmental trends, as well as (2) relate these trends to marketing decision making.

Competitors make up a visible and dynamic portion of a firm's external environment. As a result, even tactical decisions such as price changes must be made partly on the basis of expected competitive reactions. Factors influencing these reactions, thus, will be an appropriate topic for discussion in the concluding portion of this chapter.

You may not be impressed yet with the importance of environmental factors on marketing strategies. But John Hansen is. And perhaps a story involving Winnebago Industries, Inc., of which Mr. Hansen is president, will do the trick for you, too.

motor homes and roller coasters

The first production models of self-powered motor homes began appearing on the market in 1962. A decade later, they were selling at the rate of 105,000 units per year at prices ranging from about $8,000 to more than $20,000, with 1972 sales 84 per cent higher than those the year before.

By 1972, Frank Industries, Inc., the manufacturer of the first units, had been joined by about 150 competitors.[1] And General Motors, described by Raymond

[1]This and other facts regarding the motor home industry are based on Greg Conderacci, "Competition Heightens, Market-Growth Slows for Motor-Home Firms," *Wall Street Journal,* (May 31, 1973), pp. 1 and 23.

Frank as the 151st entrant into the industry, had announced its intention to manufacture a medium-priced line of motor homes and market the vehicles through certain of its 13,200 dealers. The leader in the field, Winnebago Industries, Inc., had been an early entrant that had grown to a market share of about 20 per cent and a sales volume of $212 million in fiscal 1973, a figure that had nearly put it on the most recent list of the largest five-hundred firms.

Buoyed by the rapidly expanding market and the knowledge that an important group of buyers, consisting of couples approaching retirement age, was increasing at a rapid rate, several manufacturers announced that they were doubling their production capacity. Investors, entranced by the industry's prospects and the growth in the earnings rate for Winnebago, among others, bid the company's stock to $48 per share. This price, approximately eighty-six times the company's fiscal 1972 earnings, at a time when all stocks listed on the New York Stock Exchange were selling at an average price equivalent to thirteen times their company's earnings, largely reflected investors' expectations of higher earnings for the company. Would you have invested in the stock of Winnebago Industries, Inc., at this point?

(1)

Early in 1973, a variety of concerns among motor home industry executives prompted some decisions. Economists were forecasting a possible downturn in the growth of the economy within a year. Other major automobile manufacturers were contemplating entering the industry. A possible shortage of gasoline, an important commodity for a vehicle requiring a gallon of gas for every six to eight miles, was forecast. Although the growth of modern campsites for motor homes had been rapid, a number of communities had passed ordinances against parking motor homes on streets and discharging waste in any but approved locations. Ralph Nader's Center for Auto Safety and Consumers Union, publisher of *Consumer Reports* magazine, had petitioned the National Highway Traffic Safety Administration to make automotive safety standards applicable to heretofore exempt motor homes, a move termed as inevitable by federal officials.

Winnebago Industries announced at about the same time that it had cancelled plans to build a second plant, had reduced its production rate by about 25 per cent, and would sponsor its first "factory sale" to reduce inventories of certain models in its line. By this time, Winnebago's stock had fallen to $5 per share, roughly $6\frac{1}{2}$ times the earnings rate for fiscal 1973.

In order to assess the attractiveness of Winnebago's stock at $6\frac{1}{2}$ times the company's current earnings, a financial analyst would have to appraise the effect of a number of environmental trends on the industry's growth and the likelihood that Winnebago would continue to be its leader. The dimensions of such a market appraisal would be demographic, economic, social, regulatory,

(2)

and competitive. Based on the preceding brief description, which of the trends cited would you associate with each of these dimensions of the marketing en-

(3)

vironment? How would you expect each of these to affect the future de-

(4)

mand for Winnebago motor homes? On the basis of this analysis, would you buy Winnebago's stock at $5 per share, or $6\frac{1}{2}$ times its most recent annual earnings?

The motor home story serves to illustrate the dimensions of the marketing environment that are of importance to the practicing manager, the focus of this chapter.

dimensions of the marketing environment

Of the residents of Miami Beach, Florida, roughly 50 per cent were over the age of sixty-five in 1972; Florida led all other states in the proportion of its residents over the age of sixty-five with 14.5 per cent. These facts represent measurements of the marketing environment along the demographic dimension. In that same year, the average gross national product (GNP) for each American was about $5,000, compared to about $1,500 for each Russian, and a little more than $200 for each Egyptian. These are economic measures. Furthermore, the average work week for Americans employed in manufacturing activities was 40.6 hours in 1972, a social measure of the marketing environment. The year was noted for a number of pieces of legislation significantly affecting the demand for, and the marketing of, a number of products and services, including nursing home care, home protection devices, and automobile insurance, examples of the importance of the regulatory dimension of the environment. Dun & Bradstreet reported that the business births exceeded business deaths, a gross measure of the competitive dimension of the environment.

We'll look at each of these in turn, focusing on their possible meanings for the marketing manager.

the demographic dimension

Several years ago, the H. J. Heinz Company introduced a special line of "senior foods"; a representative of General Motors indicated that the company probably would be making fewer station wagons in the future; the Gerber Products Co. ceased to publicize the motto that "Babies are our only business"; and several toy manufacturers announced plans to diversify into "less seasonal" products. How would you associate these actions with the information shown in Figure 3-1 and Table 3-1?

(5)

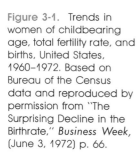

Figure 3-1. Trends in women of childbearing age, total fertility rate, and births, United States, 1960–1972. Based on Bureau of the Census data and reproduced by permission from "The Surprising Decline in the Birthrate," *Business Week*, (June 3, 1972) p. 66.

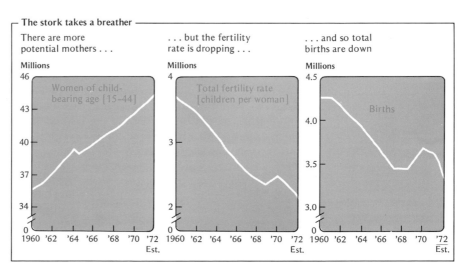

65

Table 3-1 **Trends in the Age Distribution of Population in the United States, 1950–1990***

Age Group	Percentage of Population In Each Age Group (by year)				
	1950	1960	1970	1980	1990
Under 5 years	10.8%	11.3%	8.4%	9.0%	8.3%
5–9	8.8	10.4	9.7	8.3	8.6
10–14	7.4	9.4	10.2	7.7	8.3
15–19	7.0	7.4	9.4	8.8	7.7
20–24	7.7	6.2	8.4	9.2	7.1
25–34	15.8	12.7	12.3	16.2	16.5
35–44	14.2	13.4	11.3	11.1	14.1
45–54	11.5	11.4	11.4	9.9	9.8
55–64	8.8	8.6	9.1	9.2	8.1
65 and over	8.1	9.2	9.8	10.4	11.0
Total, in percentages	100.0%a	100.0%	100.0%	100.0%	100.0%
Total, in thousands of people	152,271	180,667	204,800	227,765	251,431

* Source: *Statistical Abstract of the United States* (Washington, D. C.: Bureau of the Census, Department of Commerce, 1974), pp. 6–7. Projections for 1980 and 1990 are based on the assumptions that (1) annual net immigration will be 400,000, and (2) the average number of children per woman at the end of childbearing will be 2.11 (the so-called series E, or lowest, estimate).

aTotals may not add to 100.0 per cent because of rounding.

The Declining Birth Rate. Among other things, these companies all were reacting to one of the most striking demographic trends to develop among any of the world's nationalities in recent years: the decline in the number of children born to each woman between the ages of fifteen and forty-four in the United States by 45 per cent in just twelve years—from 3.8 in 1960 to 2.1 in 1972, graphed in Figure 3-1. Because of previously higher birth rates and the presence of a relatively high number of women of childbearing age in the population, it will take some time for the United States population to stabilize in size even at the present rates of change in family size. For example, even at a continuing rate of 2.1 births per woman of childbearing age—interestingly, the exact number of children per woman required to replace their parents' generation—it would take seventy years for the country to reach zero population growth. In contrast, the over-sixty-five group in the United States population is increasing twice as fast as those who are under sixty-five. It now spends two to three times as much for goods and services as the so-called youth market. What products and services other than foods, automobiles, and toys could these demographic trends affect significantly?

Clearly, demography, the science of vital statistics having to do with such things as births, deaths, diseases, and the location of members of a population, is of significance for marketing management. Are these statistics of greater importance for determining day-to-day actions or longer-term strategy?

(6)

(7)

66

Regionalization of Population.   Another factor of great potential interest to marketing managers is the location of population. Information in Figure 3-2 indicates the rate at which population in various regions of the United States has changed over the past forty years. It suggests why companies long since have structured marketing strategies to include the markets of the western states. Which region of the country shown in Figure 3-2 would you expect to have the highest rate of poulation growth during the decade of the 1970s?

If the percentages shown in Figure 3-2 are applied to the fact that the total population of the United States has grown from about 123 million in 1930 to about 205 million in 1970, it suggests that even the regions with the smallest proportion of total population have become markets capable of supporting the mass production of goods in economic manufacturing facilities. Furthermore, within various regions, continuous urban regions or "strip cities" have been formed by the growth of formerly separated cities, thus concentrating population even more. By 1970, the thirty three largest Standard Metropolitan Statistical Areas (SMSA),[2] those with more than one million persons, contained 57.9 per

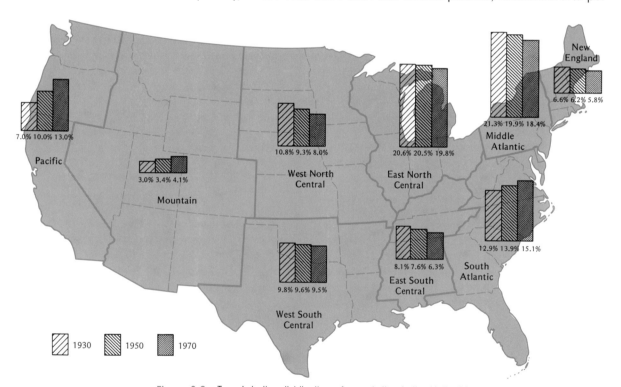

Figure 3-2. Trends in the distribution of population in the United States, 1930, 1950, and 1970. Percentages shown represent the proportion of the total United States population residing in each region for each year. Source: *Statistical Abstract of the United States* (Washington, D.C. Bureau of the Census, Department of Commerce, 1974).

[2]SMSA is defined by the Bureau of the Census as a county or group of contiguous counties with a total population of at least 100,000 and one or two central cities with a combined minimum population of 50,000.

cent of the total United States population. Thus, with the growth of regional markets, such patterns as the movement of freight transportation are changing in the country. For example, truck transportation, suitable to hauls of short, "regional" length, has increased much more rapidly than rail transportation, which is more economical for longer, interregional movements. In the past, many firms with manufacturing facilities in the East quoted "prices slightly higher west of the Rockies" on their products in order to defray additional freight costs of serving the western markets. Would you expect this practice to be increasing?

(9)

Concentration of Consumer Segments. Explanations for demographic phenomena may be more important than the mere facts themselves. For example, along with Florida, other states that have the highest proportion of their respective populations over sixty-five are Maine, Rhode Island, South Dakota, Nebraska, Iowa, and Missouri, as shown in Figure 3-3. Previously, it was suggested that one of the major markets for motor homes was among this group of potential buyers. With this in mind, in which of the preceding states would you concentrate new motor home dealerships if you were the marketing manager for a motor home manufacturer? Similarly, in which of the states would you want to concentrate your service and repair shops for such vehicles? Figure

(10)

(11)

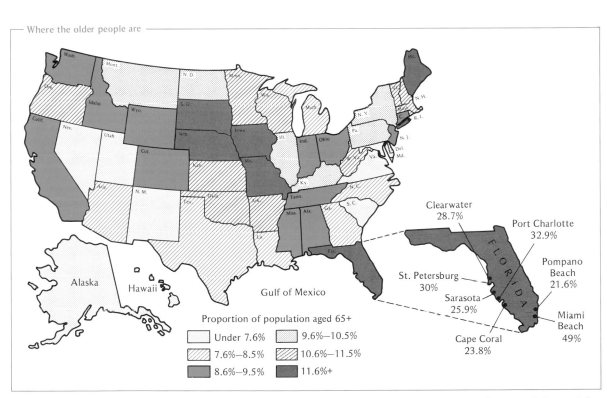

Figure 3-3. Relative proportions of people over age sixty-five in the populations of the individual states of the United States, 1970. Reproduced by permission from "The Power of the Aging in the Marketplace," *Business Week*, (Nov. 20, 1971) p. 57.

3-3 contains interesting information, but the development of more effective marketing plans requires an understanding of why patterns have developed as they have.

Urbanization.   Other trends of interest in the location of population have included the relative concentration of people in urban, suburban, and rural areas. These trends, shown in Figure 3-4 for the last twenty years, of course emphasize the fact that a sizeable number of people have left rural locations for urban and suburban residences. They suggest as well that the rate of growth in urban populations has been less than that for suburban locations.

General trends in the location of population on a regional, urban, or some other basis disguise the fact that what we see in Figures 3-2, 3-3, and 3-4 is the net result of a number of often offsetting interregional and rural-suburban-urban migrations. For example, the composition of the population of New York has changed markedly as migrants from Puerto Rico and other rural areas have moved into the city at the same time that many former residents have moved to the suburbs. Simultaneously, other couples, their families grown and away from home, have begun moving back to certain city centers in order to enjoy the cultural and other benefits of a metropolitan location. On balance, families and individuals with lower incomes have become more predominant in city-center populations. This has been of great significance to businesses oriented to city centers.

For example, over a number of years, the nation's largest retailer of foods, A&P, operated more than four-thousand retail outlets, nearly all of them located in city centers. As A&P's former customers moved to the suburbs, the company steadfastly maintained its existing retailing locations. As the grocery retailing business increasingly became a business oriented around the larger supermarket

Figure 3-4. Trends in the concentration of population in urban, suburban, and rural areas, United States, 1950–1970. Source: *Statistical Abstract of the United States* (Washington, D.C.: Department of Commerce, Bureau of the Census, 1974), p. 17. (Note: According to the 1970 census definition, the urban population comprised all persons in incorporated and unincorporated cities, villages, boroughs, and towns with 2,500 inhabitants or more. Slightly different definitions were used for the 1950 and 1960 census.)

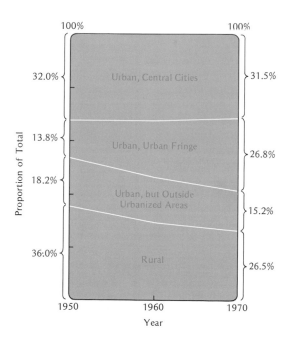

69

with high sales volume and rapid inventory turnover, A&P continued to operate stores of modest size. The buying behavior of city-center residents is, of necessity, oriented to the purchase of items in small quantities. How would you expect these trends to affect the operating performance for A&P? Now that its former competition has located its supermarkets in the most favorable suburban locations, often shopping centers, what strategy alternatives are open to A&P? What would you suggest it do?

Population Mobility. Residents of the United States are the most mobile on earth. On the average, one in five families moves during a given year. This, too, obscures the fact that mobility is concentrated among smaller "restless" segments of the population. For example, more than half of all persons five years old and over in 1970 lived at the same address they had five years previously. These facts are of great significance to business.

Studies have shown that a family in the process of moving from one location to another is especially prone to changes in its spending patterns, changes in the products and services it purchases, and even brand-switching among products. Furthermore, a large proportion of families on the move are those whose breadwinners are associated with middle-management levels of American business. As such, they are relatively affluent. Do these findings suggest to you the basis for creating a valuable service to companies marketing their products and services on a regional basis, or for companies with national marketing strategies introducing new products from time to time? What form might this service take?

family life cycles

Families experience life cycles, defined in terms of the stages shown in Figure 3-5. Reduced to a working level for practical use, profiles of family life cycles assist in the understanding of consumer behavior.

Those who have studied family life cycles have established predominant buying patterns for families at each stage in the cycle. The level and proportions of family income spent for various categories of goods and services may change significantly during the family life cycle.

For example, with increasing emphasis on preschool training or activity for small children, educational expenses for families at the full-nest 1 stage have risen. Although such expenditures for the next stage are moderate, given the widespread availability of public education, they rise for the family at the full-nest 3 stage—the family with children in public or private universities. It is in the later years of full-nest 3 and the early years of empty nest 1 that educational expenditures recede and are directed primarily toward the retraining of the senior female member of the family.

How would you expect the proportions of expenditures for other basic commodities such as food, medical care, and recreation to vary as a family passes through its life cycle? You may want to check your preconceptions

70

Figure 3-5. Stages in
family life cycles, defined
in terms adapted from
those established by the
Survey Research Center of
The University of Michigan,
Ann Arbor.

	Stage Number	Stage Name	Stage Description
Younger	1.	Single breadwinner	Young, single
Average Age of the Head of the Household	2.	Newly married couples	Limited to those with no children
	3.	Full nest I	Limited to families with youngest child under six
	4.	Full nest II	Families with the youngest child between six and high school graduation
	5.	Full nest III	Includes older married couples with dependent children
	6.	Empty nest I	Comprising older married couples with no children living with them but with breadwinner still in the labor force
	7.	Empty nest II	Older married couples with no children living with them and with breadwinners retired
	8.	Solitary survivors I	Older single people still in the labor force
Older	9.	Solitary survivors II	Older single people retired

(18) against the information shown in Table 3-2. In doing so, note that this information is based on a survey of a cross section of families at one point in time. What difference would this make for the purpose for which you are using the information?

Studies of consumer behavior suggest that the family life cycle can be used to organize our understanding not only of *what* people buy at various points in time, but also of *how* they make such purchases. For example, several studies have suggested that young newlyweds facing the need to equip a new household tend to buy a houseful of furniture at moderate prices, often buying suites (matched sets) for various rooms of the house, and relying heavily on relatives, friends, and information provided by salesmen and advertising to make the "right" style and color decisions. Often, families do not enter the market for medium- to higher-priced furniture until they reach the full-nest 3 or empty-nest 1 stages. At this time, prospective furniture buyers often have less pressure on them to make a decision, are more confident about their ability to make the right decisions concerning style and color, often are less concerned about matching sets of furniture, and buy more of it on a "one piece at a time" basis. Still, buyers may lack a great deal of knowledge at these stages because they may not have bought much furniture for many years.

(19) How could you use research information such as that in Table 3-2 in connection with demographic data generated by the census of population every ten years, which includes information about age, marital status, size of family, location, income, and the like? This perhaps suggests the greatest practical contribution of family life-cycle theories.

Table 3-2 **Proportions of Income Spent for Various Categories of Goods and Services at Different Stages of the Family Life Cycle***

| | | Stage in Life Cycles | | | | | |
| | | Families with Children Under 6 | | Families with All Children Over 6 | | Families with No Children | |
Item	Total	All Under 6	Some Under 6	All 6 to 11	Any 12 or Over	Husband and Wife	Other
Share of							
All families	100.0%	12.7%	14.5%	4.6%	25.7%	24.1%	18.4%
Total expenditures	100.0	13.3	17.1	5.4	33.4	21.3	9.5
Average family size	3.2	3.6	5.5	3.7	4.1	2.1	1.2
Expenditures for current consumption[a]							
Food	24%	22%	27%	24%	25%	23%	24%
Alcoholic beverages	2	1	1	2	2	2	2
Tobacco	2	2	2	2	2	2	2
Housing and household operations	24	26	24	23	21	25	31
House furnishings and equipment	5	7	5	5	5	6	4
Clothing and accessories	10	9	11	11	12	8	8
Transportation	15	16	14	15	15	16	12
Medical care	7	7	6	6	6	8	7
Personal care	3	3	3	3	3	3	3
Recreation and equipment	4	4	4	5	4	3	3
Reading and education	2	1	2	2	3	1	2
Other expenditures	2	1	2	2	3	2	2

* Source: Adapted from Fabian Linden, ed., *Expenditure Patterns of the American Family* (New York: National Industrial Conference Board, 1965), p. 17.

[a]Expenditures for current consumption represent the cost of all goods and services (including finance charges and sales taxes) for family living that were bought during the survey year, even if payments were not completed during that year. Durable goods such as automobiles and household equipment were considered as consumption items, but purchases and sales of homes and outlays for improvements represent changes in assets and are not included. Family expenditures for items used partially for business, such as the home or car, were adjusted to exclude the amount chargeable to business use.

the economic dimension

The combination of demographic and economic information can produce further insights into the structure of a market. For example, in 1970 there were approximately 205 million people in the United States. Of greater economic significance is the fact that they were distributed among nearly 63 million households, each comprising a housing unit representing separate living quarters. Because purchasing patterns vary less between households than between individuals, the household typically is of greater interest for marketing management. (Why is this the case?)

(20)

Personal Income. Of greater significance yet is the fact that in 1970 these 62.9 million households realized a total personal income (the income received by persons from all sources net of contributions for social insurance) of $803 billion, or $12,439 per spending unit. Not all of this money was available for immediate expenditures. For example, 14.4 per cent of it was paid out (or deducted in advance) for such items as income and other taxes. The remainder, or $10,650 per household, is referred to as disposable personal income.

In addition, families may save some portion of their incomes. In 1970, the rate of saving approximated 6.7 per cent of personal income, or an average of $830 per household. At the same time, families paid interest on money borrowed in the amount of $17.9 billion, or $270 per household. The remaining amount, $615.8 billion, or $9,550 per household, represented personal consumption expenditures in 1970. This is documented in Table 3-3, along with a list of items for which personal consumption expenditures were made.

Expenditure Patterns. As shown in Table 3-3, the largest single category of expenses for households as a group in 1970 was food, for which $114.0 billion, or $1,810 per household, was spent during the year. Other major items, in order of importance, included housing, transportation, clothing, medical care, furniture, and household operations. Which of the relationships between amounts shown in Table 3-3 are surprising to you?

(21)

It is logical to expect the types of goods and services for which expenditures were made to vary from spending unit to spending unit, depending on their location and income levels, among other factors. For example, results from one study of the spending patterns of United States families according to income levels are shown in Table 3-4 along with the size of the family in each category. In looking at Table 3-4, why does the proportion of expenditures made for food decline for families with higher incomes? Why do other expenditures show increases, as proportions of the total, with increases in family incomes?

(22)
(23)

The first widely reported studies of consumer behavior were conducted in 1857 by a German statistician named Ernst Engel. As a result of his work, he was able to make several observations that have come to be known as Engel's laws. Paraphrased to some extent, they suggested that families with higher incomes tend to spend for current consumption (1) more money in absolute terms, (2) a smaller proportion of their total expenditures for food, (3) roughly the same proportion of their total expenditures for housing and household operations, and (4) a higher proportion of total expenditures for such items as clothing, transportation, recreation, health, and education, in comparison to families with lower incomes. Furthermore, families with higher incomes were observed to save more. How do Engel's laws compare with the data shown in Table 3-4? Are differences explained by changing conditions between the Germany of 1857 and the United States of 1960 and 1961 (when the survey shown in Table 3-4 was actually taken)?

(24)
(25)

The dollar amounts that the figures in Table 3-4 represent may be of significance to companies providing goods and services to the United States market. For example, if we translate the percentage for expenditures for recreation and equipment by families with incomes of $15,000 and over into a dollar amount, it comes to $597 per year. Of what significance would this be to a manufacturer of motor homes planning to sell its product for from $9,000 to $13,000 per unit?

(26)

Expenditure Patterns and Buyer Psychology. The level of expenditures by consumers for end-use products (products not purchased for resale or other

Table 3-3 **Profile of GNP, Income, and Expenditures, United States, 1970***

	Total (in dollars)	Per Person	Per Household	As % of Personal Income
GNP	974.1 billion			
Less capital consumption, indirect business taxes, and other items	(178.2 billion)			
National income	795.9 billion			
Less corporate profits and contributions for social insurance	(128.4 billion)			
Plus government payments for salaries, interest, and other items to persons, and corporate dividends	136.2 billion			
Personal income	803.6 billion	$3,920	$12,760	100.0
Less personal taxes and other payments	(115.9 billion)	570	1,840	(14.4)
Disposable personal income	687.8 billion	$3,350	$10,920	85.6
Less net personal savings	(54.1 billion)	260	850	(6.7)
Less interest paid and transfers	(17.9 billion)	90	290	(2.2)
Personal consumption expenditures	615.8 billion	$3,000	$ 9,780	76.7

	Total (in dollars)	Per Person	Per Family	As % of Personal Consumption Expenditures
Personal consumption expenditures for				
Food	114.0 billion	$ 555	$ 1,810	18.5
Alcoholic beverages	17.7	86	280	2.9
Tobacco	11.2	55	179	1.8
Clothing, accessories, and jewelry	62.3	304	991	10.1
Personal care	10.1	49	160	1.6
Housing	91.2	445	1,451	14.8
Furniture, equipment, and household supplies	43.3	210	684	7.0
Household operations (utilities & services)	42.3	206	672	7.0
Medical care expenses	47.3	230	750	7.7
Personal business	35.5	173	564	5.8
Transportation	77.9	380	1,238	12.6
Recreation	39.0	190	618	6.3
Private education and research	10.4	51	166	1.7
Religious and welfare activities	8.8	43	140	1.4
Foreign travel and other	4.8	23	75	.8
	615.8 billion	$3,000[a]	$9,780[a]	100.0[a]

* Source: "Survey of Current Business" (Washington, D. C.: Bureau of the Census, Department of Commerce, Feb. 1972), pp. 11–12.

[a] Totals may not add exactly because of rounding.

business purposes) is an important determinant of the level of economic activity. In particular, discretionary (postponable) expenditures for products that meet other than basic needs are more important in the United States than in other countries where the proportion of income spent is not as high. The United States economy rises or falls, so to speak, on the level and pattern of discretionary spending by its citizens. For this reason, a great deal of effort has been

74

Table 3-4   **Average Annual Family Expenditures by Family Income, 1965***

Item	Total	Family Income before Taxes					
		Under $3,000	$3,000– 5,000	$5,000– 7,500	$7,500– 10,000	$10,000– 15,000	$15,000 and over
Per cent distribution of							
All families	100.0%	22.4%	20.8%	26.2%	16.1%	10.7%	3.7%
Total expenditures	100.0	8.9	15.6	27.1	21.2	18.0	9.1
Average persons per family	3.2	2.1	3.0	3.5	3.7	3.9	3.8
Expenditures for items of current consumption[a]	$5,152	$2,043	$3,859	$5,315	$6,788	$8,679	$12,687
Proportion of expenditures for							
Food	24.4%	29.4%	26.3%	24.8%	23.9%	22.7%	20.1%
Alcoholic beverages	1.6	1.0	1.4	1.5	1.7	1.8	1.9
Tobacco	1.8	2.1	2.2	2.0	1.8	1.5	1.1
Housing and household operations	24.0	30.4	25.1	23.8	23.0	21.8	23.7
House furnishings and equipment	5.2	4.1	4.8	5.3	5.6	5.5	5.5
Clothing and accessories	10.2	7.1	9.0	9.9	10.6	11.6	12.3
Transportation	15.1	8.6	14.5	15.9	16.1	16.7	14.9
Medical care	6.6	8.5	7.0	6.6	6.3	6.2	6.1
Personal care	2.9	3.0	3.1	2.9	2.9	2.8	2.5
Recreation and equipment	4.0	2.4	3.4	3.8	4.3	5.7	4.7
Reading and education	1.9	1.3	1.4	1.7	1.9	2.5	3.5
Other expenditures	2.2	2.3	1.8	1.8	2.2	2.3	4.0
Totals	100.0%[b]	100.0%[b]	100.0%[b]	100.0%[b]	100.0%[b]	100.0%[b]	100.0%[b]

* Sources: Fabian Linden, ed., *Expenditure Patterns of the American Family* and *Market Profiles of Consumer Products* (New York: National Industrial Conference Board, 1965 and 1967, respectively).

[a]Expenditures for current consumption represent the cost of all goods and services (including finance charges and sales taxes) for family living that were bought during the survey year, whether or not payments were completed during that year. Durable goods such as automobiles and household equipment were considered consumption items, but purchases and sales of homes and outlays for improvements represent changes in assets and are not included. Family expenditures for items used partially for business, such as the home or car, were adjusted to exclude the amount chargeable to business use.

[b]Totals may not add to 100.0 per cent because of rounding.

expended to determine the reasons why people make purchases when they do. One of the most reliable predictors is the Index of Consumer Sentiment developed by the Survey Research Center of the University of Michigan. The basic philosophy underlying the Index of Consumer Sentiment is that consumers' discretionary demand is a function of both ability to buy and willingness to buy. Based on quarterly interviews in about 1,300 homes, the index has linked future expenditure patterns, particularly for so-called big-ticket, durable goods such as automobiles, to consumers' optimism or concern about the environment in which they live.

The Survey Research Center has found that persons delay making expenditures for durable goods when they are pessimistic about their individual economic futures. On the other hand, if pessimism stems from a concern about inflation and future higher prices for goods and services, this can stimulate current buying to beat further price increases. Such was the case in early 1973, when concerned consumers pushed prices even higher in an effort to buy goods and services in advance of higher expected prices.

It is interesting that George Katona, the architect of the index, relates the high rate of expenditure to personal income in the United States to the relatively high level of long-range optimism about the future among American consumers. For example, working with two associates, he found recently that

> Close to two thirds of the many Americans who have experienced improvement in their financial situation over the past few years expect it to continue in the future. Only one third of the Germans, French, and Dutch think that their progress will continue, although they, too, have enjoyed substantial and steady improvement in the past.[3]

(27)
(28)
At the present time, how would you characterize the buying intentions for durable goods, including appliances and automobiles, of those you know? Could you explain these intentions in terms of expectations about the future?

The Use of Credit. A basic optimism about the future is cited as a contributing factor to the willingness of United States consumers to borrow for current expenditures. For example, it has been found that about one half of all Americans both approve of and use installment credit. Lower proportions of approval and use of credit are found among consumers of Western European countries. Among these groups, Germans represent the extreme, with only one fourth approving of the use of credit and only about 10 per cent actually making use of it. In fact, the German word for debt, *schuld,* is the same as the (29) word for guilt.[4] Do you think the two meanings of *schuld* reflect an old-fashioned, outmoded philosophy?

The Trend Toward Services. The composition of the United States work force both reflects past trends and provides implications for the future for marketing management. For example, if there is any doubt that the United States represents a postindustrial society, in which nonindustrial jobs, such as service-oriented occupations, grow at a much faster rate than industrial jobs, it should be dispelled by the trends in employment shown in Figure 3-6. Here, we see that the proportion of people employed in service and trade (including retailing and wholesaling) has increased at a much faster rate than that for manufacturing. All have grown at the expense of extractive occupations such as farming, mining, and fishing.

In total, the value of services produced (including government) constituted 64.5 per cent of the GNP (the value of all goods and services produced) in the United States in 1970. Putting it another way, the value of manufactured goods produced in the United States is barely one half the value of services, and it is declining in importance from year to year.

Employment Trends. The number of women entering the work force has increased at a much faster rate than that for men. For example, between 1960 and 1971, the number of women in the work force increased 38.8 per cent, from 23.2 million to 32.1 million. That of men increased 12.1 per cent, from

---

[3] George Katona, Burkhard Strumpel, and Ernest Zahn, *Aspirations and Affluence* (New York: McGraw-Hill, 1971), pp. 3 and 48–49.

[4] "Why Consumers Buy—or Hoard," *Business Week,* (Feb. 13, 1971), p. 54.

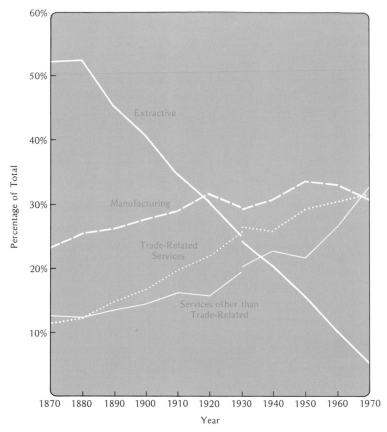

Figure 3-6. Trends of employment in manufacturing, extractive industries, trade, and services, United States, 1870–1972. Each category is stated as a percentage of the total employment allocated to all groups. Extractive occupations include agriculture, forestry, mining, and fishing. Manufacturing occupations include manufacturing and contract building construction. Trade-related occupations include wholesaling and retailing, finance, real estate, transportation, and other public utilities. Service occupations, other than those of a trade-related nature, include education, other professions, domestic services, personal services, and government. Source: *Survey of Current Business and Historical Statistics of the United States* (Washington, D.C.: Department of Commerce, Office of Business and Economics, Jan. 1973 and 1960 respectively), pp. 5–13 and 74, respectively. Note: The break in the trend lines at 1930 indicates a change in the estimating method at that time.

48.9 million to 54.8 million. This remarkable increase in women in the working force took place during a period of rapidly rising incomes in the United States, suggesting that large numbers of women are taking jobs for reasons other than economic survival. Of what significance would this be to a marketing manager responsible for the long-range planning for a chain of neighborhood, low-budget restaurants? Or a home-delivery service for groceries purchased by telephone from a catalog revised weekly?

Major factors in the importance of the United States among the world's markets are its size and the buying power per capita of its citizens. In Table 3-4 the populations, per capita incomes, and the relative rates of consumption

Table 3-5   Demographic, Economic, and Social Indicators for Selected Nations of the World*

Item	Country							
	Brazil	Canada	Egypt	France	India	Japan	U.S.	U.S.S.R.
Demographic								
Population, mid-1970 (in thousands)	95,305	21,848 (1972)	33,329	50,777	537,047	103,386	204,800	242,768
Annual rate of population increase	3.2%	1.6% (1972)	2.5%	.9%	2.1%	1.1%	1.1%	1.1%
Number of households (in thousands)	19,104	5,589 (1966)	1,992 (1960)	14,562 (1968)	83,523	24,687 (1968)	62,874	n.a.[a]
Average number of people per household	4.8	3.7 (1966)	4.8 (1960)	3.1 (1968)	5.2	3.9 (1968)	3.2	n.a.[a]
Average number of people per square mile	11	2	33	93	164	280	22	11
Proportion of people living in urban areas	n.a.	92.2%	42.1%	70.0%	n.a.	72.2%	73.5%	56.3%
Economic								
Per capita average annual rate of growth of gross domestic product	2.7% (1965–1968)	4.0% (1963–1971)	.4% (1965–1969)	4.9% (1965–1970)	n.a.	11.5% (1965–1969)	2.2% (1965–1970)	n.a.
Energy consumption, in kilograms per person	472	10,757	268	3,794	191	3,210	11,144	4,445
Number of people per tractor	1,003	34	2,081	41	993	831	43	386
Social								
Average weekly hours of work in manufacturing	48	39.7	49.0 (1967)	44.8	n.a.	43.3	39.8	40.5
Number of people per passenger car	48	3	254	4	886	12	2	n.a.
Number of people per telephone	48	2	92	6	458	4	2	22
Number of people per teacher (all levels)	131	81	199	91	268	101	90[b]	82
Expectation of life at birth, in years (for men and women)	60.7[c] (1965–1970)	69–75 (1965–1967)	51.6–53.8 (1960)	67.6–75.3 (1969)	41.9–40.6 (1951–1960)	69.0–74.3 (1968)	70.8[c] (1970)	65–74 (1968–1969)

* Unless indicated otherwise, the statistics shown are for the year 1970. Source: 1973 *United Nations Statistical Yearbook* (New York: United Nations, 1974).

[a] Not available.

[b] Does not include university teachers.

[c] Both sexes.

78

(32)

of energy for selected nations of the world are compared, along with other selected data about each. Looking at Table 3-5, how would you expect the average family size in various countries to affect their respective growth rates in the future for population, per capita income, and economic indicators?

the social dimension

Social trends help to explain demographic trends, and indirectly affect the economic performance of a country. They reflect a nation's culture, defined years ago by cultural historian Edward B. Taylor as "that complex whole which includes knowledge, belief, art, morals, law, custom, and any other capabilities and habits acquired by man as a member of society."[5]

Figure 3-7. Average weekly hours worked by production workers in selected occupations, 1930–1970. Sources: *Statistical Abstract of the United States* and *Historical Statistics of the United States* (Washington, D.C.: Department of Commerce, Bureau of the Census, 1974 and 1960, respectively).

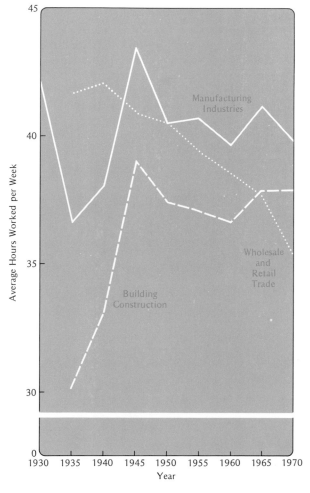

[5] Edward B. Taylor, *Primitive Culture* (London: J. Murray, 1871), p. 1.

Social indicators reflecting the way of life in several countries of the world are presented in Table 3-5. They suggest, for example, that even though the number of telephones and automobiles per person, educational opportunities, and other measures of social development for United States residents are much higher than for residents of most other countries, the length of life expectation at birth is significantly lower than that for other well-developed economies.

(33)
(34)
Which of these social trends and indicators seems most remarkable to you? Which of them do you think holds the greatest long-term significance for the future standard of living in the United States?

Figures 3-7 through 3-9 document several social trends in recent years in the United States. They suggest that, among other things, since 1945 the length of the work week has become shorter; the level of education (measured by the number of years the average individual spends in formal education) has increased; and the proportion of total expenditures of the federal, state, and local governments devoted to education and public welfare has increased while that devoted to natural resources and space research and technology has declined.

(35)
Of what importance would the trends suggested by Tables 3-1 and 3-5 and Figures 3-7 through 3-9 have for International Latex Corp., a manufacturer of
(36)
(37)
(38)
ladies' undergarments? For Club Méditerranée, an organization offering low-cost travel to various resorts around the world? For the further development of shopping centers as opposed to neighborhood stores? For the operator of a chain of franchised preschool play-learning centers for three- to five-year-old children?

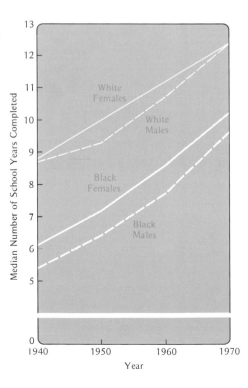

Figure 3-8. Median school years completed by persons twenty-five years old and over, by sex and race, United States, 1940–1970. Source: *Statistical Abstract of the United States* and *Historical Statistics of the United States* (Washington, D.C.: Department of Commerce, Bureau of the Census, 1974), p. 116.

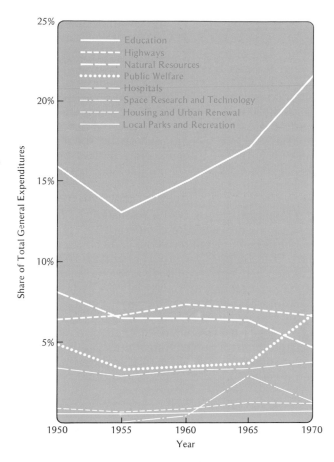

Figure 3-9. Trends in the share of general expenditures of federal, state, and local governments spent for selected socially oriented programs, United States, 1950–1970. Source: *Statistical Abstract of the United States* (Washington, D.C.: Department of Commerce, Bureau of the Census, 1974), p. 246.

Legend (chart):
— Education
----- Highways
— — Natural Resources
••••••• Public Welfare
– – Hospitals
–·–·– Space Research and Technology
- - - - Housing and Urban Renewal
—— Local Parks and Recreation

Y-axis: Share of Total General Expenditures — 5%, 10%, 15%, 20%, 25%
X-axis: Year — 1950, 1955, 1960, 1965, 1970

the regulatory dimension

In December 1972, the U. S. Center for Disease Control imposed regulations on the sale of live turtles based on evidence that such pets were carriers of salmonella poisoning for humans. In the following months, the center urged the public to stop buying pet turtles. Overnight, this action virtually eliminated the market for the leading "shut-up" pet sold by the nation's largest supplier of live pets, the Hartz Mountain Industries, Inc.; the situation is described here by the company's president:

> A kid goes into a store and says, 'I want a pet.' The mother says, 'Shut-up.' The kid says, 'But I want a pet.' The mother says, 'OK, we'll get you a turtle.' (Although Hartz's turtle business has collapsed, hamsters are replacing turtles as shut-up pets. Hartz hamsters not only sell for far more money than Hartz turtles, but also eat several times more Hartz pet foods.)[6]

[6] Roger Ricklets, "How Hartz Mountain Corp. Makes a Bundle Selling Canaries and Dog Yummies and Stuff Like That," *Wall Street Journal,* (June 21, 1973), p. 40.

When the Food and Drug Administration (FDA) invoked a ban on the sale of products sweetened with cyclamates in October 1969, it foreclosed the annual sale of about $34 million in cyclamates and such items as cyclamate-sweetened diet cola, worth about $300 million annually at wholesale prices. Ironically, findings of the study leading to the ban conducted for Abbott Laboratories, the largest United States cyclamate producer, by an independent research laboratory, have since been contradicted by more extensive tests. This led to the speculation that the original ban subsequently may be lifted.

These are two specific examples of the immediate effect that the enforcement of government regulation may have on the marketing of products and services. Of more long-term importance are those landmark laws that set limits on corporate strategy and marketing alternatives. They are outlined in Table 3-6.

(39) Dominant themes in the regulation of business practice in this country concern the protection of competitors or consumers. They stem from a strong emphasis on competition as the cornerstone of a free enterprise economy and the protection of competitors, particularly smaller or less able ones, as a necessary step in the preservation of competition. As you look over Table 3-6, which of the important pieces of legislation listed there reflect the philosophy of "let the buyer beware" or "let the seller beware"?

As a seller, of what regulation must you be beware? The Interstate Commerce Act in 1887 created the first major caveats by restricting railroad marketing managers from offering different prices to various customers for similar services provided under essentially similar conditions. Through the years, various pieces of legislation have been enacted to restrict practices of importance for product and product-line development, pricing, distribution channel relationships, and promotional practices.

Product and Product-Line Development. New products or processes can be patented by the Federal Patent Office to be protected from copying by would-be competitors for seventeen years. Similarly, copyrights are granted to authors, song writers, and others for essentially the same purpose. This protection, made possible by Article I, Section 8 of the Constitution, is intended "to promote the progress of science and useful arts, by securing for limited times to authors and inventors the exclusive right to their respective writings and discoveries." It rewards innovators by giving them a head start in the commercialization of their ideas.

Product-line development by means of merger or acquisition subjects a company to scrutiny under provisions of the Sherman Antitrust Act, the Clayton Act, and the Antimerger Act, all essentially intended to preserve competition by preserving competitors and preventing the concentration of an industry's business in the hands of a few firms. Product contents and product-labeling practices are controlled in various industries by pieces of legislation as diverse as the Federal Food and Drug Act and the Federal Cigarette Labeling and Advertising Act. Production processes themselves can be controlled by legislation for which the Meat Inspection Act of 1906 can provide the model. And, to an increasing extent, nonfood and nondrug items may be banned from the market, as was the case with toys considered to be dangerous under the Toy Safety Act of 1972.

Looking to the future, there is every indication that legislation will be passed converting the basic weights and measures in the United States to the metric system. Not only will this measure force companies to change product design features ranging from the threads on bolts to the measures used for package sizes, but it will allow firms selling products in multinational markets to standardize their products on one system of weights and measures.

Pricing. With the Interstate Commerce Act as a model, legislators have, in a number of ways, restricted pricing practices, typically when such practices would tend to substantially lessen competition and create a monopoly. The Sherman Act of 1890 dealt with conspiracy to control prices. And with prohibitions against discriminatory pricing practices not supported by differential costs raised in the Clayton Act (1914), and especially in the Robinson-Patman Act of 1936, pricing freedom has been restricted. Does this legislation benefit competitors or consumers? Furthermore, in certain states, would-be price-discounting retailers may be prevented from selling "fair-traded" merchandise at other than manufacturer-suggested prices by the Miller-Tydings and McGuire Acts of 1937 and 1952, respectively. More recently, emergency federal price controls have been imposed for the first time since World War II.

Channel Relationships. Marketing managers for products or services sold in interstate commerce have been prevented from (1) requiring the exclusive purchase of all of a customer's goods from a single source or (2) offering a noncost-justified price incentive to encourage a trade customer to do so. The former was prohibited by the writers of the Sherman Act, who were concerned about conspiracies to control distribution channels; the latter is forbidden under the Clayton Act (1914). Marketing managers are prohibited from offering promotional support, such as money for advertising or product display or demonstration, to wholesale or retail customers on a discriminatory basis not justified by cost differences under the ever-present and important Robinson-Patman Act (1936). They have, under the Antimerger Act of 1950, been prevented from buying companies with which they do or could deal, where such purchases would substantially lessen competition. In certain industries, such as under the Auto Dealers' Act of 1956, they have been restrained from imposing specific sanctions on customers, sanctions often designed to force customers to refrain from carrying competing products.

Beginning in 1953, a Uniform Commercial Code began to be adopted and used by various states. The code resulted from a review and synthesis of laws pertaining to commercial transactions in the various states of the United States. Developed by the National Council of Commissioners on Uniform State Laws and the American Law Institute, and adopted by the legislatures of forty-nine states, the Uniform Commercial Code has become perhaps the most useful piece of legislation of all in facilitating the transfer of goods and services from sellers to buyers. It sets forth practical uniform statutory provisions for a wide range of commercial activity, including sales contracts, title, warranties, various practices for financing exchange, physical transfer, and bills of lading provided by transport carriers to shippers. On the subject of warranties alone, for example, provisions of the Uniform Commercial Code include warranty—that is, guarantee by the seller—(1) of title, (2) that goods sold by description are

(40)

Table 3-6 **The Regulatory Dimension in the Marketing Environment, as Reflected in Important Pieces of Legislation**

Name of Legislation	Nature of Legislation	Parties Protected	Protected from
Art. I, Sec. 8 of the Constitution (1776)	Protected writings and inventions for limited periods of time to encourage "the progress of science and useful arts"	Authors and inventors	Would-be copiers
Interstate Commerce Act (1887) and Elkins Act (1903)	The first federal regulation of interstate commerce; outlawed rebates and special concessions and set forth penalties for discriminatory practice and the quotation of rates other than those in published tariffs by transportation firms, especially railroads	Farmers and other shippers Railroads	Discriminatory railroad pricing practices Illegal pricing practices of other railroads
Sherman Antitrust Act (1890)	Prohibited "monopolies or attempts to monopolize" and various actions, including "contracts, combinations, or conspiracies" intended to restrain trade	Small competitors	Large competitors with actual or attempted monopolies
Federal Food and Drug Act (1906)	Made unlawful the manufacture, sale, or transport of adulterated or misleadingly labeled foods and drugs in interstate commerce	Consumers	Illegal production and labeling practices of manufacturers, wholesalers and retailers of foods and drugs
Meat Inspection Act (1906)	Facilitated the federal inspection and enforcement of standards for sanitary conditions in processing plants packing meat for shipment in interstate commerce	Consumers	Unsanitary processing practices of meat processors
Federal Trade Commission Act (1914)	Facilitated the enforcement of antitrust matters by creating a body, the Federal Trade Commission (FTC), with powers to require offenders to cease and desist from "unfair methods of competition"	Consumers, competitors	Unfair competitive practices, such as deceptive advertising and pricing and unfair distribution policies
Clayton Act (1914)	Broadened the scope of the Sherman Act to prohibit practices "where the effect may be to substantially lessen competition or tend to create a monopoly," specifically citing such acts as price discrimination, forcing of the sale of some products with others (tying contracts), requirements of purchases from only one source, intercorporate stock holdings, and interlocking (overlapping) directorates	Competitors	Specific competitors' acts (such as price discrimination and exclusive dealing) intended to lessen competition

84

Legislation	Purpose	Who Is Protected	Who Is Regulated
Robinson-Patman Act (1936)	Prohibited specific trade practices where the effect might be "to substantially lessen competition or tend to create a monopoly" such as discriminating pricing practices and promotional allowances	Competing (typically smaller) manufacturers, wholesalers, and retailers	Competitors (typically larger) using discriminatory promotional allowances and price discounts not substantiated by cost differentials
Miller-Tydings Act (1937) and McGuire Act (1952)	Allowed manufacturers to sign resale price-fixing agreements with wholesalers and retailers in states permitting such agreements (in essence, exempting such agreements from antitrust legislation) and allowed manufacturers to enforce such agreements in states in which only one buyer had signed an agreement	Manufacturers, wholesalers, and nondiscounting retailers	Retailers offering price discounts against manufacturers' wishes
Wheeler-Lea Amendment (1938) to the Federal Trade Commission Act	Made possible prosecution for deceptive sales and advertising practices without proof of restrictions on competition under basic powers provided in the Federal Trade Commission Act	Consumers	Manufacturers, wholesalers, and retailers employing deceptive practices
		Consumers	Manufacturers, wholesalers, and retailers employing deceptive practices
Antimerger Act (1950)	Prohibited mergers that *might* substantially lessen competition, either horizontally (by acquiring competitors) or vertically (by acquiring channels of distribution used by competitors)	Competitors	Large competitors with *potential* (as opposed to actual or attempted) monopolies
Uniform Commercial Code (adopted by 49 states between 1953 and 1969)	Set forth a uniform set of rules of law regarding business transactions in the various states of the United States	All parties to business transactions	Fraudulent or illegal practices
Automobile Information Disclosure Act (1958)	Required the posting of prices for vehicles and accessories on each new automobile and truck	Consumers	Manufacturers' and dealers' misleading pricing of new automobiles and accessories
Federal Cigarette Labeling and Advertising Act (1967) and Public Health Cigarette Smoking Act (1971)	Required warnings regarding the effects of cigarette smoking to be placed on packages and prohibited the advertising of cigarettes on TV after January 1, 1971, respectively	Consumers	Manufacturers' failure to notify users about the harmful effects of, and TV advertising on behalf of, cigarette smoking
Consumer Credit Protection Act (1968)	Provides for full disclosure of the true interest rate charged for bank loans on trade credit	Consumers	Lenders' statements regarding the actual rate of interest on loans

as described, (3) that goods sold by sample conform to the sample, and (4) that goods intended for consumption are fit for consumption. Disputes concerning matters covered by the Uniform Commercial Code are decided in the courts of the state in which any offenses are alleged to have occurred.

Promotional Practices. Deceptive representation of products, services, or financing arrangements have been prohibited by legislation extending from the Federal Trade Commission Act of 1914 and the Wheeler-Lea Amendment to the act of 1938. In addition, a marketing manager can be prevented from making advertising claims that cannot be substantiated, even when such claims compare a product with unspecified competition. Or, as under the Public Health Cigarette Smoking Act of 1971, he or she may be prevented from using a certain medium (in the case of cigarettes, television) for advertising products.

The penalties for practices prohibited by legislation cited in Table 3-4 traditionally were quite light until, in an electrical industry price-conspiracy investigation, several marketing executives were handed jail sentences in 1961 and their companies forced to pay to complaining customers what may have exceeded $500 million in damages. More recently, more creative penalties have been enforced. For years, sponsors of misleading advertising were forced merely to withdraw such advertising by the FTC. In 1971, the first of several consent decrees was enforced by the commission requiring an advertiser to spend 25 per cent of its respective budget for a period of one year for ads designed to correct alleged misrepresentations.

In recent years, consumer spokesmen such as Action for Children's Television (ACT), Ralph Nader, Betty Furness, Esther Peterson, Bess Myerson Grant, and Virginia Knauer have worked hard for further legislation to provide consumer protection. In its first public policy stand, the board of directors of the leading United States association of professional marketers, the American Marketing Association, in 1972 voted overwhelmingly in favor of obligatory unit pricing (the statement of prices on a per pound as well as a per package basis) on grocery products in all large stores.[7] These forces, as well as sharply rising food prices, combined to make the supermarket the focal point of much of the consumer movement. Based on past experiences, this may well be an indicator of the type of legislation of greatest importance to marketing managers that we can expect in the near future. As a marketing manager in a potentially (41) affected company, assuming an ability to anticipate at least the general nature of upcoming legislation to regulate marketing practice, would you recommend that your firm (1) take steps to anticipate the legislation and alter its product, pricing, channel, or promotional policies to conform to expected legislation; (2) attempt to organize firms in the industry to do so; (3) wait until the legisla-(42) tion is passed before acting; (4) attempt to defeat the legislation; or (5) take some other course of action? If you find it difficult to answer these questions without knowing what the nature of the legislation might be, ask yourself the same questions about unit pricing under the assumption that you are a senior executive of a large supermarket chain responsible for the pricing of its products.

[7] Hans B. Thorelli, "AMA Board Approves Unit Pricing in Taking First Public Stand," *The Marketing News*, **5**:1, 7 (Aug. 1, 1972).

Admittedly, there is a confusing array of laws and regulatory policies of importance for marketing. As a general rule of thumb in our discussions, and as a practitioner of marketing, it is useful to assume that any marketing action intended to mislead customers or reduce competition or, in fact, having those effects, is in violation of one or more laws.

the competitive dimension

The overriding economic philosophy governing the attitude of the United States government toward business has been that of Adam Smith's reliance on "the unseen hand" of competition as the means to achieving the most efficient manufacture and distribution of goods responsive to customers' needs.[8] Government regulatory policy has stressed the need to preserve competition and often has pursued this objective by seeking to preserve competitors. It has done so by preventing larger companies from running their smaller competitors out of business by merger, acquisition, or marketing practices such as predatory pricing or disciminatory distribution.

What is competition? Agreeing on the need to preserve competition (at least among "the other guys") is one thing. Agreeing on what competition is, or how it is measured, is another. For example, the following have all been used as evidence of the presence of competition, or an atmosphere supportive of it, in various industries: (1) the presence of many firms, each with a small share of the market, as in the trucking industry; (2) the presence of only a few financially strong firms with somewhat equal marketing powers and abilities, as in the cereal manufacturing industry; (3) constantly fluctuating prices, hopefully reflecting changing relationships between demand and supply, as in the paper manufacturing industry; (4) identically priced bids by competitors for a major contract, as in the steel industry; and (5) constant entry and exit of firms from an industry, as in the retailing of most types of merchandise. Which of these, if any, appears to you to be the most logical measure of competition? Which might be the most workable measure for regulatory purposes?

Competition versus Concentration. The Department of Justice is charged with the enforcement of acts intended to prevent the substantial lessening of competition. It has turned to measures of industry structure, such as the number of competitors and the share of market concentrated in the hands of a few, as a means of detecting the actual or potential presence or absence of competition. Trends in the concentration of market share (and the accompanying lack of competition and need for Justice Department scrutiny that it represents) are shown for selected industries in Table 3-7. In which industries is competition, using measures of structure, most intense? What common characteristics do such industries possess? Which industries display trends toward more competition? What assumptions regarding the markets for various products (and,

---

[8] Adam Smith, *An Inquiry Into the Nature and Causes of the Wealth of Nations* (New York: Modern Library, 1937).

Table 3-7 Measures of Concentration in Selected Manufacturing Industries, 1947 and 1967*

SIC^a Code	Industry	1947			1967		
		Number of Companies	Value of Shipments (in $ millions)	Proportion of Industry Sales, Four Largest Companies (in %)	Number of Companies	Value of Shipments (in $ millions)	Proportion of Industry Sales, Four Largest Companies (in %)
2011	Meat-packing plants	1,999	977	41	2,529	2,220	26
2041	Flour and other grain mill products	1,084	2,526	29	438	2,457	30
2042	Prepared feeds for animals and fowls	2,372	2,112	19	1,835	4,797	23
2051	Bread, cake, and related products	5,985	2,404	16	3,445	5,103	26
2082	Malt liquors	404	1,316	21	125	2,930	40
2086	Bottled and canned soft drinks	5,169	748	10	3,057	3,173	13
2092	Soybean oil mills	105	586	44	60	2,148	55
2111	Cigarettes	19	1,132	90	8	3,045	81
2221	Weaving mills, synthetics	432	1,003	31	272	2,290	46
2511	Wood household furniture	2,208	899	7	2,934	2,439	12
2711	Newspapers	8,115	1,891	21	7,589	5,757	16
2721	Periodicals	2,106	1,060	34	2,430	3,096	24
2731	Book publishing	635	464	18	963	2,060	20
2821	Plastics materials and resins	94	478	44	508	3,474	27

SIC	Industry					
2834	Pharmaceutical preparations	1,123	941	28	791	4,696	24
2844	Toilet preparations	692	381	24	628	2,515	38
2911	Petroleum refining	277	6,624	37	276	20,294	33
3141	Shoes, except rubber	1,077	1,727	28	676	2,780	27
3312	Blast furnaces and steel mills	n.a.	2,845[b]	55	200	8,910[c]	48
3321	Gray-iron foundries	1,554	1,173	16	969	2,638	27
3411	Metal cans	102	679	78	96	2,891	73
3494	Valves and pipe fittings	436	634	24	575	2,275	14
3541	Machine tools, metal-cutting types	312	494	20	865	2,127	21
3621	Motors and generators	224	996	59	320	2,402	48
3722	Aircraft engines and engine parts	54	465	72	205	5,290	64
3731	Shipbuilding and repairing	272	803	43	389	2,518	42
3861	Photographic equipment and supplies	346	458	61	505	3,665	69

* Source: *1967 Census of Manufacturers* (Washington, D.C.: Bureau of the Census, Department of Commerce, 1971), pp. 9–9 to 9–42. Industries were selected on the basis of size (the largest), and availability of comparable 1947 and 1967 data.

[a]Standard Industrial Classification.

[b]This figure represents the value added from manufacture rather than the value of shipments.

[c]This figure represents the value of work done rather than the value of shipments.

consequently, the share possessed by various competitors) are implicit in the measures shown in Table 3-6?

The somewhat arbitrary set of measures shown in Table 3-7 has not escaped dispute. A number of questions have been raised, for example, about methods of measuring the relevant market for a product. For example, motor home producers compete with a range of purveyors of leisure-time goods and services as well as each other for the dollars of potential motor home purchasers. And yet, the "relevant market" against which a firm's share is measured is only the total of motor home sales. Even within an industry, firms may not compete in all price ranges or geographic territories. What do these comments suggest about the adequacy of concentration ratios as structural measures of competition?

Competitive Reaction. Of much greater relevance to the marketing strategist in most cases are questions of a more immediate nature, such as "How and when will the competition act if we don't change price or introduce a new product, or react if we do take such actions?" and "What effect will our competition's decision have on my company's sales and profits?"

Factors influencing competitors' abilities and inclinations to react include (1) the complexity of the reaction process required, (2) the patentability of a new product or process, (3) the current share of market held by the competitor's product or service, (4) the impact of change on a competitor's share of market, (5) the competitor's cost structure and the relative profitability of the product or service in question, and (6) the competitor's general financial, production, research and development, and marketing strengths.

As shown in Figure 3-10, the potential for competitive reaction may be greatest for responses involving noncomplex decisions or processes, unpatentable products, competitors with relatively large shares of the market, competitors with products or services similar to the one in question (suggesting a great impact on customers' buying decisions as a result of the contemplated change), relatively profitable products, and competitors with roughly comparable or

Figure 3-10. Factors influencing competitors' abilities and inclinations to react to marketing decisions.

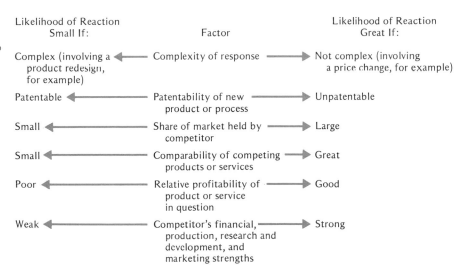

greater financial, production, research and development, and marketing strengths.

To illustrate, we might consider hypothetical actions contemplated by a struggling Diners' Club in its competition with other credit card systems in mid-1971.

Diners' Club was founded by the late Frank X. McNamara, who developed the idea of a credit card system in 1950 from a scheme employed by a customer of his small-loan company.

> The customer maintained a number of charge accounts at retail stores. He would lend his charge plates to his neighbors, exacting a high rate of interest and financing their purchases with loans from McNamara. Eventually he defaulted on his debt and McNamara referred the matter to his lawyer. . . .
>
> While they were discussing the clever operation at lunch one day, Mc-Namara was struck with the thought that, rather than renting out a dozen or so charge plates, the sensible thing would be to distribute a single charge card that would be accepted at many establishments. . . . The credit-card company would bill cardholders once a month and pay the restaurants—less a discount for the collection service. The cardholders, in turn, would presumably generate enough new business to justify the discount.

By mid-1971, consumers carried over 275 million credit cards of all types:

> 55 million bank cards, 90 million oil-company cards, 120 million retail-store cards, 5 million car-hire cards, 1.8 million air-travel cards, and 5 million "travel and entertainment" (T and E) cards.[9]

Some 9,300 banks, primarily offering Master Charge and Bank Americard, were in the business. And Diners' Club was joined by American Express and Carte Blanche in the T and E category.

Bank cards differed from T and E cards in that they were distributed free with the expectation that cardholders would allow payments to lag longer than the interest-free period, thus producing interest income to banks at the rate of $1\frac{1}{2}$ per cent of the outstanding balance at the end of each month. T and E cards typically were sold for $15. Initially, bank cards were usable primarily at retail establishments and T and E cards at restaurants and hotels. More recently, the distinction between the types of outlets accepting the two types of cards had lessened.

As the first into the business, Diners' Club expanded slowly, enjoying eighteen years of profits until, with the great boom in business in the late 1960s and an outmoded information processing and control system, the company ran up losses in excess of $70 million during a 27-month period prior to June 30, 1971. Of the newer cards, all suffered several years of losses as they built their volumes of cardholders and lists of participating business establishments. In addition, banks experienced unusually heavy losses from the unauthorized use of cards distributed en masse to customers through the mails. All except Diners' Club, however, either were exceeding or approaching break-even operations by mid-1971.

---

[9] This example is quoted from, and based on, Irwin Ross, "The Credit Card's Painful Coming-of-Age," *Fortune*, (Oct. 1971), pp. 108–111 ff.

Assume that several possible actions were under consideration by Diners' Club executives in mid-1971 to increase its card's share of the market and profitability. These might have included (1) the introduction of a totally original magnetically foolproof device that would invalidate a card used by someone other than the owner in possession of a magnetically coded "activator," (2) the introduction of a new service allowing cardholders to pay their utility bills automatically by registering their Diners' Club card numbers with their utility companies, or (3) a reduction in the annual cost of the card from $15 to $5 with an accompanying introduction of a 1 per cent interest charge on the outstanding balance at the end of each month.

(50)   How would you rate the potential for competitive response to the actions contemplated by Diners' Club executives in our hypothetical example, assuming a continuing fear of credit card "crimes" by users and the financial conditions of
(51)   major credit card companies? What impact on Diners' Club profits would you
(52)   expect from possible competitive reactions to each of the proposals? Of what significance would the factors shown in Figure 3-10 be to General Foods in the introduction of its new freeze-dried coffee, which we considered in Chapter 2?

the role of environmental analysis in the development of marketing strategy

It is easy to forget that, in all of its dimensions, the environment and its measurement is only a part of the process of formulating a marketing strategy. Customer behavior and motivation are equally important factors. For example, as a result of its observation, among other things, of (1) the growing market among older consumers and (2) the tendency of many "senior citizens" to purchase baby food, the H. J. Heinz Co. introduced the line of "Senior Foods" mentioned earlier, with characteristics much like baby food. In doing so, the company perhaps failed to take note of the fact that, although they consumed the products themselves, many of the senior purchasers of baby foods were careful to point out that they were buying them for their grandchildren. What does this suggest to you about the potential success of the line of Senior Foods?

□ □ □

As you might guess, you would have a hard time finding Senior Foods on the market today. Even though they represented a growing market for specially prepared foods in a demographic sense, senior citizens resented being identified with "baby" or "soft" foods for their own consumption.

summary

A number of environmental forces influence the relative desirability of markets, the success or failure of products and services, and an organization's strategy and decisions regarding its line of products and services. In the broadest sense of the term, the environment is the context in which products or services exist. In return, such products or services, in and of themselves, change the environment for better or worse for future generations of both people and products.

Factors external to the firm that influence marketing decisions concern customers and market segments, environmental conditions, and potential competitive responses. In this chapter, we have concentrated on external considerations other than those concerning product-customer fit. They include the demographic, economic, social, regulatory, and competitive dimensions of the marketing environment. Each of these can affect industries, companies, and the markets for products or services differently. Each poses a number of questions, some of which are illustrated in Figure 3-11.

Among the important demographic variables in assessing a product-environment fit are the declining birth rate, regional shifts in population to areas of more favorable

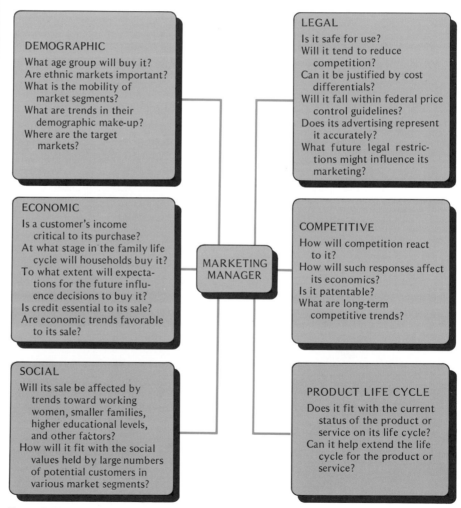

Figure 3-11. Questions a marketing manager might ask regarding various dimensions of the marketing environment.

climate or living conditions, the concentration of population with particular age and other characteristics in certain regions of the country, the increasing proportion of consumers residing in urban and suburban areas, the continuing high mobility of the American population, and changing patterns of expenditures for families passing through various stages of their respective life cycles.

Economic trends of interest include the continuing increase in personal income and discretionary spending by American spending units, a growing ability to forecast consumers' tendencies to part with discretionary funds, a continuing increase in the use of credit, a rapid rate of growth in services as opposed to tangible products, and a continuing increase in the female share of the total work force.

On the social dimension, shorter work weeks, increasing levels of education, and growing proportions of total government expenditures for education and public welfare have created a favorable climate for some products and services and problems for others.

Every facet of a marketing decision is addressed by one or more types of legislation, designed primarily to preserve competition and often to protect customers as well as competitors. Here there has been a marked trend away from the old philosophy of caveat emptor, "let the buyer beware," to one of caveat venditor.

Finally, the level of competition and the nature of potential competitive responses are important determinants of any marketing decision.

The visibility of competitors and their actions as well as the measurability of their results often invite more attention to this environmental dimension than to others. However, the rise in recognition of the importance of other environmental forces in the last decade has been remarkable. General concerns for ecology, with its concentration on the limited quantities and the use of resources, various forms of pollution, and population control, have sensitized us to the importance of environmental matters that are nonetheless important for the slow, inexorable change in market conditions that they produce.

The objectives of this chapter have been to review, in sum, a wide range of environmental influences, to introduce some comparative measures of demographic and other indicators for selected countries, and to attempt to relate these measures to the product strategies developed by individual companies in response to their analyses of the product-environment fit. From here, we can move to a less global question: "How does a product fit into a company's existing line of products and its strategic marketing and business plans?"

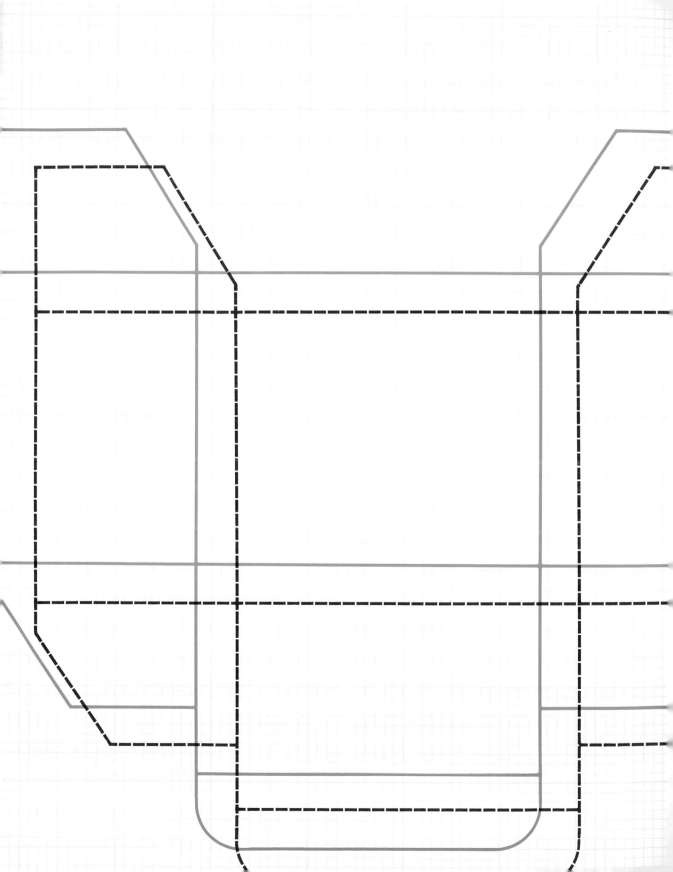

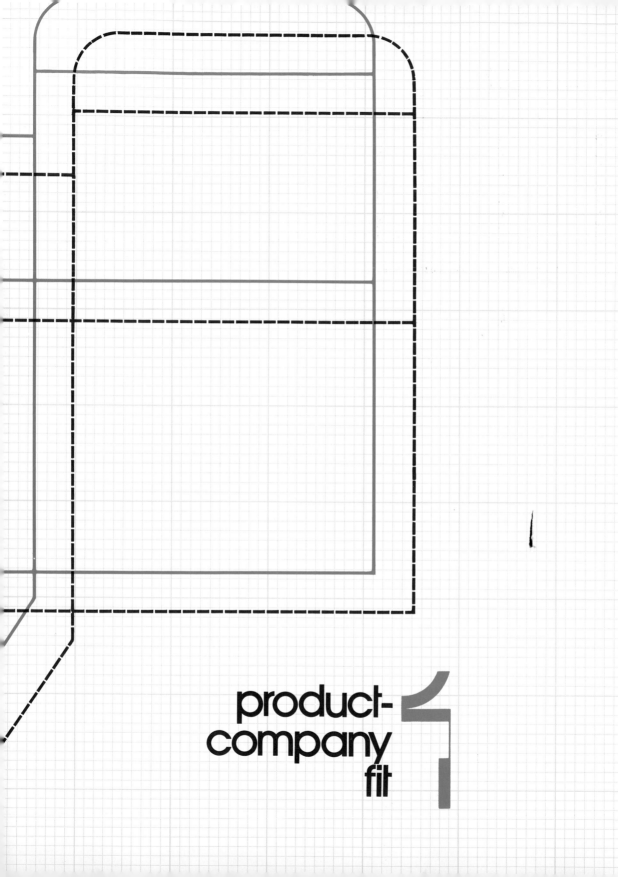

product-
company
fit

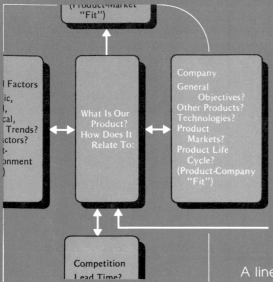

(Product-Market "Fit")

l Factors
ic,
l,
cal,
Trends?
actors?
t-
onment
)

What Is Our Product? How Does It Relate To:

Company
General
    Objectives?
Other Products?
Technologies?
Product
    Markets?
Product Life
    Cycle?
(Product-Company
    "Fit")

Competition
Lead Time?

A line of products or services can be like children in a family hurrying to a school program. All may walk quickly and in an orderly fashion toward their objective under the watchful eyes of their parents. On the other hand, two may fight. Another may decide to play "kick the can." And yet another may turn around and head back for home. The only recourse to the parents may be restricted to some form of threats and discipline.

In the process of developing a fit between product and parent, we are much more fortunate. It may be regarded as inhumane to kill an "undisciplined," unprofitable product only by its designer. Or a product that isn't behaving may be redesigned. And we have a great deal more control over the kind of product family we get in the first place.

Nevertheless, the problems of compatibility are just as great in product families as in human families. And as we'll see, the problems of cannibalization are much greater. That's why it's important at this point in our discussion to (1) explore factors external and internal to a firm that account for the increasing rate of new product introductions, (2) consider criteria for the selection of new candidates for a product line, (3) examine processes by which products or services are developed and killed, and (4) understand common life-cycle patterns and their implications for the management of an organization's line of products or services.

rolling in green

As you drive through the rolling hills of central Ohio, you come upon a small country town called Marysville. A summer traveler through the town invariably is struck by the beauty of its lawns. Exploration of this phenomenon with one of the local citizens can lead the curious traveler into a most fascinating marketing story. For Marysville is the home of The O. M. Scott & Sons Company.

Scott was founded in 1868 as a producer of the nation's first clean, weed-free grass seed. A meager beginning with an uninteresting product? Perhaps. But after fifty-odd years, the company added a lawn fertilizer to its line. By 1945, after seventy-seven years of producing and selling seed and fertilizer, the company's annual profits reached $30,000. Still not interested?

In search for improved growth, company executives began to redefine their products. Were they appropriately defined in terms of the products of their laboratories and processing plants—seed and fertilizers? Is that what customers were seeking and buying? Scott's management asked customers, and concluded that Scott's products were regarded as the means to a common goal, green lawns. As a result, Scott's management defined its product as green lawns instead of a line of seed and fertilizer. Things began to happen.

The delivery of green lawns required many kinds of seed and fertilizer to meet different soil and climatic conditions in various geographic areas. It also required products to provide ways of controlling pests. This led to the development of new weed and garden pest control chemicals and special-purpose lawn fertilizers—and to a sevenfold increase in profits to $210,000 by 1955.

But other things thwarted many customers in their search for green lawns. They knew nothing about how to determine the appropriate combination of seed, fertilizer, and pesticides for their lawns. Their sources of information, often next-door neighbors, were not reliable. In fact, they felt their local dealer often knew little more about particular lawn care problems than they did. They were bewildered by the wide array of equipment produced for lawn care. And they could not bring themselves to purchase the necessary ingredients of their lawn development programs in advance of one or two sunny weekend days in spring, increasing the chances that they would encounter empty shelves, hasty advice, and general frustration.

This prompted the company to expand its sales force, increase the number of retail dealers, and provide education for dealers, motivated by the increasing profitability of their sales of lawn care products. Scott further emphasized the distribution of its free magazine, *Lawn Care*, to home owners and others. It increased the line of products distributed under the Scott brand to include various types of equipment such as mechanical spreaders and lawn mowers. Not just any spreaders and mowers, however.

A spreader was developed that would help insure the proper application of the company's seeds and fertilizers, an important factor in a successful lawn program. A lawn mower was developed in response to research that had indicated that noise was one of the most annoying matters to "do-it-yourselfers" (and their neighbors) in mowing lawns. Hence, the development and introduction, not of just a quiet lawn mower, but the Silent Scott Mower.®

Scott undertook a program to encourage dealers to build stocks of a size sufficient to meet the needs of the unthinking customers exhibiting sheeplike behavior on certain fine spring days. This was supplemented with a strict quality-control effort and a national advertising program that assured prospective and past buyers of Scott's products that they were buying not just the finest products, but a lawn care program designed to maximize the probability of success for an amateur in producing a green lawn.

By 1970, shortly before the time the company was sold to a larger, diversified corporation, the company's profits after taxes reached $3,390,000, rewarding those who had invested $1,000 in 1945 with stock valued at more than $300,000 twenty-five years later. Scott also began emphasizing its programs for large users of the company's products, such as golf course operators, universities, and companies developing tracts of new homes and even new towns. To focus these efforts, the ProTurf® program was established and manned with forty-one specialist consultant-salesmen to foster the development of markets among potentially large users.

(1) How did the redefinition of Scott's products help the company expand its (2) sales? Does the company's latest product line reflect its product definition?

factors influencing new-product development

Clearly, by asking and answering the question: "What business are we in?" Scott's management provided itself with strong guidelines for the development of its product line. These guidelines resulted from a careful consideration of customer needs, at least among a segment of the population described most typically as middle- or upper-middle-income home and apartment owners placing a relatively high value on having an attractive, green lawn.

Factors influencing new-product development may come from outside or inside an organization. We'll move here from the former to the latter in considering some of the more important ones. Together, they have produced a constantly increasing stream of new product introductions that some claim have reached flood stage.

attention to customer needs

A stream of new products is produced primarily in response to real or perceived customer needs. Among those that we have discussed thus far are Six-Footer college scarves, the Volunteer Army, General Foods' freeze-dried coffee, and Scott's spreader. Many of these represent the cornerstone for a line of products. A successful product—one that becomes identified through need, use, or both in a customer's mind—typically spawns others. Thus, we saw the development of Six-Footer fashion scarves, General Foods' freeze-dried decaffeinated coffee, and the Scott Silent Mower.

Consider the example of Max Karl's little business.[1] In 1957, mortgage lenders and home builders were finding federal mortgage insurance, obtained mainly through the Federal Housing Authority (FHA), less desirable as a means of making and obtaining loans for new homes. The FHA imposed maximum loan-interest rate limits on lenders, rates below those on conventional mortgages. As a result, commercial lenders were making smaller proportions of their loans to FHA-insured builders. Not only was it becoming more difficult for people of moderate income to obtain financing on their homes with a small down payment—a feature of an FHA loan—but the FHA required four to eight weeks to process a loan-insurance request.

At about this time, Max Karl founded a Milwaukee-based company, MGIC Investment Corp., to provide private mortgage insurance to individuals able to make minimum down payments on loans, and without interest limits to lending banks and other institutions. Because it could rely on the credit investigations conducted by the prospective lenders, MGIC processed mortgage-insurance requests in only one or two days. Because the rate of foreclosures on mortgage loans had been so low in the post-World War II years, MGIC's insurance was priced as much as 50 per cent below that of the FHA, an agency whose rates were based in part on the experience of the Great Depression when foreclosures were common.

[1] Harlan S. Byrne, "How Mr. Karl Created a Booming Industry from Little Company," *Wall Street Journal,* (March 14, 1973), pp. 1, 23.

The company insured four home mortgages in March 1957. Sixteen years later its volume of business was about twenty-five thousand mortgages a month, $7.5 billion of insured home loans per year, 68 per cent of all residential mortgage insurance sold in the United States, and nearly double the amount written by the government's FHA. Foreclosures over this period of time were negligible.

Encouraged by its success, the company expanded its line of services over the years. It began offering commercial mortgage insurance to allow developers or building owners to get financing on more liberal terms than would be the case without mortgage insurance. Next came mortgage insurance for mobile home buyers.

This was followed by the establishment of a service to provide temporary construction financing to builders whose projects were a potential source of home mortgage insurance. Next came a mortgage buying and selling unit to provide a market for persons wishing to deal in mortgages and a service to insure bonds issued by small municipalities to help them sell bonds to the public.

MGIC profits in 1972 reached $27.2 million, a fourfold increase over the previous five years and a continuation of fifteen years of annual increases in profits. In contrast to the great difficulty that Max Karl experienced in 1957 in persuading investors to put up $250,000 to begin the company, the company's stock was a favorite of investors in intervening years. Its market value at one point reached about $2 billion, or about eight thousand times the original investment before the company began to experience new competition, the effects of high interest rates, and a reduction in new home construction.

At times, an entire line of products may be introduced simultaneously to meet customer needs. For example, Texaco several years ago announced the introduction of a line of gasolines blended in response to driving conditions experienced in different parts of the country.

At roughly the same time, the Sun Oil Company, through its Sunoco brand, offered customers the option of ordering their own "custom" blend of gasoline by means of a pump that mixed as well as dispensed gasolines with eight different octane ratings at different prices.

(3)
(4)
(5)

Which of the product-line extensions discussed in this section would you characterize as being in response to real customer needs? Perceived customer needs? No need at all?

One particular custmer need, that for variety, has had a profound effect on product-line development by supporting a growing stream of new-product introductions. Data presented by researchers of the breakfast cereal industry suggest, for example, that there is only about a 50 per cent chance that a customer will buy the same brand of cereal two times running.[2] This perhaps suggests why the stalwart brands of the past such as Corn Flakes, Post Toasties, Wheaties, and Puffed Wheat have been joined not only by presweetened cereals such as Sugar Frosted Flakes, Cap'n Crunch, and Froot Loops, but also by other "fun" brands such as Lucky Charms, Wackies, and Count Chocula.

Similarly, a study of cookie and cracker buying preferences concluded that

The opportunity for new flavors, types, and sizes is great. . . . The women in our depth interviews reacted favorably to the idea of new kinds of cookies

[2]Robert S. Headen and James W. McKie, *The Structure, Conduct, and Performance of the Breakfast Cereal Industry: 1954–64* (Cambridge, Mass: Arthur D. Little, 1966).

and crackers which offered them the opportunity to add some excitement to the ordinary routine job of purchasing food and preparing meals for their families. New kinds and flavors also seem to provide an additional chance to remind their families of the affection and interest in them. They practically demanded variety, particularly in cookies.[3]

competition—"me-too" products

In recent years, we have witnessed the introduction of many products designed to emulate and capture a share of the market held by the leading product in a field, often one that was the first of its kind and the one around which primary demand for a product category was built. Sometimes a "me-too" product surpasses the leading brand. More often it performs just as it was intended and obtains for its manufacturer a small, sometimes profitable share of the market.

For example, among liquid cleaners, Lestoil was joined by a product marketed in a similarly shaped glass container, Mr. Clean. Over the years, these leaders were joined by such me-too brands as Top Job and Lysol, whose package shapes and product capabilities were hardly distinguishable from the leaders. A more recently introduced product, Janitor in a Drum, packaged in a distinctive drum-shaped container and aimed at the customer with heavy cleaning jobs, has set a new pattern for competition by capturing a significant share of the market from the leaders as well as from other me-too's.

In part, as a result of me-too product strategies, there recently were twenty-two soft drinks advertised on network television, as opposed to seven just eight years earlier. What does this suggest to you as a potential marketer of a new cola drink? To what extent are me-too strategies customer-oriented?

(6)

(7)

Lest we conclude that me-too product strategies are confined to consumer packaged goods, consider the following description of a portion of the marketing strategy for the Caterpillar Tractor Co., the leading manufacturer of earth-moving equipment:

> The company will almost never be the first to introduce a new product if it can possibly avoid doing so. It lets others take the glory of becoming pace-setters; it also lets them make the mistakes, sweat out the "bugs," and endure the inevitable customer complaints that attend the introduction of anything new. After Caterpillar has patiently sifted the bittersweet experiences of the innovators, it will decide whether or not to follow. And when it finally comes out with a new product, it usually manages to sweep the competition to one side. . . .[4]

Holiday Inns, Inc. calls itself the world's largest innkeeper. But its position did not allow it to ignore the challenge represented by potential competitors who began building chains of budget motels offering rooms at less than half

[3] A study by the American Viscose Division of FMC Corp., reported in "Consumer Buying Habits," *Biscuit and Cracker Baker,* (July 1965), pp. 31–32.

[4] Sanford Rose, "The Going May Get Tougher for Caterpillar," *Fortune,* (May 1972), pp. 160–165 ff. Quote on p. 162.

of the normal Holiday Inn rates. Thus, several years ago its management seriously considered opening a chain of budget motels.

It is useful to distinguish the development of me-too products from the simultaneous development and introduction of new competing products by two companies.

competition—preemptive strategy

A market leader with a successful product may develop new or improved products out of a fear that if it doesn't, its competition will. Thus, although its instant coffee brand held 50.3 per cent of the national market, General Foods launched the introduction of its new freeze-dried coffee, in part because of the knowledge that a competitor, Nestlé, was readying a similar product for the market. Nor did a dominant position in coffee and important shares of the market for instant and freeze-dried coffee deter General Foods from introducing yet another convenient form of making coffee, Max Pax—measured portions for making consistently good perked coffee.

A preemptive strategy may have at least two beneficial results for its sponsor. It allows a company to establish the initial, and potentially the strongest, position for the product in the market. Often this position can support a relatively high price for the product. For example, Heinz ketchup for years held by far the largest share of the ketchup market (more than 30 per cent) with a product priced significantly higher than the competition.

Or the strategy may discourage competition from entering the market entirely. This may especially be true where the cost and resulting risk associated with entry by a competitor is high.

The always-present risk of a preemptive strategy is that it was, after all, unnecessary. This could result in a less economic and profitable process of production and marketing by the market leader of two products sharing the same market one held previously.

competition—share of the market

Among many products sold through point-of-purchase display, such as grocery products, the number of products offered by a company may influence the portion of shelf space allocated to the company's products as opposed to that of its competitors by a retailer. For certain product categories, this, in turn, influences the customer's choice. Thus, Headen and McKie show that the market share of competing companies in the breakfast cereal industry is closely correlated with the degree to which each has introduced new brands.[5] What does this conclusion assume about customer buying behavior in the retail store? For what types of products is this likely to be the case?

(8)

(9)

[5] Headen and McKie, loc. cit.

market growth

As a market grows, we have seen that it offers more potential opportunities for new products. Clearly, its actual or potential size must exceed the minimum needed to offer potential profits to a single supplier even before it can be regarded as a viable market. The rate of entry of new competing products or services can be determined not only by the rate of market growth, but also by the level of sales needed to support production, marketing, and logistical efforts.

The largest segment of the European market for automobiles grew out of the need for autos that (1) could be purchased on a postwar, restricted budget, (2) required a minimum amount of 90-cent per gallon gasoline, and (3) could negotiate the narrower, curvier European roads. The segment was large enough to support the manufacture and marketing not only of Volkswagens but of many other brands of small cars.

(10) And although many may regard the growth of Volkswagen purchases in the United States as due to a serious error on the part of American manufacturers, at what point should the latter have entered production? For example, assuming a requirement of a $250 million investment for retooling, a $50 million investment in introductory marketing, and a potential contribution (remember this from the Six-Footer example: sales price less variable costs per unit?) to investment and profit of $600 per automobile sold, at what point should General Motors have responded to the Volkswagen challenge? In 1949, when VW sold two autos in the United States? A year later, when 330 VWs were sold? Or in 1969, when Volkswagen continued to command the largest share of the market with sales of 569,000 units?

internal economics—investment and contribution

If the contribution to General Motors for each compact car sold were only $300, would the company even today be producing a Vega? Probably not. The market size and contribution per unit *in relation to the large investment* might continue to deter the development, production, and marketing of a new compact produced in America by an American manufacturer not currently offering a compact model. Other things equal, how would the relationships between market size, contribution per unit, and the investment required to introduce a new product affect the decision?

(11)

internal economics—available capacity

An organization invests its capital a number of ways. Many investments increase both available capacity and fixed costs.

A company may invest its money in a factory. The factory is capable of producing up to its rated capacity. And whether or not the factory produces anything, the act of building commits the company to fixed obligations (costs) for such things as interest on the money invested, property taxes, insurance, maintenance, utilities, and a minimum labor force. Relatively heavy "factory" investments are typical among auto manufacturers, for example, and service enterprises such as bowling alleys, railroads, educational institutions, and others.

A company may invest its money in a sales force as well. The investment here is used for training, initial experience until the individual salesperson pays his or her way, and even a short-term commitment to pay his or her salary for some period of time required for the decision to be made as to whether he or she should stay with the company. A sales force has a reasonable capacity, often stated in terms of sales calls per day, dollars of sales per call, or simply dollars of sales per year. And its development and maintenance commits a company to fixed costs. Computer manufacturers and insurance companies, for example, invest relatively large amounts of money in this manner. What do these types of businesses have in common? What other businesses does this suggest as having potentially high requirements for investment in a sales force?

A company may invest money in trucks and drivers for the physical distribution, by route, of the company's product to wholesalers, retailers, or even individual users. This creates a capacity, stated in stops per day, volume of sales per stop, or sales per month per driver and truck. And it represents a commitment to pay the fixed costs, regardless of volume, of equipment registration, maintenance, depreciation, and interest on investment as well as driver salaries in the shorter term. Institutional food products delivered to fast-food outlets, various products delivered to supermarkets on a "store-door" basis, and dairy items and cleaning and cosmetic "products" sold on a door-to-door basis all require relatively high investments in physical distribution activities.

Or a company may choose to invest money in a product brand such as Ivory, Rinso, or Lux, primarily in the form of advertising. Often this offers the opportunity to introduce other products under the same brand (sometimes referred to as a franchise in the consumer's mind) up to what some would call the capacity of a brand to support products of increasingly varied characteristics. And a major advertising campaign requires a fixed commitment of money over a period of time if it is to have a chance to provide a significant impact on sales. The soap manufacturing business is a prime example of this type of enterprise. Anyone can make soap in their sink, bathtub, or garage, and a soap manufacturing facility need not be complex or expensive. This emphasizes the desirability of, and suggests the potential availability of funds for, investment in a product brand and its advertising. What other types of business might have similar characteristics?

Organizations that plan ahead often provide for capacities in excess of current needs to provide for growth. These excess capacities, in turn, offer a strong incentive for the introduction of new products. The additional, or incremental, costs of utilizing idle factory capacity are confined largely to direct labor and materials used in making a product. As an extreme example, the incremental costs to an airline of flying a scheduled flight with or without one extra passenger may be limited to costs of ticketing; coffee, tea, or milk served enroute; and a few drops of fuel.

Similarly, it costs little extra for a salesman to sell two products rather than one on a sales call. Or for a truck and driver to deliver 500 pounds of two products as opposed to 250 pounds of one product at a given route stop. Or for three rather than two products to share a brand.

Of course, the cost to accommodate one more passenger once a plane is fully loaded (its capacity is fully utilized) may be substantial, requiring the scheduling of an additional 110-seat aircraft. Is this true for each of these types of marketing investments after capacity has been reached?

(15)

internal economics—contribution to investment

In a performance-oriented economy, many organizations plan to have some portion of their investment committed to new products for which there may be less price competition and higher contribution per unit of product or investment. This may be especially true where capacity limitations on a company's ability to produce or customers' abilities to consume its products may exist.

For example, the amount of food that customers in a given market area physically can consumer, regardless of income, is limited. But by more extensively processing and freezing foods, many manufacturers have created new products such as a wide variety of prepared dinners that at the same time (1) meet customers' needs for convenience, (2) are priced at a much higher amount per unit of volume of ingredients, and (3) return a higher contribution per unit of product, per unit of sale, or per customer than their predecessors. The baking industry, beset by the dreary combination of a stagnant market and declining profits in relations to sales, discovered Fritos and its many successors. All of these so-called snack foods are sold at much higher per unit prices and contribution rates than their poor country cousin, bread.

internal marketing organization

In the last fifteen years the product manager has come to be a familiar figure in the marketing organizations of many large companies. Often his or her job is described as involving responsibility for coordinating all aspects of marketing for a product or product group, from design and development through market introduction to continuing marketing programs. Where previously jobs were defined in terms of functions such as advertising, research, and sales, the product manager's title contains brand names such as Crisco or Crest. The identification of a marketing job with a product has facilitated the measurement of performance in terms of increases in sales, contribution, or profits for a product or product family.

(16)

(17)

If you were a product manager for products marketed under the Crisco brand, would you be likely to look toward the development and introduction of new products for improved performance? How objectively would you view the potential benefits to the company of a new product to be marketed under the Crisco brand?

the result

What is the result of these pressures for new-product development? One indicator is that in the ten years between 1962 and 1972, the number of trademarks registered annually with the U. S. Patent Office rose from 17,000 to 34,000, with another doubling predicted by the supervising examiner by 1982.[6] And this doesn't include the countless millions of trademarks and brand names in use that no one has bothered to register.

Another indicator, shown in Figure 4-1, is that the number of different items handled in an average supermarket increased from about 3,700 in 1950 to 7,950 in 1972. During this same period of time, the physical size of the average supermarket, defined by the Supermarket Institute as any food outlet with annual sales in excess of $500,000, did not grow proportionately. Nor, we are told, has the average length of time for a shopper's visit to a supermarket increased from its estimated twenty-five to thirty minutes. Nor, for that matter, have the available minutes of national and local advertising time on television stations serving a given market increased significantly during the last decade. These facts have produced some interesting phenomena.

As shown in Figure 4-1, food sales through supermarkets increased 337 per cent between 1950 and 1972, reaching a level of $46.8 billion (of 1950 dollars) in 1972). The number of supermarkets sharing in this sales volume increased about threefold during this same period of time, producing an average annual

Figure 4-1. Trends in the average number of items per supermarket, number of supermarkets, sales in supermarkets (in 1950 dollars), and average sale per SKU per store, United States, 1950–1972. Source: ''Annual Report of the Grocery Industry,'' *Progressive Grocer*, (issue published annually in April).

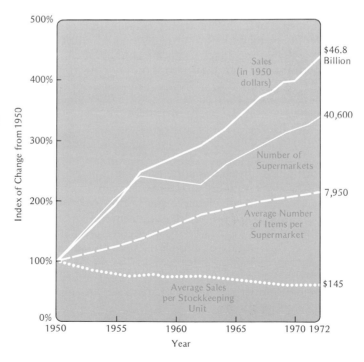

[6]''The Growing Tug of War over Trademarks,'' *Business Week*, (Nov. 4, 1972), pp. 64, 66. Quote on p. 64.

volume of sales per supermarket of $1.5 million (of 1950 dollars) in 1972. But because the number of different stock keeping units (SKU)—counted as different brands, flavors, and package sizes and types—has more than doubled in this same period of time, the annual sales volume per SKU declined from $238 in 1950 to $145 in 1972.

(18)
(19)

From the standpoint of the customer, how much time does an average visit of twenty-five to thirty minutes allow for a review of the SKUs on display at the local supermarket? What does this suggest for the manufacturer of products sold in supermarkets?

One alternative to a manufacturer to gain visibility for its product is to advertise. But if the medium selected is network or local TV, the amount of time available for advertising, as determined by the Federal Communications Commission (FCC), the National Association of Broadcasters, and the limit that viewers will tolerate before complaining—or, worse yet, "tuning out"—has not grown proportionately. Instead, the number of slots, or "spots," has been increased by making thirty seconds the standard for longer-length commercials, rather than the previous sixty seconds. Thus, a viewer of network television can now be bombarded with messages for between fifteen and twenty different products by means of ten- to thirty-second messages in the space of fewer than

(20)
(21)

eight minutes. What does this suggest for the manufacturer of products sold in supermarkets? Or for the manufacturer of a me-too product?

We have considered basic reasons why an organization might want to introduce a new product. Next we'll turn to factors influencing a manager's decision to add a particular product of all potential alternatives to his company's product line or to delete an existing product from the line. The following discussion assumes that a potential product fits customer needs as well as the competitive and other environmental trends considered earlier.

product-line management

Among the criteria for selecting new product-line candidates are the extent to which a product or service (1) conforms to a stated purpose, (2) reflects an organization's capabilities, (3) complements a company's current product line, (4) helps meet customers' needs for a complete product line, and (5) enhances a company's return on investment. These same criteria can be used for that most distasteful of all marketing jobs, product-line pruning, as well.

does it fit our business plans?

In recent years, professor Theodore Levitt has posed in a number of ways the question: "What business are you in?" to readers of his books and articles. Because he is one of the country's most widely read and remembered business authors, there is some evidence that the question is sinking in. The types of answers that Levitt seeks to his simple question are those that are sufficiently broad in nature to allow an organization to meet all customer needs associated with a product or service. Answers of this sort are stated not in terms of product or service names, but in terms of customer benefits and end results. They are not product-oriented, but rather customer-oriented. Among classic examples provided by Levitt are the following:

> Had Hollywood been customer-oriented (providing entertainment), rather than product-oriented (making movies), would it have gone through the fiscal purgatory that it did? . . . [Railroads] let others take customers away from them because they assumed themselves to be in the railroad [product-oriented] business rather than in the transportation [customer-oriented] business.[7]

This question should lead to a statement of business purpose that can provide a basic guideline for product-line management. For example, recall the statement of its basic business purpose by The O. M. Scott & Sons Company. How well does it stack up against the philosophy expressed by Levitt? Now look at a recent ad for Scott's ProTurf® products, shown in Figure 4-2. Against what competition is this ad directed? What does it tell us about the limits that Scott's management has placed on its product-line definition? Do you agree with such limits?

Or return again to the world of MGIC Investment Corp., the private home mortgage insurer described earlier. How do you think this company should define its business? Do its current services reflect this definition? What further products or services would fit within your definition of the business? Several years ago, MGIC acquired two home-building and land-development companies in Florida. Do these acquisitions fit within your definition of the business?

Within a basic business definition, individual or collective management philosophies may prevent an organization from following specific courses of action. This perhaps explains, for example, why the Gillette Co., manufacturer of the leading deodorant, elected not to market a feminine hygiene spray long before such sprays attracted medical criticism. In the words of a former Gillette marketing man:

> There's a $50 million market out there for feminine sprays. And Gillette, even though it probably has the best aerosol technology in the country, is ignoring it. Why? It's simple. They can't bring themselves to use the word "vagina" in their business conversations.[8]

For perhaps related reasons, Gillette has not advertised in *Playboy* magazine.

Figure 4-2. (On opposite page). An advertisement for ProTurf® products manufactured by O. M. Scott & Sons, an ITT company, that appeared in *Business Week*, (June 2, 1973) p. 33.

[7]Theodore Levitt, "Marketing Myopia," *Harvard Business Review*, **38**:45–46 (July–Aug. 1960). Quote on p. 45. By 1976, this had become one of the most widely read business articles of all time.
[8]William M. Carley, "Gillette Co. Struggles As Its Rivals Slice at Fat Profit Margin," *Wall Street Journal*, (Feb. 2, 1972), pp. 1, 14. Quote on p. 14.

To golfers, this landscape is nothing but trouble.
To others, it is life itself.

This is the famous 120-yard seventh hole at Pebble Beach on California's Monterey Peninsula—one of the greatest par 3 challenges a golfer can face.

But, at times, we see it differently.

One of our companies, O.M. Scott & Sons, has been working with grass for over half a century.

You probably know Scotts through their complete line of home-lawn products.

Scotts now helps groom 3,000 U.S. golf courses year round.

Scotts now also specializes in products for well-groomed golf courses like Pebble Beach. Today they supply ProTurf* products to some 3,000 courses, from the Sahalee Country Club in Washington to the Waterville Country Club in Maine to the Royal Poinciana Golf Club in Florida.

We also help green other parts of the world.

Scotts products used in the world's largest covered stadium.

The 1972 Munich Olympics were played on Scotts-fed turf.

When construction of the stadium started—and it's now the largest covered stadium in the world, seating 80,000—turf was installed.

It was a blend of grasses suitable to the Bavarian climate and able to stand up to the stress of continuous hard wear.

Grass removes pollutants, and is a vital green environmental shield.

To ensure maximum development, it was stimulated to an elegant beauty with Scotts ProTurf products.

Expanses of grass are sorely needed, whether for sports events,

on the Great Plains or in your front yard. And not only for their recreational value.

Grass removes pollutants from the air and releases life-sustaining oxygen. It cools the earth by releasing water vapor. It fights noise pollution by deflecting and absorbing sound.

Americans today are caring for five million acres of lawn. Their aim, basically, is to help beautify their homes.

But what they're also doing is caring for a great green environmental shield, vital to life itself.

International Telephone and Telegraph Corporation, 320 Park Avenue, New York, N.Y. 10022.

*Trademark of O.M. Scott & Sons

SERVING PEOPLE AND NATIONS EVERYWHERE

does the proposed product reflect
our capabilities?

An audit of an organization's strengths includes, in its simplest form, an assessment of its capabilities to finance, develop and produce, and market new products or services. Even though compatibility with financial and production expertise is important for a new product or service, many failures are explained by the fact that new-product adoptions did not consider the need for relevant marketing capabilities as well. The following examples are typical of many that could be considered.

For years, the Ampex Corp. developed and produced a successful line of tape recorder-players for the TV and radio industry. In addition, it adapted its pioneering technology to the manufacture and installation of closed-circuit video systems for schools and other customers. In selling to these markets, Ampex acquired a reputation for high quality and dependability. Then it decided to become the nation's largest producer and marketer of home tape recorders and prerecorded tape, featuring a wide range of artists. The market for prerecorded tape had risen from 4 per cent of total recorded music sales in 1966 to more than 30 per cent of the total by 1970 and had reached a sales volume of $500 million. Ampex became the largest in the field.

However, in addition to contracting with music artists for large sums of money, the company found itself facing marketing problems with which it was not familiar. For example, at the time of a recession in 1970, distributors and retailers found it difficult to pay bills on time and invested as little as possible in inventory. Ampex, as a result of its liberal return policy and generous trade credit terms, found itself taking back much of the tape shipped to retailers that remained unsold. In addition, it became more and more difficult to collect on deliveries made to distributors and retailers.

> It soon became apparent that Ampex was out of its sphere in the mass marketing of consumer goods. Japanese manufacturers, most notably Sony Corp. and the makers of Panasonic products, proved more innovative than Ampex, producing machines that many buyers found to be easier to use, better styled and lower priced. The Japanese also proved more efficient salesmen. Ampex had to stretch its resources thin to set up national sales and service operations as well as to advertise the recorders, which were its sole consumer product aside from tapes. Competition, of course, were already well-entrenched with consumer equipment like television sets and radios. One outcome was poor customer services.[9]

Ampex was forced to drop its line of home tape recorders and announced a loss of nearly $90 million in fiscal 1972.

The Monsanto Company, a well-known manufacturer of industrial chemicals, plastics, and synthetic fibers, has had a difficult time diversifying out of commoditylike industrial products such as ethylene and acetylene into commercial products with higher margins and less cyclical demand fluctuations. A weakness in marketing skills has been cited as a major reason why it has

---

[9]James E. Bylin, "How Ampex Saturated Recorded Tape Market and Got Soaked Itself," *Wall Street Journal*, (March 9, 1972), pp. 1, 19. Quote on p. 19.

failed to achieve much success in diversifying into less-cyclical consumer products such as Krillium (a soil softener) and All (a detergent).[10]

(30) (31)

Do you see a pattern in these examples? How would you explain it?

□□□

The diagram in Figure 4-3 is a simplified explanation of basic ways in which a product's compatibility with a company's capabilities can be assessed. It illustrates relationships in which a proposed product may be compatible with either technological or marketing capabilities, or both. Which of these patterns describes the Ampex and Monsanto examples?

(32)

In contrast to Ampex and Monsanto was the Schlage Lock Co., a manufacturer and marketer of a premium line of commercial and residential door locks. The company's expertise was characterized by its president as follows: "Our strong suit . . . is the precise engineering of interlocking parts."[11] Schlage was planning to market a new electronic lock. The lock, opened by waving a card that activated it by means of a radio transmitter mounted in the wall beside the door, was much less prone to lock picking than its pin-tumbler predecessor. It would appeal to the same markets currently served by Schlage. But it required a totally different production technology:

Today, its 1,200-man work force in San Francisco consists largely of highly-skilled metalworkers tending long banks of machines in a sprawling factory. But neither these workers nor the machinery would be needed in any major

Figure 4-3. Major factors in judging a new product's desirability in terms of company capabilities in an engineering- as opposed to a marketing-oriented company.

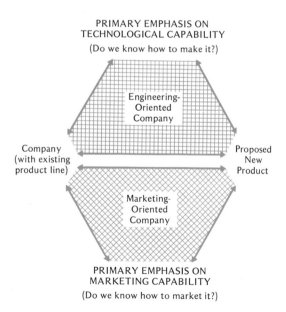

PRIMARY EMPHASIS ON
TECHNOLOGICAL CAPABILITY
(Do we know how to make it?)

Engineering-
Oriented
Company

Company
(with existing
product line)

Proposed
New
Product

Marketing-
Oriented
Company

PRIMARY EMPHASIS ON
MARKETING CAPABILITY
(Do we know how to market it?)

[10]"A Tough New Boss at Monsanto," *Business Week,* (Nov. 4, 1972), pp. 70–71.
[11]"A Lock That Opens at the Wave of a Hand," *Business Week,* (June 16, 1973), pp. 100, 102. Quote on p. 100.

113

shift to electronics. . . . A concern expressed by the company's president was: . . . "One thing that scares me about our new electronic lock is that I really don't know what's going on inside that black box."[12]

(33)
(34)
(35)
(36)

How would you characterize the Schlage example in terms of the diagram in Figure 4-3? Does the company define its business in a production- or marketing-oriented fashion? What success would you predict for Schlage with its new product? What additional information would you want to have before making such a judgment?

will it complement our current product line?

The extent to which new products extend the existing line rather than duplicate current products in the line may determine the degree to which new products add to current sales and returns on investment.

The Melville Shoe Corporation offers an interesting example of a company that has positioned its various chains of retail outlets to complement one another. For years, Melville sold its products primarily to men through its wholly owned Thom McAn stores offering low- to medium-priced shoes. In fact, in certain markets, Thom McAn was the dominant retailer of men's shoes. Several years ago, for example, nearly one in every four pairs of men's shoes sold in El Paso, Texas were Thom McAn. But Melville's management realized that Thom McAn was not reaching customers interested in low-priced shoes, high-priced shoes, women's shoes, or fashion shoes. As a result, the Thom McAn line was upgraded, and a chain of discount stores offering shoes to the entire family, Meldisco, was created. More recently, the Vanguard chain has been created to sell a high-priced line of shoes retailing at $50 per pair or more, and a Miles chain of 286 stores, originally oriented to the family trade, has been converted into a women's fashion operation. These shoe-retailing operations enable Melville "to compete across the whole spectrum of price, and in every major market in the United States," not an insignificant accomplishment in a market where people buy on the average more than five pairs of shoes per year.[13]

In fact, Melville's management concluded several years ago that it wasn't in the shoe business after all, but that its business was the delivery of fashion to the American public, including coats and dresses, jewelry, watches, toiletries, and hairpieces, among others. The company opened a chain of Foxwood Casuals stores selling clothing to girls and women between the ages of fifteen and twenty-five, started a chain called Chess King catering to a similar market among men, and purchased a chain of Consumer Value Stores selling health and beauty aids in New England. As the ultimate in product complementarity:

One Melville executive even talks of the day when the company may take a whole mall in a shopping center, creating a "total environment" for its young customers, complete with movie theaters, cafes, and discotheques.[14]

[12]Ibid., p. 102.
[13]Roger Beardwood, "Melville Draws a Bead on the $50 Billion Fashion Market," *Fortune,* (Dec. 1969), pp. 110–114 ff. Quote on p. 111. The information for this example is drawn from this source.
[14]Ibid., p. 158.

Rather than complement their older sister products, some new products cannibalize them. They eat into existing sales of a company's products. And it happens to the best of companies, as suggested by IBM's introduction of the 370 series of computers several years ago. The 370 computers were designed to be competitive with their predecessor 360 series so that reprogramming would not be necessary for current customers. But they were much faster, thus providing increased computing capacity. Company executives expected results similar to the introduction of the 360 series previously, a net income gain of 20 per cent. But the product was introduced at the height of a recession in 1971. According to one source:

> Not only did the big net gain on the 370 fail to materialize, but the strategy of upgrading the customers backfired. Computer users, more sophisticated than ever, quickly discovered that they could turn in, say, two or three old 360s for one 370 of equivalent power and thereby save money in rental fees—at the expense of IBM. The wave of "downtrading" that hit IBM, plus the discontinuances, or outright cancellations, of rental agreements, and the return of equipment to IBM were mainly responsible for the corporation's poor showing at home last year.[15]

(37)   What effect did IBM's new product have on the primary demand for computers? As you might guess, this can have a significant impact on a company that, as of 1972, had manufactured 70 per cent of the world's estimated 142,000 computers.

will the proposed product help meet customer needs for a complete line?

Regardless of their profitability, new products may have to be introduced and old products retained to provide a complete line of offerings to current or prospective customers. This was Ford's primary motivation in introducing the ill-fated Edsel. The Edsel was intended to fill a hole in the Ford product line between the Ford and Mercury on the one hand and the Lincoln on the other. It was not intended to have been one of Ford's highest money makers, but was to have provided the long-desired competitive alternative for the Oldsmobile and other medium-priced competitors' autos. Instead it offered more chrome to a market saturated with it and one of the largest single product losses in business history to Ford.

After Holiday Inns, Inc. had defined its business as travel, it was logical that it would acquire the nation's second largest interstate bus line, Continental Trailways, Inc. But interstate bus service, although an integral part of the product line necessary to meet Holiday Inns' objective, offers a significantly lower rate of growth than that of the motel business, a fact duly noted by several investment analysts.

[15]Gene Bylinsky, "Vincent Learson Didn't Plan It That Way, But IBM's Toughest Competitor Is—IBM," *Fortune*, (March 1972), pp. 55–58 ff. Quote on p. 58. The information for this example is drawn from this source.

The ability to provide a complete line of products may be particularly critical to manufacturer and dealer alike, as each strives to maintain customer interest by offering a complete range of products. The product line and distribution strategy of the Caterpillar Tractor Co. offers a case in point:

> While the competition vacillated in the early postwar years, Caterpillar expanded its product coverage and strengthened its relationship with its dealers. Caterpillar and its dealers are today linked in a highly profitable symbiosis. Since the company makes the most complete line of equipment in its class, its dealers can prosper by selling Caterpillar products almost exclusively. Dealers for International Harvester and Allis-Chalmers cannot survive without other franchises from competing equipment makers. As a result, Caterpillar dealers make effective salesmen for the company's products, while dealers for International Harvester and Allis-Chalmers have far too many distractions.[16]

In contrast to this strategy is the one that attempts to foster specialization in one or a few items generally considered to constitute a manufacturer's or distributor's product line. Thus, the Maytag Co., headquartered in Newton, Iowa, the "washing machine capital of the world," has consistently performed better than other major appliance manufacturers by building only high-quality washing machines and selling them at premium prices.

(38)   What are the major benefits of each of these product-line strategies?

what effect will the proposed product have on return on investment?

A company's return on investment before and after the introduction of a new product is of concern to its managers and shareholders. Both the potential success of the proposed product in relation to existing products in the line and the extent to which a new product may enhance or cannibalize the sales of other items in the line must be examined carefully.

Where enhancement or cannibalization is not a possibility, the decision is simplified. For a proposed product offering the highest return on investment of all alternatives under consideration, and higher than most or all of a company's existing products, a favorable decision may be easy to defend.

By a simplified example, we can explore management thinking in a situation in which the proposed product may offer a lower rate of contribution to investment but may enhance the sales of existing products. If, by introducing a higher-quality, higher-priced calibrator to the top of its line, the Ace Calibrator Company can encourage more customers to buy more units of the item that formerly carried the highest price tag, Ace may be able to justify the introduction of the new product even though the return on the product itself is low. This is illustrated in Table 4-1. Here, we see that Ace has $10 million invested in its current product line, on which it realizes $20 million in annual sales, a $12 million contribution (after subtracting variable costs of doing business), and

---

[16] Rose, op. cit., at p. 163.

Table 4-1 **Estimated Contribution to Profit for a New Product Enhancing Sales of Existing Products, Ace Calibrator Company**

	With No Increase in Sales for Existing Products		With an Estimated 10% Increase in Sales for Existing Products	
	Existing Products	Proposed New Product	Existing Products	Proposed New Product
Investment required	$10 million	$5 million	$10 million	$5 million
Annual sales	$20 million	$5 million	$22 million	$5 million
Contribution (sales less variable costs) as a proportion of sales	60%	30%	60%	30%
Contribution	$12 million	$1.5 million	$13.2 million	$1.5 million
Fixed costs	$9 million	$1.0 million	$9 million	$1.0 million
Contribution in excess of fixed costs (profit)				
from previous sales	$3 million		$3.0 million	
from new sales		$.5 million	$1.2 million	$.5 million
Rate of profit resulting from each investment	$\dfrac{\$3.0 \text{ million}}{\$10.0 \text{ million}} = 30\%$	$\dfrac{\$.5 \text{ million}}{\$5.0 \text{ million}} = 10\%$	$\dfrac{\$3.0 \text{ million}}{\$10.0 \text{ million}} = 30\%$	$\dfrac{\$1.7 \text{ million}}{\$5.0 \text{ million}} = 34\%$
Combined profit on investment	$\dfrac{\$3.5 \text{ million}}{\$15.0 \text{ million}} = 23.3\%$		$\dfrac{\$4.7 \text{ million}}{\$15.0 \text{ million}} = 31.3\%$	

an annual contribution in excess of fixed costs of $3 million, or 30 per cent on investment. The new high-quality, high-priced calibrator proposed for introduction promises to offer only a 10 per cent contribution to investment in excess of fixed costs (equivalent to profit). Without additional information, we might not decide to introduce the new product.

But if it is estimated that the introduction of the new calibrator model will increase sales of existing products by 10 per cent, the economics of the new product introduction changes considerably, as shown in Table 4-1. Here we see that a 10 per cent increase in sales of existing products represents $2 million, of which 60 per cent, or $1.2 million, is realized as contribution (assuming that fixed costs will remain the same with the increase in volume). Adding this $1.2 million to the $.5 million expected as contribution to profit from the new calibrator itself provides an incremental contribution to profit of $1.7 million, or 34 per cent of the $5 million investment required for the new product. This level of expected contribution is higher than Ace currently is realizing on existing products.

(39)   To what extent do you think this type of reasoning influenced the management at Holiday Inns, Inc. in its decision to acquire an interstate bus line with a lower rate of growth (and quite possibly a lower return on investment)?

(40)   If, instead of increasing the sales of existing products, it was expected that the new model of calibrator would cannibalize (replace) existing sales by 10 per cent, would the rate of profit on investment for the proposed product have

(41) to be higher or lower than that for existing products? What rate of profit on investment would be required to make the proposed product a desirable financial investment?

Cannibalization was expected, for example, by General Foods' management in the introduction of freeze-dried coffee. In advance of a market test, it was expected that the new product would draw freeze-dried coffee users proportionately from users of existing products being sold both by General Foods and its competitors. This was an important consideration, because regular Maxwell House and General Foods' other brands held 24.9 per cent of the regular coffee market—and Instant Maxwell House, Sanka, and Yuban (all General Foods' brands) 50.3 per cent of the instant coffee market—in the United States at the time. Thus, in order to make the new investment desirable, freeze-dried coffee had to be priced at a level in relation to existing products that would produce a 20 per cent higher margin per unit than instant coffee and a 33 per cent higher margin per unit than regular coffee. Market testing later confirmed the initial assumption regarding cannibalization and the appropriateness of General Foods' pricing decision for freeze-dried coffee.

(42) What other considerations would lead you to recommend that General Foods introduce freeze-dried coffee, in spite of an expected reduction in the rate of return on its over-all investment, if you expected sales of a new product to cannibalize sales of existing products in the manner described here?

(43) Returning to the Ace Calibrator Company, how would your requirements for a minimum return on investment on a new product be affected by the expectation that if Ace did not introduce a new calibrator, its competition would, with the same resulting 10 per cent decline in the sales of Ace's existing

(44) products? Under these circumstances, what minimum rate of return on investment would you require for the new product?

the product or service development process

A look at the entire process of developing new products or services provides us with an opportunity to review relationships between a product or service, its prospective markets, other elements of its environment, and the company that makes or distributes it. Questions posed in Chapters 2, 3, and 4 are arrayed in a form suggesting the nature of the process in Figure 4-4.

The process depicted in Figure 4-4 may encompass several weeks or a number of years; it may cost from a few hundred dollars to hundreds of millions of dollars; and it may involve the consideration of only one or several thousands of ideas. Once begun, it may be difficult to speed up or slow down, particularly for large, complex projects involving the investment of a great deal of time and money. For example, one reason why the timing of the introduction of IBM's 370 series of computers was poor, as we saw earlier, was that the company had invested, according to its president, "a few hundred million dollars" in it over a period of at least six years.[17] For this reason and the need to provide a steady stream of new products to its sales force to maintain its morale, IBM's executives decided to go ahead with the venture as originally planned, in spite of a downturn in the economy.

There are two things especially worth noting about Figure 4-4. First, we start

[17]Bylinsky, op. cit., p. 58.

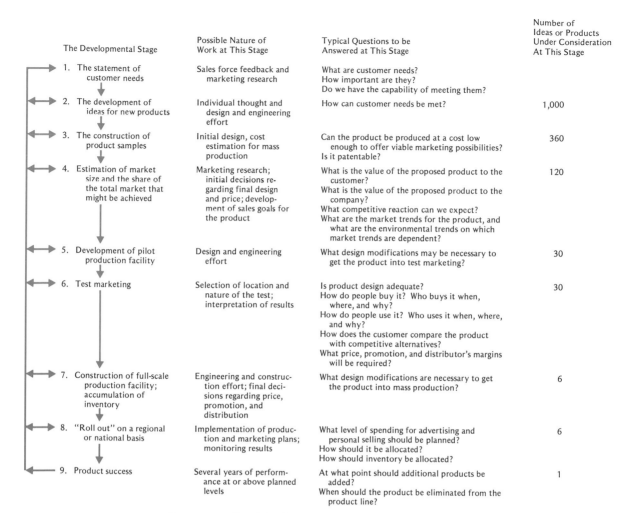

The Developmental Stage	Possible Nature of Work at This Stage	Typical Questions to be Answered at This Stage	Number of Ideas or Products Under Consideration At This Stage
1. The statement of customer needs	Sales force feedback and marketing research	What are customer needs? How important are they? Do we have the capability of meeting them?	
2. The development of ideas for new products	Individual thought and design and engineering effort	How can customer needs be met?	1,000
3. The construction of product samples	Initial design, cost estimation for mass production	Can the product be produced at a cost low enough to offer viable marketing possibilities? Is it patentable?	360
4. Estimation of market size and the share of the total market that might be achieved	Marketing research; initial decisions regarding final design and price; development of sales goals for the product	What is the value of the proposed product to the customer? What is the value of the proposed product to the company? What competitive reaction can we expect? What are the market trends for the product, and what are the environmental trends on which market trends are dependent?	120
5. Development of pilot production facility	Design and engineering effort	What design modifications may be necessary to get the product into test marketing?	30
6. Test marketing	Selection of location and nature of the test; interpretation of results	Is product design adequate? How do people buy it? Who buys it when, where, and why? How do people use it? Who uses it when, where, and why? How does the customer compare the product with competitive alternatives? What price, promotion, and distributor's margins will be required?	30
7. Construction of full-scale production facility; accumulation of inventory	Engineering and construction effort; final decisions regarding price, promotion, and distribution	What design modifications are necessary to get the product into mass production?	6
8. "Roll out" on a regional or national basis	Implementation of production and marketing plans; monitoring results	What level of spending for advertising and personal selling should be planned? How should it be allocated? How should inventory be allocated?	6
9. Product success	Several years of performance at or above planned levels	At what point should additional products be added? When should the product be eliminated from the product line?	1

Figure 4-4. Consideration of the product-market fit, the product-environment fit, and the product-company fit in the development process for new products or services. (Estimates of the number of ideas on products under consideration at each stage are based on a composite of industry experience.)

with a statement of customer needs. Secondly, nearly all of the stages of development are strongly marketing-oriented. One recent survey has concluded that new-product thinking is shifting from a technological to a marketing base.[18] This is occurring at a time when industry is spending an estimated $12 to $15 billion each year on new-product development, an effort that may get six products to market out of every one thousand ideas, only to see five out of the six fail.

Several points are emphasized repeatedly by those engaged in the development of new industrial and consumer products. Among them are the need today

[18]"New Products: The Push Is on Marketing," *Business Week,* (March 4, 1972), pp. 72–77. Much of the material in this section is based on this source.

to (1) be ruthless in weeding out new products that fail to meet a specific market need, (2) reduce the time required for market testing, (3) reduce the time required for a new product to become profitable in the market place, (4) be prepared to spend greater amounts of money and incur greater risks in the product-development process than several years ago, (5) maintain a steady flow of new products to the market, (6) look to the customer's customer, where necessary, for a measure of potential market success, and (7) develop new products as system components or interrelated items to facilitate end use.

emphasis on meeting a specific market need

Comments produced by one survey included the following:

> "The critical factor in the success or failure of new-product development today is making sure your research people are marketing-oriented," says one industrial goods executive. This means, adds Eugene W. Helms, manager of advanced corporate planning for Texas Instruments, Incorporated, "that research should be approached from the standpoint of a problem to be solved, and then developing a program to solve it. If you solve a real problem, you can be confident that the product will have a market. . . ."[19]

the reduction of time lags

With an increasing flood of new products into the market, it is often necessary for a company to develop new methods for shortening market tests and even deleting such tests to speed up the introduction process. Of course, the gains from being first into the market may be offset by a higher failure rate.

A classic example of a recent "race" to market is provided by Gillette's Trac II razor, the razor with two blades. In only six months, it moved from an unnamed, handmade prototype to a finished product with enough production capacity for a national "roll out" by World Series time. The initial promotion alone cost $4 million for this product. And Gillette, as a result, beat Schick's double-blade razor to market by fewer than six months.

Because of general perceptions that the average life for products is becoming shorter, many companies are shortening the period of time in which a new product is expected to pay back the investment in it. This may help explain the relatively high failure rate for products that do reach the market; managements of many companies are killing them sooner.

[19] Ibid., pp. 73–74.

growing investment and risk in the product-development process

Information reduces the likelihood of a poor decision and the risk associated with new-product development. But the cost of information often is high and is getting higher. For example, the market testing alone of General Foods' freeze-dried coffee required more than a year and the expenditure of hundreds of thousands of dollars. Nor did this guarantee a good decision. As one marketing executive put it:

> Don't think it is easy to read even a very successful test market. When we entered our first area, Albany, New York, almost half of our shipments were bootlegged outside of the territory . . . had we relied solely on shipment information, . . . we might have built a plant twice as big as it should have been.[20]

maintaining a steady flow of new products

In an age of reduced product life expectancies, the shifting nature of a market and competitive pressures may require a continuing new-product development effort. This can make it more difficult to maintain a minimum level of effort and expertise in product development in a company's organization. Finally, as we saw in the IBM 370 example, a continuing flow of new products can boost sales force morale, if they are successful.

looking to the customer's customer

The end user of a product often is the judge of its acceptability. This may require looking beyond a firm's immediate customer to the ultimate consumer to get a true measure of a product's potential. It is especially critical for the manufacturer or distributor of industrial products used in the manufacture of other products for end use. A failure to do this, for example, is given as one major reason why Du Pont had to absorb a $100 million loss in discontinuing Corfam, its synthetic shoe leather.

Corfam had many advantages for the shoe manufacturer, including a more stable price structure than natural hides. It offered consumers low care and long life in exchange for relatively high price. Unfortunately, after Corfam was introduced, shoe-buying patterns shifted to the purchase of low-priced but fashionable shoes, with little value placed on Corfam's advantages by the ultimate consumer.

[20] Ibid., p. 74.

developing product "systems" to facilitate end use

The age of the computer pointed up the need for a systems approach not only to marketing, but to product development as well. Many companies have found that it is difficult to sell a central computing unit without compatible peripheral equipment for the input, output, storage, and conversion of information. This must be accompanied by other elements of a product "package," including programming support, assistance in fitting the equipment into an existing system, and educational programs in the use of equipment and programs. More recently, the same requirements have arisen in the development of cash-transfer systems that replace the old cash registers in department stores and supermarkets.

Several years ago, the Monsanto Company developed a material that could be used for bottling carbonated beverages. But before it could even induce the Coca-Cola Co. to test the material, Monsanto had to develop machines to manufacture, sterilize, fill, and cap bottles made of the new material.

Birth is a much more pleasant prospect than death. But with a constant flow of new products coming to market, the death of other products becomes an economic necessity. Like a tree, the product line must be pruned if it is to continue to bloom and grow.

product-line pruning

In most organizations it is much easier to give birth to a product or service than to kill one. Old products remain because they are defended, often in terms of the need to offer a complete line to customers, primarily by marketing executives. Or their presence may result from the absence of a periodic, organized review utilizing the criteria discussed here.

Typically, product-line pruning takes place when a company's profit performance is declining, perhaps as a result of generally poor economic conditions. Thus, American Standard, Inc. eliminated 20 per cent of the shower heads, faucets, and other items in its line of bathroom fixtures during a recent period of depressed earnings.[21] Westinghouse Electric Corp., at about the same time, decided to sell off or close down the manufacturing operations of its portable products division, which produced toasters, coffeemakers, and other small appliances.

Other causes of nonroutine pruning may include the rise of competition. The capture of 75 per cent of the United States market for bicycle tires by foreign competition, coupled with poor prospects for being able to regain it, led Uniroyal, a leading United States tire producer, to drop the item from its line. Or an existing product may require a larger continuing investment in its

---

[21] Ralph E. Winter, "More Companies Drop Products That Make Unsatisfactory Profit," *Wall Street Journal*, (Oct. 15, 1971), pp. 1, 31. Quote on p. 31. Much of the information in this section is based on this article.

further development than a company's management is willing or able to provide. For example, when faced with the need to invest $500 million more in its line of computers, RCA's management decided to discontinue computer manufacturing operations at a $250 million after-tax loss. The price of continued operation, in the words of one executive, "was simply too high for RCA."[22]

Nonroutine pruning often results in unusually severe and unwarranted cutbacks in product-line offerings. It may be required by the absence of a more systematic, periodic procedure. One such procedure is that instituted by the Mead Paper Division of the Mead Corp. several years ago. It provides an unusual insight into the way in which the process can work:

> Mead Paper officials . . . went through their whole product list, evaluating each grade, size, color, finish and package three different ways. They looked at Mead's share of market for the product, the company's production costs in relation to other producers, and the expected future of the product itself.
>
> "If we had a good market share, were a good low-cost producer and the type of paper was expanding its markets, obviously it stayed in the line," explains an official. "In other items where we had a good market share and the product was growing, but we had low cost effectiveness, we tried to move the product to another paper-making machine where we could make it cheaper. But if we didn't have either a good market position or good cost effectiveness and the product wasn't growing, we just decided we wouldn't make that item anymore."[23]

As one Mead executive put it, "You don't hear that talk about being 'papermaker to America' around here anymore."[24] As a result of the conclusion by its management that it did not need to carry a number of marginal and unprofitable items in order to maintain sales of its profitable products, the Mead Paper Division's management reduced the number of types, colors, and sizes of its paper products from six-thousand to about three-thousand.

Professor Philip Kotler has proposed that a systematic appraisal of a product line be carried out on a two-stage basis following the organization of a product-pruning group.[25] First, simple criteria would be developed by which a computer could scan all products, particularly in a line encompassing many items, to identify candidates for further review. Signs of weakness that could be reflected by such criteria might include declining gross margin, declining sales in relation to total company sales, or low contribution to fixed costs, among others.

In a second stage, the product-pruning group could then select items to be eliminated on the basis of more extensive and less quantifiable criteria. These might include (1) the future market potential for the product, (2) gains to be realized by product modification, (3) gains to be realized by modifying the marketing strategy for the product, (4) useful executive time to be gained by abandoning the product, (5) the attractiveness of the firm's alternative opportunities, (6) contribution by the product in excess of the variable costs associated with its production and distribution, and (7) contribution of the product to the sale of other products.

[22] Ibid.
[23] Ibid., p. 31.
[24] Ibid.
[25] Philip Kotler, "Phasing Out Weak Products," *Harvard Business Review*, **43:**107–118 (March–April, 1965).

(45)
(46)
(47)

Should such a product-pruning group be formed within an organization's marketing department? Which functions within an organization should be represented on such a group? What would determine the frequency with which such a group should conduct its product-line investigations?

product life cycles

The birth, life, and death of products have become the interest of those who have formulated theories regarding product life cycles. After their development and introduction, there is a great deal of evidence that individual products and product categories follow life-cycle patterns, illustrated in Figure 4-5.

product life-cycle stages

Four stages characterize the cycle through which a product or product category passes: introduction, rapid growth, maturity, and decline. There are few products for which the life-cycle pattern has been as dramatically drawn as that for the pocket electronic calculator.

Introduction. The development of integrated circuits, combining as many as several thousand transistors and diodes on a "chip" no larger than one-quarter-inch square, paved the way in the late 1960s for the redesign and miniaturization of a number of products, including the development of pocket electronic calculators.

The pioneer of this story was the Bowmar Instrument Corp., which began marketing a pocket calculator in 1971 manufactured from purchased integrated

Figure 4-5. Stages of the life cycle for competing products in a typical industry.

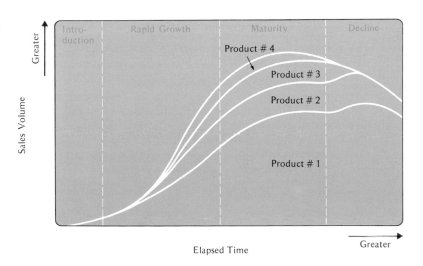

circuits. Like their counterparts in other industries, Bowmar executives were willing to bear the initial risks of failure in exchange for a ground-floor position and perhaps the dominant market share if the product could catch on. Their hopes were based on the ability of the pocket calculator to meet needs totally different than its predecessor—the standard-sized four-function (addition, subtraction, multiplication, and division) calculator selling for about $400.

(48)

(49)

(50)

At an initial price of $240 for its lowest-priced model, it was necessary that Bowmar develop a marketing strategy that would provide for a great amount of customer education and a reduction of perceived purchase risks. How could Bowmar best meet this need, putting aside considerations of the costs of various efforts? For example, would you expect expenditures for direct-selling effort, and margins paid to wholesalers and retailers, in relation to sales to be higher or lower than in later stages of the product life cycle? What about costs of advertising in relation to sales?

As you might expect, because of the lack of competition and the desire to recover its investment in its product- and market-development effort, a pioneering company often will ask a relatively high price for its product.

Market Growth. The developer of a successful product or service rarely enjoys the loneliness of its position for long. However, early competition can have its benefits. Recently, for example, the new product director for Alberto-Culver's new feminine hygiene spray, FDS, welcomed a competitor, Pristeen, which FDS had beaten to market by about three months:

> When you wage a competitive campaign that demands consumer education, you and the competitor share the educational expense. And what you get is 20 per cent of a $100 million market instead of 50 per cent of a $20 million market.[26]

(51)

How would you explain this?

Early competition, especially in the form of Texas Instruments, Incorporated (TI) also had its drawbacks for Bowmar in the pocket electronic calculator market. For TI, a manufacturer of integrated circuits, realized a desire long held by its executives to get into the production and marketing of a consumer product by introducing its four-function pocket electronic calculator at a price of $149, $30 less than Bowmar's, but a price that Bowmar met. Bowmar continued to be the market leader, selling more than 25 per cent of the 2.5 million units sold in 1972.

Both Bowmar and TI offered the bulk of their product for sale through office machine outlets, department stores, and outlets for electronics products. Such retailers were offered margins of about 50 per cent, or half of the price to final buyers. Introductions were accompanied by extensive advertising that, in some cases, outlined the steps needed to perform various calculations. How would you explain these actions? Are they about what you expected?

(52)

(53)

With the rapid development of the market, more than fifty other United States and several Japanese companies introduced models of pocket electronic calculators. Even so, sales volumes for the industry leaders were doubled and

---

[26]"New Products: The Push Is on Marketing," *Business Week,* (March 4, 1972), pp. 72–77. Quote on p. 75.

redoubled in the space of a few months. This allowed TI to practice its theory that with every doubling of production, reductions in costs obtained through the "learning effect" enabled it to reduce its prices 25 to 30 per cent in order to build a larger market and reduce costs and prices even more. As a result, it quickly reduced the price for its standard unit to $119, a price that Bowmar again met. Newer competitors, in order to make themselves known and gain a share of the rapidly growing market, began stressing standard product features at lower and lower prices. Both Bowmar and TI continued to reduce prices in response to competitive moves.

Electronic calculators began appearing in discount and variety stores, some priced as low as $49.95. One entrant to the market, Hewlett-Packard Co., centered its marketing efforts around a mail-order business supported by advertising that encouraged potential customers to order directly from the company, a firm with a respected name in measurement devices and desk-top computers. Advertising in general began to stress price at least as much as product features.

By 1974, nearly 12 million pocket calculators were sold in the United States, nearly equal to the number that had been purchased in the three previous years, and 50 per cent more units than were sold in 1973.

Because of the rapid decline of distribution and production costs on a per unit basis, profits during the period of rapid growth increase rapidly and often reach their peaks, at least for those competitors commanding the largest shares of the market. At the same time, results from one comprehensive study suggest that, at least in certain industries, costs for promotional efforts, when compared with sales, remain roughly the same.[27]

Maturity. Although industry sales continued to increase rapidly, the best estimates early in 1975 were that the over-all demand for pocket electronic calculators in the United States would level out at about 20 million per year in 1978. Foreign markets were expected to mature several years later at about the same figure. In total, one estimate expected worldwide ownership eventually to reach about 160 million, with perhaps a four-year replacement cycle for existing owners.

By this time, TI had surpassed Bowmar in sales and had captured nearly one fourth of the United States market. Rockwell International, a high-volume manufacturer of integrated circuits for other calculator assemblers, entered the market in 1974 with a complete line of well-designed calculators priced beginning at $29.95. It was thought that this line would gain wide distribution among leading retail stores in which salespeople might use the low price for the basic model to "trade up" prospects to more expensive items in Rockwell's line.

In yet another development, the Gillette Co. announced that it would begin marketing pocket electronic calculators at relatively low prices through many of the 500,000 outlets handling its well-known shaving products and toiletries, including drug and grocery stores.

One estimate indicated that twenty-nine North American and Japanese producers and distributors of pocket electronic calculators dropped out of the

---

[27] Robert D. Buzzell and Robert E. M. Nourse, *Product Innovation, the Product Life Cycle, and Competitive Behavior in Selected Food Processing Industries, 1947–1964* (Cambridge, Mass.: Arthur D. Little, 1966).

market in a twelve-month period in late 1973 and early 1974. Another opinion suggested that only those competitors who manufactured their own integrated circuits, rather than assembled circuits purchased from other sources, would survive the competition. As one student of the industry put it:

> Calculator makers that produce their own chips [integrated circuits] can save up to $1 per machine with volume output . . . . Such savings can be crucial in a $30 calculator that wholesales for $15.[28]

By now, Bowmar Instruments was making every effort to bring a new plant "on stream" for the production of its own integrated circuits.

In the study cited previously, it was found that during the maturity stage, the ratio of advertising and other marketing expenditures to sales declines substantially and then stabilizes at a rate much lower than that prevailing in the introductory and rapid-growth stages.[29] Would you expect this?

A basic characteristic of product maturity is suggested by one executive as follows: "If you can't put 'new' on the label, it had better say ' 7 cents off.'" It is at this point that a company most likely may make efforts to rekindle or extend the growth in sales for its product by (1) introducing variations on the original product designed to increase purchases by existing users, (2) designing promotional campaigns to increase the frequency of use among existing customers, (3) seeking out new users for existing products, possibly by marketing new versions of existing products at lower costs and prices, and (4) searching for new uses (new markets) for a product or service. What efforts, if any, of this type have you observed among producers of pocket electronic calculators?

Levitt has argued that a strategy for prolonging the rapid growth stage of the life cycle, or for returning a product from maturity to rapid growth, by one of the preceding means should be planned, if possible, shortly after its introduction on the market. He cites several benefits from this practice:

1. It generates an active rather than a reactive product policy.
2. It lays out a long-term plan designed to infuse new life into the product at the right time, with the right degree of care, and with the right amount of effort.
3. [It] forces a company to adopt a wider view of the nature of the product it is dealing with.[30]

Decline. Although the pocket electronic calculator may not yet be in the declining stage of its life cycle, we can anticipate what will happen in this industry in a few years. It is likely that the number of competitors will drop. As a result, the companies remaining in the market may be able to maintain reasonably profitable businesses by selling to larger shares of a declining market. Also, continually lower costs for marketing and production offer the potential for higher profit for those companies able to avoid severe price competition. This leads to the creation of so-called cash cows in a firm's product line. These

[28]"The Semiconductor Becomes a New Marketing Force," *Business Week,* (Aug. 24, 1974), pp. 34–39. Quote on p. 38. Much of the material in this section is based on this article.

[29]Buzzell and R. Nourse, op. cit., p. 4.

[30]Theodore Levitt, "Exploit the Product Life Cycle," *Harvard Business Review,* **43**:81–94 (Nov.–Dec. 1965). Quote on pp. 91–92.

are products in mature or declining markets requiring little investment and produced at low cost, to be "milked" over time for as much profit as they may be able to produce. Products such as "Jello" gelatin and "Quaker" rolled oats offer classic examples of cash cows. Can you identify others that are likely to have similar characteristics?

(56)

(57)

As a means of reviewing the effect of product life cycles on various aspects of marketing strategy, review once more how you would expect the following to vary as a product moves from the stage of introduction through that of decline: (1) knowledgeability and self-confidence of the customer in purchasing a product or service, (2) the need for sales effort at the point of purchase, (3) the relative importance of informative versus "image-creating" content in advertising, (4) the relative importance of price in the buying decision, (5) the need for product availability in the channel (in part a function of a customer's willingness to wait for the availability of a particular brand rather than substitute another), (6) the ratio of marketing expense to sales, (7) price per unit, and (8) competition.

As a final footnote on the status of the life cycle for pocket electronic calculators, early in 1975 the Bowmar Instrument Corp. announced that it lost as much as $20 million in 1974, that it had replaced its founder and chairman, and that it had filed for court protection under the Federal Bankruptcy Act.

trends in product life-cycle length

The work of Buzzell and Nourse indicated that, for companies developing and marketing such products as cold breakfast cereal, cake mixes, dog food, frozen dinners and specialties, and margarine, the average time required from initial research and development activities to limited distribution was about thirty-two months, with five additional months required to achieve "full" distribution.[31] They found also that 61 per cent of all new products had achieved "break even" (that is, cumulative sales equal to or more than the cumulative variable costs) by the end of the third year following their distribution. Thus, for two products out of three, up to three years were required to move the product past the introductory stage in the product life cycle. Many of the remaining products never made it to the stage of rapid growth.

Although there is little evidence to support it, it has been suggested that the length of the product life cycle is becoming shorter, primarily because of the more rapid rate of new product introduction. For example:

> During the last ten years, while new brand introductions more than doubled in the frozen food and dry grocery business, average product "life expectancies" fell from thirty-six months to twelve months. This means you would have only ninety to one-hundred days to make a product stick.[32]

[31] Buzzell and Nourse, op. cit., p. 89.
[32] "New Products: The Push Is on Marketing," op. cit., p. 72.

128

What implications would you expect this assertion, combined with the information given in Figure 4-1, to have for the ratio of a company's marketing expenses to its total sales?

There may be a considerable difference, too, between the length of product life cycles for goods and services purchased by industry as components for other products (often called *industrial goods*) as opposed to products purchased for end use by individuals (termed *consumer goods*). For example, how would you expect the length of the product life cycle to vary for a new type of cold-rolled stainless steel as opposed to a new style of ten-key electronic calculator? Or for a new type of lift truck for handling materials in a company's warehouse as opposed to a new style of motor home?

the importance of product life-cycle concepts

A knowledge of life-cycle patterns in a particular industry can provide a manager with the basis for managing a company's line of products or services in much the same way as a portfolio of stocks. A diversified portfolio may include products at each stage in their respective life cycles. Products in later stages may generate the funds needed to develop and introduce new products. New-product introductions, because they may hasten the decline of existing products, may have to be timed carefully. The manner in which the product portfolio is managed, taking into account interrelationships among products, their markets, their competition and other environmental conditions, and a company's goals and capabilities, in total is often the most important fact in building investor confidence in a company's ability to realize profitable performances with some degree of assurance over the long run.

In addition, product life-cycle theories can provide us with many insights into what is going on in an industry, or how a particular product should be marketed at various stages in its life. For this reason, we'll return to them from time to time.

time marches on

To bring us full cycle from the story about The O. M. Scott & Sons Company with which we began this chapter, it is interesting to note that several years ago the Monsanto Company developed a synthetic, ribbonlike material and hit on the idea that it might make a substitute for grass. The company's chemical engineers then designed a mounting, a padded base, and finally a drainage system. The finished product was Astroturf, known to every football fan. How does this help explain the advertisement shown in Figure 4-2? How might it affect the product life cycle for Scott's Proturf services and products described earlier? What implications does the development of Astroturf have for a company defining its product line as green lawns?

summary

A definition of the basic purpose of an organization is necessary to the effective match of product to a company's product line. This is typified by asking the question: "What business are we in?" The question is becoming more and more important with the increasing volume of new products introduced into the marketplace—a trend resulting from a continuing attention to customer needs, competition through new products that are intended either to emulate or preempt competitors, increasing market size, and factors internal to the firm such as the desire to improve return on investment and individual performance.

In selecting from a myriad of potential new products, a number of criteria may be developed for matching products to companies. These include the extent to which a prospective product conforms to a company's business plan, reflects its capabilities both in terms of technology and marketing, complements its current product line, helps meet its customers' needs for a complete service or product line, and enhances the company's return on investment.

The new-product development process today is characterized by the need to (1) select only products that meet specific market needs, (2) reduce the time required for market testing, (3) reduce the time required for a new product to become profitable in the marketplace, (4) be prepared to invest heavily and incur greater risks, (5) maintain a steady flow of new products to the market, (6) look beyond immediate customers' needs to those of ultimate buyers, and (7) develop new products as elements in interrelated systems that facilitate end use.

Many of the same preceding criteria developed for matching products to companies can be employed in pruning old products from the line. This requires a systematic, almost ruthless, examination and an adherence to previously agreed on guidelines for dropping existing products.

There is a great deal of evidence that products follow somewhat common life-cycle patterns, leading to the generalization that product life cycles can be defined in terms of four stages: introduction, rapid growth, maturity, and decline. Each of these stages may call for a different marketing strategy. It may be desirable for a company to offer products in each of these stages at a particular point in time in order to maintain a diversified product-line portfolio.

In the last three chapters, we have considered (1) the manner in which products can be matched with markets in general and customer needs in particular; (2) demographic, economic, social, regulatory, and competitive aspects of the environment; and (3) company and product-line strategies. With this foundation, we will turn next to elements of marketing strategy, including those of pricing, advertising, personal selling, and channels of distribution. In a sense, we already have begun our discussion, because a product or service is often the most important of the mix of elements that makes up a marketing strategy.

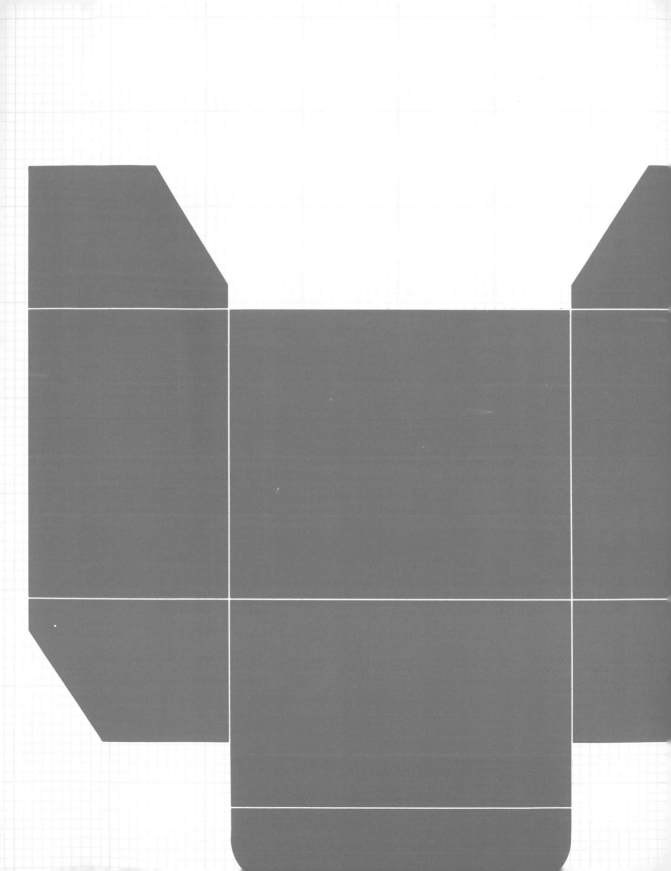

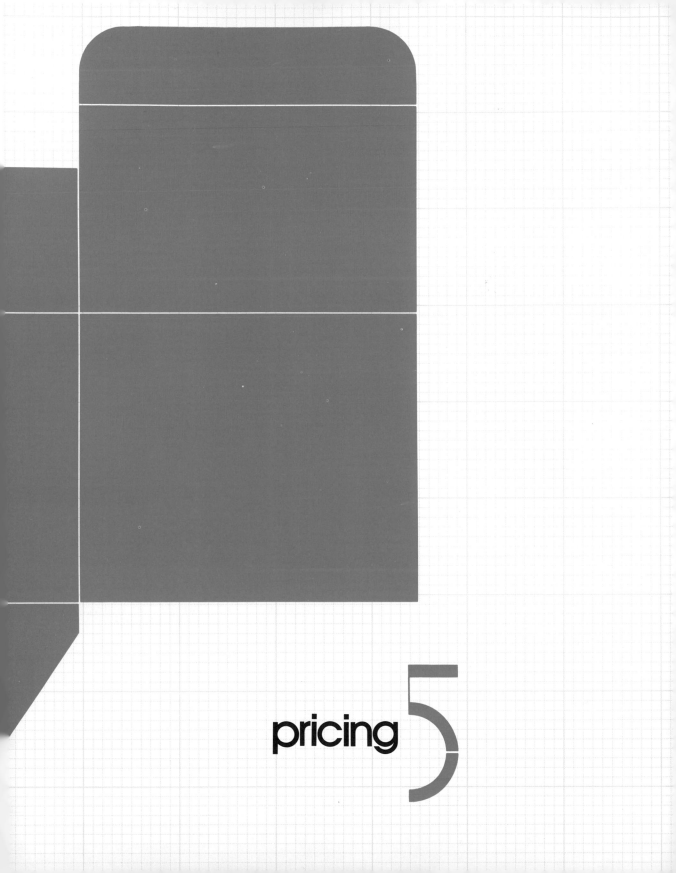

pricing 5

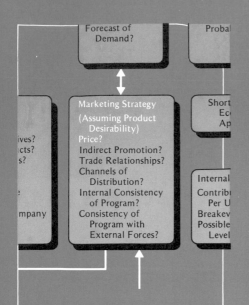

Forecast of
Demand?

Probal

Marketing Strategy
(Assuming Product
Desirability)
Price?
Indirect Promotion?
Trade Relationships?
Channels of
Distribution?
Internal Consistency
of Program?
Consistency of
Program with
External Forces?

Short
Ec
Ap

ives?
cts?
s?

Internal
Contribu
Per U
Breakev
Possible
Level

mpany

When an elephant hunter, besieged by a three-ton beast with a killer's instinct hurtling toward him in a Tarzan movie, needs quick, dramatic results, he reaches for his elephant gun. Price and pricing policies are the manager's elephant guns. Weapons with the size and force of an elephant gun are banned for use in certain parts of the world. Similarly, industries have reached "arms pacts" to shift competitive emphasis away from price, precisely because it can have such immediate and important effects on a company's and an industry's business performance and structure.

It is perhaps natural that such an interesting, powerful weapon as price should have fascinated early scholars developing a field of study that later would be called economics. This led to a natural evolution of a vast amount of work that we label *price theory*, a systematic description of some of the things that managers take into account intuitively in arriving at pricing policies and decisions. Starting with some of the elements of price theory, our objective is to look into the many factors that may influence a manager's pricing decisions.

Here we want to try to understand how prospective travelers may have regarded Eastern Airlines' efforts to introduce a low-priced air shuttle service, why steel company executive Roger Blough behaved the way he did during his confrontation with President Kennedy, and why the manager of Dubrow's Cafeteria at a time of declining business and rising costs reduced the price of a steak platter from $3.05 to $1.99.

the customer's view of price[1]

Early in 1961, executives of Eastern Airlines were contemplating the introduction of an air shuttle service over the most heavily traveled of the world's airline routes, those connecting New York's LaGuardia airport with Washington, D. C., and Boston. In contrast to regular airline service between these cities, the plan called for Eastern to replace its regular service with one that would guarantee a seat to every prospective passenger who appeared prior to flight time on a nonreservation basis. Air shuttle flights would feature in-flight ticketing and would offer none of the usual in-flight food or beverage service. Terminal facilities used for the air shuttle, at least at LaGuardia and Washington's National airports, would be spartan.

The service would be offered on an hourly basis in each direction between LaGuardia and Washington between the hours of 7:00 A.M. and 10:00 P.M. Under the guaranteed-seat plan, Eastern would have to provide standby aircraft for each scheduled departure for use in the event that the first section filled up and one or more extra passengers appeared. Older aircraft owned by the airline would be used on the air shuttle at the outset. Eventually, it was hoped that older aircraft would be used only for standby service.

It was estimated that the total costs, including ground services and administrative overhead, of operating one 95-seat aircraft in the air shuttle would be about $400 per hour. This was significantly less than the competition, and resulted from the reduction in services and the use of fully depreciated, older equipment. Because the basic plan required two planes and crews to be ready at each airport at each departure time (one for first section and one for standby), the total daily cost of the air shuttle operation between Washington and New York could be as much as $25,600 ($400 × four planes and crews × 16 hours), a figure that could be higher with the need for additional airplanes or lower to the extent that standby aircraft were not flown (resulting in total costs of only $270 per hour for planes requiring no fuel and utilizing standby crews at half pay).

[1]Much of the information in this example is based on "Eastern Airlines (A)," (Boston: Intercollegiate Clearing House, copyright 1962 by the President and Fellows of Harvard College).

135

On the assumption that a one-way trip between the cities required ninety minutes for passenger loading, flight, unloading, and aircraft preparation, each of the planes could make as many as eleven one-way trips per day, providing at least a capacity of 4,180 seats (4 planes × 11 trips × 95 seats per plane) per day between New York and Washington. The percentage of available seats filled (called load factor) on Eastern's flights over this route during 1960 had been roughly 60 per cent. At the same ratio, the total cost per filled seat on the air shuttle would be about $10.

The 4,180 available seats per day represented an increase of about 37 per cent over the number available (3,040) on Eastern's existing sixteen hourly flights per day in each direction between Washington and LaGuardia that the air shuttle would replace. To maintain its average load factor on this route, Eastern would have to (1) persuade people to fly who had never flown before, (2) persuade those who had flown to fly more often, or (3) attract passengers from its major competitors on the route.

Costs of transportation by various alternative methods between New York and Washington were $8.50 by bus, $10.65 by rail coach, $16.14 by air coach, $19.14 by first-class air, and about $20 by private auto (regardless of the number of passengers). Total transit times varied from about two hours by air to five hours or more by surface methods from city center to city center.

The mode of travel between the two cities, as between most major cities in the United States, was dominated by the private automobile, with more than 90 per cent of the people traveling by this method. Nevertheless, more than 1,300,000 had traveled between the two cities by air during 1960. Of these, roughly 630,000 had traveled on Eastern; 370,000 on American Airlines; 220,000 on Northeast Airlines; and 80,000 on National Airlines. Eastern's share of the total had, however, fallen from about 54 per cent during the first quarter of 1960 to about 43 per cent during the last quarter of the year as competitors introduced more frequent service on the route.

Basic questions confronting its planners were "Should we go ahead with the air shuttle?" and "What fares should we charge for it?" How would you respond to these queries?

As a New York resident planning a one-month vacation in Washington, D. C., how important would the price of air shuttle service be in your decision to use one mode of travel or another? Would your answer be the same if you were going to Washington for the weekend? How would your views regarding price change if you were a business executive planning a one-day business trip?

What kind of customer needs–customer segment matrix would you draw for the proposed air shuttle service? What would it suggest to you about the pricing of the service in relation to existing airline services?

On April 30, 1961, Eastern Airlines introduced the air shuttle service between LaGuardia and Washington at a fare of $14 one-way for an adult. Within a period of several years, during which time Eastern also instituted a comparable air shuttle service between Washington and Newark (within the New York City Port Authority), Eastern's share of scheduled airline passengers between Washington and New York rose to 85 per cent. During the same period, the total volume of air passenger traffic between Washington and New York increased at a rate less than the national average of 41 per cent.

(7)
(8) (9)
(10)

Surveys, among other things, indicated that 40 per cent of all air shuttle travelers made their trip on the day they decided to go. What types of travelers are these? What does it suggest about the make-up of the market? How important is price to these travelers? In view of your responses to these questions, how would you evaluate Eastern's pricing decision for the air shuttle?

(11)

To what extent do you think price may have stimulated the increase in the number of passengers flying between Washington and New York after the introduction of the air shuttle? To what extent did it influence Eastern's market share? What other influences may have been at work here?

(12)
(13)

Air shuttle equipment and manpower requirements largely were governed by peak travel volumes that occurred each morning and late afternoon. As a result, a proposal was made several years after the initiation of the service to reduce the one-way fare for off-peak (midday and late evening) travel by $3. Based on what you have concluded about the sensitivity of the air shuttle's customers to low prices, how would you regard this proposal?

(14)

□ □ □

After the proposed fare reduction was implemented, an Eastern executive estimated that the fare reduction had raised the company's off-peak business only 1 to 2 per cent, and that the reductions had reduced revenues about $2.5 million over what would have been collected on regular fares.

price and value concepts

The seller may regard price as the amount for which he or she needs to sell a product or service in order to make a profit. A buyer, on the other hand, often views price in a different way, as one of the costs of acquiring and owning a product or service.

In real estate marketing, there are a number of axioms, including (1) the market value of a house is the price that someone is willing to pay for it, and (2) any house sold cannot have been overpriced, because at least one customer was willing to pay for it.

Why is a house sold? Probably because the customer perceived the house as providing a package of potential values greater than the figure at which the house was priced. These values include not only economic values associated with a convenient location and the provision for sufficient income-producing work space, but also noneconomic, or psychic, values such as status. Looking at it this way, how many "market values" might a house have?

(15)

(16)

What proportion of the time do you pay more for candy bars at your local "mom and pop" corner tobacco or drugstore as opposed to buying them in quantity for a lower price at a more distant supermarket? Why? Why are prices higher at small grocery outlets that provide staples such as bread and milk and stay open twenty-four hours per day? Is it totally because of higher costs

(17)

resulting from their small size and small unit of sale? Price must be only one of several factors that determine a customer's willingness to buy a product or service.

Perhaps this explains in large measure the difficulties that many large communities have encountered in marketing mass transit for urban transportation to the public. What, besides price or cost, determines a customer's decision to use public transportation as opposed to a private automobile? Why will he or she drive an automobile ten miles to work at a total cost of twelve cents per mile rather than ride the bus for a 30-cent fare? If the bus fare were to be reduced to 20 cents, would many of these drivers take the bus? Would you expect a greater increase in traffic from a 10-cent reduction in the bus fare or a ten-minute reduction in transit time for the one-way trip between home and place of work? Why, in the face of faster transit time, might some people continue to drive?

One sizeable test of the influence of price on the demand for public transportation was conducted in Rome, Italy in 1971. For one week, at a cost of the equivalent of some $6 million to the city, public transportation was made free to all. This represented an attempt to measure whether a sufficient number of people could be discouraged from driving their automobiles into the center of Rome and thus reduce public expenditures for new roadways, road maintenance, and the restoration of crumbling historic structures damaged by automobile exhaust by more than the "cost" of the fare reduction. What would your expectations for the success of this test be?

□ □ □

The volume of users of public transportation in Rome increased by about 60 per cent during the test period. Although this was somewhat less than expected, and included many former walkers rather than drivers, the increase in volume was sufficiently encouraging to bring the city's commissioner of transportation to recommend permanent adoption of the plan. Does this example suggest a set of conditions in which nonconventional approaches to pricing are more likely to be attempted?

Although price has a direct and important influence on potential transactions, it rarely stands alone as the sole determinant. Customers consciously or subconsciously evaluate products or services in terms of the cost-value inventory shown in Figure 5-1, based in part on our study of the buying process illustrated in Figure 2-1, p. 34. Such a cost-value inventory places price in perspective. How many of the costs and values listed in Figure 5-1 are price-oriented? How would you construct cost-value inventories for actual and potential users of conventional air transport and air shuttle services between Washington and New York at the time of our appraisal? Based on Figure 5-1, how would you explain the difference between the terms *price* and *value*?

This suggests why a product or service with the lowest price, or even the lowest total cost to the buyer, rarely commands the entire market. Its importance among costs and perceived values associated with a transaction does, however, influence relationships between price, primary demand, and selective demand. Such relationships, often expressed by the term *price-demand elasticity,* are important to a manager planning future pricing strategies.

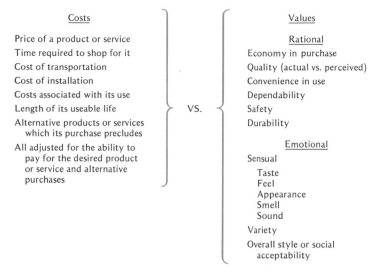

Figure 5-1. The customer's view of a price, cost, value, and the relative desirability of a prospective purchase—a cost-value inventory.

Costs VS. Values

Costs
Price of a product or service
Time required to shop for it
Cost of transportation
Cost of installation
Costs associated with its use
Length of its useable life
Alternative products or services
 which its purchase precludes
All adjusted for the ability to
 pay for the desired product
 or service and alternative
 purchases

Values

Rational
Economy in purchase
Quality (actual vs. perceived)
Convenience in use
Dependability
Safety
Durability

Emotional
Sensual
 Taste
 Feel
 Appearance
 Smell
 Sound
Variety
Overall style or social
 acceptability

price-demand elasticity

Under most circumstances, as prices (and total acquisition costs) are reduced, producing a more favorable relationship between cost and value for customers of alternative goods and services, we expect sales to rise. In situations where lowered prices create sufficiently favorable cost-value relationships for new groups of customers, we have said that primary demand has been affected. The announcement on March 19, 1908 that the Ford Model T, with features comparable to other autos priced at $2,000 or more, would be priced at $825 undoubtedly affected primary demand for automobiles as potential customers diverted expenditures out of other products and services.

In addition, Ford's action may have persuaded Buick owners or potential buyers to switch their allegiance to Ford, stimulating selective demand through a shift in the existing market for automobiles from one competitor to another.

positive elasticity

Price-demand elasticity is a shorthand method of describing relationships between price and demand. It is calculated as follows:

$$\frac{(\text{percentage change in demand}) \, (-1)}{(\text{percentage change in price})}$$

(Note: The "−1" is accounted for by the inverse relationship between price and demand implied in measures of price-demand elasticity.) If, when Ford reduced its prices in 1908 by about 20 per cent, its demand doubled, its price-demand

(28)

elasticity at that point was $\dfrac{100\%(-1)}{-20\%} = 5.0$. Had demand increased only 10 per cent, what would the price-demand elasticity for Ford automobiles have been at that time? We say that the second result indicates a lower price-demand elasticity than the first. Products with price-demand elasticity ratios of more than 1 are said to have elastic demand, those with elasticity ratios of less than 1 are said to have inelastic demand, and those with ratios equal to 1 are said to be "at unity." The concept is illustrated in Figure 5-2. Here we see that a change in price upward or downward from $100 produces a comparable inverse change in demand, measured on a percentage basis. Would the same be true if our starting price on the demand "curve," *DD'*, in Figure 5-2 were $120?

(29)

negative elasticity

(30)

There are less common situations in which an increase in price may produce an increase in demand. Recently, a manufacturer of expensive-looking fur coats made from rabbit pelts found that its product sold much better at a $300 price than at the $125 price at which it was introduced. Why does this happen? When it does, we say that there is a negative price-demand elasticity, referring to the nature of the value produced by our elasticity formula.

Figure 5-2. Price-demand elasticity relationships. (The demand "curve," *DD'*, in this case reflects demand levels that we might expect if we were to alter our price from $100 per unit.)

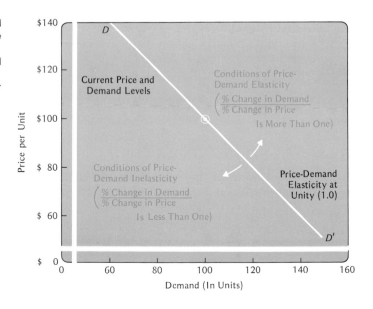

. . . and internal company economics

(31)

(32)
(33)
(34)
(35)

Three possible views that Henry Ford may have held regarding price-demand elasticity for Ford automobiles in 1908, although he probably had never heard of the term, are presented in Table 5-1. If Henry Ford, selling automobiles in 1908 priced at $1,035, was convinced that the demand for his product was relatively inelastic with regard to price, as indicated in case A in Table 5-1, would he have been so anxious to reduce the price? Might he have considered even further price increases? What more would you need to know to respond with any assurance to these questions? How would you respond if you knew that each automobile manufactured, regardless of the total number, cost $600? Or that the costs associated with each automobile were $400—but in addition the company had to meet $2,000,000 in fixed overhead costs each year?

□□□

(36)

Table 5-2 provides useful information in forming a response to the last of these questions. Which view of his market do you think Henry Ford had, judging from his decision? There is some evidence that Ford's intent was to use reduced prices not only to expand the market for automobiles but to make possible significant economies in manufacture as well (finally resulting in the construction of the most advanced plant for mass production techniques yet known). This intent undoubtedly broadened the range of perceived price-demand relationships within which Ford would have advocated reduced prices.

Table 5-1 **Three Possible Views Henry Ford May Have Held Regarding the Price-Demand Elasticity for Model T Fords in 1908**

	Case A	Case B	Case C
	Price-Demand Inelastic	Price-Demand Elasticity at Unity	Price-Demand Elastic
Demand increase: Units demanded at current price	5,000	5,000	5,000
Units to be demanded at future price	5,505	6,010	10,050
Unit change in demand	+505	+1,010	+5,050
Percentage change in units demanded	+10.1%	+20.2%	+101.0%
Price cut: Current price per auto	$1,035	$1,035	$1,035
Future price per auto	825	825	825
Dollar reduction in price per auto	$ 210	$ 210	$ 210
Percentage change in price per auto	−20.2%	−20.2%	−20.2%
Elasticity ratio $\left(\dfrac{\% \ \Delta \text{ in demand} \times -1}{\% \ \Delta \text{ in price}}\right)$	+.5	+1.0	+5.0

141

Table 5-2 Operating Implications of Three Views of the Influence of Price on Demand, Ford Motor Company, 1908

Item	Current Operations	Case A Price-Demand Elasticity at .5	Case B Price-Demand Elasticity at 1.0	Case C Price-Demand Elasticity at 5.0
1. Units of sale	5,000	5,505	6,010	10,050
2. Price per unit	$ 1,035	$ 825	$ 825	$ 825
3. Total dollar sales (1 × 2)[a]	$5,180,000	$4,550,000	$4,960,000	$8,300,000
4. Costs associated with each unit sold	$ 400	$ 400	$ 400	$ 400
5. Total unit-associated costs (4 × 1)	$2,000,000	$2,200,000	$2,410,000	$4,020,000
6. Contribution to fixed overhead costs (3 − 5)[a]	$3,180,000	$2,350,000	$2,550,000	$4,280,000
7. Fixed overhead costs	$2,000,000	$2,000,000	$2,000,000	$2,000,000
8. Profit (6 − 7)[a]	$1,180,000	$ 350,000	$ 550,000	$2,280,000

[a]Numbers rounded to the nearest $10,000.

Price-demand elasticity concepts have been used as justification for pricing decisions in industries facing investigation by government agencies. For example, steel company economists introduced testimony into hearings on questionable steel industry price increases to the effect that, because the elasticity of demand for steel is low with respect to price, it is only natural that steel company executives, experiencing depressed company performance, would turn to price increases as a possible solution. Even at a time of a recessionary decline in demand and rising import competition, steel industry executives maintained their conviction that steel was price-demand inelastic. This, coupled with high fixed costs and the assumption that major competitors would follow U. S. Steel if it raised its prices, may have provided Roger Blough, president of the company at the time, with additional resolve in his initial defiance of President Kennedy's admonition to rescind the price increases announced for steel products by U. S. Steel in 1961.

translating price-demand relationships into decision guides

Executives think in terms of the total size of the market (primary demand) and their company's share (selective demand). A price change may affect one or the other or both. More important, a price change may provide a manager with a useful handle in translating price-demand elasticity concepts into useful estimates of the desirability of various possible pricing actions in an individual company.

Take the case of John "Jock" Frane, president of United Blockhead, Inc., manufacturers of engine blocks, under exclusive license from the German developer, for use in various types of small-scale industrial applications. Frane would view price-demand elasticity concepts with some amusement if he were exposed to them. "I'm interested in profits, not sales results," he would say. "My company's goals are stated in terms of return (profits) on investment, not on achieving a certain dollar sales level or share of the total market. It's return on investment that my company's shareholders are most interested in too."

In fact, this view is typical of that held by most aggressive, thoughtful, and well-schooled managers today. The problem is that of translating views of the market, or past experiences in the market, into a basis for pricing decisions.

price-primary demand elasticity

In order to convert Frane's intuitive knowledge of the market into a bank of information for systematic decision making, a recent business school graduate who had taken the job as his assistant engaged Frane in the following conversation:

> "How would the over-all market for engine blocks of comparable materials and capabilities [currently selling for $100 per unit] be affected if prices were raised or lowered by $10?"
> "With our competitors, we might lose a small number of sales if we raised price by $10. It would take more than a $10 price cut to interest new groups of potential users to begin using engine blocks of our design, however. Now if we all were to do something drastic, like cut prices by $30, it might put us all into a position to double the over-all market by making our engine blocks suitable for new uses."

(37)

(38)

(39) (40)

(41) (42)

Frane's response undoubtedly resulted from his composite estimate of a number of possible forces influencing price-primary demand elasticity. For example, what would be your prior expectations about the price-primary demand elasticity for a product such as bread, relatively late in its life cycle, as opposed to Pernuts (a peanutlike product made from soybeans, introduced in recent years)? Would the price-primary demand elasticity be the same for umbrellas in the middle of the dry as opposed to the wet season in California? For motors as opposed to hub caps for use in assembling new automobiles? Or for Harvey's *Bristol Cream* fancy sherry as opposed to *Joe's Jug* "proof-for-penny" wine? Or for sugar as opposed to fur coats? What about the primary demand for an expensive plumber for routine plumbing repairs as opposed to the repair of a broken pipe spouting water onto a new carpet on Christmas morning?

By now you have concluded that price-primary demand elasticity may vary with such things as the stage of a product in its life cycle, time, the importance of the dollar cost of the product to a customer, the prestige of a product in the eyes of a prospective customer, the ability of a seller to differentiate a product or service from competitors, or the degree of need on the part of the customer, among others.

1	2	3	4	5	6
Price Per Unit	Dollar Change in Price from $100 per unit	Percentage Change In Price from $100 per Unit	Total Market Demand (in 000's of Units)	Unit Change in Total Market Demand from That at a $100 Price (in 000's of Units)	Percentage Change in Total Market Demand from That at a $100 Price
$115	+$15	+15%	900	−100	−10%
110	+$10	+10%	950	−50	−5%
105	+$5	+5%	1,000	0	0
100	$0	0%	1,000	0	0
95	−$5	−5%	1,000	0	0
90	−$10	−10%	1,000	0	0
85	−$15	−15%	1,100	+100	+10%
80	−$20	−20%	1,300	+300	+30%
75	−$25	−25%	1,600	+600	+60%
70	−$30	−30%	2,000	+1,000	+100%
65	−$35	−35%	2,500	+1,500	+150%
60	−$40	−40%	3,100	+2,100	+210%

[a]Underlined figures represent estimates made by the president of the company.

On the basis of information he had obtained, Frane's new assistant prepared the information in Table 5-3 for Frane's review and approval. It shows, in effect, a series of data points constructed from the bare outlines sketched by Frane in his response. In total, it describes the price-primary (industry) demand elasticity for engine blocks of the design manufactured by United Blockhead and its closest competitors. Perhaps the use of "elasticity" in the singular form is incorrect. For example, what's the price-primary demand elasticity of a $30 (30 per cent) price reduction from current prices? What is it for a $20 reduction from $100? Or for a $20 reduction from $80?

(43)
(44)
(45)

price-selective demand elasticity

Next, Frane's assistant solicited information about the share of the total market that United Blockhead might obtain by pricing above or below its direct competitors.

"How much below the immediate competition, like General Gear Box, Inc., do we have to price to get some of their engine block business?"
"There are always a few customers that would switch suppliers if they could

save a nickel. But I suppose it would take a differential like $25 to produce a really significant switchover."

"I understand we have about a 10 per cent share of the market at present. What share would a $75 price produce for us?"

"I would guess it could go to 20 or 30 per cent under those circumstances, assuming our competitors wouldn't follow."

"What is the likelihood that competitors would reduce prices too?"

"We don't think they're very high, because we think our costs are the lowest in the business; that's basically why we took on the German license arrangement."

"What would happen if we raised prices by $10 or $15?"

"Small price increases should affect our share about like small price cuts."

"And if we lowered prices by more than $25 in relation to competition?"

"After you open up a price differential of more than $25 in this business, the increases in business begin to taper off as customers start to wonder how you can price your product so low and competitors begin to react out of desperation with price cuts of their own."

Based on his conversations with Frane, his staff assistant constructed the graph of price-demand relationships shown in Figure 5-3 from information calculated in Table 5-4.

In looking over Table 5-4, Frane commented: "This looks fine, but what about the guts of what we're getting at? What about profits? What about the bottom line?"

Figure 5-3. Primary demand curve for engine blocks and selective demand curve for United Blockhead's engine blocks.

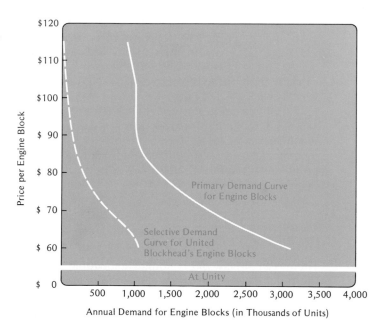

145

Table 5-4 Price-Demand (Both Primary and Secondary)
Relationships for Engine Blocks Prepared on the Basis
of United Blockhead's Top Management Estimates[a]

1	2	3	4
Price Per Unit	Total Market Demand (in 000s of units)	United Blockhead's Estimated Market Share	United Blockhead's Estimated Demand (in 000s of units)
$115	900	4%	36
110	950	7%	66
105	1,000	9%	90
100	1,000	10%	100
95	1,000	11%	110
90	1,000	13%	130
85	1,100	16%	176
80	1,300	20%	260
75	1,600	25%	400
70	2,000	29%	580
65	2,500	32%	800
60	3,100	34%	1,054

[a]Underlined figures represent estimates made by the president of the company

price-demand-profit relationships

Cost and capacity information provided the basis for estimating the influence of price-demand relationships on United Blockhead's profits. Among the pieces of information collected and used by Frane's assistant were (1) costs of making each engine block, $60; (2) fixed costs regardless of the volume of output, $1,000,000 per year; (3) the capacity of United Blockhead's $10,000,000 plant, 200,000 units per year; and (4) the cost of subsequent 200,000-unit annual capacity additions to the plant, $10,000,000 (adding $1,000,000 to fixed costs each year) each.

This information allowed Frane's assistant to construct the analysis shown in Table 5-5. In looking it over, identify the prices at which United Blockhead would maximize (1) its share of the market, (2) its dollar sales (total revenue), (3) incremental revenue, (4) incremental costs, (5) total dollar profit, (6) incremental profit, and (7) annual return on investment. Based on this analysis, what pricing decision would you make? Why?

(46)

profit maximizing

(47)

There is an old law of economics stating that dollar profits can be maximized at the point at which incremental revenue equals incremental cost. It's a brief, simple, powerful statement. Where is this point in Table 5-5? Why did you have trouble finding it? It may suggest some of the frustration that managers encounter in attempting to apply price theory in its pristine form.

Table 5-5 Estimated Economics of Engine Block Pricing by United Blockhead, Inc.

1	2	3	4	5	6	7	8	9	10	11	12	13	14	15
Price per Unit	Total Market Demand (in 000s)	United Blockhead's Estimated Market Share	Units Sold (in 000s)	Total Revenue (in 000s)[a]	Incremental Revenue (in 000s)[b]	Variable Costs (in 000s)[c]	Contribution (in 000s)[d]	Fixed Costs (in 000s)[e]	Total Costs (in 000s)[f]	Incremental Costs (in 000s)[g]	Total Profit (in 000s)[h]	Incremental Profit (in 000s)[i]	Total Investment (in 000s)[e]	Annual Return on Investment[j]
$115	900	4%	36	$4,140	$−3,175	$2,160	$1,980	$1,000	$3,160	−$1,630	$ 980	−$1,345	$10,000	9.8%
110	950	7	66	7,315	−2,135	3,990	3,325	1,000	4,990	−1,410	2,325	−725	10,000	23.2
105	1,000	9	90	9,450	−550	5,400	4,050	1,000	6,400	−600	3,050	+50	10,000	30.5
100	1,000	10	100	10,000	0	6,000	4,000	1,000	7,000	0	3,000	0	10,000	30.0
95	1,000	11	110	10,450	+459	6,600	3,850	1,000	7,600	+600	2,850	−150	10,000	28.5
90	1,000	13	130	11,700	+1,250	7,800	3,900	1,000	8,800	+1,200	2,900	+50	10,000	29.0
85	1,100	16	176	14,960	+3,260	10,560	4,400	1,000	11,560	+2,760	3,400	+500	10,000	34.0
80	1,300	20	260	20,800	+5,840	15,600	5,200	2,000	17,600	+6,040	3,200	−200	20,000	16.0
75	1,600	25	400	30,000	+9,200	24,000	6,000	2,000	26,000	+8,400	4,000	+800	20,000	20.0
70	2,000	29	580	40,600	+10,600	34,800	5,800	3,000	37,800	+11,800	2,800	−1,200	30,000	9.3
65	2,500	32	800	52,000	+11,400	48,000	4,000	4,000	52,000	+14,200	0	−2,800	40,000	0
60	3,100	34	1,054	63,240	+11,240	63,240	0	6,000	69,240	+17,240	−6,000	−6,000	60,000	Neg.

[a]Total revenue = price per unit (column 1) × estimated market share (column 3).

[b]Incremental revenue produced by each successive change in price per unit away from $100.

[c]Obtained by multiplying $60 (the variable cost per unit) by the number of units sold (column 4).

[d]Obtained by subtracting variable costs (column 7) from total revenue (column 5).

[e]Fixed costs largely result from the need to supply and maintain production capacity, in increments of 200,000 units, representing an investment of $10,000,000 per increment and an annual cost of $1,000,000 per increment.

[f]Total costs = the sum of variable costs (column 7) and fixed costs (column 9).

[g]Incremental cost produced by each successive change in demand away from 100 units.

[h]Total profit = total revenue (column 5) less total costs (column 10).

[i]Incremental profit produced by each successive change in price per unit away from $100.

[j]Calculated as the total profit (column 12) divided by total investment (column 14).

147

capacity limits

(48)

Why did the price point for United Blockhead's maximum return on investment differ from that for maximum dollar profits? This points up the need to consider capacity limits and the investment requirements of various price-demand levels in arriving at a pricing decision.

pricing objectives

(49)

(50)

(51) (52)

Your analysis of Table 5-5 may have suggested the need for the definition of one or more corporate objectives by general management, the design of controls to support the achievement of such objectives, and the adherence to those objectives by the marketing manager in charge of price. If you were marketing manager for United Blockhead, for example, and you knew that the size of your year-end bonus depended on the number of engine blocks sold by the company, what pricing decision would you make? How do the likely results of this decision square with Jock Frane's previously stated objective of maximum return on investment? Where does the problem lie? What would you suggest be done about it?

quantity discounts

Economies of making, handling, or shipping products in greater quantities may warrant the quotation of quantity price discounts designed to encourage the purchase of products in economic quantities. For example, it may cost little more to pick one case of a product off the shelf and carry it to an order assembly area in a warehouse than to pick up and transport by means of a lift truck fifty cases strapped together. Similarly, the per unit cost for transporting truckload quantities is much less than for smaller shipments. Order processing costs often do not vary with the quantity of a particular item ordered. Quantity price discounts that reflect distribution cost savings can improve profits for manufacturers, wholesalers, retailers, warehousemen, and transport carriers while they contribute to lower prices for ultimate buyers.

action implications

(53)
(54)

Having had your perceptions of the market for engine blocks quantified, what action, if you were Frane, would you take? Why? To what extent was your decision influenced by the uncertainties (such as your estimate of a 20 to 30 per cent market share with a $75 price) that you perceived in forecasting the future?

For example, what range of results would performance at the limits of your market-share estimate produce?

At this point, managers with different perceptions of risk and different degrees of aversion to risk might take different actions. But it's not difficult to see why, under the circumstances, a former "take charge" captain of his university basketball team and action-oriented executive like Jock Frane might adopt a "don't rock the boat" attitude, and leave the price charged by United Blockhead for its engine blocks at $100.

contribution and other useful concepts in review

Several useful concepts and terms are presented in Table 5-5. We've used some of them already and will use all of them again. You'll recall that variable costs are those that vary directly with the number of units of product or service manufactured·and sold. The most important of variable costs usually are for production. labor and raw material. For engine blocks, we see that these amount to $60 per block.

Subtracting variable costs for all units from sales revenues, we get a figure for contribution, the amount of money available to cover fixed costs and perhaps provide some profits. Contribution is a handy concept that provides us with a measure of return for each unit sold before we get into the sticky business of allocating fixed costs of doing business to individual items or transactions.

Fixed costs are those that do not vary with the number of units of product produced or sold. Important fixed costs are administrators' salaries, depreciation on plant and equipment, and interest on debt. If there is anything left when we subtract them from contribution, we call it profit. The point at which total contribution equals fixed costs (inclusive or exclusive of profit) often is referred to as the break-even point.

Now if you'd like to review your understanding of these concepts, you might want to answer the following questions for certain levels of price shown in Table 5-5: Would your decision have changed, if you were Frane, if variable costs for engine blocks were $80 instead of $60 per unit? Or $40 per unit? Or if there had been no variable costs? Can you think of any business operation that would have no variable costs? Additional examples of contribution, break-even, and return on investment calculations can be found in Appendix B under these three headings.

pricing the product line

The relationships of prices of related products or services are of great importance in determining the sales and profits realized for each. Relationships may produce damaging effects such as cannibalization or positive effects as a result of careful price lining, the planning of prices to allow for trading up, the use of loss-leader tactics, and attention to the profit implications of pricing interdependent products.

149

cannibalization

Often, a new product is just one of a family, a product line. Like any new member of a family, its arrival can have disruptive effects. It attracts attention away from other members of the family. In business this is represented by sales diverted from an old to a new member of the line, sales cannibalized by the new product.

Cannibalization may be desirable when the product cannibalized is near the end of its life cycle, under severe competition from other companies' products, or producing a relatively low contribution. In most situations, however, a major consideration in pricing potentially competing items in a product line will be to minimize the amount of demand diverted from an old to a new item.

At United Blockhead, for example, you'll recall that the price and variable costs of our existing product were $100 and $60, respectively. Assume that a new design developed by United's engineers would allow the company to produce engine blocks at $10 per unit less than variable costs for our existing model, and the new product would produce economies in use for the user in comparison to the existing one. Fixed costs would increase by an amount comparable to those for our current model if we were to produce and sell both. With no existing member of the product line to be cannibalized, we might calculate the relative desirability of introducing the new model as shown in Table 5-6.

The possibility of cannibalization requires prior estimates of its potential and amount. In the case of United Blockhead, our Product Planning Department has estimated that with a price equal to that for competing products on the market ($100), our new product should achieve a 10 per cent market share, gaining equally from our existing product and from those of competitors. At a price of $75 for the new product, there is general agreement that we could obtain as much as 40 per cent of the total market for existing products, including our own.

If we base a pricing decision for a new product on the incremental effects stemming from its introduction, then the burden for losses of contribution for the existing product falls on the new one. This is the assumption underlying calculations in Table 5-7. Would you make the same assumption if you thought a competitor would introduce within a year a new product comparable in production cost and features to the one you could place on the market?

price lining

A company seeking to offer a range of product items and prices to potential customers may seek out a product to be sold at a particular price to fill out its line. In some industries such price lines become almost a part of tradition. For example, women's blouses may range from $3.95 to $7.95 in the low price range, $7.95 to $15.95 in the medium price range, to more than $15.95 for expensive blouses. A manufacturer offering a complete line of low-priced blouses will attempt to have items suitable for pricing at retail at $3.95, $4.95, $5.95, $6.95, and $7.95.

Table 5-6 First-Year Economics of a New, Improved Engine Block, Assuming No Cannibalization, United Blockhead, Inc.

Items	Price per Unit	
	$100	$75
1. Total market (from Table 5-5): *New Product*	1,000,000	1,600,000
2. Market share (from text)	10%	40%
3. Units of sale (2 × 1)	100,000	640,000
4. Sales (3 × price)	$10,000,000	$48,000,000
5. Variable costs ($50 × 3)	$ 5,000,000	$32,000,000
6. Contribution (4 − 5)	$ 5,000,000	$16,000,000
7. Fixed overhead (9 × 10%)	$ 1,000,000	$ 4,000,000
8. Profit (6 − 7)	$ 4,000,000	$12,000,000
9. Investment (3 divided by 200,000 × $10 million)	$10,000,000	$40,000,000
10. Return on investment (8 divided by 9) *Existing Product*	40.0%	30.0%
11. Market share (from text)	10%	25%
12. Units of sale (11 × 1)	100,000	400,000
13. Sales (12 × price)	$10,000,000	$30,000,000
14. Variable costs ($60 × 12)	$ 6,000,000	$24,000,000
15. Contribution (13 − 14)	$ 4,000,000	$ 6,000,000
16. Fixed overhead (18 × 10%)	$ 1,000,000	$ 2,000,000
17. Profit (15 − 16)	$ 3,000,000	$ 4,000,000
18. Investment (12 divided by 200,000 × $10 million)	$10,000,000	$20,000,000
19. Return on investment (17 divided by 18) *Product Line*	30.0%	20.0%
20. Profit (8 + 17)	$ 7,000,000	$16,000,000
21. Investment (9 + 18)	$20,000,000	$60,000,000
22. Return on investment (20 divided by 21) *Change As a Result of New Product Introduction*	35.0%	26.6%
23. Profit (8)	+$ 4,000,000	+$12,000,000
24. Investment (9)	+$10,000,000	+$40,000,000
25. Return on incremental investment (10)	40.0%	30.0%

trading up

Anyone who has ever become the owner of a boat, regardless of the size, knows that quite often he or she immediately begins planning for the next larger and more versatile model. This phenomenon, based on a rising level of expectation, has been capitalized on by manufacturers offering a line of products, particularly those whose prices begin at a level within the reach of a large segment of the population desirous of owning the product.

Manufacturers of sailboats priced beginning at about $2,000 found that the market for such boats for many years was extremely limited. The size of the market was broadened greatly by the introduction of low-maintenance, high-performance sailboats made of fiberglass and priced to sell at $500. Within

Table 5-7 **First-Year Economics of a New, Improved Engine Block, Assuming Cannibalization, United Blockhead, Inc.**

Items	Price per Unit	
	$100	$75
1. Total market (from Table 5-5):	1,000,000	1,600,000
New Product		
2. Market share (from text)	10%	40%
3. Units of sale (2×1)	100,000	640,000
4. Sales ($3 \times$ price)	$10,000,000	$48,000,000
5. Variable costs (50×3)	$ 5,000,000	$32,000,000
6. Contribution ($4 - 5$)	$ 5,000,000	$16,000,000
7. Fixed overhead ($9 \times 10\%$)	$ 1,000,000	$ 4,000,000
8. Profit ($6 - 7$)	$ 4,000,000	$12,000,000
9. Investment (3 divided by 2,000,000 $\times$ $10 million)	$10,000,000	$40,000,000
10. Return on investment (8 divided by 9)⁻	40.0%	30.0%
Existing Product		
11. Market share (from text)	9%	15%
12. Units of sale (11×1)	90,000	240,000
13. Sales ($12 \times$ price)	$ 9,000,000	$18,000,000
14. Variable costs (60×12)	$ 5,400,000	$14,400,000
15. Contribution ($13 - 14$)	$ 3,600,000	$ 3,600,000
16. Fixed overhead ($18 \times 10\%$)	$ 1,000,000	$ 2,000,000
17. Profit ($15 - 16$)	$ 2,600,000	$ 1,600,000
18. Investment (12 divided by 200,000 $\times$ $10 million)	$10,000,000	$20,000,000
19. Return on investment (17 divided by 18)	26.0%	8.0%
Product Line		
20. Profit ($8 + 17$)	$ 6,600,000	$13,600,000
21. Investment ($9 + 18$)	$20,000,000	$60,000,000
22. Return on investment (20 divided by 21)	33.0%	22.6%
Change As a Result of the New Product Introduction		
23. Profit ($20 - 17$, Table 5-6)	+$ 3,600,000	+$ 9,600,000
24. Investment ($21 - 18$, Table 5-6)	+$10,000,000	+$40,000,000
25. Return on incremental investment (23 divided by 24)	36.0%	24.0%

several years, a large group of new $500 sailboat owners became actively interested, potential customers for $2,000 models.

Given the existence of a product line comprising products of varying qualities, capabilities, and prices, a salesman may induce a customer to trade up during the purchasing process. For example, what new car salesman would neglect the opportunity to demonstrate a Ford LTD to a customer initially interested in looking at a lower-priced Pinto?

Several years ago, a West Coast manufacturer marketed two models of a machine designed to be sold to large retail stores that would allow them to make their own professional-looking signs for in-store use. A basic model was produced to sell for $900, with a more versatile model offering a greater variety of type styles and controls for more flexible layout planning priced at about $1,500. A major consideration in the decision to bring out a model priced at $2,100 was the effect that this might have on customers' decisions to buy not the $2,100 model, but the $1,500 model, given the fact that the latter would now be

152

the "medium-priced" item in the line. Subsequent to the introduction, about 90 per cent of the machines sold were of the $900 model. After the introduction of the $2,100 model, it was found that almost no stores bought it, but the proportion of $1,500 units sold rose quickly to about 40 per cent of the total unit sales. What was happening here?

In some cases there is a fine line between trading up and the so-called bait-and-switch tactics practiced by some retailers. In the latter situation, the retailer may have only one or a very few demonstration models of a low-priced item designed to entice the customer into the store, with no intention of selling it if a sale can in any way be avoided. Rather, the intent is to sell the customer a higher-priced model once the limitations of the lower-priced model are demonstrated. In some extreme cases, the one or two units of the lower-priced model may be sold, the advertising continued, and subsequent customers told that the advertised item has been sold out before the initiation of the effort to get the customer to look at a more expensive model.

Bait-and-switch tactics are now outlawed nationally by the Federal Trade Commission. The guidelines for identifying this illegal tactic vary, but typically include (1) one or a small number of units of "bait" held in stock as opposed to many units of other items to which the customer is to be "switched" and (2) the out-and-out unwillingness of a seller to part with a unit of bait stock.

loss-leader pricing

Dubrow's, a large cafeteria in the garment district in New York, suffered the extreme effects of the recession of 1970 and 1971 on the garment manufacturing and wholesaling businesses. Furthermore, along with other cafeterias—at one time the current-day equivalent of the fast-service, low-priced restaurant—it faced growing competition from lower-priced fast-food franchise operations. With a seating capacity of 450 and a large staff of bakers as well as cooks, the volume of sales necessary just to provide a break-even operation for Dubrow's was about $125,000 per month. Anything over this amount yielded nearly fifty cents of each dollar to profit. By September 1970, the monthly volume had fallen to about $117,000. Mr. Leo Martin, the manager and part-owner, had to alter his thinking about pricing.

"Every time my costs went up, I would try to pass it onto the customer. Each time I raised my prices I served fewer and fewer customers,"[2] he explained. Because of Dubrow's high overhead and food quality, it was perhaps easy for Mr. Martin to fall into this habit of thinking. Finally he had an idea.

Dubrow's would price certain of its short orders and dinners as specials, perhaps below the full cost of the food and its preparation and presentation. For example, a hamburger and coffee at lunch, instead of being priced at $1.02, would be priced at 69 cents. A dinner consisting of soup, a sliced steak platter, baked Idaho potato, tossed green salad with dressing, hard roll and butter and coffee would be reduced from $3.05 to $1.99, tax included.

[2] This quote and example is drawn from "Loss Leaders Draw Cafeteria Customers," *New York Times,* (Oct. 26, 1971), pp. 59 and 69, quote from p. 59.

When the specials were offered, volume increased immediately from a low of 4,300 customers per day to between 5,500 and 5,600 customers per day. The cafeteria's volume rose to about $140,000 in October, enough to produce bottom-line net profits of nearly $7,000 for the month.

In retrospect, Mr. Martin admitted that, if his customers had bought nothing else but specials, it would have put him out of business. It didn't work that way, as is often the case. Actually, only about 25 per cent of the customers actually ate specials, even though a higher percentage may have intended to do so when they entered the cafeteria.

"A customer comes over to the counter and says, 'I want a sliced steak sandwich.' The counterman tells him to go to the other line to get the 99-cent special. The customer, often as not, says, 'Never mind, I'll have a roast beef sandwich,' or he makes some other selection at the regular prices.

"During the higher-price era, the customer would buy a cup of coffee to go with his hamburger. Now he also buys a dessert to go with his special, but at the regular price."[3]

Similar loss-leader tactics are employed on a continuous basis by many food retailers. Typically, items selected for such pricing treatment are often well-known items such as one-pound tins of Maxwell House coffee or a popular cut of meat, comparable in popularity to Leo Martin's sliced steak sandwich. What criteria might you establish for selecting a candidate item for use in a loss-leader pricing strategy?

(62)

deal pricing

A company may engage in deal pricing in order to stimulate demand, to clean out existing stocks of a product prior to dropping it, or to obtain initial product trial. A "deal" price may be structured in such a way that customers know it will not be maintained, thereby allowing the effective price to be raised after the introductory period.

An extreme example of this occurred in 1971 when Wilkinson Sword Ltd. introduced on a national basis its bonded blade, the most serious challenge to Gillette's 60 per cent share of the blade market in several years. It attached a $2 refund coupon to its $2.95 package of a razor and five blades. In some areas, consumers were able to buy the package for as little as $1.39 and, by cashing in on the $2 coupon, in effect got paid 61 cents to try the Wilkinson product. But there was no doubt in customers' minds in this case that Wilkinson intended eventually to sell its razors and blades at higher prices.

pricing of interdependent products

Pricing strategies sometimes must be developed for interdependent products. Examples of these are Polaroid cameras and film, certain machines and machine tools, and automobiles and special customer accessories. This family of decisions has come

[3] Ibid., p. 69

154

to be known as the "blade-razor" problem, or even the "Gillette" problem in reference to perhaps the most famous of all of these situations.

Basic questions concerning this problem are (1) do you price each of the interdependent items to achieve the same percentage of contribution in relation to price; in other words, price both the blades and razor in relation to their variable costs or (2) should one be priced to yield a higher percentage of contribution than the other?

In cases where replacement parts for machines represent a small proportion of the cost of the original machine and seldom are used, a manufacturer may price them to yield a large margin in the belief that customer need will support such a price.

In other cases, the continuing sale of expendable supplies may represent a major source of a company's prospective flow of income, thereby tempting a marketing manager to nearly give away the tool, whether it might be a camera or a razor, to encourage the use of expendables.

(63) For example, as a manager in charge of pricing Gillette's Techmatic razor and its Trac II blades, what relative prices would you establish for each if the direct, variable costs for producing the Techmatic were 30 cents and those for producing a pack of five
(64) Trac II blades were 15 cents? What additional information would you want to know to
(65) reach a decision? How would you respond if you assumed that (1) a 60-cent price (to wholesalers) for razors would result in annual sales of eight million units and a 30-cent price in sales of twelve million units (a price-demand elasticity of 1.0), and (2) a shaver using Gillette Trac II blades exclusively would consume four packs of
(66) blades, on the average, per year? Would your response be different if, perhaps, 80 per cent of the demand for Trac II blades would be diverted from conventional platinum blades with variable costs of approximately 20 cents for a pack of five, consumed at the rate of about six packs per year, and selling to wholesale
(67) distributors and large retail accounts for 45 cents per pack? Or if razors were purchased, on the average, every three years instead of every other year?

Given the number of razors that the Gillette Co. either has passed out free or sold at "sale" prices, and the fact that the company traditionally has ranked as one of the most profitable in the United States, there should be little doubt about where that company's executives stand on the issue.

(68) Would your views regarding the pricing of interdependent products change if you were pricing the Polaroid Square Shooter camera (1) with variable production costs of approximately $9 per camera and variable production costs for film packs of about $1 per pack, (2) under the assumption that the usage rate for film would be about eight packs during the first year of usage and four packs per year thereafter, and (3) under a price-demand elasticity similar to that for Gillette Techmatic razors,
(69) starting at a base of an $18 price to wholesale distributors for the camera? How would your decision be affected by the belief that 50 per cent of Polaroid camera owners typically trade up to a higher-priced camera every five years on the average?

(70) As a competitor of Polaroid, at Kodak, how would you price (1) an Instamatic camera thought to be in some ways competitive with the Square Shooter, costing $3.50 per camera; (2) a cartridge of 126 film (containing twelve exposures versus eight offered by the Polaroid Square Shooter), costing $.75 per cartridge to produce; and (3) film processing services, with the knowledge that the variable cost to process a film of twelve exposures is about $.50 per cartridge and that about 80 per cent of all Kodak camera owners use Kodak film, of which about half have their films processed by Kodak film processing centers?

(71)   Looking over the prices that you have established as a representative, first, of Polaroid, and then of Kodak, how would you assess the relative attractiveness of the prices of these two products, assuming you are now a potential camera buyer?

longer-term pricing policies and strategies

Up to now, we have spent most of our time considering the pricing of individual products in the context of customer expectations, product economics, and other products in a company's line, among others. In fact, these are important considerations. Often, however, a product's price must pass examination not only on these criteria, but also in terms of general corporate objectives, often stated in terms of average margins, shares of markets, and profits.

pricing policies

Studies of pricing policies have shown that, regardless of their objectives, companies typically take two basic approaches to pricing across a broad line of products. These can be termed the *cost-plus* and *price-minus approaches.*

Cost-Plus Pricing.   The cost-plus approach to pricing policy is one in which the costs, usually the direct, variable costs of production or acquisition (in wholesaling or retailing), for a product are established and an amount added to cover marketing, administrative, and other overhead costs and contribute to a targeted profit figure. Under such a policy, a company producing a machine tool with variable costs of $40 and pricing its product line at twice variable (or direct) costs would establish a price of $80 for the item. Given the complexities of establishing prices, such as those we experienced earlier, a pricing policy of this type can simplify the job somewhat. Even so, prices established on such a basis often are adjusted to reflect conditions both internal and external to the firm.

Perhaps the most famous examples of cost-plus pricing were those used for the pricing of supplies and weapons to the United States government during and after World War II. Many contracts were written on a "cost-plus-fixed-fee" basis that allowed suppliers to add specified fixed fees to the actual costs of fulfilling a contract, no matter how much higher than originally estimated the (72) actual costs might be. What kind of incentives may this arrangement have provided to the supplier?

Retail stores often establish target margins for groupings of products that determine the amount by which individual items are "marked up" as they are received. For example, a drug department of a retail outlet may have as its objective for over-all margin 30 per cent of retail sales, or 30 cents on every $1 worth of drug products sold. Because of loss, pilferage, and reduced prices on slow-selling items, it may be necessary to price products initially with a 33 ⅓ per cent margin in order to achieve eventually an average margin of 30 per cent. Thus, items costing seventy cents may be priced initially at $1.05 and those costing 30 cents may be priced initially at 45 cents. In either case, the margin (calculated on the sale price) would be 33 ⅓ per cent.[4] Under what circumstances could a company most successfully maintain a cost-plus pricing policy?

Price-Minus Pricing. At times it may be desirable to estimate the price at which a product or service might achieve a market share or volume objective and then attempt to produce the product or service at a cost sufficiently below the price to yield a satisfactory margin and profit. Once again, competitive forces, customer expectations, or company product policies may suggest the need for such an approach.

For example, as the car-washing business became more and more price competitive with the introduction of machinery to replace human effort in the car-washing process, it became more and more difficult to produce car-washing machines capable of doing a satisfactory job at a price that would yield an acceptable margin or profit both to the manufacturer and the operator. In the case of operators, many finally despaired of obtaining an acceptable margin from car washing and began using the service as a loss-leader to attract customers to, for example, auto service stations where other products with higher margins could be sold as well.

Price-minus pricing may be employed in bidding situations in which a bidder has a good idea of the price at which the prospective buyer expects to "let" a contract (accept a bid) or the price at which a competitor is likely to bid. This is quite typical, for example, in the consulting business, where a large number of contracts are "let" on the basis of bids. How does the emphasis on price-minus pricing vary in relation to the importance of price in the decision to let a contract?

In 1961, the Department of Defense began using "total package procurement" (TPP) as the basis for awarding some of its major contracts. TPP had many features, among them "fixed price-incentive fee" contracts in which a prospective contractor (1) bid at the outset on all phases of the project from research and development to production and (2) shared a portion of unexpected costs or profits with the government. By 1970, the largest government contractor, the Lockheed Aircraft Corp., was on the brink of bankruptcy from an inability to absorb risks inherent in several contracts, chief among them the TPP contract for the C-5A giant military transport. Why might the difficulty of shifting from cost-plus to price-minus contracting have been one of the causes of Lockheed's crisis?

A belief that customers harbor preconceptions about acceptable prices often governs, for example, the large clothing retailer who will ask a manufacturer to produce a large order of shirts "designed to sell for $7.95." The price is established and, from it, the acceptable cost calculated.

Are you conscious of any trends in the incidence of cost-plus or price-minus pricing?

[4]See Appendix B under "margin" and "markup" for other examples illustrating the arithmetic of margins.

sequential pricing strategies—
new product pricing

Our company, Arroyo Laboratories, Inc., has spent $500,000 developing its new drug. It is thought that it has perhaps a one-year lead on its competition. Competing drugs performing the same function, not manufactured by our company, sell at wholesale for $1.20 per gram and are estimated to have variable costs of about 30 cents per gram. Our new product has variable costs of only 15 cents per gram and is more conveniently consumed by the user. Promotional and administrative costs assigned to the new product would probably amount to about $100,000 the first year.

We estimate that the current market for competing drugs is about three million grams per year. At one third of the current wholesale price, the market might increase to four million grams per year. A wholesale price comparable to current competition might win us shares of market variously estimated at 2 to 20 per cent by the end of our "year of grace." On the other hand, a wholesale price of one third that of the current price could produce shares of the larger primary market estimated to range from 10 to 40 per cent by the end of the first year. Furthermore, such a strategy could dissuade some potential competitors from reacting by rapidly developing comparable products. On the other hand, it could encourage other competitors to push their research, testing, and development efforts harder, particularly those currently possessing the largest shares of the market. Clearly, our pricing decision now would have some influence on future prices charged by our competitors when they might introduce their comparable products. At that time, our share, because of our lesser name in the market, could once again recede from its peak without an increasingly large promotional effort. Such an effort, representing a total of some $200,000 per year in relatively fixed costs for salaries for "detail men" (drug product salesmen calling on wholesalers, retailers, and doctors), samples, trade advertising, and administration could help preserve much of the peak share of market attained by the product.

(77) (78)

What would you recommend as a pricing strategy for this product? On what assumptions did you base your decision?

Skimming. Of alternative pricing strategies we could follow, one is a skimming strategy, under which we would charge high prices at first and then lower prices as we captured sales from one market segment after another.

Did you know that the first ball point pen brought on the market in 1947 was priced to sell at $12.95? I bought one. It wasn't long before the same or better ball point pens were selling for $4.95, $2.95, and then 99 cents. And several years ago Monsieur Bich of France began selling his Bic ball points to the world for a price so low that it could just as well be quoted by the pound or bushel.

In contrast, when color television sets first were introduced to the market at a price of about $1,200 in 1958, sales were so low as to discourage some manufacturers. I didn't buy one. Clearly, the skimming price was considered too high by nearly all potential customers. Perhaps, like me, they had all bought $12.95 ball point pens or other products under similar circumstances and were waiting for the price to come down. Or perhaps they figured that their old television set plus a vacation in the Virgin Islands offered a more attractive entertainment package. In any event, it wasn't until prices of color television sets reached $600 about six years later that they touched off a bonanza of sales.

Penetration. At the other extreme, we could practice a penetration strategy designed to maximize unit sales and gain a large share of the market rapidly by introducing a new product at an attractively low price. In addition to advantages already cited in our discussion of Arroyo's alternative strategies, a penetration strategy can encourage an immediate volume of sales necessary to achieve the most economic production quantities.

Henry Ford's penetration pricing went hand in hand with the construction of the most wondrous mass production facilities in the world in the early 1900s. Having achieved one level of volume and production economies with his $835 Model T, he topped both several years later by introducing a $465 model of new design and comparable quality, constructing even more sophisticated production facilities for it.

(79)

(80) (81) Where, on the spectrum of pricing strategies bounded by skimming and penetration strategies, would your recommendation for Arroyo's new drug product fall? What results would you expect? Would your recommendation be different if it looked as if we could get seventeen-year patent protection for our product, preventing direct replication by competitors, except under license from us, for this period of time? How would it differ if, instead of having currently none of the market to be served by the new product, another of our products already possessed a 20 per cent market share at the current prices? Putting aside the "what ifs" and getting back to our original situation, how fast would you expect Arroyo to make profits equal to its original investment under your recommended course of action?

(82)

(83)

Based on our peek at Arroyo's problem, you should be able to construct a set of critical factors affecting a new-product pricing decision and conditions favoring skimming or penetration strategies, or some combination of the two extremes.

(84)

(85) How would you apply this set of factors to the problem of pricing United Blockhead's new engine block? What type of new-product pricing strategy would you recommend to Jock Frane as a result?

potential for competitive reaction

Pricing rarely can be done on an existential basis, without regard for tomorrow. For tomorrow, in the form of a competitive reaction, can come back to haunt a pricing decision maker. A longer-term view of pricing requires an appraisal of the nature and probability of competitive reactions as well as an estimate of their possible impact on the total size and division of a market.

For example, we could appraise a first-year pricing strategy for the new drug being introduced by Arroyo Laboratories in terms of the analysis presented in Table 5-8. It indicates that the range of contribution, after allocated costs for promotion and administation, might extend from a loss of $37,000 to a gain of $530,000 during the first year of a skimming pricing strategy. Comparable results for a penetration pricing strategy are estimated to range from contributions of $0

Table 5-8 **First-Year Economics of Skimming and Penetration Pricing Strategies for a New Drug Being Introduced by Arroyo Laboratories, Inc.**

| | Pricing Strategy | |
	Skimming	Penetration
High Market-Share Estimate		
1. Total annual market	3,000,000 grams	4,000,000 grams
2. × Arroyo's share	.20	.40
3. Arroyo's sales	600,000 grams	1,600,000 grams
4. Arroyo's price per gram	$1.20	$.40
5. − Variable cost per gram	.15	.15
6. Contribution per gram	$1.05	$.25
7. Total first-year contribution (3 × 6)	$630,000	$400,000
8. Less $100,000 promotional cost	$530,000	$300,000
Low Market-Share Estimate		
1. Total annual market	3,000,000 grams	4,000,000 grams
2. × Arroyo's share	.02	.10
3. Arroyo's sales	60,000 grams	400,000 grams
4. Arroyo's price per gram	$1.20	$.40
5. − Variable cost per gram	.15	.15
6. Contribution per gram	$1.05	$.25
7. Total first-year contribution (3 × 6)	$ 63.000	$100,000
8. Less $100,000 promotional cost	− $37,000	0

(86)

(87)

to $300,000 for the first year. On the basis of this information, which you might have calculated already for yourself, what decision would you make regarding the initial price for Arroyo's new drug? What does your decision tell you about yourself?

The probability of a competitor's reacting to a price cut will vary directly with factors such as (1) the share of market that it may have currently, (2) its research and development capabilities, (3) the importance of the threatened item in its product line, and (4) a past history of price leadership and followership in an industry. The probability of a competitor's reaction most often will vary inversely with (1) the level of its costs, particularly its variable costs per unit, (2) the degree to which competing products can be differentiated in terms of either their physical, performance, or psychic characteristics, and (3) the degree to which the price of the threatened item is tied to the price of other items in a competitor's product line.

To the extent that price cuts competitively are more threatening than price increases or identical pricing, the probability of competitive reaction to the first of these actions probably is greater than that in response to the latter actions in most cases.

(88)

If Arroyo's major prospective competitor is a company with a 40 per cent share of the market, thought to have variable costs of production of about forty cents per gram and an annual marketing budget of about $250,000 for its product, and with total company sales for all products of about $100 million per year, how would you assess the chances of its reacting with a price cut to possible skimming or penetration strategies by Arroyo? What are the possibilities that, instead of a price cut, it might increase its promotional budget to $400,000 per year for the product? If the low first-year market-share estimates in Table 5-8 for Arroyo's new product assume both competitive price cutting and increased promotion, high estimates assume neither, and midpoint estimates assume a price cut but no increase in promotion, how would you assess the relative attractiveness to Arroyo of skimming and penetration pricing strategies?

The tree diagram in Figure 5-4 provides a handy method of organizing thoughts about the value of alternative decisions in the context of potential competitor reactions. It shows possible combinations of actions by both Arroyo and its major competitor in the second and succeeding years after the introduction of Arroyo's new product, with a set of estimated probabilities of occurrence attached to each. Dollar contribution values that each hold for Arroyo also are calculated and shown. Multiplying the probability by its value for each possible combination of occurrences and adding the results for each family produces a weighted contribution figure for each for Arroyo. What strategy does it suggest? Is this compatible with your conclusions regarding the best strategy for the first year? Perhaps you don't agree with the estimated probabilities shown in Figure 5-4. If not, what probabilities would you attach to each of the branches at the right side of Figure 5-4? How would it affect your selection of a long-term pricing strategy for Arroyo?

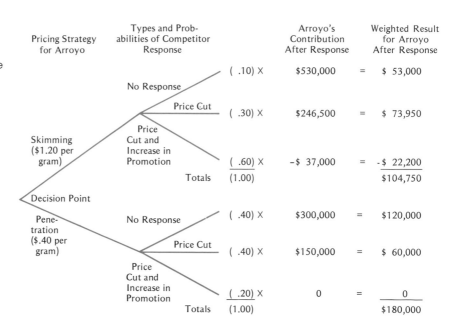

Figure 5-4. A tree diagram of several combinations of pricing decisions and competitive responses for Arroyo Laboratories' new drug.

Pricing Strategy for Arroyo	Types and Probabilities of Competitor Response		Arroyo's Contribution After Response	Weighted Result for Arroyo After Response
	No Response	(.10) X	$530,000	= $ 53,000
	Price Cut	(.30) X	$246,500	= $ 73,950
Skimming ($1.20 per gram)	Price Cut and Increase in Promotion	(.60) X	-$ 37,000	= -$ 22,200
	Totals	(1.00)		$104,750
Penetration ($.40 per gram)	No Response	(.40) X	$300,000	= $120,000
	Price Cut	(.40) X	$150,000	= $ 60,000
	Price Cut and Increase in Promotion	(.20) X	0	= 0
	Totals	(1.00)		$180,000

Decision Point

161

industry structure and customs

An industry, its make-up, and its customs provide an important context for pricing decisions.

perfect competition

To the classical economist, so-called perfect competition conjures up visions of a large number of competing producers unable or unwilling to control the total output of a product or the entry of new competitors, the production of non-differentiated (or standardized) products, the absence of price-influencing mechanisms other than supply-demand relationships, and prices seeking a level that will (1) clear the market of an oversupply or (2) ration inadequate supplies among possible buyers.

To the manager, perfect competition means the inability to differentiate his product from his competitor's, the acceptance of a market-determined price regardless of the amount of his production, and over long periods of time greater price fluctuations in relation to industries experiencing "less perfect" competition. Perfect competition helped create the following conditions for Charlie Stephenson, operator of a 420-acre farm near Sadorus, Illinois, in 1971: (1) a profit of $6,000, or about $550 less than the previous year, as a bumper crop drove prices to two thirds of their level the year before; (2) the lack of money either for a replacement for Stephenson's 1949 Studebaker truck or for a hoped-for Arizona vacation; and (3) the need for both Stephenson and his wife to take extra jobs when not putting in sixteen-hour days in farm work. Until 1973, when farm surpluses in the United States began their decline, farmers in general had family incomes about three quarters of the size of blue-collar family incomes, rapidly increasing debt from capital expenditures, and a departure rate of two thousand per week from the business.

The semantics lesson for the day follows: What's perfect for one party to a transaction may not be perfect for another. The term *perfect competition* is a loaded one. Unfortunately for the customer, but perhaps fortunately for the supplier, perfect competition in its pure form is hard to find. Can you think of any examples? Even agricultural controls are introduced to allow a government's Department of Agriculture to buy and store surplus quantities of agricultural commodities grown during a given season. Such controls have been used less frequently with declining agricultural supplies, increasing demands, and sub-stantially increased prices for many agricultural commodities in recent years.

(95)

oligopoly structure

A large proportion of the volume of business in the United States is transacted by industries with few sellers, called oligopolies, representing imperfect competition to the economist. Characteristics of this condition, in addition to the

162

limited number of sellers, are implicit control over output and price stability, difficulty of entry into the industry for potential new competitors, and prices that may reflect profit goals to a greater extent than they do levels needed to produce full use of an industry's producing capacity. Oligopoly industries may deal either in products with largely standardized (steel, aluminum, chemicals) or largely nonstandardized (automobiles, typewriters, machine tools) features.

Some industries generally considered to be oligopolies might experience effects similar to those typical of "more perfect" competitive conditions. For example, the market for certain types of paper products grows at a rather constant rate. But efficient paper-making machines, larger than ten railroad locomotives laid end to end, typically can spit out enough paper to fill a moderately sized living room in ten minutes. And like the proverbial restaurant operator who "throws away the key" and stays open twenty-four hours, there isn't even much point in including a turn-off switch with a paper-making machine. It costs so much, resulting in such a high level of fixed costs for interest and equipment depreciation, and is so time-consuming to start up once it is shut off, that a company can rarely afford to shut it off and have it out of production. Furthermore, one new, modern, efficient machine produces so much paper that, when it is put into production by its owner, it seriously affects supply-demand relationships and price levels for most companies producing similar paper products.

Penalties to an industry from "unstructured" pricing behavior on the part of its competing participants can be great, leading to informal, implicit efforts to structure pricing actions through price leadership and other mechanisms.

price leadership

Price leaders generally are regarded as companies whose prices for products or services set the pattern for competing products or services offered by other companies. A price leader may establish its position by virtue of (1) the non-differentiated or standardized nature of a product, creating a need for "organized" pricing in an industry; (2) an important position in the market, indicated by market share, among other measures, (3) a willingness in past actions to use punitive pricing tactics on competitors not following its lead; and (4) its assembly of a respected group of business economists or managers responsible for pricing. When it changes a price, a price leader has a reasonable expectation that competitors will follow.

A high degree of price leadership discourages the shifting of market share, or selective demand, by means of changing price relationships. It allows an industry with several or, in some instances, many smaller competitors to behave as if there were none, at least from the standpoint of price.

It is not difficult for one competitor to "lead" an industry downward in price. In fact, the hungriest competitors often do it in desperation. The real test of price leadership for a company is that of getting its major competitors to follow it in increasing prices, resisting the temptation not to follow and perhaps thereby gain a larger market share. Bethlehem Steel and United States Steel, for example, have assumed price leadership for certain types of steel products from time to time. Other companies in the industry have assumed price leadership for products in which they specialize, such as stainless steel.

When price leadership can be effected by one competitor, competition in an industry may shift to forms other than price, such as promotional allowances, advertising, new product development, increased services, or equipment financing.

(96)

(97)

What are some industries in which you would expect the need for price leadership to be high? What characteristics do they have in common?

pricing customs

Unwritten industry pricing customs, perhaps established by a price leader, may provide informal limits on pricing decisions. For example, for years the maximum quantity discount allowed by manufacturers of consumer paper products was 4 per cent for the purchase of "carload" quantities (typically about 30,000 pounds or more) by wholesalers or retail food chains. One large manufacturer determined that savings approximating $100 per carload, or an additional 1 per cent of the price, in handling and other costs were achieved when very large customers ordered single-product carloads as opposed to those made up of orders for ten or more product-line items.

A group of executives within the company argued that an appropriate incentive to prospective single-product carload customers would be a $4\frac{1}{2}$ per cent quantity discount. Because of past pricing customs in the industry, however, this was rejected in favor of a decision to maintain the maximum quantity discount at 4 per cent for carload orders, but to offer an additional $25 per car loading allowance to those customers ordering single-product carloads.

(98) (99)

Was this double talk? Did it violate industry custom?

when price leadership fails

The failure of price leadership efforts may lead to price competition so severe as to drive many producers out of an industry. Symptoms of such situations are the quotation of "list" prices, usually in published form, by competitors, all of whom proceed to sell at varying prices below list. Attempts alternately may be made to insure adherence to list prices, to ignore them, and to establish list prices again at lower levels.

Industries in recent years suffering from the failure to stabilize prices through vehicles such as list prices include those producing tubes, transistors, and various electrical apparatus. The failure of price-stabilizing efforts such as price leadership raises the temptation to collude, almost as a last resort, to fix prices illegally. This brings us to a brief review of some of the major legal and social issues in pricing.

As the purchasing agent for a soap manufacturer, you enjoyed a situation in which suppliers of your major ingredient were engaged in severe price competition, depressing prices for the ingredient to all-time lows. First one competitor would lower its price, then another would exceed the price reduction of the first. But recently, you've noticed that all suppliers of this product are quoting exactly the same prices, and that two recent price increases have been announced by all competitors on the same day.

In your job as purchasing agent you receive information through competing sales representatives, with whom you meet regularly, that leads you to believe that your largest competitor is purchasing a basic chemical for the manufacture of soap powder in the same sized shipments as you but is receiving a lower base price for the product, excluding transportation costs.

Picture yourself now as a shopper for a list of grocery products. You notice that one store has a "one-cent sale" which, among other things, is featuring soap powder at $1.45 per box, with two boxes for one cent more, or $1.46. The $1.45 price is printed on the package. At a competing store you notice that the same item is being sold, without special promotion, for seventy cents, again with the price printed on the box. Although you're not in need of soap powder on this particular day, you do reflect on the situation because you often do your grocery buying at the first store.

Now you are the owner of a small retail store. You know that your competitor down the street pays the same price for its powdered soap as you do. It is using the item as a loss leader to draw business into its store. In fact, at the price at which it is advertising the product, you know that your competitor has to be selling it below the amount it paid the manufacturer for it. Your only alternative may be to retaliate, perhaps using other items. But you fear the eventual results, including relatively higher prices on other items sold in your store and, if price competition becomes too pronounced, bankruptcy for one or both of you.

Or you are marketing manager for the manufacturer of Glen Falls soap. Your marketing strategy has been to maintain a higher price to retailers for Glen Falls than for another brand in your line that is designed to be sold at a lower price. You have invested time, effort, advertising dollars, and laboratory research to create real and imagined differences between your premium product, Glen Falls, and its lower-priced sister item. Your sales representatives are reporting more and more frequently that in some areas Glen Falls, perhaps because of its widely known name and high reputation, is being used by certain grocery outlets as a special, sometimes selling it for less than your lower-quality, lower-priced (to retailers) item.

Once again, you are a shopper. You're battling for position in the aisle of your local supermarket during a rush hour, with a shopping list in one hand, pushing the shopping cart with the other. The next item on your list is Glen Falls dishwashing soap powder. You find two box sizes of the product. The regular size weighs two pounds, three ounces and is priced at 68 cents a box. The family economy size weighs three pounds, ten ounces and is priced at $1.20. Although you know how to use a slide rule, you didn't think to bring it to the supermarket with you.

In any of these situations, do you feel that you should have legal protection? If so, of what type? If you were the ultimate consumer of the product in each case would you feel differently about the need for legal protection for the parties to each situation? Would you desire different types of legal protection in each case? In which of these cases do you think legal protection exists today?

These vignettes illustrate situations that have led to debate and, in some cases, legislation regarding conspiracy in restraint of trade, price discrimination among customers, deceptive pricing, pricing practices destructive to retail competitors or to products, and unit pricing. Like all powerful weapons, pricing policies can be constructive or destructive, used well and misused. At this point it is useful to mention briefly some current legal limits on the use of the pricing elephant gun.

conspiracy in restraint of trade

Conspiracy to control prices, or the achievement of the same result through the formation of a monopoly, is prohibited by the Sherman Act, the first major federal law affecting pricing practices, passed in 1890. The recent pricing behavior of the suppliers of raw materials for soap powder mentioned earlier would be cause for further scrutiny under this act.

Would you expect conspiracies to have occurred more frequently in industries selling consumer or industrial goods, nonstandard or standardized goods, branded or unbranded products? Check your preconceptions against this list of industries in which conspiracy charges have been filed over the years by the Justice Department: railroad wheels, pipe flanges, carbon sheet steel, plumbing fixtures, carbon dioxide, steel rings, aluminum cable, asphalt, salt, electrical equipment, and drugs.

Conspiracy among competitors is illegal in all industries except the transportation industries, where it is specifically exempted for pricing by the Reed-Bulwinkle Act of 1948.

price discrimination

Perhaps the most frequently applied law addressing, among other things, pricing policy, is the Robinson-Patman Act of 1936. It is designed to prevent price and other forms of marketing discrimination between customers purchasing commodities of like grade and quality in interstate commerce when (1) such price differences are not based on demonstrable differences in cost and (2) the effect may tend to injure competition (presumably by injuring competitors).

The difficulty of interpreting and establishing the presence and degree of these necessary conditions for application of the Robinson-Patman Act has aborted many actions brought under this law. For example, in a case extending over several years in the 1960s, Borden Inc., indicated that its canned milk sold under the Borden label was exactly the same (in ingredients and cost) as that of the canned milk it sold to grocery chains at lower prices, to be marketed under their individual private labels, most often also at lower prices than the Borden brand. And although the Supreme Court, in upholding the position of the FTC, which had brought the charges, held that a different label doth not a different product make, a United States court of appeals found that there was no evidence of injury to competition and would not be until Borden's price differentials exceeded the "recognized consumer appeal of the Borden label" —whatever that means.

(106)

Based on what you know about the situation, would our small manufacturer of soap powder who has been led to believe that it is paying more for a basic ingredient than its competition have cause for complaint under the Robinson-Patman Act?

deceptive pricing

Deceptive pricing typically leads a customer to think a product or service is being sold at a "bargain" price when in fact it isn't. Under the FTC's "Guides Against Deceptive Pricing"—an attempt in 1958 to clarify the wording of the original Wheeler-Lea amendment of 1938, which made illegal "unfair or deceptive acts in commerce"—manufacturers, distributors, and retailers were required to "in every case act honestly and in good faith on advertising a list price, and not with the intention of establishing a basis . . . for a deceptive comparison in any local . . . trade area." Our favorite outlet for soap powder does, indeed, appear to be deceiving customers, with the cooperation of its supplier, under these guidelines. But things are rarely as clear-cut as this. Much effort may be required to distinguish situations in which customers are and are not deceived.

destructive retail pricing practices

Two major series of legislative and judicial actions have encouraged some states to establish similarly named laws regarding prices charged by retailers: unfair trade practices and fair trade legislation. The first of these, now enforced in varying degrees by perhaps half of the states, typically prevents a retail store from reselling merchandise for less than it paid for it or for less than the purchase price plus a minimum specified margin (or, more typically, markup). Because of the potential for frequent violation of this law among stores using loss leaders over sufficiently long periods of time to threaten the viability of competitors relying heavily on the sale of such items, states rely on competing retailers, through a complaint process, to call violations to the attention of regulatory authorities. The mere threat of prosecution usually leads to conformance on the part of violators, although the need for these laws is perceived to be much less now than in the 1930s, when many were passed as a defense for the small, independent retailer against the "creeping evil" of the chain-store movement in its early growth. (It's hard to believe that we lived so recently in an era when one of the greatest threats in our society was perceived by many to be the chain store.)

(107)
(108)
As the retailer of soap powder described earlier, do we have a case against our competitor offering a loss leader? Assuming we do business in a state that still has unfair trade practices legislation on its books, should we initiate a complaint against our competitor down the street?

Fair trade legislation has permitted one of the few examples of legal price fixing, a manufacturer's right to prescribe the price at which its products will be sold at retail. Under the McGuire Act, passed in 1952, individual states were allowed to permit manufacturers to enforce prescribed retail prices, even if retailers had not signed an agreement with the manufacturer to do so. Although fair trade legislation, including such a "nonsigner's clause," at one time was on the statutes of forty-five states, the burden and cost of enforcement by manufacturers restricted its use. More recently, conclusions that fair trade has outlived its useful life and constitutes a questionable practice had led to its repeal in all but twenty-two states late in 1975 and to an expected repeal by Congress
(109)
eventually. As the manufacturer of soap powder described earlier in this section, should we initiate action against our offending customer?

unit pricing

Increasing emphasis on consumer protection and the proliferation of package shapes and sizes in recent years have led to the call for unit pricing, under which prices, particularly of food items, are translated into prices for standard quantities, such as the price per pound, dozen, or quart, for purposes of display for sale to ultimate consumers. Although such requirements have not become law, many supermarket chains have instituted unit-pricing practices in which shelf-price stickers are prepared, often by computer, to show the actual as well as the unit price of each item on the shelf. In doing so, many retailers have corrected errors of the sort illustrated in our soap powder example: higher unit prices for larger than for smaller packages.

price controls

For the first time in 1971, peacetime price controls were instituted in the United States to slow the rate of inflation. Among the major features of these controls were the requirements that (1) price changes reflect no more than changes in the costs of product or service components, (2) manufacturers submit proposals for price increases to a price board for approval, and (3) prices of selected lists of popular items be posted in each outlet where items were sold at retail, with deviations from a precontrol-base price noted. As in wartime, the success of such programs depends on the spirit with which consumers and others identify, report, and follow up on possible violations. Their complexity makes them impossible to enforce without the cooperation of the public and business enterprise.

pricing latitude

Lest we overemphasize price-oriented legislation at this point, the fact remains that managers still possess a wide latitude of authority in establishing prices and retain various alternatives for limiting the use of price, as opposed to other elements of marketing strategy, as a competitive weapon.

A price based on cost, established without consultation with competition or a central price-coordinating agency within an industry, established without an intent to restrain competition, and not deceptive to customers, will be hard to prove illegal. Furthermore, through price leadership or the quotation or alteration of prices in a manner intended to meet (not beat) competition, identical prices for competitors can be justified.

pricing and customer behavior

It is appropriate that the first and last sections of our discussion of pricing deal with customers. We've come full cycle, beginning and ending with the true objective of almost all pricing machinations. It gives us a chance to tie together loose ends concerning customer perceptions regarding prices. It is an opportunity as well to introduce one final set of external influences on a pricing decision, the needs of wholesalers and retailers, as well as ultimate consumers, in a channel of distribution.

consumer price "psychology"

We often are tempted to portray relationships between price and demand as capable of being described by continuous lines or curves on a graph. Curves of this sort are convenient as well for mathematicians, econometricians, and management scientists, because they can be described and manipulated by means of mathematical statements.

Does the real world often work this way? Probably not. Managers, for example, often envision the results of possible pricing decisions in a form similar to that in Figure 5-5. Here we see that large price changes at certain points on the price curve for an individual product produce no changes in demand, whereas smaller changes at other points may result in great changes in demand.

The psychology of pricing, particularly of goods bought by ultimate consumers for individual use, embodies a number of old wives's tales, few of which have been substantiated by marketing research tests. Whether substantiated or not, they influence pricing decisions. The following are included among them:

1. Consumers often drop the cents from a price stated in dollars and cents. Therefore, an item priced at $1.95 becomes "about a dollar" in the consumer's mind both at and after the time of the purchase.

2. Consumers associate odd prices more readily with low-quality or less-important purchases and even prices with high-quality and more-important

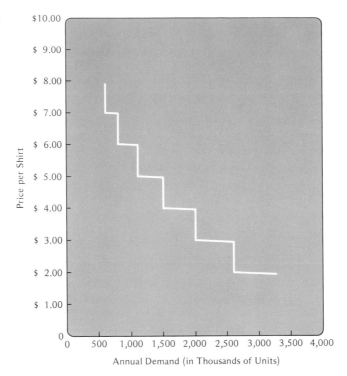

Figure 5-5. Price-demand relationships for men's shirts.

Price per Shirt

Annual Demand (in Thousands of Units)

purchases. Thus, the same consumers that might regard as quite natural a $1.95 price for a paring knife would be surprised to see a Cadillac priced at $9,999.95.

3. Consumers react differently to varying differences in price between competing products. Small price differences may be regarded as a natural product of competition. Large price differences may be suspected of being associated with basic quality differences.

4. Price differentials between competing products vary directly in their effectiveness in redistributing demand from the highest- to the lowest-priced competing product with the amount of knowledge and assurance about their essential similarity that the consumer possesses. We could go on. In fact, you may want to extend this list.

For example, if you, as marketing manager of a company manufacturing men's shirts, subscribed to the conception of price-demand relationships shown in Figure 5-5, how would you price your product? Which of the rules of thumb described above are most likely at work in this situation and most likely to lead you to view price demand relationships for men's shirts as they are shown in Figure 5-5?

How do you explain, in terms of our previous discussion, the fact that American Motors' small-sized Gremlin was priced several years ago at $1,999? Does this violate any of the rules of thumb expressed earlier?

(110)

(111)

(112)

(113)

170

prices and margins to resellers

Prices to retailers and wholesalers—organizations involved in the resale of goods—are based not only on the price to the ultimate individual consumer for which it is thought a product should sell, but also on the amount of margin—the difference between purchase and resale prices—it is thought that resellers must have to perform their functions effectively.

Margins are payments to resellers for performing the functions of buying, assembling, selling, advertising, sorting, extending credit, and others. As such, they should vary directly with the extent and importance of such functions. A manufacturers' representative who only sells typically receives a much smaller margin than a full-service wholesaler who performs all of the functions listed here in addition to those of risk absorption in the ownership of inventories and the possible generation of marketing information to be passed on both to suppliers and customers.

(114)
(115)
(116)
(117)

What happens when margins become too small to support the provision of such functions as those listed previously, expected of the full-service wholesaler by the manufacturer? Or conversely, what happens when retail margins become much greater than the cost of providing the functions expected of the retailer, especially when the latter situation is typical for two or more retailers competing in the same market? Do so-called discount stores provide the same functional services to customers and suppliers that full-service retailers do? What happens when a manufacturer's merchandise is distributed through both types of outlets reaching many of the same customers in a metropolitan market area?

factors in reaching a pricing decision

As a means of summarizing our discussion of pricing, many possible internally and externally oriented influences on a pricing decision are diagrammed in Figure 5-6, along with references to examples that have been used in discussing each one. Not all are applicable to every situation.

(118)
(119) (120)
(121)

For example, which are most relevant for a company determining a price for its first product or service? For a company with a number of items in its line? Or for a company altering the price of an existing product as opposed to pricing a new product? In reviewing your understanding of the implications of each of these influences, ask yourself this question about each factor displayed in Figure 5-6: What conditions for each of these factors would favor an initial price at, or a price increase to, a level higher than the competition?

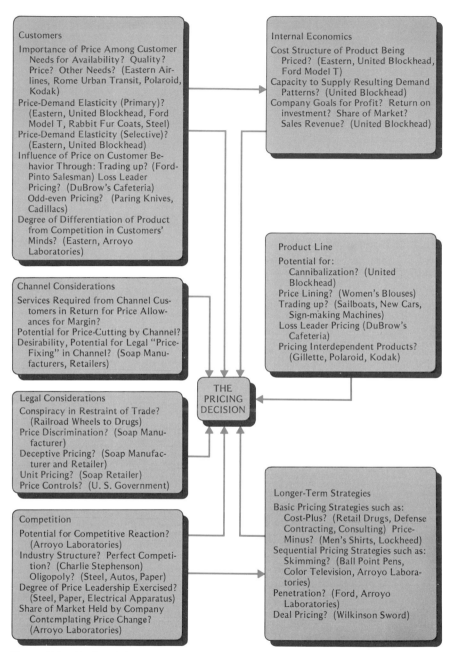

Customers

Importance of Price Among Customer Needs for Availability? Quality? Price? Other Needs? (Eastern Airlines, Rome Urban Transit, Polaroid, Kodak)

Price-Demand Elasticity (Primary)? (Eastern, United Blockhead, Ford Model T, Rabbit Fur Coats, Steel)

Price-Demand Elasticity (Selective)? (Eastern, United Blockhead)

Influence of Price on Customer Behavior Through: Trading up? (Ford-Pinto Salesman) Loss Leader Pricing? (DuBrow's Cafeteria) Odd-even Pricing? (Paring Knives, Cadillacs)

Degree of Differentiation of Product from Competition in Customers' Minds? (Eastern, Arroyo Laboratories)

Internal Economics

Cost Structure of Product Being Priced? (Eastern, United Blockhead, Ford Model T)

Capacity to Supply Resulting Demand Patterns? (United Blockhead)

Company Goals for Profit? Return on investment? Share of Market? Sales Revenue? (United Blockhead)

Channel Considerations

Services Required from Channel Customers in Return for Price Allowances for Margin?

Potential for Price-Cutting by Channel?

Desirability, Potential for Legal "Price-Fixing" in Channel? (Soap Manufacturers, Retailers)

Product Line

Potential for:
   Cannibalization? (United Blockhead)
Price Lining? (Women's Blouses)
Trading up? (Sailboats, New Cars, Sign-making Machines)
Loss Leader Pricing (DuBrow's Cafeteria)
Pricing Interdependent Products? (Gillette, Polaroid, Kodak)

Legal Considerations

Conspiracy in Restraint of Trade? (Railroad Wheels to Drugs)

Price Discrimination? (Soap Manufacturer)

Deceptive Pricing? (Soap Manufacturer and Retailer)

Unit Pricing? (Soap Retailer)

Price Controls? (U. S. Government)

THE PRICING DECISION

Competition

Potential for Competitive Reaction? (Arroyo Laboratories)

Industry Structure? Perfect Competition? (Charlie Stephenson) Oligopoly? (Steel, Autos, Paper)

Degree of Price Leadership Exercised? (Steel, Paper, Electrical Apparatus)

Share of Market Held by Company Contemplating Price Change? (Arroyo Laboratories)

Longer-Term Strategies

Basic Pricing Strategies such as: Cost-Plus? (Retail Drugs, Defense Contracting, Consulting) Price-Minus? (Men's Shirts, Lockheed)

Sequential Pricing Strategies such as: Skimming? (Ball Point Pens, Color Television, Arroyo Laboratories) Penetration? (Ford, Arroyo Laboratories)

Deal Pricing? (Wilkinson Sword)

Figure 5-6. Factors influencing the pricing decision, with matching citations of illustrative examples used in this chapter.

summary

A seller may regard price as the amount for which he or she needs to sell a product or service in order to make a profit. A buyer, on the other hand, often views price in an entirely different way, as one of the costs of acquiring and owning a product or service, including the time required to shop for it, the attendant cost of transportation, installation costs, costs associated with its use, costs implied by the length of its useful life, and costs of foregoing alternative expenditures. A product or service may have a value to its owner or a prospective buyer that is based on real or perceived needs, a figure not necessarily synonymous with its price.

Profits produced by pricing decisions are based on the demand levels generated by various prices as well as product costs. Products or services for which prices and demand levels are related inversely are said to have positive price-demand elasticities. Percentage changes in price creating greater inverse percentage changes in demand are price-demand elastic. Those that lead to smaller inverse percentage changes in demand are price-demand inelastic. Price-demand elasticities can be measured for both primary and selective demand. Of even greater importance to a manager is the profit implied by various price-demand relationships.

Profits are maximized at the point at which incremental revenue equals incremental costs associated with sales at successively lower price levels. Often one of the goals of management is to achieve this point, subject to limits on the capacity to produce products for sale.

In pricing items in a product line, a marketing manager must take into account interrelationships among sales, prices, and profits for each item. These interrelationships may produce damaging effects of cannibalization or more positive effects as a result of careful price lining, the planning of prices to allow trading up, the use of loss-leader tactics, deal pricing, and attention to the profit implications of pricing interdependent products.

The extremes of longer-term pricing policies can be characterized as cost-plus and price-minus pricing. The cost-plus approach is one in which an amount is added to cost to contribute to a targeted profit figure. Under price-minus pricing, a target price is established and costs cut to allow the sale of a product or service at the target price.

Other longer-term pricing strategies may include skim or penetration pricing. Price skimming involves the pricing of a product or service at successively lower prices over time, essentially opening up new markets at each price level. Penetration pricing may be designed to sell as much volume in as short a time as possible, possibly to preempt or discourage potential competitors.

The potential for competitive reaction is one of the most important factors in establishing pricing policies as well as individual pricing decisions.

Prices under perfect competition are determined solely by demand-supply relationships. Industries in which the sellers are few are called oligopolies. In oligopoly industries, supplies and profits can be controlled to a greater extent through price leadership and pricing customs.

Legal limits have been placed on the control of prices within industries. Various laws exist to prevent conspiracy in restraint of trade, price discrimination, deceptive pricing, and destructive retail-pricing practices. From time to time, other laws have established federal price controls as part of national economic policy.

The pricing decision may include the desire to convey a particular product image through the level of its price, a situation in which a price becomes an integral product characteristic. In other cases, prices to ultimate buyers, retailers, and wholesalers are based on the need to provide sufficient margins (differences between purchase and sale prices) to compensate middlemen for their services and to provide appropriate selling incentives.

The means by which price information is conveyed to prospective buyers is our next interest, as we turn to indirect and direct forms of promotional effort, the next stops in our tour of the elements of a marketing strategy.

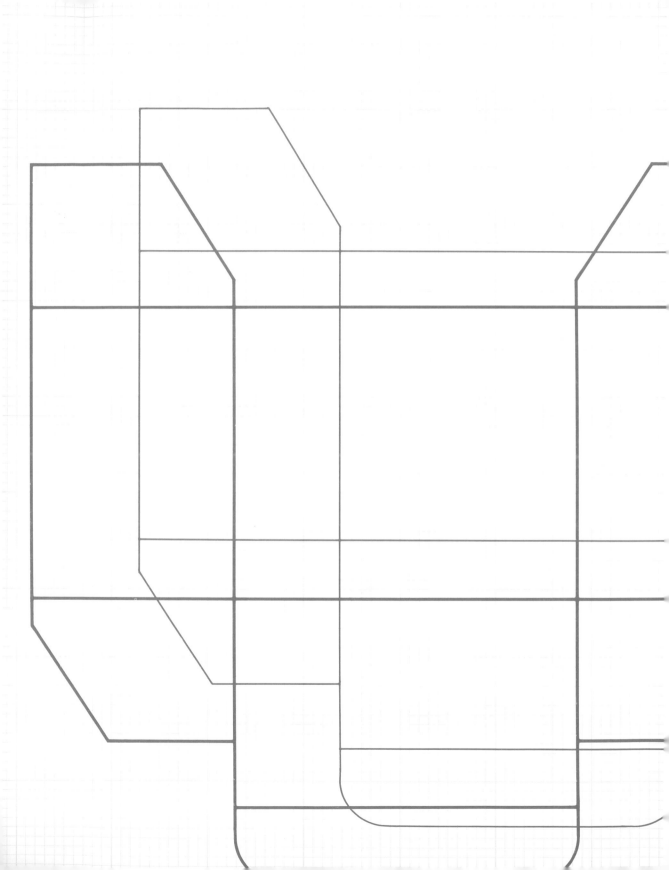

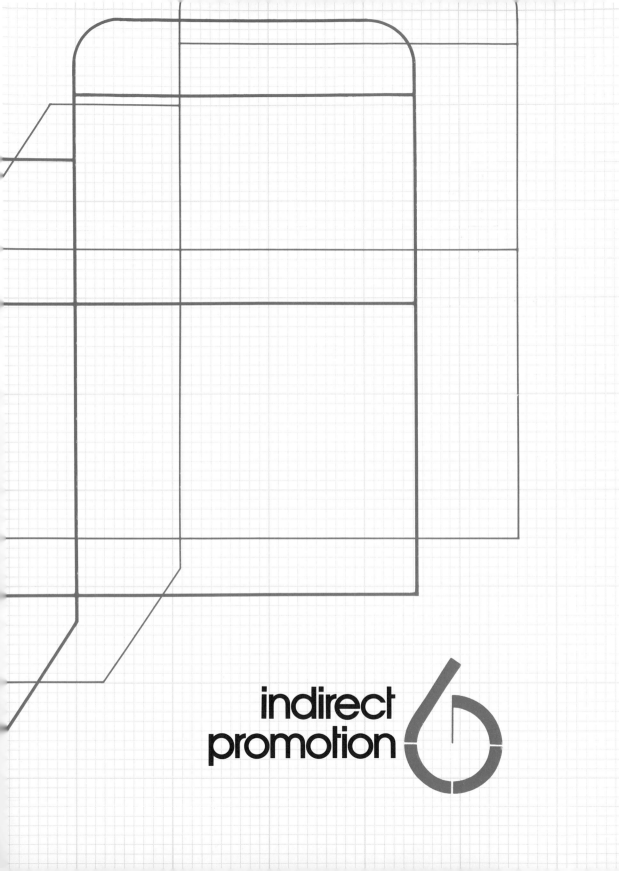

indirect
promotion 6

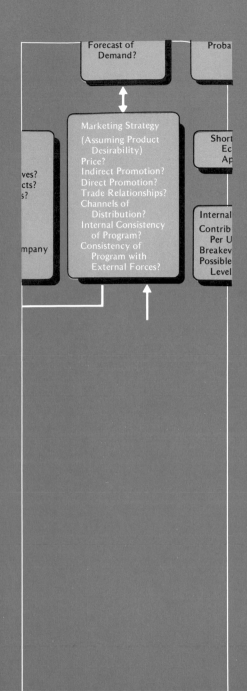

Forecast of
Demand?

Proba

Marketing Strategy
(Assuming Product
Desirability)
Price?
Indirect Promotion?
Direct Promotion?
Trade Relationships?
Channels of
Distribution?
Internal Consistency
of Program?
Consistency of
Program with
External Forces?

Short
Ec
Ap

Internal
Contrib
Per U
Breakev
Possible
Level

ves?
cts?
s?

mpany

American industry currently spends about $400 per American each year for promotion. Does it get its money's worth?

Our major objective in this and the following chapter will be to understand how and why this money is spent. This will require an exploration of the promotional process and the elements of communication on which it is based. Of more immediate importance is an understanding of the elements of promotional strategy involving indirect communication, including advertising, branding, and packaging.

I'll try to accomplish these aims while communicating some of the excitement of the field. It would be criminal to suppress the colorful and exciting aspects of an activity that can produce a zany promotional campaign such as that for the Bic Banana. At the same time, we have a responsibility to identify patterns, islands of order in a sea of creative chaos, useful in structuring the use of indirect promotional methods.

This chapter introduces the first of several marketing institutions with which we will become familiar, the advertising agency. It offers an opportunity to consider the nature of relationships between advertisers and their agencies as well as the output of such relationships. For this purpose I've chosen to focus on a classic relationship between Volkswagen of America, Inc. and its advertising agency, Doyle Dane Bernbach.

Given the fickle character of advertiser-agency relationships, it's possible that even this one will have been severed by the time you read this. In any event, the extent to which the product has influenced consumers and the agency and its advertising have influenced the advertising world give the relationship a timeless quality.

As an American citizen or resident, you spend an average of about $400 per year for promotion. Do you get your money's worth?

going bananas

(Scene: Modestly furnished dining room. A large bowl of fruit is on the table. An elderly woman is seated at the table in front of a large piece of paper. Voice-over: comedian Mel Brooks.)

"Don't write with a peach. If you write with a peach, you'll get a very wet letter. Nor should you write with a prune. Words will come out wrinkled and dopey. And blueberries? Worse yet. It would take you two boxes to write one postcard. That's how small they are. Let's face it, the only fruit you can write with is a banana. The Bic Banana. A fine line marker. Not to be confused with a ball point."

With this commercial, shown on four network television programs, the Bic Pen Corp. and its new agency, Wells, Rich, Greene, launched a $3 million, six-month ad campaign in June 1972 for Bic's new 29-cent fine line marker, a soft-tipped pen billed as a "different way to write." The expenditure would exceed the previous year's total advertising expenditures for all other marker manufacturers combined.[1]

Bic's goal with the campaign was to do the same thing for the marker business it had done for ball pens ten years previously, when it set out to make its 19-cent throwaway stick ball pen a household word. In that year, 1962, Bic sold $1.8 million worth of pens in a fragmented industry producing and selling 750 million pens worth $80 million a year with little advertising. Partly because of Bic's massive advertising, in ten years annual ball pen production had risen to 1.3 billion units per year worth about $160 million, of which nearly $40 million were sold by Bic.

During this same period of time, the sales of markers had been growing at an annual rate of 20 per cent as ball pen sales fell off to 5 per cent annual increases. Gillette's Paper Mate Division had captured 50 per cent of the $60 million marker market with its Flair marker. Meanwhile, according to the president of Bic's United States subsidiary, Robert Adler, his company stayed out of the market until it had a quality product at a low price. At the time, 90 per cent of the markers sold carried a price of forty-nine cents, although Scripto recently had introduced a 19-cent marker and Paper-Mate® one selling for 29 cents.

According to Adler, "Our marketing strategy is very basic, and is governed by the fact that we are coming into the market late and long after everyone else. Our tactic has always been to mass market a price. . . . But if price and product were all we had, we wouldn't go anywhere."[2] Bic's vice-president of sales explained, "Where we have the edge is in our distribution—200,000 retail outlets and more than 12,000 commercial-dealer outlets. We also have the Bic name, which says quality."[3] And there was Bic's advertising.

The advertising task was described by Charlie Moss, president and creative director of Wells, Rich, Greene:

> They came to us with this huge board filled with fifty or so different markers that were then being sold. These went by dozens of different names: fiber-tip pens, porous pens, soft-tip markers, Magic Markers®, etc. There was no one generic name to fit this whole product category. The result was that when you put the Bic marker in there, it just disappeared into all the confusion. It became a commodity. We had to make this thing not a commodity but a product bought for its own sake. And we had to come up with what we hoped would become a generic term for writing markers. Because this is an established product category and the product awareness had already been created, our job was to try and expand the market.[4]

While Adler liked the idea of the Bic Banana, Bic's vice-president of sales was fearful: "From a marketing standpoint, I could see one-hundred reasons why it wouldn't work. While the name had to grab the consumer, it also had to appeal to a sophisticated purchasing agent at AT&T or Chase Manhattan. And how do you get them to buy something called a Banana?"[5] Finally, as the appeal of the

[1] This example is based largely on "A Zany Campaign to Sell the Bic Banana," *Business Week*, (May 27, 1972), pp. 76–78. Quote on p. 76.
[2] Ibid.
[3] Ibid.
[4] Ibid., pp. 76–77.
[5] Ibid., p. 77.

concept grew on Bic's senior management, it decided that it just had to make the idea work through heavy merchandising implemented by the company's ninety-man sales force.

(1)
(2)

How well did the proposed campaign respond to the problem posed by the introduction of a new Bic marker? What chances for success would you have associated with this effort in 1972?

communication

Each day we are confronted with literally hundreds of marketing communications. These are messages sent and received that are intended primarily to influence our behavior. This excludes only those messages intended primarily to convey information, or those that are transmitted unintentionally. Few of them are effective, if we define effective marketing communications as those that (1) make the intended impression at destination, and (2) influence the recipient's behavior in a predetermined way. But this should not be too surprising in view of the relatively complex nature of the communication process.

The nature of the communication process is diagrammed in Figure 6-1. It suggests that the extent to which a particular marketing communication may have its desired effect on us depends on the attitude that we may have toward the source of the message, the way in which it is encoded or translated for us, the probability that we will encounter the message, the strength of the "signal" with which we receive it, and the way in which we decode or interpret it. Having reached its destination, a message will influence our behavior only to the extent that it is relevant to our needs or interests.

Figure 6-1. The nature of the communication process. Source: Adapted from Wilbur Schramm, ed., *The Process and Effects of Mass Communication* (Urbana: University of Illinois Press, 1954), p. 6.

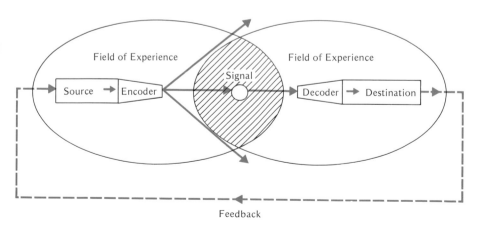

source

Message sources influence our interpretation of a message and our subsequent actions. This is called the source effect in communications.

We associate a variety of sources with the marketing communications that reach us. For example, in the purchase of a marker, we may encounter advertising such as that proposed for the Bic Banana. In this case, we may perceive the source of the message to be the Bic Pen Corp.

The medium carrying the message also may contribute to the source effect. Thus, the television station or magazine carrying the message may enhance or detract from the message, according to a recipient's views of the various media. Do you think the broadcast media, such as television or radio, or the print media, such as newspapers or magazines, contribute the greatest amount of source effect to marketing communications? Is this equally important for a product such as a 19-cent marker as it is for a brand of fine table crystal?

Similarly, sources of direct communications include salesmen and friends. We may perceive them as being more or less expert, more or less biased in their views of a product or service. In general, would you tend to hold a higher regard for a salesman or a friend as a source of communication?

encoder

It is the responsibility of the encoder to translate a message in such a way that it will be received in the intended manner. This requires that the encoder first understand what the intent or objective of the message is. In the case of the Bic Banana campaign, who was the encoder?

At one point in the development of the promotional campaign, problems developed. According to Bic's vice-president of sales, John Paige: "The agency had somehow gotten completely off-track. The pitch of their message was don't write with a ball pen, write with a Bic Banana. Hell, we do $40 million a year in ball pens, we don't want to work against ourselves."[6] How would you explain what had happened in terms of the communication process?

the signal: transmission

The strength of a communication signal, as shown in Figure 6-1, is dependent on an overlapping field of experience between the encoder and decoder as well as the degree to which a particular marketing communication or campaign is able to compete with all others for our attention.

The simplest examples of the need for an overlapping field of experience occur in the transferability of advertising campaigns from one language to another. American campaigns based on slang peculiar to our culture or the

[6]Ibid.

182

English language don't "travel" because of the lack of a common field of experience between the encoder and the decoder when the latter's language is other than English. Similarly, the ad shown in Figure 6-5, page 201, would have seemed peculiar to its audience if used in Germany where the Volkswagen was not considered to be a small car in 1960.

Given a common field of experience between the sender and the receiver, the strength of a message's signal may depend in part on the frequency with which it is transmitted or the variety of methods by which it is transmitted to the same destination.

decoder and destination

A popular theory of advertising strategy holds that a consumer can hold only a limited number of positions for a particular product category in mind at any one time. Furthermore, as a possible reaction to the growing number of marketing communications directed at him, the consumer is thought to be developing more and more selectivity in the types of messages that actually register any impact at their destination. Regardless of the strength of the signal, the decoding process may filter out many messages that find their way to the decoder. This may be due, for example, to poor judgment on the part of the source, which results in a marketing communication being received at the wrong time by the wrong person. As a result, its recipient may have no perceived need for the package of benefits promised by the action recommended in the message.

is anybody listening?

Finally, an effective communication process is two-way in nature. In a telephone conversation, for example, try remaining absolutely silent as a caller relates a story to you. Odds are that your caller will ask if you're still there even though no response has been required during the story. The same is true for marketing communication. Only through feedback and measured responses can we obtain the information necessary for more effective subsequent communications.

promotional strategy

A number of methods are available in formulating a promotional strategy. These include methods of indirect (impersonal) promotion such as advertising, branding, packaging, and publicity. They also encompass forms of direct promotion such as personal selling and so-called word-of-mouth recommendations passed between friends. The extent to which each may be appropriate and the manner in which each might be employed in a particular promotional strategy

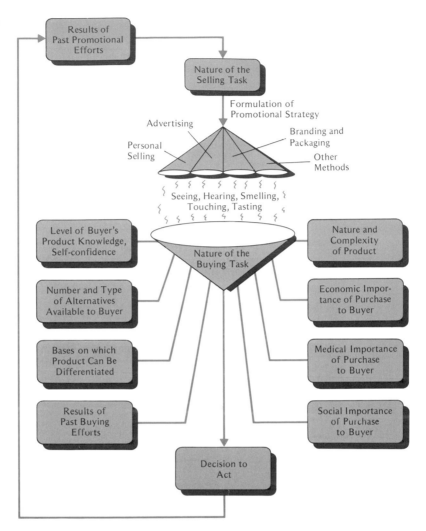

Figure 6-2. Determinants of the buying task, the selling task, and the promotional strategy.

depend on the nature of the promotional task. The promotional task in turn is dependent on the nature of the buying task. These relationships are diagrammed in Figure 6-2.

the buying task: a process of risk reduction

One of several explanations of the buying task is that which views the customer as being involved in a problem-solving process typified by behavior designed to reduce risk. This can be used to explain not only the manner in which customers buy new products with which they are relatively unfamiliar but also why they repeat their purchases of products or services with which they have had satisfactory experiences.

184

Risk reduction in buying requires that the problem solver turn to various sources of information. The extent to which this behavior is engaged in for a particular product purchase decision will depend, according to the theory, on such factors as (1) the complexity of the product; (2) the level of a buyer's knowledge about the product and self-confidence in buying it; (3) the economic, social, and medical importance of a decision to a buyer; (4) the number and type of alternative products available; (5) the nature of the bases on which alternative products might be differentiated; and (6) a prospective buyer's perceptions of the results of past buying efforts.

Nature and Complexity of the Product. The problem-solving task, and a prospective buyer's willingness to engage in it, is likely to vary directly with the complexity of the product. Try this on yourself. Would you seek out a greater amount of information from a wider variety of trusted sources in the purchase of a ready-made stereo set or a set of individually purchased stereo components? Because of the nature of either these products, you might be reluctant to make a purchase without hearing various demonstration units, thereby restricting the use of indirect methods of communication in the promotion strategy.

(8)

Buyer's Knowledge and Self-confidence. Two buyers' knowledge about, and self-confidence in buying, a product will be different. The amount of additional information required from trusted sources tends to vary inversely with such product knowledge and self-confidence. For example, a salesclerk in a sporting goods store might have less need for professional advice in the purchase of a tennis racket for personal use than a person with less opportunity to work with such products on a day-to-day basis. Indirect and less personal forms of promotion might be sufficient to provide the salesclerk with all of the information necessary on which to base a purchase decision.

Importance of Purchase Decision. The importance of a purchase decision varies directly with the perceived risks in making the wrong decision. Such risks may be economic, social, or medical. For example, would your search for risk-reducing information be greater for a new kitchen or a new easy chair for the living room? For a new easy chair for the living room or an occasional chair for a bedroom never seen by friends? Or for a new easy chair of conventional design or one designed to alleviate a back ailment with which you might be afflicted?

(9)

(10)
(11)

Number and Type of Alternative Products. Have you ever been so overwhelmed by the number of types of a product available in a retail store that you left without buying, even though you needed the product? You were unable to complete what suddenly became a much more complex problem-solving process than you had anticipated when you walked into the store. Because this is a common experience, few stores featuring large product assortments display them all without having a clerk available to assist in the decision-making process. A smart retail clerk will limit the number of items displayed before a customer at any one time, removing some items as others are presented for consideration.

The task of information collection and the reduction of uncertainty most often varies directly in magnitude with the number and type of alternative solutions to a buying problem.

Bases for Product Differentiation.　Differences between competing products may be real or perceived, tangible or intangible, visible or invisible. Each combination of product differences presents a different set of problems to the prospective buyer.

For example, golf balls all look pretty much alike. In fact, only recently did one manufacturer depart from industry practice and produce a ball with only 324 dimples (indentations on the white surface) on it, as opposed to the 336 dimples on other balls. However, golf balls are constructed with different types of centers, an invisible difference. And it is very difficult for a golfer to measure the effect of various balls on his or her golf game. In contrast, automobiles possess both visible and invisible differences. Styling and accessories comprise visible differences. However, what is "under the hood" may be much less visible, and more important, to many drivers. And what's under the hood describes real, tangible differences in product alternatives to the automobile buyer.

Aspirin-based products provide another interesting set of examples. All essentially do the same thing: they kill pain. But competing manufacturers have done a number of things to differentiate their aspirin-based products. They have added ingredients to provide other types of relief. And they have given their products different names, whether or not the products have any tangible or visible differences.

(12)　How do you think the buying process is influenced by the way in which competing products are differentiated, using golf balls, automobiles, and (13)　aspirin-based products as specific examples? How does the information-collection and risk-reduction process vary with each combination of differences between alternative products?

Perceptions of Past Results.　Trial and error may be a predominant mode of purchasing behavior for many products. Over time, a buyer learns by means of his past mistakes and zeroes in on a preferred product. Because of the complexity of the purchase process, and the frequency with which we are required to engage in it, we seek ways of simplifying the task and making it more routine. Past experience with a product, good or bad, is an important means for doing this. We become, in the term of consumer-behavior theorists, product loyal, less likely to switch products or brands from one purchase to the next.

The importance of previous buying results varies directly with the frequency with which a product is purchased or the frequency with which it is used. For example, we might be much more conscious of this factor in the purchase of a regularly used coffee than in the purchase of a decaffeinated coffee served occasionally to friends who request it.

The ease with which product performance can be measured by potential or previous users also influences the information-seeking and risk-reducing processes in which they engage. This may vary greatly, for example, as between automobiles and refrigerators. The prospective buyer of a refrigerator has nothing comparable to the "test drive" on which to base his or her decision.

Where possible, manufacturers have sought to obtain trials of their products by prospective buyers. In certain cases, such as the automobile test drive, attempts may be made to influence the perceptions obtained from such trials by presenting the product in its most favorable light.

(14) (15)　Try, if you will, to remember the last time you purchased either a ball pen or a marker. How complex was the nature of your buying task? On what sources of

(16)
(17)

information did you rely to carry it out? How would you account for this in terms of the factors influencing the processes that are cited in Figure 6-2? Does this offer any basis for judging the likely success of a far-out scheme to market a product such as the Bic Banana?

the buying task: a hierarchy of effects

A view that complements the risk-reduction philosophy in explaining the buying task and buying behavior is that based on the so-called hierarchy of communication effects. This holds that buyers experience three stages of mental processing, or response levels, in a purchase decision and action. The first of these involves learning, including the development of awareness, knowledge, and understanding of product attributes. The second concerns attitude change, encompassing the development of interest in, and evaluation of, possible purchase alternatives and the adoption of a conviction that a particular decision is right. The third stage concerns more overt behavior, the establishment of an intent to act (buy) and the buying action itself.

There is some agreement among researchers about the existence of this hierarchy. But there is also considerable debate about the order in which the stages occur for a particular buyer confronted with a particular decision. For example, does learning always occur before attitude change and behavior (or action)? Or do buyers sometimes act and then experience attitude change and learning? Or do buyers learn, act, and then experience attitude change? What hierarchy of effects do you think would be most typically associated with the purchase of a golf ball, an automobile, or a ball pen marker?

(18)

the gatekeeper phenomenon

We have assumed up to now that the buyer and user of a product are the same person. But in many marketing situations, perhaps most, it is not true. Buyers and users are differentiated every time someone buys you a gift, an adult makes a purchase decision for children or other members of a family, or a purchasing agent buys supplies used by personnel in various departments of a large organization. Equally typical is a situation in which the illusion is created in the minds of children or the specifying engineers that they have made purchase decisions when in fact their decisions have been controlled through the selective transmission of information by parents or purchasing agents, respectively. The process of selectively filtering information to influence or control a purchasing decision by someone else is called the gatekeeper phenomenon. The gatekeeper determines the nature of the information to be used in the purchase decision, or—figuratively—who may pass through the gate, who must wait, and who will be denied passage.

Gatekeepers can be recognized as a mother influencing her children's preferences for breakfast cereal as well as a data-processing manager filtering information about alternative computers under consideration for purchase by less well-informed senior managers. It is just as important to establish their identity as it is to identify the decision makers themselves in formulating a promotion strategy.

the promotional task

The promotional task at least involves (1) the identification of decision makers and decision influences on buyers, (2) the development of awareness of needs on the part of buyers, (3) building interest in a product or service, (4) assisting in the buyer's risk-reducing process, (5) making the product physically available, (6) obtaining buyer action and trial, and (7) encouraging a repurchase of the product. These steps are shown in the context of a broader marketing strategy in Figure 6-3. Reviewing Figure 6-3 and the elements of the buying task that we discussed previously, to what extent does the promotional task anticipate or precede the buying task?

Identification of Decision Makers and Decision Influences. In a given purchase, the individual making the purchase may or may not be the individual deciding what is to be bought. For example, in the purchase of a jet airplane for business use, a company's treasurer may actually make the purchase by preparing the check. But it is quite likely that at least the president and the company's pilot will have participated in the decision. In this situation, who is the decision maker likely to be? What roles do the others play? What other decision influences may be present?

In general, is the task of identifying decision makers more difficult in the marketing of consumer or industrial goods?

Development of Awareness of Needs. An old story is told about the farmer demonstrating how to work with a mule. Beginning his demonstration by hitting the mule over the head with a two-by-four board, the farmer explains that first you have to get the mule's attention. The same is true for promotional effort. It

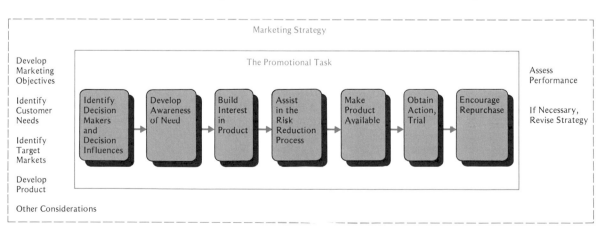

Figure 6-3. The promotional task in the context of a marketing strategy.

is not enough at this stage to develop an awareness of the availability of a product or service, a possible solution to a buyer's need. It may be necessary to develop an awareness of the need itself through an understanding of the problems confronted by prospective buyers.

Building Interest. It may be important to build interest in a particular product to the point where, when a decision to buy is made, the product is considered a viable alternative. This may be accomplished by means of an advertising program in which successive ads feature different advantages of a particular product. In some cases, interest is built before the identity of the product is disclosed. For example, an automobile dealer may advertise, "Coming on September 27, the all-new economy car from Chevrolet".

Repeated promotional messages from a variety of sources may be necessary to build interest to the desired level.

Assisting in the Risk-Reducing Process. Promotional effort can provide the information and assurances necessary in helping a buyer engage in his or her risk-reducing activities. In some cases, through the provision of a guarantee or a penalty clause in a construction contract for assurance against delayed perform-ance, risk essentially may be eliminated for a buyer. Most other times, the task involves providing information on which the buyer can make a more knowl-edgeable decision among alternative products or services.

Making the Product Available. In some cases, the demonstration of a product is essential to its sale. In others, it is necessary to gain distribution or retail display of a product in anticipation of buyer demand. Failure to do so can result in a waste of promotional effort and buyer badwill. Various forms of promotional effort, either to end users or others, can encourage wholesalers and retailers to stock a product in anticipation of the effects of such efforts.

In the case of the Bic Banana, this presented a particular problem. According to John Paige, Bic's vice-president of sales:

> Our message to our sales force was that, "Fellas, retailers will not be sitting there with open arms. They are doing a healthy 49¢ business today, and here we come with a 29¢ marker. So let's be honest with the customer. While this is just another marker and the retailer may not really need it—especially at a lower price—the important thing is what we are going to make of this marker.[7]

How were Bic's ninety salesmen to deal with this problem? At a critical point in their sales pitch, they were to play the Mel Brooks commercials on small cassette players with which they had been equipped, afterward explaining that starting on June 1, Bic would spend $500,000 on advertising for the month of June and another $2.5 million between August 7 and October 16 for the back-to-school business. The idea, according to Bic's ad manager:

> was that the retailer just couldn't afford not to carry it. This advertising was bound to expand the market, and thus expand his own sales and profits. After all, this is exactly what we did when we introduced our crystal-stick ball pen.[8]

[7]Ibid., p. 78.
[8]Ibid.

As a result, Bic Bananas began selling briskly at retail as much as a month before the beginning of the advertising campaign. What were the relative roles of advertising and personal selling in developing an awareness of need, building interest in the product, assisting in the risk-reduction process, and obtaining product distribution for the Bic Banana?

Obtaining Action or Trial. Perhaps the most challenging stage in the promotional task is that of stirring the potential customer to action. Nothing short of physical force may at times be sufficient to motivate a television viewer to vacate his easy chair in front of the set. The ease with which action or trial is obtained is at least a function of the strength of the customer's need, the memorability of the promotional message, and the nature of the product.

It has been shown that advertising messages have a certain "decay rate." That is, their ability to produce sales diminishes with the passage of time after their communication. By the same token, it is possible that the strength of a promotional communication in a buyer's mind decays with the passage of time between the realization of a need, the exposure to the promotional message, and the exposure to the product itself. The more important the need and the more forceful the promotional communication, the slower the decay rate. Certain products may naturally whet the curiosity of the buyer, thus lending themselves to more memorable promotional communication and a greater likelihood of purchase or trial. For example, how would you compare a new bath soap and a new battery-powered automobile in terms of the decay rates for the promotional communications transmitted for each?

Sampling, involving the mailing or personal distribution of product samples to prospective users, has been employed to encourage product trial. Sampling, however, is limited to those products that can be produced and mailed or otherwise distributed economically in sample form. Furthermore, some argue that the most effective trial is one that involves the purchase of the product rather than the receipt of a gift.

Encouraging Repurchase. A good product, offering better value than its competitors, is the best stimulant to repurchase. But promotional effort can help by confirming the "rightness" of his decision in the buyer's mind. This may be done by showing the product being used by people with whom the buyer would like to be associated. It may be done by means of a service sales call, in which the purpose is to let the buyer know that someone is interested in his or her experiences with the product. In its simplest form, postpurchase reinforcement designed to encourage repurchase is typified by the waiter asking you if you enjoyed your restaurant meal, particularly if the question is asked after you've left your tip.

Recalling our earlier discussion of the hierarchy of effects in buying on page 187, which order of effects is assumed in Figure 6-3? Would you expect it to be the same for all buyers and products?

Having explored the nature of the buying and promotional task in a general sense, we turn now to the specific methods of communication around which a promotional strategy can be structured. In our discussion we will return several times to questions concerning the stages in the promotional task at which each method can be employed most effectively. Among the promotional methods utilized are such indirect methods as advertising, branding, and packaging. They rely on methods other than person-to-person communication.

190

advertising

Few influences are so pervasive on our way of life as advertising. In return for recent expenditure levels of approximately $27 billion per year, or about $125 for every man, woman, and child in America, we receive messages intended to inform, entertain, motivate, or brainwash us, depending on your point of view. Because of its visibility, few people are without a point of view on the subject of advertising.

Advertising is treated as an expense of doing business by accountants. In many respects, however, it resembles an investment on which a return is expected. Money is spent or committed for an advertising campaign months in advance of its expected impact. And the return on such expenditures may be spread out over some period of time.

In another sense, advertising is the closest thing to automation that the field of marketing can claim. As reporter Martin Mayer has put it:

> The relative efficiency of advertising as a selling tool is arguable on the national scene and within specific industries. But advertising to the millions is unquestionably more efficient—less expensive per dollar of sales produced—than the old methods which saw individual salesmen working over individual customers.[9]

What are the means by which paid, nonpersonal communications designed to inform or persuade, otherwise called advertising, are brought to us?

the media

The media available to advertisers can be categorized in terms of print, broadcast, outdoor, and other types. As shown in Table 6-1, print and broadcast media contained nearly 79 per cent of the dollar volume of advertising placed in 1972, with newspapers leading the way. For the ten-year period shown in Table 6-1, which medium has exhibited the most rapid growth in the share of total expenditures captured? Which has exhibited the greatest decline in share of the total?

Potential advertisers often appraise media alternatives in terms of the means of communication that they offer, and the clutter, decay rate, type and size of audience, and cost associated with each.

Means of Communication. Until television came along, the only means of combining sight and sound for advertising purposes were provided by motion picture theaters and sound trucks displaying print advertising. These are advertising media that are still used extensively in some countries of the world. More recently, advertisers have been offered the potential for color advertising by newspapers and the communication of smell and sample textures (feelies), particularly by magazines. We are told that in the future smellevision, combining an appeal to three of our five senses, may be technically possible.

[9] Martin Mayer, *Madison Avenue, U. S. A.* (New York: Harper, 1958), p. 22.

(28)

(29)

Table 6-1   Trends in Expenditures for Advertising in the United States, by Medium*

Medium[a]	By Percentage of Total (Unless Indicated Otherwise)	
	1962	1972
Print		
Newspapers		
National advertising	6.3%	5.4%
Local advertising	23.3	24.8
Total	29.6%	30.2%
Magazines		
Weeklies	4.2%	2.6%
Women's	1.6	1.6
Monthlies	1.8	2.0
Farm	.5	.3
Business	4.8	3.3
Total	12.9%	9.8%
Direct mail	15.5%	14.5%
Total, all print	58.0%	54.5%
Broadcast		
Television		
Network	7.8%	7.7%
Spot	4.9	6.0
Local	2.5	4.1
Total	15.2%	17.8%
Radio		
Network	.4%	.3%
Spot	2.3	1.7
Local	3.7	4.6
Total	6.4%	6.6%
Total, all broadcast	21.6%	24.4%
Outdoor	1.3%	1.3%
Miscellaneous[b]	18.9%	19.7%
Total	100.0%[c]	100.0%[c]
Total dollars spent (in millions)	$12,440.8[d]	$23,060,0[d]
Dollars spent as a proportion of GNP	2.247%	2.00%

* Sources: Advertising Volume Finally Tops $12 Billion," *Printer's Ink*, **5** (Feb. 15, 1963), for 1962 data; ''Advertising Volume in the United States in 1971 and 1972," *Advertising Age,* **64** (Feb. 19, 1973) for 1972 data.

[a]For definitions of each of these media categories, see pages 578–580.

[b]Including transportation (transit), point of purchase, specialty, and directory advertising.

[c]Totals may not add to 100.0 per cent because of rounding.

[d]Excluding nonpaid forms of advertising such as publicity and word of mouth.

Media may lend themselves particularly well to the presentation of products that benefit especially from the use of various combinations of methods of communication. For example, the Polaroid Corp., the manufacturer of a camera for which a simple but dramatic demonstration was possible, found that television provided a particularly effective combination of communication methods for the presentation of its product to a potentially disbelieving market.

Clutter. Advertising messages compete with one another for our attention. Billboards may compete with car radio advertising for the commuter by automobile, for example. In recent years, competition for attention has been heightened by the development of new media, such as television.

Perhaps of greater importance is the competition of ads within a particular advertising medium. This competition, to the extent that it reduces the effectiveness of an individual message, is called clutter. For example, by moving from a standard module of sixty seconds to one of thirty seconds for their standard network spots, NBC, CBS, and ABC added to the number of advertisements per hour and the clutter on a particular television channel. Because two thirty-second spots sell for more than one sixty-second spot, the networks benefited financially from the action.

As a means of reducing clutter and competition for the attention of a potential customer, advertisers have a number of options open to them. They may simply buy more time or reserve more space. They may pay more per exposure to have their messages positioned in such a way that the effects of clutter are reduced, as an advertiser does in buying the inside front cover spot in a leading magazine. Or they may utilize media that minimize clutter. In your opinion, how do the various media rate on this score?

(30)

Decay Rate. As we have seen, decay rate refers to the rate at which the ability of an advertisement or advertising campaign to produce intended results declines. The process begins immediately after exposure. Its rate may depend on such factors as the size of the ad or campaign, the effectiveness of the message, the nature of the advertised item and its targeted market segments, and the clutter of competitors' advertising and other messages in general. Which do you think would have a faster decay rate, a given color ad placed in a newspaper or magazine?

(31)

Type of Audience. Magazines "deliver" different audiences. We wouldn't, for example, expect to reach a large number of businessmen at a time and place when they are in a decision-making mood through the children's magazine *Jack and Jill.* Radio and especially television networks and stations deliver different audiences at various times of the day. It is the advertiser's task to match a medium with a desired audience before assessing the relative value of using a particular advertising medium.

For example, several years ago *Reader's Digest* had a circulation (copies purchased) of more than 15 million, an audience (estimated number of readers) of more than 37 million, a cost per thousand circulation of $2.81, and a cost per thousand audience of $1.17 for a full-page black-and-white ad. *Business Week,* in contrast, had a circulation of about 550,000, an audience of about 3.4 million, a cost per thousand circulation of $12.20, and a cost per thousand audience of

$1.99 for the same type and size ad. Which would represent the most economical medium for an advertiser of an instant breakfast? An advertiser of oil drilling equipment? Why does *Business Week* have a higher cost per thousand audience than *Reader's Digest* for an advertiser?

Size and Cost of Audience. The cost of all media can be measured on some basis such as that used here for magazines. Although this may provide a reasonable means for measuring alternatives within a particular medium, cost comparisons between media are difficult, as suggested by the data for costs and circulation (or audience) of selected media shown in Table 6-2.

Table 6-2 **Rates and Circulation for Advertising in Selected Media**[a]

Media	Rate and Circulation Information		
	Rate per Page[b]	Circulation[c]	Frequency of Publication
Newspapers (1974)			
Wall Street Journal	$22,431	1,313,000	Daily
New York Times	9,816	878,000	Daily
Chicago Tribune	6,051	682,000	Daily
St. Louis Post Dispatch	3,522	317,000	Daily
Los Angeles Times	6,048	1,010,000	Daily
Magazines (1974)			
American Home	10,687	3,448,000	Monthly
Better Homes and Gardens	38,375	7,797,000	Monthly
Cosmopolitan	8,800	1,804,000	Monthly
Vogue	6,200	542,000	Monthly
McCall's	29,000	7,508,000	Monthly
Ladies Home Journal	26,250	7,008,000	Monthly
Business Week	9,940	744,000	Weekly
Progressive Grocer	2,950	82,000	Monthly
Time	25,560	4,506,000	Weekly
Reader's Digest	51,375	18,591,000	Monthly
The New Yorker	5,000	482,000	Weekly

Direct Mail (1973)	Cost per Thousand Mailings	Circulation
	$60–$80[d]	Controlled by user

Network Television (1974)	Rate per Broadcast
Network one hour program 17 weeks	$578,000–$1,870,000

Spot (Local) Television (1974)	Rate per 60-Second Commercial
WNBC–TV, New York City	
The 7:25 A.M. news	$ 300
The Eleventh Hour News (11 P.M.)	3,600

Table 6-2 (Continued)

Media	Rate and Circulation Information	
WLS–TV, Chicago:		
Kennedy and Company (7–8:30 A.M. news program)	$ 120	
Eyewitness News (10 P.M. news)	3,200	
Dick Cavett Show (after 10:30 P.M.)	550	

Radio (1974)	Rate per 60-Second Announcement[e]	
WCBS, New York City	$60–180	
WGN, Chicago	75–225	
KMOX, St. Louis	65–170	
KNX, Los Angeles	75–150	

Outdoor Advertising (1973)	Cost per Month	Potential Number of People Exposed
No. 100 showing (top 10 markets)[f]	$203,319	34,600,000
No. 50 showing (top 10 markets)[g]	$105,230	34,600,000

Yellow Pages Directories (1971)	Rate	
10 Largest markets	$700–$7,500[h]	
50 Largest markets	$2,900–$25,600[h]	

[a]Rates do not include production costs.

[b]Based on a one-time insertion. Rate and circulation information for newspapers, magazines, radio, and television was obtained from Standard Rate and Data Service, Inc.

[c]Equivalent to the number of copies sold nationally unless indicated otherwise; these figures do not reflect readership, the fact that a magazine may be read by more than one person.

[d]A typical range; actual costs would vary with the nature of the piece.

[e]Based on a single broadcast, with the lowest rate representing an airing after 8 P.M. and the highest rate representing an airing before 10 A.M.

[f]A No. 100 showing in the top ten markets provides 1,746 panels (billboards approximately 8 × 20 feet, of which 451 are illuminated), enough to reach approximately 93 per cent of the population an average of 21 or 22 times during a 30-day period.

[g]A No. 50 showing in the top ten markets provides 895 panels (billboards approximately 8 × 20 feet, of which 234 are illuminated), to reach approximately 85 per cent of the population an average of 10 or 11 times during a 30-day period.

[h]The lower of these figures represents a rate for bold-faced (dark-print listing), the higher the rate for a one-quarter-column (equivalent to one eighth of a page) advertisement.

(35)

(36)

For example, which would represent better value for the Bic Pen Corp. in the introduction of its Bic Banana, two full-page ads in *Reader's Digest* or one full-page ad in each of the newspapers in the top ten markets? An equivalent amount of money spent on one-minute network television spots or local thirty-second radio spots in all major cities?

the advertisers

The ten largest advertisers in the United States spent a total of about $1.6 billion, or about 6 per cent of the national total of about $27 billion in 1973. The companies, examples of their more famous brands, and their expenditures in relation to sales are shown in Table 6-3. What patterns, if any, do you see in Table 6-3 regarding the types of products sold or manufactured by the firms listed there? Which group ranked highest in terms of advertising to sales (or more commonly A/S) ratios, the standard measure used for the level of advertising employed by many firms? Does this suggest product characteristics or differences (tangible, intangible, visible, or invisible) for which advertising is thought to be particularly important as a part of the promotional strategy?

Advertising is pervasive. It is employed by all types of commercial and public enterprises, as suggested in Table 6-4. Of particular interest is the fact that the federal government moved up to tenth on the list of major advertisers in 1973 with a total expenditure of nearly $100 million, primarily for increased promotion in support of armed services recruiting and other public service messages. The volume of advertising in Russia was estimated to have increased to $52 million in 1971, with further significant increases predicted for the future.[10]

Table 6-3 **Estimated Advertising Expenditures of Ten Largest United States Advertisers in 1973***

Advertiser	Well-Known Brands	Total 1973 Expenditures (in millions of dollars)	Expenditures As a Percentage of 1973 Sales
Sears, Roebuck and Co.	Kenmore; Allstate; Coldspot		
National advertising		$215	1.7%
Local advertising		230	2.0
Total		$465.0	3.7%
Proctor and Gamble Co.	Crest; Tide	310.0	6.3
General Foods Corp.	Jell-O; Maxwell House	180.0	8.1
General Motors Corp.	Chevrolet; Cadillac	158.4	.4
Warner-Lambert Pharmaceuticals	Listerine; Bromo-Selzer	141.7	14.6
American Home Products Corp.	Anacin; Chef Boy-Ar-Dee	133.0	9.9
Bristol-Myers Co.	Clairol; Excedrin	132.0	12.7
Ford Motor Company	Ford; Continental	127.2	.6
Colgate-Palmolive Co.	Ajax; Baggies	120.0	12.2
United States government	Volunteer Army	99.0	n.a.[a]

* Source: Merle Kingman, "Top 100 National Advertisers Hike Ad Total to $5.68 Billion," *Advertising Age* (Aug. 26, 1974), pp. 1 and 28. Totals are for domestic operations only. For all companies except Sears, Roebuck (for which local store advertising is most important) only expenditures for national advertising are estimated.

[a] Not applicable

[10] Lyman E. Ostlund, "Russian Advertising: A New Concept," *Journal of Advertising Research,* (Feb. 1973), pp. 11–19. Quote on p. 12.

Table 6-4 Percentages of Sales Invested in Advertising for Selected Products or Services, Fiscal 1969–1970*

Industry	Percentage of Sales Invested in Advertising
Manufacturing	
Soap, cleaners, and toilet goods[a]	10.09
Drugs	9.10
Tobacco	5.36
Canned and frozen foods	2.38
Household furniture	1.08
General industrial machinery	.90
Concrete, gypsum, and plaster products	.41
Aircraft, guided missiles, and parts	.22
Transportation	
Air[a]	2.45
Railroad	.12
Retail Trade	
Furniture, home furnishings, and equipment stores[a]	3.13
Apparel and accessory stores	2.12
Building materials, hardware, and farm equipment	.79
Wholesale Trade	
Motor vehicles and automotive equipment[a]	.86
Metals and minerals, except petroleum and scrap	.13
Finance, Insurance, and Real Estate	
Subdividers, developers, and operative builders[a]	3.06
Personal credit agencies	2.35
Life insurance	.26
Services	
Educational[a]	6.51
Motion picture	5.51
Legal	.36

* Source: "Percentage of Sales Invested in Advertising in 1969–70." *Advertising Age* (July 16, 1973), p. 34, based on IRS data.

[a]Product or service in the over-all category for which the highest proportion of sales was spent for advertising.

(40)

(41) (42)

How do you explain the differences in advertising to sales ratios shown in Table 6-4 for manufacturers of soap and manufacturers of general industrial machinery? Between air transportation and railroad transportation firms? Between retailers and wholesalers?

advertiser-agency relations

After a three-month search, Carl Hahn and Paul Lee, the president and advertising manager, respectively, of Volkswagen of America Inc., in July, 1959 entered into a relationship with an advertising agency, Doyle Dane Bernbach, that was to set new trends in advertising for years to come and break many of the existing rules for the creation of advertisements in the process. Up to that time, Volkswagen had spent small amounts of money to advertise its transporters in the United States in a manner shown in Figure 6-4. This was typical of much of the automobile advertising at that time, which featured drawings of automobiles, structured if possible to enhance their size or length in a way impossible to achieve with photographs, in fine settings.

Prospective customers were waiting up to six months to purchase a Volkswagen sedan in 1959. However, the decision was made to spend $400,000 on advertising for transporters and $800,000 on advertising for sedans to prepare for

Figure 6-4. A 1958 advertisement for Volkswagen products.

The full of sun, full of fun Station Wagon

A Volkswagen DeLuxe Station Wagon, to be sure! It's the growing American family's
pride and joy — roomy as can be — and carefree as the whole outdoors with sliding sun-roof, skylights and
big picture windows. And with all this fun ... Volkswagen quality,
Volkswagen dependability, Volkswagen economy.

Famous VW Service and Genuine VW Spare Parts available in all 49 states

For free full-color
illustrated brochure, write
P. O. Box 2502, New York 17, N. Y.

VOLKSWAGEN

the day when competition from other importers and from small cars manufactured by United States firms would increase.

The Volkswagen account was sought by a number of advertising firms. According to Helmut Schmitz, then assistant to Volkswagen's advertising manager:

> We were led into meeting rooms that had about a hundred speculative ad concepts pinned to the wall, and we were bewildered because we thought: How can anybody just make up ads before they know enough about the product? All we saw were presentations which showed Volkswagen ads exactly like every other ad—an airline ad, a cigarette ad, a toothpaste ad. The only difference was that, where the tube of toothpaste had been, they'd placed a Volkswagen.[11]

At a time when Volkswagen's executives were about to conclude that advertising agency people "were all a bunch of phonies," they encountered Bill Bernbach, a partner; Julian Koenig, account executive; Helmut Krone, art director; and Bob Levenson, copywriter from Doyle Dane Bernbach. According to Stuart Perkins, at that time an assistant to Hahn but destined to become president of Volkswagen of America:

> Doyle Dane weren't big then, not what they are now, at least, and they were all young guys. They were quick to sense that this was a different car, so how could you write standard copy about it? These were people who wanted to do something different. . . .[12]

In the words of one of Doyle Dane's executives:

> In the world of 1959 we were ten years old, three hundred people, and billing around twenty-five million dollars. For the first time we'd begun to climb steeply. VW was not perceived as a small account. It was not a charity case. It was an account we wanted, and a car. We were still suffering then from a kind of small-agency, soft-goods-agency reputation—a department store, rye bread, fibers. We were not reluctant. VW was a fine hard-goods account, and a *car*.[13]

The combination of creative agency people presenting an advertising concept for acceptance or rejection by their advertiser-client is one that typically produces conflict. In describing their relationship later, Helmut Schmitz of Volkswagen wrote:

> I think that the creative people in this agency are willing and eager to show us all their ideas. They are not afraid, nor are the account executives. They don't do what is so common: rejecting an idea before it ever reaches the client because they think the stupid so and so won't buy it anyway. They show us all the ideas they think have merit. We don't accept all of them, but those we refuse we turn down for sound reasons, not just for a vague feeling.[14]

[11] Frank Rowsome, Jr., *Think Small* (Brattleboro, Vt.: The Stephen Greene Press, 1970), p. 60. Much of the material in this section is based on this source.
[12] Ibid., p. 66.
[13] Ibid.
[14] Ibid., p. 88.

On the agency's part, it typically insisted that an ad be run as proposed or not at all.

The result of this relationship was the production and publication of advertising that violated then-existing rules of thumb by utilizing humor, including vast expanses of white space, utilizing photographs instead of drawings for automobiles, emphasizing in great detail the mechanical features of the product, and poking fun at the product's shape and its shortcomings as well as the manufacturer's policies. It was some of the best-read and best-remembered advertising ever created, and included the ad shown in Figure 6-5. How would you contrast the advertisements in Figures 6-4 and 6-5? To what type of potential customer would the ad in Figure 6-5 have the most appeal?

Bob Levenson, who wrote the copy for Volkswagen for three years, described the process by which the ads were created:

> In other agencies more often than not a rather rigid strategy is laid down and the "creative" people are instructed to implement it. In our place, if that happens, the first thing you do is question the strategy. Okay, so suppose we say what you say, prove what you want proved, will that really make any difference in how people perceive this product, or in their purchase patterns?
>
> Typically an ad begins with an art director and a copywriter sitting down together in a room, with or without direction from the client or the account people. Together they develop a picture-and-headline combination that seems promising. The picture doesn't always come from the art director nor the headline from the copywriter. The two guys may modify or reexamine that combination a hundred times, but there's generally no copy written at that point, though there's a pretty good idea of where the copy would lead. The combination, which we grandiosely call a concept, is what gets shown to Volkswagen for initial approval. Not having copy at the time of concept approval prevents you from getting into the wrong arguments—the kind of horror meeting where the copy is finally approved but the ad gets killed.[15]

Agency Organization. Julian Koenig, as the account executive for Doyle Dane at the beginning of its relationship with Volkswagen, had the responsibility for coordinating the activities of the agency on behalf of the account as well as acting as a liaison between Volkswagen and his firm. Typical of most account executives, he was also expected to attract new accounts to the agency. Figure 6-6 shows a typical advertising agency organization and the nature of the relationships between its personnel and those of a major account. In addition to account and creative services, it suggests that advertising agencies typically perform other services such as media selection (the actual purchase of time or space), marketing research, and related sales promotion effort on behalf of advertisers. Looking at the organization chart in Figure 6-6, what possible difficulties that an account executive might encounter in the performance of his or her job are suggested to you?

Agency Income. The bulk of advertising agency income is produced by a rebate received from media. Typically, this amounts to 15 per cent of the value of advertising purchased by the agency, referred to in the industry as "billings." If, at the time it received the Volkswagen account, its billings were about $25

(43)
(44)

(45)

(46)

[15] Ibid, pp. 86 and 87.

Think small.

Our little car isn't so much of a novelty any more.

A couple of dozen college kids don't try to squeeze inside it.

The guy at the gas station doesn't ask where the gas goes.

Nobody even stares at our shape.

In fact, some people who drive our little flivver don't even think that about 27 miles to the gallon is going any great guns.

Or using 5 pints of oil instead of 5 quarts.

Or never needing anti-freeze.

Or racking up about 40,000 miles on a set of tires.

That's because once you get used to some of our economies, you don't even think about them any more.

Except when you squeeze into a small parking spot. Or renew your small insurance. Or pay a small repair bill. Or trade in your old VW for a new one.

Think it over.

Dealer Name

5-058-2

AUTHORIZED
DEALER

Figure 6-5. An early advertisement produced for Volkswagen of America Inc., by Doyle Dane Bernbach.

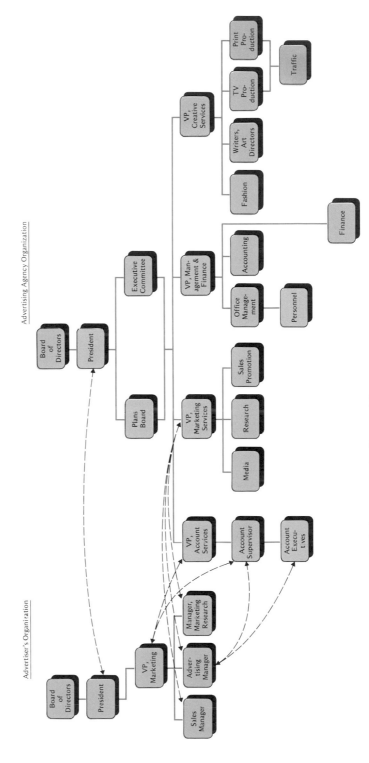

Advertiser's Organization

Advertising Agency Organization

Figure 6-6. Organizational relationships between an advertiser and its agency.

(47)

million, what would the income from these billings have been for Doyle Dane? What potential conflicts are created by this method of compensation?

For additional services not involving the purchase of advertising, such as marketing research, advertising agencies typically charge their clients separate fees.

Structure and Performance. In 1973, Dentsu Advertising, the largest advertising agency in the world, billed about $922 million worth of advertising, of which 97 per cent was in its home country, Japan. The next ten largest agencies, all based in the United States, billed about 11 per cent of all of the advertising purchased in the United States. The international character of the business is illustrated by the fact that these same United States agencies obtained 41 per cent of their billings from advertising placed in non-United States markets.

(48)

Trends in the financial performance and the "profit models" of advertising agencies are shown for a sample of firms in Table 6-5. Based on Table 6-5, what appear to you to be the most significant of these trends?

By 1972, Doyle Dane had risen from its ranking as the eightieth largest advertising agency, in terms of United States billings, at the time of the beginning of its relationship with Volkswagen, to become the fifth largest agency. Its billings had increased from about $25 million to $323 million, worldwide. The Volkswagen account had grown in size from $800,000 to more than $20 million per year in billings.

Table 6-5 **Advertising Agencies' Composite Profit and Loss Statements, 1962 and 1971***

	Income and Costs, As a Percentage of Gross Income	
	1962[a]	1971[b]
Billings	556.0%[c]	513.0%[c]
Gross income[d]	100.0	100.0
Expenses:		
Rent, light, and depreciation	7.5%	7.8%
Taxes (other than U. S. income)	2.3	3.0
Other operating expenses	13.9	15.9
Total payroll	68.5	65.3
Payments into pension or profit-sharing plans	1.4	1.9
Insurance for employee benefit	.7	1.1
Total	94.3%	94.9%
Profit before U. S. income tax	5.7	5.1
U. S. income taxes	1.7	1.8
Net profit after tax	4.0	3.3

* Source: Adapted from "Four A's Agencies Costs, Profits: 1962–1971," *Advertising Age* (July 31, 1972), p. 68.

[a] Based on a sample of 239 advertising agencies.

[b] Based on a sample of 215 advertising agencies.

[c] Based on a subsample of incorporated agencies only.

[d] Gross income includes commissions, agencies' service charges, and fees.

branding and packaging

In a sense, brands provide the basis for much of today's advertising effort in that they provide a product name on which to focus attention and around which to build an "image" of experiences and types of people with which the product can be associated in people's minds. Packaging may supplement advertising in the image-building effort centered on the brand.

Perhaps the epitome of a brand-image relationship is the "Marlboro man." We are told by consumer behaviorists that consumers select products, in part, because their perception of a brand's image conforms with their perceptions of what they are or would like to be. One such opinion is that consumers (1) buy products consistent with the self-image, (2) avoid products inconsistent with their self-image, (3) trade up to products that relate to an improved self-image, (4) purchase products that relate favorably to group norms of behavior, and (5) avoid products that show a radical departure from accepted group norms.[16]

Thus, brands can provide a method by which a manufacturer can differentiate products for which tangible differences may be hard to identify or communicate. At the same time, they provide an additional basis on which the consumer can identify and select products. They also may serve to encourage consistent product quality to the extent that a company's reputation, as well as that of its brand, may be jeopardized when products consistently fail to live up to the expectations of brand-loyal or new customers.

(49) The seven brands most heavily advertised in 1972 are listed in Table 6-6. Do the products represented by these brands have anything in common?

Packaging serves to communicate and build brand imagery as well. It has grown in importance with the growth of self-service merchandising, because it provides the only means of communicating at the point of sale when more personal forms of communication are not possible. Packaging may be especially critical for products that typically are purchased on impulse, or without any previous plan to do so before seeing them on the retail store shelf. For these products, which customers are unwilling to seek out on a preplanned basis,

Table 6-6 **The Seven Most Heavily Advertised Brands in 1972 in the United States***

Brand	Manufacturer	Amount Spent for Advertising
Anacin	American Home Products	$26,200,000
Bayer	Sterling Drug	24,388,000
Alka-Seltzer	Miles Laboratories	23,600,000
Pepsi	Pepsico	21,000,000
Dristan	American Home Products	18,468,000
Coke	Coca-Cola	17,600,000
Marlboro	Philip Morris	14,000,000

*Source: Merle Kingman, "Top 100 National Advertisers' Ad Total Reaches $5.27 Billion," *Advertising Age* (Aug. 27, 1973), pp. 1 and 167, quoted from p. 167.

[16] C. Glenn Walters and Gordon W. Paul, *Consumer Behavior, An Integrated Framework* (Homewood, Ill.: Irwin, 1970), p. 234.

packaging may carry the main burden of attracting attention and inducing the final sale. It is estimated that $29 billion was spent on packaging materials alone in 1974, with over 60 per cent of it going for other than shipping containers.[17] How does this compare with the figure for advertising quoted earlier?

(50)

the formulation of strategy for indirect promotion

The development of strategies for indirect promotion first requires the formulation of objectives as a means of defining the promotional task. Once the promotional task is defined, subsequent efforts to design and implement advertising, branding, and packaging efforts may be carried out. For advertising, this may involve the selection of an advertising theme, the selection of media, the development of the advertising budget, the preparation of the packaging budget, the creation of package graphics, and the execution of the program. Hopefully, the result of these often concurrent efforts will be advertising, branding, and packaging efforts that are coordinated around a common objective. The relationship of these efforts is illustrated in Figure 6-7.

make or buy?

An issue arising early in the development of a program for direct promotion will be whether a company should design and implement the program on an in-house basis or contract with outside agencies for such efforts as marketing research, the design and placement of advertising, and brand and package design.

Those firms that perform such efforts in house ("make") claim that they can (1) maintain greater control over the effort; (2) eliminate the need to communicate company needs, goals, and "character" to outsiders; (3) use such projects to develop their own marketing personnel; and (4) eliminate the payment of fees for outside support.

Other firms, which "buy" such services, maintain that they (1) can't afford to maintain an expert staff on a full-time basis to do work that is of a some-time, project nature; (2) can't attract creative personnel to work on promotional programs for only one type of product or product category (as opposed to a variety of products sold by advertising agency accounts); and (3) obtain greater objectivity and critical appraisal of new products and promotional programs from outside agencies than from their own personnel.

Even though the decision to make or buy such services may be delayed until after initial marketing research has disclosed the potential for various types of strategies for advertising, branding, and packaging, it may be wise to resolve it early to allow for the possible execution of the research by an outside agency entrusted with the program design effort.

[17] "Encyclopedia and Planning Guide," *Modern Packaging,* **47** (Dec. 1973), p. 12.

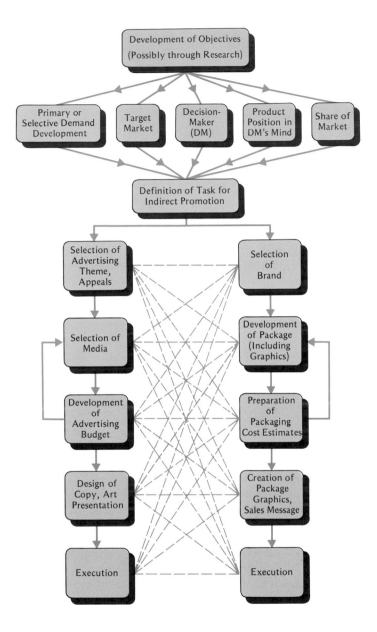

Figure 6-7. Steps in the design of a program for indirect promotion.

Development of Objectives (Possibly through Research)

Primary or Selective Demand Development

Target Market

Decision-Maker (DM)

Product Position in DM's Mind

Share of Market

Definition of Task for Indirect Promotion

Selection of Advertising Theme, Appeals

Selection of Brand

Selection of Media

Development of Package (Including Graphics)

Development of Advertising Budget

Preparation of Packaging Cost Estimates

Design of Copy, Art Presentation

Creation of Package Graphics, Sales Message

Execution

Execution

development of objectives

Basic to the definition of the indirect promotional task is the development of objectives. At this point, it may be necessary to determine whether an organization's strategy calls for the promotion of specific products or services or, more generally, ideas or the organization's name alone.

From time to time, many organizations turn to so-called institutional advertising, which features ideas or art work intended to maintain a corporation's public profile without necessarily stimulating sales of products or services in short supply, to improve "bad guy" images, or to foster employee morale, among other objectives. During the recent shortage of petroleum products, for example, institutional ads such as those shown in Figure 15-9, page 510, appeared with increasing frequency.

More often, objectives may be formulated in terms of the potential for the development of primary or selective demand for a product or product category, as shown in Figure 6-8. Recalling our discussion in Chapter 2 (pages 42 through 44), primary demand development can be thought of as expanding the market pie. Selective demand development seeks to cut a larger slice of the existing pie for a particular product or brand by diverting demand from competing brands.

Marketing research often provides information around which objectives can be structured.

Figure 6-8. Basic questions to be answered in the development of promotional objectives. Source: Adapted from Charles E. Overholser and John M. Kline, "Advertising Strategy from Consumer Research," *Journal of Advertising Research,* (Oct. 1971), pp. 3–9. See p. 7.

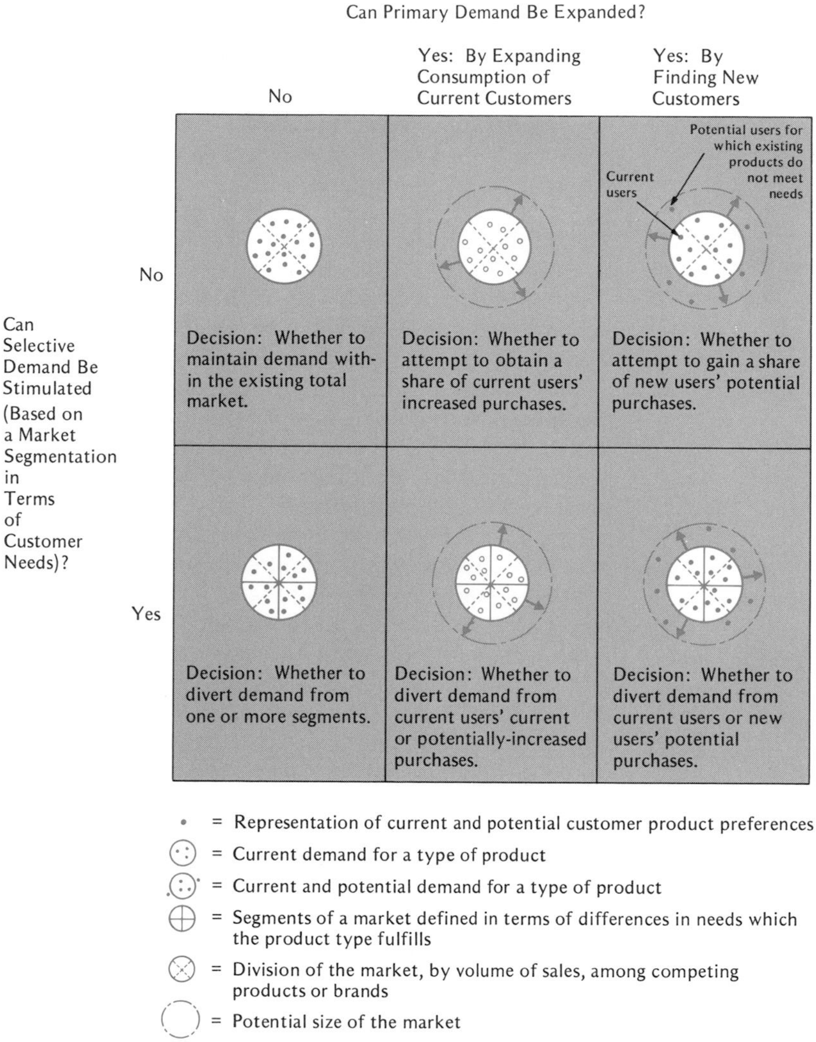

Can Primary Demand Be Expanded?

Can Selective Demand Be Stimulated (Based on a Market Segmentation in Terms of Customer Needs)?

• = Representation of current and potential customer product preferences

⊙ = Current demand for a type of product

⊙ = Current and potential demand for a type of product

⊕ = Segments of a market defined in terms of differences in needs which the product type fulfills

⊗ = Division of the market, by volume of sales, among competing products or brands

( ) = Potential size of the market

Research. The task of research can be accomplished by executing its design to determine whether actual and potential customers for a product (1) recognize differences in existing products; (2) harbor unsatisfied needs regarding products they use, thus restricting their purchases; or (3) avoid purchasing various types of products because they are perceived not to meet customer needs. The means by which this can be done will be taken up in Chapter 11. The implications of various types of findings are of importance to us here.

Studies disclosing (1) current users cannot recognize differences in competing products within a product category and (2) neither users nor nonusers register strong complaints or can identify important unmet needs by existing competing products suggest that a company may enter such a market only with great difficulty. Those already sharing such a market may find it difficult to identify needs through which their existing share can be expanded. Few products, such as various brands of sugar, are perceived in this manner. Can you think of others?

(51)

At the other extreme, research may suggest that (1) current users recognize and describe what to them are important differences in competing products within a product category and (2) both users and nonusers express serious concerns about products available to them. This type of product category may offer the widest range of alternatives for establishing objectives, including (1) whether to divert demand from existing products by emulating their characteristics and market appeals, (2) whether to expand the market by increasing the amount of use among current users, or (3) whether to expand the market by attracting new users by means of a product that is perceived as meeting previously unmet needs. Most often these characteristics are associated with actual or potential markets for newly developed product categories, such as water pics for tooth care or various types of home humidifiers.

Most often, products or product categories fall at neither of the extremes of the spectrum described here. For example, surveys of beer drinkers have suggested that although beer drinkers may have strong brand preferences and perceive distinct brand differences, beer as a product category meets their perceived needs. Furthermore, those who are not beer drinkers register such strong objections (unmet needs) regarding the product category that they offer much less desirable opportunities for the expansion of primary demand than do heavy beer drinkers. This latter group comprises 15 per cent of all beer drinkers who consume 85 per cent of all beer and have oppressed desires to consume more. Assuming this to be the case, where would you position beer in Figure 6-8? Among other factors, this perhaps explains why attempts to market low-calorie beers have failed. Actual customers don't drink beer to control their weight (other than perhaps to correct an underweight condition). Potential beer drinkers shun it for strong reasons other than its fattening characteristics. On the other hand, both primary and selective-demand increases may have been achieved by campaigns such as the "It's an unexpected pleasure" campaign by Anheuser-Busch, Inc. on behalf of its premium brand, Michelob. To whom is this campaign directed?

(52)

(53)

Marketing research should help answer questions regarding the most effective appeals to be used in promoting new or existing products, the effects that such efforts should have on the total size of the market, and the share of the resulting market that a product might be expected to attain. The latter represents a tangible statement of an objective against which performance can be measured.

For example, in 1969 Hanes Corp. paid about $400,000 for marketing research to determine how it could market its panty hose through supermarket and drugstore outlets. Up to that time, Hanes had sold its hosiery only to department store outlets. Hosiery was offered by supermarkets mostly under private, or store, brands. As such, it had been featured in supermarket promotions for as little as 39 cents a pair compared with $1.39 per pair and more through other stores. Even so, Hanes' research disclosed that in 1968, only 12 per cent of hosiery sales were realized in supermarkets. By contrast, about 50 per cent of health and beauty aids, products introduced into supermarkets at about the same time as hosiery, were being purchased in supermarkets.

Respondents to the studies displayed little awareness of brands of hosiery marketed through supermarkets and drugstores. The research further suggested that women were not particularly impressed by supermarket price promotions for hosiery. Instead, they were disgusted with the variable quality and fit of such hosiery, deficiencies that Hanes was equipped to correct and control. What type of situation, among those illustrated in Figure 6-8, does this one parallel? What opportunities does it suggest to you?

Positioning. It can be useful to state advertising program objectives in terms of the position that the advertiser wants to achieve for its product, in relation to competitors, in the customer's mind. Positioning may emphasize positive product characteristics or, more recently, statements designed to establish a product's position in totally different, memorable terms.

An example of the first of these positioning approaches is provided by consumer needs regarding toothpaste. Research has suggested that toothpaste consumers can be divided into four groups, those placing relatively high priority on (1) maximum cavity prevention, (2) whitening and brightening, (3) mouth and breath freshening, and (4) flavor satisfaction. A statement of promotional program objectives for a manufacturer of toothpaste ranking high in several of these qualities would identify product characteristics and the market segment, in terms of age or other characteristics, around which to formulate a strategy. For example, which of the tooth paste appeals would you associate with stages in consumers' life cycles?

More recently, a number of products have been advertised successfully by positioning them more directly in relation to competition by seeking unorthodox, memorable appeals that may or may not utilize product features. Many of these have violated former taboos by mentioning the competition. This strategy has been prompted by recent research suggesting that consumers are able to keep only one or two brands in mind for each type of consumer product. Typically, these are the brands with the largest market shares. Positioning theorists suggest that an also-ran can make use of firmly entrenched brands or their characteristics to establish consumer identity for its products.

Recent examples of this trend are campaigns featuring ads such as

Avis' "Avis is only No. 2 in rent-a-cars. So why go with us?"
Volkswagen's "Ugly is only skin-deep."
Seven-Up's "The uncola."

209

Sports Illustrated's "The third newsweekly."
Honeywell's "The other computer company."

In contrast, this type of positioning theory holds that market leaders, instead of proclaiming themselves as No. 1, need to devote more effort to the development of primary demand and the adoption and preempting of as much new technology as necessary to keep their products current.

How would you rate the early Volkswagen ad recommending that customers "Think Small." and a more recent one that said, "Volkswagen introduced a new kind of Volkswagen. Big." in these terms?

Six questions formulated by advocates of the "new" positioning concepts are (1) What position, if any, do we already own in the prospect's mind? (2) What position do we want to own? (3) What companies must be outgunned if we are to establish that position? (4) Do we have enough marketing money to occupy and hold the position? (5) Do we have the guts to stick with one consistent positioning concept? and (6) Does our creative approach match our positioning strategy?[18]

definition of the task of indirect promotion

The process of establishing marketing goals may suggest the magnitude of the task for indirect promotion. In addition, the findings of the research should provide inputs to a determination of the most critical roles for indirect promotion in a promotional program. Going back to Figure 6-3, page 188, must brand awareness be created? Must interest be developed? Will such efforts primarily encourage retailers to stock the product? Or will it have to be designed with the primary objective of reducing customer perceptions of risk, stirring the potential customer to action, or encouraging repurchase? Finally, research results should suggest ways in which the promotional task can be carried out.

Once goals for the effort, and the task itself, have been defined, efforts to design advertising, branding, and packaging can proceed most effectively. Although such efforts may proceed sequentially, as shown in Figure 6-7 on page 206, the work on advertising, branding and packaging often will be carried out concurrently, sometimes by the same person or group. This was the case at the Hanes Corp. in its efforts to introduce a hosiery product to be sold by supermarkets and drugstores.

branding and packaging

The development of a branding and packaging program involves the selection of a brand, the development of a package, the preparation of a packaging "budget," the creation of package graphics and copy, and the implementation of package production.

(57)

Figure 6-9. A typical supermarket display for L'eggs pantyhose.

[18]Jack Trout and Al Ries, "The Positioning Era," *Advertising Age* (May 8, 1972), pp. 114, and 116. Quote on p. 116.

At Hanes the selection of the brand and the package was based on the decision to emphasize the fact that Hanes panty hose would offer a better fit than its supermarket competitors. This proposition led to the idea that the word *leg,* in addition to playing a prominent part in the promotional theme, might also be worked into the brand for the product. At about the same time, it was determined that if Hanes' panty hose were to be distinguished from its competitors in a buying situation devoid of salesclerks, it would have to be offered in a distinctive, esthetically pleasing package. This would support the decision to price the product at a premium to competitors' products, perhaps as high as $1.39 per pair. Almost concurrently the brand name L'eggs and the idea of packaging the product in white, egg-shaped plastic containers for display, as shown in Figure 6-9, were developed.

In the case of L'eggs, the initial concept evoked such enthusiasm and the higher price provided sufficient margin so that the problem of redesigning the package to meet a particular cost requirement was not particularly critical. This may not be the case for products with low margin or little reliance on the package to differentiate or "sell" the product. In such cases, cost may be an overriding concern. How would these concerns differ, for example, in the packaging of milk as opposed to Coca-Cola or a gift fruit pack?

Once the basic design of the package has been completed, remaining details concerning its graphics and copy can be completed and the program for producing it executed.

As a footnote to the matter of branding, Adolf Hitler displayed little talent for such activities when, during the days of the Third Reich, he proclaimed that the automobile that was to become the Volkwagen should be called the *Kraft-durch-Freude Wagen,* or "strength-through-joy car." Can you imagine what Doyle Dane Bernbach could have done with that?

advertising

The design of an advertising strategy requires the selection of an advertising theme and appeals, the selection of media, the development of an advertising budget, the preparation of art and copy, and the execution of the program.

Selection of Theme and Appeals. Advertising themes and appeals should reflect the objectives and task defined for a promotional program. They may be based on product or company attributes that are thought to be important to customers, product or company attributes that research has suggested are important to customers, product or company attributes identified as important but not covered by competition, or consumer needs more or less related to the product.

Some product attributes and related customers' needs are so obvious that the product may be marketed with little research. Even under these circumstances, it may be useful to test advertising to see if the intended message is being communicated.

Products that are thought to reflect a person's self-image may utilize appeals totally divorced from the product or company marketing it. For example, adver-

(58)

211

tising for Marlboro, the world's leading selling brand of cigarette in recent years, rarely mentioned product or company attributes, as illustrated by the ad shown in Figure 7-9, p. 251. Why was it successful?

(59)

Shortly after the Hanes Corp. adopted the L'eggs brand and the egg-shaped package for its product, an advertising program centered around the theme, "Our L'eggs fit your legs," was designed.

Selection of Media and Budget. Ideally, advertising media and the frequency with which they are used should be planned to achieve a predetermined goal and the budget based on the type and amount of advertising needed. More often than not, however, the budget is predetermined as an advertising-to-sales ratio assumed in the annual budget projection. The media plan must be tailored to fit within the budget. This suggests that questions of media and budget are closely interrelated. Media strategies and budget levels must take into account (1) the need for "reach" and "frequency," (2) varying needs during the introduction and sales sustaining periods of a product's life cycle, and (3) the pattern of expenditures during the sales sustaining period.

Reach and Frequency. The task of selecting media within budget constraints often requires a trade-off or balancing between what is called reach and frequency. Reach refers to the breadth of coverage of an advertising program, expressed in terms of the number of different people or market segments exposed to a message. Frequency concerns the number of times that any selected group of customers will be exposed to the campaign. Reach may be particularly important for products with broad-ranging market segments, requiring the use of a relatively large number of media. How is the need for reach related to the ability to identify market segments?

(60)

Frequency, on the other hand, may be desired for products for which (1) a customer shops frequently, (2) competition employs a similar strategy, and (3) selling appeals are sufficiently indistinct to be recalled by customers only over short periods of time.

Introductory and Sales Sustaining Programs. A campaign may require a different medium and higher expenditures during an introduction than the sales sustaining period following product introduction. For example, what relative importance would you assign to sampling activities in the budget for the introductory as opposed to the sales sustaining period?

(61)

Timing During Sales Sustaining Periods. Various patterns of expenditures may be warranted during the sales sustaining period. For example, a great deal of research has been conducted, without definitive results, to determine whether "pulsing" strategies, in which advertising expenditures are made in periodic waves, are more effective than strategies that employ more constant expenditures. One thing does appear to be clear. The most successfully advertised products are those for which continued advertising efforts are programmed and followed over long periods of time.

In marketing seasonal products one may face a peculiarly difficult problem in deciding whether to maintain sustaining promotional efforts for his or her products on a year-round basis or to "reintroduce" them each year.

Advertising frequency was given high priority in the development of the

212

L'eggs campaign by David E. Harrold, who was hired to design and manage the product's introduction. With more than six hundred brands of hosiery available to American consumers, it was thought that a sizeable effort would be required to establish the L'eggs brand in consumers' minds and to encourage retailers to stock it. Furthermore, the nature of the product called for the use of media offering visual presentation. Finally, it was important that potential customers try the product to experience its improved quality and fit. As a result, Hanes budgeted $10 million for its introductory advertising campaign, an amount double that spent by the rest of the hosiery industry. In addition, it decided to spend $5 million more on coupons worth 25 or 35 cents off on each L'eggs purchase, which were mailed directly to a large number of consumers.

(62) Putting yourself in David Harrold's position and assuming that the media alternatives shown in Table 6-2 were available to you in planning the introductory promotional campaign for L'eggs, how would you allocate your funds among the specific media?

Within eighteen months after the introduction of its product, Hanes' L'eggs had become the largest selling brand of hosiery in supermarkets and drugstores, due in part to Hanes' extensive newspaper and television advertising.

Other Steps. Once the selection of media and the campaign budget are agreed on, the development of copy and art for specific advertisements can begin in earnest. This, in turn, leads to the approval of the program, the production of finished advertising, and the purchase of time or space.

(63) Reviewing the examples concerning the development of indirect promotional strategy for the Bic Banana and the Volkswagen, to what extent did they appear to follow the format shown in Figure 6-7?

summary

Whether we employ indirect or direct promotional effort, the extent to which a marketing communication may have its desired effect on us depends on the attitude that we have toward the source of the message, the way in which it is encoded or translated for us, the probability that we encounter the message, the strength of the signal with which we receive it, the way in which we decode or interpret it, and the extent to which it is relevant to our needs or interests.

The nature of the customer's buying task influences the necessary selling task and the seller's promotional strategy. The buying task can be viewed usefully as a problem-solving process in which the buyer attempts to reduce the risk of a wrong decision through the collection of information from friends, experts, advertising, and other sources. The magnitude of the task will depend on factors such as the complexity of the product, the buyer's knowledge and self-confidence, the importance of the decision to the buyer, the number of alternatives available, the ease with which alternative products can be differentiated, and the availability of results of past buying efforts.

The resulting promotional task concerns itself with the identification of decision makers and decision influences, the development of a buyer's awareness of a need for a product or service, efforts to build interest, provision of assistance in the risk-reducing process, making the product available, obtaining action or trust, and encouraging repurchase.

Among the indirect methods of carrying out the promotional task, advertising is by far the most important. Print, broadcast, outdoor, and other types of advertising media offer varying means of communication, degrees of clutter, decay rates, types of audiences, and sizes and costs of audience.

In developing an advertising program, a firm may employ its own personnel or hire the services of an advertising agency. The latter typically helps formulate a marketing strategy, performs marketing research, develops copy and art work for advertisements, prepares advertising budgets, and purchases space and time from the media. The advertiser's decision to make or buy services performed by outside advertising agencies often is based on the degree of control that he may desire over the process, the desire to develop skills in-house, the relative need for expertise and objectivity provided by outside agencies, and the willingness to pay the costs for such purchased services.

Branding and packaging offer (1) a means of differentiating products, (2) a "franchise" justifying the investment of advertising funds by a manufacturer of branded merchandise, (3) a means by which customers can identify goods of a desired quality, and (4) an incentive to a manufacturer to maintain a consistently high quality. They have grown in importance with self-service retailing.

In formulating a strategy for indirect promotion, marketing research can help in the development of program objectives. This may disclose opportunities for stimulating primary demand. Or it may suggest customer needs currently unmet by existing products, or a niche in the existing market for a properly positioned product by which its manufacturer might attract (selective) demand from competing products. Product positioning can be accomplished through perceptions or images developed by means of indirect promotion as well as through new product design.

Once objectives are defined, the task for indirect promotion, through branding, packaging, and advertising, can be defined. Using this as a base, a brand can be selected if necessary, a package developed, a packaging budget prepared, the package graphics created, and the packaging produced. Similarly, advertising themes and appeals can be selected, media chosen and a budget developed, advertising copy and art prepared, and the advertising program implemented.

Next we turn to the subject of direct promotion, to which one of America's most famous philosophers might as well have been referring when he said:

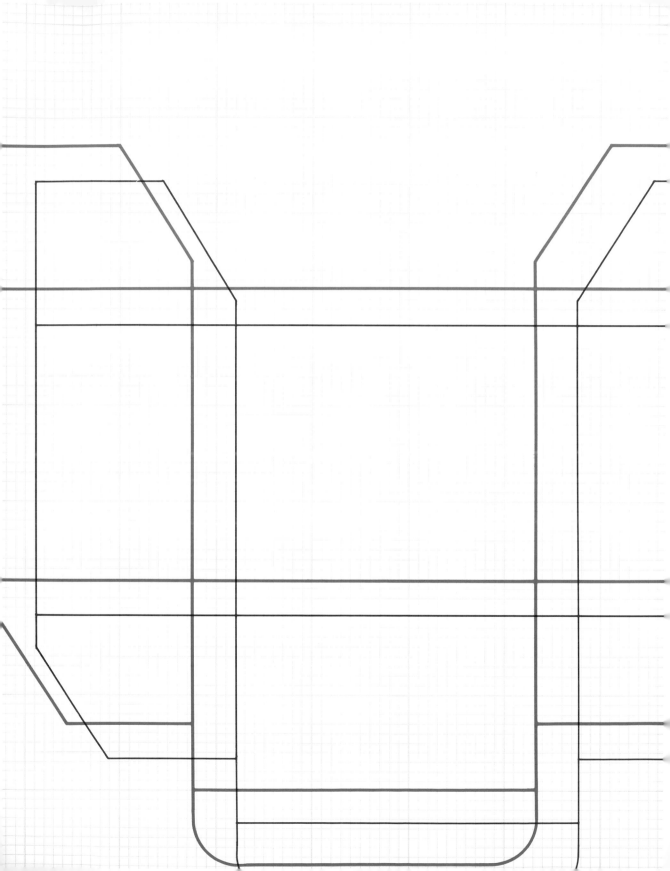

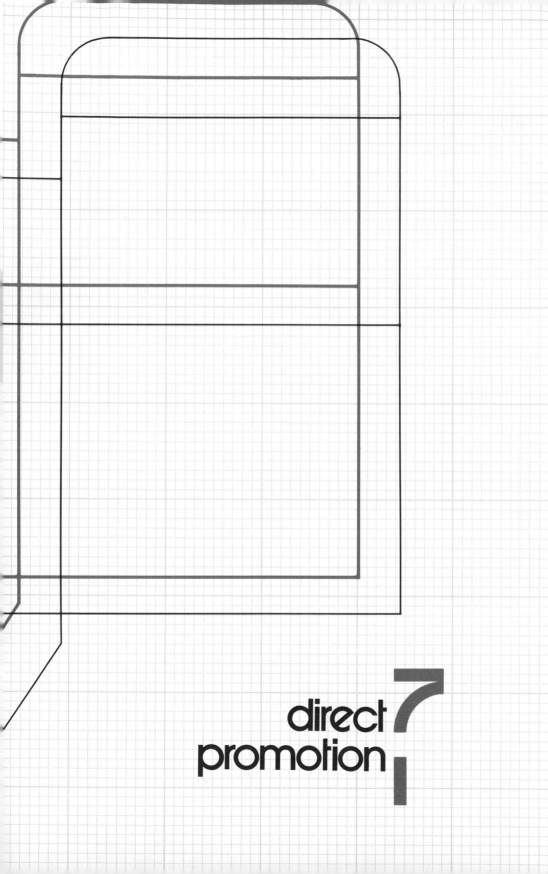

direct
promotion 7

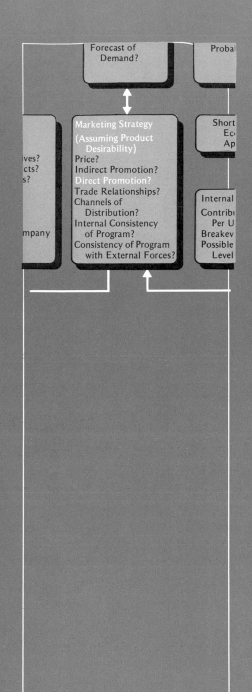

Forecast of Demand?

Proba[...]

Marketing Strategy
(Assuming Product
    Desirability)
Price?
Indirect Promotion?
Direct Promotion?
Trade Relationships?
Channels of
    Distribution?
Internal Consistency
    of Program?
Consistency of Program
    with External Forces?

Short
    Ec[...]
    Ap[...]

Internal
Contrib[...]
Per U[...]
Breakev[...]
Possible
Level

ives?
cts?
s?

mpany

"No woman was ever seduced by a letter." This comment by Mark Twain graphically suggests why most promotional strategies require both indirect and direct efforts.

Direct promotion by means of personal selling, either in person or by telephone, is the backbone of marketing strategies for most industrial and many consumer goods producers. The Kim Kelleys and Roberta Wells of this chapter are both striking contrasts and distant cousins to Elmer Blurt, the vacuum cleaner salesman of early radio fame whose knock on the door and timid "I hope, I hope, I hope" became the personification of salesmanship to many listeners.

By looking in some detail at the activities of individual sales representatives, we can gain some understanding of the needs, motivations, and elements of success of individuals engaged in direct promotional activities; examine trends that have characterized their work; and develop an understanding of the problems of managing their efforts. An exploration of possible problems faced by Honeywell, Inc. and Philip Morris Inc. allows us to study steps in the design of a direct promotional program. A final objective of this chapter will be to explore the relative roles of in-

direct and direct promotional methods in marketing strategies with the help of George McGovern
and Richard Nixon.

The scheme of this chapter takes us, in terms of
the scope of the issues considered, up through
the marketing organization and from the specific
to the broad.

But as we focus in on Kim Kelley, he is hurrying to
the office of Hank Malkus, division administrator in
the office of the secretary of state of Illinois, where
he will learn whether or not his firm, Honeywell,
Inc., and his efforts of the past three years will be
rewarded with the sale of an $8.1 million com-
puter installation to the state. Kelley pauses only
long enough to vomit into an office wastebasket.

Kim Kelley

On his way to learn of the results of his sales effort, Kim Kelley recalled how he
had spent a year at the University of Iowa and cooked pizza, sold shoes, and
hustled in California pool halls before returning to Iowa to marry his high school
sweetheart.[1] How he had held one sales job after another for four years after he
had decided to follow in the footsteps of his late father, a tire salesman. And
how, after having sold three shirts to a Honeywell, Inc. regional manager the
manager had concluded that anyone who could sell him three shirts that he
needed but hadn't intended to buy could sell computers.

He remembered having been sent to Springfield, Illinois in 1970 from his
initial training at Honeywell with the intention to follow his instructions to keep
four or five big sales simmering but to put only one at a time "on the front
burner." He picked his first major target immediately, the largest potential

[1] Based on material in Thomas Ehrich, "To Computer Salesmen, the 'Big-Ticket' Deal Is the One
to Look For," *Wall Street Journal* (Jan. 22, 1974), pp. 1 and 41, and on a personal interview with Kelley.

customer in his territory, the Illinois state government. In pursuit of this goal, he recalled having made daily rounds of important state offices for three years, pausing to drop off literature about Honeywell's computing equipment or just to chat. One of the purposes of these efforts had been to seek out responsible, objective people with whom to deal, something that would prove to be critical at the time that these potential customers had to choose between equipment manufactured by Honeywell and its much larger competitor, IBM. He remembered the six or seven hours of preparation that had gone into each sales call at the state office building, and the extent to which he had become involved in the concerns of a number of the state employees, ranging from one person's afflicted wife to another's house painting project.

During this time, his income rose from $18,000 (1970), to $22,000 (1971), to $25,000 (1972) from the 1 per cent commissions paid by Honeywell on the value of sales he had made to nonstate customers.

He reviewed how he had molded his personal life to meet the needs of his job. How he had bought a Buick and expensive suits to appear prosperous, but had resigned from the country club to avoid appearing too prosperous. How he had met frequently with his potential government customers after hours at the American Legion Hall because of his conviction that a computer sales representative had to develop a mutual trust with potential customers, a trust that would have to endure a long relationship.

He remembered the care he and his company had taken to respond to questions posed by Malkus and members of a technical committee assigned by the state to evaluate bids that would be requested on the new computer installation. How he had answered within forty-eight hours the difficult questions that arose daily, hand-delivered replies to obtain several additional minutes of selling time, and concentrated on committee members rather than

sell to more senior state administrators or old friends. How he had had Honeywell experts and top marketing officials flown in from Boston, Minneapolis, Phoenix, and Chicago, a result of his personal program of spending nearly two thirds of his time negotiating for, and coordinating, customer sales support provided by other offices of his own company as opposed to about a third of his time selling to customers.

He recalled how, in spite of his dislike of flying, he had flown the six buying committee members and their bosses to Atlanta and Houston to meet Honeywell users, and to Phoenix twice to see performance tests at a Honeywell facility. On these trips, everything had been arranged in advance by Kim and his secretary, right down to the use of a slow-propeller company plane to allow more selling time in the air. In planning the important trip to Houston, Kim had made the trip in advance to familiarize himself with such details as the best restaurants and ways to avoid rush-hour traffic. He made arrangements for members of the state's buying committee to interview at their request executives of a company that they believed (mistakenly) was a dissatisfied Honeywell customer. He had provided pretrip agendas, including dates, addresses, and telephone numbers, all part of an effort to communicate to his prospective customers how much Kelley valued their time and would try to make good use of it.

He recounted the stake he had in this potential sale, including the toll it had taken on his family life over the last three months, during which he had worked six days a week, often fourteen hours a day. He remembered having snapped at his three-year-old daughter, Brook and having heard his wife recount his daughter's daily question about whether Daddy would be home that night. During this time, his wife Sandy had assumed the task of managing the family and a new home construction project. He recalled his wife having awakened in the middle of the night worrying about what Kim would do it he didn't get the order, worth $32,000 in commissions upon the signing of a sales contract and about $48,000 more when the computer installation might be completed more than a year later.

Roberta Wells[2]

In the settling dusk, Roberta Wells emerged from the Euclid Avenue Drug in Arlington Park, Illinois, her ninth call of the day as one of a growing number of saleswomen out of a total sales force of nearly one thousand employed by Philip Morris Inc. for the sale of its various brands of cigarettes. Her final call had resulted in the placement of two check-out counter displays for Benson & Hedges 100's (in return for a $1 payment to the store), the sale of an eleven-carton Product Promotion Plan (in return for a five-pack premium incentive to the store for purchasing the plan), and the booking of a free-standing floor display (requiring about six square feet of floor space) for cartons of Benson & Hedges 100's, to be put up the following week and left up for at least two weeks (in return for a $5 payment to the store). In addition, she had been able to check

[2] In our discussion of Philip Morris, names other than Roberta Wells, Joe Karner, and Doris Berendt are disguised, along with selected data concerning the company's operations.

and straighten Philip Morris stock displayed along with all other brands on a large carton rack supplied by a competitor, making sure that space assigned to Philip Morris was not infringed on. In the process, she had noted two competitive stand-alone "deal" displays that she would report in writing later that evening to her district manager. Finally, she had overheard a customer buying a pack of Pall Malls (a competing brand); talked her into putting out the cigarette she was smoking, lighting a Marlboro, and exchanging the pack of Pall Malls just purchased for a pack of Marlboros; and ended the "switch sale" by buying the customer a complementary pack of Marlboros from the drugstore pack dispenser to encourage an even longer trial of the product. All in twenty minutes.

Roberta was particularly pleased, because she had been able to do on this call something her district manager, Joe Karner, had emphasized during jointly made calls the previous day: how to maintain "quality" in sales calls without sacrificing "quantity."

Roberta knew as she left the Euclid Avenue Pharmacy that she had just time to make the twenty-mile drive home to feed her three cats and change clothes for a dinner date with friends from a previous job. Because she lived alone, she would often get a bite to eat after finishing her last call. Recently, she had worked until 9 P.M. constructing a Pack Master single-pack dispenser at a soon-to-be-opened discount drugstore. As she put it:

> It wasn't until I put up my first Pack Master that I knew what Joe Karner was getting at when he asked me in the process of interviewing me for the job how good I was with tools. Because in setting up the Pack Master, it helps to be

handy with a drill and a screwdriver. Fortunately, I had had a chance to become familiar with tools when, after graduating from the music conservatory at Lawrence University and concluding that I couldn't make a living playing the violin, I became interested in archery, found that I could teach it well, and was hired by a friend to give lessons and run his archery pro shop. That job included making and repairing equipment, which got me into woodworking. Subsequent jobs as a reference librarian and inside (telephone) salesperson for an electronics distributor further broadened my background. The Philip Morris job came along just after I had lost my inside sales job to a woman with more seniority. And the opportunity to get into outside sales, where I could enjoy the freedom and even the driving, make friends on the job, and get a raise of $900 per year even as a Philip Morris sales trainee was too attractive to turn down.

On a typical sales call, Roberta would first check the Philip Morris merchandise appearance and location, putting it in order and noting quantities of product in stock. What she did next depended on whether the account was "controlled" or "noncontrolled." At a controlled account, typically a chain outlet at which a manager had limited latitude, she would check the store's order book to make sure that adequate stocks had been ordered from a jobber or the store's warehouse, then seek to increase the order if desirable. One means of accomplishing this was by making a brief presentation to the store manager of one or more of the current promotions, previously approved at chain headquarters for field presentation, requiring increased orders in exchange for payments to the chain. At a noncontrolled account at which she dealt with a manager or owner requiring no outside authorization for action, she had more latitude in selling special promotions. In addition, she might sell small quantities of product from stocks maintained in the trunk of her company car, receiving cash payments for them. Larger quantities were ordered, as in controlled accounts, from the jobber.

She made it a point to know all of the managers of the 267 accounts on which she made regular calls on a first-name basis.

Although she had not yet achieved her personal sales goals, with continued improvement she hoped to be promoted from a sales trainee to a sales representative at a salary increase. She was confident that her ability and interest in teaching eventually would qualify her for a division manager's job.

Few of Roberta's retail accounts had been surprised to encounter a woman representing Philip Morris.

On balance, it helps being a woman on this job at this point in time. I'm able to kid with most men and smooth over difficult situations. A little flirting once in awhile doesn't hurt a bit. Then, too, a growing number of people I deal with are women. And let's face it. When you walk into a store that's short on Marlboros, they're glad to see you whether you're male or female.

The Euclid Avenue Drug, as one of Roberta's 60 "double high" accounts, received a call every three weeks from her. Her 84 "high" accounts, mostly smaller drug and liquor stores, saw her once every six weeks. And another 123 medium accounts, such as small newsstands and tobacco counters, were visited four times per year. In order to complete ten to twelve calls on a given day, Roberta had to leave the house by 7:30 A.M. and grab a cup of coffee and a donut before stopping at her base distributor, a tobacco wholesaler, in order to replenish stock that she had sold from the trunk of her car the previous day. If things went according to plan, she could spend approximately twenty to thirty minutes at each call and complete her day by 5:30 P.M. This required, however, that she spend another hour or two each evening going over her reports and planning the next day's activities. Did this sour her on the job?

> Not on your life. I control what I do. If I screw up or exceed my goals, it's because of something I do. I'm on my own. And yet my division manager, Joe Karner, is there every so often to provide advice when I need it.

(1)
(2)
(3)

How would you contrast the sales jobs held by Kim Kelley and Roberta Wells? How does the role played by each relate to the nature of the product each sells? For which of these persons would it be most difficult to measure performance?

direct communication in the promotional process

Direct communication, largely involving personal selling, may be most effective in assuring the delivery of a marketing communication to a decision maker, describing complex product features, reaching prospective customers at the time and place they use a product, obtaining merchandising effort necessary to support a promotional program, allowing for buyer-seller interaction, and inducing and influencing buyer actions.

assuring delivery of a marketing communication

In many major industrial purchasing decisions, such as for a conveyor system for an assembly line, the purchasing agent may be responsible for carrying out the transaction, often involving the collection and opening of competing bids from suppliers. But the purchase process may actually involve the engineer as the individual establishing the specifications for the conveyor system, a consulting engineer to review the specifications, the plant manager as the person recommending a particular supplier from among those competing for the business, and the treasurer or even president as the executives placing the final stamp of approval on the purchase.

Where this is the case, direct sales effort can pinpoint the decision maker, identify those individuals who might exert influences on the decision, and provide each with the type of information in a form that each may prefer. For example, the information communicated to the engineer often would be more technical than that communicated to the purchasing agent, treasurer, president, or even the plant manager.

(4)

What types of questions would each of these executives be most likely to ask? The nature of the questions asked by each can provide a good indication of the most effective appeals to be used in a competitive marketing situation.

describing complex product features

The end user of the output of an office copier may be interested only in the quality of the copy, cost, and speed, features that can be communicated effectively by advertising. The operator of a duplicating service contemplating the purchase of such a machine will require much more information about specific operating, maintenance, and service features. These may be communicated effectively only by direct sales effort, most often by means of a physical demonstration of the machine.

A large trucking company may be able to inform potential customers of its rates and routes by means of a tariff book and other printed reference materials. But the planning of a particular, important shipment invariably requires direct contact between a shipper and the carrier's sales representative, either in person or by telephone.

reaching customers where and when they use a product

So-called point-of-sale advertising material carries the sales message to the store location where a product is purchased. Similarly, direct sales effort can carry the message to the point of use, particularly for a number of products used in the home. This perhaps explains why such a large proportion of vacuum cleaners are still sold on a door-to-door basis. Or why salesmen for manufacturers of china and silver have had success by showing their products on a prospective buyer's dining room table.

obtaining supporting merchandising effort

Advertising that is successful in drawing potential customers to a store or other point of sale will be wasted if the product is either unavailable or displayed poorly. Sales effort directed to the retailer, perhaps using the lever provided by the prospective results of an advertising campaign, can insure product availability, good shelf location, the possible use of point-of-sale material to draw attention to the product, and education and training of retail sales personnel.

allowing for buyer-seller interaction

Most successful salesmen maintain that it is most desirable that a customer raise objectives during the selling effort. In fact, many claim it is essential. An objection to a product or service characteristic shows that the prospective customer is serious enough about purchasing to object and provides the next important selling point for the salesman, assuming that the objection can be answered. Without the personal interaction afforded by direct sales effort, the buyer-seller interaction would be impossible.

inducing and influencing buyer actions

Many purchases are postponed, particularly for products or services for which the need may not be immediate or particularly great. For such items, it may be much more difficult for a potential buyer to treat a salesman, as opposed to advertising, with passive indifference. The former will often force a decision, even if it is negative.

Direct promotional effort may be most effective when the desired buyer action is complex. It may be easier to induce a customer to buy something at a local store by means of indirect communication. To get a retailer to stock your product, provide favorable shelf location, and post a "shelf talker" (a strip of advertising placed above or below the product display) may require more direct communication.

(5)
(6) Which of the particular strengths of direct promotional effort explain Kim Kelley's job? Roberta Wells' job?

trends in selling

Sales representatives can be particularly effective in establishing social relationships and a basis for human interaction with prospective customers, communicating especially complex product features, adapting a standard sales message to meet the needs of a selling situation, and in identifying and helping to solve potential customers' problems. Although all of these dimensions have characterized much of the selling effort exerted through the years, each has risen to prominence to characterize a different "era" in selling, as shown in Figure 7-1.

selling eras

From time to time, selling has been characterized in terms of its reliance on social relations, product benefits, cookbook or programmed sales effort, and customer problem solving.

Social Selling. A slap on the back and a big cigar have come to characterize the social selling approach that rose to prominence during the early years of the twentieth century described by the River City High School band with its 76 trombones and new uniforms sold to them by Professor Harold Hill, "The Music Man." The social salesman had to know the "territory." But knowing the

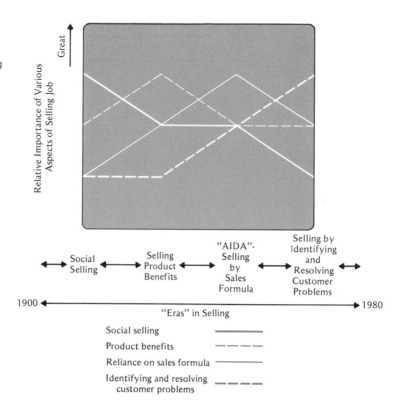

Figure 7-1. Eras in selling, and the relative emphasis on various selling approaches during each era.

Relative Importance of Various Aspects of Selling Job

Great

Social Selling

Selling Product Benefits

"AIDA"- Selling by Sales Formula

Selling by Identifying and Resolving Customer Problems

1900 ←→ 1980

"Eras" in Selling

Social selling	—————
Product benefits	– – – –
Reliance on sales formula	———————
Identifying and resolving customer problems	– – –

territory really didn't mean knowing where potential customers were located and how to reach them. It meant the establishment of relationships with them sufficiently strong to discourage competitive salesmen.

Social selling isn't dead. A common modern day vehicle for the social salesman is the golf course, whether or not business is discussed during a serious golf game. And it is said that the most successful golfing salesmen are those who can play a good game and yet lose.

(7)   What emphasis, if any, did Kim Kelley place on social selling?

Communicating Product Benefits. Between World Wars I and II, as products became more and more complex, emphasis shifted from knowing the territory to knowing the product and the product line. Sales training emphasizing product knowledge became popular. During this era, a great deal of responsibility was placed on the customer to interpret product benefits in terms of his needs. The predominant sales philosophy was that the product would sell itself if its features were communicated properly.

Programmed Selling. Along with the rise in interest in psychology came the notion that because all customers, whether ultimate consumers or industrial purchasing agents, were humans, they would respond favorably to standard sales techniques designed to take them through a logical progression of buying steps. Programmed sales approaches, using extensive training literature or predesigned and printed flip-chart presentations, became popular. Selling

227

philosophies characterized by "ten easy steps" or acronyms such as AIDA (based on obtaining a customer's attention-interest-decision-action) came into vogue.

Programmed sales approaches were particularly useful in bringing poorer salesmen up to speed and in assuring some uniformity in, and control over, the sales effort. At the same time, they were merely points of departure for more creative, effective salesmen.

Identifying and Solving Customers' Problems. In recent years, a great deal of emphasis has been placed on the need for sales effort to involve the identification and solution of customers' problems through the correct application of a product or service. On occasion, this approach has led to the recommendation by a salesman of his competitor's product. Titles for sales jobs have changed from ordinary salesman to sales engineer, technical sales representative, market analyst, or even sales consultant. No longer is the task of matching needs and the features of increasingly complex products and services left to the customer.

Most firms can afford this selling approach only for potentially large sales transactions. The costs of training sales representatives to the point where they can identify customers' problems can be great. The large amounts of time and effort invested in each sales situation increase the risks of losing a sale or of making a small one. This has led some firms to assess charges for such a sales effort.

(8)   Which of the sales philosophies described here best portrays the efforts of Kim Kelley and Roberta Wells?

team selling

Teams of sales representatives, composed of individuals with complementary skills, have been formed to sell products of increasingly complex design, those requiring custom design to a customer's specifications, or those for which the seller is responsible for installation and continuing maintenance.

For example, Waukesha Motor Co., a manufacturer of internal combustion engines sold to manufacturers of construction machinery, petroleum equipment, and marine products, recently reorganized its selling efforts to assign sales teams to customers in each of these industries. Each team is composed of a specialist salesman and an engineer. According to Peter A. Ford, manager of construction and industrial sales at Waukesha:

> The new system puts sales and application engineering support in one group for each industry area. This insures that nobody is going to sell a customer an engine and then just step back and say, "Put it in." There's going to be an application engineer around to stay in touch with the customer's engineer and to make sure the equipment is installed properly and is performing satisfactorily."[3]

(9)   Does this concept have any applicability to the sale of either computer systems or cigarettes?

[3]"Specialist Selling Makes New Converts," *Business Week* (July 28, 1973), pp. 44 and 45.

multilevel selling

Products and services for which the purchase decision is a complex one may require a sales approach at several levels in a customer's organization. For example, the purchase of a $10 million pollution control system for one of its factories may require a company to obtain opinions on competing devices from its engineers, consulting engineers from outside the company, and representatives of pollution control agencies in local, state, or federal government. The senior production executive may have to evaluate competing systems from a cost standpoint. The legal department may have to assess the threat of legal action if a device is or is not installed. And the final decision may be made by the president. Each may have to be contacted personally during the process of evaluation and purchase decision, either by one or several representatives of a prospective seller's organization.

(10)   In planning a multilevel selling campaign for a pollution control system, would it be more effective to have one sales representative call at various levels in a customer's organization or to have various individuals in the seller's organization, beginning with the president, call on their counterparts in the buyer's

(11) organization? If the latter were to be done, how could a company coordinate, maintain continuity, and avoid contradictory claims in its over-all selling efforts to a particular customer?

     Multilevel selling for an advertising campaign is illustrated in Figure 6-6.

(12) Turning to Figure 6-6, page 202, with what types of questions would the president, the vice-president of marketing services, the vice-president of account services, the account supervisor, and an account executive have to deal in selling an advertising agency's services to a prospective advertiser?

     According to a marketing executive at Honeywell, Inc., the president spends more time in the field selling computer systems than most branch (sales)

(13) managers and perhaps even the poorer sales representatives. Do you think this is a good use of the president's time in a company like Honeywell?

sales management

As a district manager for Philip Morris Inc., Doris Berendt's job (regardless of how it was described in her written job description) required her to (1) serve as the channel for communicating company policies and objectives to the five sales representatives and trainees reporting to her and then report their needs to her section manager, (2) see to it that company marketing policies were implemented, (3) set sales goals and motivate sales representatives to attain them, (4) reallocate sales effort when necessary, (5) diagnose poor sales performance, (6) train new sales representatives, (7) maintain her sales reps' morale and loyalty to the company, (8) monitor the activities of competing cigarette manufacturers, and (9) assume sales responsibility for a small chain headquartered in her territory. In line with company policies, she spent only a few hours each week at the desk provided for her at a regional office. In her words, "The field is where the action is. That's where we belong. I feel caged up after I've spent an hour or two at the office." The nature of her task is outlined in Figure 7-2.

channeling communications

To her salespeople, Doris Berendt was their link with Philip Morris. At occasional formal and more frequent informal meetings, she devoted time to a review of new company policies or old policies that she had observed being ignored, to new products, to upcoming advertising campaigns and sales promotions, and to a discussion of complaints or suggestions volunteered by members of her sales force. Of greater importance were the three days or so that she spent every six weeks with each of her sales representatives. Each of these efforts involved going over a salesperson's objectives, including shortcomings to be corrected; observing the person making several sales calls; determining other things to be corrected; demonstrating proper techniques; once again observing; and finally drawing up revised objectives and methods for achieving them for future follow-up with the sales rep. Much of the process was carried out in the auto enroute to the next sales call, over coffee, or while preparing a set-and-sell display from stock that filled the trunk of each sales representative's company automobile.

implementation of company policies

Most of a sales manager's responsibilities are related to the implementation of company policies. It can be most difficult if such policies conflict with each other or penalize the incomes of those salespeople who adhere to them.

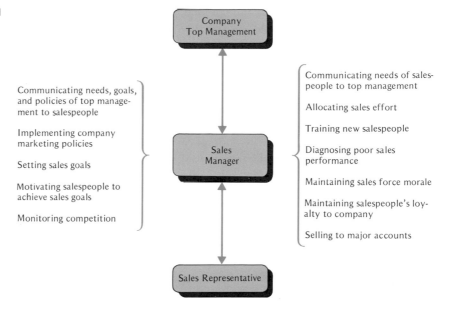

Figure 7-2. Elements and results of the sales management task.

Company Top Management

Communicating needs, goals, and policies of top management to salespeople

Implementing company marketing policies

Setting sales goals

Motivating salespeople to achieve sales goals

Monitoring competition

Sales Manager

Communicating needs of salespeople to top management

Allocating sales effort

Training new salespeople

Diagnosing poor sales performance

Maintaining sales force morale

Maintaining salespeople's loyalty to company

Selling to major accounts

Sales Representative

For example, assume you are a sales manager in a company establishing rigid guidelines for the type of outlet through which its line of fishing tackle gear should be sold and discouraging sales through discount stores. The company places responsibility for carrying out this policy (and the selection of all small retail outlets) on its sales managers. Its sales managers realize about 20 per cent of their income on bonuses based on the attainment of a sales quota; its salespeople realize all of their income from commissions. Based on several hours spent making joint calls with your best salesman, who consistently is producing sales well over his quota, you suspect that two of his best accounts may be buying merchandise for resale to discount outlets. Although the company's merchandise has appeared mysteriously from time to time in discount outlets outside your sales territory, none has been traced to your territory. In fact, you wonder whether senior marketing executives have as yet made much effort to trace it. What would you do? Assuming you revealed your concern to your top salesman and he indicated that he had no evidence that any of his accounts were "fronts" for discounters, what would you do? If you expected a crackdown from your firm's top management intended to stop such practices, what action would you take?

(14) (15)

(16)

setting and achieving sales goals

The most successful efforts to set sales goals that are achieved subsequently have employed inputs not only from the salesperson but also his or her manager and perhaps marketing research efforts. This is a so-called bottoms-up approach.

231

At the same time, a management planning its activities for the coming period might set sales goals on the basis of the volume needed to attain a corporate profit objective, essentially taking a top-down approach. When these are in conflict, which should take precedence? At what level in the organization should they be resolved? How?

Sales personnel may be more supportive of goals that they have had a hand in formulating. The fact that their natural optimism often produces goals that may have to be reduced by their more objective superiors may produce what, to them, appears to be even more reasonable goals. However, the success of this approach may depend on the way in which sales personnel are compensated. For example, how would you adjust for bias a sales goal produced by a salesperson compensated on a straight commission (percentage of sales) as opposed to a salesperson compensated by means of a salary plus a bonus based on the extent to which he or she exceeds the sales goal?

It is important to distinguish a sales goal from a sales estimate. A sales goal may be a figure that the firm or a salesperson would like to see attained; a sales estimate should be a more realistic appraisal of what the company or the salesperson will attain. Firms confusing the two often end up with very optimistic sales estimates.

Once set, it should be in the best interests of a sales manager to see his or her salespeople's sales goal and the territory sales goal achieved. This may require various efforts to help sales representatives motivate themselves to achieve their objectives. Some of the more successful of these efforts have employed positive devices such as training, demonstration selling, and subtle assistance in achieving successful sales calls.

allocating sales effort

Several times in recent years, Philip Morris' sales territories had been reorganized and condensed to accommodate a larger sales force and provide more intensive coverage, particularly in important markets. Each time this was done an effort was made to divide territories in such a way that each represented approximately the same work load as the next.

Between territorial reorganizations, district sales managers could make minor changes in accounts assigned to each of their sales representatives. It was just such a change that Doris Berendt was contemplating in order to improve results in the northern end of her division's territory, a territory that extended north and west from downtown Chicago, as shown in Figure 7-3.

Available information on which to allocate effort included the compilation of data from daily call reports, some of which are presented in Figure 7-3. This was distributed weekly from Philip Morris' central data-processing facility. However, all of this data reflected sales accomplishments, as reported by sales representatives, rather than the proportion of over-all sales potential being realized. Perceptions regarding the latter had to be based on a division manager's observations during frequent sales calls with each representative as well as the goals agreed on between a division manager and each sales representative, as shown in Figure 7-3.

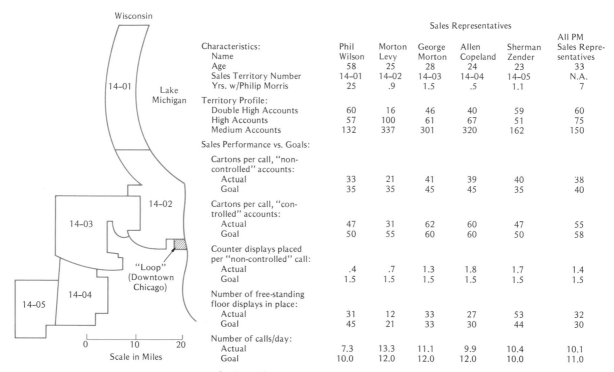

Figure 7-3. Profile of Philip Morris sales representatives, their sales goals and their performances, five Chicago area territories and nationally, for the second eight-week period in 1976. (Note: All names and statistics presented here have been disguised.)

Characteristics:	Phil Wilson	Morton Levy	George Morton	Allen Copeland	Sherman Zender	All PM Sales Representatives
Name						
Age	58	25	28	24	23	33
Sales Territory Number	14–01	14–02	14–03	14–04	14–05	N.A.
Yrs. w/Philip Morris	25	.9	1.5	.5	1.1	7
Territory Profile:						
Double High Accounts	60	16	46	40	59	60
High Accounts	57	100	61	67	51	75
Medium Accounts	132	337	301	320	162	150
Sales Performance vs. Goals:						
Cartons per call, "non-controlled" accounts:						
Actual	33	21	41	39	40	38
Goal	35	35	45	45	35	40
Cartons per call, "controlled" accounts:						
Actual	47	31	62	60	47	55
Goal	50	55	60	60	50	58
Counter displays placed per "non-controlled" call:						
Actual	.4	.7	1.3	1.8	1.7	1.4
Goal	1.5	1.5	1.5	1.5	1.5	1.5
Number of free-standing floor displays in place:						
Actual	31	12	33	27	53	32
Goal	45	21	33	30	44	30
Number of calls/day:						
Actual	7.3	13.3	11.1	9.9	10.4	10.1
Goal	10.0	12.0	12.0	12.0	10.0	11.0

(21)

The sales representatives in the two northernmost of the five sales territories that comprised Doris Berendt's division consistently had performed below what she believed their potential to be, rarely had achieved their goals, and generally detracted from her division's performance. Alternatives she was contemplating to deal with the matter included (1) the reassignment of several accounts away from each of these sales reps to enable them to realize greater proportions of potential sales in reduced territories, (2) working intensively with the reps to help them improve their performance, or (3) replacing them with new people. Based on the information in Figure 7-3, what would you do if you were in Doris Berendt's position?

diagnosing poor sales performance

Doris Berendt was aware of some of the possible factors associated with the substandard performance of two of her sales representatives. For example, Phil Wilson was counting the months until he could take an early retirement at sixty-two. Several years earlier, after having been transferred into his current territory, he had purchased a tract of land that he intended to place into

233

cultivation as a "gentleman farmer." His future plans distracted him from his work.

Excerpts from Doris's notes regarding the remaining four, taken from reports filed on the basis of joint sales calls with them, included the following comments:

> Morton Levy—lacks self-confidence; as a result, he fails to get cooperation on our display campaigns from a number of his accounts; may get a high call rate, but takes too many shortcuts during calls; has been a sales trainee for several months more than most; should we go along with him any longer?
>
> George Morton—handles people well; father has sold for a career; wants to go into sales management; not aggressive enough; too nice to retailers, often favoring them too much in their dealings with Philip Morris.
>
> Allen Copeland—creative, imaginative guy, but tends to be a perfectionist in his calls.
>
> Sherman Zender—has good ability to communicate; holds attention; presents product on "brand merit," not on the basis of incentives; deserves to be designated for Management Action [training] Program as a potential district manager.

(22) Given these diagnoses, what action would you recommend Doris Berendt take regarding the improvement of sales effort in territories staffed with the sales representatives described here?

sales training

The typical orientation program for sales trainees at Philip Morris was two weeks in length, involving a week of morning orientation sessions and afternoon sales calls with a division manager. During a second week of sales calls, responsibility for selling gradually was shifted from the division manager to the sales trainee. From the third week on, a sales trainee received only periodic coaching from his or her division manager. Those with potential to become division managers subsequently were designated for the company's Management Action Program. In this program, candidates for promotion were given extra assignments corresponding to those for which they would be responsible after promotion, some as little as a year after joining the company.

At Honeywell, the sales training program was about six months in length and consisted of a series of two-week segments involving orientation to the company, programming and computer logic, field sales policies, and customer system-audit procedures interspersed with periods of time in which the trainee would observe Honeywell sales representatives and systems engineering teams in selling and servicing actual accounts. Those demonstrating good sales abilities and administrative potential might become managers after a period of several years of solid performance.

(23) How would you explain the differences in these sales training programs?

maintaining sales force morale and loyalty

A problem confronted by many sales managers is that of helping salespeople to achieve and maintain a balance in their loyalties to their company and their customers. At the one extreme, sales representatives overly loyal to their employer may assume an undesirably hard line in dealing with customer complaints, essentially taking the attitude that the customer is always wrong. The opposite of this attitude is illustrated by the salesman who "goes native," identifying so completely with the needs and views of his customers that he not only manages to resolve questions in favor of them but takes delight in criticizing his employer in the process. How does this latter attitude differ from the often expressed marketing philosophy that "the customer is always right"?

(24)

At Philip Morris, Doris Berendt never reversed a commitment or decision made by her salesmen in regard to customer concerns. But she tried to monitor them by direct observation and to counsel those of her salesmen exhibiting extreme company or customer loyalties in conversations held between sales calls. Would a system of call reports, written summaries of what transpired during each sales call, prepared by all salesmen be an aid to Doris Berendt in monitoring this aspect of sales performance?

(25)

monitoring competition

Either personally or through her salesmen, Doris was asked to collect information to document sales promotion activity, either in the form of deals or point-of-sale promotions, being conducted by Philip Morris' competition. On occasion, when she became concerned about the quantity or quality of her company's programs, she would collect such data on her own initiative to support a recommendation to her regional sales manager.

selling to major accounts

Doris called occasionally on buyers associated with a small retail chain headquartered in her territory. At these meetings, she outlined upcoming deals, in-store promotional programs, and Philip Morris' advertising plans. She attempted to secure approval from the buyers that would help her salesmen in selling deals to individual chain store managers or placing point-of-sale material in their stores.

designing the direct promotional program

Steps in designing the sales effort include the development of objectives for the effort, the identification of potential accounts, the establishment of salespersons' qualifications, a determination of the size of the necessary sales force, the allocation of sales effort, the establishment of a method and expected level of compensation, the development of a budget, a decision to make or buy necessary sales effort, the organization of the sales force, and the development and executiion of programs for direct promotion.

development of objectives for the effort

In developing objectives for a direct promotional effort, it is necessary to determine the relative emphasis to be placed on achieving primary or selective demand increases, the nature of the communication task to be carried out, which target market segments should be given highest priority, individuals within customer organizations to whom direct sales effort should be directed, and specific sales goals. These questions must be considered in the context of factors shown in Figure 7-4, which include the nature of the product package, the general needs of customers in considering its purchase, the nature of competition and other aspects of the environment, and the general policies of the company for which the program is being developed. As in the development of indirect promotional programs, these factors help define the nature of the promotional task and the relative role that direct selling effort can play in it.

Honeywell, Inc. and Philip Morris Inc. provide convenient examples for a discussion of these questions.

The market for computers of the types manufactured by Honeywell could be divided into actual and potential purchasers of large, medium, and small computers. Competition for the existing market in 1974 was intense, with IBM commanding nearly 70 per cent of the United States market. As we have seen, the selling process was complex, the needs of customers for risk reduction very great, and the role of the salesperson all-important in the over-all company promotional strategy. Several of the largest firms in the industry emphasized only large- and medium-sized computers in their marketing programs. Although small computers might require only one to four weeks of selling effort, there was a belief that they represented one-shot sales at a price below $20,000 per unit. Large computer installations, those generally considered to be priced above $2 million, often led to the sale of additional central processing or peripheral equipment. However, their sale might require from several months to up to three years of selling effort.

Owners of competing computers were considered potential customers. Their purchasing decisions often reflected constantly changing needs and dissatisfaction with their current supplier. Over all, the market for central computing units had increased at the rate of about 15 to 20 per cent for a period of some five years prior to 1974; during this time, Honeywell's share had risen to about 9 per cent of the $8 billion of central computing units sold in the United States in 1974.

In contrast to computers, cigarettes were sold through more than 500,000 retail outlets, not including machines operated by vending companies. In total, the number of cigarettes sold in the United States was increasing at about a 3 per cent annual rate in spite of a TV advertising ban and the publication of a statement by the surgeon general that cigarettes were detrimental to the health

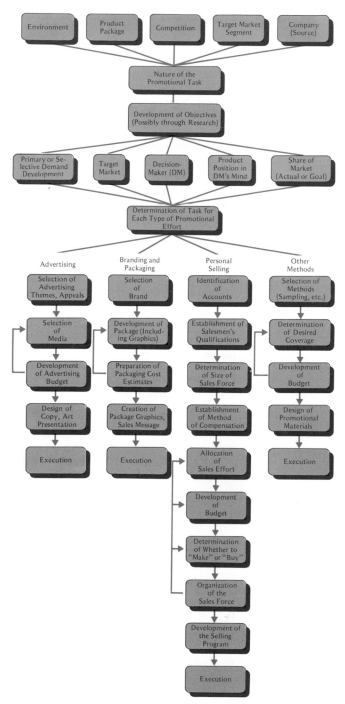

Figure 7-4. Factors determining, and steps in, the design of a direct promotional program.

of smokers. Philip Morris was the second largest of the six cigarette manufacturers dominating the United States market. By 1974, its share of total unit sales had risen to a new high of about 23 per cent, and its products were sold through all outlets selling cigarettes. Although much of the communication task was achieved by means of advertising, direct selling could have an influence on sales, particularly through the 60,000 largest retail outlets, including all supermarkets and larger drug outlets. Thus, all sales representatives were encouraged to call every three weeks on these accounts, while perhaps visiting another 75,000 outlets once every six weeks and perhaps 150,000 other outlets four times per year. Calls on the smallest 215,000 retail outlets were left to sales representatives of tobacco jobbers (wholesalers) handling Philip Morris products in each market in return for margins approximating 4 to 6 per cent of the value of the cigarettes sold to retailers. Thus, based on a typical twenty- to thirty-minute sales call, a Philip Morris sales representative might spend the equivalent of two working days per year with a major account.

(26)
(27)
Which of these situations offers the greatest potential for the expansion of primary demand? How does this influence the nature of the communication task required of promotional effort?

identification of potential accounts

At Honeywell, sales representatives specializing in the sale of small- and medium-sized computers received print-outs of addresses of firms with more than one hundred employees from the Dun & Bradstreet reporting service. Large computer sales reps concentrated most of their efforts on the thousand largest companies in the United States as well as on major government organizations and educational institutions. Whether or not an organization with these characteristics owned a computer, it was considered a potential account.

In contrast, Philip Morris relied on its sales representatives and those of its brokers to physically identify store renovations, shopping center construction projects, and other indicators of potential outlets for the sale of cigarettes. Grocery, drug, and tobacco outlets of any type automatically became potential accounts for the sale of Philip Morris products.

allocation of sales effort

How much sales effort is enough on a companywide basis? Factors influencing a response to this question include the complexity of the selling task, the minimum level of effort required to maintain contact with a customer, the relative desirability of targeted accounts, and a company's sales goals. A company rarely will be able to provide what everyone would agree is "enough" sales effort. Therefore, allocation is necessary. Because this is a matter that must be resolved in relation to the method of compensation, sales budget, the decision to make or buy effort, and the organization of sales effort, we'll come back to it.

establishment of salespersons' qualifications

Sales representatives often are evaluated on several major dimensions, reflecting the complexity of the sales task and those who perform it. Elements of a candidate's background of interest to a potential employer might include his or her age (or, more important, maturity), health, previous experience, technical training and ability, and marital and family status. Fair employment and civil rights legislation has prohibited the inclusion of sex or race on this list for firms engaged in interstate commerce.

In addition, aspects of a candidate's basic intelligence, such as his or her memory, problem-solving ability, and quickness of thought may be explored. Human skills, including a candidate's interest in people, ability to work in groups, and reactions to adverse situations (important in countering customers' objections) often are carefully reviewed. And, finally, indicators of character, such as honesty, integrity, the ability to exercise good judgment under stress, and even such surface indicators as personal appearance and mannerisms may be important in evaluating potential sales representatives.

(28)
(29)
Are there any important dimensions, such as managerial ability, that you feel are eliminated from this list? How would you compare the relative importance of each of these dimensions for potential Honeywell and Philip Morris sales representatives?

determination of sales force size

Factors influencing the desired size of a company's sales force are the number of potential customers with which contact might be maintained at any one time, their density (proximity to one another), and the level of effort to be devoted to each in terms of the frequency and length of sales contact or problem-solving activity.

For example, a Philip Morris sales representative averaging ten calls per day and an average of eighteen selling days per four-week period (allowing for scheduled nonselling activities) would be capable of performing 180 calls per four-week period. As in Roberta Wells' case, these calls could be allocated as follows:

Account Potential	Number of Customers	Number of Calls per Four-Week Period per Customer	Number of Calls per Four-Week Period
Double High	60	1.33	80
High	84	.75	56
Medium	123	.33	41
Total	267		177

(30)
(31)
Given this distribution of the 285,000 largest customer accounts nationally, how many sales representatives would Philip Morris need if it were to sell directly to all retail accounts of medium or larger size? What result would you get if you performed the same analysis for Honeywell?

establishing a method and expected level of compensation

Sales representatives may be paid on the basis of commissions, bonuses, salaries, or some combination of the three. The method selected should be consistent with the selling task, a company's marketing strategy and policies, salespeople's needs, and the ability to identify sales results with sales efforts.

Common beliefs among marketing executives are that a heavy reliance on sales commissions (based on a percentage of dollar sales) in the compensation scheme produces a greater incentive for a salesperson to engage in aggressive selling activity, makes it more difficult for a company to control a salesperson's activities, provides an automatic means of discouraging and weeding out poor performers, creates a temptation for a salesperson to engage in "cherry picking"—in which he or she concentrates effort on only the customers with the best potential—and is most workable when a salesperson can be identified easily with a sale. An added feature of commission schemes are that they make selling cost a variable with sales, thus allowing their users to budget future sales costs with certainty and shift risk from the company to the individual salesperson.

Much the opposite of these characteristics are associated with compensation plans based heavily on salaries. Unfortunately, research results to date have been unable to document relationships between various schemes and the results they produce.

In recent years, there does appear to have been a trend away from the total reliance on either commissions or salaries in favor of salaries plus bonuses based on sales performance in relation to plan. Presumably, this will offer some combination of the strengths and weaknesses associated with more "extreme" alternatives.

(32) What methods of compensation, stated in terms of the proportion of a salesperson's income to be derived from commission, bonuses, and salaries, would you feel to be most appropriate for Honeywell and Philip Morris sales (33) representatives? How do you explain the differences between your recommendations and the compensation methods actually employed by these two companies?

The level of compensation to be paid often depends on the amount required to attract desired sales talent as well as the amount that a company might be able to afford in its budget. Current salaries for different types of full-time selling jobs may range from $9,000 to $30,000 per year, with a company often spending an equivalent amount for travel expenses, training, supervision, and other activities in support of the direct selling effort. Salespeople compensated heavily on the basis of commissions, in contrast, literally can receive from nothing to several hundred thousand dollars per year for their efforts. Under these schemes, there is often a constant turnover among less successful salespeople unable to meet their income needs. When training and sales support costs are low, some companies pay a straight commission and literally regard the size of the sales force they can support and afford as unlimited, thereby reducing or eliminating the allocation problem.

development of a budget

By combining estimates of the necessary selling effort with compensation schemes and levels of compensation, a budget for sales activity can be prepared. Results of this computation falling outside acceptable limits may require a recycling of thinking regarding the desired level and allocation of direct sales effort.

For example, if all 500,000 outlets selling Philip Morris products were to be visited every three weeks by company sales representatives, it would require a sales force of 2,779 (500,000 accounts × 1.33 calls per month ÷ 240 calls per salesperson per month). At an average salary of $11,000 per salesperson and an equivalent amount for training, supervision and other costs, this would result in an annual direct promotional budget of more than $61 million, or nearly 7 per cent of Philip Morris' domestic cigarette sales. Given the fact that Philip Morris currently might be willing to budget approximately $30 million for such activities, something would have to give.

Under these circumstances, Philip Morris could adopt a compensation program based totally on commission and designed to result in $15 million in commissions and an equal amount for sales support. By doing so, the company could convert half of its costs to those variable with sales, thus shifting a portion of the risk for poor sales performance to its sales representatives. But at current sales levels, if 2,779 sales representatives had to share $15 million in commissions, it would mean an average compensation of only about $5,800 per salesperson, too low to attract anyone, let alone individuals of the type that the company might seek.

Two other alternatives would be to reduce the frequency of sales calls, either selectively or across the board, or hire organizations such as wholesalers to sell to small accounts, possibly passing their sales commissions (referred to as margins by wholesalers) on to small retailers in the form of higher prices. As we can see, Philip Morris did adopt a variable sales call frequency, essentially eliminating visits by its representatives to nearly one half of its accounts. At the present time, is Philip Morris understaffed or overstaffed? What results would you get if you applied similar logic to the Honeywell sales effort?

At Honeywell, given the vast nature of the potential market and accompanying sales effort. a sequential allocation of salespeople to accounts was necessary to develop the market over time and allow the development of a stable sales force with long-run opportunities with the company.

decisions to make or buy sales effort

At an expected call rate of 2,400 per year (200 per month) and a total average cost of $22,000 per sales representative, Philip Morris's average cost per call would be about $9.17. At this rate, how many calls per year could the company afford to have made on the 215,000 smallest (out of 500,000 total) United States retail accounts averaging $300 per year in sales of Philip Morris products? This suggests the need to buy the services of an organization offering a line of products sufficiently broad to support regular sales calls to such accounts. Thus, even though nearly all Philip Morris products are physically distributed through candy, tobacco, and drug wholesalers, as well as through chain store distribution centers, small retail accounts are visited only by the wholesalers' sales representatives. Would this be a practical decision for Honeywell to make as well?

organization of the sales force

The variable of greatest importance in the allocation of sales effort and the determination of sales force size and budget is that of the use of generalist or specialist salespeople. The former typically sell the entire product line to anyone located in a given geographic territory. The latter may sell only certain products to companies with carefully selected operating characteristics. Coverage of a given number of accounts may require more salespeople when they are organized as specialists because of the need to assign large, often overlapping geographic territories containing accounts corresponding to the specialties of each group of salespeople.

factors in the development of promotional strategies

We now turn to strategic decisions about the relative amounts of indirect and direct promotional efforts to employ in marketing a product or service. Factors influencing such decisions include (1) the nature of the buying task from the viewpoint of the potential customer, (2) a company's ability to pinpoint market segments, (3) the availability of appropriate promotional media, (4) the potential size and concentration of targeted market segments, (5) the size of the promotional budget available, (6) competitive practices, (7) the willingness of firms in a channel of distribution to share the promotional burden, (8) the life-cycle stage of the product or service being marketed, (9) the stage in the innovation diffusion process for the product in question, (10) whether the product is a consumer or industrial good, and (11) the relative stages of the selling process to which various promotional efforts are to be directed.

nature of the buying task

The determinants of the buying task that we discussed in Chapter 6 are arrayed in Figure 7-5 in relation to the relative amounts of direct and indirect promotion that might appropriately be employed in a marketing strategy for corresponding products or services. These are generalizations that might be expected to prevail in most marketing situations.

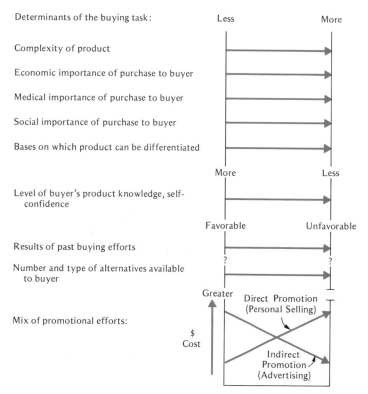

Figure 7-5. The relationship between the nature of the buying task and the relative importance of indirect and direct methods in a promotional strategy.

Determinants of the buying task:

Complexity of product

Economic importance of purchase to buyer

Medical importance of purchase to buyer

Social importance of purchase to buyer

Bases on which product can be differentiated

Level of buyer's product knowledge, self-confidence

Results of past buying efforts

Number and type of alternatives available to buyer

Mix of promotional efforts:

Figure 7-5 is intended to be read as follows: as the complexity of a product increases, the relative importance of direct promotion (personal selling) in its marketing strategy increases; as the level of a buyer's product knowledge and self-confidence declines, the relative importance of direct promotion increases. Do you agree with the generalizations shown in Figure 7-5? What headings, if any, would you apply to the spectrum of possibilities for the number and type of alternatives available to the buyer shown in the figure? Where would you position products marketed by Honeywell and Philip Morris on the scales in the figure? We'll gain some idea later of the extent to which these companies fit the generalizations shown in Figure 7-5.

(38) (39)

(40)

ability to pinpoint market segments

The potential markets and channels of distribution for a new vegetable juicer may be much harder to define than those for a piece of equipment used in petroleum refining. This may require that a higher proportion of funds be devoted to advertising for the former than for the latter. If nothing else, the advertising of a vegetable juicer may help identify market segments through the use of a coupon or other form of reader or viewer response. Direct sales effort can be utilized in larger relative quantity in the promotion of petroleum refining equipment to identified firms and decision makers within those firms. At the same time, relatively efficient media may exist for the promotion of products for which market segments have been pinpointed, allowing a lower expenditure per level of exposure for advertising. This is particularly true in the promotion of industrial goods for which well-defined markets and trade journals directed to decision makers in specific industries (market segments) exist.

availability of efficient media

Trade journals may thus represent efficient media, in terms of the potential for exposure to a marketing message that they offer for specified executives in well-defined industries. By the same token, mass media have attempted to respond to the increasing capability of advertisers to identify target market segments by positioning themselves to "deliver" audiences with particular, measurable profiles. Thus, radio stations have geared their programming to attract teeny-bopper, black, or non-English language audiences. *The Wall Street Journal* is read by individuals with average incomes of $37,000. *Vogue* appeals to a more select, fashion-conscious segment of female readers than *Ladies Home Journal*. Various types of television programs, often grouped by evenings of the week on network television, deliver audiences with different profiles. Regional editions of nationally distributed magazines and newspapers not only offer an opportunity to direct an advertising message to geographic market segments, but may offer services such as a roll-out program under which an advertiser may duplicate its introductory advertising program in successive regional editions.

Efficient advertising media may not be available. When this is the case, it may warrant a shift in the promotional mix for a product or service. When denied the use of television for the promotion of its products, the cigarette manufacturing industry directed an estimated $150 to $175 million of the $225 million it had been spending on television to such media as newspapers, magazines, billboards, point-of-sale promotion, premium offers, cigarette-sponsored sporting events, and the purchase of shelf position in supermarkets.

Before the TV ad ban, Philip Morris had only 450 salespeople, the smallest field force in the industry. Several years later, the force had been increased to more than 900, the pay for individual salespeople increased an average of 20 per cent, and a sales training program featuring week-long seminars instituted. Why were these changes in promotional strategy adopted by Philip Morris?

(41)

potential size and concentration of the market

The number and geographical concentration of potential customers may suggest the use of a particular blend of indirect and direct promotional effort. For example, a supplier to the automotive industry might find itself with only four major potential customers and a relatively small number of decision makers to which to direct its efforts. It could well be able to obtain a high level of personalized sales effort with a modest expenditure for direct promotion.

Retail markets for consumer goods in a major metropolitan area may encompass hundreds of thousands of prospective spending units (families). Few types of retail outlets, however, have the ability to draw potential customers from an area of much more than several miles in radius. Thus, only a small share of the total market may be available to the operator of a single outlet, making the purchase of advertising time or space in media with metrowide coverage relatively wasteful and expensive. For example, in its rush to open new Burger Chef fast-food outlets, General Foods sought to enter as many new markets as possible, often with only one or two outlets serving a major metropolitan area. As a result, it wasn't possible to make efficient use of local mass media. After reorganizing its strategy at considerable cost to the company, it adopted the policy of clustering its remaining outlets in selected regions. For operators of individual retail outlets, a more selective medium such as direct mail may be a more efficient method of pinpointing customers.

size of promotional budget available

The cost of certain promotional media make their use prohibitive for many firms. For example, for the cost of one full-page ad in the national edition of *The Wall Street Journal,* most firms could keep a salesperson in the field for a year.

competitive practice

Firms in particular industries may adopt parallel promotional strategies. In fact, there is a basic underlying rationale for firms in industries dominated by several competitors to do so. A firm may be able to spend fewer dollars or a smaller proportion of sales dollars for promotion in relation to its competitors only at the risk of losing market share.

Consider the following example: Assume that two firms, the Savon Corp. and Sopa Industries, are competing for the market for soap products, which largely are indistinguishable in use except by means of promotional appeals. Increases in the total spent for promotion by competing firms cannot influence primary demand, the total size of the market. The price of soap is fixed at $1 per unit and is produced at a total variable cost of $.20 per unit, yielding a contribution before fixed overhead and promotional expenses of $.80 per unit. Fixed overhead for both firms is about $10 million per year, and will support capacity to allow each firm to sell 100 million units if necessary. The total market is 100 million units, with each firm selling 50 million units and budgeting $10 million for promotion. Past experience has suggested that the two competitors have divided the market in relation to the volume of their relative promotional expenditures.

(42)
(43)

As a marketing executive at Savon preparing your 1976 promotional budget, how much would you budget for promotion? What would the result be for Savon and Sopa if the latter budgeted $10 million against your budget for 1976?

(44) (45)

If Sopa matched your budget? How would the results differ if the total demand for soap was thought to be related to total industry (Savon plus Sopa) advertising expenditures in a way such that the expenditure of each industry promotional dollar more than $20 million would result in one additional unit of soap being sold by the industry, and the expenditure of each promotional dollar less than $20 million would result in one less unit of soap being sold? What type of competitive promotional budgeting would a situation involving unchanging primary demand encourage? Returning to Table 6-3, page 196, do you see any evidence that competitors adopt somewhat parallel promotional stategies? Based on your calculations here, how would you guess most executives in the cigarette manufacturing industry regarded the government's ban on cigarette advertising on television after January 1, 1972?

(46)
(47)
(48)

willingness of the channel to share the burden

It may be common practice in the distribution of certain goods for wholesalers and retailers to share advertising expense under a cooperative arrangement in which a manufacturer may match dollars to be spent by middlemen for advertising its products. Where *detailing*—involving the arrangement of product displays in retail outlets—is required, it may be necessary for either wholesalers' or manufacturers' sales personnel to do it. This is becoming particularly necessary in discount retail outlets lacking personnel for such activities.

product life-cycle stage

(49)

Possible roles played by indirect and direct promotional effort at various stages in a product's life cycle are outlined in Figure 7-6. How would you think the relative emphasis on each type of promotional effort might vary from one stage to the next for a product such as the ball pen discussed in Chapter 6?

stages in the diffusion process

In the innovation-diffusion process, the adoption (through purchase) of new-product innovations often occurs on a geographic basis, takes place among individuals who are in close communication with each other on a word-of-mouth basis, and spreads from so-called early adopters to those who are influenced by them and eventually to late adopters. The results of several studies have suggested that the relative effectiveness of indirect and direct promotional effort may be different in communicating with early adopters, the majority of adopters, and later adopters. For example, in the adoption of a new drug, the sources of information on which each group of physicians relied are shown in Table 7-1. What significant changes in emphasis do you see as you

(50)

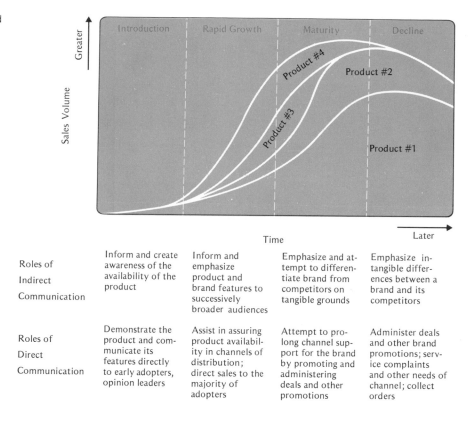

Figure 7-6. Roles played by indirect and direct promotional efforts at various stages in a product's life cycle.

	Introduction	Rapid Growth	Maturity	Decline
Roles of Indirect Communication	Inform and create awareness of the availability of the product	Inform and emphasize product and brand features to successively broader audiences	Emphasize and attempt to differentiate brand from competitors on tangible grounds	Emphasize intangible differences between a brand and its competitors
Roles of Direct Communication	Demonstrate the product and communicate its features directly to early adopters, opinion leaders	Assist in assuring product availability in channels of distribution; direct sales to the majority of adopters	Attempt to prolong channel support for the brand by promoting and administering deals and other promotions	Administer deals and other brand promotions; service complaints and other needs of channel; collect orders

Table 7-1 Sources of Information Mentioned by Physicians Adopting a New Drug at Various Points in Time in the Innovation Diffusion Process*

Sources of Information	Proportion of Total Mentions by Physicians Adopting the Drug at Each Stage in the Diffusion Process		
	Stage 1 (Early Adopters)	Stage 2 (Majority of Adopters)	Stage 3 (Late Adopters)
Salesmen	52%	27%	5%
Colleagues and meetings	13	19	36
Direct mail	22	16	14
Journal articles	6	21	21
Drug house periodicals	3	11	21
Other media	4	7	3
Total	100%	100%	100%

* Source: Adapted from Elihu Katz, "The Social Itinerary of Technical Change: Two Studies on the Diffusion of Innovation," in *Advertising Management: Selected Readings* ed. Harper W. Boyd, Jr., and Joseph Newman (Homewood, Ill.: Irwin, 1965), p. 139.

(51)

move from the left- to the right-hand columns in Table 7-1? What implications might these findings have for a drug manufacturer in the design of its promotional strategy?

consumer versus industrial goods

(52)
(53)

Differences in the promotional strategies employed by manufacturers of industrial, consumer durable, and consumer nondurable goods, as suggested by one extensive study, are shown in Table 7-2. What important relationships do you see there? How would you explain them?

stages in the selling process

(54)

Functions of indirect and direct promotional effort at various stages in a marketing relationship with an individual customer are shown in Figure 7-7. It is important to note here that both types of effort can play an important role at each stage of the process. What are the relationships, if any, between the relative importance of indirect and direct promotion in the early stages of a product's life cycle, the diffusion of an innovation among early adopters, and the early stages of the selling process with an individual customer?

Table 7-2 The Relative Importance of Elements of Communication Strategy*

Elements of Communication Strategy	Allocation of Relative "Points" by Type of Product		
	Industrial Goods	Consumer Durables	Consumer Nondurables
Advertising			
Printed media	12.5	16.1	14.8
Broadcast media	.9	10.7	20.9
Sales management			
Personal selling	69.2	47.6	38.1
Branding and promotional packaging	4.5	9.5	9.8
Special promotional activities	9.6	15.5	15.5
Other	3.3	.6	.9
Total	100.0	100.0	100.0

* Source: Jon Udell, "The Perceived Importance of the Elements of Communication Strategy," *Journal of Marketing*, **32** (Jan. 1968) pp. 34-40. Quote on p. 38. The data are the average point allocations of 336 industrial, 52 consumer durable, and 88 consumer nondurable goods producers. Each respondent was asked to allocate 100 points among the activities according to the estimated contribution of each to the marketing success of his product.

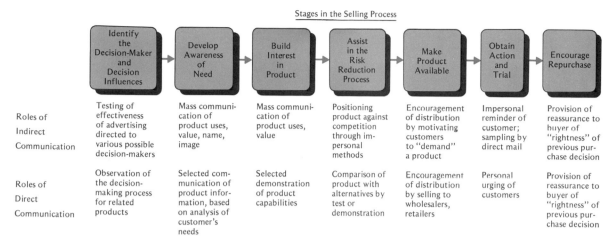

	Identify the Decision-Maker and Decision Influences	Develop Awareness of Need	Build Interest in Product	Assist in the Risk Reduction Process	Make Product Available	Obtain Action and Trial	Encourage Repurchase
Roles of Indirect Communication	Testing of effectiveness of advertising directed to various possible decision-makers	Mass communication of product uses, value, name, image	Mass communication of product uses, value	Positioning product against competition through impersonal methods	Encouragement of distribution by motivating customers to "demand" a product	Impersonal reminder of customer; sampling by direct mail	Provision of reassurance to buyer of "rightness" of previous purchase decision
Roles of Direct Communication	Observation of the decision-making process for related products	Selected communication of product information, based on analysis of customer's needs	Selected demonstration of product capabilities	Comparison of product with alternatives by test or demonstration	Encouragement of distribution by selling to wholesalers, retailers	Personal urging of customers	Provision of reassurance to buyer of "rightness" of previous purchase decision

Figure 7-7. The roles of indirect and direct promotion in the buying-selling process.

push versus pull

Two shorthand terms have come to be used to describe basic alternative strategies of promoting and distributing: push and pull. A classic push strategy is one in which a wholesaler is convinced to stock and resell a manufacturer's product through the latter's sales effort and other incentives. Consequent sales effort by the wholesaler and the wholesaler's retail customer to an ultimate consumer describes the promotional effort devoted to the product. In contrast, a manufacturer may take its sales message directly to the ultimate consumer, relying on him or her to request the product from their local retail outlet and "pull" it through the channel of distribution. These basic differences are diagrammed in Figure 7-8.

The 1972 presidential campaign provided another test for the so-called new politics spawned by supporters of Senator Eugene McCarthy several years earlier. Instead of relying on a large advertising budget, George McGovern's campaign was based on an unusually large force of volunteers who made house-to-house visitations to collect information about voters' views and to

Figure 7-8.
Communication strategies emphasizing push and pull in channels of distribution for consumer goods.

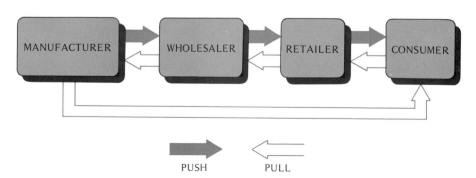

persuade them to vote for Senator McGovern. The candidate himself spent a good deal of time in personal campaigning. In contrast, President Nixon's campaign utilized what had come to be more traditionally heavy inputs of advertising in relation to personal canvassing. The president largely refrained from campaigning. Would you associate "new politics" with push or pull promotional strategies? Was the 1972 presidential political campaign a good test of the relative effectiveness of either?

(55)
(56)

(57)
(58)

What is the relative importance of a push or pull strategy in the promotional efforts planned for Honeywell computers and Philip Morris cigarettes? How would you describe the promotional process for the drug for which information was collected in Table 7-1? (In dealing with this question, it is important to remember that the physician is not the ultimate consumer.)

It is a mistake to assume that push strategies are associated only with personal selling or pull strategies only with advertising. Direct and indirect promotional effort are used more often to complement each other in both push and pull strategies.

For example, the sales organization for Du Pont's Teflon has for years practiced the strategy of concentrating direct sales effort not only on Du Pont's customers but also on its customers' customers. By helping the latter solve their problems by suggesting the specification of Teflon-coated products manufactured by Du Pont's customers, its sales organization has been able to deliver ready-made sales to Du Pont's direct customers. This has further enlisted customer support for the promotion of products containing Teflon and provides a good example of a pull strategy implemented by means of direct promotion.

Similarly, the Bic Pen Corp.'s large advertising budget discussed in Chapter 6 was justified in part by the argument that the prospect of such a volume of indirect promotional effort to ultimate buyers of the product would encourage reluctant retailers to stock the Bic Banana. Thus, the advertising budget fostered retailer push for the Banana, at least to the extent that it provided retailers with an incentive to stock it, as well as the subsequent pull experienced from TV and radio advertising aimed at ultimate consumers.

integrated promotional strategies

The successful design of promotional strategies invariably features equal care in devising complementary direct and indirect promotional efforts.

Philip Morris Inc.

Philip Morris' total marketing budget for each of its brands was determined by multiplying the brand's sales forecast by a dollar amount per thousand cigarettes. Although the total marketing expenditure averaged 90 cents per thousand cigarettes in 1972, including about 53 cents per thousand for indirect promotion, the amount spent for advertising varied a great deal from brand to

Figure 7-9. A recent advertisement for Marlboro cigarettes.

brand. Only about 40 cents per thousand was spent for advertising for a strong, established brand such as Marlboro, whereas a new brand might receive up to $1.40 per thousand in advertising support.

In 1972, this produced a total United States domestic marketing expenditure of $99.4 million, of which about $30 million was spent for sales salaries, bonuses, and the support of direct promotion efforts and the remainder for indirect promotional activities. The latter were designed to reinforce a brand's image. For example, advertising for Marlboro had varied little over the years from the format suggested in Figure 7-9. Other indirect promotional activities for this brand included the distribution of 10.5 million copies of *Chuckwagon Cooking from Marlboro Country* and a heavy magazine promotion of the "Marlboro Country Store," offering fourteen items ranging from Chuckwagon coffee cups to sheepskin coats for sale by direct mail.

In the promotion of Virginia Slims, Philip Morris sponsored such events as an annual "Virginia Slims American Women's Opinion Poll," based on four thousand interviews by Louis Harris & Associates, and the Virginia Slims Women's Tennis Circuit, featuring matches between the top female players in the world (at rates of pay equal to the leading male players).

Similarly heavy emphasis was placed on the design of the cigarette package, even to the extent of incorporating the package into previous advertising lyrics

Figure 7-10. A recent advertisement for Honeywell computers.

At the Sign of the Cat, we're adding to their kitty.

The Cougar, the Mercury, the Comet—we're helping all parts of Ford Motor Company because we're helping Ford with their parts.

We're helping them reduce their inventories, reduce their production losses and improve the quality of the parts they buy.

At Ford Motor Company's General Products Division, Honeywell computer systems are keeping track of hundreds of parts—

those on order, those on hand, and those on the factory floor.

At the Automotive Assembly Division, other Honeywell computer systems match each part to a specific car—and handle the production scheduling, control receipts and shipments, and project future parts requirements.

Then a Honeywell communications system gives Ford Motor Company headquarters instant status reports on inventory and production.

And Ford is saving time and

money in the process. For example, at model changeover time, Ford can switch production without losing time or wasting parts.

Now you don't have to be in a big business like automobiles to profit from a Honeywell information system. You can be in banking, education, health care, distribution—almost anything.

In fact, if you have a business with things like payroll, accounts receivable and accounts payable, Honeywell can help keep your business purring.

The Other Computer Company:
Honeywell

Honeywell Information Systems (MS 061)
200 Smith Street, Waltham, Massachusetts 02154

such as "You get a lot to like with a Marlboro. Filter. Flavor. Flip-top box." George Weissman, Philip Morris' president, was quick to point out that among smokers no product is purchased more frequently than a pack of cigarettes, adding:

> And if you're an average smoker, that package comes out of your pocket twenty times a day. That means twenty times a day that package will be visible and other people will see it. So this is one of the biggest pluses going for us.[4]

(59)   What are the relative roles played by the advertising, packaging, direct selling, and other promotional programs designed by Philip Morris in marketing a product like Marlboro cigarettes?

Honeywell, Inc.

Similarly, although the major thrust of Honeywell's promotional effort was centered around sales representatives such as Kim Kelley, the company had for several years also sponsored an eye-catching advertising program featuring fierce looking animals sculptured from computer components, such as the one shown in Figure 7-10. In 1973, the company had budgeted about $1 million for award-winning advertising positioning it as "The Other Computer Company." This compared with an estimated expenditure of $48 million for sales support, including demonstrations and a multilevel selling effort, in addition to the 1 per cent commission that it had paid its sales force on a 1972 United States sales volume of $600 million.

(60)   What function could advertising such as that shown in Figure 7-10 perform in supplementing direct sales efforts for Honeywell's computers?

In spite of various types of support that his company had made available to him, Kim Kelley knew, as he approached the office of the division administrator for the secretary of state of Illinois to learn the outcome of three years of selling effort, that he represented the basic element in his company's promotional program.

Within minutes, he had been informed by a grinning Hank Malkus, division administrator, that Kelley and Honeywell had indeed won the contract. Kelley's pent-up emotions caught up with him and he cried tears of joy and relief as he was hugged by Malkus' secretary.

But the story doesn't end here. For, as you might guess, the twenty-nine-year-old Kelley was recently rewarded with a promotion to a salaried position as sales manager of an eighteen-man office, a promotion he refused initially in order to stay on commission. Instead, he negotiated a small salary as a sales manager plus the opportunity to remain on commission as a sales representative. According to Kelley, although he expects eventually to move higher in the Honeywell marketing organization, "I can't afford the pay cut."

[4]"Why Philip Morris Thrives," *Business Week* (Jan. 27, 1973), pp. 48–54. Quote on p. 54.

summary

Direct communication, largely involving personal selling, can be employed most effectively in assuring the delivery of a marketing communication to a decision maker, describing complex product features, reaching prospective customers at the time and place they use a product, obtaining merchandising effort necessary to support a promotional program, allowing for buyer-seller interaction, and inducing and influencing buyer action.

Early selling efforts emphasized the importance of social relations. In subsequent periods, primary emphasis in personal selling was placed first on the communication of product benefits (regardless of customer need) and then cookbook, or programmed, sales effort. More recently, and concurrent with more complex customer needs and product features, personal selling has come to rely to a greater extent on customer problem solving, at times employing team selling or simultaneous selling efforts at several levels in a customer's organization.

Among the many dimensions of the sales manager's job are those of serving as a two-way channel of communication between salespeople and their company's top marketing management, seeing to it that the company's marketing policies are implemented and adhered to, setting sales goals and motivating salespeople to

Table 7-3 **Factors Determining the Mix of Promotional Effort in a Marketing Strategy**

Factors	Characteristics Suggesting a Heavy Reliance on Indirect Promotion (Advertising)	Characteristics Suggesting a Heavy Reliance on Direct Promotion (Personal Selling)
Determinants of the Buying Task		
Complexity of product	Less?	More?
Economic importance of purchase to buyer	Less?	More?
Medical importance of purchase to buyer	Less?	More?
Social importance of purchase to buyer	Less?	More?
Bases on which product can be differentiated	Less?	More?
Level of buyer's knowledge, self-confidence	More?	Less?
Results of past buying efforts	Favorable?	Unfavorable?
Number and type of alternatives available to buyer	?	?
Other Factors		
Ability to pinpoint market segments	Less?	More?
Availability of efficient media	More?	Less?
Potential size of the market	Great?	Small?
Concentration of the market	Less?	More?
Size of promotional budget available	More?	Less?
Competitive practice	?	?
Willingness of channel to share burden	More?	Less?
Product life-cycle stage	Late?	Early?
Stages in the diffusion process	Late?	Early?
Consumer versus industrial goods	Consumer?	Industrial?
Stages in the selling process to an individual customer	Late?	Early?

attain them, allocating sales effort, diagnosing poor sales performance, training new salespeople, maintaining their morale and loyalty to the company, monitoring competitive activities, and perhaps assuming sales responsibility for some major accounts.

At a higher level in the marketing organization, direct promotional effort must be designed. Included among the stages of this process are the development of objectives for the effort, identification of potential accounts, establishment of salespeople's qualifications, determination of the size of the necessary sales force, allocation of sales effort, establishment of a method and expected level of compensation, development of a budget, a decision to make or buy necessary sales effort, organization of the sales force, and development and execution of programs for direct promotion.

At an even higher, more strategic, level in the planning process, the promotional strategy is formulated. This requires decisions regarding the relative emphasis to be placed on indirect and direct methods of promotion and the manner in which each might be employed in a broad strategy framework.

Various factors influencing the relative emphasis to be placed on indirect or direct promotional efforts are arrayed in Table 7-3. Although this is one means of assembling various factors discussed in this chapter, you'll note that the list is long and the incidence of question marks great. You might want to engage in the intriguing game of ''marketing theory'' by seeing how many of the question marks you would be willing to remove from the dimensions listed in Table 7-3.

The next stop on our tour of elements in a marketing strategy is the channel of distribution and one type of marketing institution in particular, the retailer.

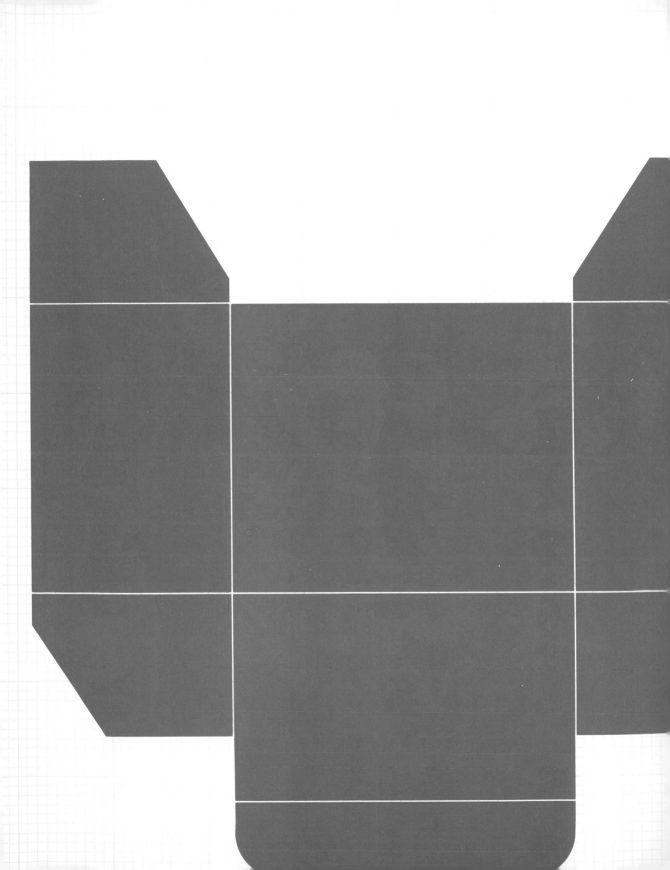

distribution: the retailer's view

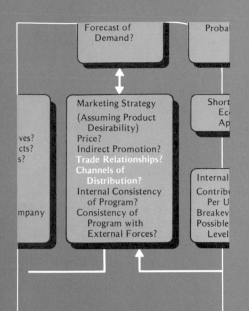

Forecast of
Demand?

Proba[

ves?
cts?
s?

Marketing Strategy
(Assuming Product
Desirability)
Price?
Indirect Promotion?
Trade Relationships?
**Channels of
Distribution?**
Internal Consistency
of Program?
Consistency of
Program with
External Forces?

Short
Ec
Ap

mpany

Internal
Contribu
Per U
Breakev
Possible
Level

Although they don't realize it, this chapter is brought to you by the merchants of Bakersfield, California and York, Pennsylvania. They'll help introduce us to concepts of retailing that relate to much of the material we will be discussing in the next three chapters concerning channels for the distribution of products and services.

One of our aims here is to find out what is important in the management of their retailing firms. Before doing that, it is helpful to see how retailers in general fit into a distribution structure that serves the needs of ultimate buyers by creating values (utilities) in goods and services that they desire. This will help us understand the basic marketing functions performed in channels of distribution and provide us with a way of describing the customer-need and supplier-response patterns that are a major concern of the following two chapters and the book in general.

So the next time you're in the vicinity of Bakersfield or York, patronize our local retailers.

thousands of miles separate Bakersfield, California and York, Pennsylvania. But these two commercial centers of about the same size provide us with an opportunity to study determinants of the retail distribution structure for several products and services.

a tale of two cities

(1)

(2) (3)

(4)
(5)
(6)

Data describing the Bakersfield and York Standard Metropolitan Statistical Areas (including population, number of families, number of selected types of retail outlets, sales for these outlets, and other data) are presented in Table 8-1. In addition to representing the basis for some sparkling dinner conversation (did you know that there is only one drugstore for every 5,500 people in Bakersfield?), the data in Table 8-1 allow us to draw some interesting comparisons about the nature of retailing within and between these two cities. For example, how do the number and average sizes of department stores, grocery stores, gasoline service stations, drugstores, appliance outlets, and liquor stores vary in Bakersfield? Is there a similar pattern for York? Are these differences more or less significant than the differences between the number and size of each of these types of retail establishments in Bakersfield and York? Why do you think these patterns emerge? Of what significance is the volume of sales for gasoline service stations, shown in Table 8-1, in the determination of these patterns? For example, how do you think these patterns might differ if gasoline sales per capita were one fourth their current level?

the nature of the distribution system

Products were made available in 1967 in the quantities shown in Table 8-1 for Bakersfield and York as the result of a complex system of distribution channels encompassing producers of basic materials and services, manufacturers, wholesalers, retailers, customers, ultimate consumers, and others. The complexity of products and product assortments prohibits all but a few products from moving directly from the manufacturer to the end consumer, for example. A number of transactions between distribution channel "members" are required to accomplish the transformation, not only of raw materials into finished products but also of single products into product assortments assembled for the convenience of buyers.

259

Table 8-1 Tale of Two Cities: Selected Census Information about Bakersfield, California and York, Pennsylvania*

	Bakersfield, Cal.[a]	York, Pa.[a]
Rank in Size Among U. S. SMSAs	91	90
Population in SMSA	329,162	329,540
Land area of SMSA (in square miles)	8,152	1,435
Proportion of total population		
central city	21.0%	15.3%
other urban areas	59.3	35.0
places with 1,000–2,500 in population	4.4	6.4
other rural areas	15.3	43.4
Total	100.0%	100.0%
Number of families	83,503	87,457
Average size of family (persons)	3.60	3.46
Average income per family	$9,946	$11,206
Proportion of families receiving public-assistance income	10.3%	3.0%
Proportion of families lacking some or all plumbing facilities	1.4%	5.5%
Proportion of families earning less than 75% of poverty level	7.8%	3.4%

Retail Trade	Number of Establishments	Sales (000s)	Number of Establishments	Sales (000s)
All establishments	3,118	$542,176	3,040	$500,730
Building material and supply stores	57	13,593	77	14,591
Hardware stores	31	2,446	28	2,421
Farm equipment dealers	38	22,810	40	9,456
Department stores	9	51,878	15	48,457
Variety stores	46	8,402	26	10,285
Miscellaneous general merchandise stores	35	5,080	67	10,121
Grocery stores	302	112,888	326	94,494
New and used car auto dealers	73	79,835	167	79,385
Tire, battery, and accessories dealers	104	10,768	50	8,051
Gasoline service stations	486	55,570	339	34,644
Women's apparel and accessory stores (total)	177	19,390	196	21,481
Furniture stores	63	9,918	72	11,021
Home furnishing stores	32	2,457	36	2,368
Household appliance stores	27	3,275	41	7,450
Radio, TV, and music stores	47	6,892	52	6,530
Eating places	467	34,633	378	24,517
Drinking places	195	9,572	156	9,285
Drug stores	60	20,715	69	11,700
Liquor stores	95	15,846	26	7,636
Antique (and secondhand furniture) stores	74	1,902	97	2,399
Sporting goods stores	21	2,442	35	2,127
Jewelry stores	41	3,613	42	2,839
Fuel and ice dealers	20	2,064	50	9,430
Florists	29	1,644	40	2,165
Cigar stores and stands	7	504	17	586

Table 8-1 **(Continued)**

	Bakersfield, Cal.[a]	York, Pa.[a]
Proportions of population 5 years old and older		
Living in same house as 5 years earlier (1965)	45.3%	61.7%
Living in different house, same county as 5 years earlier	26.0%	22.4%
Living in different county than 5 years earlier	19.5%	10.4%
Living in different state than 5 years earlier	7.8%	5.3%
Living in different country than 5 years earlier	1.5%	.5%
Number of workers	111,129	137,305
Proportion of workers getting to work by		
private auto, as driver	80.8%	71.5%
private auto, as rider	8.0%	13.2%
Proportion of males 16 and over included in labor force	75.6%	81.0%
Proportion of females 16 and over included in labor force	36.4%	44.8%
Proportion of labor force in professional, technical, and kindred work	14.6%	11.0%
Proportion of labor force in farm and nonfarm labor, service work, and private household work	27.4%	15.7%

* Sources: *1970 Census of Population* and *1967 Census of Business* (Washington, D. C.: Bureau of the Census, Department of Commerce, 1973 and 1971, respectively).

[a] All information is for calendar 1970 except that describing retailing activity, which is for calendar 1967.

product and service flows

This transformation of raw materials and service components into goods and services can be pictured in the form of flows of ownership of products and services from such basic sources as agriculture, the extractive industries (mining and fishing), and public utility and other service industries to individual households. Such flows for the entire economy of the United States for one year are shown in Figure 8-1.

Now before writing Figure 8-1 off as an academician's nightmare, invest just five minutes in reviewing it. It will be well worth your while in terms of the over-all picture of the distribution system and the understanding of Chapters 8, 9, and 10 that it may provide.

In reviewing Figure 8-1, note that the width of each line represents the volume of transactions between groups of buyers and sellers. Furthermore, purchases are diagrammed as lines entering each block (representing groups of buyers and sellers) from the left. Sales are diagrammed as lines leaving each block at the right. The numbers beside each line represent sales, in billions of

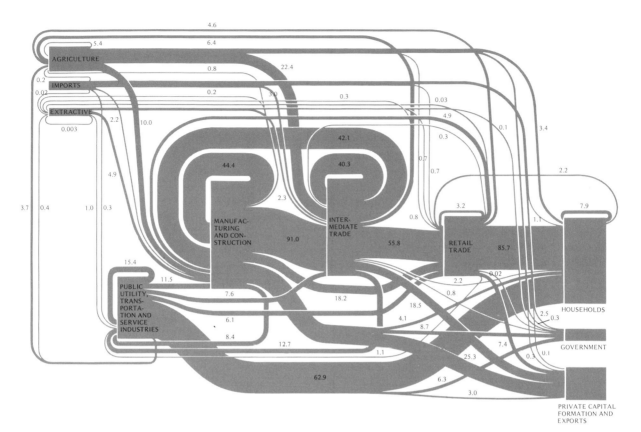

Figure 8-1. The flow of ownership for the United States economy in 1947. Figures shown are the dollar values, in billions, of all of the purchase and sale transactions involving goods and services. Purchases enter each block at the left; sales emerge at the right. The total of purchases and sales shown here is $676 billion. Source: Reavis Cox, Charles S. Goodman, and Thomas Fichandler, *Distribution in a High Level Economy* (Englewood Cliffs, N.J.: Prentice-Hall, 1965), cover leaf.

dollars. For example, to test your understanding of Figure 8-1, what was the volume of sales by agricultural institutions to manufacturing and construction firms? Did you identify it as $10 billion? Similarly, purchases and sales for the entire economy can be identified.

channels of distribution

At the center of Figure 8-1 are the traditionally regarded flow patterns for manufactured goods. They can be diagrammed in abstract form as shown in Figure 8-2. More often, the means by which such products or services move from original producers to final buyers, such as households, are called channels of distribution. It's the purpose of this and the next two chapters to examine the

(7) (8)

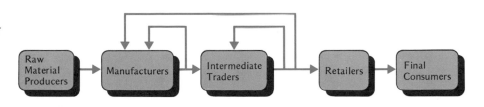

Figure 8-2. Important channels of distribution for manufactured goods.

strategies used by major participants in such channels—ultimate consumers, retailers, wholesalers, and manufacturers—in dealing with one another.

Look once again at Figure 8-1. Notice the flows of ownership to end users (households and the government, in particular) for the output of manufacturing and construction firms on the one hand and public utility, transportation, and service industries on the other. Basically, how do they differ? Why do you think this is the case? It may help explain why most of our examples in this and the next two chapters dealing with distribution channels and the firms of which they are composed will feature channel strategies for products rather than services.

Another fact of interest in Figure 8-1 is emphasized by its creators:

> for every dollar of value [final sales to final buyers in Figure 8-1] delivered by the economy there were three dollars of buying and selling—one in the final sale and two in the earlier stages of these complex flows. . . . [this] should not be taken as indicating the relative importance of the costs involved in getting goods through any category of buyers or sellers. Nevertheless the 2-to-1 ratio has some utility as indicating the mass, scope, and complexity of the intermediate trading that lies behind retail operations.[1]

The ratio of total sales in channels of distribution to sales to final buyers, cited here, suggests that goods and services are bought and sold several times during their journey from original producers to final buyers. Why is this the case? Is it just a scheme to cut parties to these transactions in on overly large profits? Or is it a means of creating value in goods? An understanding of the rationale for frequent channel transactions requires that we review the nature of functions that must be performed by one or more organizations in a channel of distribution. These traditionally have been referred to as marketing functions, although the components of the list vary from one author to another.

marketing functions performed in channels of distribution

Marketing functions performed in channels of distribution can be grouped as those that are necessary to a transaction, those that are required for the physical exchange of goods, and those that facilitate both the transaction and the physical exchange. In short, these groupings can be termed *transactional,*

[1] Reavis Cox, Charles S. Goodman, and Thomas C. Fichandler, *Distribution in a High-Level Economy* (Englewood Cliffs, N. J.: Prentice-Hall, 1965), p. 40.

263

logistical, and *facilitating functions.* In order to provide a context for our discussion, let's assume we are shoppers in a supermarket. What functions are being performed and who performs them?

Transactional Functions. Transactional functions include buying, selling, and risk assumption. The supermarket chain sells, and as consumers we buy, a wide range of products. Without the mutual willingness to buy and sell, there would be no transaction. But when we buy anything we must perform another function essential to a transaction. We must be willing to assume the risk of ownership. Even if that risk is nothing more than the chance that the oatmeal cookies we purchased will become stale over time and have to be thrown out because our family consumes them at a slower rate than we anticipated.

Logistical Functions. Logistical functions encompass assembly (assorting), storage, sorting, and transportation. More than any others, logistical functions help explain the existence of the so-called middlemen in a channel of distribution. At certain points in the channel, goods have to be assembled in sufficient quantity to constitute an efficient selling and shipping quantity. For example, in the process of transforming wheat into the bread purchased at the supermarket, grain elevators located in wheat producing areas assemble the production of individual farms into sufficient quantities for economical shipment in rail carload quantities to processors. Similarly, a central distribution warehouse maintained by a supermarket chain will assemble items ordered by individual stores into single truckload quantities which are much less expensive to deliver than a number of separately shipped items.

Just as goods are assembled to achieve economical quantities for shipping and other purposes, they may be gathered together to provide an assortment of items desired by buyers. This is the nature of the assorting function.

As a means of focusing on the importance of the assembly and assorting functions, consider the nature of the channel of distribution that brings to the Bakersfield consumer an assortment of grocery items offered by our supermarket. We know from our discussion in Chapter 4 that a typical supermarket offered, as of 1972, 7,900 items. These might be obtained from as many as 1,000 suppliers. Based on information in Table 8-1, we see that there is an average of 1,090 people (a population of 329,162 divided by 302 grocery stores) and perhaps 303 families of average size (3.60 persons) served by each grocery store in Bakersfield. If, as we see in Figure 8-3, each of the 303 families purchased items directly from each of the supermarket's suppliers, this would require 303,000 transactions (1,000 $\times$ 303). However, with just 1,000 transactions between the supermarket and its suppliers, and another 303 transactions between the supermarket and its customers, we can accomplish the same complex job of distribution at a fraction of the cost with a little left over for supermarket operating expenses and profits.

It might be argued that this example is dramatic, but irrelevant. After all, on a typical trip to a supermarket, a consumer may purchase no more than ten items supplied by perhaps seven or eight different suppliers. What do you think of this argument? Would it apply equally to (1) the consumer who carefully decides the items and brands to be purchased before leaving for the supermarket and who does not deviate from the plan and (2) a consumer who makes no such plans,

Figure 8-3. Transactions required in the channel of distribution for grocery products sold in Bakersfield, California with and without grocery retailers.

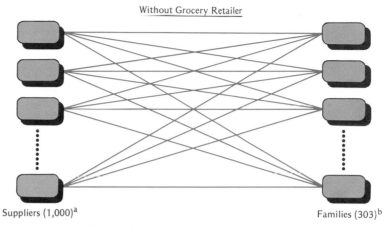

Without Grocery Retailer

Suppliers (1,000)[a]

Families (303)[b]

Total number of transactions:

Supplier–family (1,000 × 303) = <u>303,000</u>

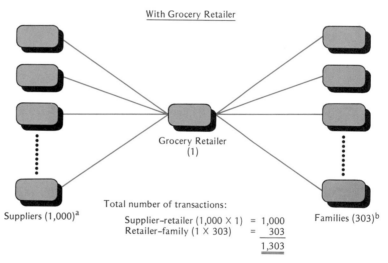

With Grocery Retailer

Grocery Retailer
(1)

Suppliers (1,000)[a]

Families (303)[b]

Total number of transactions:

Supplier–retailer (1,000 × 1) = 1,000
Retailer–family (1 × 303)   =   303
                              <u>1,303</u>

[a] Assumed to be the number to supply the typical grocery retailer.

[b] Computed as the average number of families per grocery retailer in Bakersfield from information in Table 8-1:

$$\left(\frac{329{,}162 \text{ people}}{302 \text{ grocery stores}} \text{ divided by } 3.60 \text{ persons per family} = 303 \right).$$

but who relies on decisions made while viewing products from the supermarket aisles?

Storage makes goods available at that *point in time* at which they are desired by buyers. Transportation similarly makes goods available at the *place* at which they are desired by buyers. Without product availability, in terms of both the time and place desired by a buyer, many transactions would not otherwise take place. As shown in Table 8-2, supermarket shoppers don't usually postpone a

265

Table 8-2 **Customers' Behavior when Confronted with a Product Stockout at a Supermarket**[a]

	Per Cent of Customers Who Would														
Product	Buy Elsewhere[b]					Switch Brands[b]					Buy Later at Same Store[b]				
	#1	#2	#3	#4	#5	#1	#2	#3	#4	#5	#1	#2	#3	#4	#5
Margarine	17%	18%	26%	36%	17%	58%	46%	66%	27%	52%	25%	36%	10%	45%	33%
Cigarettes	75	82	81	83	80	10	4	17	17	5	15	14	2	8	15
Gelatin	13	11	27	10	21	61	50	60	40	49	26	42	13	60	32
Liquid starch	6	9	27	11	28	50	39	54	44	53	44	52	19	56	19
Hand soap	30	21	33	45	30	43	43	53	36	49	26	36	15	27	23
Toothpaste	39	36	63	60	43	52	40	28	30	36	9	24	10	20	21
Cereal	30	28	28	20	24	61	59	58	30	57	9	17	15	60	20
Dog food	61	62	39	25	41	39	38	50	50	44	0	0	11	50	19
Baby food	40	60	48	20	59	40	33	46	40	33	20	7	9	60	7
Deodorant	59	54	67	56	58	36	19	25	33	26	5	27	10	22	16
Shampoo	61	54	66	67	57	26	21	27	33	23	13	25	8	17	20
Regular coffee	46	48	36	27	36	32	28	57	18	33	23	28	6	64	33
Catsup	30	7	26	40	19	57	59	67	40	63	13	35	8	30	19
Mayonnaise	52	7	39	22	27	26	55	51	22	59	22	41	13	67	14
Instant coffee	33	14	44	11	29	52	36	53	33	50	14	55	4	67	23
Canned tuna	30	19	22	9	18	52	56	67	46	53	17	26	12	55	29
Canned peaches	9	10	11	9	18	73	52	81	36	55	18	38	8	64	27
Peanut butter	17	18	26	20	27	67	46	61	50	58	17	36	14	40	18
Jam	9	21	15	36	21	77	48	77	27	64	14	31	8	46	16
Tomato juice	27	15	17	11	17	68	56	76	44	66	5	30	7	56	17
Toilet tissue	26	28	24	25	22	65	52	63	33	61	9	21	13	50	18
Facial tissue	22	19	19	0	19	70	52	67	33	64	9	30	14	78	19
Aluminum foil	17	18	13	33	15	78	46	80	33	68	4	36	8	44	19
Salad oil	26	11	24	38	20	57	50	67	38	62	17	39	10	38	20
Solid shortening	13	12	27	18	20	65	35	65	50	56	22	54	8	46	27
Canned soup	32	14	33	25	25	46	45	51	33	50	23	41	17	50	25
Canned milk	20	14	15	30	13	70	43	77	30	68	10	43	8	50	20
Canned corn	27	7	18	9	19	55	65	73	55	57	18	31	10	46	24
Canned green beans	18	11	17	29	19	64	61	78	57	57	18	32	6	29	24
Laundry detergents	46	36	51	50	52	38	29	43	30	23	17	43	9	30	27
Waxed paper	13	12	13	20	14	78	65	74	40	73	9	23	13	50	14

* Source: *Progressive Grocer: The Magazine of Super Marketing* (Oct. 1968).

[a] Out-of-stock, a big problem to supermarket operators, is also a big factor in the minds of consumers when selecting a favorite store. In answer to a question about how they would react to an out-of-stock situation on their favorite brands of 31 types of grocery products, they show some interesting unanimity of opinion. A dominant percentage of customers in all neighborhoods say they will go to another store to buy their favorite brands of cigarettes, coffee, deodorant, dog food, laundry detergent, and shampoo. High-income shoppers and Negroes show strong brand loyalty to toothpaste. Young marrieds and small-town customers will go out of their way to get their favorite brands of baby foods.

In nearly all but the few categories mentioned above, better than half the customers in all neighborhoods say their reaction to an out-of-stock situation on their favorite brand would be to choose a substitute.

The percentages sometimes add up to more than 100 per cent due to the fact that some respondents checked "buy elsewhere" and "buy later at the same store," indicating that they would do one or the other but will not switch brands.

[b] Key to store neighborhood numbers: #1 = young married, #2 = blue collar, #3 = high income, #4 = Negro, #5 = small town.

(11)
(12)

purchase because of the nonavailability of the goods they had planned to buy on entering the store. They often substitute competing brands or other products. Would this be of greater concern to a supermarket operator or his manufacturer-supplier? To a manufacturer of tooth paste or liquid starch (based on information in Table 8-2)?

The failure of storage and transportation to make goods available at the time and place they are desired can produce a combination of disappointed customers and reduced sales for suppliers. Disappointed customers willing to try alternative products or brands under such conditions become potential new, regular customers for competing suppliers.

Facilitating Functions. Facilitating functions include postpurchase service and maintenance, financing, information dissemination, and channel coordination or leadership. Mechanically complex products ranging from small appliances to automobiles may require installation or periodic maintenance. For buyers of such products, the availability and proximity of high-quality postpurchase services may be the most important determinant of their buying decision. Several foreign automobile manufacturers who were unable to build an effective service network in the United States discovered this to their great dismay.

In addition to being willing to assume the risk of owning a product, the buyer must be able to finance his or her ownership. Whether it's oatmeal cookies or a $10,000 automobile, for example, a purchase by a consumer represents a commitment of funds that might otherwise be used for other purposes, including interest-earning savings. Assuming that they are not free goods, the ownership of products requires financing. Any potential home buyer who has had a loan request refused at the bank knows that financing facilitates transactions.

Information dissemination, by facilitating planning and management decision making within a channel of distribution, can improve the performance of a channel, measured in terms of the degree to which the needs of buyers, sellers, and other parties to the channel are met. For example, the more rapidly the supermarket communicates information about the quantity and type of products it has sold, the more opportunity a supplier may have to respond to the supermarket's need for product replenishment. This, in turn, can reduce the out-of-stock situations that frustrate the transactional process. Similarly, longer-term buying trends, shifts in the share of the market held by competitors, and seasonal purchasing patterns can be measured and communicated by retailers, wholesalers, manufacturers, and specialists in marketing research to other channel members.

Finally, coordination may be required to organize channel members to help themselves and perhaps to develop and distribute systematically information and knowledge about management techniques designed to help channel members improve their performance. Typically, a large firm with an unusually high stake in the success or failure of an important channel of distribution in which it operates may have a great deal to gain by assuming responsibility for the coordination and leadership needed to facilitate the more effective performance of other channel members and functions.

Marketing functions performed at each of several stages in the distribution of products sold by supermarkets are arrayed in Figure 8-4. As you see there, the ultimate consumer, as a participant in the channel of distribution, is primarily responsible for performing certain marketing functions. Do you agree with the assessment of who performs which functions at each of the channel stages shown in Figure 8-4? If you were to construct a similar assessment for the channel of distribution for haircuts, substituting a barber shop for the supermarket shown in Figure 8-4, how would it look?

(13)

(14)

Figure 8-4. The performance of marketing functions in a channel of distribution for certain products sold through supermarkets.

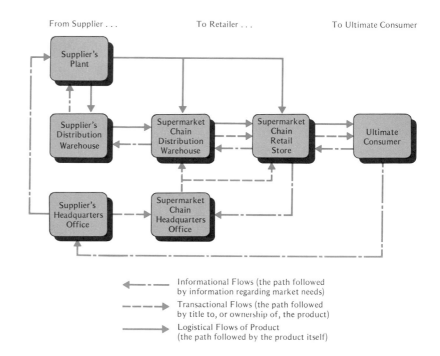

Functions:	Functions Performed By:			
	Supplier	Retailer's Warehouse	Retailer's Store	Ultimate Consumer
Transactional				
Selling	X		X	
Buying		X	X	X
Risk assumption	X	X	X	X
Logistical				
Assembly (assorting)	X	X	X	X
Storage	X	X	X	X
Sorting		X	X	X
Transportation	X	X		X
Facilitating				
Post-purchase				
service & maintenance				
Financing	X	X		
Information dissemination	X	X	X	
Coordination		X	X	

268

the creation of value—product utility

(15)
As a resident of Bakersfield, which experiences a rainy season confined to the months of January through March, would an umbrella be of more value to you
(16)
in Bakersfield in August or February? Would it be of value to you if it were
(17)
available in February in York, Pennsylvania instead of Bakersfield? If you owned
(18)
it instead of your neighbor on a rainy morning in February? If it were pink with yellow polka dots, instead of black, and you were preparing to go into the rain to lunch with an important business client?

These four questions illustrate the four important dimensions of product value, or types of *utilities,* as they are referred to by economists. They include time, place, ownership, and form utility.

For example, we say that time utility is created when umbrellas are made available in Bakersfield when they are needed—in February as opposed to August. Of course, for these purposes, availability in August would be more desirable than availability in April. The fact that you probably would be willing to pay more for a given type of umbrella on a rainy morning in February than on a sunny one in August is a reflection of the value of the services that make the product available when you want it. Thus, marketing activities, if performed effectively, are said to result in added value, not just added costs, for products and services.

(19)
To what extent are marketing activities as opposed to production activities
(20)
responsible for each of these types of utilities? Which of the marketing functions shown in Figure 8-4 would you associate with each of the utilities mentioned here?

determinants of retail distribution strategy

Customer needs, as in other aspects of marketing, are the primary determinants of retail distribution strategy. These can be grouped into transactional, logistical, and post purchase service needs. They influence the way in which consumers view products and services as well as retail outlets. This, in turn, may shape other aspects of retail distribution strategy.

customer needs

Although you might want to add to this list, important transactional needs concern matters such as price and assistance, information, and perhaps trial during the purchase process. Logistical needs concern the proximity of retail outlets, the availability of a variety of merchandise that they are expected to stock, and the delivery of merchandise to the point of use.

Postpurchase service needs may involve matters such as installation, continuing product maintenance, ease of replenishment, financing, and certain types of postpurchase information that may reinforce the confidence of the buyer that he or she has made a good decision.

(21)　　How would you relate each of the needs outlined here to the marketing functions listed in Figure 8-4 on page 268?

(22)　　Customer needs may help explain the amount of effort that consumers invest in the purchase of a product or service. For example, how much effort are you willing to expend in buying a tube of tooth paste as opposed to a new dining room table? Answers to these questions may explain further retail distribution strategies.

the consumer's view of products or services

A number of years ago, a pioneering marketing scholar, Melvin T. Copeland, developed a classification system of so-called consumer goods, goods bought by individuals for their ultimate consumption.[2] This system employed three categories: convenience, shopping, and specialty goods. Despite dispute and elaboration,[3] this method of categorization has survived. For our purposes, the following headings serve as useful descriptions of each category.

(23)　*Convenience Goods.*　Convenience goods are those for which a consumer is willing to expend little effort in their purchase, perhaps substituting brands rather than making the additional effort required to buy a particular item or brand. Thus, if a manufacturer of convenience goods wants to avoid the loss of potential sales, what retail strategy must it adopt concerning the location,

(24)　number, and stock levels of the retailers handling its product? Based on the information in Table 8-2, which products appear to fit the description?

Shopping Goods.　Shopping goods are those for which the consumer has developed no strong preferences, requiring the initiation of a search to obtain information and develop preferences.

Specialty Goods.　Specialty goods are those for which a consumer is willing to expend the effort required to purchase a most preferred item rather than to buy a more readily accessible substitute.

(25)
(26)　　Where would you place the tube of tooth paste and the dining room table, mentioned previously, among the categories of consumer goods? Can this
(27)　categorization be used for services as well as products? For example, where would you place a shampoo and manicure, a major furnace repair job, and a car wash in these categories?

　　The amount of effort that a consumer is willing to expend in purchasing a product or service may have some bearing on the number and proximity to
(28)　consumers of retail outlets selling certain products or brands. Looking back

---

[2]Melvin T. Copeland, "Relation of Consumers' Buying Habits to Marketing Methods," *Harvard Business Review,* **1** (April 1923), pp. 282–289.

[3]Among the most constructive elaborations on Copeland's classification is that of Louis P. Bucklin, "Retail Strategy and the Classification of Consumer Goods," *Journal of Marketing,* **27** (Jan. 1963), 51–56. Descriptions of the categories that follow are based on those set forth by Bucklin.

(29)
(30)
(31)
again to Table 8-1, on page 260, which types of retail establishments do you think would be most likely to sell predominantly convenience goods? Shopping goods? Specialty goods? Now compare the number of outlets predominantly selling each type of good, in your opinion, in Bakersfield or York. What is the relationship, if any, between the number of outlets and the type of goods sold?

(32)
Determinants of a Product's Categorization. Why are consumers willing to expend more effort purchasing some kinds of goods than others? For example, how would you expect convenience, shopping, and specialty goods to differ in terms of price? In terms of the amount of additional knowledge that the consumer is likely to require in advance of a purchase? In terms of the level of risk perceived in making the purchase? In terms of the frequency with which each type of product typically is purchased? In terms of a product's position on the product life cycle shown in Figure 4-5 on page 124?

(33)
(34)
(35)
(36)

(37)
There may be other determinants of the way in which consumers view and purchase goods. For example, how would you categorize a $15 portable radio if you were a teen-ager working part-time for $5 per week and making your first major purchase with your own money? Would your answer be the same if you were the head of the household earning $80,000 per year, and the family's only portable radio was found to have a faulty transistor on the morning of an outing to the beach? This perhaps suggests the elusive nature of the concept.

(38)

the consumer's view of retail outlets

The things consumers need and expect from retail outlets might include a broad assortment from which to choose; the ability to buy "on terms," using credit extended by the retailer, his financing agency, or a credit card organization; the availability of a money-back guarantee on unsatisfactory purchases; the ease with which shopping can be accomplished (especially the availability of convenient parking); a location convenient to the consumer's home or work place; goods or services in a certain price category; enjoyment, perhaps provided by a store's atmosphere; highly knowledgeable salesclerks; or impressive store "image," perhaps to impress friends or reinforce the "rightness" and reduce the perceived risk of a potentially questionable purchase.

Categorization of Retail Outlets. The importance of each of the preceding needs and a store's ability to meet them may determine the way in which a consumer views a store as well as a product. Thus, a store at which a consumer buys goods primarily because the store is most accessible can be termed a *convenience store*. A *shopping store* may be one for which the consumer has not yet developed a preference, requiring a search and comparison of alternative retail outlets. Finally, a *specialty store* may be one from which a consumer is willing to buy without surveying alternative outlets, even though it is not the most accessible.

The Product-Store Patronage Matrix. Consumers' views of products and retail outlets can be combined, as suggested by Bucklin, into the type of

Table 8-3   The Product-Store Patronage Matrix for Consumer Goods*

Consumers' Perceptions of Products	Consumers' Perceptions of Stores		
	Convenience Store	Shopping Store	Specialty Store
Convenience Product	Consumer buys most readily available brand of product at most accessible store	Consumer is indifferent to brand of product but shops among stores	Consumer prefers to trade at a particular store but is indifferent to the brand of product purchased
Shopping Product	Consumer buys from among the assortment carried by the most accessible store	Consumer makes comparisons among both products and stores by shopping	Consumer prefers to trade at a certain store but is uncertain about product to buy before examining the store's assortment
Specialty Product	Consumer buys favored brand from the most accessible store that has the item in stock	Consumer has strong brand preference but shops among stores to satisfy other needs associated with his or her purchase	Consumer has both a preference for a particular store and a specific brand

* Source: Based on Louis P. Bucklin, "Retail Strategy and the Classification of Consumer Goods," *Journal of Marketing,* **27** (Jan. 1963) pp. 51–56. See p. 55.

(39)

product-store patronage matrix shown in Table 8-3.[4] Can you identify buying experiences (by product brand and retail store name) that you have had recently that meet, for you at least, the specifications in each cell of the matrix in Table 8-3?

This concept of product-store relationships will be useful to us when we return later to the consideration of specific retailing strategies.

consumers' needs and retail location

Some retailing executives maintain that the first three factors in the success of retail stores are location, location, and location.

Earlier, we related the number of retail outlets of various types in Bakersfield and York to the nature of the products that each sold and the consumer's willingness to expend effort to buy a product from a particular retail outlet. This

[4] Ibid., p. 55.

is no small matter, considering the fact that one study found that a family of four in the course of the year 1954 probably made 1,700 purchases from just nineteen lines of retail trade for which estimates were possible.[5] In order to accomplish this chore, did someone make 1,700 different trips to buy for our average family? Although up to now, our discussion implicitly has assumed this, clearly it wasn't the case. To reduce the task of buying, as consumers we cluster our purchases. This has given birth, for example, to the slogan, "one-stop shopping."

The clustering of purchases is of great importance for the location of retailing activities. It suggests that stores cannot be located only with regard to consumer work and living places. The location decision must take into account the relative locations not only of actual or potential competitors, but also of stores that, in the lines of products they carry, complement each other. It helps to explain why city centers, and more recently shopping centers, have been important concentrations of retailing activities. It helps to explain why people crowd into concentrations of retailing outlets knowing that they will encounter traffic congestion and perhaps personal discomfort. As stated by Cox in the form of a "Principle of Efficient Congestion":

congestion means contacts, and contacts are what people seek when they crowd into the city in the first place.[6]

And the tendency of consumers to cluster purchases also helps explain why already crowded locations, even those containing competing retail outlets, may be attractive for a new store location. Because stores build consumer "traffic" for one another if they are located in close proximity, they can contribute to each other's profitability. Regional scientists call this phenomenon agglomeration. Retailers call it good business. According to Robert Brooker, the former chief executive officer of Montgomery Ward, one of the largest mass merchandising organizations in the United States at the time:

We like to go into a [shopping] center with two other strong [mass merchandising] stores, even when they are as competitive with us as Sears and Penney are. The traffic we can draw together is worth more than the business we take from each other.[7]

The clustering of purchases may obscure theories regarding consumer behavior in the purchase of various types of goods from various retail outlets. For example, convenience goods may be purchased from a convenience store on the same buying trip that specialty goods are purchased from a specialty store. This may require us to base our judgments on the way in which consumers perceive products and stores on the amount of incremental effort they are willing to put forth to buy a product or visit a store.

[5] Reavis Cox, "Consumer Convenience and the Retail Structure of Cities," *Journal of Marketing,* **23** (April 1959), pp. 355–362. See p. 359.

[6] Ibid., p. 362.

[7] John McDonald, "The Strategy That Saved Montgomery Ward," *Fortune* (May 1970), pp. 168–172 ff. Quote on 234.

retailing as a business

Theory is one thing; practice is another. We need to find out more about what retailing is really like, and how managers develop strategies for successful retail businesses.

structure

(40)
Our first stop is an examination of the relative importance and trends in the importance of various types of retail outlets presented in Table 8-4. Looking at Table 8-4, which segments of the industry have the highest and lowest growth
(41)
rates? Based on our discussion of information in Table 3-4 on page 75, are you
(42)
surprised that food stores have a relatively low growth rate? And why, in a period of rising incomes and increasing wealth, do consumers appear to have turned to discount department stores for a rapidly increasing share of their purchases?

The relative sizes and rates of growth are shown also for selected services in Table 8-4. This list excludes the many services to ultimate users or consumers, such as telephone service and various utilities, that are not sold through typical retail places of business.

organization of effort

The organization of effort in a typical retailing organization is illustrated by the organization chart shown in Figure 8-5. Several characteristics distinguish it from a similar chart for a typical industrial firm. First, there is no need for a production manager, although some retailing organizations producing their own merchandise do have such managers. Secondly, is there a great emphasis on merchandising, suggested not only by the organizational position of the function, but also by the fact that merchandising typically is regarded as the most important training ground for a store's and a retail chain's top management positions.

(43)
How do you relate each of the tasks shown in Figure 8-5 to the basic marketing functions listed in Figure 8-4?

At the level of the individual store, merchandising managers may be assigned by major department groupings, such as jewelry, cosmetics, men's clothing, and so on (hence, the name department store for outlets offering complete lines of men's, women's, household, automotive, and sporting furnishings). Many of these department merchandise managers may report directly to the store manager, depending on the nature of the store's merchandise. For example, in a typical supermarket, separate managers of the produce, meat, delicatessen, and grocery departments all report to the manager or his or her assistant. Thus, a good portion of a store's as well as a retailing organization's effort is devoted to the merchandising effort.

274

| | Retail Sales (in billions of dollars) | | | | |
| | 1963 | | 1969[a] | | Compound Annual Growth Rate, 1963–1969 (in %) |
	Sales All Products	%	Sales	%	
Food stores	$ 59.1	24.0	$ 75.9	21.7	3.8
General merchandise stores					
Conventional department stores	13.9	5.6	21.9	6.0	4.8
Discount department stores	6.2	2.5	20.6	5.9	28.8
Variety stores	4.1	1.7	4.7	1.3	2.5
Mail-order houses (with department store merchandise)	2.0	.8	3.5	1.0	7.4
All other	2.7	1.1	3.3	.9	1.8
Total	28.9	11.7	53.1	15.1	8.5
Nonstore retailers (general merchandise only)	n.a.	n.a.	5.5	1.6	n.a.
Apparel stores	14.5	5.9	20.2	5.7	4.4
Furniture and appliance stores	11.6	4.7	16.7	4.7	4.5
Lumber and building materials stores	15.5	6.3	19.3	5.5	3.0
Passenger car dealers	43.2	17.6	62.0	17.7	6.3
TBA (tires, battery, and accessory) dealers	2.8	1.1	4.7	1.3	6.7
Gasoline service stations	19.4	7.9	25.1	7.1	4.3
Drug and proprietary stores	8.2	3.3	11.7	3.3	5.3
Bars and restaurants	18.1	7.3	25.8	7.3	5.2
Liquor stores	5.7	2.3	7.4	2.1	4.8
All others	19.4	7.9	24.2	6.9	3.8
Total, products	$246.4	100.0	$351.6	100.0	5.2
Selected services					
Hotels, motels, tourist camps	$ 5.1	11.4	$ 8.3	11.7	8.6
Personal services	9.2	20.3	13.4	18.9	6.4
Miscellaneous business services	15.2	34.2	27.6	39.0	10.4
Auto repair, auto services, garages	5.4	12.1	8.0	11.3	6.6
Miscellaneous repair services	3.0	6.7	4.3	6.1	6.1
Motion pictures	2.6	5.8	4.0	5.6	7.7
Amusement and recreation services except motion pictures	4.0	9.0	5.3	7.5	4.9
Total, selected services	$ 44.5	100.0	$ 70.9	100.0	8.0

* Sources: *1963 Census of Business* (Washington, D. C.: Bureau of the Census, Department of Commerce, 1967) for the 1963 retail sales, and The Center for Advanced Studies in Distribution, Columbus, Ohio, for 1969 sales estimates.

[a] To arrive at these figures, compound annual growth rates documented by the 1963 and 1967 *Census of Business* were applied to 1967 sales for each type of outlet.

alternative profit models

Every business should have a profit model, a plan suggesting the manner in which it hopes to succeed. As suggested by Table 8-5, there are as many paths to profit as there are types of retail businesses. Here we have fiscal 1971 operating figures for three different types of retailing operations: (1) the Zayre Corp., which operates primarily discount department stores, (2) Federated Department

Figure 8-5. A typical organization chart for a retailing organization.

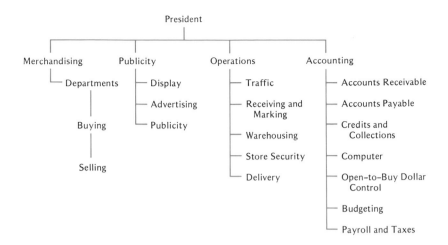

Table 8-5 **Profit Models for Three Leading Retailing Organizations, Fiscal Year, 1971***

	Zayre Corp.[a]	Federated Department Stores, Inc.[b]	Safeway Stores, Inc.[c]
Ratio of $\frac{\text{net sales}}{\text{total assets}}$	2.52	1.84	5.57
× Ratio of $\frac{\text{net profits}}{\text{net sales}}$	×1.25%	×4.08%	×1.49%
= Ratio of $\frac{\text{net profits}}{\text{total assets}}$	= 3.16%	= 7.51%	= 8.31%
× Ratio of $\frac{\text{total assets}}{\text{net worth}}$	×3.59	×1.60	×1.76
= Ratio of $\frac{\text{net profits}}{\text{net worth}}$	= 11.32%	= 12.00%	= 14.68%
Annual inventory turnover rate[d]	4.49	6.76	11.30
Net margin realized on goods sold[e]	21.5%	26.6%	22.2%

* Source: Based on information in *Moody's Industrial Manual* (New York: Moody's Investers Service, Inc., 1973).

[a] For the year ending January 29, 1972, Zayre Corp. operated 204 self-service discount department stores and various lesser numbers of apparel specialty stores, fabric shops, discount toy stores, promotional ladies apparel stores, and gasoline stations, and realized net sales of $797,550,000.

[b] For the year ending January 29, 1972, Federated Department Stores, Inc. operated 113 department stores, 23 discount department stores, and 68 supermarkets, with the former representing by far the greatest share of the business, and realized net sales of $2,353,095,000.

[c] For the year ending January 1, 1972, Safeway Stores, Inc. operated 2,291 grocery supermarkets and realized net sales of $5,358,836,000.

[d] Computed as the ratio of the cost of goods sold to the average inventory on hand (computed as half of the sum of year-ending inventories for 1970 and 1971).

[e] Computed as follows: net sales − cost of goods sold divided by net sales.

Stores, Inc., the largest United States operator primarily of full-line, full-service department stores, and (3) Safeway Stores, Inc., the largest in sales volume among supermarket chains in the United States.

To understand the operating ratios arrayed in the so-called profit model in Table 8-5, consider only the figures for the Zayre Corp. First, we see that Zayre's net sales were 2.52 times its total assets (all of the money invested by stockholders and lenders alike in its real estate, stores, fixtures, merchandise, and transportation equipment). Secondly, Zayre realized net profits on sales of 1.25 per cent, or 1.25 cents on every dollar of sales. This produced net profits to total assets of 2.52 × 1.25 per cent, or 3.16 per cent. Zayre's owners contributed a relatively small amount of the total money invested in the company's real estate, stores, fixtures, merchandise, and transportation equipment. All the money invested was 3.59 times the amount contributed by the company's owners. This high rate of "leverage," when multiplied by the amount of net profits to total assets, produced a return on the owners' investment (net worth, exclusive of borrowed money) of 11.32 per cent for the year, a figure comparable to that for the other two retailing organizations shown in Table 8-5. Other elements of Zayre's profit model were a relatively low net margin of 21.5 per cent on sales, which you would expect in a discount department store business, and an annual inventory turnover rate of 4.49 times.

Now compare the sets of figures shown in Table 8-5 for Zayre and Federated, operating discount and primarily full-service department stores, respectively. (44) (45) Which realized the highest net margin on goods sold? How is this reflected in (46) the relative ratios of net profits to net sales realized by each? If Federated realized distinctly superior results on both of these dimensions, how is it that Federated's profits on net worth (the money invested by its owners as opposed to lenders) was only slightly higher than that for Zayre?

Next look at the relative figures for Federated and Safeway Stores, Inc. Here we see that Safeway realized a lower net margin on goods sold than Federated and a distinctly lower ratio of net profits to net sales, which we might expect as a result of a low-margin pricing policy. Also, the relative amounts of money invested by the owners, as opposed to the total investment required from all sources, were roughly comparable for these two organizations (a ratio of total (47) assets to a net worth of 1.60 for Federated and 1.76 for Safeway). How is it then that Safeway managed to earn a higher rate on net worth (ratio of net profits to net worth) than Federated? As a graphic illustration of the rationale behind the supermarket business, the next time you visit your local supermarket, you might want to ask a stock clerk how often he or she restocks the store shelf for a particular item of merchandise.

(48) How would you position each of these types of retailing operations, and the predominant categories of consumer goods that each sells, on the matrix in Table 8-3?

which profit model to follow?

The manager's decision regarding the particular profit model to use as a guideline for a retailing strategy will depend, among other things, on (1) his or her assessment of his interest in, and capability for, offering different types of goods;

(2) trends in customer interests and needs, as he or she sees them; and (3) the implications of both product and customer needs for location, pricing, product-line selection, promotional activity, store fixturing (design and decoration), and staffing (the amount of sales personnel per $1,000 of sales, for example).

Once a category of product has been identified, Bucklin suggests that the classification shown in Table 8-3 can be used to (1) associate potential customers in a designated market or area with each of the matrix "cells", (2) determine the relative importance of customer needs associated with various matrix cells containing relatively large proportions of the total market, (3) assess the extent to which these needs are being met by current retailers, and (4) relate customer needs to the ability of the proposed operation to meet them (for example, in terms of the investment required to meet a given set of needs) as a means of reaching a decision regarding a particular profit model for operations.

(49)

For example, as you move from the upper left-hand corner to the lower right-hand corner of Table 8-3, how would you expect consumers' needs or expectations to change regarding such matters as the relative importance of price in a purchase decision; the importance of the number of different items of merchandise offered for a particular type of product (typically known as the depth of assortment); the amount and type of sales assistance, measured in terms of the number and caliber of sales clerks; location; and the elaborateness of store facilities and fixtures?

It is possible to relate each of these needs or expectations to one or more of the elements of the profit model shown in Table 8-5. For example, a low-margin pricing policy similar to that employed by Zayre and Safeway requires either a relatively low investment in relation to sales (as in the case of Zayre) or a relatively high turnover of inventory (as for Safeway) to produce acceptable returns on investment. The greater the depth of assortment offered by a retailing operation, the slower the inventory turnover. Thus, you would expect a store with such characteristics to price its products to produce a higher net margin per

(50)

dollar of sales to compensate for slow inventory turnover. Similarly, how would the other dimensions of number or caliber of sales clerks, location, or the elaborateness of store facilities be reflected in Table 8-5?

pricing and the profit model

The average margin achieved as a part of a store's profit model rarely results from the establishment of a margin common to all items and then selling them at that price. So-called markdowns from the original price are posted to sell slow-moving merchandise. Furthermore, the merchandising policies of most retailing institutions are built around the concept of a pricing strategy that will, variously, in the eyes of a cynic or a retailer, lure customers or build traffic, respectively. Thus, the average margin on cigarettes in a supermarket may be 8 per cent, whereas that for fresh produce may be 40 per cent. In spite of these differences, the supermarket may realize higher profits on the former than on the latter. In a department store, drug items may sell for a 20 percent margin, whereas gifts may bring a margin of 50 per cent. Recalling our discussion in Chapter 5, what will determine the nature of items selected for bargain prices as traffic builders?

(51)

Much of the creativity in the management of a retail store or department is associated with pricing as well as with assembling and displaying merchandise in an attractive and timely fashion.

consistency in formulating a retailing strategy

Some basic elements in retailing strategy are shown in Figure 8-6. The most successful retailing operations have been able to combine all or some of these elements in an internally consistent manner at the same time that they meet consumer needs. The most obvious example of this is that many of the elements shown in Figure 8-6, such as the availability of parking, the offering of stamps and premiums, the use of expensive store fixtures, the availability of credit, the depth and breadth of merchandise assortments, and advertising, involve costs that must be reflected in the margin realized on sales and, consequently, price. To the extent to which pricing policy does not recover these costs, perhaps because of competitive pressures or consumer objections, a retailing organization may suffer losses as a result of an inconsistency in its strategy. Conversely,

Figure 8-6. Some basic elements in retailing strategy.

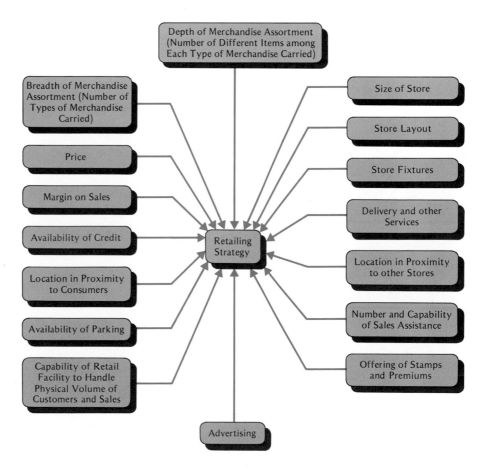

high prices and high margins typically are not compatible with cheap fixtures and shabby surroundings in a store.

(52)

How would you organize the elements of retailing strategy in Figure 8-6, based on our categorization of marketing functions in Figure 8-4 on page 268 or on our discussion of consumer transactional, logistical, or postpurchase needs on page 269?

In the spring of 1972, the Great Atlantic & Pacific Tea Co., Inc. (A&P) initiated one of the most momentous changes in retailing strategy ever attempted by a single firm in United States retailing history. It initiated its Where Economy Originates (WEO) discount pricing strategy and within a year had converted all of its 4,200 grocery stores and supermarkets (defined by the Supermarket Institute as any food store with more than $500,000 in annual sales) to the new program.[8]

Founded by George Hartford in 1859 as a tea store in Manhattan, A&P was built into the nation's largest retailing organization by successful promotional efforts including brass bands, free dishes, and imaginative decorative effects. However, in 1961 A&P was surpassed in size by Sears, Roebuck and Co., a milestone in a long period of stagnating sales and profits that saw Safeway Stores replace the company as the second largest retailer in 1972.

The company's decline was attributed generally to a succession of management teams that (1) maintained relatively small stores (averaging 14,000 square feet against more than 20,000 square feet for many other major food chains), (2) failed to follow consumers to the suburbs, refusing to pay the higher rents demanded by shopping-center owners, (3) allowed many of its stores to become poorly lit and badly kept, and (4) moved slowly and half-heartedly to adopt such competitive devices as trading stamps when they became popular early in the 1960s. As a result, A&P found itself in 1972 with many of its stores realizing only one fourth to one third the sales of its competitors' stores, with many locations in free-standing neighborhood stores in crowded city-center areas, and a customer profile described by one supplier as "usually old or retired people" served by employees described by one A&P executive as including "too many irritable old ladies."

Enter William J. Kane (a new chairman) and his program, WEO. Under WEO, the company reduced prices on 90 per cent of its merchandise items, reduced the number of items offered from an average of eleven thousand in a conventional A&P store to as few as eight thousand in a WEO, reduced average margins from 21 per cent to an estimated range of 9 per cent to 13 per cent, placed distinctive green WEO signboards on its stores, and allocated a substantial amount of money to advertising. Kane described the rationale for the program in these terms:

> We have to start the growth factor in this company right now. This is a business based strictly on volume, with sales measured in tonnage . . . this is a tonnage recovery program.[9]

(53)

Based on the internal consistency of the WEO strategy, what success would you predict for the program?

[8] Sources for the information in this section are "Lethargic Food Giant Has Glamorous History —And Balance Sheet," *Wall Street Journal* (Feb. 14, 1973), pp. 1 and 12; and "A&P's Ploy: Cutting Prices to Turn a Profit," *Business Week* (May 20, 1972), pp. 76–79.
[9] "A&P's Ploy: Cutting Prices to Turn a Profit," ibid., p. 76.

retailer needs: determinants in selecting suppliers

Just as ultimate consumers or users perceive transactional, logistical, and post-purchase needs that are met by successful retailers, so do retailers perceive similar needs in their relationships with the wholesaling and manufacturing companies from which they obtain their merchandise. These needs help determine the suppliers selected by an individual retailing organization. A representative sample of them is arrayed on the left side of Figure 8-7.

Transactional Needs. Once the nature of a store's business and product line has been determined, its transactional needs for supplier support may encompass a wide range. A broader (more types of items) or deeper (more kinds of a given product-line item) assortment in a supplier's product line may allow a retailer to buy more from a supplier, with attendant benefits in shipping costs and bargaining power commensurate with the importance of a retailer to its supplier.

The margin that a retailer can obtain on its products is its compensation for assuming responsibility for the performance of marketing functions discussed

Figure 8-7. Needs exhibited by retailers in dealing with suppliers and met by retailers in dealing with consumers.

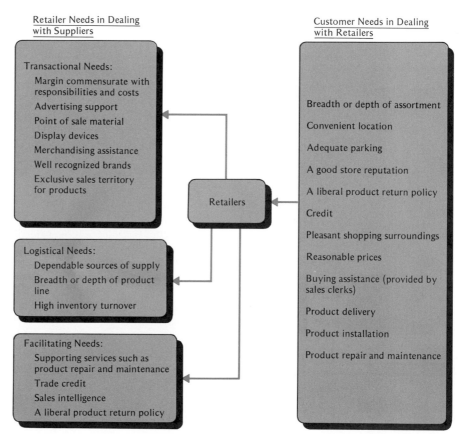

Retailer Needs in Dealing with Suppliers

Transactional Needs:
  Margin commensurate with responsibilities and costs
  Advertising support
  Point of sale material
  Display devices
  Merchandising assistance
  Well recognized brands
  Exclusive sales territory for products

Logistical Needs:
  Dependable sources of supply
  Breadth or depth of product line
  High inventory turnover

Facilitating Needs:
  Supporting services such as product repair and maintenance
  Trade credit
  Sales intelligence
  A liberal product return policy

Retailers

Customer Needs in Dealing with Retailers

Breadth or depth of assortment

Convenient location

Adequate parking

A good store reputation

A liberal product return policy

Credit

Pleasant shopping surroundings

Reasonable prices

Buying assistance (provided by sales clerks)

Product delivery

Product installation

Product repair and maintenance

281

earlier and listed in Figure 8-4. Low margins offer limited incentives to retailers to perform marketing functions. However, retailers may accept low margins on well-advertised, well-known branded merchandise because such merchandise often "sells itself." When margins are high and retailers' responsibilities low, on the other hand, what would you expect to happen?

Many retailers expect and receive a variety of sales-supporting services from their suppliers. These may include the preparation and stocking of displays and shelves on a regular basis by "detailers" (manufacturers' sales representatives who provide sales assistance to the regular wholesalers' salesmen who are entrusted with actually taking orders for the product). Merchandising assistance also may be provided by wholesalers' sales representatives and by wholesalers called "rack jobbers" (referring to their major chore of keeping display racks stocked on a regular basis). Often assistance to retailers may include product and sales information, the training of salesclerks, and the provision of display devices and other point-of-sale material.

Suppliers may be willing to "cooperate" in sharing expenses, within preset limits, of advertising featuring the supplier's products and the retailer's name. This practice has come to be known as cooperative advertising.

Logistical Needs. Among retailers' logistical needs are dependable sources of supply and the rapid response by suppliers to retailer orders. These are conditions that can produce a high rate of inventory turnover by retailers, in turn allowing them to minimize their investments in inventory and devote their money to other purposes. What are the implications of these factors for Pier 1 Imports, a Fort Worth based retail chain that chiefly sells household furnishings, decorative items, accessories, and novelties from around the world? In 1973, about 90 per cent of its merchandise came from foreign sources, 70 per cent of which was bought directly from foreign suppliers by Pier 1's traveling buyers. For many of these purchases, buyers had to commit themselves to buy and pay for merchandise four to twelve months in advance.[10]

A retailer may rely on its supplier for the assumption or full responsibilities for the delivery of merchandise involving warehousing, material handling, and transportation. This may include the processing of claims on damaged merchandise.

At times, retailers may desire or even demand so-called exclusives on products or services, involving a guarantee by the supplier that he will not sell to other retailers in an agreed on market area. Exclusives often are granted to retailers expected to provide strong promotional effort, or may be a means of obtaining distribution through stores possessing strong reputations among consumers in certain markets.

Prepackaging and the premarking of price on merchandise in advance of delivery to retail stores has been sought by retailers as a means of reducing costs of in-store labor for such activities. What does a retailer sacrifice for such benefits?

Postpurchase Needs. Faulty postpurchase services, such as product repair and maintenance, reflect unfavorably in the consumer's mind not only on a

---

[10]"Pier 1: Sets Pattern for Imports Merchandising," *The Discount Merchandiser* (April 1973), pp. 89–90.

manufacturer's product but also on the store that sold it. For this reason, a manufacturer's service policy often is an important determinant in the selection of a supplier by a retailer for those types of goods requiring periodic maintenance and repair.

A retailer may seek suppliers offering liberal policies regarding the return of unsold goods for a refund of the purchase price of a credit against future purchases. This is particularly critical for certain lines of merchandise such as fashion, seasonally sold, or easily damaged items.

Most purchases by retailers are made on *terms*. Terms of sale include not only the price, but also a statement of the credit policy of the supplier. For example, terms of "2/10, net 30" indicate that a supplier will grant a 2 per cent discount for payment within ten days of the date on the invoice (bill) and that he expects payment in full within thirty days of that date. The incentive for early payment is a means by which suppliers can maintain a relatively rapid turnover of capital. Typically, grocery products are sold under terms that allow a relatively brief credit period. In contrast, jewelry often carries a relatively long credit period, extending up to several months. What explanation could you offer for this difference?

(57)

(58)

In reviewing Figure 8-7, how would you array the needs of consumers in dealing with retailers against comparable retailer needs in dealing with suppliers that are listed there?

trends in retailing

Among the interesting trends in retailing are structural changes that are taking place in the business; changes in store size, assortment, and location; the role of private or retailers' brands; the renewed interest in franchising; and changes in the environment that exert an effect on the nature of retailing activity.

structural changes—circles or cycles?

Conceptually, changes in the structure of retailing have been represented both as circular and cyclical. Professor Malcolm P. McNair first suggested the concept of the "wheel of retailing,"[11] illustrated by the following example:

> Remember when motels were Spartan, $7-a-night places that beckoned you with a "Kleen Kabins" sign and offered you little more than a bed and a shower?
> Then they got fancy, with bellhops, room service, and plush cocktail lounges—and the price shot up to $20 a night.
> Now here's the latest thing in the motel business: Spartan, $7-a-night places (without a Kleen Kabins sign) that offer you little more than a bed and a shower.

[11] Malcolm P. McNair, "Significant Trends and Developments in the Postwar Period," in *Competitive Distribution in a Free, High-Level Economy and Its Implications for the University*, ed. A. B. Smith (Pittsburgh: University of Pittsburgh Press, 1958), pp. 1–25. Quotes on pp. 17–18.

283

Lured by single-room rates between $6 and $9.90, bargain-hungry travelers are flocking to so-called budget or economy motel chains, and in the process they are igniting a boom in a brash industry that's taking on the established motel chains on their own turf.[12]

(59) Why have economy motels, featuring full-sized rooms but no swimming pools, restaurants, television, convention facilities, or big lobbies, been such a success?

Eugene Ferkauf, a small retailer who began selling all types of appliances for $10 over wholesale cost from his fourth-floor luggage store, called E. J. Korvette, Inc., in New York City in 1948, started another turn of the wheel of retailing that became known as discount merchandising. According to one description of the early growth of Korvettes:

> In the 1950s, a group of thirty-eight men, almost all Brooklyn high school pals of Ferkauf, ran the fast-growing chain. Called "the open-shirt crowd" or "the boys," Ferkauf's management operated from a dingy old building on 46th Street in Manhatten, where Ferkauf presided at a beat-up desk in a corner of the board room.[13]

As the chain grew, however, Korvette's administrative costs increased so rapidly that it was forced to increase its margins on the very hard goods (durable goods, such as appliances) on which it had established its low-price, high-value reputation. Consumer interest turned to other lower-priced competitors, cutting drastically into the company's profits, until in 1973 Korvettes' new management indicated that its future strategy would be to establish Korvettes in the consumers' minds as a "promotional department store" chain emphasizing leisure and fashion goods sold in pleasant, shopping center-oriented locations. According to Kenneth Kolker, chairman of Korvettes' merchandising committee: "We want to make Korvettes trendy and chic too, by having some real high-fashion items from time to time at low prices."[14]

(60) Could you predict what the basic elements of McNair's wheel-of-retailing concepts are, based on these examples?

Circles. Once new retailers enter a business with low-cost, low-margin enterprises offering few or no services but selling goods or services at low prices, why eventually do they abandon this successful strategy to other retailers? A number of opinions have been advanced. These include (1) temptations presented by more conventional competition and pressures from customers to move around the "wheel" toward more services, more elaborate facilities, and higher prices; (2) deterioration in a firm's management; (3) a loss of enthusiasm for the original, sometimes less-glamorous concept; (4) the difficulty of maintaining effective price competition (because of its visibility and ease of emulation by competitors) over a period of time; and (5) the entry of emulators into the business until excess capacity makes all competitors marginally profitable.

[12] Urban C. Lehner, "Economy Motels Lure Travelers with Prices As Low as $6 a Room," *Wall Street Journal* (Dec. 26, 1972), pp. 1 and 17. Quote on p. 1.

[13] This quote, and much of the information in this example, appears in "Korvettes Tries for a Little Chic," *Business Week* (May 12, 1973), pp. 124–126. Quote on p. 124.

[14] Ibid., p. 126.

An example in the evolution in a retailer's strategy is provided by Sidney Cooper, the chief executive of a highly successful chain of discount appliance stores, Silo, Inc., based in Philadelphia:

> Now, Cooper is even talking about spending something more than "rock bottom" dollars for a lease on a new location in center-city Philadelphia. "I used to say that we didn't need it and couldn't afford those rentals," he says. "Now we see that we can't afford not to be there. Maybe," he adds, "we're becoming more establishment."[15]

Characteristically, established retailing institutions will use various means, including legislation and ostracism from trade associations, to discourage the development of new types of businesses. For example, the French government, in order to protect small shopkeepers (who represent many votes) has been slow to grant building permits for so-called *hypermarchés* (discount stores, some of which are more than 200,000 square feet, or five acres, in size) in France. In one extreme case, a disgruntled small competitor was suspected of setting fire to a Carrefour *hypermarché* south of Paris several years ago.

Cycles. Unfortunately, not all developments in retailing structure conform to the wheel concept. For example, marketing historian Stanley C. Hollander cites the development of automatic merchandising, or vending, that began as a high-cost, high-margin, high-convenience form of retailing.[16] In view of these conceptual difficulties, it is perhaps more useful to return once again to life-cycle concepts, such as those illustrated in Figure 4-5 on page 124, to illustrate the idea of structural change in retailing.

In applying life-cycle theory to institutional change in retailing, Professor Bert C. McCammon, Jr., has concluded that institutional life cycles are accelerating, as suggested by information in Table 8-6. He estimates that department stores moved from early growth to maturity in a period of about one-hundred years from the opening of the first department store by a Parisian merchant in 1852 to the mid-1960s. But such newer types of retailing ventures, such as furniture warehouse showrooms and catalog showrooms, will move over the same cycle in no more than just ten years.

A retailer can employ life-cycle concepts in modifying his company's priorities over the cycle. According to McCammon:

> Expansion programs are vigorously pursued during the initial stages of the life cycle, administrative and operating issues are stressed during maturity, and greater emphasis is placed on strategic reprograming toward the end of the cycle.[17]

(61)

What are the implications of accelerated life cycles for retailing management?

[15]"An Appliance Dealer with a Real Clout," *Business Week* (Nov. 6, 1971), pp. 76 and 78. Quote on p. 78.

[16]Stanley C. Hollander, "The Wheel of Retailing," *Journal of Marketing,* **24** (July 1960), pp. 37–42. See p. 41.

[17]Bert C. McCammon, Jr., "The Future of Catalog Showrooms: Growth and Its Challenges to Management," Working Paper no. P-69-C, (Cambridge, Mass.: Marketing Science Institute, 1973), pp. 1–11. Quote on p. 4.

Table 8-6 **Trend in the Length of Life Cycles for United States Retailing Institutions***

Type of Retail Institution	Examples	Time of Early Growth[a]	Time That It Reached Maturity[a]	Total Elapsed Time (in yrs.)
Department stores	May Company Macy's J. Magnin	Mid 1860s	Mid 1960s	100
Variety stores	Woolworths Kresge S. S. Kress	Early 1900s	Early 1960s	60
Supermarkets	King Kullen Jewel Winn-Dixie	Mid 1930s	Mid 1970s	30
Discount department stores	Korvette K Mart Arlens	Mid 1950s	Mid 1970s	20
Fast-food service outlets	McDonald's Kentucky Fried Chicken Shaky's	Early 1960s	Mid 1970s	15
Home-improvement centers	Grossman's Plywood Ranch	Mid 1960s	Late 1970s	15
Furniture warehouse showrooms	Levitz J. Homestock Wickes	Late 1960s	Late 1970s	10
Catalogue showrooms	Best Products Wilson Service Merchandise	Late 1960s	Late 1970s	10

* Source: Bert C. McCammon, Jr., "The Future of Catalog Showrooms: Growth and Its Challenges to Management," Working Paper no. P-69-C, (Cambridge, Mass.: Marketing Science Institute, 1973), pp. 1–11. See p. 3.

[a] The dates shown are valid for types of retail institutions, not for the particular companies used as examples.

store size, assortment, and location

Although a number of factors have influenced trends in store size, assortment, and location in various retailing enterprises, perhaps no influence is more pervasive than that of the private automobile. It has simultaneously created downtown congestion and made suburban stores more accessible to greater numbers of consumers. Thus, it has fostered a trend toward larger supermarkets, larger discount department stores, and larger home-improvement centers (formerly regarded in the strict sense as lumber yards or hardware stores). Quite often, these stores offer either broader or deeper assortments of immediately available merchandise than their more conventional competitors. To a growing extent, they are being located in suburban areas adjacent to limited access, peripheral highways and in areas of moderate to high average incomes.

A remarkable illustration of the growing store size, increasing assortment, changing location, and significantly altered retailing concepts made possible by the automobile is the furniture warehouse showroom, which has risen in prominence in recent years. This type of facility typically is composed of two parts: (1) a large showroom in which as many as several hundred "rooms" of furniture are displayed in their entirety, and (2) an attached warehouse, in which pieces of furniture in their shipping containers are stacked seven and eight levels high in racks for immediate access. Customers picking their furniture have the option of hauling it away immediately in their own automobiles at perhaps 6 per cent less than the delivered price. A typical furniture warehouse showroom stocks about $1 million worth of furniture, delivered from manufacturers in railcar and truckload quantities. It can support a heavy volume of advertising, directed to a wide audience.

> The ads get results. On a recent Sunday afternoon at the Wickes warehouse-showroom here in Itasca, about 40 miles northwest of Chicago in a fast-growing suburban area, throngs of customers, children in tow, wander through the aisles of furniture. Blue-blazered salesmen, order pads clutched under their arms, hover behind the wanderers, hoping to snag the occasional customer who buys an entire room display right down to the ashtrays on the tables. . . . Outside, the parking lot is jammed, and potential customers are trapped in traffic backed up for several miles. Those who've come prepared to haul away their purchases jockey for a position at the loading docks.[18]

(62) (63)

(64)

How would you explain the success of this concept? What responsibilities for the performance of marketing functions does this place on the retailer and the customer? How would you evaluate this retailing strategy in terms of the consistency among the elements shown in Figure 8-6?

scrambled merchandising

How large can retail stores become, especially on one level as opposed to the multilevel downtown department store? There is some indication that certain types of retailers feel that they may be approaching the practical limit within which they can offer an adequate assortment of merchandise without subjecting the customer to an endless search and an exhausting hike. Thus, rather than expanding in size, many supermarkets are limiting the depth of the assortments offered (the number of kinds or brands of one product type) in order to be able to offer a growing breadth of assortment (more product types). Even for fast-selling product types, many supermarkets have adopted the policy of offering only two or three brands. The ultimate extension of this may be the superstore, designed to offer the customer many of the most *routinely* purchased products and services, including certain foods, in a store of 30,000 to 35,000 square feet, about the size of the largest supermarkets today.[19]

[18]Susan B. Miller, "Furniture Warehouses That Sell to Public Spring Up and Do Well Across the Land," *Wall Street Journal,* (May 30, 1972), p. 34.

[19]For a more detailed description of the superstore, see Walter J. Salmon, Robert D. Buzzell, and Stanton G. Cort, *The Super-Store—Strategic Implications for the Seventies* (New York: Family Circle Magazine, 1972).

The tendency of many retailers to offer a growing number of product types, such as would be the case in the superstore, inevitably has produced overlapping assortments between new and traditional retailing establishments. It has been termed *scrambled merchandising*. Scrambled merchandising has created a number of stresses in supporting channels of distribution that we will consider in the following chapters.

(65)   As an alternative to the superstore, what would you think of a proposal to open a chain of "new-product" stores, in which knowledgeable salesclerks would display, demonstrate, and sell only products on the market six months or less? Presumably, such products would be sold at relatively high prices with high margins, perhaps with the protection of a short-term "exclusive" territory

(66)

(67)   granted by the manufacturers. How would this concept contrast with that of the superstore? What marketing functions would each emphasize?

branding: private brands

Private, or retailers', brands have played an important role in the merchandising policies of certain retailers for a number of years. A pioneer and major proponent of private brands, A&P, for example, produces merchandise carrying its private Ann Page, Jane Parker, and other labels in its own twenty-four manufacturing and processing plants and twenty-two bakeries that employed twelve-thousand people in 1972. These items were estimated to comprise 12 per cent to 15 per cent of A&P's total sales. In the general merchandise field, private brands such as Kenmore and Cold Spot offered by Sears, Roebuck and Co. command large shares of local markets for appliances and television sets. Typically, such products are manufactured for Sears by manufacturers selling well-known brands of their own, such as the Whirlpool Corporation.

Private brands can be retailed at higher margins and yet lower prices than their competing manufacturers' brands. Typically, they are purchased at much lower costs, reflecting the fact that they need not support large advertising or sales expenditures. Furthermore, they are purchased in large, economic quantities, typically under long-term contracts. Often, manufacturers of both private and their own brands regard private label merchandise sales as a means of utilizing excess available capacity at relatively low incremental costs.

(68)   Why is it that private label merchandise is offered by A&P, Sears, and others but not by your corner convenience store?

renewed interest in franchising

Although franchising may seem new because of the proliferation of fast-food outlets (such as McDonald's, Arby's, and Kentucky Fried Chicken) that have employed this strategy in recent years, the concept began at about the time of World War I when automobile dealerships were first formed. By 1970, retail sales made by franchised outlets were estimated by the Department of Commerce to have reached $156 billion, or more than one fourth of all retail sales. Included among the wide range of goods and services provided at retail under franchising arrangements were automobiles, gasoline, fast foods, carpets, car-rental services, income-tax advisory services, motion picture entertainment, business education, community greeting services, and high-rise combined one-stop mausoleum-funeral homes. Interestingly, although fast-food franchisers are perhaps the most visible of all, they comprise only about 2 per cent of sales by franchised retail outlets of all types.

Under a typical franchising arrangement, a franchising organization will agree with a franchisee (an aspiring entrepreneur) to grant the right to sell a product or service; provide advice on site location and construction planning; provide intensive training in the operation of the business; and supply signs, promotional material, business forms, bookkeeping and information systems, the assistance of continuing management consultants, and a national or regional advertising campaign. In return, the franchisee often pays a franchising fee, a monthly percentage of its sales or profits, and an advertising charge. Where appropriate, food and other supplies needed to run an individual outlet are made available through a central purchasing system by the franchising organization.

At its best, franchising has enabled franchising organizations to grow more rapidly, by using capital and acquired management talent and motivation supplied by franchisees, than otherwise might have been possible. It has enabled many franchisees to become managers and owners of successful businesses with the reduced risk made possible by professional advice and a well-formulated plan.

At its worst, franchising has been a vehicle attracting the money of individuals with little potential management skill, for forcing franchisees to purchase supplies from a central source at inflated prices, and for selling franchises at a faster rate than the franchising organization could service in order to inflate its earnings and stock price. Although franchising failures have gained a great deal of attention in recent years, there are indications that the problems caused by rapid growth in the use of the concept in the 1960s are being resolved in some cases by means of class-action lawsuits by groups of franchisees against franchisers. A number of protective organizations, including the National Association of Franchised Businessmen, the Ford Dealers Alliance, and the Chicago Independent Gasoline Retailers Association have been formed at various times to protect the interests of franchisees.

(69)   What are the conditions, or types of businesses, that lend themselves particularly well to franchising? It has been said that franchising enables an
(70)   individual to become an independent entrepreneur. To what extent do you think this is the case?

environmental trends

Environmental trends, which have become important to retailers in recent years, influence shopping behavior and store opening hours, costs of operation, and the growth of consumerism.

Shopping Behavior and Store Opening Hours. Several factors have combined to induce retailers to extend the hours that their businesses are kept open to the public. A greater number of potential shoppers are working four-day work weeks. Others have been given an opportunity to work on a "gliding" time schedule, in which they may begin and end their work days over a range of times. Although Sunday blue laws, passed by state and city legislators to prohibit the sale of certain types of merchandise on Sunday, have come back into vogue since a Supreme Court decision in 1961 upholding their validity, many are so badly written that they are difficult to enforce. Some shopping centers, the focus of much of the pressure for longer opening hours, now have come to be social centers, attracting people at all hours for entertainment, community politics, and even church going. In response, a number of retailers, particularly supermarket chains, have begun to remain open on Sunday. Some outlets now require no keys, remaining open literally 168 hours per week.

A study made several years ago by the International Council of Shopping Centers of thirty-six retail chains operating 666 shopping centers that had begun to remain open on Sunday reported that the chains realized an average sales increase of 9 per cent over their previous six-day per week operation.[20] Does this suggest to you that longer operating hours should be more profitable?

Costs of Operation. Minimum-wage legislation and the 1963 Equal Pay Act have increased the costs of labor for retail operations significantly. And even though new technology is being introduced into retailing, it has not been sufficient to offset rising labor costs.

By 1976, Congress had voted to raise the minimum wage to $2.30. Because many retailing employees are paid at the minimum-wage level, any increase in this figure can raise labor costs more significantly than in other industries.

In 1972, full-time women workers in retailing received an average wage of $4,062 per year; full-time men workers received $8,639. The 1963 Equal Pay Act has been interpreted as requiring equal pay for jobs requiring equal skill, regardless of the sex of the employee. On the basis of this legislation a number of lawsuits have been filed which, through their settlement, may well narrow the gap in salary between women and men. In a landmark case, one retailer sought to justify its differential payment for men and women on the basis of the fact that different departments of a store constitute different selling establishments and, therefore, may differentiate their salary structures. Specifically, men fitting suits in a men's clothing department were paid more than women fitting women's suits in another department of the same store. Knowing what you know about the 1963 Equal Pay Act, as a retailer what do you think the chances are that this argument would hold up? Would your answer be the same if the two departments involved were a jewelry department paying its male employees more than the female employees of a women's clothing department?

To combat rising labor costs, retailers are seeking means to increase employee productivity. One of the most effective advances in recent years has been the adoption of the electronic cash register, which is capable of capturing data at the point of sale that a retailer can use to verify credit, count and control inventory, and forecast sales. Perhaps of more immediate importance, early

(71)

(72)

(73)

[20]"Retailers Move Toward the 168-hour Week," *Business Week* (Oct. 16, 1971), pp. 96 and 98. See p. 96.

users of electronic cash registers report that the rate of processing an average sale at the check-out counter has been speeded up by 20 per cent.

Of equal importance for supermarket retailing is the development of the Universal Product Code, a symbol for a ten-digit number identifying all manufactured and processed items, which can be scanned automatically by passing an item over an optical scanner, thereby triggering the input of data to an electronic information system that includes the cash register. The availability of this code, now agreed on, makes possible significant savings in retail labor costs and the generation of data for automatic inventory replenishment and marketing planning throughout a channel of distribution.

Growth of Consumerism. Retailing, and particularly the supermarket, represents the battleground of consumerism. Although we will discuss it at greater length later, it is important to consider the effect of consumerism on the retailer and some of the responses it has provoked.

Consumers always have acted in their own individual interests. But to a growing extent in recent years, they have organized themselves around various issues to bring pressure to bear on businesses and legislatures to change business practices thought to be unfair to consumers. Efforts to take direct action often involve the most easily accessible and visible institution, the retailer. Thus, consumer boycotts and picketing invariably have been carried out on or near retailing establishments, most often supermarkets. Among the responses that they have prompted are a number of actions by Congress and state and city legislatures as well as retailers themselves.

As a result, many grocery supermarket chains have instituted programs to better inform consumers of the prices they are paying, the contents of the products they are getting, and the values available to them. To a growing extent, supermarkets display unit-pricing information, in which the cost of various packages, regardless of size, are equated back to a standard unit, such as a pound. Retail chains are encouraging manufacturers to begin to display not only the contents of their products on packages (required by law), but also to present the nutritional values associated with the contents. Several large manufacturers already have adopted such nutritional labeling. Still other manufacturers and retailers employ "open dating," in which the last date on which an item should be sold is displayed on the package. Others have instituted consumer education programs based on periodic publications of "value planners"—advertising with a strong informational content—and store demonstrations.

Finally, what the automobile has brought it can take away. The continued threat of shortages of gasoline could influence buying behavior, and particularly the willingness of the consumer to assume marketing functions. This could be important for a retailing structure based in large part on the automobile and ample supplies of inexpensive energy.

Which of these environmental trends do you feel will be of the greatest importance for retailers?

summary

The distribution system of any nation is made up of firms performing basic marketing functions. These include the transactional functions of buying, selling, and risk assumption; the logistical functions of assembly, storage, assorting, and transportation; and facilitating functions such as postpurchase service and maintenance, financing, information dissemination, and channel coordination and leadership. The performance of such functions creates utilities (or value) in goods by placing them in buyers' hands in the form and at the time and place in which they are desired.

Customer needs are the primary determinants of retail distribution strategy. At the heart of these needs, a customer's willingness to put forth incremental effort to purchase various types of goods influences the number and location of types of retail outlets as well as the breadth and depth of assortment of goods each might display and sell. This has led to a categorization of types of consumer merchandise as convenience, shopping, or specialty goods and retail outlets as being convenience, shopping, or specialty stores.

There are a number of paths to success in retailing. Regardless of the prices charged, margins earned, or the relationship of the size of a store to that of its parking lot, all successful retailers have one thing in common: an internally consistent retailing strategy sensitive to customer needs, competitive trends, and supplier capabilities.

Life cycles for types of retail outlets are becoming shorter and shorter, a phenomenon brought on by such things as the mobility and access to competitive retailing concepts and sites provided by the automobile, increasing consumer education and self-confidence, and changing customer needs and shopping patterns. Thus we have seen a growing number of large-scale specialty stores with deeper assortments, and discount department stores and superstores with broader assortments, than have been assembled for immediate availability to customers in the past. Many of these have relied on consumers' increasing willingness and ability to assume responsibility for marketing functions in exchange for lower prices. In the process, we have witnessed the growth of a number of retailing concepts that probably will outlive their originators and major proponents. These include scrambled merchandising, private branding, and franchising.

Environmental trends, not the least of which has been the recent threat of shortages to our automobile-based retailing structure, will, if anything, accelerate the life cycles for retailing institutions. Included among these are basic changes in buying behavior, internal operating costs and productivity in retailing, and consumer movements.

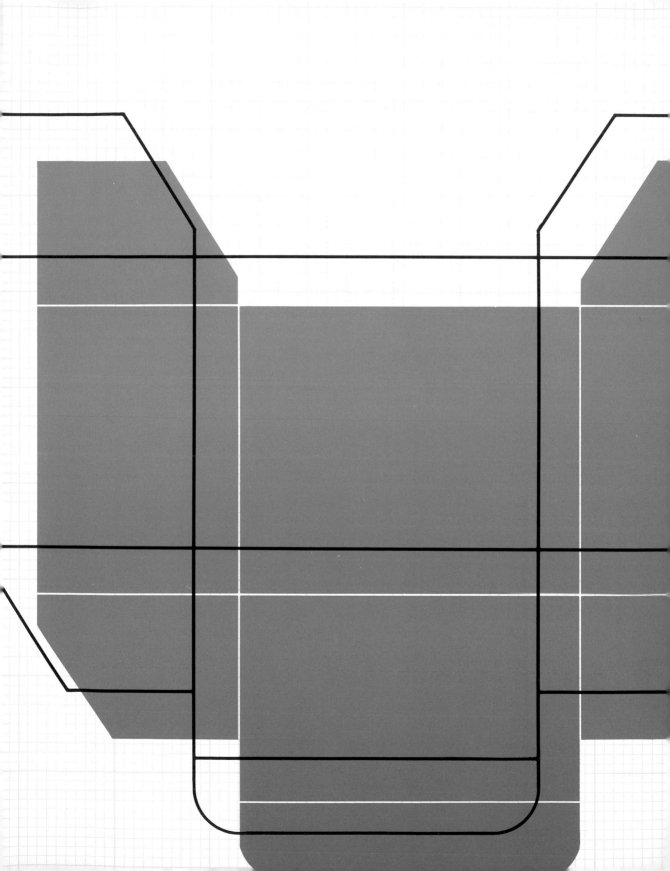

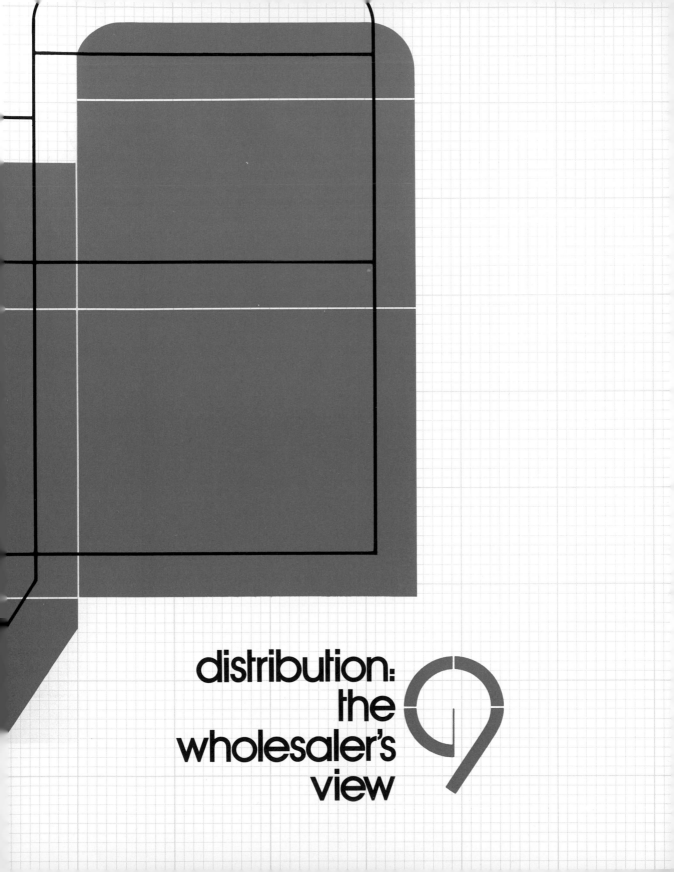

distribution:
the
wholesaler's
view

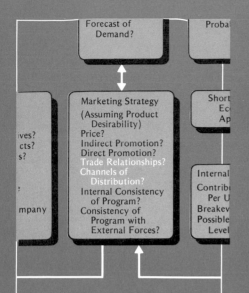

Forecast of
Demand?

Proba

ives?
cts?
s?

?

mpany

Marketing Strategy
(Assuming Product
    Desirability)
Price?
Indirect Promotion?
Direct Promotion?
Trade Relationships?
Channels of
    Distribution?
Internal Consistency
    of Program?
Consistency of
    Program with
    External Forces?

Short
    Ec
    Ap

Internal
Contribu
    Per U
Breakev
Possible
    Level

This topic is the perfect candidate for an encyclopedic treatment replete with a complete listing of
names, definitions, and primary functions of each
of an endless variety of institutions serving as intermediaries between manufacturers and retailers in
channels of distribution. At this point, however, I
believe it's more important that we understand
something about the organization, methods,
hopes, and concerns of one such intermediary. To
do this, it's useful to look at the world through the
eyes of a wholesaler, in this case, Dale Johnson,
president of Johnson Mill Supply of Bakersfield,
California. Based on the insights Johnson may
provide, we can perhaps (1) better appreciate
the role that wholesalers and channel intermediaries in general play in the marketing system
of the United States and other countries, (2) understand the way in which channel intermediaries
adapt to changing customer and manufacturer-
supplier needs, and (3) gain some notions about
the future of a type of business that the popular
press would have us believe is either an enduring
evil or a dying enterprise.

arly in 1973, at a time when food prices in general and meat prices in particular were rising rapidly in the United States, consumers took things into their own hands and organized a "meatless" week during which families were asked to eat no meat. Several government agencies organized informal investigations into the distribution channels for meat to determine what portion of the high prices could be identified with inefficiencies or excessive margins charged by middlemen—retailing and wholesaling institutions linking consumers with sources of raw materials and products. In one public statement, the president identified the food industry's middlemen as the prime villains. The chairman of the federal government's price commission proposed that dollar margins realized by wholesalers and retailers be fixed, regardless of the extent to which prices might be increased by farmers and meat producers.[1]

(1)　　As a result of these concerns, the United States government froze retail prices (to consumers) but not farm prices for a number of food products. What general attitude toward middlemen does this action reflect?

At other times, cries of "eliminate the middleman" and almost joyous predictions of the demise and eventual death of wholesaling in various industries have appeared in print.

Nor are these views of modern origin. They reflect the distrust and suspicion that has been directed toward the "trader" at various times and places throughout history in no less venerable volumes than the Holy Bible, views that have been most pronounced in agrarian or nonindustrial societies. For example, we are told that

> in Egyptian Thebes, [only] by abstaining from market transactions for ten years . . . could [a trader] become eligible for office. . . . But prevailing prejudices were all against the trader. If he rose socially it was by renouncing his ignominious occupation.[2]

Indeed, if the middleman is so unnecessary and, at his worst, parasitic, why do we bother to devote time to him here? A look at Figure 8-1 may suggest why. In Figure 8-1, page 262, notice the relative volume of sales for the retail trade and (2) (3)　　the intermediate trade (wholesalers and others). Which is greatest? Why is this the case?

If the predictions of various business and economic prophets are true, the intermediate trade should be declining in importance relative to other segments of business. Figure 9-1 shows the relative rates of growth for United States population, personal income, national income generated by manufacturing and construction firms, and sales by retailers and intermediate traders (wholesalers (4)　　and other middlemen). Does it confirm the predictions of the end of the middleman?

Although a number of factors may have influenced trends in the importance of wholesaling activities, Bucklin has proposed that the major reason is the increasing prosperity in the economy of the United States. At such times, customers are able to afford more purchasing convenience and a greater variety

[1]John A. Prestbo, "A Food Price Rollback Would Not Be Simple—Too Many Middlemen," *Wall Street Journal* (April 3, 1972), pp. 1 and 18.

[2]Miriam Beard, *A History of the Business Man* (New York: Macmillan, 1938), p. 18.

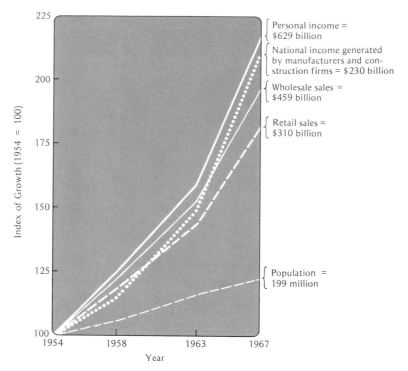

Figure 9-1. Relative rates of growth in population, personal income, national income generated by manufacturers and construction firms and sales by retailers and intermediate traders (wholesalers and other middlemen) in the United States, 1954–1967. Source: *Statistical Abstract of the United States* (Washington, D.C.: Bureau of the Census, Department of Commerce, 1974), p. 14.

of goods and services in changing assortments requiring the services of intermediaries to facilitate the coordination between manufacturers and retailers. According to Bucklin: "the mature economy offers significant opportunity for the growth of wholesaling, probably more than retailing.[3]

Trends in the relative growth of wholesaling and retailing activities in the United States may suggest the need to revise our opinions about the worth of the activities carried out by intermediate traders and the spirit in which such activities have been regarded for centuries in societies relying heavily on trade as opposed to agriculture for their livelihood. For example, in Holland:

> The merchant there is honored and regarded as a member of a class which is the strongest pillar of the Republic. The road to honors and to the highest dignity in the state is open to him.[4]

Little wonder that the middleman at times suffers an identity crisis, given the wide range of attitudes with which he has been regarded at various times in history and among various cultures.

What does he do to incur such wrath and enjoy such adulation? In modern times, the wrath has been concentrated on the costs that middlemen—particularly wholesalers—experience, whereas the adulation has resulted from the services that they perform, services based on the needs of retailers, other wholesalers, and manufacturers.

[3] Louis P. Bucklin, *Competition and Evolution in the Distributive Trades* (Englewood Cliffs, N. J.: Prentice-Hall, 1972), p. 207.
[4] Herbert Heaton, *Economic History of Europe,* rev. ed. (New York: Harper, 1948), p. 223.

roles that wholesalers play

Johnson Mill Supply in Bakersfield, California is one of about 213,000 full-function, full-service industrial distributors in the United States. Dale Johnson probably doesn't know it, but the firm he founded thirty-five years ago is known as a merchant wholesaler, one that buys, sells, and takes title to (thereby assuming the risk of owning) the goods it sells. It is a type of firm that provides a range of other services, such as assembling in one place, storing, and delivering an assortment of thirty-thousand items ranging from small grinding wheels to large replacement parts for industrial machinery. It offers its products for sale to customers ranging from small machine shops to large manufacturing firms. It may finance the goods its customers buy by offering them trade credit, allowing them several days or weeks in which to pay for their purchases. It collects and passes on trade information to customers and suppliers alike.

At the same time, Johnson Mill Supply is the sales arm of its suppliers and the purchasing agent for its customers. It provides the warehouse and principle inventory control point for the products it sells. On occasion, it is banker to both suppliers and customers. And it serves as a message center for information to suppliers about customers and their needs and to customers about suppliers, their competitors, and their products. As sales arm, purchasing agent, warehouseman, inventory controller, banker, and information center Johnson Mill Supply retains a margin (the difference between the amounts for which it buys and sells goods respectively) of about 27 cents of every dollar of sales it realizes.

the anatomy of a wholesaler— functions performed

Additions to the California-Spanish-style stucco home of Johnson Mill Supply accommodated the growth of the firm to its current size of $3,254,000 in annual sales and forty-six employees. Although Dale Johnson "would have no use" for such a chart, his organization could be diagrammed as shown in Figure 9-2. Managers of the four major functions of the firm, purchasing, operations (receiving, warehousing, and inventory control), sales, and accounting, reported most frequently to Johnson, although any member of his organization could take advantage of his "open-door policy" to see him about any matter, business or personal, at any time.

Buying. Johnson had built his organization carefully over the years. The average length of time that his four buyers had been with the company was twelve years, suggesting general job satisfaction and reflecting the high level of morale that was characteristic of Johnson's personnel. These four buyers divided the responsibility for purchasing a total of 115 product groupings, such as coated abrasives (sandpaper), high-speed steel cutting tools, and fasteners (screws and bolts). This required that they place orders with more than five hundred manufacturer-suppliers or other wholesalers. In addition, they had to monitor the offerings of perhaps another 1,500 potential suppliers. They accomplished this

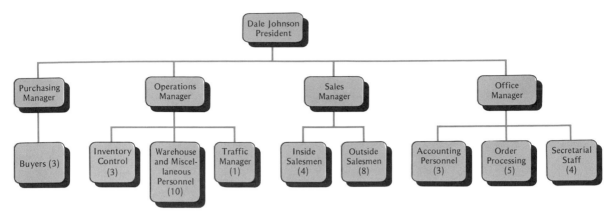

Figure 9-2. Organization chart, Johnson Mill Supply.

task by hosting some two hundred sales representatives each month and by maintaining files for the mountain of sales literature that was sent to the firm each week.

Transportation, Storage, and Inventory Maintenance. The firm's operations manager, Rod Bryant, presided over the 60,000-square-foot warehouse in which the firm received, inventoried, and picked orders from the 12,000 different items for which the firm maintained some stock. (The remaining 18,000 items were purchased for direct delivery to Johnson's customers, alleviating the need to maintain such items in stock.) What would you suspect might be the nature of items purchased for direct delivery to Johnson's customers?

(5)

During the most recent year, Bryant's crew of ten warehousing personnel had picked from stock some or all of 28,000 of the firm's 36,200 orders that year. The average size of these orders, each comprising an average of four separate items, was about $90 in sales value. The operations group also contained a staff of three inventory controllers, responsible for preparing sales forecasts on an item-by-item basis, reviewing and changing inventory management rules when necessary, and preparing information to be sent to the computer service bureau that processed inventory information for Johnson Mill Supply.

Selling. Jack Brandon, Johnson's sales manager, supervised a force of two inside salespeople and ten outside salespeople. Each inside salesperson occupied a desk with two telephones. These provided links with an assigned group of customers who preferred to place orders or request occasional "rush" orders by phone, often for products they had ordered before and with which they were familiar. Although inside salespeople did business on a first-name basis with most of their assigned customers, they rarely met such customers face to face. An outside salesperson, on the other hand, was assigned an average of about eighty accounts, each of which he or she attempted to call on no less frequently than every month. This required about four sales calls during a typical working day. An outside salesperson not only had to maintain some knowledge of the range of items stocked by Johnson, but also had to be prepared to offer advice to customers concerning the proper selection and application of items with which they were not familiar. In addition to supervising his sales force, Brandon sold to some twenty of the firm's larger accounts and was responsible for training new salesmen and coaching the existing ones in proper sales methods and the application of new-product information.

The responsibility for accounting, order processing, and payment of suppliers; preparation of invoices (bills to customers); and the secretarial needs of the business rested with Maxine Anderson, office manager. In addition, she was responsible for drawing up estimates of the future cash needs of the business.

Financing. Given the estimates of future cash needs, Dale Johnson could arrange for a line of credit from the bank to meet the company's working capital needs. Working capital was used for accounts receivable, resulting from trade credit extended to customers, and the inventory that the company was required to maintain in stock in advance of the time when it might be sold. By the end of 1973, the company's accounts receivable had mounted to $410,000, and its investment in inventory totaled $780,000. Although partially offset by credit extended to Johnson Mill Supply by its suppliers, these needs produced a requirement for about $900,000 in short-term financing of Johnson's working capital needs at all times. And the figure grew with the volume of Johnson's sales.

Information Exchange. In addition to his general duties of providing leadership for, and coordination of, his employees, Dale Johnson had instituted a program designed to improve the company's relationships with its suppliers. Each month, he gathered the firm's salespeople and buyers for a two-hour meeting devoted to presentations of new products by sales representatives of one or two of Johnson's major suppliers. This was followed by a discussion of customer needs regarding the products demonstrated, often led by Johnson's salespeople and buyers. The program not only improved the coordination internally between salespeople and buyers but also generated valuable information for suppliers' representatives. It had resulted from Johnson's conviction that unless a wholesaler could meet customers' and suppliers' needs more efficiently than such organizations could do so by dealing with each other directly, the very existence of wholesaling companies such as Johnson Mill Supply would be threatened.

Service, Service, and More Service. In his efforts to make sure that Johnson Mill Supply would continue to justify its existence to the customers and suppliers it served, Dale Johnson monitored closely the methods that his fellow industrial distributors had adopted to improve their services. For example, a number of such wholesalers had instituted "stockless purchasing" programs for their customers, allowing customers to minimize or even eliminate inventories that might be required for items they used in their businesses. One method by which this was achieved was by consignment selling by the distributor, in which items shipped by a distributor to its customer did not have to be paid for until they were used.

Other distributors had actually established fully stocked storerooms on the premises of their major customers, often on the floor of a plant operated by a manufacturer-customer. These were manned by distributors' personnel, who charged the customer for those tools, wire, or grinding wheels actually dispensed after they were requested and obtained by the customer's employees.

Still other industrial distributors had provided their larger customers with data-transmitting terminals so that requests for products could be transmitted by direct wire to the wholesaler's computer. Dale Johnson had read of one such case in which Beals, McCarthy & Rogers, a large Buffalo-based industrial distributor, had installed a Data-Phone® transmitter at the Towanda, Pennsylvania plant of one of its customers, Sylvania Electric Products, to allow immediate inquiry of the distributor's inventory, the elimination of purchasing procedures, the preparation of all documentation by the distributor, and next-day delivery of shipments. As a result of this system, Sylvania was able to reduce its number of order clerks by 25 per cent. Within a year after the installation of the program, Beals, McCarthy's sales to Sylvania increased by more than fifty times to about 25 per cent of the purchases of the Pennsylvania plant.[5]

Among other services provided with increasing frequency by wholesalers of industrial supplies were (1) systems engineering, in which a wholesaler's sales engineer would help customers identify problems and design systems of component parts and controls to meet customers' needs; (2) guidance on occupational safety hazards resulting from the use of various types of industrial supplies and machine tools; (3) advice regarding pollution-control problems; (4) light fabrication or assembly of parts to a customer's order; (5) preventive maintenance programs in which a wholesaler's representative would provide routine maintenance, such as greasing, for the wholesaler's products; and (6) the training of those hired by a customer to operate a machine sold by the wholesaler.

problems and opportunites

Although day-to-day management problems occupied a good deal of his time, Dale Johnson's major concerns were about the future. The growing number of plaques, such as his distinguished service award from the National Industrial Distributors Association (NIDA), with which he had decorated the wall behind his desk in his modest oak-veneer paneled office, supplied evidence of the dwindling amounts of time he had to devote to his business. Each new flare-up of his arthritis reminded him that he wasn't getting any younger, and that he would have to think more seriously about a successor.

Competition from Other Wholesalers. The loss of a potentially large sale to an old customer on what appeared to be strictly price was the latest evidence that Johnson would face increasingly difficult competition in the future. In this case, a Fresno-based special-line distributor had offered a price 2 per cent below that quoted by Johnson. Increasingly, special-line industrial distributors, who concentrated their efforts on a relatively narrow range of products as opposed to the wide (general) line carried by Johnson, were gaining business by offering lower prices on that portion of a customer's needs that they could supply. It was

[5] Lassor Blumenthal, "How To Cut Purchasing Costs," *Dun's Review* (March 1964), pp. 53–54 and 66–69.

distressing to Johnson that some of his firm's old customers were willing to trade with several special-line distributors instead of Johnson in order to gain lower prices. The latest compilation of operating measures for general- and special-line industrial distributors, shown in Table 9-1, provided little comfort to Johnson. Reviewing the measures shown in Table 9-1, how would you contrast the operating characteristics of general- and special-line distributors? How does Johnson's firm compare with the usual general-line distributors? Would you expect general- or special-line industrial distributors to grow more rapidly in the future?

(6)
(7)
(8)

Customer Relations. Johnson was concerned about growing demands for improved service, through reduced response times, from customers who were ordering in smaller and smaller quantities, undoubtedly to reduce their own commitments of capital to inventory. As a Detroit-based industrial distributor had put it, "You can't deliver a $5 item with an $18,000 truck and a $10,000 a year driver."[6]

Table 9-1 **Comparative Operating Measures, Johnson Mill Supply, General- and Special-Line Industrial Distributors, 1972**

	Johnson Mill Supply	Averages for General-Line Distributors[*]	Averages for Special-Line Distributors[*]
Gross sales	$3,254,000	$1,657,000	$975,000
Average percentage margin on sales	29%	27%	44%
Dollar margin for wholesaling activities	$943,000	$447,000	$429,000
Operating expenses	$790,000	n.a.[a]	n.a.[a]
Net profit after taxes, in dollars	$153,000	n.a.	n.a.
Net profit after taxes, as a percentage of gross sales	4.7%	n.a.	n.a.
Assets employed for			
Inventory	$745,000	$294,000	$ 95,000
Receivables less payables	155,000	186,000[b]	210,000
Fixed facilities and equipment	750,000	n.a.	n.a.
Total	$1,650,000	n.a.	n.a.
Net profit after taxes, as a percentage of assets employed	9.3%	n.a.	n.a.
Average number of product lines	123	111	26
Average dollar value per invoice (sale)	$79	$42	$81
Average dollar value per item ordered (order-line item)	$18	$10	$22
Number of invoices (bills) per year	42,700	33,200	14,600
Size of warehouse (in square feet)	56,500	33,777	13,143
Ratio of annual sales to average inventory (inventory turnover)	4.4	4.4	5.2

[*] Source "27th Annual Survey of Distributor Operations." *Industrial Distribution* (March 1973), pp. 33–39. Figures shown were those reported by distributors in the Pacific and Mountain region.

[a] Not available.

[b] The figure shown is for receivables only.

[6] John Cavnar, "They Buy, They Sell—Here's What They Tell," *Purchasing* (May 8, 1973), pp. 32–37. See p. 35.

Although Johnson had been a leader in responding to customer service needs, some of these same customers had purchased from Johnson's competitors when offered a lower price and comparable service on a particular order. Over all, Johnson's concerns were reflected in the results of a poll of industrial distributors regarding their problems with customers that had appeared recently in a trade publication. The results are shown in Table 9-2. What possible responses to these problems could you suggest to Johnson?

Supplier Relations. On the other hand, it seemed to Johnson that the level of service provided by manufacturer-suppliers had declined in recent years. This was characterized by the declining dependability with which orders were received. Manufacturers in increasing numbers were failing to offer various forms of support ranging from formal training programs for sales personnel to the rather basic product literature needed to represent adequately a manufacturer's line to prospective customers. Declining supplier support inevitably led to a decline in the sales of that company's products by Johnson. In several instances, Johnson had substituted one supplier's line of products for another's for reasons of lack of support.

Johnson's experiences with suppliers were confirmed by additional results from the previously mentioned survey, which is shown in Table 9-3. In this study, two thirds of all wholesalers surveyed mentioned their concerns about undependable deliveries provided by their suppliers. Other complaints centered around the failure of manufacturer-suppliers to "protect" their wholesaler-distributors by refusing to sell their products through competing wholesaling organizations. Competition from other distributors, as a result, was the second greatest concern expressed by wholesalers responding to the survey. How might a wholesaler deal with the supplier-oriented problems cited in Table 9-3?

Of perhaps greatest concern of all to Johnson was the perpetual threat, experienced to some degree by all types of middlemen, of losing his largest potential sales, or entire customer accounts, to direct sales efforts by his sup-

Table 9-2 **Industrial Distributors' Problems with Customers***

Problem	Proportion of Total Surveyed Mentioning Problem (in %)[a]
Too much emphasis on price	60
Too many small orders	45
Too many rush orders	44
Slow pay	41
Buyers lack technical knowledge	26
Excessive customer demands that distributors carry their inventories	19
Customers' buyers roadblock distributors' salesmen	14
Customers' buyers won't visit the distributors' facilities	7
Excessive technical-service demands	3

*Source: Adapted from results reported in John Cavnar, "They Buy, They Sell—Here's What They Tell," *Purchasing* (May 8, 1973), pp. 32–37. See p. 35.

[a]Percentages do not add to 100 because respondents may have cited more than one problem.

**Table 9-3   Industrial Distributors' Problems with Manufacturer-Suppliers*

Problem	Proportion of Total Surveyed Mentioning Problem (in %)[a]
Undependable deliveries	66
Competition from other distributors	32
Poor communication in general	27
Lack of formal training programs (provided by manufacturer-suppliers)	18
Lack of technical help (from manufacturer-suppliers)	13
Insufficient product literature (supplied by manufacturer-suppliers)	7
Lack of advertising support (provided by manufacturer-suppliers)	5
Poor contract terms	3

*Source: Adapted from results reported in John Cavnar, "They Buy, They Sell—Here's What They Tell," *Purchasing* (May 8, 1973), pp. 32–37. See p. 37.

[a]Percentages do not add to 100 because respondents may have cited more than one problem.

pliers. Often these were customers whom Johnson had introduced to his suppliers' products and carefully nurtured to significant sales volumes.

Over the years, Johnson had become able to predict the point at which a supplier might become a potential competitor by selling direct to one of Johnson Mill Supply's customers. For example, it was estimated that a sales call on a potential buyer of industrial products cost anywhere from $40 to $50 in sales salaries, sales commissions, and selling expenses. A typical call pattern might produce twelve calls per year on a customer, resulting in $480 to $600 in selling costs. On sales to a larger customer, Johnson Mill Supply might receive a (11)   margin of 25 per cent on sales. (Why is this significantly less than Johnson's average margin of 29 per cent on sales to all customers mentioned earlier?) About 40 per cent of Johnson's margin, or 10 per cent of its sales, was spent for sales and promotional activities. Thus, at an annual volume of sales of any one supplier's product line in excess of $4,800 to $6,000 (sufficient to defray selling expenses equal to 10 per cent of sales to a single customer) it became potentially less expensive for the manufacturer-supplier to use its own sales force in dealing with the customer.

More often, on potentially large single sales to prospective customers, Johnson's salesmen faced low price quotations made directly by Johnson's suppliers to its customers. At times, the quotations, if met by Johnson, would completely eliminate Johnson's margins on the sales. The suppliers' typical responses to complaints from Johnson were that if they did not quote such a low price on a "direct" basis, the business would go to some competing distributor's supplier quoting a similarly low price on a direct basis. Thus, Johnson would be better off losing a sale to its supplier than to the supplier of (12)   a competing product line (sold through a competing distributor). As Dale Johnson, how would you deal with a situation such as this?

the relative importance of wholesalers

Dale Johnson's concern that his firm would exist only so long as it provided services to customers and suppliers more efficiently than they could supply such services themselves basically reflects the underlying rationale for the relative importance of wholesalers (and all middlemen) in the distribution of various types of goods. The extent to which channel intermediaries are able to justify their existence depends in large part on the nature of the product or service being distributed and the relative capabilities of customers (buyers) and suppliers (sellers) in performing the marketing functions required by the product or service.

nature of the product or service

Wholesalers are involved to a greater extent in the distribution of nonperishable products, items that are purchased from stock rather than custom designed "to order," products of a relatively noncomplex nature, and those that are part of a relatively narrow or small product line. Why is this?

Certain perishable products may neither be able to survive the extra handling nor support the duplicated special low-temperature facilities required for their physical distribution through wholesalers. Even so, brokers, limited-function wholesalers who buy and sell at wholesale perishable products such as fruits and vegetables that are shipped directly from producers to retailer customers, may participate in the distribution of products of which they rarely, if ever, see or take physical possession. Similarly, transactional functions have been disassociated from logistical functions in the apparel and footwear trades, where product perishability has led to an emphasis on nonstocking, wholesaling methods such as those of manufacturers' agents and selling agents.

Products that are designed or assembled to order are those for which the ultimate buyer often is known before the product is assembled and shipped by its manufacturer-supplier. By contrast, other items bought in standard shapes, sizes, color combinations, or other specifications can be placed in a wholesaler's stocks in anticipation of their eventual resale. Such items may be picked from a wholesaler's shelves or, in the case of warehouses operated by wholesalers of steel products, may undergo light manufacturing such as cutting, bending, or welding in the wholesaler's warehouse. For such items, the wholesaler can perform the assembly and sorting functions with a minimum of capital investment in heavy manufacturing equipment and in the duplication of manufacturer-supplier activities.

Wholesalers have been more successful selling products of a less complex nature, particularly those requiring little technical knowledge or custom engineering. Thus, plumbing supplies are sold through wholesale middlemen whereas computers for the most part are not. In large part, this is due to the inability of a wholesaler's sales representative to obtain the knowledge needed to specialize in the sale of a complex product because of the need to be a generalist with some knowledge about a broad range of products offered by many manufacturers.

relative supplier and customer capabilities

Returning once again to our discussion in Chapter 8 of functions performed in a channel of distribution, we can trace the importance of wholesalers to their capability relative to their potential suppliers and customers in performing transactional, logistical, and facilitating functions.

Transactional Capabilities. A wholesaler often can sell a line of products more efficiently than its manufacturer-supplier when the products in question are sold in small quantities to individual customers. Thus, tobacco products in general and cigars in particular, sold in small quantities often to small retailers, are distributed most efficiently through various types of wholesale middlemen rather than directly from manufacturers. The importance of this point may depend literally on the gap between manufacturing practice (related to the economies of scale) and consumer buying behavior for various products.

Manufacturers of one or a limited number of products selling in relatively small quantities to any one customer may not be able to justify the expense associated with a "captive," in-house sales force. A wholesaler, by contrast, can spread selling costs over a broader range of products purchased from several manufacturers. On one sales call, a wholesaler's sales representative can make a sale of a number of complementary products of sufficient dollar amount to defray the costs of the call. (Remember Dale Johnson's estimates of the range of volume within which he might lose his comparative advantage in serving as an intermediary between suppliers and customers?)

Because nearly all wholesalers receive a fixed margin (percentage of resale volume) or a fixed commission (percentage of sales) for their selling efforts, a manufacturer-supplier can assure itself of selling costs directly variable with sales by utilizing a wholesaler. This may be important for a producer of a small- or low-volume product line unwilling to incur the risk of a fixed investment associated with the recruitment, training, and support of its own sales force, regardless of the volume of sales.

Wholesalers typically are intimately familiar with the needs of customers in a particular type of commercial business, industry, or geographic region in which they do business. They provide benefits of local entreprenuership to a more distant manufacturer-supplier. They employ localized marketing strategies that might escape the notice of an organization devoting its primary efforts to manufacturing rather than marketing.

Wholesalers can buy broad assortments of products more efficiently and with greater expertise than smaller retailers that cannot afford an expert staff of buyers. For these customers, wholesalers not only provide one-stop but also low-cost buying requiring only a small portion of the time of a busy, small retail entrepreneur.

Logistical Capabilities. Wholesalers assemble, sort, and offer assortments of lines of products on behalf of many small manufacturers producing related products sold to many small customers. By buying and selling in larger quantities than individual suppliers dealing directly with individual customers might be able to do, wholesalers not only reduce transactional costs but also the logistical costs associated with transportation. In this respect, would they be more effective in serving as intermediaries between geographically concentrated or dispersed customers and their suppliers? Between geographically concentrated or dispersed suppliers and their customers?

Because few wholesalers engage extensively in basic manufacturing activities, their efforts and costs are divided between buying, physically stocking, and selling goods. The success of their businesses, as opposed to those of manufacturer-suppliers, depends to a much greater extent on effective buying, stockkeeping, and inventory control. This perhaps explains why such a large proportion of wholesalers has adopted computerized inventory-control methods. Methods for accomplishing this have included the purchase or lease of computer facilities or the use of outside service bureau organizations (companies offering to share time on large, central computers with access from the wholesaler by means of electronic information input devices and high-speed data-transmission lines).

Wholesalers often are market-oriented, and thus are able to position a manufacturer's products close to the market in terms of both time and distance. This may be of great significance for a small manufacturer (or one selling in small quantities to individual customers) who wants to develop markets distant from its manufacturing facilities. For example, compare the potential customer service (relative response time) as well as the distribution cost achieved by Johnson Mill Supply as opposed to direct sales by eastern United States manufacturers to western United States industrial customers for average transactions of $19, as illustrated in Figure 9-3. What are the relative response times and logistical costs achieved by each of the three alternate channels of distribution?

Some wholesalers justify their existence by their ability not only to maintain market-oriented stocks but also to convert them into the quantities, sizes, or shapes desired by individual customers. Thus, steel warehousemen purchase standard products in large quantities from manufacturers, holding them in stock in anticipation of customer orders, and cut or bend standard products to order for customers. By delaying such light manufacturing operations to the last possible stage in the channel of distribution, the wholesaler (steel warehouseman) is able to minimize inventories and reduce the amount of buying based on mistaken assumptions about what customers eventually might order.

Capabilities in Fulfilling Facilitating Functions.   Financing, information dissemination, postpurchase service or maintenance, and channel coordination or leadership can be provided more effectively by wholesalers than either their suppliers or their customers.

A wholesaler's familiarity with a particular geographic region or group of customers may allow it to make fewer mistakes in extending trade credit, or establishing limits on trade credit extended, to potential customers. In doing so, a wholesaler can relieve a manufacturer of the burden of investing its limited funds in distribution as well as manufacturing activities, a matter of no small significance to a small manufacturer with limited sources of financing.

Wholesalers, by dealing with a wide range of manufacturer-suppliers, can transmit useful information among them. This type of information often is not available to a manufacturer from its own sales force, whose contacts are limited largely to customers.

As an adjunct to their distribution activities, wholesalers can maintain service

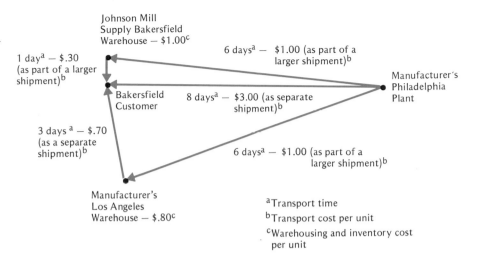

Figure 9-3. Logistical alternatives for a Philadelphia manufacturer distributing its industrial product to a Bakersfield customer.

Johnson Mill Supply Bakersfield Warehouse — $1.00[c]

1 day[a] — $.30 (as part of a larger shipment)[b]

6 days[a] — $1.00 (as part of a larger shipment)[b]

Bakersfield Customer

8 days[a] — $3.00 (as separate shipment)[b]

Manufacturer's Philadelphia Plant

3 days [a] — $.70 (as a separate shipment)[b]

6 days[a] — $1.00 (as part of a larger shipment)[b]

Manufacturer's Los Angeles Warehouse — $.80[c]

[a]Transport time
[b]Transport cost per unit
[c]Warehousing and inventory cost per unit

or maintenance facilities, again of a type that no small manufacturer could maintain for buyers of its products.

Wholesalers have proven themselves to be particularly effective in providing channel coordination or leadership for independent retailers operating one or several stores in competition with large retail chain-store organizations. Wholesalers, for example, have offered economies of chain-store buying, warehousing, inventory control, and consolidated store delivery to independent retailers of such products as groceries, hardware, and variety merchandise by taking the initiative to organize the efforts of such independent entrepreneurs.

(16)   Based on our discussion of the factors influencing the relative importance of wholesalers in the distribution of various types of products, what reasons would you cite to explain your expectations regarding the importance of wholesalers in the distribution of (1) wet yeast, a highly perishable product for which stringent regulations regarding freshness are imposed by the government; (2) candy and gum products sold to small retailers; (3) automobiles, typically assembled to customer order; or (4) electrical apparatus, equipment, and supplies, which often involve products of considerable complexity?

Data supplied by the Census of Business allowed Bucklin to calculate the share of total sales at wholesale of some fifty categories of products that merchant-wholesalers (comparable to full-service wholesalers with which we have been dealing here) as opposed to manufacturers' sales branches and offices handle. Information for a number of these product categories is shown in Table 9-4. Although these are not measures of the relative importance of wholesalers in general, in the distribution of various types of goods, they do allow us to compare the relative use of less-direct wholesaling methods (merchant-wholesalers) as opposed to direct wholesaling methods (manufacturers' sales

(17)   branches and offices) for the distribution of products in various categories. Do they bear out your preconceptions regarding the roles of merchant-wholesalers in the distribution of wet yeast, candy and gum, automobiles, and electrical

(18)   apparatus, equipment, and supplies? How do you explain the wide use of merchant-wholesalers in the distribution of iron and steel scrap, or waste and secondary materials?

Table 9-4 Relative Strength of Merchant Wholesalers (as Opposed to Direct Sales Through Manufacturers' Sales Offices and Branches) for Selected Product Lines, 1967*

Product Categories in which Merchant Wholesalers Occupied the Strongest Positions			Product Categories in which Manufacturers' Sales Offices and Branches Occupied the Strongest Positions		
Product Category	Sales ($billion)	Percentage Share	Product Category	Sales ($billion)	Percentage Share
Iron and steel scrap	2.4	96.8	Auto	25.3	80.7
Waste and secondary materials	2.0	94.2	Chemicals	13.7	80.1
Metal service centers	7.9	93.3	Metal sales offices	17.8	76.4
Tobacco	5.3	87.9	Commercial machines and equipment	6.2	73.6
Beer and ale	4.3	86.7	Farm machinery and equipment	2.9	70.2
Fish and seafood	.9	85.4	Paint and varnishes	1.0	64.9
Art goods	.8	79.8	Electrical apparatus, equipment, and supplies	10.8	60.8
Jewelry and precious stones	1.6	77.9	Tires and tubes	1.8	55.7
Professional equipment and supplies	2.9	76.5	Construction materials	4.5	55.5
			Industrial and personal service papers	3.1	51.5

* Source: Adapted from Louis P. Bucklin, *Competition and Evolution in the Distributive Trades* (Englewood Cliffs, N. J.: Prentice-Hall, 1972), pp. 221 and 223.

types of channel intermediaries—what you call them depends on what they do

Up to now, we have centered much of our attention on wholesaling businesses referred to as full-function wholesalers (and in particular, one type of full-function wholesaler, the industrial distributor). Full-function wholesalers offer the broadest range of services to customers and suppliers, and as such provide a convenient base from which to explore a number of types of channel intermediaries specializing in fulfilling a subset of these functions.

the big three of wholesaling

Merchant wholesalers (including, but not limited to, full-function wholesalers) are one of two types of wholesaling institutions differentiated by functions performed for customers and suppliers that the U. S. Census of Business identifies in the economic data it collects. The other type encompasses a category called agents and brokers. The functions most often performed by each, along with a typical range of margins that each receives, are outlined in Table 9-5.

Based on information in Table 9-5, what are basic differences between the two? What relationships do you see between the functions performed and the margins received by each?

Perhaps the most important difference between merchant wholesalers and agents and brokers, as the U. S. Bureau of the Census views them, is that the former buy and sell goods for their own account, taking possession of such goods, whereas agents and brokers more often buy and sell for others without taking title to, or in many cases without taking physical possession of, goods purchased. Both, however, represent independently owned companies not controlled by organizations engaged primarily in manufacturing or other operations.

The third major group of wholesaling institutions identified by the Census of Business is sales branches and offices owned and operated by manufacturing companies for the sale of their products at wholesale. In concept, these may be operated either like merchant wholesalers or agents and brokers, but in either event the sales branch or its parent manufacturing company maintains title to goods held in the stocks of the sales branch.

The relative growth and importance of merchant wholesalers, agents and brokers, and manufacturers' sales branches and offices is shown in Figure 9-4. Which of these basic wholesaling forms has exhibited the most dynamic growth? How might you explain this?

Table 9-5 **Typical Functions Performed and Margins Received by Merchant Wholesalers and Agents and Brokers**[a]

Functions	Merchant Wholesalers	Agents and Brokers
Transactional		
Selling		
Personal sales effort	X	X
Advertising	O	—
Buying	X	X
Risk (title) assumption	X	—
Logistical		
Assembly	X	X
Storage	X	O
Assorting	X	O
Transportation	X	O
Facilitating		
Financing (providing credit)	X	O
Postpurchase service and maintenance	O	—
Information dissemination	X	O
Channel coordination	O	—
Range of margins received (as a percentage of sales)	5–30%	3–10%

[a]X = function typically performed; O = function occasionally performed; — = function not performed.

311

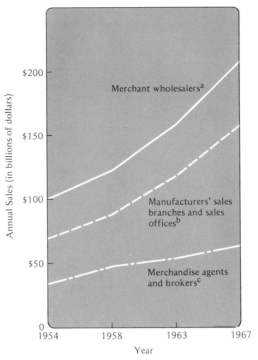

Figure 9-4. Wholesale trade by three major types of wholesalers. Source: *Census of Business* (Washington, D.C.: Department of Commerce, Bureau of the Census, 1971) p. ix. Other categories of wholesalers separately identified by the *Census of Business* are (1) petroleum bulk stations and terminals and (2) assemblers of farm products. Together, these make up about 8 percent of all wholesaling activity. (a) Merchant wholesalers are defined by the *Census of Business* as establishments primarily engaged in buying and selling merchandise on their own account, including wholesale merchants or jobbers, industrial distributors, voluntary group wholesalers, exporters, importers, cash-and-carry wholesalers, wagon distributors, retailer cooperative warehouses, terminal grain elevators, wholesale cooperative supply associations, and metals service centers. (b) Manufacturers' sales branches are defined by the *Census of Business* as establishments maintained by manufacturing and mining companies apart from their plants or mines for marketing their products at wholesale. (c) Merchandise agents and brokers are defined by the *Census of Business* as establishments whose operators are in business for themselves and are primarily engaged in selling or buying goods for others.

a more detailed look

Census of Business data lump together information about a number of distinctly different types of wholesaling activities within each of the categories described here. A catalog of functions performed and typical margins received by each type is presented in Table 9-6. It is useful to explore briefly the nature of some of the more important types of wholesalers without running our categorization into the ground. More formal definitions of each category of business are presented in the glossary in Appendix B.

Full-Function Merchant Wholesalers. As we see in Table 9-6, full-function merchant wholesalers comprise general-line wholesalers, similar to Johnson Mill Supply; specialty wholesalers, comparable to some of Johnson's competitors concentrating in fewer and more limited lines of industrial supplies; and rack jobbers or service merchandisers, an important category that we have not discussed as yet. These three types of wholesaling institutions perform the broadest range of transactional, logistical, and facilitating functions.

In a sense, rack jobbers, or service merchandisers, offer the most comprehensive service of all. They not only buy, sell, assume the risk of ownership, assemble, store, assort, deliver, finance, disseminate information, and coordinate channel activities to some extent. Their most distinguishing feature is that they create, place, and stock on a periodic basis displays containing merchandise (hence the term *rack jobber*) located on the premises of their retailer customers, particularly supermarket and drug outlets. Rack jobbers maintain current assortments of such items as phonograph records, taking careful note of what is hot and what is not by means of weekly or even more frequent visits to each display. Or they may insure fresh supplies of potato chips by carefully and frequently rotating the stock contained in self-standing displays. They deliver, supply displays, take inventory, rotate and replenish stocks, in some cases own the merchandise until it is sold, and invoice the retailer for the amount actually sold.

Limited-Function Merchant Wholesalers. Other wholesalers who buy and sell for their own account nevertheless offer a much more limited range of services to their customers and suppliers.

Cash-and-carry wholesalers require customers to (1) call at the wholesaler's place of business, (2) order their needs across the counter, (3) pay cash for their purchases, and (4) carry away the goods bought. Hence the term *cash-and-carry.* Drop shippers, in contrast, typically direct manufacturer-suppliers to ship orders directly to customers so that the drop shipper need not take merchandise into his possession. In total, these types of limited-function merchant wholesalers are of much less importance than several categories of agents and brokers.

Agents and Brokers. Of the various kinds of agents and brokers listed in Table 9-6, four types are worth mentioning here because of their continuing importance: manufacturers' agents, brokers, selling agents, and export and import agencies.

Manufacturers' agents are individuals, or organizations comprising relatively small groups of salespeople, who represent several manufacturers in selling often complementary lines of products to prospective customers in a particular geographic region. They are of particular importance in the sale of industrial and automotive products, iron and steel products, footwear, and piece goods. They most often confine their activities to selling, and in return are paid a commission based on the value of goods they sell.

Brokers may represent suppliers in the same manner as manufacturers' agents, and most extensively involve themselves in the sale of grocery items typically bought and sold in small quantities, such as candy, gum, and food specialties. In other cases, brokers more often bring together buyers and sellers on an ad hoc, or one-time, basis. This is particularly true in the distribution of agricultural raw materials. In selling perishable fruit and vegetables, a broker

313

Table 9-6 Functions Performed and Other Characteristics of Wholesalers and Other Channel Intermediaries[a]

Type of Channel	Transactional				Logistical							Facilitating				Examples of Typical Goods Handled	Typical Gross Margins Earned on Goods (in %)
Intermediaries Between Manufacturers and Retailers	Selling: Personal sales effort	Selling: Advertising	Buying	Risk assumption (taking title to goods)	Assembly	Storage: Storage only	Storage: Storage and inventory control	Assorting: Broad assortment	Assorting: Deep assortment	Assorting: Private brands	Transportation	Financing (providing credit)	Postpurchase service and maintenance	Information dissemination	Channel coordination		
Merchant wholesalers																	
Full-function wholesalers																	
General-line wholesalers	X	O	X	X	X		X	X		O	X	X	X	O	O	Groceries; hardware	7–20
Special-line wholesalers	X	O	X	X	X		X		X	O	X	X	X	O	O	Frozen foods	12–25
Rack jobbers or service merchandisers	X	X	X	X	X		X		X	O	X	X	X	X	X	Cosmetics; hosiery	12–16
Limited-function wholesalers																	
Cash-and-carry wholesalers	X		X	X	X		X	X								Groceries; drugs	8–10
Drop shippers			X	X								X				Construction materials	5
Agents and brokers																	
Manufacturers' agents	X							O								Industrial goods; clothing	5–7

314

Type of intermediary	Products	Number of functions[a]
Brokers	Food specialties	3–6
Commission merchants	Farm products	5
Selling agents	Textiles; industrial goods	5
Export and import agencies	All products	4–10
Auction companies	Agricultural products	2–3
Purchasing agents and resident buyers	Hardware; electrical products	3–4
Manufacturers' sales branches and offices	Industrial goods	6–12
Other intermediaries		
Public warehouses	All products	1–2
Central market facilities	Furniture	n.a.
Trade shows and exhibits	All manufactured products	n.a.
For-hire transportation carriers	All products	1–5
Distribution companies	All products	1–10
Factors	Textiles; other products	1–2
Banks and other financial institutions	All products	1–2
Advertising agencies	All products	1–2
Marketing research organizations	All products	.5

[a] X = functions typically performed; O = functions sometimes performed.

may seek out buyers for carloads of product already moving in the general direction of its market territory.

Selling agents contract to assume responsibility for all sales of a manufacturer's product and typically are given a wide latitude in determining promotional policies. Often they confine their efforts to the product line of only one or a limited number of manufacturers and are compensated on a commission basis. The largest proportion of selling agents is comprised of those who specialize in the sale of dry goods and apparel.

Export and import agencies maintain buying contacts abroad and perform a number of specialized functions involving the preparation and processing of documentation needed to transport products across international borders. They may perform these functions on behalf of other wholesalers who buy and sell imported goods in the United States market.

other intermediaries between manufacturers and retailers

A serious shortcoming of the Bureau of the Census data is that they include only those channel intermediaries who perform transactional functions, participating in the exchange of title for goods and services. This excludes a number of important intermediaries performing only logistical or facilitating functions. Among the more important of these types of organizations are for-hire freight transportation carriers, public warehouses, advertising agencies, and marketing research organizations. Of importance to certain industries are central market facilities and factors. Of interest because of their future potential are the so-called full-service distribution companies and in-store servicing firms. Information concerning all of these is arrayed in Table 9-6.

For-hire freight transportation companies by rail, highway, air, water, and pipeline generate the largest revenues by far of all nonwholesaling channel intermediaries by performing only one basic function, transportation, either at the behest of shippers or receivers of goods. Goods in transit may be owned either by buyers or sellers, depending on the terms of sale associated with the transportation movement, but rarely by the for-hire carrier. In recent years, the transportation of freight in manufacturer-owned vehicles, called private transportation, has grown in popularity to challenge, particularly, for-hire truckers.

Public warehouses contract to receive, store, ship, and sometimes deliver to destinations near the warehouse, products owned by others. In addition, they may control inventories, prepare bills of lading (documentation) for subsequent shipment by means of for-hire transportation companies, and prepay freight bills. As such, they provide useful and flexible alternatives to manufacturer-owned and operated warehouses.

Advertising agencies may perform marketing research, help plan campaigns, provide creative services associated with the design of advertising material, and contract for advertising time or space in various media, typically for a commission of 15 per cent of all advertising space or time purchased. They attempt to maintain contact with clients to provide such services over a period of time.

In contrast, marketing research organizations hold themselves out to perform investigations of customer attitudes, buying behavior, or new-product acceptance on a project basis.

Central market facilities are utilized heavily in furniture distribution, for example. Buyers and manufacturers alike congregate for several days each year at such important furniture markets as those in High Point, North Carolina; Grand Rapids, Michigan; and Chicago. Here the manufacturers display their new lines and write a substantial volume of orders for future delivery. Why would central market facilities be particularly useful to the furniture industry, which is made up of a large number of relatively small manufacturers?

In industries where manufacturers may not have sufficient working capital to finance their accounts receivable until such time as customers see fit to pay for their products, factors have played a useful role. Typically, they stand ready to "buy" at a substantial discount a manufacturer's accounts receivable, assuming responsibility for their subsequent collection. They represent an alternative, often an expensive one, to banks who may make loans that are secured by such accounts receivable. Historically, these factors have been prominent in financing receivables of garment manufacturers, among others.

Of potential future importance are full-service distribution companies. These companies contract literally to take physical possession of a manufacturer's products at the end of its production line, making such products available at the time, at the place, and in the quantities and form in which the manufacturer's customers desire them. Thus, while the manufacturer retains responsibility for transactional functions, the full-service distribution company, for a fee, assumes responsibility for all logistical functions. The first of these types of companies has been organized only in recent years and has yet to gain much prominence. They represent a response to the inability of small- to medium-sized manufacturers to obtain economies of scale in their logistical operations, for example, through the consolidation of shipments, and to acquire expertise in managing logistical as opposed to transactional (promotional) activities.

Of interest because they illustrate the development of channel intermediaries in response to need are in-store servicing firms. As one consumer products sales executive put it: "We're losing sales because retail shelves have never been shabbier nor stockout gripes more acute. Why? Because chains are slashing personnel to stay in the discount race."[7]

As a result, in-store service firms have been created to offer services to manufacturers, including the tidying of displays, the replenishment of in-store shelf stocks, and the checking of backroom supplies in retail outlets, often producing a doubling or tripling of retail sales for their manufacturer clients. Fees received by in-store service firms in total are miniscule compared to revenues of other types of channel intermediaries, and changing conditions may eliminate the need for their services just as rapidly as they were created. But the in-store service firm is an interesting example of the ever-changing subculture of channel intermediaries that springs up to meet needs at particular points in time.

(24)   Looking back over Table 9-6, do the conclusions you developed earlier regarding the relationships between functions performed and margins received by full-function wholesalers as opposed to agents and brokers (from Table 9-5) generally hold true for the more detailed summary of wholesalers and other

(23)

---

[7]James D. Snyder. "In-store Servicing Catches Fire," *Sales Management* (April 17, 1972), pp. 28–30. Quote on p. 28.

317

channel intermediaries? Competition among wholesalers, and the ever-present possibility that suppliers or customers might perform certain marketing functions more efficiently than channel intermediaries, should provide some assurance that such relationships will continue into the future.

At this point, you may be reeling from our brief discussion of the confusing array of intermediary institutions that serve manufacturers and retailers. Even though an exposure to the various types, neatly arrayed and defined, provides useful background information, you may take some comfort in the following comments by a marketing executive:

> Certainly too much is said about channel relationships in published textbooks for businessmen and students, if one is to look for proof in current marketing practice. The picture usually given is one of long lists of various types of middlemen and facilitating agencies, which differ minutely but precisely in functions performed. Alignments of particular types are presented as "right" or "customary" for a given commodity or type of producer.

> Yet hybridity is too common among marketing firms to be ignored. For example, almost any wholesaler will do some business at retail; similarly, it is not uncommon for a broker to find himself holding title to a given lot of goods, thus becoming temporarily a merchant middleman.[8]

In spite of these remarks, the never-never world of Table 9-6 will provide some confidence in dealing with the contradictions of the real world.

wholesaler needs: determinants in selecting manufacturing-suppliers

(25)
(26)

For some years, marketing practitioners and scholars have argued the question of whether it is in the best interests of a wholesaler to think of itself primarily as a buying agent for its customers or as a selling agent for its suppliers. What has our discussion suggested up to this point? What are your views on this question?

If we are to follow the precedent set in preceding chapters, we should conclude that a wholesaler's primary role is to satisfy its customers' needs. In doing so, it may in turn make its needs known to suppliers, particularly at times when it is considering dropping or adding product lines in which it might trade.

customer needs as a determinant of wholesaler needs

It can be argued that once a wholesaler establishes the basic line of products it will sell and initiates trade relationships with one or more suppliers, its basic strength most often is derived from its customers rather than the reputation of

[8] Philip McVey, "Are Channels of Distribution What the Textbooks Say?" *Journal of Marketing,* **24** (Jan. 1960), pp. 61–64. Quote on p. 61.

its products or suppliers. As we have seen, the primary means of building customer relations is by offering the products and services that a customer may need and come to expect at a competitive cost.

This may lead a wholesaler to select new lines of products and new manufacturer-supplier relationships on the basis of whether they are desired by its existing or a desired customer group. For example, several years ago, McDonald's, the franchiser of fast food outlets, decided to test the capability of one supplier to provide a McDonald's franchisee with its entire line of food and nonfood supplies.[9] At the time, the total annual bill for these products purchased by McDonald's franchisees was about $400 million. In order to participate in the experiment, Golden State Foods Corp., a Los-Angeles-based distributor, realizing 80 per cent of its annual $66 million in sales by supplying burgers, buns, potatoes, and other nondairy items to 432 of McDonald's 2,200 outlets, had to take on a complete line of paper goods and other nonfood supplies.

Similarly, wholesalers have had to adjust the services they provide to meet customer needs. For example, as the product lines offered by individual wholesalers dealing with relatively small retailers have become more complex, wholesalers have begun to take a more active role in monitoring and controlling retailer inventories through in-store merchandising, automatic computer-controlled replenishment systems, or education programs designed to help retailers help themselves. In the case of Golden State Foods Corp., in order to get the business of a new franchisee, Golden State typically trained the staff of a new McDonald's franchise. What are some other relatively recent service innovations that we have discussed in this chapter? What customer needs does each meet?

(27)
(28)

wholesaler needs in selecting manufacturer-supplier relationships

In turn, wholesalers must make sure that certain fundamental needs are met in their dealings with manufacturer-suppliers. Among these are (1) the adequacy of the product line they offer; (2) exclusivity in representing a supplier—or the avoidance, if possible, of competing directly with another wholesaler for the sale of a line of products; (3) the continuity of trade relationships; (4) the adequacy of various means of marketing support provided by prospective suppliers; and (5) the relationships between wholesaler rewards (margins or commissions) and responsibilities (functions to be performed).

Adequacy of Product Line. In developing a product line, we have said that a wholesaler must be most concerned about customer needs. In addition, a wholesaler's offerings must be great enough to at least produce margins sufficient to defray the variable costs of a sales call. Unrelated products sold to basically different customer groups do not meet this need. At the same time, manufacturer-suppliers offering an extensive line of related products often are

[9]"A Fight for All of McDonald's Business," *Business Week* (Feb. 17, 1973), pp. 42 and 46.

able to justify having their own selling personnel and direct sales to at least larger retailing organizations or industrial customers. Thus, most wholesalers have a continuing need to seek out suppliers with complementary, but limited, product lines or those with extensive product lines seeking distribution to smaller potential customers.

Exclusivity. Concerns about competition from other wholesaling organizations have led many wholesalers to seek means of restricting such competition to at least a reasonable level. Among those that have been attempted are the assembly of unique lines of products through exclusive distributorships. The ability to gain an exclusive distributorship from a supplier may depend on the relative strength of a wholesaler's reputation and the selling ability of the supplier in the market place. Even where exclusive agreements have existed between wholesalers and manufacturers, the acquisition of one wholesaler organization by another may alter the geographic territories served by wholesalers and throw two organizations with exclusive agreements with the same manufacturer-supplier into competition with one another.

Continuity of Relationships. At the time of the introduction of Volkswagen automobiles in the United States, the German manufacturer was willing to sign agreements providing exclusive distributorships for various regions of the country. Major functions of these distributors were to seek out desirable retail dealers for Volkswagen automobiles, help coordinate promotional efforts designed to introduce Volkswagen products to the American public, and maintain inventories of replacement parts on a regional basis. Having performed the first of these two tasks so well that within several years Volkswagen was a household name whose products (and dealerships) were eagerly sought out, the role of the distributor was reduced largely to administering an existing dealer system at costs far below the margins originally agreed on. The protection of their contractual agreements provided an early incentive for distributor effort and prevented Volkswagen from assuming these functions and most of the margin once the effort had succeeded.

It is perhaps in the nature of the business that wholesalers who are particularly effective inevitably work themselves out of the task of representing a manufacturer-supplier unless they can obtain contractual agreements or build such a franchise of customer loyalty that a supplier can terminate a distributor relationship only at some cost in lost sales. And yet, wholesalers must devise means of assuring that their costly efforts to develop a market will not go unrewarded once the market is developed.

Manufacturer-Supplier Support. Wholesalers of consumer goods may rely on suppliers to fund advertising programs sufficient to familiarize consumers with their products and convince potential retailer customers that an effort is being made to promote such products to consumers. In other cases, manufacturers are relied on to devise special promotions for their products. One piece of evidence of the selectivity employed in screening various manufacturer-supplier promotions, and the proportion of such promotions that is perceived as being potentially successful by wholesalers in four industries, is presented in Table 9-7. How would you regard the proportions of acceptable promotions? Do they vary significantly by industry?

(29) (30)

320

Table 9-7 **Comparison of Wholesale Promotions Offered and Those Actually Accepted by 400 Wholesalers***

	Average Number of Promotions		
Product Line	Offered to Each Wholesaler	Accepted by Each Wholesaler	% Accepted
Electrical	56	8	14.3
Plumbing, heating, and cooling	36	8	22.2
Drug	3,700	390	10.5
Food, candy, and tobacco	244	39	16.0

* Source: Based on a survey of 400 wholesalers conducted in 1966 in conjunction with the National Association of Wholesalers and reported in Richard S. Lopata, "Faster Pace in Wholesaling," *Harvard Business Review,* **47** (July–Aug. 1969) pp. 130–143. See p. 141.

Wholesalers dealing in industrial goods most often stress the need for technical support ranging from extensive sales literature to consultation by manufacturers' sales engineers on particularly difficult customer problems. As industrial product lines and individual products become more complex, this need increases. It is virtually impossible for a general-line distributor such as Johnson Mill Supply to take up the slack when inadequate technical support is provided; special-line distributor-wholesalers are in a much better position to do so.

Margins Commensurate with Responsibilities. The most tangible form of manufacturer-supplier support is the margin provided on wholesaler sales. Margins that do not reflect the fact that wholesalers may act as order takers for some products and must employ intensive technical sales effort for others are harbingers of wholesaler-supplier conflict. A wholesaler confronted with such a situation can (1) reduce its sales effort, a possibly unfortunate action if the product in question requires (and customers desire) extensive selling effort; (2) raise its prices, a questionable decision for products in limited demand; (3) request either more extensive supplier sales support or greater margins (through lower supplier prices), thereby reducing the value of its service to its supplier; (4) discontinue the relationship, a possibly unfortunate decision if customers perceive a need for products of the type in question; or (5) seek means of accomplishing the required level of selling effort at lower cost, a universally attractive action but one difficult to achieve for an already well-run distributorship. The problem often is made more difficult for suppliers who want to avoid Robinson-Patman prosecution for offering discriminatory prices or services to two competing wholesalers purchasing essentially in the same quantities. At times, a wholesaler may be forced to follow a course that represents the lesser of evils in improving its profitability.

Many wholesalers are just beginning to develop the information systems that allow them to identify the most and least profitable of their customers, product lines, and suppliers. As the result of recent efforts, Johnson Mill Supply had found that 20 per cent of the items that it stocked produced 80 per cent of its total sales volume. In addition, it had correlated relatively unprofitable product lines with several types of measures: (1) low percentage margin on sales, (2) low inventory turnover, and (3) low average dollar sale per order line item. Products

(31)

registering low marks on two of these three criteria invariably were unprofitable. With the never-ending growth in the number of items carried by Johnson, a growing number of products were flunking the profitability test. Having identified this problem, what steps might Johnson Mill Supply take to correct it?

trends in wholesaling

Available statistics, both because of their aggregate nature and the limited relevance of measures of wholesaling activities employed by the Census of Business, do not reflect the substantial changes at work in wholesale distribution activities today.

structure and concentration

(32)

(33)
(34)

The world of wholesaling is populated by businesses of modest size, as suggested by the data in Table 9-8. In fact, the sales of the largest wholesaler, Foremost-McKesson, a diversified wholesaler of drugs, grocery products, liquor, and health and beauty aids, recently exceeded $2 billion per year. But, referring to Table 9-8, what do you find regarding the relative concentration of wholesalers compared to retailers in the United States? Would you regard Johnson Mill Supply as a big business? About what proportion of the wholesaling establish-

Table 9-8   **Relative Concentration of Wholesalers and Retailers, 1967***

Item	Wholesalers	Retailers
	1967	1967
Sales	$459 billion	$310 billion
Number of establishments[a]	311,000	1,763,000
Average sales per establishment	$1,470,000	$176,000
Proportion of total sales by firms with the following number of establishments		
1	40.9%	60.2%
2	4.8	5.8
3–5	7.2	2.0
6–10	5.4	2.7
11–25	6.7	3.6
25–50	7.4	7.0
51+	27.6	18.6
Total	100.0%[b]	100.0%[b]

* Sources: *1967 Census of Business* (Washington D. C.: Bureau of the Census, Department of Commerce, 1971), Vol. III, p. xx for wholesaler statistics and Vol. I, pp. 4–8 for retailer statistics.

[a] An establishment is defined as a separate place of business.

[b] Totals may not add to 100.0 per cent due to rounding.

ments shown in Table 9-8 would you estimate had annual sales volumes in 1967 that exceeded Johnson's most recent figure of $3,245,000?

(35)

Concentration. In recent years wholesaling chains have been organized in the paper and industrial supply trades by investors seeking to achieve competitive advantages over independent, single-branch wholesalers. For example, a former Gulf & Western executive, Joel Roth, has organized a chain of industrial distributorships located in a number of major cities and called Industrial Distributors of America, Inc., an organization that eventually may be in direct competition with Dale Johnson's. What advantages will Joel Roth's organization achieve over Dale Johnson's with such a strategy?

Growth of Special-Line Wholesalers. Special-line wholesalers have grown at a particularly rapid rate, not only in the industrial supply trade but in others such as those for hardware and drug items. In the case of industrial supply wholesalers, the phenomenon has been a response to the large number of new products developed in recent years by manufacturer-suppliers that have proven to be such a burden for Johnson Mill Supply, for example. In this regard, a recent article directed at independent, general-line distributors titled, "Don't Look Now—But You're Obsolete" was particularly disturbing to Dale Johnson.[10] It predicted the eventual replacement of independent, general-line distributors, with their outdated management and excessive investments in slow-moving inventories, by better-managed, more efficient special-line industrial distributor chains.

Hardware and drug wholesalers have turned to special-line operations in response to the growth of large-scale retailers and the advent of scrambled merchandising.[11] Specialization has provided opportunities for great wholesaling efficiencies, particularly in inventory control, as a means of forestalling the tendency of manufacturers to deal directly with large retailers through their sales branches. As certain hardware and drug items have moved into supermarkets and discount department stores, special-line wholesalers have been able to seek out retailers of hardware items wherever they are to be found in an age of scrambled merchandising in which, as one exasperated wholesaler put it, "every retailer seems to be selling everything."

Growth of Voluntary Wholesalers. Retailers operating one or several outlets in the grocery, drug, hardware, automotive "home and auto," and variety merchandise trades have turned to voluntary wholesaling through contractual agreements with wholesalers as a means of combating the competition of chain stores and large retailing organizations.

In return for an agreement from a retailer to buy a certain volume or proportion of its total merchandise from a voluntary wholesaler, a voluntary wholesaler passes on lower prices made possible by central buying; makes available private-brand merchandise; and provides financial, merchandising, advertising, and promotional assistance.

---

[10] Paul T. Nelson, "Don't Look Now—But You're Obsolete," *Industrial Distribution* (Feb. 1973) pp. 40–41.

[11] James C. McKeon, "Conflicting Patterns of Structural Change in Wholesaling," *Economic and Business Bulletin* (Winter, 1972), pp. 37–48.

In the food field in particular, independent retailers purchasing from voluntary wholesalers such as Super Value and Independent Grocers' Association (IGA) have grown at a much faster rate than chain retailing organizations. In recent years, voluntary wholesaling plans offered by such organizations as the wholesale divisions of the Rexall and Walgreen companies and McKesson & Robbins have served nearly half of all drugstores. Voluntary wholesaling in this trade has been spurred by the growth of drug discounting among larger retailing organizations.

Services provided by voluntary wholesaling organizations have been broadened to meet changing needs. For example, according to McCammon: "many drug wholesalers, sponsoring voluntary programs, routinely sign shopping center leases to secure prime locations for their accounts, and others provide a centralized accounting service."[12] Well-known trade names of voluntary wholesalers such as National Automotive Parts Association (NAPA) in auto parts; Western Auto, Gamble-Skogmo, and Coast-to-Coast stores in home and auto merchandise; and Ben Franklin in variety store merchandise attest to the success of their efforts.

shifting emphasis on functions performed

In an effort to meet customer needs within acceptable cost limits, many wholesalers have altered their emphasis on functional tasks and the manner in which they perform them. They have turned to selective selling methods, selective stocking, and changing service programs.

Selective Selling. Because of the rapidly rising costs of personal sales calls, many wholesalers lavish such attention on their largest or most profitable retailer customers. Others are served, where possible, by automatic reordering programs in which replenishment shipments are based on retailer reports of sales and other inputs, telephone or "inside" selling, and catalog selling. Salesmen, thus freed from routine order taking functions, can spend time diagnosing current customer problems.

Selective Stocking. Given the rapid proliferation of available products in many trades, more powerful wholesalers have demanded that manufacturer-suppliers reduce the size of their product lines. Others have eliminated many slow-selling items from stock and reduced the level of service provided for others. The margin freed up by these actions has been used to provide badly needed services.

Changing Service Programs. Functions typically performed by wholesalers in many trades are in a constant state of flux. Consultant Richard S. Lopata offers one of many possible illustrations of this:

In the grocery field, credit extension used to be a prime function of the wholesaler. Today almost all wholesale grocery products flow into retail stores

[12]Bert C. McCammon, Jr., "The Emergence and Growth of Contractually Integrated Channels in the American Economy," in *Marketing and Economic Development,* ed. Peter D. Bennett (Chicago: American Marketing Association, 1965), pp. 496–515. Quote on pp. 508–509.

on a cash basis, for all intents and purposes. Here service has shifted from credit extension to merchandising support, inventory management counseling, and profit analysis on behalf of the retailer.[13]

profitability

Given the changing and conflicting forces besetting many wholesaling operations, how are wholesalers faring? Ratios of net profit to tangible net assets shown for wholesalers and manufacturers in selected lines of trade in Table 9-9

Table 9-9 **Profits of Selected United States Merchant Wholesalers and Manufacturers, 1967 and 1973***

| | Percentage of Net Profit on Tangible Net Worth[a] | | | |
| Product Category | Merchant Wholesalers (in %) | | Manufacturers (in %) | |
	1967	1973	1967	1973
Durable goods				
Auto parts and accessories	6.85	10.39	11.05	n.a.[b]
Electrical parts and supplies	8.65	10.52	14.83	14.28
Furniture and home furnishings	8.90	8.48	7.87[c]	11.32[c]
Hardware	3.87	7.48	9.51[d]	11.62[d]
Plumbing and heating supplies	6.23	8.41	8.41	9.16
Lumber and building materials	6.73	13.87	7.55[e]	15.44[e]
Metals and materials	8.33	13.44	9.23[f]	8.95[f]
Nondurable goods				
Groceries	6.42	8.84	11.25[g]	11.83[g]
Drugs and drug sundries	6.50	7.56	10.38	13.40
Chemical and allied products	7.43	14.70	8.35[h]	14.25[h]
Paper	6.92	9.68	8.50	10.81

* Source: *Key Business Ratios* (New York: Dun & Bradstreet, Inc., 1968 and 1974), pp. 6–11 in both editions.

[a] Median percentages after taxes.

[b] Not available.

[c] Wood and upholstered household furniture.

[d] Cutlery, hand tools, and general hardware.

[e] Average of concrete, gypsum, and plaster products and sawmills and planing mills.

[f] Iron and steel foundries.

[g] Canned and preserved fruits, vegetables, and seafoods.

[h] Average of agricultural and industrial chemicals.

[13] Richard S. Lopata, "Faster Pace in Wholesaling," *Harvard Business Review,* **47** (July–Aug. 1969) pp. 130–143. Quote on p. 136.

(36)

may provide some indication. Based on Table 9-9, how well do you think wholesalers have fared in comparison with manufacturers in comparable lines of trade? In comparison with what you might have expected?

(37)

a final question

We have explored factors influencing the importance of wholesaling in general in distribution systems and various types of wholesaling in particular. What do these forces hold for the Dale Johnsons of the business world? If Johnson Mill Supply is to survive, what changes, if any, will it be forced to make in its operation?

(38)
(39)

summary

I've attempted purposely to write this chapter as might an owner of a wholesaling organization with a somewhat inflated view of the importance of his firm's services to customers and manufacturer-suppliers, concerns about the relative power of those with whom he does business as well as his competition, and above all a more independent attitude toward suppliers than toward his customers. In the process, hopefully this material has reaffirmed the unchanging nature of the basic transactional, logistical, and facilitating functions that must be performed by someone in the distribution process.

Although merchant wholesalers realize the greatest volume of sales of any of the big three of wholesaling (as opposed to agents and brokers and manufacturers' wholesale sales branches and offices), other channel intermediaries such as for-hire transportation firms probably realize greater net revenues and play important roles in the distribution process.

In devising the most effective means of achieving its primary goal, the satisfaction of customer needs, a wholesaler must, in its dealings with manufacturer-suppliers, assure itself of (1) an adequate product line; (2) no more than a reasonable level of competition from other wholesalers, by offering a product line differentiated from that of its competitors, (3) continuing relationships with both customers and suppliers; (4) supplier support appropriate to the nature of the product and the difficulty of the selling task; and (5) most important, margins commensurate with responsibilities such that it can continue to prosper and perform needed marketing functions.

Wholesaling is practiced by many relatively small businesses in the United States. These organizations occupy a strategic place in channels of distribution—figuratively speaking at the crossroads of product flows from suppliers to retailers. They are beset by the pressures created by scrambled retail merchandising, the relative growth of retailing institutions capable of performing many functions formerly performed by wholesalers, and the desire of retailers further to reduce inventories and engage in "stockless purchasing." Competition, in the form of wholesaling specialists and wholesaling chains, threatens particularly the general-line distributor of many types of products. And growing product and product-line complexity, coupled with a perceived lack of selling support, have created stresses in wholesaler relationships with suppliers.

The continuing importance of wholesalers and other channel intermediaries depends on their ability to devise new ways of performing certain of the unchanging marketing functions more effectively than their customers or their suppliers. As a result, wholesalers have placed their stocks in customers' facilities to make stockless purchasing even more convenient for customers, have established direct means of electronic order input for important customers, have employed radio-controlled fleets of vehicles for servicing and maintaining the equipment that they sell, have instituted better methods of communicating market trends to suppliers, and have devised many other new ways of performing basic marketing functions. Judging from the relative rate of growth of wholesaling volume in the United States, their efforts have not gone unrewarded. If sales volume is a rough indication of the value of services performed (what would be a better measure?) customers and suppliers in large numbers apparently have been willing to pay the margins necessary to have a number of basic functions performed by channel intermediaries.

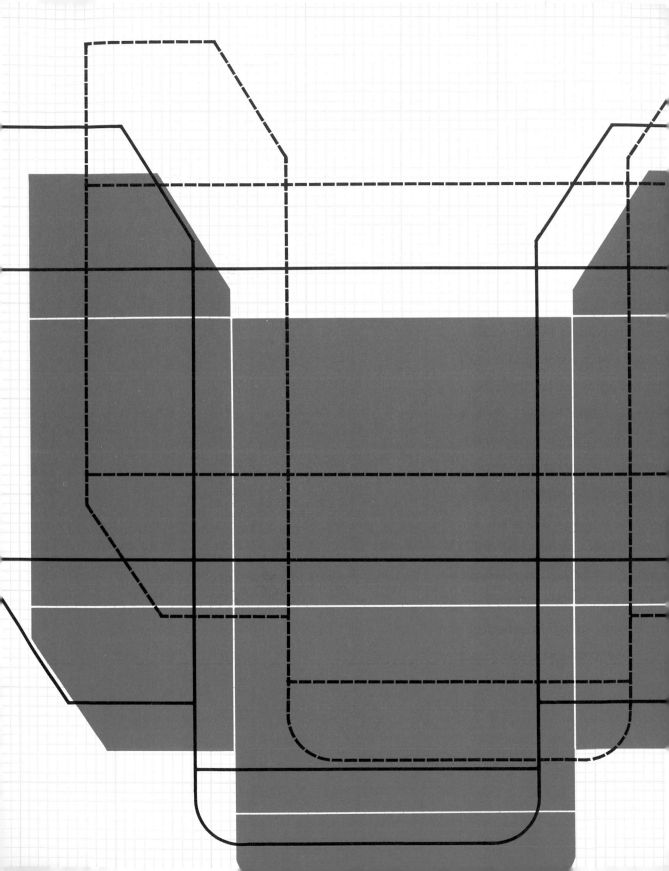

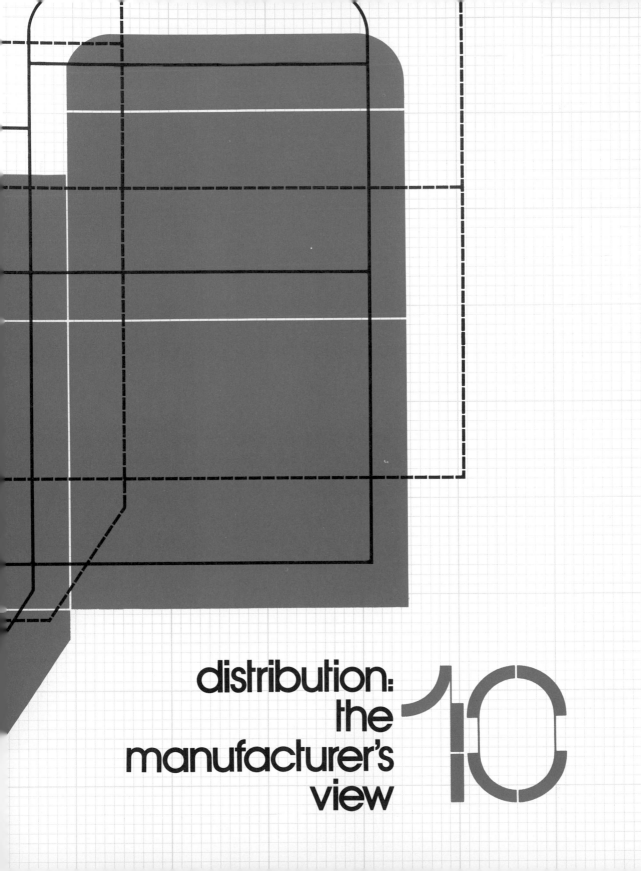

distribution: the manufacturer's view

10

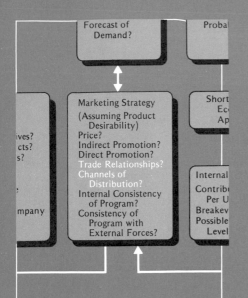

Forecast of
Demand?

Proba

Marketing Strategy
(Assuming Product
Desirability)
Price?
Indirect Promotion?
Direct Promotion?
Trade Relationships?
Channels of
Distribution?
Internal Consistency
of Program?
Consistency of
Program with
External Forces?

Short
Ec
Ap

ives?
cts?
s?

mpany

Internal
Contribu
Per U
Breakev
Possible
Level

Our objectives here are twofold, to look at channels of distribution from the manufacturer's point of view and to take an over-all view in order to draw together the material of Chapters 8 through 10. As always, the goal is to develop a point of view through a decision-making process. What better way to start than with three manufacturer-oriented channel problems? I'll refer to each of them later in the discussion.

It's easy to get hung up and cowed by the complexity of channels of distribution. Because it can be extremely confusing to discuss channels in general, I'll attempt to be example-specific as much as possible. Our discussion will involve patterns rather than rigid rules of channel relationships. Some would suggest that even this is going too far. Scholars remind us that every time a consumer buys something he or she is served by a particular combination of specific firms that may never have been put together before and may never be put together again. In a strict sense that may be true, but it provides little guidance for the development of manufacturers' channel strategies and policies.

A word of clarification: throughout our discussion, we'll use the terms manufacturer and product in their broadest sense, whether the "manufacturer" produces nuts and bolts or trucking services. It's imprecise, but handy.

Many marketing scholars define channels of distribution only in terms of the flow of title to goods, essentially focusing on transactional functions. Others admit logistical and facilitating functions to the club, but treat them like lepers, isolating them in an unrealistic fashion. Here transactional, logistical, and facilitating functions are, to the extent possible, discussed in parallel. Throughout the discussion, I've made an attempt to follow through with the structure of customer needs and marketing functions developed in Chapters 8 and 9.

Toro's surprise

At its annual marketing conference in August 1972, John C. Norton, group vice-president for the Toro Co., a Minneapolis-based manufacturer of lawn and turf-care equipment sold to home owners and golf and country club operators, surprised the company's sixty-five independent distributors. He announced to them that, beginning the following month, they would be able to give their large customers the option of buying lawn mowers direct from Toro at a 12 per cent margin to the distributors instead of the 40 per cent margin they had been receiving.[1]

Toro's action was based on a belief that the trend toward consumer buying from mass merchandisers would continue beyond its current rate of 40 per cent of the market. At the time, Sears, Roebuck alone sold one out of every seven power mowers sold in the United States at prices that did not allow margins for

[1] Based on information supplied by company executives in addition to material appearing in Sally Scanlon, "Toro Takes the Bull by the Horns," *Sales Management* (Feb. 19, 1973), pp. 25–26.

distributors but required direct distribution from the manufacturer to Sears' distribution warehouses. In contrast, Toro's consumer products had been sold primarily through smaller retail accounts at higher prices that provided both higher retailer and higher distributor margins. The company had relied entirely on its sixty-five independent distributors and six company-owned distributorships in major markets, which it had acquired during the past two years to bolster market share in these areas. Even so, its sales growth had lagged behind that of its competitors. In fact, Toro, with 1972 sales of $85 million, employed only five sales people (all district managers) for its consumer lawn products marketing effort.

At the same meeting, Mr. Norton announced that Toro would train two hundred selected dealers, who might or might not sell Toro products, to do warranty service and repair work. These dealers, who would be required to stock adequate supplies of Toro parts, would provide the supporting services that mass merchandisers refused to do. In a third action, Norton indicated that Toro would spend $2.25 million for advertising in 1973, nearly double its expenditures for 1972.

These supporting programs, however, did not allay distributors' concerns regarding the "direct accounts" program. Those most seriously affected were among Norton's top sales producers. As one distributor put it, "I don't blame Toro for putting in the new program. The other big brands, Outboard Marine's Lawn-Boy and Allegheny Ludlum's Jacobsen, already had them. Toro had to compete. But it didn't consult us beforehand. I'm going to have to take on other lines to get my profits back in shape."

(1)
(2)

What factors would you take into account in evaluating Toro's decision to institute its direct accounts program? Based on what you know, would you have announced it?

Unimarket[2]

As part of its effort to reduce its dependence on sales to the government, the Raytheon Company's Distributor Products Division developed the Unimarket concept. Under Unimarket, Raytheon closed its six strategically located distribution centers and began shipping all products directly to its seven hundred franchised distributors from one inventory located in Westwood, Massachusetts. Products included replacement tubes and transistors, which were sold in turn by distributors to many of the 125,000 television and radio repairmen in the United States. Nearly all of the distributors carried two of more lines of competing replacement tubes and transistors.

Prior to the introduction of Unimarket, Raytheon's products were ordered by phone or mail from the nearest distribution center. Here they were either picked

[2] Based on information in John T. Thompson, "Physical-Distribution Management in Raytheon Company," in Management of the Physical-Distribution Function, AMA Management Report No. 49 (New York: American Management Association, 1960), pp. 179–188; "Raytheon Revisited," Traffic Management (March 1962), pp. 46–47; Donald J. Frederick, "Unimarket, An Interim Report," Air Cargo (July 1961), p. 15; and Albert M. Joseph, "How Packaging Affects Your Total Distribution Costs," Handling & Shipping (Aug. 1962), p. 19.

from stock, or subsequent orders for unavailable items were sent on to the company's plants in Massachusetts. Shipments from distribution centers largely were made by truck. The entire process usually took four to twelve days from the time a distributor placed its order until it received its shipment.

The dispersion of inventories among six distribution centers (DCs) often created more product availability problems than it solved. The DCs sometimes delayed transmitting their needs to Raytheon's plants. In addition, added investment was required as more DCs were added to the network in response to the demands of the sales force for better service.

Under Unimarket, all DCs were closed in favor of the factory-oriented center at Westwood. Dealers' orders were phoned or mailed to a Raytheon district sales office from which they were transmitted by wire to Westwood for sale-day processing. All shipments were shipped by air freight to fifteen regional break-bulk points, from which they were sent on to individual dealers by truck. The entire process was designed to provide a 48- to 72-hour response time from the time a dealer's order arrived at a Raytheon sales office. As a result, Raytheon became one of the first firms to distribute an entire product line by air.

Cost savings reported for the first year of Unimarket's operation resulted mainly from a $2 million reduction in inventory:

Item	Amount
Decreased costs	
Interest on capital	$100,000
Warehousing	237,000
Protective packaging	100,000
Taxes	48,000
Total cost decrease	$485,000
Increased costs	
Transportation	$124,000
Net cost decrease	$361,000

Customers generally reacted favorably to the change. Some comments included: "Excellent service—best of any tube manufacturer"; "Good service, keep it up"; and "Best delivery yet." There was some minority reaction: "Terrible! Amazed you can operate this way" and "Somebody goofed."

(3)
(4)
Do the figures shown here accurately reflect the impact of Unimarket on the performance of Raytheon's Distributor Products Division? How would you assess the long-run potential for success under Unimarket?

the go-go gambit

Late in 1965, the regional commodity manager for a major stock brokerage firm and a university professor began efforts to register with the Securities and Exchange Commission (SEC) a mutual fund that would be the first authorized to trade not only in stocks but also in highly speculative and volatile commodity futures contracts. This was in response to the increasing popularity among investors of so-called go-go glamour stocks and mutual funds, in part a result of general prosperity and generally rising stock prices.[3]

After a long period of negotiation, as the result of its founders' efforts, the Comsec (for commodities and securities) Fund, Inc. was registered in 1970 by the SEC and cleared for trading in thirty-seven states. By this time, however, a period of economic recession and stock market losses had soured many investors on go-go funds. In addition, several studies had indicated that mutual funds, by pooling investor purchases of mutual fund shares and reinvesting their money in a portfolio of securities, did provide an opportunity to the small investor to diversify his investment and reduce risk. However, they were found not to have performed as well as the average for all stocks. As a result, sales of mutual fund shares had declined rapidly.

By the end of its first year of operation, the Comsec Fund was one of the best performing mutual funds in the United States. However, only $600,000 in Comsec Fund shares had been purchased by investors, far short of the $5 million needed to defray the costs of the fund's management. To defray the sizeable legal costs involved in its registration, its founders were forced to sell the Comsec Fund to an insurance company early in 1972, although one of them continued to serve as its president.

Up to 1970, most mutual fund shares were distributed through local offices of regional and national stock brokerage houses. A small investor, for example, would surrender $8\frac{1}{2}$ per cent of his initial investment as a "load," or sales charge. Most of this was paid as a sales commission to the brokerage house and the individual employee making the sale to his or her investor-customer. Some fifteen major brokerage organizations had authorized personnel in their branches to sell shares of the Comsec Fund on this basis. This constituted the only major promotional effort on behalf of the fund other than that put forth by its president in contacting brokers' salesmen as well as individual investors. Because of the unique nature of the fund, its objectives and methods had to be explained in detail not only to potential investors, many of whom were totally unfamiliar with the nature of commodity futures markets, but also to the brokers' representatives responsible for recommending one investment as opposed to another. Although several funds were advertised rather heavily, with two even advertised extensively on television, most were advertised by means of small ads in financial publications or newspaper financial sections. Advertising on behalf of the Comsec Fund consisted of a twice-monthly ad, one column inch in size, announcing the latest prices of the fund's shares in *The Wall Street Journal.*

By early 1972, the fund's president was contemplating a proposal to file for permission to change Comsec to a "no-load" fund. This type of fund, for which no sales charge is assessed, would, it was thought, be more favorably received by investors. Sales loads had been cited as a further factor limiting the performance of mutual fund shares for those who invested in them. Several load funds already had been converted to no-load funds, and most new mutual funds being introduced were of the no-load type. Sales of no-load fund shares were far outpacing those for load funds.

(5)
(6)
As president of the Comsec Fund, Inc. would you take action to convert the fund to a no-load status? Why?

[3] Based on bitter experience.

(7)

We know what Toro and Raytheon did. And the Comsec Fund was converted to a no-load status. How do you think each of these decisions affected the performance of the respective companies in which each was made? We'll review the evidence later in this chapter.

What do these vignettes have in common? They all concern a manufacturer's or producer's attempt to build or maintain sales for its "product," possibly by providing incentives for retailers or wholesalers to devote substantial effort to its sale. They provide us with a variety of illustrations of manufacturers' or producers' decisions regarding the design of channels of distribution for their products. And they introduce us to the manufacturer's view of the channel of distribution.

the manufacturer's view of the channel

If we think of a channel of distribution for a manufacturer's product as a river or pipe line, the manufacturer stands at the head looking downstream. What does he see? Figuratively speaking he may see a delta at the far end, representing the sale of the product to ultimate buyers through a variety of different types of retail or other outlets. Or there may be no delta. He may see a long stream involving many channel intermediaries, or a short stream. He may see a stream with a fork, where the flow of title to, and physical possession of, product are separated. Or there may be no fork. What the manufacturer sees depends, at least in part, on a number of decisions that he may make regarding the division of responsibility for performing the basic marketing functions that, by now, should be imprinted indelibly on your mind.

breadth of the channel

Questions concerning the breadth of a channel of distribution include those of the number and number of types of outlets through which to sell to ultimate customers and the number of types of intermediaries through which to reach these outlets.

Number of Selling Outlets. Products and services can be sold through all available outlets, some selected subsets of these, or as few as one outlet per defined market area. We refer to distribution policies employing each of these alternatives as intensive, selective, and exclusive, respectively.

The nature of the policy selected may depend primarily on the nature of the product, perceived market segments for the products or services in question, the strength of the name of the product or its producer, the manner in which customers in each segment buy the product, available outlets and their interest in selling the product or service, and competitive forces. This takes us back to our discussion in Chapter 8 of the comparative nature of convenience, shopping, and specialty goods and retail outlets, as diagrammed in Table 8-3 on page 272.

(8)

(9)

How would you relate convenience, shopping, and specialty goods to intensive, selective, and exclusive distribution strategies? One possible relationship is suggested in Figure 10-1. Recalling our use in Chapter 8 of a tube of toothpaste and a new dining room table to illustrate differences in products, the manner of their purchase, and the types of outlets through which they are sold, what type of distribution strategy would you be most likely to associate with each?

Number of Types of Selling Outlets. As suggested in Figure 10-1, the degree to which a product is perceived as being a convenience good may depend on the frequency with which it is purchased, the perceived importance or risk associated with its purchase, and the need for added information about the product. These factors influence the willingness or reluctance of a customer to (1) plan the purchase in advance as opposed to making an impulse purchase by a chance contact with the product in a store, (2) expend effort in its purchase, (3) substitute one brand or product for another, and (4) rely on the retail sales effort as opposed to his or her own judgment in making a purchase.

Historically, markets have associated consumer products with store-product types such as drug, grocery, and hardware stores. Each was serviced by a group of wholesalers reflecting the same set of specialized product lines. But to an inceasing extent, consumers have come to value one-stop shopping and the purchase of several types of products on a single buying trip with a minimum expenditure of *incremental* effort for the purchase of each item. In part, this has been a response to the increasing burden and complexity of the buying task for an average family. It has led consumers, as Professor Eugene J. Kelley has suggested, to seek an acceptable balance between commodity costs, those paid to a seller for goods purchased, and convenience costs, those associated with the incremental time, energy, and expense of making a purchase.[4] Consumers have become better educated through the frequency of their purchasing and other means. As a result, they have gained self-confidence in buying more and more types of goods. Self-confidence, combined with economic affluence, have increased their willingness to buy grocery items, certain frequently purchased drug items, and even small appliances on the same buying trip, from the same retail outlets, and even to a degree on impulse at the time of contact with the product in the store.

Figure 10-1. Types of consumer goods, the level of incremental efforts that customers are willing to put forth to acquire them, and the distribution strategy each might suggest.

Types of Consumer Goods	Incremental Efforts which Customers Might Expend for Them	Suggested Distribution Strategy	Pattern of Retail Outlets in a Given Market
Convenience	Little	Intensive	
Shopping	Moderate	Selective	
Specialty	Great	Exclusive	

[4]Eugene J. Kelley, "The Importance of Convenience in Consumer Purchasing," *Journal of Marketing,* **22** (July 1958), pp. 32–38.

Consumers, with their usual wisdom, intuitively have come to regard retail stores as outlets for convenience, shopping, or specialty goods. Operators of grocery, variety, and department stores, sensing this, have added items such as frequently purchased drug products to their stocks. This has created what has come to be known as scrambled merchandising and intertype competition among retailers and the wholesalers who serve them. As a result, the number of types of outlets in which many products are sold has increased, whether or not this has been accompanied by an increase in the number of outlets.

(10)   We might ask ourselves by whom the new forms of merchandising were perceived as being "scrambled"—manufacturers, wholesalers, retailers, or consumers?

(11)   How would you characterize Toro power lawn mowers on the spectrum of
(12)   types of consumer goods? How would you describe Toro's distribution strategy?
(13)   Are these consistent, given the relationships suggested in Figure 10-1?

length of the channel

The length of a distribution channel is a figure of speech enabling us to refer to the number of times that a product changes ownership, is physically handled, comes to rest, and is assembled and assorted in its course from its producer to its ultimate buyer. Channel length often varies directly with the extent of the differences between the quantities, assortments, and locations in which products or product lines are produced and ultimately purchased.

For example, Sears, Roebuck and Co., until recently, purchased the entire output of lawn mowers of the Roper Corporation of Kankaki, Illinois. Sears' sales volume was such that it could receive at its distribution centers (warehouses) truckloads of lawn mowers moving directly from the end of Roper's production line. In this channel, the transactional functions of buying and selling were minimized. Many of the logistical functions normally performed by wholesalers were assumed by Sears, who assembled assortments for display and sale in small units to ultimate consumers.

In the sale of stock to the public, a corporation desiring to sell the stock often will contract with an underwriter to sell the entire amount of the stock issue at a discount. The underwriter, in turn, will sell "blocks," or small quantities, of the stock to brokerage houses, often known in the securities trade as retailers of securities. Brokers' representatives, or salesmen, will then endeavor to interest their individual customers in the stock at the retail price established for the underwriting before the stock is traded on the open market.

(14) (15)   Which of these products requires longer channels? Is this true both for transactional and logistical functions? If we apply this logic to services, what do
(16)   we often find? For example, what is the relative length of the channels for transactional and logistical functions performed by H & R Block at its 6,500 (as of 1974) income tax computation centers located in all communities of any size
(17)   in the United States. Or for the services produced by your neighborhood shoe
(18)   repair shop? Similarly, how would you expect the channel length for industrial goods sold by one manufacturer, which are used ultimately in the production process or as product components by another manufacturer, to compare with that for most consumer goods?

An extreme example of channel length is provided by the typical distribution system for frequently purchased consumer items sold in Japan. Here, channels must accommodate the fact that "the average Japanese housewife shops every-day within 500 yards of her home," spending an average of $3.25 each time in one or more small neighborhood shops.[5] Either as a cause or result, Japan has about the same number of retail stores as the United States, even though the latter has twice the population and twenty-five times the land area. To reach these outlets, manufacturers must sell to large wholesalers who sell to regional wholesalers who sell to neighborhood wholesalers. Only the latter possess the intimate knowledge and relationships necessary to sell to small groups of retailers. In this example, what are the determinants of the length of the channel for transactional functions? For logistical functions?

(19)
(20)

"multiplicity" of channels

Our preceding discussion should suggest that the performance of transactional, logistical, and facilitating functions can take on distinctly different character-istics in a channel of distribution. Thus, a manufacturer may have at its disposal different channels for having each of these groups of functions performed. In addition, any one group of functions may be performed by two or more channels.

Different Channels for Different Functions. The transactional aspect of a channel is described by the separate institutional entities buying and selling a product—the flow of its "title." The logistical aspect depends on the number of points at which products are handled, moved, stored, and assorted, regardless of the number of transfers of title or the number of institutional entities involved in performing these activities. Facilitating functions often are performed through totally different channel patterns. For example, recall the Toro Co.'s plan to train two hundred retail lawn mower dealers to service the company's products, regardless of whether or not a particular dealer sold new Toro lawn mowers.

The breadth and length of the manner in which transactional, logistical, and facilitating functions are performed in channels of distribution can be differ-entiated, in a sense describing three separate types of channels. Whether forks occur in the flow of title, physical exchange and facilitating functions can be to some extent controlled by a manufacturer in establishing its distribution stra-tegies. The potential for differentiation of these flows is illustrated for lawn mowers in Figure 10-2. What additional alternatives are suggested by our listing of channel intermediaries in Table 9-6?

(21)

Dual Channels. Any one group of functions can be performed by two or more types of channels. The Toro Co.'s decision, you'll recall, was to sell directly at one price and set of distributor margins to mass merchandisers and to sell through distributors at higher prices and margins to traditional lawn mower

[5]William D. Hartley, "Cumbersome Japanese Distribution System Stumps U. S. Concerns," *Wall Street Journal* (March 2, 1972), pp. 1 and 12. Quote on p. 12.

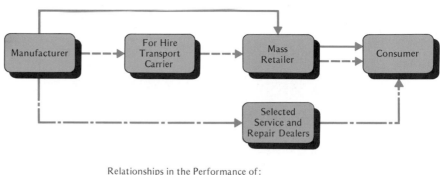

Figure 10-2. An example of differentiation of relationships in the performance of transactional, logistical, and facilitating functions in selected channels of distribution for power lawn mowers.

Relationships in the Performance of:

→ Transactional Functions

--→ Logistical Functions

-·-→ Selected Facilitating Functions

dealers. As such, it elected to employ a dual channel for the performance of transactional functions. To the extent that customers served by each transactional channel required goods in basically different quantities, shipped by different transportation methods, from different warehouses, this decision may have required dual or multiple logistical channels as well.

As we have seen, the growth of specialized retail outlets selling large volumes of products at relatively low (discount) prices has been one of the more significant developments of the age of consumer mobility. It has resulted from the consumer's ability to perform more and more of the logistics task (including home delivery for goods ranging up to furniture in size). It has stimulated the development and use of dual channels of distribution. What impact would a severe, five-year shortage of automobile fuel have on this series of developments?

(22)

locus of performance of functions

Assuming we could adopt "channel vision," we might pose questions such as those suggested in Figure 10-3. They generally raise the issues of where functions should be performed, and by whom, in channels of distribution (in this case, for a lawn mower), as well as those points in the distribution process at which the greatest opportunities for improvement may exist. Because of the complexity of the problem, much of the theoretical work done to date on these questions has been limited to economic considerations. When in doubt, we typically revert back to the stand-by common denominator, money. For example, what are the nature of cost and margin relations as we move from left to right in Figure 10-3? What does this suggest in terms of the greatest points of opportunity for the long-run improvement of economic performance through channel change?

(23)

(24)

Two of the most useful pieces of theoretical work regarding the locus of functional activity in channels of distribution are those of the influential mar-

Figure 10-3. Cost and margin relationships as a factor in the development of channel vision for power lawn mower distribution.

Questions raised by "channel vision":
Where in the channel should each marketing function be performed?
Who should perform it?

Item:	Manufacturer	Distributor	Mass Retailer	Consumer	Total
Sales per unit to customer:	$120	$135	$185	$220[a]	$220
Purchase price per unit from supplier:		120	135	185	
Production costs per unit:	60				60
Gross margin per unit	$ 60	$ 15	$ 50	$ 35	$160
Actual per unit costs of performing marketing functions (and probable costs for those not performed at a given level):					
Transactional:					
Buying				$ 20	$ 20
Selling to consumers	– ($20)[b]	– ($15)[b]	$10[b]		$ 10
Selling to retailers	$5 ($15)	$8	n.a.		$ 13
Selling to distributors	$10	n.a.[c]	n.a.		$ 10
Advertising	$15	– ($20)	$10 ($20)		$ 25
Logistical:					
Storage	$ 2	– ($4)	$ 3 ($6)		$ 5
Transport	$ 4[d] ($14)	– ($6)	– ($8)	$ 10[e]	14
Inventory (assortment) maintenance	$ 3	– ($5)	$ 3 ($7)		6
Facilitating:					
Financing	$ 1	$2 ($2)	$ 3		6
Service and repair	– ($8)[f]	– ($6)[f]	– ($5)[f]		
Total costs	$ 40	$10	$29	$30	$109
Net profit before tax	$ 20	$ 5	$21	$ 5	$ 51

[a] The assumed "value" of the product to the consumer, as perceived by the consumer.

[b] To be read as: the manufacturer and distributor actually spent nothing for the direct sale of the power lawn mower to consumers. Had either assumed the full responsibility for this, it would have cost them $20 and $15 respectively. The mass retailer actually was able to perform this function for a cost of $10 per unit.

[c] Not applicable.

[d] For transport directly to the mass retailer.

[e] Consumer costs of searching out and carrying home the lawn mower.

[f] Service and repair functions are assumed to be performed outside the channels shown here.

keting theorists Wroe Alderson and Bucklin. Alderson first set forth a principle of postponement, which holds that an organization should

> postpone changes in form and identity to the latest point in the marketing flow; postpone changes in inventory location to the latest possible points in time.[6]

[6] Wroe Alderson, *Marketing Behavior and Executive Action* (Homewood: Ill.: Irwin, 1957), p. 424.

(25)   Based on variations in marketing costs as goods move toward markets, as suggested in Figure 10-3, which types of costs could be minimized by a manufacturer postponing its commitment of stocks by inventorying its products only at its plant and producing many items only on the receipt of orders from customers? What types of risk would this incur?

(26)   Bucklin later formulated the converse of this, the principle of speculation, which proposes that

> changes in form, and the movement of goods to forward inventories, should be made at the earliest possible time in the marketing flow in order to reduce the costs of the marketing system.[7]

Combining these two complementary ideas gives a principle of postponement and speculation:

> A speculative inventory will appear at each point in a distribution channel whenever its costs are less than the net savings to both buyer and seller from postponement.[8]

(27)   How would you assess the relative levels of postponement and speculation for a manufacturer and its customers in (1) a channel of distribution in which the manufacturer inventories products only at its plant, producing many items only to customer order as opposed to (2) one in which the manufacturer might maintain many extensively stocked inventories near major markets?

The relative desirability of postponement or speculation for either the manufacturer or customers would be based on possible cost levels associated with each strategy. The combined principle views an intermediate inventory as an effective means for both manufacturers and their customers to increase postponement and reduce the risks associated with speculation only when the costs of the intermediate inventory don't exceed the benefits.

channel design decisions

From a manufacturer's point of view, the channels through which its products or services may flow will be determined in large part by such factors as the needs of customers regarding its product in target market segments it might select, company objectives regarding such matters as control over various functions performed by the channel, the margin available to support the performance of necessary functions, and the availability of alternatives for the performance of such functions.

[7]Louis P. Bucklin, "Postponement, Speculation, and the Structure of Distribution Channels," *Journal of Marketing Research,* **2** (Jan. 1965), pp. 26–31. Quote on p. 27.
[8]Ibid., p. 28.

customer–product needs in target market segments

A number of customer needs of a transactional, logistical, and facilitating nature are listed in Table 10-1 along with target market (customer) and product characteristics contributing to high- or low-level needs of each type. Using the approach suggested in Table 10-1, how would you describe the transactional,

(28)

Table 10-1 Customer Needs and Product Characteristics in Market Segments

Customer Needs in Acquiring Product	Customer-Product Combinations for Which Needs May Be Low or High	
	Low	High
Transactional		
Price	Low-priced products; high-income customers	High-priced products; low-income customers
Information, orientation, expert advice, and physical inspection	*Products that are* noncomplex frequently purchased late in life cycle bought to specification, according to explicit standard *Perceived by customers to* have well-known brand be sold by trusted outlets be manufactured by well-known companies represent low-level risk in purchase	*Products that are* complex infrequently purchased early in life cycle custom-designed according to particular requirements *Perceived by customers to* have unknown brand be sold by unknown outlets be manufactured by unknown companies represent high-level risk in purchase
Logistical		
Variety	Need for product comparison low; need to make socially right purchase low	Need for product comparison high; need to make socially right purchase high
Proximity of purchase point	Customer willingness to expend effort to purchase high	Customer willingness to expend effort to purchase low
Availability of product	Low stock-out penalty; noncritical need for product; highly differentiated product; customer willingness to substitute another product low	High stock-out penalty; critical need for product; nondifferentiated product; customer willingness to substitute another product high
Shelf location (for goods sold through retail outlets)	Customer willingness to seek out product high; customer tendency to purchase on impulse low	Customer willingness to seek out product low; customer tendency to purchase on impulse high
Postpurchase delivery	Heavy, bulky	Light, small
Facilitating		
Installation	Noncomplex product; customer capability high; little or no installation required	Complex product; customer capability low; installation important
Postpurchase servicing	Noncomplex product; customer capability high; customer expectation of continued performance low	Complex product; customer capability low; customer expectation of continued performance high
Financing	Low-priced product; well-financed customer	High-priced product; poorly financed customer

logistical, and facilitating needs of the Toro Co. in the purchase of (1) paper supplies for company washrooms by the purchasing department; (2) a standard fastener for the company's lawn mowers, bought in small quantities to specification over the course of the year by the purchasing department; and (3) a new plastic molding machine, capable of molding parts of a material that has never been used in Toro's products before, to be purchased through the purchasing department after concurrence by the company's manufacturing, marketing, and engineering personnel? Was the level of need you identified for transactional and logistical functions comparable for paper supplies? For the plastic molding machine?

(29)
(30)

desirability of maintaining control over the marketing process

The desirability of maintaining control over transactional, logistical, and facilitating functions as well as price may vary markedly with customer-product needs as well as the complexity of performing each set of functions.

Transactional Functions. The desirability of a manufacturer's controlling transactional aspects of the marketing process quite likely will vary directly with the magnitude of the task, largely determined by product-customer transactional needs. A complex, new product for which the customer's perceived risk is high, such as the new plastic molding machine being considered by Toro, typically requires selling expertise. The manufacturer of this machine will want to take steps to insure that it receives the proper transactional support, perhaps by assuming responsibility for selling through its own sales force or by establishing a comprehensive training program for distributors' sales personnel and rewarding them highly for successful sales efforts. In contrast, a fastener manufacturer might be much more willing to entrust the sale of its product to a distributor's salesmen representing a number of manufacturers and products to their industrial customers.

Logistical Function—Industrial Goods. Because of the nature of the product, and the lack of alternatives to Toro, the logistical needs associated with the plastic molding machine may be relatively high but the task itself simple. Under these circumstances, its manufacturer may be able and willing to assume direct responsibility for logistical functions.

For fasteners, too, logistical needs may be high if Toro's purchasing personnel readily accept substitutes in the event of the nonavailability of fasteners made by its current supplier. But if the total volume of fasteners sold to Toro is small, the logistical task of bridging the gap between efficient production and shipping quantities for a manufacturer and those bought by Toro may be complex. Here the logistical needs of the ultimate customer are high, but the manufacturer's ability to assume direct responsibility for meeting them may be limited; instead, it may be necessary to distribute such items through full-function wholesalers.

Logistical Functions—Consumer Goods. Manufacturer responses to customer-product needs for goods sold to ultimate consumers through retail outlets often are somewhat different from those for industrial goods. Consider, for example, problems experienced by the Quaker Oats Company in the introduction of 100% Natural Cereal, a product made of natural ingredients.

Up to the time of its introduction late in 1972, cereals appealing to the "health food crowd" had been manufactured by a number of small companies and distributed through a limited number of health food stores to potential customers willing to expend some effort to seek out such a store, and possibly a particular kind of cereal. A growing interest in nutrition and balanced, healthful diets led Quaker's management to introduce a natural cereal of potentially broad appeal, supported with a more extensive advertising campaign than any such cereal ever had received.

The potential for the success of this effort to broaden the primary demand for natural cereals required more intensive distribution and the introduction of the product to many supermarkets that never had sold a granola-type natural cereal. Because of its strong relationship with supermarket outlets through the distribution of its other cereal products, including the most widely accepted of all cereals, Quaker Oats, the company was able to obtain shelf space in a high proportion of the grocery outlets located in the regions where 100% Natural Cereal was introduced originally.

Thus, the ability to obtain distribution for the product justified Quaker's advertising expenditure. The advertising expenditure, once planned, required intensive distribution to create retail stocks in close proximity to a new group of consumers perhaps less willing to travel long distances (and somewhat self-conscious about doing so) to seek out health food stores.

Supermarket managers, confronted with this new type of product, basically could locate it in several places on their stores' shelves; with the high-volume ready-to-eat cereals, with "hot cereals" (even though 100% Natural Cereal required no cooking), or with other ready-to-eat nutritional cereals, such as those basically designed for babies and small children. Which of the preceding locations do you feel would be most desirable for the new product? How would your response differ if you felt that Quaker's new product would (1) be the object of a planned purchase, in which a shopper would determine in advance of the buying trip that it would be sought out by brand, or (2) result from an impulse purchase, in which the shopper would buy it without prior intent by seeing it on the store shelf?

As it turned out, some supermarket managers, because of similarities in box size and their perceptions of the way in which shoppers would regard the new product, located it with other nutritional cereals designed basically for babies and small children. Quaker's sales force, modest in size when compared with other cereal producers and with responsibility for selling a variety of cereal products, were not, in some cases, able to persuade store managers otherwise.

Nevertheless, as the result of media and word-of-mouth advertising, consumers in large numbers were willing to seek out Quaker's new product—in such large numbers, in fact, that Quaker immediately exceeded its sales estimates by several times in certain areas. It began to experience stock-outs in a number of stores, eventually had to allocate its limited stocks to retail stores, and failed to realize some of the potential for early sales of its product.

How much control was Quaker able to exert over logistical functions in its introduction of 100% Natural Cereal? How important did this turn out to be?

Facilitating Functions. The need for manufacturer control over the manner in which facilitating functions are performed may vary directly with such factors as the complexity and sale price of the product, customer expectations regarding continuous product performance, and customer capabilities for financing, installing, and servicing the product. For which of the types of products—paper supplies, standard fasteners, or a new plastic molding machine—would control over the manner in which facilitating functions are performed be most critical to a manufacturer-supplier of the items?

In response to such needs, manufacturers have, among other things (1) sponsored training programs for those responsible for the installation or service of products; (2) assumed direct responsibility for such functions by establishing separate manufacturer-owned outlets to provide such support; and (3) created, in the case of the major automobile and appliance manufacturers, financial organizations to provide consumer credit to finance purchases of "big-ticket" items.

Even these types of efforts have failed to stem the rising costs and deteriorating quality of the manner in which facilitating functions are performed. In response to growing complaints from angry consumers expecting better product support, several manufacturers of small appliances have begun packing more popular replacement parts and more extensive "do-it-yourself" instruction booklets with their products to encourage in-home repair.

Pricing for Ultimate Sale. The need for control by manufacturers over the prices at which some products are ultimately sold is of special importance to warrant attention here. A deterioration of price levels below those suggested by manufacturers is most likely to occur for those items (1) representing established, well-known values (often because of their well-known brands) to customers; (2) requiring seasonal clearance from stocks; (3) for which insufficient demand exists; (4) for which retail margins are sufficient to permit price cutting; (5) distributed through two or more transactional channels with different price structures; and (6) for which manufacturers seek "discount" retail outlets capable of generating a volume of retail sales consistent with efficient manufacturing and shipping quantities. Thus, after the "seller's market" subsequent to World War II, manufacturers who had geared their capacity to catch up with consumer demand found that they possessed too much capacity. Consequently, several turned to volume selling to discount retail outlets to generate demand. As a result, traditional retail outlets such as department and nondiscount appliance stores either had to establish discounting operations or discontinue sales of certain appliances and brands.

Manufacturers may be desirous of controlling retail prices for their products where (1) they have invested large amounts of money in promotional efforts to establish a perception of high product quality among consumers, (2) price maintenance is perceived to be essential to the maintenance of a quality image, (3) price maintenance is important to the preservation of retailer or wholesaler support for a product and its distribution, and (4) consumer loyalty to a product is thought to depend on stable prices.

An interesting problem of this nature developed for owners of National Football League (NFL) professional teams late in 1973 with the implementation of a rule whereby games sold out 72 hours in advance of game time could be televised in the cities in which they were being played. A local discount store chain bought the last 1,400 tickets to a championship game between the Dallas Cowboys and the Minnesota Vikings at the regular price of $12 each so that the game could be shown on television in the Dallas area. It then stunned league officials by advertising them for sale in its stores at $10 each. League commissioner Pete Roselle charged such a practice with "lessening the aura or mystique of the game." The NFL's executive director complained that "It's a cheapening of our product. . . . We've always sold tickets at full price."[9]

(36) (37) What was happening here? What could the NFL, or the individual teams, do about it?

As the result of manufacturers' desires to control retail prices, and perhaps to a greater extent the desire of smaller retailers of products such as drug items to have prices controlled, so-called fair-trade laws were enacted. As we know from a previous discussion, these laws essentially gave manufacturers hunting licenses with which to police the maintenance of retail prices and to punish violators by withdrawing products from their shelves or threatening to do so. However, many manufacturers have found them so expensive and time consuming to patrol that they have abandoned retail price maintenance policies.

(38) Would it be more difficult for a manufacturer to control retail prices for products sold by means of intensive or exclusive distribution strategies?

The Case for Functional Differentiation. High transactional needs requiring complex efforts thus suggest direct distribution, or other methods by which a manufacturer can maintain control over the transactional activities. High logistical needs, on the other hand, may be met more effectively by less direct logistical methods when the complexity of the task is great. This suggests that a product-customer combination may produce different levels of transactional, logistical, and facilitating functional needs. And a manufacturer's response to a high level of each type of need may be totally different in terms of the number and type of channel intermediaries enlisted to help meet such needs. This suggests once again the desirability of a manufacturer's approaching the task of channel design differently for each type of marketing function, and possibly utilizing a different channel for each.

available margin—the value added by marketing

The total dollar margins available to manufacturers and the institutions dealing in their products determine, and may place constraints on, the types of responses that can be made to customer-product needs. Total dollar margins for a channel are a function of the total volume of a product that can be sold at a particular level of margin. The volume that can be sold at a particular level of margin in turn depends on the willingness of the ultimate buyer to pay for a "package" comprising the product (and, as we have said, its value in use) and a

---

[9]"NFL Fears Being Sold Short by Discount Store," *Boston Sunday Globe* (Dec. 30, 1973), p. 29.

variety of transactional, logistical, and facilitating marketing functions. The willingness—essentially the sensitivity of the customer to price—varies with such matters as the nature of the product, the nature of the use to which it will be put, the time at which a need for it may arise, and the customer's ability to pay. The price that a customer is willing to pay for a product or service is the best indication of its value in a particular transaction. Similarly, the margin (sales price less manufacturing or purchase costs) obtained for products or services can be said to reflect roughly a customer's willingness to pay for marketing services, sometimes termed *value added* by marketing advocates.

Examples of margin relationships for power lawn mowers sold by small dealers and mass merchandisers, not unlike those experienced by the Toro Co., are shown in Figure 10-4. Here some customers are willing to pay $210 for lawn mowers sold through home and garden stores operated by department stores, staffed with sales personnel able to explain the features of competing models, and offering such services as delivery. To a growing extent, however, they are buying the same models (manufactured at the same average cost) through mass merchandisers at perhaps $185 (as in Figure 10-3), relying to a lesser extent on information provided by store sales personnel, and they are willing to transport their purchases from the store. In this example, how does price paid reflect differences in the product "package"? How does it reflect differences in the value added by marketing activities?

(39)
(40)

(41)

Price competition may force the total margin available to a channel downward. What effect would this have on the number of available alternatives for the distribution of a particular product open to a manufacturer?

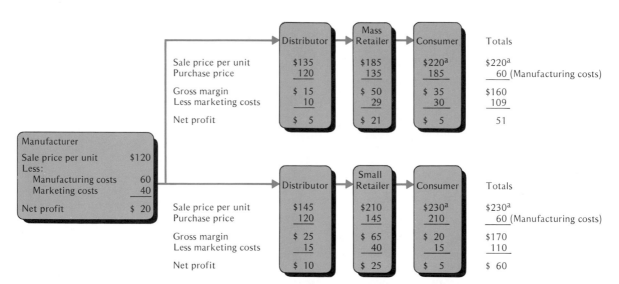

a Value of the product to the consumer at the time and place of purchase, as perceived by the consumer.

Figure 10-4. Prices, margins, and costs associated with the distribution of power lawn mowers through mass retailers and small retailers.

dollar margins required by channel intermediaries

The distribution of available margins to channel intermediaries will influence their behavior and the amount of effort expended to sell a manufacturer's product. Although margins expressed as a percentage of sales provide a handy comparison of relative margins offered by competing manufacturers, the total dollar margin realized through the sale of a manufacturer's product line is of much greater practical importance to a channel intermediary.

> Because he sells products that have almost unique market acceptance and are usually 5 to 10 per cent more expensive than comparable machinery, the average Caterpillar dealer has grown richer than other distributors of earth-moving equipment. His net worth totals about $4 million to $5 million (versus less than $1 million for a typical International Harvester dealer). . . . He can, therefore, afford to stock more parts, buy more testing equipment, and, what's most important, do more machinery leasing than can the International Harvester dealer. All this means, of course, more business and still better market penetration.[10]

When faced with the need to diversify into less cyclical consumer-oriented products several years ago, Cooper Industries acquired five small manufacturers of widely-recognized brands of hand tools. This provided a single sales representative with five lines of hand tools to sell instead of one, required that customers deal with only one sales representative instead of five, and increased the importance of Cooper's products to its customers by increasing the total margins they realized from the sale of the entire line.

(42) Regardless of percentage margins provided in the pricing structure of the small dealers and mass merchandisers of power lawn mowers illustrated in Figure 10-4, how much loyalty and effort could Toro expect from a small dealer selling two Toro units per year?

Often, dollar margins realized on sales per square foot of selling space are used by retailers as measures of the relative desirability of stocking a particular product. Products failing to meet such standards often are replaced by other items that do. This factor alone may foreclose certain channel alternatives to the manufacturer.

available channel alternatives

The availability of existing channels may further influence the channel design decision. Channels may never have been developed to handle certain new products. Existing channels may be preempted by competition, requiring the development of new ones. Or traditional channel intermediaries may be regarded as unable to provide the marketing effort required by a new product or a new marketing program.

[10]Sanford Rose, "The Going May Get Tougher for Caterpillar," *Fortune* (May 1972), pp. 161–165 ff. Quote on pp. 163–164.

At the time of its development, for example, there was no one obvious channel of distribution for the skimobile. As a result, franchises for the sale of various brands of skimobiles were awarded to retailers ranging from farm equipment dealers to service station operators, and including some newly developed outlets specializing in selling and servicing skimobiles. Firms entering skimobile manufacturing relatively late in the introductory stage of the product's life cycle found that many of the most desirable types of outlets had been preempted by the competitors that preceded them. They were forced to rely to a greater extent on marginal or newly developed retail dealerships.

In addition to the factors discussed here, the freedom with which a manufacturer can approach its channel design decisions will be determined by the locus of control and leadership within the channel, the closing topic of this chapter. Before taking this up, however, let's review some of the ways in which manufacturers have improved distribution practices within existing channels of distribution.

trends in manufacturer distribution

Trends in manufacturer distribution can be reviewed in terms of their primary transactional, logistical, or facilitating orientation.

performance of transactional functions

In addition to those trends in communication practices that were discussed in Chapters 6 and 7, there is an additional development of some significance for the performance of transactional functions by manufacturers: the growth of vertically integrated, or corporate, marketing entities.

Corporate marketing entities have been formed by the acquisition of firms at one level in a channel of distribution by those in another. McCammon provides us with some examples of this:

> Sherwin-Williams, for example, operates over two thousand paint stores; Hart Schaffner and Marx, a long established manufacturer in the men's wear field, owns over one hundred clothing outlets; Sears has an ownership equity in production facilities that supply over 30 per cent of the company's inventory requirements; and, large food chains obtain almost 10 per cent of their requirements from captive manufacturing facilities, many of which were acquired in the 1950s.[11]

Further evidence is provided by the growth of manufacturers' sales branches and offices, illustrated in Figure 9-4, page 312. This rivals the growth in the use of a

---

[11] Bert C. McCammon, Jr., "The Emergence and Growth of Contractually Integrated Channels in the American Economy," in *Marketing and Economic Development,* ed. Peter D. Bennett (Chicago: American Marketing Association, 1965), pp. 496–515. Quote on p. 497.

second method of channel integration, the contractual approach typified by voluntary wholesalers' relationships with the retailers they serve. What impact have both of these developments had on the relative importance of transactional as opposed to other marketing functions in channels of distribution typified by corporate and contractual channel relationships?

A third method of channel integration, that involving so-called administered relationships, typified by efforts by one independent organization to influence the behavior of another for the good of both, has perhaps had greater importance for the performance of logistical functions.

performance of logistical functions

In the last two decades, remarkable changes have occurred in the management of logistical activities, particularly among manufacturers. Included among these changes are the development of total cost concepts for management, new organizational arrangements for the management of logistics or physical distribution activities, and new programs to utilize rapidly changing technology in logistics.

Reasons for Significant Change. Among the opportunities and pressures that have led to changes in the management and performance of manufacturer logistics are (1) the development of new operations research techniques highly applicable to logistics problems, (2) the ascendancy in the use of computers capable of handling data-laden logistics problems, (3) the development of new technologies for transportation and material handling, (4) the increasing costs of logistics activities in channels of distribution, and (5) the pressures created by the large-scale adoption of the marketing concept as a way of life, with increasing emphasis on wider lines of products and improved customer services.

Beginning with the application of economic lot-size formulas in computing the most efficient product runs at the time of the growth of interest in Frederick B. Taylor and his scientific management techniques late in the nineteenth century, logistical functions have long lent themselves particularly well to the application of operations research techniques. Techniques such as linear programming and queueing theory, developed at the time of World War II, have gained their greatest acceptance and practical use in the management of logistics activities. This development, which occurred parallel to the development of large-scale computing devices, insured basic changes in technical approaches to the analysis of logistics problems.

In recent years, manufacturers have shifted their emphasis from that of designing computers for the more effective analysis of problems to those with the data-storage capacity to recall and manipulate the large masses of data associated with the day-to-day control of inventories, scheduling of shipments, processing of shipment-related data, and other logistics tasks.

In the last two decades, we have seen the development of air freight as a viable means of transportation; the introduction of the modern era of containerization, featuring the transfer between ships, trucks, rail cars, or planes of products moving in room-sized containers of standard dimensions; the rebirth of methods of coordinated transportation involving such forms as piggybacking, the carriage of truck trailers on railroad cars; and a twenty-fold expansion in the size of ships for carrying products in bulk form. In addition, increases in material handling capabilities during this period of time range from tenfold increases in the rate of handling materials in bulk to the implementation of standard pallet sizes and methods for handling products in palletized form, stacked on wood, plastic, or cardboard sheets and moved as a unit by lift trucks.

One estimate of trends in costs of performing logistics activities is shown in Figure 10-5. It breaks such costs down into two major components, movement (transportation) and inventory (including costs of warehousing, interest on money invested in inventory, property tax and insurance on inventory in storage, and the spoilage and obsolescence of goods held in inventories). Such costs, combined with the estimated costs of managing such activities, approximated 26 per cent of the tangible GNP (the value of products as opposed to services created) in the United States in 1970. Thus, of every dollar spent for products, approximately 15 cents went to transportation, another 9 cents for the costs of inventorying the product at various levels in channels of distribution, and a fraction of a cent for the management of these activities. What factors do you think account for the trends shown in Figure 10-5?

(44)

We implied in our earlier discussion that the adoption of the marketing concept by a growing number of American businesses has led to an expansion in the choice of products available to the public. This was illustrated in Figure 4-1, p. 108. Of equal importance for the management of logistics activities is that the concept has highlighted the importance of customer service in marketing strategy and the need for improvements in physical service that can lead to more rapid response times and greater product availability. The combination of wider product lines, reduced sales per product-line item (or stockkeeping unit), and pressures either to locate products closer to their ultimate markets

Figure 10-5. Trends in estimated movement (transportation), inventory holding (warehousing, interest on investment, insurance, property tax, and damage and obsolescence), and logistics management costs, as a percentage of tangible GNP, 1950–1970. Source: James L. Heskett, Nicholas A. Glaskowsky, Jr., and Robert M. Ivie, *Business Logistics* (New York: Ronald, 1973), p. 19.

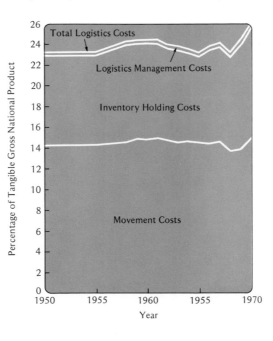

351

or to employ more rapid forms of transportation in their distribution have accounted not only for higher costs of distribution in relation to the value of products distributed, but also for the need for more effective management.

Manufacturer Responses. Management responses to the pressures cited here have included the development of total cost concepts in selecting logistics strategies, new organizational arrangements for the effective implementation and control of such strategies, and new strategies making effective use of improved logistics methods.

Total cost concepts for logistics management emphasize the (1) identification of transportation, warehousing, inventory control, and order entry and processing costs associated with various logistics strategies and (2) the trading of certain types of costs for others with the objective of determining the least total cost strategy. The concept is illustrated graphically in Figure 10-6.

(45) Using the total cost concept, how would you describe the cost trade-offs made by the Raytheon Company in altering its logistics strategy, discussed on page 332? In contrast to the Raytheon Company, whose products averaged $10 per pound in value, a growing number of steel manufacturers, with products selling for perhaps 30 cents per pound, have increased the number of steel

(46) warehouses through which their products reach customers. Using total cost concepts, how would you explain the contrast in trends suggested here in the distribution of electronic tubes and steel?

By spending more for transportation, Raytheon reduced its expenditure for the performance of all logistical functions. At the same time it was able to provide improved customer service on an over-all basis. This was a matter of some importance for a line of tubes and transistors that were rapidly becoming difficult to differentiate from those of competitors on any other basis.

Adopting total cost concepts for the analysis of logistics strategies is one

Figure 10-6. The total cost concept of logistics management showing hypothetical trade-offs among transportation, inventory, and order-processing costs. Source: James L. Heskett, Nicholas A. Glaskowsky, Jr., and Robert M. Ivie, *Business Logistics* (New York: Ronald, 1973), p. 35.

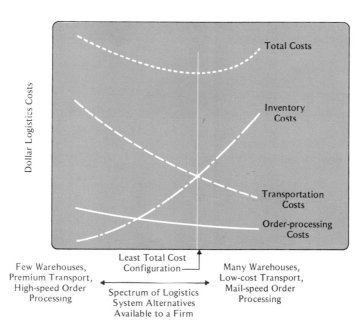

thing; implementing them is another. The effective management of logistics activities as related tasks has led many large organizations to consolidate all or some of the responsibilities for the management of traffic and transportation, warehousing, inventory control, production planning, and order entry and processing under logistics or physical distribution managers. This has required that such responsibilities be shifted within a manufacturer's organization as suggested by the example in Figure 10-7. Looking over Figure 10-7, what do you think might have led to the assignment of responsibilities as shown before the adoption of a more fully integrated organization for the management of logistics activities?

(47)

The Raytheon example is perhaps an extreme one, but typical of a tendency for many firms to distribute their products through fewer, strategically located distribution centers (warehouses at which orders may be accepted, stock picked for shipment, and inventory controlled by means of communication with central information-processing units). In doing so, they have taken advantage of the improved transit times and delivery dependability resulting from the construction of the interstate highway system and the introduction of improved transportation methods.

Other firms, making use of the fact that in many product lines 20 per cent of the items may represent approximately 80 per cent of the unit or dollar sales, have centralized the stocks of slower-selling items to make such items available for sale to wider market areas and thus to minimize their inventories. Other higher-volume items may be stocked at a greater number of market-oriented distribution centers. This has been termed *inventory echeloning,* and recognizes the fact that customers may have higher service needs for high-volume as opposed to low-volume product-line items. Why might this be the case?

(48)

Still other firms have begun to apply the principles of postponement and speculation by holding products in bulk or semiassembled form in market-oriented inventories, delaying their packaging or final assembly until the receipt of firm orders for particular product-line items. This essentially is a principle that automobile manufacturers have applied for years by assembling automobiles to detailed customer specifications after the receipt of orders from dealers at market-oriented assembly plants. Regardless of what such facilities have been called, they have functioned as distribution centers at which some assembly is performed. Similar strategies have been adopted by the manufacturers of packaged chemical products, shipping such products in bulk to distribution centers for packaging to order. How would you describe such strategies, in terms of principles of postponement and speculation discussed on pages 339–341?

(49)

As total cost methods of analysis and integrated logistics management are adopted by increasing numbers of firms, we can expect many more creative logistics-oriented responses to marketing pressures.

performance of facilitating functions

As (1) a growing proportion of merchandise is sold through low-price, low-margin retail outlets offering limited services, (2) products become more complex, and (3) craft labor for product repair becomes more difficult to find, headaches associated with facilitating functions grow for manufacturers.

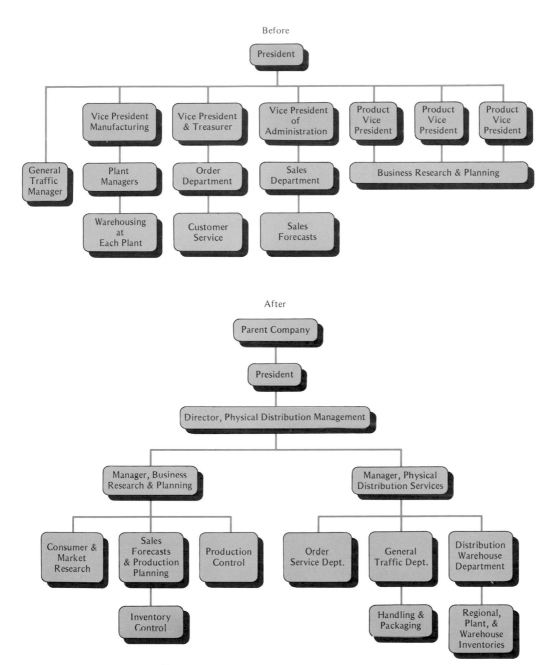

Figure 10-7. Organizational relationships in the Norge Division of the Borg-Warner Corporation before and after the adoption of a more fully integrated organization for the management of logistics activities. Source "From Red to Black," *Handling & Shipping,* (Sept. 1966), pp. 69–72.

As a result, a conscious effort has been made by some manufacturers and retailers to shift responsibilities for the performance of facilitating functions to customers. This has been accomplished by manufacturers, for example, through the publication of more extensive service manuals illustrated for ease of use by consumers. Retailers have offered lower prices to those customers willing to forego delivery or financing.

In other industries in which the complexity of products sold or leased does not facilitate customer servicing, manufacturers have performed service and maintenance through technical service representatives. For example, Xerox and IBM products are maintained through extensive manufacturer-managed service organizations that provide on-the-spot equipment service.

Entire product lines have been redesigned for simplified servicing. These range from cameras to watches, with the latter designed in some cases to sell for prices that discourage repair as opposed to the purchase of a new watch.

Finally, television set and automobile manufacturers, among others, have designed products around modules to facilitate the replacement of faulty or damaged parts by service personnel with limited ability.

Often the implementation of new strategies by manufacturers for the performance of transactional, logistical, or facilitating functions has required them to exercise channel control and leadership.

channel control and leadership

The concept of channel control concerns the ability of a manufactuer or other channel entity to influence the behavior of those with whom it deals. Channel leadership relates more to the willingness of those with whom the ability to control rests to take action on behalf of the well-being of cooperating channel intermediaries.

An example from the early days of packaged oil distribution may serve to illustrate these concepts. At the time of the introduction of packaged oil products, service station operators dispensed oil by pumping it in small quantities from barrels into pouring cans. Many consumers, although relying on the advice of service station personnel, often suspected them of mixing new oil with used oil that had been drained from other automobiles and selling it from their dispensing barrels as new oil. Aware of this common perception, petroleum companies introduced packaged oil with the appeal to prospective consumers that, by buying packaged oil, they could assure themselves of getting clean oil. The new product introduction failed.

Service station operators, sensitive to the implications of the promotional campaign, reacted by ignoring packaged oil in their selling efforts. As a result, petroleum producers had to withdraw their promotional campaign and sell service station operators and consumers instead on the amount of time they could save by selling and buying oil in measured, packaged form. This approach worked.

(50)
(51) (52)
(53)

At the time of the first packaged oil promotion, who had control of the channel of distribution for this product? Why? In what way, if any, did the successful introduction of packaged oil shift control? In what way, if any, was channel leadership employed here?

channel control

The ability of a manufacturer, wholesaler, retailer, or other channel intermediary to exercise channel control may reflect the relative perceived strength of its customer "franchise," the combination of supporting activities and margin that it is willing to offer other intermediaries, and the "stake" that others have in the success of its products, services, or marketing efforts.

Customer "Franchise." A customer franchise represents the relative reputation and saleability that a company, its brands, and its products or services possess in the minds of customers. A manufacturer's franchise classically is built around the design and introduction of good products, representing good value (reasonable price in relation to value in use), promoted and distributed effectively. However, a channel intermediary may use the same means for building a franchise for its products, company name, or store name. In fact, its close proximity to ultimate buyers often provides an intermediary with a good strategic position from which to do so. At that moment of truth at which the motorist had to weigh the reputation of Standard Oil of New Jersey against that of his neighborhood service station operator, greasy hands and all, whose advice did he follow? Why?

Supporting Activities and Margin. The responsibilities that a channel institution may be willing to assume will be related to the rewards with which they might be associated. Both are closely related to the idea of customer franchise. Recall that in our discussion of pull and push promotional strategies from Chapter 7, the former often relieves channel intermediaries of the responsibility for a good deal of the selling effort, making channel relationships attractive even at lower margins (rewards) than might be required under the latter strategy. To the extent that a pulling strategy helps build a franchise with the ultimate customer for a product or service, it may enhance the potential profitability of handling the product for a channel intermediary even at a low margin. For example, the typical voluntary wholesaler of grocery products conducts its purchasing, storage, and delivery activities at a margin of only about 6 per cent of its sales volume. In contrast, for relatively unknown products requiring a great deal of selling effort, it may be difficult to buy distribution at any price (margin).

Remember the Comsec Fund, the first mutual fund authorized to deal in commodity futures contracts, that was featured in one of our opening examples? Its management found to its regret that it had neither a customer franchise for its new concept nor sufficient supporting activities and margin after it decided to change the fund to a no-load status, eliminating the sales commission formerly offered to brokerage house representatives for the sale of the fund's shares. Although the product may have been enhanced with the elimination of the customer sales charge, the loss of sales effort reduced the sale of the fund's shares drastically. It was little consolation to the fund's management that many other funds suffered a similar fate.

"Stake." Stake is a concept used to measure the relative importance of one channel institution to another.[12] Channel intermediaries, for example, with a

[12]Wroe Alderson, *Dynamic Marketing Behavior* (Homewood, Ill.: Irwin, 1965), pp. 37–45.

356

high stake in the success of a firm's products are those for which such products represent a high proportion of their total sales. Presumably, a firm's willingness to respond to the desires of a supplier or customer depends in part on its stake relative to either.

(56)

What would you anticipate regarding the relative control that (1) the Toro Co. could exercise over its smaller dealers, for which it might be one of several suppliers, (2) the Roper Corporation, selling a large proportion of its total production of power lawn mowers to Sears, Roebuck for sale under Sears' private brand might enjoy, or (3) Cooper Industries might be able to exercise in doing business with its dealers? How were your comparisons explained by the basic determinants of channel control?

(57)

Generally speaking, channel control tends to gravitate to that level at which the transactional functions might be concentrated in the fewest hands. Thus, retailers of furniture, manufactured by some five thousand firms, are in a position to exert much greater control over channels of distribution for furniture than are automobile dealers, supplied essentially by only four manufacturers.

channel leadership and interorganization management

Channel leadership depends on the willingness of a firm to use its hard-won control to induce change that may be beneficial to those with whom it does business. At times, these actions may benefit competitors as well. Firms whose managements are willing to assume such roles have come to be referred to as channel captains. The process by which they have achieved improved channels of distribution has come to be known as interorganization management.

As an example, several years ago the Armstrong Cork Co., a well-known manufacturer of floor coverings and related items, instituted a program in which it

> signed up 1,200 of its 30,000 dealers and made them "Armstrong Floor Fashion Centers." The dealers, who pay a $1,250 initiation fee and $250 a year, agree to set aside part of their floor exclusively for Armstrong products and arrange their displays exactly as Armstrong prescribes. For the first time, they must also guarantee their installation work, while Armstrong guarantees the floor material. In return, dealers receive a series of . . . promotional aids.[13]

According to an executive employed by one of Armstrong's major competitors, "It has forced dealers to clean up their showrooms and advertising, and that's good for all of us."

In addition to a willingness to exercise the power that it may possess for the good of a channel, a channel captain also must (1) be able to identify the channels of distribution for its products or service, (2) adopt channel vision, and (3) be willing to trade short-term profits for longer-term economic benefits in the application of interorganization management.

[13]"Armstrong Cork Gets Off the Floor," *Business Week* (Sept. 8, 1973), pp. 68–70. Quote on p. 69.

Identification of Channels. Channel leadership is easiest to exercise for those products or services with well-defined channels. We have discussed a number of forces that have produced scrambled merchandising in recent years. This has obscured the nature of channels for many products, offset any concentration in consumer goods producing industries, and made the exercise of channel leadership more difficult.

Adoption of Channel Vision. In Figure 10-3, we identified questions asked by those firms with channel vision, questions concerning responsibility for the performance of marketing functions throughout channels of distribution. The willingness to ask the questions is not enough, however. To follow up, it is necessary to collect data regarding the costs and benefits of performing marketing tasks at each stage of the distribution process. A job of this size can be performed only for proposed shifts in responsibility of large magnitude.

Willingness to Trade Short-Term for Long-Term Benefits. The concept of trade-offs, this time between firms and over time, can be put to work in exercising channel leadership. Rarely can the investment required, and the returns from that investment, be spread evenly among the participants in a major shift in responsibility for the performance of marketing functions within a marketing channel. It is at this point in the process that a channel leader must be willing to absorb the uncertainty associated with change and accept a lower short-term return to insure the success of the change and the longer-term increases in profitability to all channel participants that such a change may create.

This is all high-sounding talk. What we need is an illustration, a final case study of great long-run significance for channels of distribution for consumer goods, and as a result, for all of us.

the universal product code and the "instrumented store"[14]

Perhaps the greatest potential for improving productivity in the performance of transactional and logistical functions in the distribution of food and other consumer products lies in the ability to implement improved methods of store operation, data capture, and communication regarding product sales and inventories. The two basic elements essential to the implementation of such methods, the Universal Product Code (UPC) and the instrumented store, are being quietly developed in the food industry, something that would be impossible without the exercise of channel leadership and interorganization management on the part of retailers, wholesalers, and manufacturers.

Basic to the development of improved methods is the electronic cash register, which is becoming more and more common in larger retailing establishments. For the first time, this device offers the potential to a retailer to find out what is being sold at the time it's being sold.

---

[14] Much of the material in this section is based on material appearing in Lawrence C. Russell, *Universal Product Code* (Scarsdale, N. Y.: National Wholesale Druggists' Association, 1973), pp. 4–33.

Much of the effort in retailing today involves relating items to prices. Product codes are necessary to identify what is being sold. Because different combinations of manufacturers, wholesalers, and retailers transact business with one another, it is vital that all use the same method of identifying products if data is to be captured efficiently. This created the need for what has come to be known as the Universal Product Code.

Comparison of Current and Proposed Methods.   Currently, most food products are shipped to wholesalers or retailers unpriced and with only a manufacturer's product number for identification. As most products are placed on the store shelf they are price marked. At the check-out stand of the supermarket, prices are read by a checker and punched into either a mechanical or an electronic cash register, both of which perform the major functions of capturing gross sales statistics for the store and providing the shopper with a listing of charges.

Under the sponsorship of several trade organizations in the grocery manufacturing and distribution trades, a study committee of senior industry executives developed a format for the most effective manner in which the functions mentioned here might be assigned, given the availability of a Universal Product Code. Essentially, this would involve the printing of a ten-digit number (the UPC) by manufacturers on each of their product packages in the form shown in Figure 10-8. Packages for products that are sold through grocery retail outlets numbered 269 billion in 1973 (even though only about 186 billion of these actually were sold through grocery outlets).

Product code numbers would be assigned by an independently financed agency called Distribution Codes, Inc. In the retail store, prices would appear

Figure 10-8. An example of the manner in which the UPC typically appears on a grocery product package.

only on the shelves, not on the packages themselves. As items would be checked through the check-out stand, they would be passed over an optical scanner in an upright position (with the UPC printed on the bottom). The code would be read by the scanner, the information communicated to a time-shared data bank of codes and store prices, and the item and price recorded in the electronic cash register.

Estimated Savings and Investments. The adoption of the proposed methods making use of the UPC could be expected to result in dramatic "hard" cost savings in retail store operations. Among these would be a 50 per cent reduction in checker-bagger time, a task currently consuming about 40 per cent of total store labor; a significant reduction in time required for the price marking of merchandise; a reduction in training expense for new checker-baggers, a job category that experiences a 100 per cent turnover rate each year; and a significant reduction in mis-rings at the cash register. (Such a large proportion of mis-rings are made in the customer's favor that the amount lost to a supermarket through mis-rings represents about 30 to 40 per cent of its current profit before tax.)

The estimated savings and investments for both retailers and manufacturers, as of mid-1973, resulting from possible widespread use of the UPC are shown in Table 10-2. Savings include both "hard" savings, relatively easy to estimate, and "soft" savings, of unknown proportions. The net annual hard savings to the industry were estimated at $200 million, about .2 per cent of current industry sales through supermarkets, about 20 per cent of profits realized by all food retailers at the time of the estimates, and more than the current profits realized by those retailers adopting the program. Reviewing Table 10-2, what types of cost trade-offs can you identify? How would you describe the shifting of marketing functions between retailers and manufacturers (or wholesalers) necessary to achieve these cost savings? What types of potential problems in implementation of the UPC does the data in Table 10-2 suggest?

(58)
(59)

(60)

Implementation. Given the estimates shown in Table 10-2, either manufacturers would have to accept lower profits or charge higher prices to both users and nonusers of the UPC, including retailers outside the food retailing industry. If retail prices for their products were to be maintained with higher manufacturer prices, retailers would have to accept lower margins. In the case of nonusers of the UPC, this would lead to reduced profits. One alternative explored was to shift the task of applying the code to individual packages to retailers, so that only those using the UPC would have to affix codes to packages. But the cost of doing this at the retail level for the volume of packages assumed in Table 10-2 was estimated to be anywhere from $190 to $380 million, a figure that could wipe out all of the estimated savings from the program.

This was a situation requiring channel leadership on the part of those manufacturers who represented channel captains in the distribution of their particular products. At the critical stages in the development of the program, larger manufacturers, led by their representatives on the UPC Study Committee, agreed to bet on the success of the program and the likelihood of being able to recover their added costs shown in Table 10-2. According to a consultant to the committee, not one of the manufacturers' members were heard to say, in the development of the program, "That's okay for you guys, but it's not a very good deal for us."

Table 10-2 An Estimate of Savings and Investments for Food Retailers and Manufacturers in the Introduction of the UPC* [a]

Item	Amount
Food Retailers	
Hard Savings [b]	
Checker-bagger labor	
Price marking and reprice labor	$495 million
Checker-bagger training	
Reduction of mis-rings	
Soft Savings [c]	
Improved inventory control	— [d]
Reduced spoilage and theft	—
Improved merchandising information	—
Improved warehouse order picking	—
Hard Costs:	
In-store symbol marking	$ 45 million
Depreciation and maintenance of new equipment	180 million
Net savings before tax to retailers	$270 million
Food Manufacturers	
Hard Savings	None
Soft Savings	
Better marketing information, including product-movement data	— [e]
Lower costs of coupon redemption on product promotions	—
Elimination of manufacturer price marking	—
Reduced stock-outs through improved inventory control	—
Hard costs	
Printing of UPC on packages, including administration	$ 70 million
Net savings before tax to manufacturers	($ 70 million)
Net savings before tax to industry	$200 million

*Source: Lawrence C. Russell, *Universal Product Code* (Scarsdale, N. Y.: National Wholesale Druggists' Association, 1973), pp. 4–33.

[a] Based on estimated full use of the UPC for products representing 21% of retail grocery sales volume. Net savings are dependent on the rate of usage.

[b] Hard savings are those that could be estimated as of mid-1973.

[c] Soft savings are those that could not be estimated as of mid-1973.

[d] Impossible to estimate.

Major manufacturers who have been assigned UPC numbers and have been proceeding to implement them in recent years represent a large proportion of the volume of manufactured products sold through grocery stores. As a result, the concept is being explored by organizations involved in the distribution of other products such as drugs.

Furthermore, the adoption of the UPC has made possible the long-run implementation of the so-called instrumented store. An instrumented store is one in which transactions would be captured electronically on an item-by-item basis, with the information used to (1) replenish stocks automatically, (2) help determine the amount of shelf space to be devoted to various items for maximum profitability, and (3) assist in maintaining an effective store layout and merchandising plans, among others.

(61) How would you compare the type of channel leadership exercised by the Armstrong Cork Co. and the grocery product manufacturers?

In the future, each visit to a supermarket should provide ample reminders (in the form of UPC markings) of channel relationships through which products reach us, and the channel coordination, control, and leadership that can reduce the amount of time that a product may spend in a channel of distribution just as it reduces the amount of time we may spend acquiring it.

summary

The development of a manufacturer's channel strategy requires attention to questions regarding the number (and number of types) of outlets through which a product or service should be sold to ultimate buyers; the number of channel intermediaries or levels that should participate in performing transactional, logistical, or facilitating functions for a product or service; the number of different channels that might be utilized for distribution; and the division of responsibility for the performance of marketing functions within channels of distribution.

Products or services regarded by ultimate buyers as convenience goods may require an intensive distribution strategy, utilizing as many outlets (and types of outlets) for retail sales as possible. Shopping and specialty goods may be distributed most effectively by more selective or even exclusive distribution strategies. Scrambled merchandising at the retail level has brought with it the distribution of many products through greater numbers and types of retail outlets.

Channel length, or the number of channel intermediaries involved in the distribution process, often varies directly with the extent of differences between the quantities, assortments, and locations in which products are produced and ultimately purchased.

Greatly differing customer needs, dependent on such factors as the size of the average purchase and the capability of the customer for performing certain marketing functions, may suggest the desirability of two or more types of channels for a particular product.

The points in the channel at which various functions are performed can be determined in part by an assessment of the relative costs for their performance at each of several levels, an assessment requiring the application of channel vision by a manufacturer or other participant in the channel.

A manufacturer's channel design decisions will be based on factors such as the customer-product needs in selected target market segments, the desirability of maintaining control over certain functions performed by the channel, the over-all margin available to support the performance of necessary marketing functions, competitors' channel strategies, and the availability of channel alternatives.

Trends affecting manufacturers' channel decisions and the improved management of functional activities within channels by manufacturers include that of channel integration by the formation of corporate, contractual, or administrative arrangements. This has reduced the burden of performing transactional functions by consolidating control over such activities in the hands of one coordinating organization.

362

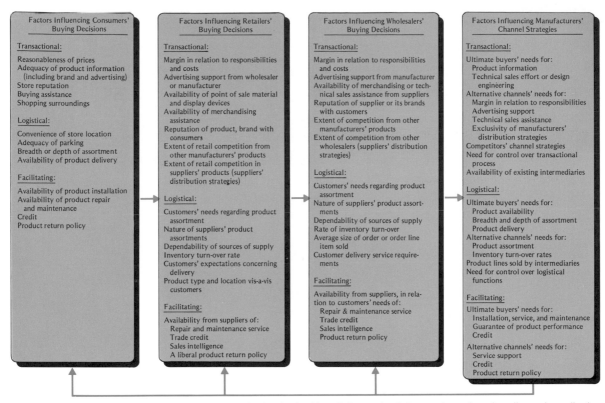

Figure 10-9. Some factors in decisions to buy or trade in goods and services through particular channels of distribution.

Of perhaps greatest significance are improvements in the management of logistical activities by manufacturers through the development of total cost concepts for management, new organizational patterns for more effective coordination, and systems designed to make use of changing technology. The most important opportunity in the performance of facilitating functions has been the improvement of postpurchase service and maintenance by (1) shifting such responsibility to the ultimate buyers, (2) training manufacturer-paid technical service representatives, and (3) simplifying product design.

The ability of a channel entity to exercise control, potentially influencing the behavior of organizations with which it deals, will depend on (1) its franchise, or that of its products, with its customers; (2) its willingness to assume direct responsibility or offer adequate rewards for the performance of critical marketing functions; (3) and the stake that other firms have in the success of its products or services. Its willingness to exercise control may determine the extent to which a channel entity leads others to adopt improved distribution programs on a coordinated basis. Such leadership may depend in part on (1) the ability to identify a channel's structure, (2) the ability to adopt a broad view of existing and potential channels, and (3) the willingness to trade short-term for long-term benefits.

In the past three chapters, we have seen how the needs of their customers not only influence retailers' and wholesalers' marketing strategies but also the requirements that such merchants place on their suppliers and the criteria by which they select them. Many of these are reviewed in Figure 10-9, along with resulting factors that influence the responses made by manufacturers in the form of channel strategies.

Having completed our discussion of the basic elements around which marketing strategies are structured—product, price, communication, and channels of distribution—we turn next to the development of data on which marketing decisions can be based.

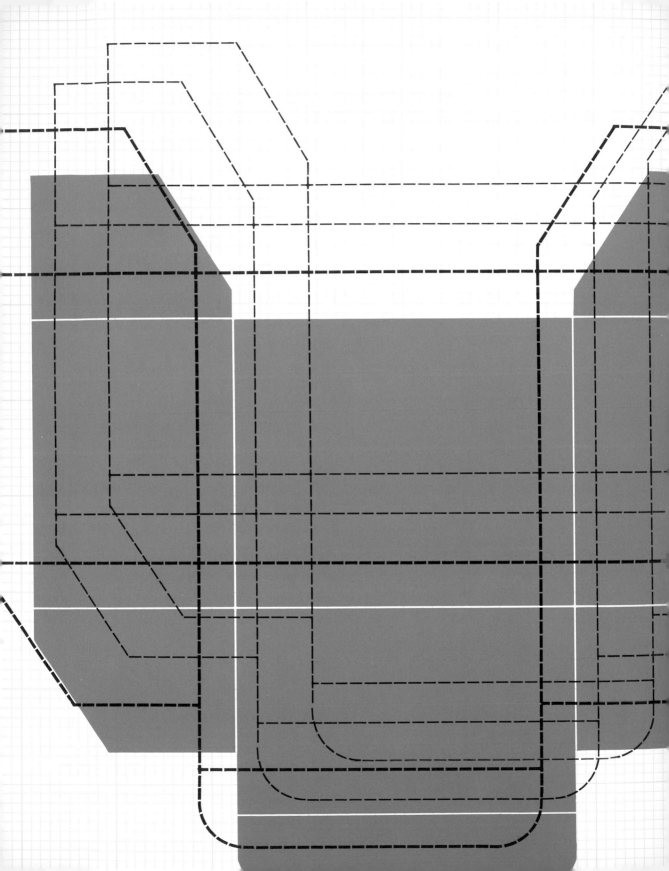

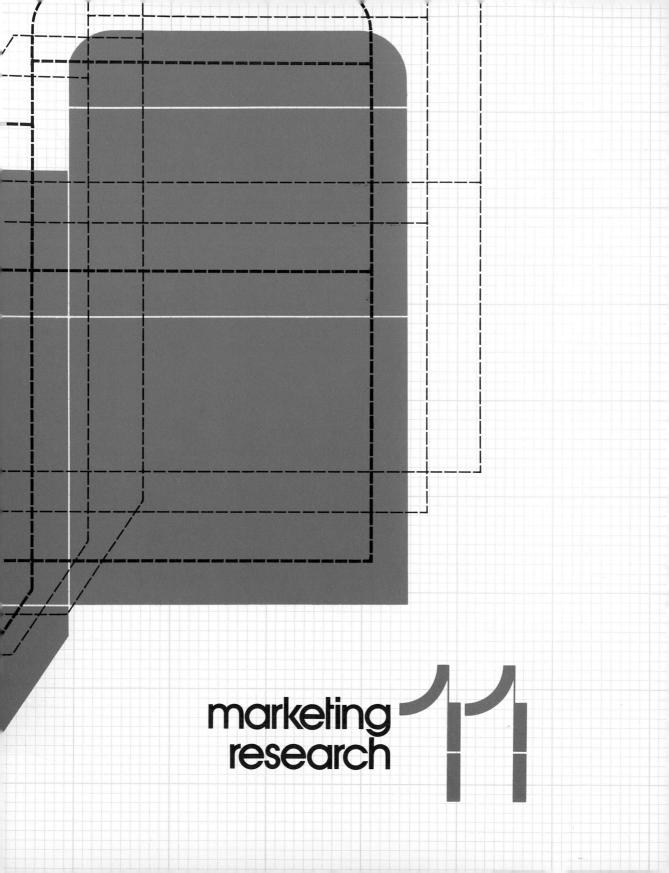

marketing
research **11**

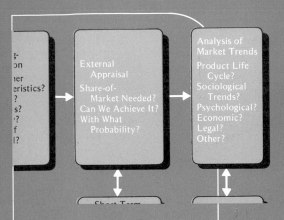

g-
on

ner
eristics?
?
s?
'?
f
l?

External
Appraisal

Share-of-
Market Needed?
Can We Achieve It?
With What
Probability?

Analysis of
Market Trends

Product Life
Cycle?
Sociological
Trends?
Psychological?
Economic?
Legal?
Other?

Short Term

If we accept as the definition of the marketing concept that it is "the determination and satisfaction of customer needs at a profit," then marketing research represents the keystone of the marketing concept. For it is one of the major tasks of marketing research to assist in the determination of customer needs. Thus, by posing several questions to 1,500 voters we may learn that their major concern is with inflation, suggesting a primary need for economic stability. Or we may learn from one-hour, in-depth interviews with one-hundred males that the major reason they object to giving blood is the subconscious fear that it may lead to a loss of virility, suggesting the need to represent to potential male donors the donation of blood as the "manly" thing to do, a method of fertilizing and giving life to other people.

Markets are analogous to moving targets.

Marketing is much like shooting at a moving target. And in this type of target shooting, it is more useful to have a general sense of the direction and velocity of the target than it is to have an extremely sensitive and accurate gunsight. Marketing research can provide the ``general sense of the target'' necessary for effective decision making.

Marketing research is as close to science as we get in this field. Perhaps for this reason, it is necessary to resist the temptation to overrepresent its capabilities and value. It can, however, provide useful inputs to the process of formulating marketing strategy.

The basic objective of this discussion is to review the ways in which various types of research can be utilized effectively in marketing decision making. This requires that we explore types of research and the translation of their results into useful decision inputs. Along the way, the discussion should provide exposure to some of the sources of data relevant to marketing that are listed in Appendix A.

pols and polls

In the spring of 1970, John Marttila, campaign manager for a candidate for the U. S. House of Representatives, was faced with a problem common to most political campaign managers, a limited budget. His candidate, Father Robert Drinan, had been encouraged by an insurgent group of Democrat party members to run in the Democrat party primary against a seventy-six-year-old incumbent who had built his reputation in twenty-six years in the House of Representatives as a supporter of military preparedness. In addition to being a strong advocate of the withdrawal of American troops from South Vietnam at a time when it was a highly controversial matter, Father Drinan was the first Catholic priest to run for national office. These factors had produced a highly motivated core of supporters, many of them of college age, and some financial support.

John Marttila carefully reviewed his facts in preparing a plan for his candidate's campaign. The voting district, the Third District of Massachusetts, contained approximately 225,000 persons who were registered to vote. Of these, about 90,000 were registered as Democrats, 45,000 as Republicans, and 90,000 as Independents. Only Democrats and Independents would be eligible to vote in the Democrat party primary. Although it was generally known that the support for Father Drinan's stand on Vietnam would come from the more populous eastern part of the district, the fact that he was a Jesuit priest made it hard to predict voting patterns among groups of registered voters.

Marttila estimated that a total of $125,000 might be raised in support of the campaign. Perhaps 40 per cent of this would be required to defray the relatively fixed, basic expenses of staffing, space rental, and telephone. The remainder, or $75,000, would be largely available for promotional activities. Of this, perhaps $40,000 would be available for direct-mail communication with voters. The average cost of a direct-mail piece was 15 cents for printing and postage. A simple calculation indicated to Marttila that he would not be able to afford the three such communications with each prospective voter, approaches he felt to be necessary for a candidate whose views might well be misinterpreted by the typical voter. He regarded this as an essential supplement to whatever direct contact that might be made with potential voters by Drinan and his volunteers.

John Marttila's organization had recruited and received offers of volunteer help from nearly three-thousand people, many of them students residing outside the Third District. His past experience suggested that unless volunteers were put to work, they often lost interest rapidly in helping out. And yet he wasn't sure how best to make use of this resource.

(1)   If you were in Marttila's position, what would you do?

□ □ □

John Marttila's first action was to commission a professional poll to determine voting preferences, current issues of interest to potential voters, and the degree to which they associated various candidates with the issues. When the poll had been completed and the results processed, Marttila found that, although more than 50 per cent of the registered voters opposed United States involvement in the Vietnamese war, more than 50 per cent also incorrectly perceived Drinan's opponent to be opposed to United States involvement.

Furthermore, only 32 per cent recognized Drinan's name, and 48 per cent were against the idea of a priest's involvement in politics. Over all, the April poll some five months in advance of the primary vote indicated that 48 per cent of potential voters favored Drinan's major opponent, 16 per cent favored Drinan, 9 per cent expressed support for a third candidate, and the remainder were undecided. According to Marttila:

> We designed the most likely strategy based on the market research. Knowing the district was opposed to the war by more than 50 per cent, we zeroed in on this viewpoint as the only possible way to overcome the incredible obstacles Drinan faced as a candidate.[1]

As a result of the poll, a questionnaire was designed that could be administered by the army of volunteers on their first calls to a large number of homes of potential voters. The questionnaire is shown in Figure 11-1. At the same time, Marttila invested about one fourth of his $40,000 promotional budget for the development and operation of a computer program that sorted out voters' responses on the basis of their opinions about the importance of various issues and their support for alternative solutions of each. In addition, the computer program allowed the sorting of respondents by name and address.

Based on information provided by the initial professional research, Marttila's organization set out to raise the recognition level for Drinan, associate his name in potential voters' minds as the candidate favoring United States withdrawal from Southeast Asia, and accomplish the first two objectives through a "low-profile" campaign that would not arouse supporters of Drinan's relatively confident and inactive opponent. This required direct contact between volunteers and potential voters as well as the careful use of direct mail as a medium of communication rather than billboards, radio, television, or other "splashy" and expensive media.

The massive canvass by volunteers, using the questionnaire shown in Figure 11-1, made it possible to identify specific potential voters and their addresses with various points of view. Based on this information, it was possible to eliminate addresses of potential voters favoring "the president's policy of Vietnamization and gradual withdrawal" or "an all-out attempt to win the war militarily" from the list of those to be contacted directly or by mail. The remainder, about 75,000 Democrat and Independent voters, were sent a major direct-mail piece reemphasizing Father Drinan's position on what was considered to be the "leverage issue" of the campaign: American involvement in Vietnam. Among these 75,000, it was possible to sort names and addresses by computer to indicate those also favoring or opposing Drinan's candidacy as well as particular issues of greatest interest to each respondent for further targeted communications. By this means, the final two mailings of the campaign were directed only to 25,000 households (with an average of 1.6 voters each) whose profiles indicated strong support for both Drinan and withdrawal from Vietnam, with the idea that this core of voters, largely in the eastern half of the voting district, would be sufficient to produce a primary victory for Drinan, based on voting totals in previous years.

Following their initial canvass of all homes of registered Democrats or

---

[1]This quote, and information in this example, are based on an interview with Mr. Marttila.

DRINAN CANVASS

15 Elm Street, Waltham 02154, 891-6624
20 Putnam Street, Fitchburg 01420, 342-9404

Name of Person Canvassed
Mr.
Mrs.
Miss _____

Household's Street Address _____

Town/City _____ Ward _____ Precinct _____ Date _____

Response (Check one below)

☐ Individual responded in person

☐ Took mail-back questionnaire

☐ Interviewed by telephone

☐ Not home_____times; left mail-back questionnaire

☐ Refused to respond (Thank anyway)

HEADQUARTERS FILLS IN THIS BOX
3-digit code _____
zip code _____
household's phone number: _____
☐ rest of questionnaire ok

1. Although it is still early in the campaign, have you previously heard of Robert Drinan's candidacy for the United States Congress?

☐ Yes

☐ No

In either case, respondent should next look at or be told about Drinan's qualifications as Dean of Boston College Law School, etc.

2. How do you generally feel about Father Drinan's candidacy?

☐ Very positive

☐ Positive

☐ Neutral

☐ Negative

☐ Very negative

Estimate response and if possible indicate why_____

_____

3. Your Congressman Philip Philbin has generally supported the war effort. Robert Drinan is for the immediate cessation of hostilities and withdrawal of U.S. forces. He would like to know how you feel. Which of the following actions would you favor most? CHECK ONE:

☐ Complete and immediate withdrawal;

☐ Complete withdrawal within 12 months;

☐ The President's policy of Vietnamization and gradual withdrawal;

☐ An all-out attempt to win the war militarily

☐ No response or other_____

Independents, volunteer workers were used to solicit funds from the strongest of Drinan's supporters and maintain contact with all eligible voters not strongly opposed to candidate Drinan. They also produced eight full-time staffers who were stationed in the eight easternmost wards in the district. Finally, as primary election day approached, volunteers were organized to insure maximum coverage of Drinan's 25,000 strongest households.

(2)
(3)
(4)
How would you relate this effort to the process of market segmentation and targeting that we discussed earlier? What was the cost of information in this example? What was the value of the information obtained?

4. Robert Drinan believes that the war is the principal cause both of inflation and of a potential recession. Has your family felt either of these economic effects?

☐ Severely,   Note how, only if volunteered

☐ Moderately, or

☐ Not noticeably   _____

5. Congressman Philbin's uncritical approval of military appropriations has encouraged wasteful spending. Robert Drinan favors reduced military spending and a re-ordering of national priorities to give attention to domestic problems. He would like to know which of these problems you feel deserves the most attention.

CHECK ONE OR NUMBER IN ORDER OF PRIORITY:

☐ Civil rights   ☐ Problems of the elderly

☐ Crime   ☐ Student unrest

☐ Drugs   ☐ Tax reform and government spending

☐ Education   ☐ Other: _____

☐ Environment

☐ Poverty   _____

THANK RESPONDENT AND ENCOURAGE VOTE FOR DRINAN IN SEPTEMBER 15 DEMOCRATIC PRIMARY

SUPPLEMENTARY INFORMATION (COMPLETE AFTER INTERVIEW)

REFER TO STREET LIST TO COMPLETE THE FOLLOWING:

VOTER REGISTRATION

☐ Democrat   Approximate age _____

☐ Republican

☐ Independent (unenrolled)

☐ Unregistered, but eligible   ☐ Male   ☐ Single

☐ Not eligible to vote   ☐ Female   ☐ Married

Profession _____   Number of Voters
In This Household _____

CHECK BELOW IF APPLICABLE:

☐ Potential volunteer

☐ Took bumper sticker   ANY OTHER COMMENT: _____

☐ Send bumper sticker   _____

Canvasser's Name _____   Canvasser's
Phone Number_____

the uses of marketing research

(5)

The following vignettes illustrate some of the varied uses of marketing research. In reading them, identify the basic questions addressed by each of the efforts described.

Several years ago the Central National Bank in Chicago decided to organize a youth club to increase its percentage of customers under thirty, which at the time represented about 20 per cent of the bank's customer accounts. Among other things, it staged expensive youth parties, featuring go-go girls dancing on the banking floor and a golf exhibition by Gary Player. It produced few results.[2] A subsequent study of the youth market by a newly hired marketing director suggested two major obstacles to patronage among younger customers: high minimum balances required on checking accounts and unfair credit standards for loans and credit cards, typified by questions discriminatory to younger customers such as, "How long have you been employed?," and "How long have you lived at your present address?" Following the introduction of low-cost checking plus easier credit terms and requirements, the bank's proportion of younger customers rose 50 per cent. And it was not necessary to employ go-go girls or Gary Player in marketing the new service features effectively.

Twice a week, six children ranging in age from three and one-half to four and one-half report to the East Aurora, New York nursery operated by Fisher-Price Toys, the largest manufacturer of toys for children under six in the United States. For two hours they play with a large number of toys designed and manufactured by Fisher-Price and other manufacturers. During their free-play period, they bang, poke, prod, and ignore various toys created by Fisher-Price designers under the watchful eyes of their teacher, the designers, and Fisher-Price marketing personnel. Many designs ignored by the children are discarded by the company. Others are altered, based on expected uses of a design under actual play conditions. According to the company's vice-president for research and development, this approach helps the company make sure that its products are designed for kids and not toy designers.

The primary political campaign strategy of Robert Drinan described earlier represented yet another use of marketing research.

Finally, early in this century, it is said that executives for a now well-known manufacturer of paper products were astounded by the sales increases being registered by a new tissue. The product had been developed and marketed for use as an easy, neat way of enabling women to remove cold cream from their faces after completing a then-popular nightly ritual of applying cold cream. Finally, by the time sales had surpassed all expectations, a study was initiated to find out why so much of the tissue was being sold. It was then that researchers found that more of the tissue was being used as disposable handkerchiefs than for face cleansing purposes. This heavily influenced the future direction of promotional and distribution efforts on behalf of the product, Kleenex.

(6) Basic marketing questions to which research efforts often are addressed were suggested as well in Figure 6-8, page 207. Which of these questions can you identify in the examples above? Answers to questions of this sort help in the structuring of new-product development efforts as well as marketing programs.

the basic research question: cost and value of the research

The decision to engage in formal marketing research is, at its most fundamental level, based on a comparison of the value and cost of such efforts, as illustrated graphically in Figure 11-2. This is much easier said than done. Nevertheless,

[2]"Now Banks Are Turning to the Hard Sell," *Business Week* (June 24, 1972), pp. 78–82. See p. 82.

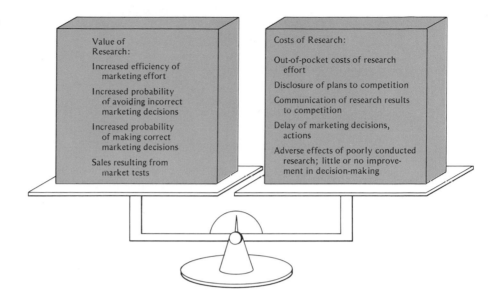

Figure 11-2. The basic research consideration requires weighing the relative value and cost of research efforts.

Value of Research:

Increased efficiency of marketing effort

Increased probability of avoiding incorrect marketing decisions

Increased probability of making correct marketing decisions

Sales resulting from market tests

Costs of Research:

Out-of-pocket costs of research effort

Disclosure of plans to competition

Communication of research results to competition

Delay of marketing decisions, actions

Adverse effects of poorly conducted research; little or no improvement in decision-making

marketing managers frequently weigh the benefits and cost of research intuitively. Others occasionally may employ a more formal means of analyzing the same problem.

an intuitive approach

Many decisions to employ marketing research are based on a manager's "feel" for the problem. They involve a nonquantitative appraisal of values and costs associated with the proposed research effort.

Value of Research—The Need to Know. Perhaps the most important value of marketing research is the improvement in marketing results that it should produce. This is a function both of the magnitude of the decision and the amount of uncertainty we may have about it. Putting it another way, it is equivalent to the extent of improvement in decision making that we are likely to experience because of the availability of marketing-research results. The Chrysler Corporation will place a higher value on marketing research in the introduction of a new luxury compact auto than a local used car dealer attempting to decide whether to take a luxury compact auto in trade for another model on his lot.

The extent of incremental improvement in decision making is difficult to measure in all but the most extreme cases. What is the value of marketing research to an executive whose attitude is epitomized by the humorous saying, "Don't bother me with facts, I've already made up my mind?" Or to the marketing manager whose available facts all strongly support a particular decision?

(7)

(8)

Other values of marketing research may be less difficult to measure. For example, in situations in which marketing research is used to segment markets for the subsequent planning of promotional effort, value can be measured in terms of the amount of expense avoided in marketing a product to a market segment with unlikely prospects for sale. What was the value of information generated by John Marttila's survey on behalf of candidate Robert Drinan in the example we considered earlier?

(9)

Tests of products or marketing programs in the market place may, by their very nature, generate sales that represent useful data. The sales may be of sufficient volume to produce tangible returns to the sponsor of the research.

It is in the borderline cases involving a great deal of uncertainty and facts supporting several different possible decisions that marketing research can be most valuable, and its value most difficult to measure.

Cost of Research. Tangible costs of marketing research may be much less difficult to measure and intangible costs easier to imagine than is the case with the measurement of value.

In many organizations, the budget of the group with responsibilities for formal marketing research often is identified separately. Costs such as those for data collection, processing, and interpretation associated with a particular project often can be calculated accurately.

In addition to such measurable out-of-pocket costs, others may arise. Marketing research takes time, thus delaying decisions and actions. Research involving the actual sale or demonstration of a product may disclose possible plans to competition as well as allow competition to monitor the results, particularly in a test-marketing situation. How do these factors help explain why dress designers rarely conduct marketing research? Why would a forest products manufacturing company with a new patented process for producing reuseable tableware from wood pulp be more likely than a dress designer to engage in marketing research in the development and marketing of its product?

(10)
(11)

There is always a risk, and in some cases a strong likelihood, that marketing-research results may be communicated to competitors. This is especially true for research efforts employing test marketing in which a new product or promotional program is tested under typical marketing conditions in one or more communities. This risk is particularly high for consumer packaged goods, for which auditing services can be hired to measure competitive sales levels, as well as certain industrial goods, about which information may travel rapidly within the engineering fraternity.

Marketing research takes time. Consequently, it can delay marketing decision making. In cases where a firm may have only a slight time lead on its competition, and such a lead is important, time may be costly.

Finally, there is always a risk that the research may be conducted in such a way that it produces few results of any real use, may have little influence on the actual marketing decision, or, worst of all, may mislead the decision maker. It is not difficult to understand how this can happen, given the pressures on the marketing researcher to obtain the most useful information possible in the shortest possible period of time. Decision makers are not always distinguished by their patience. Useful marketing research may require the testing of one variable, or change in a product or marketing program, at a time. Under the time pressures created by managers, researchers are tempted to measure the effects of two or more variables at the same time. Without appropriate care, this can result in an inability to judge the effects of any one variable, or different combinations of variables, thus negating the value of the information collected.

(12)

Based on our discussion, how would you explain the findings of one study that disclosed that many marketing research department budgets amount to about .2 per cent of sales, or $200,000 for every $100 million in sales, in contrast to product (research and development) design budgets that sometimes repre-

(13)

sent 5 per cent to 10 per cent of sales dollars? What types of marketing problems might these firms face?

a formal approach

Assume that our company, American Cleansers, Inc., currently is marketing a soap-impregnated pad of steel wool, "Little Red," which is losing marketing share and experiencing declining contribution levels in competition with the products, "Pink Pad" and "Big Blue," manufactured by competitors. We have developed an improved product, Big Red, but have not decided whether to invest the $2 million that we have estimated will be necessary to launch the product on the market. We think our product is superior to the competition but are not sure that consumers will perceive it as such. On balance, we think there is about a 60 per cent chance that they will. If they do, we think that increased sales of Big Red will increase our contribution from this product by about $5 million. If they don't, our contribution may increase by a much smaller amount, perhaps $500,000 per year.

If we were to decide not to introduce the new product, we might expect the contribution to fall by about $1 million a year anyway. The potential results of each of our two possible decisions under each of the two sets of conditions, or "states of reality," are shown in Table 11-1.

Table 11-1 **An Evaluation of the Effects of Marketing Actions in a Formal Appraisal of the Value of Marketing Research**

Decision	Possible States of Reality ("State of Nature") and Probability of Each		Expected Pay-off
	New Product Superior to Competition (60%, or .6, probability)	New Product Inferior to Competition (40%, or .4, probability)	
Introduce new product	Increased contribution = $5 million Cost of marketing program = −$2 million Net result = $3 million	$.5 million −$2.0 million −$1.5 million	(.6 × $3 million) + (.4 × −$1.5 million) = $1.2 million
Don't introduce new product	Increased contribution = −$1 million Cost of marketing program = 0 Net result = −$1 million	−$1.0 million 0 −$1.0 million	(.6 × −$1 million) + (.4 × −$1 million) = −$1.0 million

Based on our expectations of reality, indicated by the probabilities that we might assign as managers to conditions we might encounter, we can compute the expected pay-off of each possible decision. This is a weighted value of each combination of condition and decision multiplied by the likelihood with which we think each will occur. Thus, the expected pay-off from introducing the new product would be $1.2 million, with a chance that our results might produce anything from a $3 million increase in contribution to a $1.5 million reduction in contribution. Regardless of conditions in the market place, we assume that we stand to lose $1 million in contribution if we don't introduce the new product, producing an expected (weighted) pay-off of −$1 million.

If we are not overly concerned about the possibility of losing $1.5 million by introducing a new product into a unreceptive market, we may introduce our product without collecting further information. If we are "risk averse," however, we may want the assurance that good marketing research can provide. There is a rationale for calculating the value of such research.

The Value of Perfect Information. Let's assume that we were able to carry out marketing research that would tell us the true state of reality. If it indicated that Big Red would be perceived by potential customers as superior to the competition, we would introduce our new product and increase the contribution by $3 million. If the findings were to the contrary, we would not introduce a new product and suffer a $1 million decline in contribution. Based on our current assessment of product and market, we attached a 60 per cent probability to the former finding and a 40 per cent probability to the latter. Thus, on a weighted average basis, the value of perfect information would be ($3 million × .6) + (−$1 million × .4), or $1.4 million in contribution. Compared with the highest value associated with our possible decisions, $1.2 million resulting from the introduction of Big Red, the added value of perfect information in this example would be $200,000 ($1.4 million − $1.2 million). Presumably, this represents the maximum amount of money that we would consider spending to obtain more information. What would the value of perfect information be if our original assessments of customer perceptions of our product were an 80 per cent chance that it would be regarded as superior to the competition and a 20 per cent chance that it would be regarded as inferior? Does this make sense to you?

The Cost and Value Trade-Off. At American Cleansers, we have two marketing research alternatives. We could conduct extensive consumer surveys by placing Big Red and one or more competitive products in the homes of a thousand consumers in several markets and returning to obtain their reactions to the competing products in actual use. This would take about a month, but would cost approximately $40,000. Or we could select four markets in which to introduce Big Red and trace the sales results. This would require about three months, but it could produce anything from a $10,000 increase in contribution to a $10,000 net decline in contribution. There is nothing about Big Red that is patentable. In fact, it is quite common for competitors in our industry to purchase, analyze, and sometimes copy products.

Under these circumstances, how would you assess the prospective values and costs of the proposed methods of marketing research? What action would you take?

378

This type of analysis illustrates the basic nature of the application of a type of decision theory utilizing Bayesian statistics to marketing problems, a branch of statistics advocating a systematic approach to decision-making based on individual beliefs (prior analysis) about the future rather than the time-consuming, costly, and most-often impossible measurement of the results of many similar experiences.[3] More important, it suggests the nature of the decision to invest in research, whether or not a formal method of appraisal is employed.

marketing research in the decision-making process

In reaching decisions, marketing managers call on a wide variety of information inputs. Included among these may be direct observations, such as store visits; past experiences; internal sales data; readily available information provided by government agencies or otherwise found in libraries; and routine external data sources such as store audits by commercial organizations of competitors' product sales. Many of these inputs can be obtained in an informal, unstructured manner. At the other extreme, surveys, product tests, market tests, and tests of various alternative marketing programs can be planned carefully and systematically executed in what represents a much more formal information-gathering and analysis effort.

Most definitions limit marketing research to the latter types of activities. If this is the case, we can conclude that most decisionmakers engage in formal marketing research as a last resort only after they have exhausted most of the quicker and less expensive methods of obtaining information inputs. As suggested in Figure 11-3, formal marketing research efforts often constitute a last step before a decision. More often than not, they are by-passed when marketing managers can obtain sufficient information for decision-making purposes from less formal sources.

What is the nature of the process? Many have likened it to a practical application of the scientific method, involving the definition of the problem, the identification of alternatives, the formulation of opinions about the best course of action, the testing of alternative courses, and a final decision based on an objective interpretation of available evidence. It is useful to explore the nature of each of these activities and information inputs most commonly employed at each stage in the decision-making process.

problem definition

Problem definition requires the identification of problem symptoms, possible causes, and alternative solutions, as well as the formulation of opinions regarding the most desirable of possible courses of action. For example, several years

[3] For a more complete discussion of these techniques, see Paul E. Green and Donald S. Tull, *Research for Marketing Decisions,* 2nd ed. (Englewood Cliffs, N. J.: Prentice-Hall, 1970), pp. 23–71. In particular, Green and Tull discuss methods of valuing research that, by its very nature, produces less than perfect information.

Figure 11-3. The role of marketing research in the decision-making process.

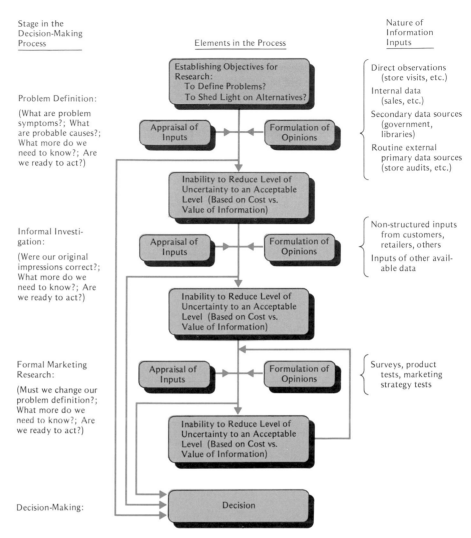

Stage in the Decision-Making Process

Problem Definition:

(What are problem symptoms?; What are probable causes?; What more do we need to know?; Are we ready to act?)

Informal Investigation:

(Were our original impressions correct?; What more do we need to know?; Are we ready to act?)

Formal Marketing Research:

(Must we change our problem definition?; What more do we need to know?; Are we ready to act?)

Decision-Making:

Elements in the Process

Establishing Objectives for Research:
    To Define Problems?
    To Shed Light on Alternatives?

Appraisal of Inputs

Formulation of Opinions

Inability to Reduce Level of Uncertainty to an Acceptable Level (Based on Cost vs. Value of Information)

Appraisal of Inputs

Formulation of Opinions

Inability to Reduce Level of Uncertainty to an Acceptable Level (Based on Cost vs. Value of Information)

Appraisal of Inputs

Formulation of Opinions

Inability to Reduce Level of Uncertainty to an Acceptable Level (Based on Cost vs. Value of Information)

Decision

Nature of Information Inputs

Direct observations (store visits, etc.)

Internal data (sales, etc.)

Secondary data sources (government, libraries)

Routine external primary data sources (store audits, etc.)

Non-structured inputs from customers, retailers, others

Inputs of other available data

Surveys, product tests, marketing strategy tests

(18)

ago the Gerber Products Co. introduced a new cereal for infants that failed to produce expected sales levels. In this case, would insufficient sales represent a problem symptom or cause?

There are several conceivable reasons why the sales of Gerber's cereal were disappointing. Among them were possible deficiencies in the product as perceived by consumers, inappropriate promotional efforts, a disadvantageous price, or insufficient product availability in retail stores. Each of these possible causes suggested a different solution and course of action.

In this case, by direct observation Gerber's marketing management assured itself that the cereal was being offered at a competitive price. Compared with other promotional programs, it was receiving a comparable quantity of support, although the quality of the effort was not measured exactly. Past experience, including consumer expressions of need during studies conducted in support of the development of other infant cereals manufactured by Gerber, suggested that the product should have been attractive to the market. And by means of the company's information system containing periodically collected data regarding product shelf space, position, mix, and movement in fifty-thousand retail outlets representing 85 per cent to 90 per cent of the total retail food sales in the United States, Gerber's director of marketing research learned an interesting fact:

> Among the stores that carried it, the product became our sixth best seller. Yet the computer told us that we had only 25 per cent distribution [product on display in only 25 per cent of the available outlets].[4]

(19)
(20)
In this case, would it be necessary to proceed to an informal investigation or more formal marketing research effort before reaching a decision? What problem cause and course of action would be suggested by the problem definitions?

Translating Data into Information. Possible causes of Gerber's sales problem were not realized until data, represented by indications of whether or not each store in the company's program was carrying the new cereal, could be collected and organized in a manner in which it defined a pattern of retailer behavior. At this moment, it became information, something of use to marketing decision makers at Gerber. This job of translating data into information is a basic task of marketing research.

To insure that the information obtained from data inputs is relevant, it is important to establish a purpose for data collection and translation. A practical way of defining the purpose is to determine the nature of the decision to be made ultimately on the basis of the information and the questions for which the decision maker must have answers. Much of the task of problem definition may concern itself with these efforts.

Primary Data Inputs. Data collected by Gerber through the direct auditing of store activities represented what is regarded by many as primary data. Generally speaking, the term is used to refer to data collected directly by the user or specifically for the user in such a manner that the conditions and assumptions under which the data was collected are well known to the user.

Sources of primary data may include informal observations, systematic auditing of store activity, or special marketing-research studies conducted for specific purposes or decisions.

Secondary Data Inputs. Secondary data, collected by those not under the direction or control of the decision maker, also can be useful in helping to define a marketing problem.

The federal government represents the largest source of secondary data about products and markets in the United States. At the heart of this data-collection effort is the Bureau of the Census, termed "the largest marketing research organization in the world" by its director several years ago.[5] In 1974, this agency had a budget of $120 million, employed 10,400 people, and gener-

---

[4]"The Low Birthrate Crimps the Baby-Food Market," *Business Week* (July 13, 1974), pp. 44–50. Quote on p. 48.

[5]This and other information in this section is based on "The Supersalesman at the Census Bureau," *Business Week* (March 23, 1974), pp. 84–85.

ated more than 1,100 reports containing more than 200,000 pages. The efforts of this agency relevant to marketing management include the collection of a large amount of data from every resident of the United States every ten years as part of the *Census of Population*. This is updated monthly in a "Current Population Survey." Every five years, the Census Bureau presents the results of its extensive collection of data concerning the number of retailing establishments of various types, their locations, their sales volumes, and their numbers of employees in the *Census of the Retail Trades*. Similar censuses of the wholesale trades, manufacturing and transportation are prepared. From all of these inputs, marketers can measure the size and composition of various actual and potential markets. And, among other uses, commercial marketing research organizations can rely on the data to prepare reliable samples of respondents representing cross sections of the United States population. In the words of the president of one of the largest commercial marketing research organizations, A. C. Nielsen Co., "census data are the keystones of all market research."[6] The price is hard to beat as well. The Nielsen organization, which considers itself a heavy user of census data, lays out about $30 per year for all of the information that it needs.

Census data is presented in summary form monthly in publications such as the *Survey of Current Business* and annually in a volume called the *Statistical Abstract of the United States*. Both of these are important starting points for a search of secondary data inputs for marketing decisions.

Nongovernmental sources of secondary data include periodic surveys conducted by newspapers and magazines, data collected and circulated by advertising agencies as an element in their service to clients, trade association reports, and data supplied on a subscription basis by firms that conduct continuing audits of consumer behavior and actual product sales.

Typical of the first of these is the annual "Survey of Buying Power," prepared and published by *Sales Management: The Marketing Magazine*, which can be used to estimate the level of discretionary spending for residents of various communities.

Advertising agencies such as J. Walter Thompson Co. hire representative groups of consumers to serve as "panels" for the testing of new products and the continuing measurement of consumer buying patterns. Some of these reports may be made generally available, but most are for the use of actual or potential clients of such advertising agencies.

A large number of trade associations, with widely varying names such as the National Association of Retail Druggists and the National Association of Purchasing Agents, publish reports prepared primarily for their members. But many of these are available to interested parties for the asking and are indexed in a volume called the *Directory of U. S. Trade Associations*. These may contain useful information concerning a particular industry.

The most timely and expensive of these three types of nongovernmental data is that supplied on a subscription basis by firms such as the A. C. Nielsen Co., the Market Research Corporation of America (MRCA), and Selling Areas-Marketing, Inc. (SAMI). The Nielsen organization provides, among other services, a continuing survey of retail sales trends for some 8,000 different drug and grocery products based on actual store visits and shelf counts at a sample of 1,600 supermarkets and 750 drugstores, selected on the basis of information

[6]Ibid., p. 85.

provided by the Bureau of the Census. MRCA, through diaries kept by members of a panel of about 5,000 families, representing a cross section of the United States population, provides data regarding the purchases of food, drugs, and other selected items. This includes not only the items purchased, but also information about the prices paid and the stores where various items were bought. SAMI offers detailed data about warehouse product withdrawals (not necessarily sold) at four-week intervals. Can you think of any reasons why a marketing manager would want to subscribe to two or more of these services, each of which can cost from $25,000 to more than $100,000 per year, depending on the information ordered?

(21)

A good deal of secondary data is as near at hand as your nearest library. For your convenience, I have listed and briefly described major sources mentioned in this section, along with others, in Appendix A. It is worth a quick look now, and perhaps continuing use, as you begin to familiarize yourself with your own favorite set of secondary data sources.

(22)
(23)

Based on our discussion, what would you cite as the general strengths and weaknesses of primary and secondary data sources? Which do you think would be relied on most heavily in the problem-definition stage of the decision-making process?

For major decisions regarding the introduction of a new product or a change in marketing strategy, problem definition may warrant the largest amount of time in the decision-making process. It is of little comfort to a marketing manager to come up with the right solution to the wrong problem.

Once a problem is defined, in terms of its symptoms, possible causes, and potential alternative solutions, the best solution may become immediately apparent. Where this is not the case, the manager may turn to an informal investigation.

informal investigation

Informal investigation may range from nothing more than a chat with a purchasing agent representing a major potential customer to the solicitation of information from a nonrandom sample of customers, retailers, or others familiar with a particular product or marketing method. Efforts at this stage of the decision-making process most often are intended to further define the problem and alternative solutions as well as eliminate the need for more formal research. They often require little time or money. Whether they produce useful information inputs depends on the representativeness of the people whose opinions are solicited as well as the nature of the questions asked.

A small number of potential buyers, for example, might possess power and wield influence out of proportion to their number. For example, in the design and marketing of loading-ramp devices to board and deplane airline passengers, the opinions of a few managers of major airports might be sufficient to determine whether the product has promise or requires redesign. A similarly small sample of airline passengers would probably produce few useable results.

Informal investigations are most productive when those surveyed are asked specific questions, shown a product or advertisement to be evaluated, or asked to compare two things. (More than two things often confuse respondents.) Even under these conditions, misleading results may be obtained. For example, wives of four advertising agency executives were shown pink and yellow versions of a new kitchen sponge mop by their husbands and asked to select the one they would prefer. Based on the selection of pink mops by three of the women, the agency ordered a large proportion of pink mops for a more systematic research effort. This effort required the selection of a mop for use in the home by a randomly selected sample of respondents in which each home in the metropolitan area studied had an equal chance of being selected for the sample. The user was then told that he or she could keep the product chosen in return for writing in a diary information about how it was used and how well it worked and submitting to a personal interview two weeks hence. As data collectors began placing the mops in various residences, they soon ran out of yellow mops. They found that more than half of all kitchens surveyed were yellow. Mops were color selected to complement the over-all decor of the kitchen. In this case the informal investigation conducted by the advertising executives with their wives did not meet the needs for a representative sample. How would you account for what happened here?

Informal investigation, in addition to helping sharpen problem definitions, may lead directly to decisions in cases where the evidence obtained from even spotty and biased sources points overwhelmingly in a certain direction. At other times, it may only point up the need for more formal research. For example, at a time when it wished to enter a new market with a broad line of process control equipment for industrial uses, Beckman Instruments, Inc. executives began in their usual fashion by soliciting design ideas from a few large potential users. But this did not produce a set of specifications for a general-purpose line of equipment, the company's objective. Furthermore, Beckman's executives suspected that answers were biased by experiences that respondents had had with other Beckman products. As a result, the company spent five years and several million dollars in developing its new major product line with the help of more formal research inputs supplied by in-depth interviews conducted by a marketing research firm with groups of instrumentation engineers. The anonymity of both Beckman and the responding engineers was maintained. As a result, the company introduced its new line of equipment that it claimed was the first to be designed by customers themselves. What do these examples suggest about important differences between informal investigation and formal marketing research?

formal marketing research

As a last resort, marketing managers may turn to formal marketing research to produce more valid and reliable inputs for their decision making. The validity of research refers to the extent to which it really measures what it purports to measure. Its reliability is the accuracy with which it portrays reality. Generally speaking, how would you compare the validity and reliability of information produced by the United States census of population and small-sample surveys designed to suggest consumer buying-behavior patterns for specific products in the allocation of national advertising budgets for such products?

(24)

(25)

(26)

Most formal marketing research involves the systematic solicitation or testing of ideas, the testing of products or services, and the testing of the market acceptance of products and marketing methods with the basic objective of determining the "market potential" for an idea, product, or service. These efforts may employ surveys, experiments, simulations, or any or all of these in different combinations. Some common relationships between methods and uses of formal research are shown in Table 11-2.

Surveys. Surveys of individuals' opinions, perceptions, or experiences may be conducted by mail, telephone, or in person. Each of these survey methods has distinctly different characteristics when compared on the basis of cost per respondent, the speed with which responses can be obtained, the response rate (percentage of requested responses actually received), the volume of information obtained per response, and the depth of probing allowed by each.

For example, given the cost of paying interviewers and obtaining cooperation from interviewees, in-person interviews are reserved largely for those projects requiring in-depth probing and a great amount of interaction between the interviewer and the respondents. A branch of marketing research called motivation research employs in-depth interviewing, psychological testing, and the interpretation of results in psychological terms to assist in product development and promotion. Studies conducted by one of the leading exponents of motivation research, Dr. Ernest Dichter, through his Institute for Motivational Research, have produced interesting and controversial results.[7] Among them are that large doorknobs help sell a house because they provide one of the few ways that potential buyers can caress the house by grasping something that allows them to fill their palms, satisfying a basic need evidenced at birth by a baby folding its thumb into its palm. The same reasoning has led to the conclusion by Dichter that the shape of a handle helps sell a tool. Based on a small number of in-depth interviews with males, Dichter's organization reached the hypotheses cited earlier about the fear of a loss of virility resulting in a reluctance among males to give blood. In this case, the interviews were followed by a psychological test in which the participants were shown pictures of males standing erect and with

Table 11-2 **Some relationships between methods and uses of formal research**

| | Methods Employed | | |
	Surveys	Experiments	Simulations
Uses			
Solicitation of ideas	X		
Testing of ideas	X	X	
Testing of products or services			
Perceived performance	X		
Price	X		X
Physical characteristics	X		X
Market testing of			
Promotional programs	X	X	
Channels of distribution	X	X	
Perceived performance of products or services	X	X	

[7] Roger Ricklefs, "Ernest Dichter Thrives Selling Firms Research on 'Hidden Emotions'", *Wall Street Journal* (Nov. 20, 1972), pp. 1 and 23.

poor posture. Invariably, blood donors were associated with the picture of the male with poor posture, leading to the conclusion that the opinions resulting from individual interviews were valid. Most such motivation research studies are based on interviews or tests involving no more than one-hundred respondents.

To reduce interviewer costs and obtain the idea-generating benefit of group interaction, group interviews have become popular where the perils of a group's influence on an individual respondent are not significant. In the marketing research performed for Beckman Instruments in the development of its process control equipment, focused or structured group interviews were held with instrumentation engineers. To encourage such engineers to participate, the researcher offered them cocktails and $40 apiece for devoting three hours to an evening interview.

Highly structured surveys may best be conducted by mail, those requiring a rapid response rate such as Gallup polls of national opinions on timely topics by telephone. Surveys encompassing a number of questions may require mail questionnaires or in-person interviewing. Those requiring a low cost per person contacted may elect mail, but those requiring a high response rate may better utilize telephone or in-person methods with several attempts made to follow up initially unsuccessful efforts to make contact.

All survey forms are subject to biases of various types. The manner in which questions are phrased may influence responses on mail questionnaires. An interviewer's voice inflections and mannerisms may influence responses by telephone and in person, respectively. The number of do's and don't's associated with survey design and administration suggest that it is best left to skilled craftsmen in the marketing research department. What types of bias, if any, might be introduced by the use of the questionnaire shown in Figure 11-1?

Survey Validity.   The nature of questions posed on surveys largely determines the validity of such efforts. In designing effective questions, it is first necessary to define the problem being addressed and determine the nature of the information that addresses the problem before turning to the design of questions that will elicit the necessary information.

Survey Reliability.   The reliability of surveys can be measured on a statistical basis only when a form of random sampling is used in the selection of respondents—that is, when all potential respondents in the entire group being measured (the "population") have an approximately equal chance of being included in the sample. The use of such techniques typically allows a researcher not only to state his or her estimate of the most likely percentage of total respondents that have bought a particular product recently, but also to state limits around the most likely percentage within which the actual (unknown) percentage is likely to fall with varying probabilities.

For example, a recent telephone survey of two-hundred homemakers in Detroit indicated that about 30 per cent of the total had a particular brand of soap powder on their shelves. Because the homemakers had been selected randomly, researchers were able to report that there was a 95 per cent chance that the true proportion of all homemakers in Detroit possessing the product was between 22 per cent and 48 per cent. A larger sample size would have produced smaller "confidence limits" around the most likely value. What factors would determine whether you would want to authorize a survey utilizing a larger sample as an executive in charge of introducing a new dishwasher reliant for its best performance on the use of the soap in question?

It should be noted that measurements of survey reliability in no way account for potential systematic biases introduced by questionnaire designers or interviewers.

(29)

(30)

(31)

How would you assess the validity and reliability of conclusions based on the motivation research techniques described earlier, for example the conclusion that large doorknobs help sell houses? Similarly, assuming that the information in Table 8-2, page 266 was collected by asking a randomly selected sample of individuals a series of questions about shopping habits by means of a mail survey, how would you assess the validity and reliability of this data? Could more valid data of this sort have been collected in some other way?

Experiments. Efforts to measure cause-and-effect relationships under controlled conditions, called experiments, may be designed, for example, to measure sales rates for products under varying sets of conditions such as different prices, promotional appeals, and combinations of competing products. The simplest of experimental designs may consist merely of measuring sales before and after the introduction of a new promotional program (sometimes called a before-after without control-group design). But this design can leave lingering doubts about whether sales increases after the introduction of a new promotional program are due to the program, a general increase in sales for all products, or a reduction in competitors' promotional efforts, to name just a few variables. Managers unwilling to live with such doubts often elect before-after with control-group designs in which two similar markets or groups of respondents are selected, the new program introduced only to one (the experimental group), and the remaining (control) group used as a basis for the comparison of sales results with and without the new promotional program. Depending on the nature of the test, it may be desirable to select experimental and control groups on the basis of similarities in the make-up of customer groups, competitors, marketing practices, weather, and other factors, and the ability to protect one group from the effects of the variable being tested. For example, Syracuse and Rochester, New York, Columbus, Ohio, and Indianapolis, Indiana have become favorite test markets for experiments requiring matched customer groups for consumer goods. As more and more marketers use these cities for marketing experiments, how attractive will they be as test cities?

(32)

Even where it is possible to find two or more markets approximately equivalent on two or more vital dimensions, it may be very difficult to insure that all variables are held constant except the one being tested in both markets. In addition to chance variances in conditions during an experiment, competitors getting wind of such an experiment have been known to sabotage results by purposely engaging in unexpected behavior in either the control or experimental market during the experiment.

By means of these and more complex experimental designs, marketers have measured the sensitivity of product sales to varying prices, promotional programs, and methods of distribution.

Simulations. Simulation is the process of modeling things, problems, or concepts, ranging from the testing of airplane models in wind tunnels to the "operation" of the United States economy by means of a model consisting of

387

mathematical equations portraying the way in which the designer of the model thinks things interact.

Forecasts may be prepared on the basis of price-demand sensitivities and other relationships observed and measured for products comparable to a new one for which no data exists. These relationships, when combined, may be formed into models consisting of a series of mathematical statements about relationships. One such statement might be

$$\Delta D = -\frac{\Delta P}{2}$$

where

Δ = the amount of change, in percentages
D = the level of demand
P = the level of price

(33)

How would you read this statement? For models much more complex than this one, computers may be employed to generate appropriate relationships from a number of observations as well as forecasts themselves.

Efforts to ask survey respondents to project themselves into the future, to identify possible product or service needs in a nonspecific context, or to indicate prices they would pay for new products or services have produced misleading results. It is perhaps unreasonable to expect respondents to be able to answer certain questions accurately. For example, the question, "How much would you be willing to pay for this (*new kind of product*)?" invariably produces distorted results. In what way would you expect the results of this question to be distorted? Why?

(34)
(35)

Instead, a simulation can be constructed in which respondents are offered a choice of items of varying values paired against the new product. The value of an existing product selected instead of the new one then is used as the upper limit for pricing the new product. This test is assumed to simulate the actual purchase process. How well do you think it succeeds?

(36)

Surveys, experiments, and simulations often are used in combination in formal marketing research efforts. An experiment may involve market surveys of results. Simulations may be based on data from experiments. And as we have seen in the pricing research example, surveys may employ simulations. All three, in turn, may be used in varying combinations in the measurement of such things as market receptivity to concepts, customer perceptions of products, and market size. The use of concept, product, and market testing can be illustrated in the context of an example involving the proposed introduction of a new line of frozen fruits by the Green Giant Company several years ago.

The Green Giant Example.[8] In the summer of 1964, executives at the Green Giant Company were exploring ways to insure the continuing rapid growth of the company through product diversification. The company's line of canned and frozen vegetables had produced sizeable annual increases in sales and profits for

[8]Material for this example is based on "The Green Giant Company, Frozen Fruits," Case 9-514-058 (Boston: Intercollegiate Case Clearing House, Copyright 1970 by the University of Minnesota).

the company. The acquisition in 1962 of a company possessing expertise in frozen fruits led Green Giant executives to speculate whether this might offer the desired opportunity for product diversification. At this point, the company's advertising agency was asked to study the fruit industry while Green Giant's research and development department began work on the development of products and packing methods.

In presenting its report, provided at no cost to Green Giant, the advertising agency cited a periodic survey by *Food Topics* magazine that estimated that consumers spent $60.1 million, or 2 per cent of expenditures on fruits of all types, for frozen fruits in 1963. Furthermore, the market for frozen fruits had increased only 8 per cent in the preceding five years compared with a 38 per cent increase for frozen vegetables during the same period. About 80 per cent of all frozen fruit purchased was frozen strawberries. A panel study published by the *Chicago Tribune* indicated that between 20 and 55 per cent of the households surveyed served frozen fruits occasionally, primarily for dessert toppings. A study conducted for *Life* magazine was cited in the advertising agency's report that indicated that the disadvantages for frozen fruits cited most often by consumers and retailers were (1) long thawing time, (2) high price, (3) quality, appearance, and flavor inferior to fresh and canned fruits, and (4) low prestige of the product. Birdseye, a brand marketed by General Foods Corp., a large, diversified grocery manufacturer, possessed the largest share of the market but had spent less than $42,000 for advertising in 1963.

Before the advertising agency's report became available, Green Giant's marketing research group assembled three discussion groups, each composed of five Minneapolis women, to taste blind samples (with brand names concealed) of Birdseye and Green Giant frozen mixed fruit. These tests suggested that the Green Giant product was preferred on "liking" and "readiness to buy" dimensions, and that the product packed in clear liquid was preferred to one packed in a colored liquid. The test cost only about $300 to conduct, primarily because it was conducted near the company's Minneapolis, Minnesota, headquarters.

Based on these findings, Green Giant executives concluded that the current market was not large enough to support a substantial investment in a frozen fruit product line. However, they were intrigued by the possibility that, by introducing frozen fruit in packages comparable to the "boil-in-the-bag pouch," which the company had developed for its frozen vegetables, the market for frozen fruit might be increased substantially. Potential consumers could reduce the necessary thawing time from several hours to fewer than fifteen minutes by immersing the frozen pouch in warm water.

(37)   How would you characterize the efforts of Green Giant executives to this point in terms of the diagram in Figure 11-3?

Concept Testing. In group discussions such as the preceding one, Green Giant representatives first let participants see the frozen fruit products and then asked them to evaluate how well they might like the product. Other tests with similar purposes have been based on pictures showing people using a particular product. Participants are then asked to describe the kind of person portrayed in the picture, thus yielding information about how they regard the product. These exercises, intended to test receptivity to the basic concept of frozen fruit usage, often are used when the actual product is not available for testing. In addition, they may elicit more objective responses to the basic idea of trying a product than an actual product test, which assumes that consumers will be willing to try the product initially in an actual market situation. How well do motivation research techniques such as these lend themselves to concept testing?

Product Testing. Following the receipt of the advertising agency's report, Green Giant conducted a series of product tests utilizing small groups. An October 1964 test of mixed fruit and sliced peaches once again indicated that Green Giant mixed fruit was preferred to Birdseye. The group, however, objected to Green Giant's mushy, messy sauce for packing peaches.

A month later, fruit packed in the conventional fibrous paper containers and the new boil-in-the-bag pouch was tested. The new package was universally preferred. In this test, participants were asked to prepare Green Giant fruit before eating it.

In February 1965, Green Giant paid a marketing research firm approximately $3,000 to test perceptions of 428 members of middle- and upper middle-income families in Denver and San Francisco regarding Green Giant mixed fruit packed in the quick-thaw pouch and Birdseye mixed fruit packed in the conventional package. Among the results of this study were that (1) 37 per cent preferred the Green Giant product and 44 per cent that of Birdseye, (2) the major complaint about the Green Giant product was that it was too sweet, (3) there was a strong preference for the quick-thaw pouch, and (4) participants expected to pay the same price for both products.

Group discussions once again were conducted in May 1965 to test reactions to both the two package types and the packing of strawberries, peaches, and blueberries in either a syrup or a cream sauce. Participants expressed a strong preference for the quick-thaw package and the product packed in syrup. Shortly after this, Green Giant executives were informed that Birdseye had begun testing frozen fruit packed in a quick-thaw pouch by placing it on sale in several stores in Los Angeles.

Throughout the remainder of 1965, Green Giant continued testing and modifying its frozen fruit products. A study costing approximately $3,000 in January 1966 of eight-hundred middle- to upper middle-income families in New York, Minneapolis, and San Francisco compared Birdseye mixed fruit, combinage (peaches and strawberries), and strawberries and Green Giant mixed fruit, blueberries, peaches, and strawberries. In general, Birdseye products scored higher on the like-dislike and readiness-to-buy scales. In particular, its raspberries scored surprisingly high. The objections to Green Giant products, and strawberries in particular, were that they were not sweet enough.

In February 1966, a marketing research company was hired for about $2,500 to test the quick-thaw package in actual in-home use in sixty homes in New Jersey and California. Again, the study confirmed the preference for the quick thaw bag, and suggested that 62 per cent of the test group definitely expected to buy frozen fruit products in the future.

At this point, would you suggest to Green Giant executives that they should begin market tests similar to those being conducted by Birdseye? How would you evaluate the value of information, cost of information, and over-all research strategy employed by Green Giant through May 1965? In your opinion, what are the relative strengths and weakness of product testing?

Market Testing. Green Giant next hired a market auditing firm to measure the sales of its frozen fruit products in ten Philadelphia supermarkets for forty-eight weeks in a test beginning in April 1966. In the fall of 1966, the decision was made to audit Birdseye quick-thaw pouch sales for six months in test markets that it had initiated—fifteen stores each in Buffalo and Miami. In addition, purchasers of Green Giant products in Philadelphia and Birdseye products in Miami were interviewed after they had used the products. These auditing and interviewing efforts were estimated to cost about $12,000.

During its test, sales of Birdseye products packed in the quick-thaw pouch leveled off at about 30 per cent of the frozen fruit dollar sales in both Buffalo and Miami. Interviews indicated that a slightly higher proportion of purchasers intended to repurchase Birdseye than Green Giant frozen fruits.

While these audits were being completed, Green Giant's marketing department authorized full-scale test marketing activities to begin in November 1966 in Cleveland and Miami, cities in which Birdseye frozen fruit products packed in the quick-thaw pouch were being sold. These tests included full-scale marketing efforts, store audits, interviews with purchasers of Green Giant products within a week of their purchases, and a telephone study to determine the relative awareness of potential consumers regarding either Green Giant or Birdseye frozen fruits. The tests were expected to cost $87,500.

At this point, a target of 2.2 million cases per year was set for national sales of the product. This was equivalent to 12 per cent of a total market that Green Giant executives estimated would be 18 million cases, 50 per cent larger than what was thought to be the size of the existing market. This increase was expected because of the widespread introduction of frozen fruit in the quick-thaw package. If national sales were to reach 2.2 million cases, annual sales in Cleveland and Miami would have to total 52,000 cases per year.

At this time, Birdseye rolled out to national distribution—a move interpreted by many Green Giant executives as one resulting from a desire to be first into the market. In addition, during its introduction in Cleveland and Miami, Birdseye priced its 49-cent packages as low as 10 to 15 cents per 12-ounce package. Most of Green Giant's sales were at 49 cents, but an effort was made to offer 10-cent price reductions through coupons to meet a similar offer by Birdseye.

Test market results in June 1967 indicated that Green Giant products had captured 16 to 24 per cent of the market for frozen fruit in Cleveland and Miami combined. This amounted to 20,000 cases in six months. In comparison, Birdseye's quick-thaw products achieved market shares varying between 30 and 57 per cent of the market. Brokers, through which Green Giant sold its products in exchange for a 2.5 per cent commission, concluded that much of Birdseye's success was due to its price cutting. In comparison, results of the ten-store market test of five Green Giant frozen fruit items in Philadelphia, in which Birdseye had only one of five items in its product line for sale, indicated that Green Giant products combined obtained an 18 per cent market share to 6 per cent for Birdseye mixed fruit.

An informal survey of Green Giant's brokers in May 1967 indicated that Birdseye had obtained good distribution nationally for its products. They were being sold generally for 49 cents per 12-ounce package, with a price to the retailer of $4.28 per case less a 5-cent advertising allowance for most of the items. Its promotional effort included spot and network television advertising in addition to some newspaper ads. Brokers noted also that the number of facings (shelf spaces) allotted to the new Birdseye frozen fruit products in supermarkets had declined to about half of what they were at the time of the product's introduction. They feared that consumers regarded the price as too high, and that less-than-expected sales had led to the reduction in facings. Several commented that they didn't think supermarket buyers were interested in another frozen fruit line at this time.

In the fall of 1967, Green Giant executives purchased the A. C. Nielsen New Product Service report on Birdseye frozen fruits for $2,000. This report, based on audits in sixty stores nationally between September 1966 and September 1967, provided the estimates shown in Table 11-3.

(42)
(43)
(44)

How would you assess the value and cost of the various market tests described here? What part could the results of concept, product, and market testing play in a final decision regarding the marketing of this product? In terms of Table 11-2, what types of marketing research techniques were employed at various stages of the formal marketing research program executed by Green

(45)

Giant's marketing department? As the executive in charge of marketing at Green Giant, would you have done anything differently?

Based on these efforts, Green Giant's marketing executives had several alternatives in December 1967. They could (1) cease all efforts on behalf of frozen fruits and drop the idea; (2) continue their previous testing in several other small markets; (3) expand their testing to include tests of alternative marketing strategies; (4) invest in further product-development efforts, estimated to cost between $50,000 and $150,000; or (5) proceed into the market with a line of frozen fruit products. If the company were to enter the market nationally with its new products, it was estimated that it would require an invest-

Table 11-3   A. C. Nielsen Co. New-Product Service Report on Birdseye Frozen Fruit, June–July 1966 and 1967

| Product | Total Retail Sales–Nielsen (60 stores) | | | No. of Stores Stocking | | Estimated Annual Volume (nationally) | |
	June–July 1966	June–July 1967	Change 1966–1967 (in %)	1966	1967	Retail Dollars (in millions)	12-Package Cases (in millions)
Total market	$25,367	$24,619	−3	60	60	$76.3	17.6
Birdseye	$ 2,087	$ 3,608	+73	44	47	$11.2	2.0
Quick-thaw		$ 2,697			38	$ 8.4	1.5
Blueberries Supreme		6			1		
Cherries Supreme		300			22		
Mixed Fruit Supreme		788			30		
Peach Combinage		335			17		
Selecte Raspberries		351			16		
Selecte Strawberries		917			36		
Birdseye other fruit	$ 2,087	$ 911	−56	44	31	$ 2.8	.5
Strawberries	1,053	421	−60	36	15		
Other fruits	1,034	490	−53	29	26		
All remaining brands	$23,280	$21,011	−10	60	60	$65.1	15.6
Strawberries	17,501	15,647	−11	60	58		
Other fruits	5,779	5,364	−7	56	53		

ment of $7 million over a five-year period for plant, equipment, initial marketing, and management costs. In addition, an undetermined annual marketing expenditure would be required. At this time, the average cost of goods sold (for all materials, processing, and packaging) for Green Giant's line of canned and frozen vegetables approximated 65 per cent of total annual sales of about $140 million. Marketing, distribution, and general expenses consumed another 28 per cent of the sales dollar, leaving about 7 per cent of sales for earnings before taxes.

(46) (47)

What would you recommend that Green Giant do? To what extent did you rely on marketing research results to reach your decision?

Now that we have some idea about how primary and secondary market data are assembled, we can consider ways of translating it into useable information for the marketing decision maker. This information invariably includes a forecast of future market size or a demand for planning purposes.

forecasting

Every decision is based on some expectation of the future, equivalent to either a formal or an informal forecast. And all forecasts are based on history. (If you challenge this last statement, try to think of a situation in which it is not true.) These two statements should suggest the importance of a familiarity with the applicability of various forecasting techniques to common marketing decision-making situations and ways of organizing and interpreting historical data or experience.

forecasting in the context of decisions

Forecasts are used most often to (1) decide whether to enter a new market or business, (2) determine how much capacity to build in advance of potential need, (3) aid in product "pruning" and product-line planning, (4) assess the effects of a proposed marketing program, (5) prepare annual budgets based on estimated sales revenues, (6) prepare standards against which to measure performance, and (7) provide inputs to operating activities such as production planning and inventory control. How would you compare the risks associated with these various uses of forecasts? To what extent does this determine the value of information provided by each and the related cost that a manager might be willing to incur to reduce uncertainty about each?

(48)
(49)

forecasting techniques

A marketing manager for a tire manufacturer may estimate future sales for a standard tire on the basis of his or her "feel" for markets and products, relying primarily on judgment and experience. Or he or she may graph sales over time, fit a line to the graph and project that line into the future, and study sales trends as a function of time. Or he or she may attempt to assess determinants of tire sales such as the rate of new automobile sales and the replacement rates for existing tires, describe their relationship to the total sales of tires and the company's share of the total in some mathematical fashion, and forecast sales on the basis of such relationships. These efforts illustrate approaches to the preparation of forecasts by means of each of three families of techniques: judgmental, time-series analysis, and the analysis of causal relationships.

Judgmental Techniques.   Judgmental forecasts may be based on opinions of individuals or groups of individuals. They may appear to consist of nothing more than pulling a number out of the air. But that number may be based on a great deal of experience, a knowledge of the effects of a number of possible future events, or the ability to equate one product's performance with a predecessor for which there is data to document its sales over a full life cycle.

Included among judgmental techniques are approaches that attempt to combine the judgments of a number of people. A "census" of the sales force or important customers may be taken to establish sales or buying intentions, respectively. A panel of experts may be assembled to combine their judgments. One variation on this latter approach is called the Delphi method, in which experts place individual predictions on paper, compare predictions, and repeat the cycle until a consensus is reached.

Judgments may be based on experiences or market research results that require interpretation for use as forecasting inputs. Methods employed and assumptions made in marketing research must be described adequately to allow an assessment of the validity and reliability of research results. This is essential to the most effective use of judgment in translating research results into decision inputs.

Time-Series Analysis.   Techniques of time-series analysis include, among others, moving averages, exponential smoothing, and trend projection. All relate sales levels to time, rather than to other causes of sales patterns.

Moving averages assume that the sales figure for the next period, for example, will be the average of sales levels for some number of preceding periods of time. For example, if monthly frozen fruit sales for January through April 1963 were 600,000, 500,000, 700,000, and 700,000 cases, respectively, the four-month moving average forecast of sales for May would be (600,000 + 500,000 + 700,000 + 700,000) divided by 4 = 625,000 cases. Exponential smoothing techniques merely give different weights to items of data. Specifically, they allow the forecaster to weight the most recent results more heavily than the rest on the assumption that the most recent results are better indicators of the immediate future. In the preceding example suggested, would this produce a forecast for May sales above or below 625,000 cases?

Trend projections involve the documentation of sales during successive time periods, the attempt to discover patterns in sales levels from period to period, and the projection of past trends (or patterns) into the future. Such relationships often are stated in arithmetic form, as in the simple example in Figure 11-4. In this example, sales data for frozen fruit between 1958 and 1963 have been plotted, a line fitted to the data, and the line projected into the future to provide the basis for estimates of future market size on which a company like Green Giant might base a decision to introduce its new frozen fruit quick-thaw product.

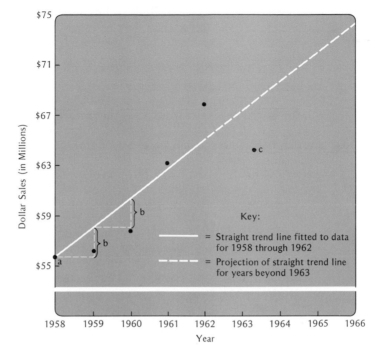

Figure 11-4. A straight-line trend projection of United States retail frozen fruit sales, 1958–1966. Source: Based on sales data presented in "FT's 14th Annual Expenditures Study," *Food Topics*, 15 (Sept., 1961) and "FT's 17th Annual Expenditures Study," *Food Topics*, 15 (Sept., 1964).

Key:

—— = Straight trend line fitted to data for 1958 through 1962

----- = Projection of straight trend line for years beyond 1963

cNot factored into trend projection, because industry sources attributed the deline in sales from 1962 to 1963 largely to weather conditions which affected the 1963 fruit pack adversely.

(51)

Lines can be described by mathematical statements. Straight lines, such as those in Figure 11-4, take the form of $x = a + by$, where x is the projected sales figure for a given year, a the sales volume during the base year (1958 in Figure 11-4), b the amount by which sales change each year, and y the number of years from the base year for which the forecast is being prepared. Thus, to estimate frozen fruit sales in 1968 by this method, we would calculate $x = 55.7$ million $+ [2.5$ million cases $\times 10$ (1968–1958)] or 80.7 million cases. Based on what you know about the Green Giant example, how suitable would a trend projection be for forecasting frozen fruit sales beyond 1967?

Actual sales levels may fluctuate regularly around a trend line. This may be due to seasonal peaks and valleys in sales or to longer-term cycles in the level of general business activity. In actual practice, seasonal and cyclical variations are measured and subtracted out of raw data to produce a true trend line. The trend line is projected into the future. And then seasonal and cyclical variations are added (or subtracted) from the trend line to create more realistic estimates of sales.

Analyses of Causal Relationships. A number of techniques attempt to relate possible causes of sales levels to factors other than time. Two of these are regression analysis and the construction of econometric models.

Regression analysis attempts to project values for an unknown variable, such as sales, on the basis of known projections for a second variable and past relationships that have been observed between the two. Either graphically or mathematically, data for each of the two variables at given points in the past can be plotted against each other and measured by the same procedure as that illustrated in Figure 11-4.

For example, instead of relating the sales of frozen fruit to time, a regression analysis might attempt to relate it to the amounts of disposable personal income in the United States. If we were to assume that frozen fruit is regarded by many as a somewhat expensive luxury, it would provide a logical basis for our analysis. Assuming we found a direct, close relationship between the sales of frozen fruit and disposable personal income in 1958 through 1963, we could then estimate disposable personal income for 1968 (possibly by means of trend projection) and calculate a forecast for frozen fruit sales on the basis of the projection of disposable personal income.

Or we could construct an econometric model based on the statistical analysis of relationships between frozen fruit sales and a number of factors that could cause them. This could represent a number of regression analyses and involve the forecasting of factors ranging from fresh and canned fruit prices to the incidence of working women, among others.

Other modeling efforts might have special applications. For example, in the introduction of a new product, it might be useful to construct a model forecasting the rate of adoption and resulting sales increases based on marketing research results showing receptivity to the product among potential customers identified as innovators, early adopters, early majority adopters, late majority adopters, or laggards.

influences on the selection of a technique

The need to reduce uncertainty determines the degree of accuracy that might be required in a forecast and represents a major influence on the technique selected. Other factors influencing the selection of the appropriate forecasting technique include the availability of historical data, the length of time for which the forecast is to be made, and the time available for the preparation of the forecast.

In addition, the nature of the forecasting task is affected by a firm's position in the channel of distribution. For example, the task of predicting sales in a retailing organization requires fewer assumptions about the behavior of channel intermediaries than the task of estimating the timing and volume of sales for a firm manufacturing components for a product later assembled for distribution through wholesalers and retailers.

The nature of decisions may change as a product passes through its life-cycle stages, suggesting a corresponding change in the emphasis placed on forecasting techniques.[9] Decisions, along with information needs, information availability, and relevant forecasting techniques associated with each stage of the product life cycle are shown in Figure 11-5.

[9] This approach is similar to that employed by John C. Chambers, Satinder K. Mullick, and Donald D. Smith, "How to Choose the Right Forecasting Technique," *Harvard Business Review,* **49** (July–Aug. 1971), pp. 45–74.

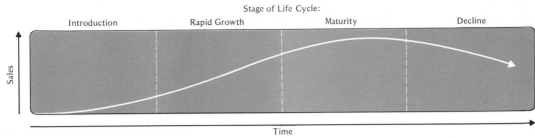

Stage of Life Cycle:

	Introduction	Rapid Growth	Maturity	Decline

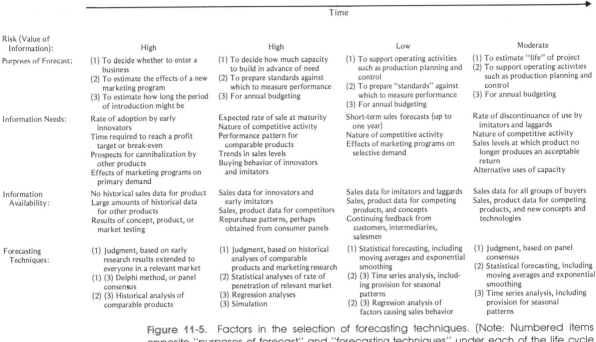

	Introduction	Rapid Growth	Maturity	Decline
Risk (Value of Information):	High	High	Low	Moderate
Purposes of Forecast:	(1) To decide whether to enter a business (2) To estimate the effects of a new marketing program (3) To estimate how long the period of introduction might be	(1) To decide how much capacity to build in advance of need (2) To prepare standards against which to measure performance (3) For annual budgeting	(1) To support operating activities such as production planning and control (2) To prepare "standards" against which to measure performance (3) For annual budgeting	(1) To estimate "life" of project (2) To support operating activities such as production planning and control (3) For annual budgeting
Information Needs:	Rate of adoption by early innovators Time required to reach a profit target or break-even Prospects for cannibalization by other products Effects of marketing programs on primary demand	Expected rate of sale at maturity Nature of competitive activity Performance pattern for comparable products Trends in sales levels Buying behavior of innovators and imitators	Short-term sales forecasts (up to one year) Nature of competitive activity Effects of marketing programs on selective demand	Rate of discontinuance of use by imitators and laggards Nature of competitive activity Sales levels at which product no longer produces an acceptable return Alternative uses of capacity
Information Availability:	No historical sales data for product Large amounts of historical data for other products Results of concept, product, or market testing	Sales data for innovators and early imitators Sales, product data for competitors Repurchase patterns, perhaps obtained from consumer panels	Sales data for imitators and laggards Sales, product data for competing products, and concepts Continuing feedback from customers, intermediaries, salesmen	Sales data for all groups of buyers Sales, product data for competing products, and new concepts and technologies
Forecasting Techniques:	(1) Judgment, based on early research results extended to everyone in a relevant market (1) (3) Delphi method, or panel consensus (2) (3) Historical analysis of comparable products	(1) Judgment, based on historical analyses of comparable products and marketing research (2) Statistical analyses of rate of penetration of relevant market (3) Regression analyses (3) Simulation	(1) Statistical forecasting, including moving averages and exponential smoothing (2) (3) Time series analysis, including provision for seasonal patterns (2) (3) Regression analysis of factors causing sales behavior	(1) Judgment, based on panel consensus (2) Statistical forecasting, including moving averages and exponential smoothing (3) Time series analysis, including provision for seasonal patterns

Figure 11-5. Factors in the selection of forecasting techniques. (Note: Numbered items opposite "purposes of forecast" and "forecasting techniques" under each of the life cycle stages are keyed to correspond with each other.)

forecasting for product introduction

At Green Giant, several pieces of data were available on which to base a possible forecast of the potential market for frozen fruits, particularly those packaged in quick-thaw pouches. You'll recall that company executives estimated a market of 12 million cases prior to the introduction of the new product, and potentially 18 million cases per year after the introduction. This contrasted with an annual growth rate in the market of about 1.5 per cent per year during the five-year period prior to 1964. Shortly after Birdseye's introduction of the new product on a national basis in the fall of 1967, A. C. Nielsen Company estimated the total market for frozen fruit to be about 17.6 million cases, with Birdseye's new product representing about 1.5 million cases of the total. If you were a Green Giant marketing executive, what would you make of this informa-

(52)

397

tion? What range of forecasts might you prepare for the five years subsequent to 1967? Which of the techniques discussed previously did you use in preparing your estimates?

forecasting in periods of rapid growth

As the sales of a product move into a period of rapid growth, the nature of questions to be answered by forecasts and research change. However, they do remain relatively critical. For example, instead of deciding whether to enter the frozen fruit business, we may be more concerned about the rate of growth of the market and the eventual size that it might reach in order to decide how many plants of what size, and where, we should build or lease. This requires an estimate of the shape of the S curve shown in Figure 11-5 and the point at which it will level out on a region-by-region basis. Decisions at this stage continue to have long-run implications for a company's performance and warrant an investment in good forecasts.

A combination of judgmental, time-series, and causal relationship methods may be employed at this stage. Judgment must be used in the interpretation of data regarding early adopters and their repurchase rates. Time-series analyses may be used to calculate rates of sales growth that can be sustained at least over intermediate periods. And causal relationships may be modeled to take into account limits on the growth of sales for a new product, including potential competitive reactions, the prices and costs of substitutable products, and the economics of various user groups or market segments.

At this stage, the availability of sales information and data regarding customer reactions and repurchase rates may be used as inputs to models that attempt to relate new-product sales experiences to others for which data is available for longer periods of time. This attempt to match product trajectories is based on the assumption that, like bullets, products have somewhat similar sales trajectories. It requires the collection of as much sales data as quickly as possible after a new-product introduction.

forecasting for mature products

Stability is the byword for mature products. Although seasonal or cyclical patterns may remain, the sales of mature products do not fluctuate rapidly. They have a full history on which forecasts can be based. At this point, it may be most important to have forecasts for relatively short-term budgeting and inventory-control purposes. But a replenishment order for inventory based on a mistaken forecast carries relatively light penalties and can be corrected more quickly than the construction of a plant of inappropriate size.

It is hard to justify a major investment in rigorous forecasting methods for this phase of a product's life cycle. Most often, statistical techniques utilizing relatively simple time-series analysis, such as moving average or exponential smoothing techniques, are sufficient here.

forecasting product decline

Forecasts for a product moving into its declining stage involve the prediction of a turning point and inputs to decisions regarding the likely death for the product. Although this is a relatively difficult task, and one most ably performed by analyses of causal relationships, the penalties of prematurely killing a product or accumulating too much inventory for a dying product often do not warrant the investment in this type of analysis. Rather, time series often continue to be used in a manner for which they are ill-suited. Product-line pruning decisions as a result often are made too late and on the basis of hindsight rather than foresight.

Forecasts are only as good as historical data and the interpretation on which they are based. This perhaps explains why so much forecasting has produced inaccurate results. However, the construction of models based on statements regarding causal relationships already has begun producing more accurate results, notably in forecasts of GNP and other important measures of economic activity. This type of effort, because of the importance of the decisions involved and its relatively high cost, must be concentrated at early stages of a product's growth and development.

research and pseudoresearch

Our discussion has assumed that marketing research is carried out in the context of a decision-making process in which the decision maker has defined his or her information needs in terms of the problem to be solved and the information needed to solve it with an acceptable level of uncertainty. The implication is that research results should influence decisions.

Recently, a marketing researcher suggested that most of his research has not influenced decisions. Much of the research he has observed has been carried out to (1) justify decisions that already have been made, (2) support the marketing efforts of advertising agencies and various advertising media, and (3) allow marketing researchers to exercise their skills and enhance their self-esteem. Results contrary to expectations and decisions already made have not been interpreted objectively. He has called this expenditure of energy "pseudo-research."[10]

It is perhaps useful for researchers and managers alike to consider ways of avoiding pseudoresearch. Among the possible ways are (1) the requirement that a decision maker specify the manner in which research results will be used in advance of the design of the research effort, (2) the establishment of guidelines in advance of the availability of research findings indicating the limits within which various decisions will be made, and (3) the submission to decision makers of both findings and their implications for decision making by marketing researchers who presumably have less commitment to a particular course of action.

[10]Stewart A. Smith, "Research and Pseudo-Research in Marketing," *Harvard Business Review,* **52** (March–April 1974), pp. 73–76.

researching the research market

In spite of the fact that requests for Bureau of the Census data had quadrupled in the previous five years, the bureau's director felt that it was reaching only a small share of its potential customers. As a result, in 1974 Director Vincent P. Barabba asked eight advisory committees representing various census statistics users to help it assemble a questionnaire to be sent to two-thousand major companies. The purpose of the questionnaire was to help the bureau determine how it could make its products more useful prior to an increased effort to promote their use. The mail questionnaire was followed up by intensive interviews with a smaller sample of potential users conducted by senior staff members.

According to Barabba:

> If you just hand somebody 4-billion pieces of information and say, "Here, do what you want with it," you're not doing him any favor. We've got to find out what information is most needed, cull that out, and then make it more graphic. That's what the survey is all about.[11]

It is especially appropriate that marketing research is being used to aid decision making in the marketing of research data.

summary

All research decisions are based on informal or formal assessments of the value and cost of obtaining more information for decision-making purposes. Value is directly related to the need to reduce uncertainty and increase the probability of making the "right" decision. Costs may include the direct costs of research as well as the costs of delayed or poor decisions and the disclosure of important data to competitors. Thus, inexpensive but inappropriate research methods can be very costly.

Research can be employed at each of the basic steps in the decision-making process. Most often, however, formal marketing research is carried out only when other information-gathering efforts have failed to provide a clear direction for a decision maker. At the outset of the process, the problem must be defined. Direct observations, internal sales data, secondary data sources (such as government reports), and routine primary data sources (such as store audits) help executives formulate opinions about the problem and its alternative solutions. If this is not sufficient to reduce uncertainty to an acceptable level for the decision maker, informed investigations can be carried out based on inputs from customers, retailers, suppliers, and other sources internal and external to an organization. If further assurance is needed, formal marketing research may be called on.

Formal marketing research efforts may include surveys by mail, telephone, or in person. Data provided by surveys must be appraised both in terms of their validity (or extent to which it really measures what it purports to measure) to the problem at hand as well as their reliability (or accuracy with which it portrays reality). Experiments offer an opportunity to single out the possible effects that might be expected when

[11]"The Supersalesman at the Census Bureau," op. cit., p. 86.

changes are made in only one element of a marketing strategy; these often involve market tests under somewhat realistic conditions. Simulations can be constructed to produce estimates based on complex relationships perceived by experts to exist among products, markets, marketing programs, and competitors. They offer an opportunity to test the effects of program changes that might be difficult or impossible to test by survey or under real market conditions.

Surveys, experiments, and simulations can be used in various combinations in concept, product, and market testing. Concept testing may employ surveys and experiments to detect customer attitudes toward new-product ideas. The products themselves may be tested by means of experiments or simulations, perhaps involving surveys. And market tests often involve experiments.

The end objective of much marketing research effort is directed toward the forecasting of future sales under varying conditions. Judgmental techniques, time-series analyses, and analyses of causal relationships represent three basic families of forecasting techniques. Judgmental forecasts may be based on opinions of individuals or groups of individuals. Time-series analyses relate sales levels and trends to time rather than their possible causes. The analyses of causal relationships concern themselves with detecting causes of sales patterns by testing relative levels of sales against those for other phenomena. Each of these forecasting techniques may be employed at different stages in a product's life cycle.

Marketing research can be employed successfully in a wide range of commercial and noncommercial situations. Among the examples cited in this chapter, it was probably employed with the most satisfying results by political candidate Drinan's campaign manager. His organization produced a voter turnout in wards favorable to Drinan that was double that of the previous congressional primary election, whereas the turnout in wards favoring Drinan's opponent was comparable to that of the previous primary. As a result, candidate Drinan won a stunning upset in his primary election campaign and went on to gain a seat in the U. S. House of Representatives. As Marttila put it:

> The professional marketing research, even though it suggested disaster for our candidate, gave us the information we needed to develop a strategy aimed at the eye of a needle. Further, an all-out campaign against the war flew in the face of conventional wisdom in 1970 that antiwar candidates had to have broader platforms to win. As it turned out, Drinan was one of the few "antiwar" candidates to win that year. Had we listened to consistent advice which admonished us to avoid the war, we would have lost. The survey research gave us the intellectual guts to pursue what many thought was a suicidal course.[12]

Marttila, too, went on to repeat his "magic" through the miracles of modern marketing research on behalf of other candidates with whose ideologies he agreed. He later founded one of the nation's leading consulting firms specializing in political campaign management.

[12] Personal interview.

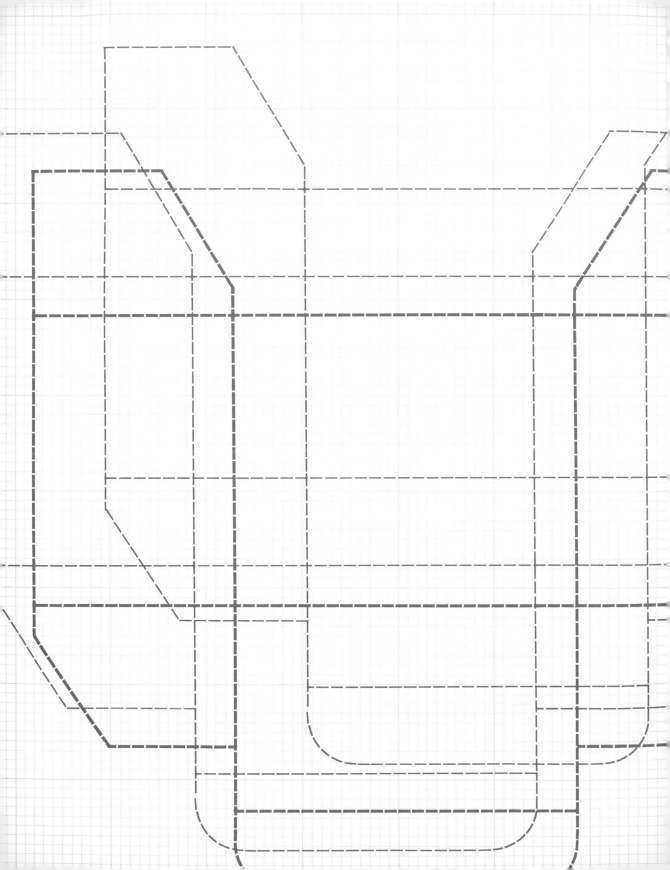

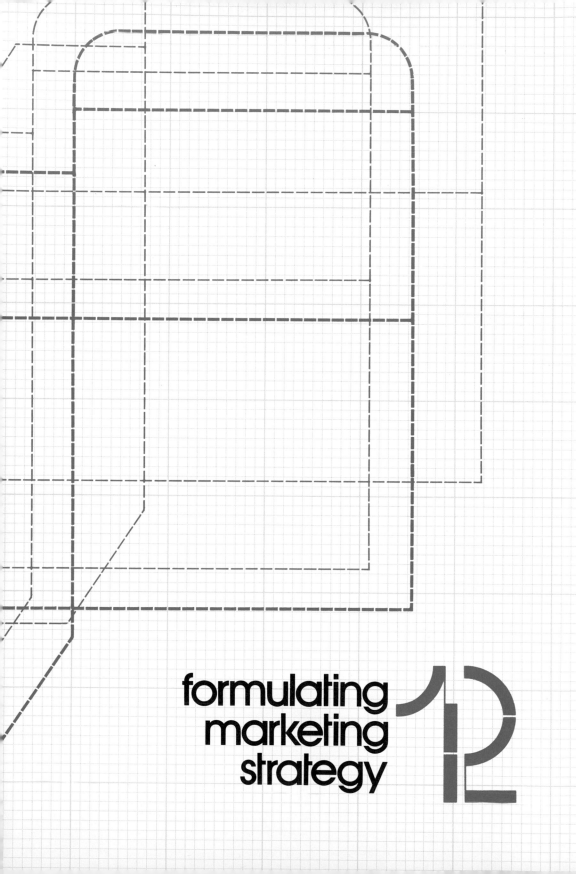

formulating marketing strategy 12

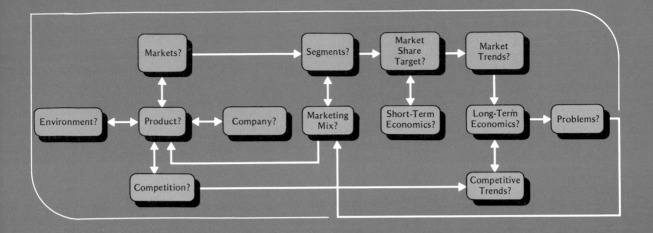

Before the introduction of automatic tuning, the user of a color TV set had to adjust knobs in order to control the picture contrast as well as basic color tints. In addition, the desired sound volume had to be selected. The mix of sound and picture selected might depend also on external factors such as the light level in the room, the size of the room, the number of people viewing the set, the noise level in the room, and even the mood of the viewers. It was a difficult task, best performed simultaneously with four hands.

This process is remarkably like that by which marketing programs are formulated and fine-tuned. Television viewers can now avail themselves of automatic tuning controls to achieve a good picture instantaneously. No such device is available to marketing managers. However, it is possible, and it is the primary objective of this chapter, to suggest ways of systematically formulating new marketing strategies or appraising existing ones.

Here we can pull together many of the concepts we have already become familiar with in the process of developing an understanding of the relationships between elements of a marketing strategy. In addition, we'll explore ways of coordinating marketing programs with organizational objectives.

The marketing program that fails is akin to the TV viewer obtaining the proper sound level without a picture, or a nicely contrasted picture of a flaming blue tree, or a well-tuned TV set in a room in which the telephone rings constantly. This chapter, however, is dedicated to the greater likelihood of marketing program success rather than better TV viewing.

the elements of a marketing strategy

On a mild summer day in 1932, Mr. Philip E. Young, founder of a company that had manufactured specialty rubber parts for twenty-five years, came home angry from a golf match. He was convinced he had lost money that day because the ball was off center. He persuaded his playing partner, a doctor, to X ray the ball to see if it was really round. It was not. So his company, the Acushnet Co., went into the business of manufacturing golf balls on the premise it could consistently make its balls round.[1]

[1] Based on information supplied by a company executive, as well as material appearing in "How Acushnet Plays to Win at Golf," *Business Week* (Feb. 17, 1973), pp. 90–91.

Over the years, Acushnet became the leading manufacturer of golf balls, with its Titleist balls regarded as of the highest quality available. It unswervingly followed some definite distribution policies as well. Its product carried a typical price for top-grade golf balls, $1.25 apiece, a price that had not changed since 1956. It sold its balls only through some eleven-thousand pro shops located at golf courses throughout the United States, flatly refusing to sell through any other retail stores, especially discount stores. Even with this policy, it was thought that about 20 per cent of all Titleist balls sold were resold by pro shops to other retailers at a small margin; the latter often resold them to the public at prices less than $1.25 per ball.

Pro shops tended to price the product to golfers at or near the suggested retail price, purchasing balls from Acushnet for $9.25 per dozen and realizing a 38 per cent margin on sales. However, in recent years pro shops had tended to discount retail prices when selling balls by the dozen. Acushnet reached these shops directly through a sales force of approximately forty salespeople.

Although Acushnet advertised its Titleist balls on television and in general news, business, and sporting magazines, the company had not followed the practice of some of its competitors of sponsoring either professional golfers or club pros. By 1968, the company had captured 40 per cent to 45 per cent of the market for top grade golf balls sold through pro shops, estimated at that time to account for 55 per cent to 60 per cent of the total volume of sales through all outlets. Unlike many other products, it was estimated that nearly two-thirds of all the money spent for golf balls was for the highest-priced, top-grade quality.

In 1968, the Acushnet Co. acquired a small manufacturer of golf clubs selling about 55 per cent of its output to Sears, Roebuck and Co., 25 per cent to pro shops, and the remaining 20 per cent to other retailers of golfing equipment. This action, plus a modest leveling off in the pro-shop share of the market and a rapid 6 per cent to 12 per cent annual growth rate for some years in the number of golfers, raised the question of whether Acushnet should go dual: that is, develop separate products, brands, and promotional programs for a pro-shop line and a retail line. In addition, a decision would have to be made regarding the continued sale of products to Sears which were branded with Sears' Arnold Palmer name. Although such sales had been profitable, it was thought that if they could be replaced by sales of products under an Acushnet brand through pro shops, they could produce even greater profits. Finally, a decision would have to be made to use a name such as Golfcraft (the name of the purchased company), Titleist, (Acushnet's well-known and well-respected golf ball brand), or some other name for golf clubs not sold to Sears.

Another possible rationale for a dual strategy was the eventual effect that the rapid democratization of the game of golf would have on outlets through which golf clubs would be purchased. However, in order to accomplish an expanded distribution program, it would be necessary to (1) expand the company's marketing organization to include a manager and separate salesforce for nonpro shop sales efforts and (2) increase its marketing budget to provide for added advertising in news magazine and other print media with mass circulation. As Richard Young, the founder's son and Acushnet's president in 1968, would you advocate a dual marketing strategy? Why?

internal elements

In settling on the appropriate marketing strategy for its new line of golf clubs, Acushnet's marketing executives naturally might be inclined to follow the success formula used by the company in selling its golf balls:

1. A quality *product* sold to actual and would-be serious amateur golfers, primarily business people and other sportsmen at
2. A relatively high *price*
3. *Distributed* exclusively through pro shops located at golf courses and provided with substantial dollar margins, and
4. *Promoted* by means of an aggressive advertising program including TV and magazine advertising and a sales force of thirty selling only to some eleven-thousand pro shops.

The product, price, channels of distribution, promotional effort, and marketing research on which their design would be based constitute the internal elements of a marketing strategy, or marketing mix, as shown in Figure 12-1.

Internal elements of the marketing mix make up the heart of a marketing

Figure 12-1. Relationships between and among internal elements of the marketing mix, marketing research, and external elements of the marketing mix.

Elements of the Marketing Mix	Scale of Measurement		
Internal			
Product			
Quality	Low	→	High
Perceived complexity of product in use	Low	→	High
Level of contribution from its sale	Low	→	High
Price in relation to competition	Low	→	High
Distribution			
Exclusivity	Intensive	→	Exclusive
Margins to trade	Low	→	High
Promotion			
Level of indirect effort (advertising)	High	→	Low
Level of direct effort (personal selling)	Low	→	High
Marketing Research			
Value of added information	Low	→	High
Cost of added information	Low	→	High
External			
Company			
Profit-sales goal	Modest	→	High
Financial capability	Limited	→	Great
Compatibility with technological capabilities	Low	→	High
Compatibility with marketing capabilities	Low	→	High
Environment			
State of product life cycle	Decline	→	Rapid Growth
Basic environmental conditions	Unfavorable	→	Favorable
Market segment characteristics			
Level of perceived risk in purchase	Low	→	High
Level of income, other demographic variables	Low	→	High

strategy. It is important that they be internally consistent. For example, relatively high prices are associated with quality products. Quality products often are distributed on an exclusive or limited basis because of their frequent need for personal sales attention and push. And high-priced products require advertising and other promotional effort targeted toward those market segments that can afford them. How would you account for the ability of Acushnet to achieve and hold a 40 per cent to 45 per cent share of all pro-shop sales of golf balls, equivalent to nearly 25 per cent of the total market for golf balls, at a time when mass merchandisers were selling larger and larger shares of standard sporting goods items?

(3)

external elements

An important influence on any proposed strategy for marketing golf clubs would be the behavior patterns of *buyers* in purchasing such products. In total, the dollar volume of golf clubs sold was about twice that for balls. About 32 per cent of all sets of clubs sold, representing more than 50 per cent of dollar volume, were top-grade clubs selling at more than $200 per set. Of these, 85 per cent to 90 per cent were sold through pro shops. Marketing intelligence suggested that buyers of golf clubs shopped considerably more, searching for the right combination of club length, weight, "feel," and price, than they did in buying golf balls.

Although there were only about eight manufacturers of golf balls, Acushnet's executives knew that they would have perhaps fifteen *competitors* in marketing golf clubs, among them several large, well-established companies such as Wilson, Spaulding, and MacGregor. All of these companies, as well as other ball manufacturers, marketed both retail and pro shop product lines with different brands for each.

In spite of the potentially stiff competition, the rapidly growing interest in golf showed no signs of slowing, and foreign markets such as Japan had increased rapidly with the democratization of the sport. Sociologists had suggested that golf, among other activities, fulfilled a basic *environmental* need for people to escape the large organizations with which they had increasingly become associated and accomplish results attributable to their individual skills. Company executives acknowledged the fact that the *company* had almost no experience in manufacturing and selling products intended for sale through mass merchandising channels.

Buying behavior within market segments; competition; other environmental trends; and the needs imposed by a company, its technological and marketing expertise, and its other products represent basic external elements of the marketing mix, as shown in Figure 12-1. Acushnet's marketing executives had no doubt of their ability to duplicate elements of the internal marketing strategy for golf clubs that had been achieved for golf balls. But they wondered whether such a strategy would be compatible with external elements. For an internally consistent marketing strategy badly out of tune with external elements would be about as successful as a TV program whose sound is obscured by noise in the room in which it is being viewed.

408

(4)
(5)
(6)

What combination of internal elements would you suggest for a marketing strategy for Acushnet golf clubs? In what ways, if any, might this be incompatible with one or more external elements of the mix? What would you do if this were the case?

marketing research

Marketing research represents the bridge between internal and external elements of a marketing strategy. The information generated by marketing research can provide the basis for assessing the basic compatibility between internal and external elements. In a general sense, how would the value of information generated by marketing research vary with each of the external elements of the mix listed in Figure 12-1?

(7)

how wrong can you be and still succeed?

Just how important is this matter of consistency within internal elements of the marketing mix? You can probably think of certain circumstances in which a company could get by without it. Lack of competition, the ability to command high prices or margins, rapidly increasing market demands, and highly favorable environmental trends may offer a sizeable margin for error in the design of marketing campaigns. But a much more common set of circumstances involves an organization with established competitors, relatively mature markets, and the inability to obtain patent or other protection from competitors or enjoy any of the marketing luxuries enumerated here.

Where the margin for error is not great, it is perhaps most important that internal elements of the mix be developed on an internally compatible basis in relation to external needs of the market. If this is done, even intense competition, unfavorable environmental trends, and a lack of product-company fit can be overcome.

additional steps in appraising a marketing strategy

A qualitative appraisal of the elements of a marketing strategy helps us narrow down alternatives. In addition, it is necessary to (1) assess the economics of alternative marketing programs, (2) estimate the potential size of the market for a product or service, (3) determine the share of the potential market needed to meet stated organizational objectives, and (4) develop some estimate of the likelihood of being able to attain stated objectives for a marketing program in either the short- or long-range future. In essence, this brings us full cycle back to Figure 1-9 on page 27. The Gillette Co., through its exploration of a new marketing opportunity, provides a convenient focus for our discussion.[2]

the Gillette cassette

In late 1970, Mr. Ralph Bingham, vice-president of new business development for the Safety Razor Division of the Gillette Co. was considering the potential for the marketing of a line of blank recording cassettes by his division. Over the years, largely through diversification, Gillette had grown from a manufacturer of men's shaving products realizing about $60 million in sales and $20.4 million in profits before taxes in 1947 to a manufacturer of such things as Toni women's hair preparations, Paper Mate writing products, Braun small home appliances, and Right Guard deodorant products for the entire family. In 1969, its profits before taxes were $119 million on sales of $609 million. The divisionalization of the company had resulted in the creation of a separate Safety Razor Division (SRD) responsible for the backbone, but also the slowest-growing portion, of the company's business. Therefore, in 1970, SRD was seeking new growth opportunities outside of the blade and razor business.

In assessing the strengths of his existing division, Mr. Bingham concluded that it was strong in both shaving technology and the high-volume manufacture of precision metal and plastic products, but particularly strong in the marketing of mass-distributed packaged goods. In 1968, Gillette razors and blades were sold through 100 per cent of all drugstores in the United States (54,000), in 96 per cent of all chain and independent food stores (256,000), in 21,000 discount and variety stores, and in 170,000 other outlets. Nearly 50 per cent of SRD sales were handled by 3,000 drug wholesalers, tobacco wholesalers, and toiletry merchandisers employing 20,000 salespeople. In addition, Gillette's SRD sold directly to large chain merchandisers through some 136 sales representatives employed by the division. In thinking about it, when is the last time you went through a supermarket check-out stand and didn't see the SRD's products displayed? Over all, approximately 60 per cent of all razor blades sold in the United States were Gillette's.

(8)

Annual marketing costs for the SRD were estimated by industry observers to be about $5 to $6 million for its sales force and about $10 million for media advertising, largely for television. Because of its low production costs, the SRD was able to offer retailers and wholesalers margins that produced high-margin per square foot results on items of relatively small unit value. How would you profile this product in the terms suggested in Figure 12-1?

(9)

Mr. Bingham's interest in the potential for blank cassettes was stimulated by several estimates of the size and rate of growth in sales of the unrecorded cassette market as well as his feeling that current products were not being marketed to take advantage of the product's full potential. A group of young

[2]This section is based on facts presented in a case problem, Gillette Safety Razor Division, The Blank Cassette Project (Boston: Intercollegiate Case Clearing House, copyright 1974 by the President and Fellows of Harvard College). Names of individuals and essential financial data have been disguised in this case example.

consultants whom he had hired estimated that in 1970 sales of all recording tapes of all types would be $650 million at retail, of which sales of unrecorded or blank tapes would reach $150 million. Of the latter, 10 per cent were represented by reel-to-reel tapes, 5 per cent by eight-track cartridges, and the remaining 85 per cent by cassettes, essentially miniature reel-to-reel systems encased in plastic. Bingham's consultants estimated in addition that (1) by late 1969, 5.9 million cassette recorders had been sold in the United States; (2) in 1970 another 7.0 million would be sold; and (3) sales of blank cassettes would grow at the rate of 30 per cent per year through the 1970s. Some industry observers believed that eventually 75 to 80 per cent of the projected 65 million households in the United States would own one or more cassette recorders. Against this background, Bingham could not remember having seen a television ad for blank cassettes.

Early cassette recordings did not possess the quality of recordings on reel-to-reel tapes or eight-track cartridges. In part, this had been due to the low quality of recording and playback devices for cassettes. It was estimated that 80 per cent of all cassette recorders sold in the United States in 1970 would retail for between $19.95 and $139.95. Only the more expensive of these could provide fidelity of sound equivalent to a good radio. According to one study cassette ownership in comparison to cartridge ownership was greatest among younger people, particularly those in higher-income families. Thirty-two per cent of all cassettes were purchased by people under nineteen years of age.

Existing blank cassettes on the market in the most popular sixty-minute size were available in three combinations of price and quality, including (1) professional quality at $2.98 per tape, (2) standard quality from $1.75 to $2 per tape, and (3) budget quality at about $1 per tape. The first two quality tapes were sold under well-known brand names such as Sony, 3M, and Mallory through audio shops, home entertainment departments of department stores, and some discount stores. Although Bingham's consultants characterized the marketing effort on behalf of these items as extremely limited, new competitors such as RCA and Capitol Records had entered the business recently, and Memorex was about to do so. In fact, reports from SRD's sales force indicated that Memorex was building a fifty-person sales force for blank cassettes and had hired the Leo Burnett Co. to develop an advertising campaign. In 1970, about 50 per cent of the dollar value of all blank cassettes sold was thought to be of budget quality, marketed under private and unknown brand labels by many manufacturers. Some of these manufacturers were selling product thought to be 100 per cent defective in some respect. The SRD sales force reported that competition in the blank cassette business appeared to be fierce and completely price-oriented.

The SRD consultants reported that current unit sales of blank cassettes were divided among retail outlets in the following manner: 40 per cent among discount and department stores, 10 per cent among drugstores, 10 per cent among variety stores, 7 per cent among catalog stores such as Sears, 18 per cent among electronics stores, 7 per cent among high-fidelity stores, and 8 per cent among other outlets. Of these, the SRD sales force and wholesalers currently called on the first four categories.

Sixty-minute blank cassettes of professional or standard quality typically were sold to retailers at a 50 per cent discount off list price. Wholesalers and rack jobbers, who handled about 70 per cent of this business, received similar discounts but typically resold to retailers at a 35 per cent discount off list price.

All discounts in the cassette business were somewhat higher than they were in the razor and blade business.

If Gillette were to enter the blank cassette market, several other matters would have to be decided. The current SRD sales force, it was thought, could squeeze in cassettes by devoting about 10 per cent of its time to them, provided that the SRD did not introduce other products. If audio and other stores were to be included in the marketing plan, it was thought that they could be reached by offering audio and electronics wholesalers 10 per cent commissions on sales to retail outlets at 50 per cent off list price. Although major product introductions such as that of the Techmatic razor had received more than $5 million in introductory advertising support, the SRD's advertising agency had proposed on a highly preliminary basis a media budget for blank cassettes of $2 million for the first year and $1.2 million per year thereafter. A virtual saturation of teen-oriented radio stations was proposed. Alternatively, the SRD could divide its budget between teen-oriented radio, adult-oriented radio, and entertainment-oriented print media.

Other questions confronting Mr. Bingham concerned whether Gillette should (1) make its blank cassette components or (2) buy and assemble them until it had achieved a sufficiently large sales volume. Another question was whether or not Gillette should put its name on the product. It was thought that one positive aspect of this would be to build an image of reliability, related to Mr. Bingham's interest in the possibility of the SRD's bringing order to the chaotic blank cassette market and contributing to its sales and profit growth objectives at the same time.

(10)
(11)

What strategy for entering the blank cassette market might make sense to you if you were in Mr. Bingham's position? How would you appraise your proposed strategy against possible alternatives in terms of the dimensions of the profile shown in Figure 12-1?

marketing by the numbers— the economic appraisal

Based on discussions with suppliers to the cassette industry, the SRD's consultants estimated that empty (unloaded) cassette cases could be purchased in large quantities for 15.9 cents each. A sixty-minute reel of tape would cost 21.4 cents for standard quality tape and 32.2 to 37.5 cents for professional quality tape. In addition, the costs of loading, packaging, and inspecting were expected to approximate 20 cents per cassette. The manufacturing manager estimated that it would require a $500,000 annual fixed cost to provide sufficient capacity to assemble cassettes at the rate of one million per month. Although there was excess capacity among suppliers, the consultants estimated that manufacturers of unloaded cassette cases realized gross margins of 25 per cent on sales, and that producers of tape received gross margins as high as 50 per cent of sales.

With this data, it became possible to draw up an economic appraisal of various possible marketing strategies that the SRD might follow. One such strategy with surface validity, for example, involved the positioning of a standard quality cassette against the lower-priced budget competition, perhaps at a slight premium of $1.30 per tape. This product could be advertised to both teens and young adults and sold through all existing Gillette SRD outlets by the division's current sales force. The format for analysis and the actual computations necessary for the appraisal of this alternative are shown in Table 12-1.

The typical sequence of steps in an economic appraisal of any marketing strategy shown in Table 12-1 includes (1) the computation of the manufacturer's price resulting from the deduction of any trade discounts from the list price to the ultimate buyer, (2) the assembly of all costs that vary directly with volume, (3) the calculation of contribution per tape by subtracting the variable costs per tape from the price to the manufacturer, (4) the assembly of all fixed costs or investments (amortized over some reasonable period of time) associated with the strategy, and (5) the calculation of a break-even sales level at which the SRD could recover its annual fixed costs by dividing the total of fixed costs by the per unit contribution. On the basis of this computation, we find that the strategy under examination would require annual sales to the budget-market segment of 39.6 million cassettes, or $51.5 million in retail sales value. What provision does this calculation make for profit on investment?

In view of the fact that the only sales estimate that Mr. Bingham had for the total budget blank cassette market in 1970 was 50 per cent of $130 million, the proposed strategy would require that the SRD capture $51.5 million divided by $65 million, or about 85 per cent, of the budget blank cassette market. This market share to break-even figure is important to a manager in determining the risk and the likelihood of the success of a venture. In addition, in this case the necessary production to achieve the sales target would far exceed the available capacity of 12 million cassettes per year. Thus, the proposed strategy would have to be rethought or the capacity expanded.

Table 12-1 An Economic Appraisal of a Strategy for Marketing Standard Quality Blank Cassettes at Premium Budget Prices

Item	Computation
Price to ultimate buyer	$1.30 per tape
Price to retailer or wholesaler (50% of list price)	.65
Variable costs per tape	
Unloaded cassette	$ .159
Standard quality tape	.214
Assembly	.200
Total	$ .573
Contribution (manufacturer's price less variable costs)	$ .077
Fixed costs for	
Assembly plant (per year)	$500,000
Sales force salaries (10% of $5–$6 million total annual budget)	550,000
Advertising (first year)	2,000,000
Total per year	$3,050,000
Break-even sales volume (fixed costs divided by contribution)	$\dfrac{\$3,050,000}{\$.077} = 39,600,000$ tapes or $39,600,000 \times \$1.30 = \$51.5$ million in retail sales

(13)   What alternatives might we consider for improving the economic potential for SRD blank cassettes: raising the list price with or without an increase in the quality of the product; reducing trade margins to retailers and wholesalers; eliminating all but a small group of salesmen and the sale of nearly all cassettes through wholesalers; reducing the advertising budget; investing in manufactur-

(14) ing facilities for unloaded cassettes and tapes? What effect would one or more of these adjustments have on the estimated break-even point for the marketing

(15) program? What additional implications would each have for other elements of the marketing mix?

One additional alternative might be to wait and let the market achieve a size large enough to support the SRD strategy analyzed in Table 12-1. Or, if the sales needs suggested by our economic analysis appeared to be attainable, this would take us to the next step in our economic analysis.

determination of market share needed to meet objectives

At this point, we could have a need for a longer-term projection of the size of the market segment relevant for a proposed product. This is one of those points at which marketing research becomes most important. Its first tasks would be to define the relevant market and the time frame for its forecast. Once the size of the target segment were known, we could calculate the share of the market needed to achieve objectives on the basis of the forecast.

The alternative analyzed in the previous section assumed that the relevant market segment was that which bought budget tapes, constituting about half of the dollar sales of the entire market. The relevant time frame for a forecast might be several years beyond the point in time when we might introduce our tapes, say five years into the future. On the basis of estimates provided by SRD's consultants, we could project total blank cassette sales at the rate of a 30 per cent annual increase from a base of $130 million. This would produce an estimate of $482 million in total blank cassette sales and $241 million in budget

(16) (17) blank cassettes in 1975. What assumptions are inherent in this projection? How

(18) much confidence would you have in it? How long would it suggest we wait if

(19) we were to enter this market? Assuming price-cost relationships had not changed, what share of the 1975 market for budget blank cassettes would the

(20) SRD need to break even? Is this a viable alternative?

estimation of the likelihood of attaining the goal

In appraising the alternative of waiting for entry into the blank cassette market, you probably took into account (1) the quality of the forecast, (2) the rate at which market conditions favorable to entry might change, and (3) the SRD's ability to penetrate other markets as extensively as it would have to penetrate the budget blank cassette market. In addition, it would be appropriate at this point to review assumptions regarding customer buying behavior in the target and related market segments and other elements of the marketing mix. Much of the process at this point is intuitive and judgmental. It is a point at which a manager must make important decisions justifying his or her pay.

adjusting marketing strategies

A person watching color TV continues the tuning process until an acceptable picture appears. Not until several unsuccessful efforts may he or she give up. So it is with the economic appraisal of marketing programs. The process is pictured in Figure 12-2. The results of its application to three alternative strategies for marketing the SRD's proposed blank cassette are shown in Table 12-2. These include the marketing of professional cassettes, standard cassettes at relatively low prices, and budget cassettes with certain adjustments in the originally

Figure 12-2. A conceptual scheme for the economic appraisal of a marketing program.

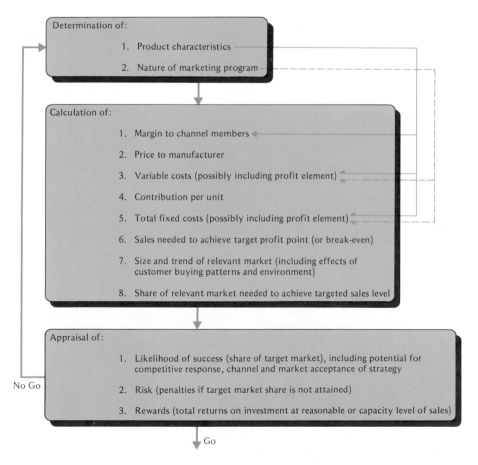

Determination of:
1. Product characteristics
2. Nature of marketing program

Calculation of:
1. Margin to channel members
2. Price to manufacturer
3. Variable costs (possibly including profit element)
4. Contribution per unit
5. Total fixed costs (possibly including profit element)
6. Sales needed to achieve target profit point (or break-even)
7. Size and trend of relevant market (including effects of customer buying patterns and environment)
8. Share of relevant market needed to achieve targeted sales level

Appraisal of:
1. Likelihood of success (share of target market), including potential for competitive response, channel and market acceptance of strategy
2. Risk (penalties if target market share is not attained)
3. Rewards (total returns on investment at reasonable or capacity level of sales)

No Go

Go

Table 12-2   An Economic Analysis of Three Alternative Strategies for Designing and Marketing SRD Cassettes

	Alternative 1
Determination of	
Product characteristics	Budget cassette, sold under a name other than Gillette
Elements of marketing program	
Price (list) to ultimate buyer	$1.20/cassette
Channels	Current Gillette retail outlets, wholesalers; total margin = 25%
Promotion	Advertising = $2.0 million per year; personal selling = $.5 million per year
Relevant target market	Teenagers for pop music; 50% of total dollar value
Calculation of	
Price to ultimate buyer	$1.20/cassette
Price to SRD	$ .90
Variable costs and profit per tape	
Unloaded cassette	$ .159
Tape of each quality	.214
Assembly	.200
Profit (20% of sales)	.180
Total	$ .803
Contribution to fixed costs	$ .097/cassette
Fixed costs for	
Assembly plant (per year)	$ 500,000
Sales force salaries	500,000
Advertising	2,000,000
Total	$3,000,000
Target sales level (units)	$3,000,000/.097 = 30,900,000
Value to ultimate customers of target sales level	$37,080,000
Estimated 1970 target market size ($ and % of $130 million)	$65,000,000 (50%)
Appraisal of	
Likelihood of success (share of target market), including potential for competitive response, channel, and market acceptance of strategy	57% share of target market required to break even
Potential risk	High fixed investment
Potential return on investment at capacity operations	Would require expanded investment in manufacturing facilities

No Go

Alternative 2	Alternative 3
Standard cassette, sold under Gillette name	Professional cassette, sold under Gillette name
$1.50/cassette	$2.50/cassette
Current Gillette retail outlets, wholesalers; total margin = 30%	Audio shops, wholesalers; total margin = 60%
Advertising = $2.0 million per year; personal selling = $.5 million per year	Advertising = $1.0 million per year; personal selling = $.2 million per year
Young adults, business people for dictation, letter writing; 40% of total dollar value	Serious audiophiles for convenient high-fidelity recording of music; 10% of total dollar value
$1.50/cassette	$2.50/cassette
$1.05	$1.00
$ .159	$ .159
.214	.322
.200	.200
.210	.200
$ .833	$ .881
$ .217/cassette	$ .119/cassette
$ 500,000	$ 500,000
500,000	200,000
2,000,000	1,000,000
$3,000,000	$1,700,000
$3,000,000/.217 = 13,800,000	$1,700,000/.119 = 14,300,000
$20,700,000	$35,800,000
$52,000,000 (40%)	$13,000,000 (10%)
40% share of target market required to break even	275% share of target market required to break even
High fixed investment	Moderate fixed investment
Would require expanded investment in manufacturing facilities	Would require expanded investment in manufacturing facilities

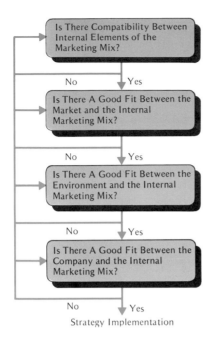

Figure 12-3. Four basic questions in the assessment of a marketing strategy.

Is There Compatibility Between Internal Elements of the Marketing Mix?

No   Yes

Is There A Good Fit Between the Market and the Internal Marketing Mix?

No   Yes

Is There A Good Fit Between the Environment and the Internal Marketing Mix?

No   Yes

Is There A Good Fit Between the Company and the Internal Marketing Mix?

No   Yes

Strategy Implementation

(21)

proposed program. Note that these calculations include an allowance for profit equivalent to the level currently enjoyed by Gillette on its over-all operation. Which of the strategies analyzed in Table 12-2 appears to be most viable, possibly with some adjustment?

In assessing the likelihood of achieving results suggested as necessary by our analysis in Table 12-2, we can ask ourselves the several basic questions posed thus far in the book. They are pictured in diagrammatic form in Figure 12-3.

is there compatibility among internal elements of the marketing mix?

Can a budget cassette of reliable quality be sold at $1.20 through drug and supermarket outlets with primary promotional support from teen-radio advertising at a total margin of 25 per cent for wholesalers and retailers combined? Or, putting it another way, are these elements of the strategy internally compatible? At this point, a question might be raised about the 25 per cent margin, higher than the average received for retailing many grocery products but lower than margins offered typically for the sale of housewares through supermarkets. A 30 per cent margin, on the other hand, would reduce the SRD's contribution from $.097 to $.049 per cassette (at a profit of 20 per cent of the SRD sales price to retailers). This would double the share of the market required to achieve the profit goal to an impossible figure, suggesting that we look to a substantially different alternative, perhaps that of offering a quality cassette for a relatively low price of $1.50. This is represented as alternative 2 in Table 12-2.

418

is there a good fit between the market and the internal marketing mix?

Will young adults and businessmen purchase blank cassettes priced at $1.50 in sufficient volume through drug and supermarket outlets to provide the SRD with the needed 40 per cent of the market for standard blank cassettes? Or will significant numbers of teen-agers trade up from budget tapes to make this strategy feasible? Your assessment of these questions would require that you formulate some opinions, if possible supported by evidence, about (1) the way in which blank cassettes of standard quality are purchased; (2) the possibility that the SRD could command prime space, perhaps near the stores' cash registers, for its cassettes as well as its razor blades; and (3) the extent to which you might think prime or high-traffic space is necessary for this type of product. What do you think?

(22)

is there a good fit between the environment and the internal marketing mix?

(23)

Environmental conditions suggested the likelihood of rapidly growing markets for blank cassettes. Did the fact that there was no formidable competition among current manufacturers bode well or poorly for the SRD? Would new entrants concern or encourage SRD marketing executives? If there was sufficient concern about actual or potential competition, it would be necessary to recycle the planning process to provide for changes in the product or other elements of the internal marketing mix to establish a competitive distinction or niche.

is there a good fit between the company and the internal marketing mix?

A reduction in the profit goal from 20 to 10 per cent of SRD sales would increase its contribution on standard cassettes from $.217 to $.322 per cassette, thus lowering the share of market necessary to attain the goal from 40 to 27 per cent ([$3,000,000/$.322 × $1.50] ÷ $52,000,000). But it would be difficult to sell a program to Gillette's top management that was not aimed at maintaining the company's current average return on sales.

Similarly, we could elect to sell much less costly budget cassettes with significantly lower quality than assumed under alternative 2 in Figure 12-2. But that wouldn't be consistent with the company's maintenance of a reputation for quality. At the other extreme, the sale of professional quality cassettes through audio shops would fail to make use of the SRD's current outlets and marketing expertise. What changes in strategy, if any, might be necessitated by the top-management view at the time that one of the SRD's great strengths was the manufacture of precision metal and plastic products?

(24)

419

sensitivity analysis

Finally, we might engage more systematically in assessing adjustments such as those suggested previously. This effort, called sensitivity analysis, seeks to measure the sensitivity of a target level or other measure of performance, in this case market share, to each of several types of adjustments in the marketing mix. For example, any one of the following would reduce SRD's necessary target market share for alternative 2 in Table 12-2 from 40 to 27 per cent: (1) a reduction in programmed profits from 20 per cent to 10 per cent of sales, (2) a reduction in first-year advertising expenses (and the extent of SRD's front-end "exposure") from $2 million to $1 million, (3) an increase in price from $1.50 to $1.70 per standard quality cassette, or (4) a reduction in retailer and wholesaler margins from 30 per cent to about 21 per cent of retail selling price. Which one of these would seem to be most feasible to you?

Once again, it could be useful at this point to obtain information through marketing research that would test the effects on demand of the most performance-sensitive of the alternative actions under consideration, either individually or in combination.

long-term implications

The appropriate time frame for assessing a marketing strategy must be chosen for purposes of analysis. For a brief advertising campaign, we might want to achieve our goal within a month. A high-fashion product might have to produce its programmed return in several months. What would be the appropriate period of time over which to expect the SRD blank cassette to meet a profit goal?

If we were to use five years as the time frame for the assessment of alternative 2 in Table 12-2, what share of the market over that time period would the SRD have to achieve if it were to spend $1.2 million for advertising in the second and succeeding years? Now how feasible does the strategy appear to be?

At this point, you might want to test the approach to strategy appraisal suggested here on another situation. For example, how would you appraise the Green Giant Company's proposed introduction of frozen fruit in terms of Table 12-2 and Figure 12-3?

relationships between elements of the marketing mix

Several concepts with which you are familiar provide a good means of illustrating relationships between elements of the marketing mix under basically different marketing strategies and conditions. We can call on Acushnet's golf clubs and Gillette's cassettes once again to illustrate our discussion.

(25)

(26)

(27)

(28)

(29)

marketing mix and the product life cycle

We saw in Chapter 4 that all products experience life cycles in which they move through stages of innovation, rapid growth, maturity, and decline. Companies have found the "fountain of youth" just as illusive for their products as did early explorers in the southeast United States who searched extensively for it.

Both internal and external elements of the marketing mix change as products mature. During the period of introduction, a product or service may require carefully controlled promotion involving a great deal of direct selling effort to wholesalers and retailers as well as ultimate buyers. This may require full-service channels of distribution and relatively high margins. At the same time, relatively high prices made possible by the innovative quality of the product and the absence of competition provide the funds for substantial margins to the channel and for an extensive and expensive selling effort.

A successful innovator, supported by favorable environmental trends and unable to secure effective patent or other protection, soon is joined by competition. This may take the form of product and price competition. By now, with customers becoming more and more knowledgeable about the product and its uses, a higher proportion of indirect promotional effort may be injected into the mix, thus relieving wholesalers or retailers of certain promotional responsibilities and allowing for lower margins made necessary by lower prices. New channels of distribution, involving mass merchandisers and self-service retailing, may be employed.

(30)
(31)

Based on our discussion, you should be able to complete the entries for the stages of maturity and decline shown in Figure 12-4. Where would you position Acushnet golf clubs and Gillette cassettes on the product life cycle shown in Figure 12-4?

An organization must be able to adjust its marketing strategy for existing products from time to time if it wants to market them on a continuing basis. The alternative is a rapidly changing product line composed only of those products or services passing through a restricted segment of the life cycle.

marketing mix and the buying process

In the introduction or special promotion of a product, internal elements of the marketing mix have a sequential relationship over time, as suggested in Figure 12-5. First, marketing research can be employed to pinpoint the best target-market segment for a product or service. Advertising to ultimate customers or wholesalers and retailers, as well as personal selling effort, should next help build the awareness of the product and its name. Through distribution the product is made available, an essential ingredient in encouraging trial. Whether an actual trial of the product is actually obtained may depend also on the promotional effort and the price and surface features of the product itself, such as its appearance. Finally, the repurchase of the product depends primarily on its performance in actual use and the price. In fact, if it performs well enough, occasionally a product may be repurchased by knowledgeable and enthusiastic customers in spite of the quality of its promotion and distribution.

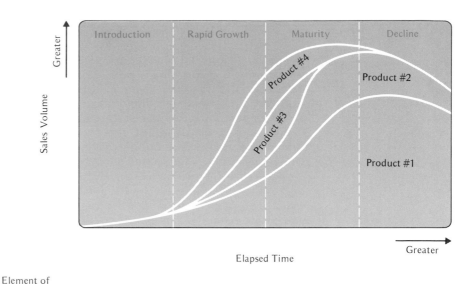

Figure 12-4. Changes in the marketing mix as a product passes through various stages of its life cycle.

Element of the Mix	Characteristics in Each Stage of Life Cycle			
Product	Regarded as innovative, requiring customer education	New to many, requiring "risk reducing" information	Relatively common, requiring little "risk reducing" information	Commodity-like in nature
Direct Communication and Promotion	Extensive selling effort to wholesaler, retailers, and ultimate buyers	Reduced emphasis on direct selling		
Indirect Communication and Promotion	Emphasis only on advertising designed to educate potential customers	Growing emphasis on advertising to increase market awareness for product		
Channels of Distribution	Exclusive distribution, high margins	Selective distribution, possibly involving mass merchandisers, lower margins		
Price	High	Lower, perhaps because of competition and economics of scale		
Competition	Nonexistent	Limited, but increasing		

Another way of viewing these relationships is in terms of the number of points at which a poorly designed and coordinated marketing program can fail. In fact, an entire program is as weak as its weakest link. The problem is illustrated by the experiences some years ago of a highly successful manufacturer of fats and oils, Corn Products Company, in attempting to break into the market for pourable salad dressings.

In speculating on the reason for the failure of later programs to gain adequate distribution and product trial, it is possible that Corn Products had lost

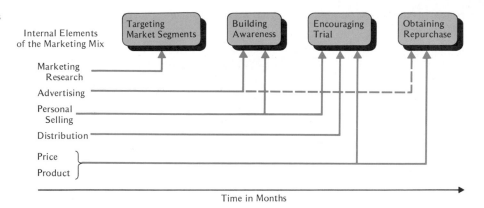

Figure 12-5. Relationships between elements of the marketing mix and the buying process.

Internal Elements of the Marketing Mix

Targeting Market Segments

Building Awareness

Encouraging Trial

Obtaining Repurchase

Marketing Research

Advertising

Personal Selling

Distribution

Price

Product

Time in Months

(32)
(33)

credibility and goodwill with retailers for its pourable salad dressings because of several previous misfires. Once trade credibility is lost, what can a company do to regain it? Would Gillette face this potential problem in marketing its cassettes through outlets selling its blades and razors?

The diagram in Figure 12-5 stresses the importance of sequence and timing in the design of a marketing program. Examples of failure in timing are legion. For example, the Polaroid Corp. suffered a severe loss of investor enthusiasm several years ago, in part because of its failure to meet the demand that its marketing program stimulated for its SX-70 camera and film. Amtrack, the National Railroad Passenger Corp., successfully promoted its product in phase with a distinct upsurge of interest in passenger travel by railroad in the United States, but before it had upgraded its service to a level regarded as acceptable by many of its riders. And a number of outstanding Broadway plays have failed for lack of apparent promotional effort.

marketing mix in push and pull strategies

As we saw in Chapter 7 and see again in Figure 12-6, manufacturers selecting push strategies for their products must provide high margins to wholesalers and retailers to support extensive personal selling efforts and costs. These efforts are required to sell relatively complex products to uninformed customers who see their purchase as representing a high element of risk. Of necessity, a manufacturer must either sell such products directly to ultimate purchasers or rely heavily on channel intermediaries to perform a large proportion of promotional efforts. This requires the incentives provided by high margins to wholesalers and retailers. It also may require methods by which the manufacturer can maintain some semblance of control over the manner in which, and the prices at which, its products are sold, suggesting exclusive or limited distribution and efforts to police prices.

In contrast, manufacturers employing pull strategies assume a much larger share of the promotional task, often by advertising directly to ultimate purchasers. By preselling customers, they are often able to offer lower margins to wholesalers and retailers who incur much lower promotional costs.

423

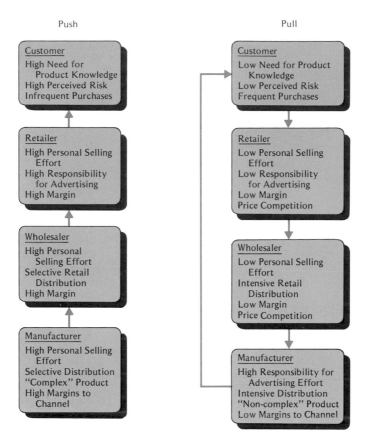

Figure 12-6. Contrasts in the elements of the internal marketing mix for push and pull marketing strategies.

Push

Customer
High Need for
    Product Knowledge
High Perceived Risk
Infrequent Purchases

Retailer
High Personal Selling
    Effort
High Responsibility
    for Advertising
High Margin

Wholesaler
High Personal
    Selling Effort
Selective Retail
    Distribution
High Margin

Manufacturer
High Personal Selling
    Effort
Selective Distribution
"Complex" Product
High Margins to
    Channel

Pull

Customer
Low Need for Product
    Knowledge
Low Perceived Risk
Frequent Purchases

Retailer
Low Personal Selling
    Effort
Low Responsibility
    for Advertising
Low Margin
Price Competition

Wholesaler
Low Personal Selling
    Effort
Intensive Retail
    Distribution
Low Margin
Price Competition

Manufacturer
High Responsibility for
    Advertising Effort
Intensive Distribution
"Non-complex" Product
Low Margins to Channel

(34)

(35)

We can test the logic of relationships between elements of the marketing mix. What would happen if we employed a pull strategy for a new, relatively complex product such as a mechanical device for achieving higher gas mileage for private automobiles? What would happen if, as a manufacturer, we advertised heavily to ultimate purchasers and yet gave wholesalers and retailers large margins as incentives to stock our new soap products?

(36)

(37)

Companies that have developed expertise in marketing products or services by one or another of these alternative strategies may find it difficult to switch to the other or simultaneously employ both. For example, how well does its experience in marketing golf balls through golf course pro shops prepare Acushnet for marketing its golf clubs through mass merchandisers? Similarly, how well should Gillette be prepared by its knowledge of razor and blade marketing for introducing a line of tape cassettes to the market?

Thus far we have confined our examples to the development of strategies under the implicit assumption that the United States represents the target market. It is useful at this point to ask ourselves whether the same general guidelines discussed previously apply as well for the development of marketing strategies for non-United States markets.

strategies for multinational marketing

In Italy, a United States company established a plant to process corn for home use, only to fail in its marketing effort to convince Italians that corn isn't "pig food." Similarly, General Foods was unsuccessful in selling Jello to the British market in the powdered form that has made it so successful in the United States for years. British homemakers prefer a solid-wafer or cake form, even though it requires more time to prepare. At the other extreme, in Asia the name Colgate has become so nearly synonymous with tooth paste that it must now compete with Coalgate, Goalgate, Goldkey, Goldcat, and Goldrat tooth pastes.[3]

(38)

(39)

Some years ago, there might have been limited interest in these successes or failures. But the importance of multinational marketing has grown rapidly in recent years. One indicator of this is the increase in foreign trade between 1962 and 1972, shown graphically in Figure 12-7. What patterns do you see in Figure 12-7? For example, what is the relationship between economic development, for which indicators are cited for selected countries in Table 3-5, page 78, and the volume of international trade between nations? Why would you expect this?

International trade is only one indicator of the importance of multinational marketing activities. One study has suggested that the output from facilities owned by foreign direct investors, mostly multinational enterprises, largely for sale in the countries in which they are located, represented about 6 per cent of the combined GNP of the non-Communist nations. Furthermore, between 1950 and 1970, the output from foreign direct investment grew at the rate of about 10 per cent annually, a rate greater than that for either GNP or international trade. The importance of these figures for United States multinational firms is emphasized by the fact that it is estimated that about 60 per cent of all foreign direct investment in the non-Communist world has been made by American companies in other countries. In turn, another 10 per cent of the total has been invested in the United States by non-United States companies.[4] Little wonder that a French publisher, author, and politician, Jean Jacques Servan-Schreiber, has predicted that by 1985, American-owned industry in Europe will rank only behind the United States and the Soviet Union as the world's third most important economic force.[5]

(40)

The decline in barriers to trade combined with increasingly attractive opportunities "abroad" have contributed to the rapid growth of multinational enterprises, particularly in advanced-technology industries such as computer, pharmaceutical, and chemical manufacture. What effort will the newly found wealth obtained by "third-world" nations through the increasing prices of petroleum and other basic commodities have on international trade and multinational marketing volume in relation to measures of over-all economic activity?

The increasing importance of multinational marketing and the frequent failure of multinational marketing programs have given rise to questions regarding the transferability of marketing strategies and concepts from one country or

---

[3]"Why a Global Market Doesn't Exist," *Business Week* (Dec. 19, 1970), pp. 140–144.

[4]Robert B. Stobaugh, "A Proposal to Facilitate International Trade in Management and Technology," Working Paper No. 73–29 (New York: Graduate School of Business Administration, New York University, June 1973), pp. 2–3.

[5]Jean Jacques Servan-Schreiber, *The American Challenge* (New York: Atheneum, 1968), p. 3.

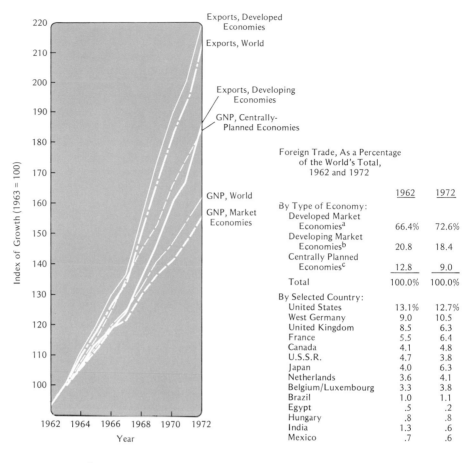

Figure 12-7. Trends in exports, GNP, and foreign trade, by selected countries and groups of countries. Source: 1973 *U.N. Statistical Yearbook* (New York: United Nations, 1973), pp. 394–410.

Exports, Developed Economies

Exports, World

Exports, Developing Economies

GNP, Centrally-Planned Economies

GNP, World

GNP, Market Economies

Index of Growth (1963 = 100)

Year

Foreign Trade, As a Percentage of the World's Total, 1962 and 1972	1962	1972
By Type of Economy:		
Developed Market Economies[a]	66.4%	72.6%
Developing Market Economies[b]	20.8	18.4
Centrally Planned Economies[c]	12.8	9.0
Total	100.0%	100.0%
By Selected Country:		
United States	13.1%	12.7%
West Germany	9.0	10.5
United Kingdom	8.5	6.3
France	5.5	6.4
Canada	4.1	4.8
U.S.S.R.	4.7	3.8
Japan	4.0	6.3
Netherlands	3.6	4.1
Belgium/Luxembourg	3.3	3.8
Brazil	1.0	1.1
Egypt	.5	.2
Hungary	.8	.8
India	1.3	.6
Mexico	.7	.6

[a] Including the U.S., Japan, countries of Western Europe, and others.

[b] Including Brazil, petroleum producing countries of the Middle East, and others.

[c] Including Russia, mainland China, Eastern European countries, and others.

national market to another. Clues to these questions can be obtained by considering those factors exerting the greatest influence on multinational marketing strategies as well as traps into which marketers have fallen in playing the multinational game.

factors influencing multinational marketing strategies

Of the many factors influencing multinational marketing strategy, perhaps four are the most pervasive and important. These concern basic levels of economic development, contrasting environmental influences, differences in customer behavior patterns, and the varying availability of mechanisms for carrying out marketing tasks.

Stages of Economic Growth. Economist W. W. Rostow has identified similarities in the economic growth patterns of various countries and suggested that they consist of five stages: (1) the traditional society, (2) the preconditions for take-off, (3) the take-off, (4) the drive to maturity, and (5) the age of high mass consumption.[6] These stages are shown graphically for the United States in Figure 12-8. At the risk of doing violence to Rostow's work, some of the important characteristics of each stage can be summarized.

The traditional society believed that there was a ceiling on the output of an individual, because "the potentialities which flow from modern science and technology were either not available or not regularly and systematically applied."[7] The work of Sir Isaac Newton in England and other scientists in the early seventeenth century brought an end to this stage in England at about the time of the first serious colonization of the United States.

During the development of the preconditions for take-off, scientific knowledge was translated into improved productivity for agriculture and industry. Britain possessed the necessary resources, strategic trading location, and social and political structure to develop first the conditions essential for take-off by the late eighteenth century. Its success in part made possible the early entry by the United States into the take-off stage of economic development by 1850.

The take-off stage is typified by (1) technological development and the creation of new industries, (2) rapid growth and high profits, (3) a tendency to reinvest a rising proportion of income in further technological development, and (4) rapidly increasing productivity.

Figure 12-8. Rostow's stages of economic growth and U.S. development. Source: W. W. Rostow. *The Stages of Economic Growth,* 2nd ed. (Cambridge: Cambridge University Press, 1971), pp. 4–12.

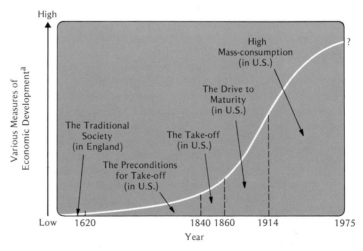

[a]Including: (1) proportion of net national product reinvested, especially during take-off and the drive to maturity, (2) the development of leading sectors of economic activity, and as cotton textiles in England and railroads in the United States, during the take-off stage, (3) the spread of technology to other industries, such as the development of post-railway technology in the United States, during the drive to maturity, and (4) the diffusion rate of the private automobile during the stage of high mass-consumption.

[6]W. W. Rostow, *The Stages of Economic Growth,* 2nd ed. (Cambridge: Cambridge University Press, 1971), pp. 4–12.

[7]Ibid., p. 4.

The drive to maturity for most economies lasts about sixty years, according to Rostow. During this period (1) technological advances are extended to all industries; (2) productivity increases far exceed population growth rates; (3) a high proportion of earnings are reinvested; and (4) the emphasis shifts from basic industries such as coal, iron, and railroads to industries such as machine tools, chemicals, and electrical equipment, which involve more complex technologies. By 1914, this period was completed in the United States, and the country was poised for the fifth stage.

The age of mass consumption is featured by (1) an emphasis on durable consumers' goods and services; (2) a declining proportion of individual incomes needed for food, shelter, and clothing; (3) a rising proportion of the working force employed in offices or skilled factory jobs; (4) declining emphasis on "the further extension of modern technology as an overriding objective"; and (5) an increasing allocation of resources to social welfare.[8] Rostow fixed the beginning of the age of mass consumption at the time of the creation by Henry Ford of the moving assembly line in 1914. Based on Rostow's work, how would you classify countries for which data is presented in Table 3-5 on page 78?

(41)

Because the economy of the United States leads the world by almost any measure, its behavior will perhaps define the nature of further stages of economic development. Interestingly enough, in writing of the possible sixth stage, "beyond consumption," in 1960 Rostow speculated that, at least with Americans, a diminishing marginal utility (value) for durable consumers' goods was setting in, with an attendant rise in emphasis on nonmaterial services and on larger families. Has our experience since 1960 borne out his hypothesis?

(42)

Contrasting Environmental Influences. The most obvious of environmental contrasts in multinational markets is that of language and the ability to communicate the intended meaning of a message in different languages. A promotional program that is effective only in the French language immediately restricts a marketer to a limited segment of the global market. Some famous slogans, such as Esso's (now Exxon) "Put a Tiger in Your Tank", translate well. But when translated from English to Japanese, for example, 3M's "Sticks Like Crazy" slogan for Scotch tape becomes "Sticks Foolishly" and GM's "Body by Fisher" becomes "Corpse by Fisher."

Language can present other types of obstacles. For example, there are fifty-seven dialects spoken in Ethiopia. In many countries the inability of many potential customers to read the national language requires that advertisers rely heavily on media such as radio, picture billboards or posters, printed ads that feature pictures rather than words, or even singing troubadors.

Constraints ranging from those imposed by religious beliefs to government regulations of marketing activity may be peculiar to various parts of the world. These would be of particular importance to a company marketing pork products in the Middle East, where religious beliefs don't permit their consumption by large segments of the population. An advertising program stressing adjectives such as "better" or "longer-lasting" to describe products could not be used in Germany, where even implicit references to competing products are prohibited.

Differences in Customer Behavior Patterns. A multinational marketer must be aware of vast differences in customer behavior patterns as well as subtle

[8]Ibid., p. 11.

differences in taste and preference. Good illustrations of this are provided by the patterns of consumption for beverages in Europe. In 1951, the average French-man drank seven quarts of wine for every quart of beer he consumed. His Belgian neighbor, who drank nearly as much volume per year, downed more than twelve quarts of beer for every quart of wine consumed. French Burgundy wine intended for Belgian export must have a higher sugar content than the Burgundy sold for French consumption. Nestlé, a Swiss multinational company, several years ago brewed more than forty varieties of instant coffee to satisfy national tastes, just as United States soft drink producers typically add more sugar to their products to be sold in the southern United States. How would you account for the fact that, in recent years, Frenchmen have begun drinking a higher proportion of beer and Belgians a higher proportion of wine?

(43)

Explanations for differences in consumption patterns require explorations in depth into history, patterns of commerce, social and other customs, and gener-ally held attitudes. What effect would you expect the rapid penetration of the European market for color television sets to have on differences in customer behavior patterns in this part of the world?

(44)

Mechanisms for Multinational Marketing. In the United States, the avail-ability of a wide range of advertising media, channels of distribution, marketing research services, transport methods, and freedom of access to vast markets are taken for granted. In other markets, more or fewer constraints and opportunities may present themselves for purposes of strategy formulation. Several indicators of the extent of the presence and use of marketing mechanisms in selected national markets are presented in Table 12-3. What relationships, if any, do these indicators have with per capita figures for GNP, which also are contained in Table 12-3?

(45)

Television rapidly is spreading to many parts of the world. But this does not insure the availability of television to advertisers in all markets. Even in Europe, many stations operated by governments do not accept advertising, and others broadcast only for several hours each evening. In Latin America, sound trucks are highly acceptable and widely used as advertising media; in New York City they are not.

The availability of professional advertising assistance in non-United States markets has increased greatly in recent years. J. Walter Thompson, for many years the world's largest advertising agency before losing its position to a Japanese agency in 1973, opened its first branch outside the United States in 1899. Today it realizes nearly half of its billings through thirty non-United States offices.

The relative roles of advertising and personal selling in marketing strategies may vary greatly from country to country. Advertising is playing a greater role than ever in the marketing of many consumer products, but the weekly public market, with its heavy emphasis on personal selling for both food and nonfood items, is still an important institution in the rural areas of most countries. Is it surprising to you that the advent of improved advertising media has coincided with the growth of supermarket retailing in many countries?

(46)

Major considerations in the development of distribution strategies are (1) tariffs imposed on imported finished products or components by countries or groups of countries; (2) the physical size of, and divisions within, markets; and (3) the availability and use of market intermediaries in various countries. Tariff

Table 12-3 **Several Indicators of the Extent of the Presence and Use of Marketing Mechanisms and per Capita GNP, Selected National Markets, 1972 (Unless Indicated Otherwise)***

	Country							
	Brazil	Canada	Egypt	France	India	Japan	U.S.	USSR
Number of retail establishments	325,000 (1959)	135,000 (1966)	n.a.[a]	482,000 (1966)	3,098,000 (1966)	1,471,000 (1970)	1,415,000 (1967)	686,000 (1972)
Number of wholesale establishments	18,000 (1959)	31,000 (1966)	1,300 (1970)	95,000 (1966)	195,000 (1966)	256,000 (1970)	311,000 (1967)	1,400 (1972)
Ratio of wholesale sales to retail sales (1.00 = equality)	1.01 (1959)	1.36 (1966)	1.18 (1970)	1.15 (1966)	1.67 (1966)	4.06 (1970)	1.60 (1967)	.88 (1972)
Employment in retail establishments	694,000 (1959)	826,000 (1966)	n.a.	1,625,000 (1966)	4,730,000 (1966)	4,926,000 (1970)	8,626,000 (1967)	4,000,000 (1972)
Employment in wholesale establishments	143,000 (1959)	329,000 (1966)	n.a.	746,000 (1966)	544,000 (1966)	2,861,000 (1970)	3,641,000 (1967)	163,000 (1972)
Radio receivers per 1,000 population	61	821	143	329	23	658	1,695	404
TV receivers per 1,000 population	67	349 (1971)	17 (1971)	237	.1	225	474	162
Newsprint consumption per person (in kilograms per year)	2.3	23.0	1.3	11.2	.4	19.6	44.7	4.1
Advertising agency billings per person[b]	$1.75	$24.10	n.a.	$13.20	$.09	$16.10	$102.40	$21 (1969)
Number commercial vehicles (mainly trucks) per 1,000 population	7 (1959)	91 (1966)	.3 (1970)	58 (1971)	1 (1966)	90 (1970)	98 (1967)	n.a.
GNP per person, 1972	$513	$4,805	$216 (1970)	$3,823	$94 (1969)	$2,823	$5,551	$1,521

* Source: For all statistics that do not appear in footnote b, see 1973 U. N. Statistical Yearbook (New York: United Nations, 1973).

a Not available.

b Based on a comparison of a compilation of advertising agency billings for 1972 appearing in Advertising Age (March 26, 1973), pp. 36 ff. with population data presented in the 1973 U. N. Statistical Yearbook, loc. cit., pp. 67–79.

barriers have been erected primarily to provide an advantage for local industry or to discourage expenditures for various categories of imports. With the rise in internationalism and the formation of cooperating economic blocks, general levels of tariffs have declined in recent years. Nevertheless, they can be an important factor in the total costs of manufacturing and shipping goods for sale in another national market. They encourage production or assembly in markets where products are intended to be sold, or in countries having reciprocal tariff agreements. For example, the Argentine affiliate of the Carborundum Co. pays no duty on refractories imported from the company's Mexican plant, compared with the 50 per cent duty it would have to pay on the same product from sources outside Latin America.

Distribution economics have been altered through the creation of economic communities of countries such as the European Economic Community (the Common Market), the Latin American Free Trade Association (LAFTA), and others. Within these communities, tariffs are being lowered or eliminated, making feasible for the first time the manufacture of products in one country for sale in another. This can have great significance in an economic community such as the European Common Market, now encompassing a population of 263 million with a total GNP of over 80 per cent of that of the United States. With the implementation of the European Common Market now in an advanced stage, is it possible to think of its members (The Netherlands, Belgium, Luxembourg, France, West Germany, Italy, Ireland, Denmark, and the United Kingdom) as a single market of approximately the size of the United States?

Particularly for new and complex products, there may be no channel intermediaries capable of providing the expertise needed to sell a product. This may require a multinational company to integrate forward in the channel through the establishment of its own wholesaling organization. At the very least, it may require the development of an extensive training program for foreign sales personnel, assistance in financing inventories, and equipment and training needed for postpurchase service support. In this latter respect, repair manuals for some of the first United States agricultural equipment sold to foreign markets were printed only in English.

At the opposite extreme, many products are sold to ultimate consumers in such small quantities and with such high frequency (up to several times daily for French bread) that many intermediaries and complex channels of distribution are required to move products from manufacturers to ultimate users. Even in Japan, where the widespread ownership of modern appliances has made possible more efficient buying and distribution, a traditional, complex network of intermediaries, many receiving commissions in return for performing no functions, has discouraged many would-be multinational firms from competing in that market.

The development of coordinated methods of transportation have made possible faster and less costly international transport. Of greatest importance has been the development and use of containers with standard dimensions that can be loaded at the point of manufacture, transported by trucks or rail cars to a port, transferred by cranes to the decks of specially constructed ships, delivered by other cranes to trucks or rail cars at the ports of destination, and transported to waiting customers. Through the use of sealed containers, costs of material handling, damage, and theft and insurance have been reduced significantly. Little wonder that this concept, developed only in 1965 for use in the North

Atlantic between the United States and Europe, accounted for the movement of 70 per cent of freight deemed capable of being handled by container on this route just seven years later.

Marketing research services are now available in most parts of the industrial world. For example, the A. C. Nielsen Co. added offices in eighteen countries between 1939 and 1970. Their effectiveness, particularly in performing customer survey work, may vary with the willingness of potential respondents to discard long-held beliefs about the confidentiality of various types of information.

pitfalls in multinational marketing

Prominent reasons why multinational marketing efforts have fallen short of expectations may include the failure to assess market needs, heed environmental differences, and apply basic marketing concepts.

Failure to Assess Market Needs. Unsuccessful multinational marketers often rely on stereotypes, inadequately controlled marketing research, and strategies tried and proven "at home." For example, using "conventional wisdom," answer the following questions:

1. Does the average French male or female use more cosmetics?
2. Do Italians consume more spaghetti than the Germans or the French?
3. Are homemakers in Luxembourg and Belgium more interested in cooking than those in France and Italy?

If your answers were the French female, yes, and no to these three questions, you would join the mass of people who rely on stereotypes of national behavior. If they were the French male, no, and yes, respectively, you probably are familiar with the results of marketing research conducted in Europe. Given the fact that the reference containing answers to these questions is more than ten years old, how much confidence would you place in this information as a multinational marketer?[9]

Companies may fail to assess market needs because adequate marketing research services are not available, the validity of their results can't be checked, or the barriers of language and meaning lead to the exploration of inappropriate questions or those producing misleading results. Those that have relied on individuals familiar with new markets, or have had the opportunity to work through an existing foreign subsidiary or partner have been most successful in this regard. For questions presenting serious problems of interpretation, the market tests may be the most valid approach to research, even though they tend to require expensive special packaging in their multinational mode.

Finally, strategies tried and proven at home may prove inappropriate elsewhere. For example, in an area as straightforward as package design, the package may require more than language translation. In Holland, for example, blue is considered feminine and warm, whereas Swedes associate it with masculinity

[9]Based on information in Robert L. Brown, "The Common Market: What Its New Consumer Is Like," *Printers' Ink* (May 31, 1963), pp. 23-25.

and coldness. In Malaysia, a green-colored consumer product failed to sell because it suggested illness and the jungle.

Failure to Heed Environmental Differences. A company attempting to market products without assessing environmental differences could face failure caused by factors noted earlier such as restrictive regulations, favored local competition, nationalism, variations in customer behavior patterns, and the lack of the necessary supporting "infrastructure." For example, a marketer of heavy, large automobiles in Europe immediately encounters a market in which large autos are punitively taxed, auto users must pay very high prices for fuel, and much of the road network (infrastructure) is not constructed or suited for comfortable use by drivers of large autos.

American manufacturers of detergent and appliances have been successful in marketing their products in South America in spite of ingrained beliefs that pounding garments on a rock represents the most effective washing technique, the absence of electricity in many areas, and generally low levels of income. They have succeeded by developing a small washing machine cranked by hand that sells for less than $10. But it has required an extensive educational program sensitive to the fact that hand-washing techniques are still highly regarded.

Failure to Apply Basic Marketing Concepts. Much of the failure to apply basic marketing concepts in "foreign" markets, particularly for American marketers, can perhaps be traced to overconfidence. After all, if a strategy or product can succeed in the most competitive market in the world, why can't it succeed elsewhere as well? This often leads to sloppy execution, sometimes based on an assumption of product superiority or inferior local competition and marketing expertise.

For example, for years stories of young Europeans offering to buy used Levi's from American tourists filtered back to Levi Strauss headquarters in San Francisco. This may have influenced company executives when they decided to expand greatly their marketing effort, particularly for more fashionable Levi garments, in Europe. Large inventories were established with inadequate controls for their management. European buyers tended to be more selective than was anticipated. As a result, some items sold very well whereas others accumulated dust at the warehouse. It took the company perhaps a year to adjust its controls, and much of Levi Strauss' decline in earnings in 1972 was traceable to a write-down in the value of European inventories. How could Levi Strauss have averted this problem?

In 1966, some eighteen years after it introduced its first camera to the American public and two years after it had begun seriously to market its products in France, the Polaroid Corp. introduced its Model 20 Swinger to the French market. The Swinger was a simple version of its many predecessor models selling for only $19.95. In the United States, Polaroid's advertising in the early years had stressed information about how to operate each successive generation of the company's cameras. For the Swinger introduction, Polaroid's French advertising campaign was almost a direct translation of its then-current American campaign. In French, consumers were told that, "You can have a photo in 15 seconds with a Polaroid that costs only 99 francs." Early sales of the Polaroid Swinger in France were a source of disappointment to the company's executives. What possible explanation could you offer for these results?

(52) Based on our brief exploration of multinational marketing practices and conditions, what conclusions have you reached about the transferability of marketing concepts and strategies from one national market to another?

summary

As a first step in appraising or developing a marketing strategy, a marketing manager must appraise the compatibility among internal elements of the strategy, including the product in relation to its price in relation to the channels through which it is to be distributed in relation to the promotional methods by which it is to be sold. Next, the relationship of the internal strategy to external factors such as markets, competitors, the general environment, and other company objectives and needs must be assessed and inconsistencies resolved. To the extent that additional information is required to complete the assessment of external elements, marketing research may be required. In a sense, it serves as the bridge or link between internal and external aspects of the marketing strategy formulation process.

An internally and externally logical marketing strategy may fail to meet the economic goals, or the limits of perceived risk, imposed by an organization. When this occurs, a recycling of the design effort to allow for the compromise of certain strategy elements may be necessary.

Marketing strategies must be designed as well to reflect changing stages in a product's life cycle, the timing of actions required by the nature of the buying process, and the relative emphasis on push or pull efforts, among others.

Multinational markets represent much larger opportunities than might be suggested by measurements of exports and imports on a worldwide basis. In determining the transferability of marketing concepts and strategies from one national market to another, it is important to note important differences in such markets. These include the varying stages of economic growth associated with national markets as well as contrasting environmental influences, differences in customer behavior patterns, and the varying degree of availability of mechanisms for marketing effort encountered in each.

Reasons why multinational marketing programs fail often include the failure to (1) assess market needs, (2) heed environmental differences, or (3) apply basic marketing concepts. In many cases this behavior can be traced to overconfidence in a product, perhaps based on its success in the United States market, and a tendency to assume the existence of inferior local competition or the absence of local marketing expertise.

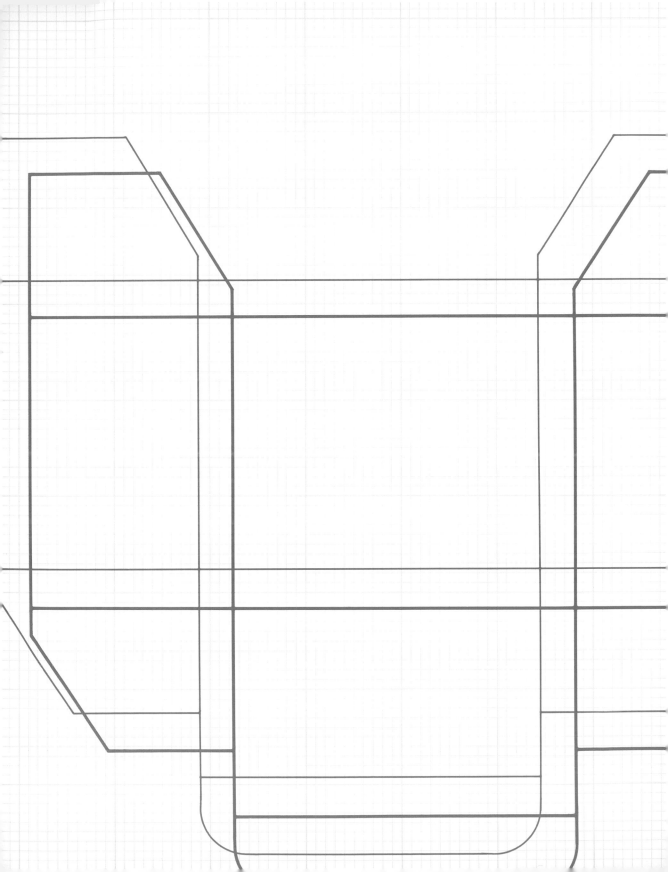

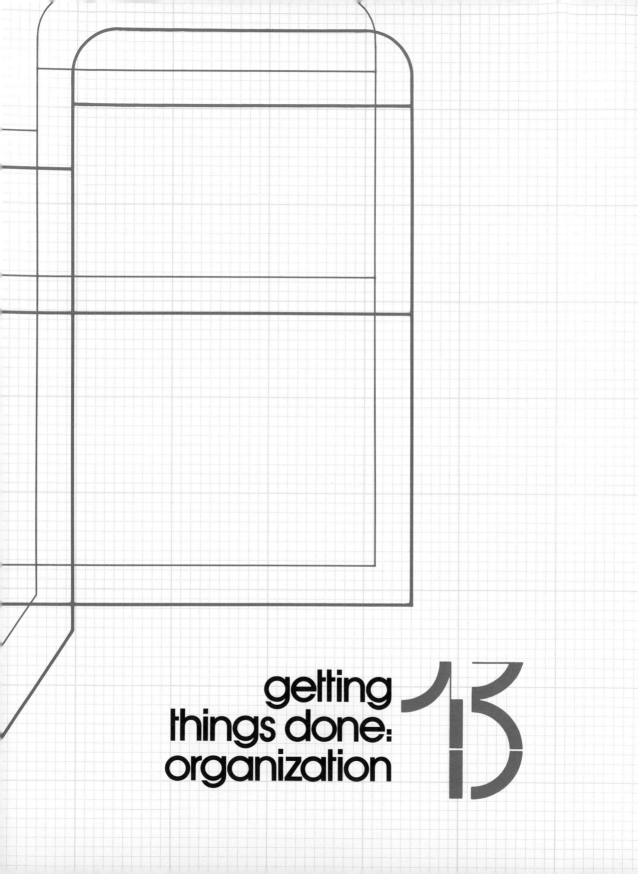

getting things done: organization 13

Marketing strategy formulation is only half the game; implementation is the other. And implementation—getting things done—is what organizing and controlling, our next two topics, are all about.

What good is a well-planned marketing strategy if the product isn't available when the advertising breaks in the market; or if a marketing organization is structured to give equal emphasis to geographic areas of low and high sales potential?

This chapter offers us the opportunity to expand our acquaintances among marketing managers. Here we'll get to know the tasks performed and problems faced by Fred Holland in his job as product manager for stainless steel sheet for the Allegheny Ludlum Steel Corporation. At the same time, we'll familiarize ourselves with relationships within the marketing organizations of consumer and industrial products, manufacturers as well as service organizations. This will supplement our previous exposure to an advertising agency organization in Chapter 6, a retailing organization in Chapter 8, and Dale Johnson's wholesaling company in Chapter 9. Furthermore, it will allow us to relate the task of product or program management in marketing to other more functionally oriented tasks, such as sales management, advertising management, and marketing research, that we have discussed previously.

Whenever people are involved, there are few absolute rules. This is true of much of the subject of organization. Our objectives here are to review the basic purpose for organizing marketing effort, to explore various organizational alternatives, and to relate organizational structures to marketing strategies, both for domestic and international markets.

The diagram at the head of this chapter was placed there purposely as a reminder that organization is a means to an end. It supports, and should be a direct reflection of, marketing strategy, which reflects marketing objectives, which reflect organizational objectives, which result from people and their ideas. Thus, the process starts and ends with people, which should be encouraging in an age of computers and numbers.

why organize?

Many residents of communal living experiments, attracted by the potential for individual freedom that such arrangements promise, will tell you that the most frequent reasons for the failure of such organizations are disputes over responsibilities for doing the dishes and carrying out the garbage for the group. This inability to delineate jobs in such a way that they get done without unnecessary duplications of effort and with a reasonable level of morale is often experienced by more formal organizations. It suggests several of the most important reasons for organizing: (1) to differentiate between jobs and allow for specialization of effort, (2) to provide for coordination between tasks and people, (3) to define responsibilities and authority held by members of an organization, and (4) to reflect and support over-all strategies.

differentiation and specialization

One of the basic purposes of organizing is to differentiate one job from another in order to foster the achievement of greater efficiency in each job by making it possible for individuals to specialize their efforts. Opportunities for differentiation and specialization often are directly related to the size of an organization.

For example, consider the opportunities for specialization in marketing at the Allegheny Ludlum Steel Corporation, a subsidiary of Allegheny Ludlum Industries, Inc., the tenth largest steel company in the United States in 1973.[1] The company manufactured a wide variety of special grades of steels in three principal product groups. The first of these, stainless and high-temperature steels, were sold to fabricators for use in various types of fabricated products ranging from large milk tanks to tableware. The second, electrical steel, was used primarily in transformers, motors, and generators. Tool and die steels were used in forgings and castings and the manufacture of tools. The company's marketing personnel were organized under the direction of the vice-president of sales, as shown in Figure 13-1.

Among the specialized activities represented in the Allegheny Ludlum marketing organization were commercial research and advertising and promotion, each of which was represented by a small group reporting to separate managers. In addition, a manager of application development was responsible for maintaining a channel of communication between customers and their needs and the company's research and development organization.

Stainless steel sheet was sold by Allegheny Ludlum's "production steel" salesmen located in eighteen district sales offices, each of which was headed by a district sales manager. These salesmen, representing about two thirds of the company's total sales force, also sold electrical steels, high-temperature alloys, and other forms of stainless. The remaining third of the sales force, which

[1] Information concerning the Allegheny Ludlum Steel Corporation is based on material contained in Allegheny Ludlum Steel Corporation (B), (Boston: Intercollegiate Clearing House, copyright 1958 by the President and Fellows of Harvard College) and a more recent interview with a company executive. Individual names used in this example are fictitious.

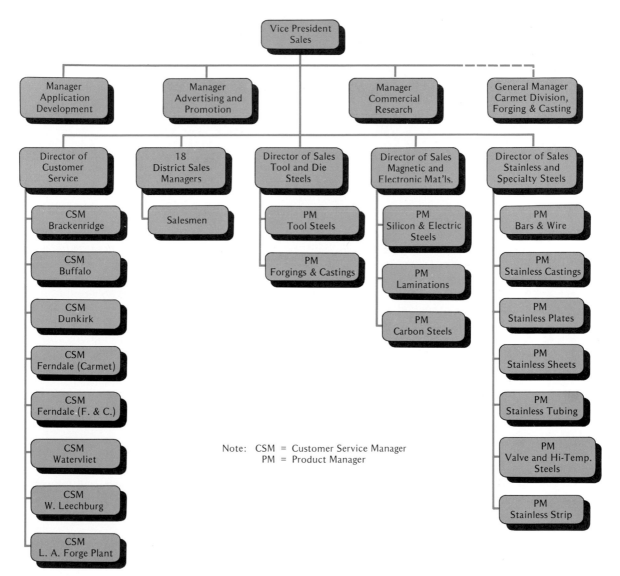

Figure 13-1. The organization of the Sales Division of Allegheny Ludlum Steel Corporation.

reported as well to the district sales manager, was responsible for selling tool and die steels. Salesmen were responsible for preparing price quotations with guidelines established by the vice-president of sales.

Eight customer service managers, reporting to a director, served as liason between the company's mills and its customers. These managers were responsible for handling customer inquiries, issuing delivery dates and other delivery information, processing changes in orders, applying finished inventory to expedite shipments, and making a follow-up of delivery performance. They "loaded" the company's mills through their authority to enter incoming orders on production schedules for promised delivery within given weekly periods.

Thus, at Allegheny Ludlum, the marketing task was differentiated into commercial research, advertising and promotion, application development sales, and customer service. Compare this degree of differentiation, for example, with that in The Six-Footer Company in Chapter 1. On this basis, how would you analyze the organization chart for the advertising agency shown in Figure 6-6, page 202?

(1)
(2)

integration and coordination—the other half of the riddle

Carried to an extreme, differentiation and specialization can lead to uncoordinated actions. On the other hand, perhaps the best-coordinated actions are those completely carried out by one person, thus requiring no communication or cooperation and allowing no specialization. In large organizations, much of the secret of success is in achieving the proper balance of differentiation and integration. A second major function of the organization is to provide for a coordinated effort by specialists, particularly where timing or a consistent approach to customers is important.

For example, to bring a marketing program to fruition at Allegheny Ludlum might require the communication of customer needs from the sales force to the Application Development group. Given the development of a new product, the Commercial Research group might attempt to estimate the size of the market for it. Advertising and Promotion would develop materials for its presentation. The sales organization would sell it. And customer service managers would be responsible for making sure that the product, once sold, could be made available by the mills.

This process requires more coordination than is likely to be achieved by individual specialists, each with their own carefully defined responsibilities. As a result, many large marketing organizations have developed jobs primarily concerned with integration and coordination. At Allegheny Ludlum, the title of product manager was assigned to these jobs, described by each of twelve products shown in Figure 13-1.

As product manager of stainless sheets, Fred Holland, a young business school graduate, was responsible for developing marketing programs for stainless sheet. One of his responsibilities included informing the sales force about these programs, attempting to encourage salesmen to sell more stainless sheet product, and controlling the inventories of semifinished stocks that could be used to reduce customers' waiting times below those required for product made from scratch at the mill. His over-all responsibility was for improving the volume and profitability of stainless sheet sales. In Fred Holland's own words:

> My objective is to sell the sheet department to each salesman. I try to get to know each man through personal visits, phone calls and correspondence. I provide a sympathetic ear, and try to assist each man as much as I can. Once a personal relation is established, it's possible to work with a salesman to realize specific targets. Better market identification, for instance. Or more calls on key customers. Or improved procedures for use in negotiating orders, and in

following up on quotations to make sure we're getting the orders we should. We also work together in formulating strategy for breaking into a new account. If it seems necessary to put together a high-level team to call on an account, I'll make preparations for that.

There are a couple of things I don't do in my relations with salesmen. One is to make profit comparisons between sheet and other company products, and use this as an argument to spend more time on sheet. The other is to argue for a reduction in the amount of time a salesman is spending on another product. What I'm after is an improved performance on sheet and not a worse job for other important company products.[2]

Holland also visited eighteen steel warehouses, equivalent to wholesalers, through which Allegheny Ludlum's products were sold. At the request of warehouse salesmen, he occasionally made calls on their accounts to help resolve questions regarding delivery, service, or product quality that may have arisen.

Allegheny Ludlum's salesmen were credited with sales made directly to customers plus warehouse fill-in orders, but not with regular stock shipments to warehouses. Thus, Allegheny Ludlum's salesmen in a sense competed with warehouse salesmen. Recently, unfavorable market conditions had made it more difficult to sell stainless sheet. And customers for stainless sheet generally ordered in smaller average quantities than customers for other of Allegheny Ludlum's product categories. What effect would these factors have on the difficulty of Fred Holland's job? To what extent could he control the sales and profit performance for stainless sheet?

(3)
(4)

Fred Holland was particularly concerned by the fact that the field sales force was devoting a declining proportion of its total time to the sale of stainless sheet. He was also concerned about the way salesmen negotiated for sheet orders. In his opinion, customer service received too many inquiries that asked for delivery "as soon as possible" instead of advising exactly when customers needed the material. Salesmen also failed in too many cases to follow up on delivery quotations to make sure that Allegheny Ludlum would get a second crack at an order if its delivery quotation was not competitive. If you were in Fred Holland's position, what would you do about each of these concerns?

(5)

definition of responsibility and authority

The third major purpose of organization is that of defining responsibility and authority. The complete description of a job includes statements of responsibilities, those matters that a manager is held responsible for, and authority, in a sense a description of the amount of power assigned for use in carrying out responsibilities.

Responsibilities of various members of the Allegheny Ludlum marketing organization have been described here. Some members of an organization are assigned the responsibility of advising others, a task often associated with so-called staff functions. Others, sometimes called line managers, hold what

[2] Ibid., pp. 14–15.

might be called action responsibilities. This is just another way of looking at the nature of the responsibility associated with a job.

Authority often is associated with the ability to hire, promote, or fire subordinates and to otherwise influence their compensation. A long-held principle of management is that authority should be commensurate with responsibility. That is, a manager should have sufficient authority to carry out his or her responsibilities.

(6)
(7)
How would you describe Fred Holland's responsibilities and authority in these terms? In his job as product manager, is his authority commensurate with his responsibilities?

organization as a means of supporting company strategies

Organizations both support and, at times, constrain company strategies, as suggested by the diagram at the beginning of this chapter. The most widespread evidence of this in marketing is the nature of organizational change associated with the adoption of the marketing concept by various enterprises. You'll recall that this involves the definition of the primary purpose of the business as "the detection and satisfaction of customer needs at a profit." Ways in which this has been reflected in organizational change include (1) the collection of responsibilities for such functions as sales, advertising, and customer service under one senior executive, (2) the creation or enlargement of the marketing research effort, and (3) a change in name for the over-all function from *sales* to *marketing*. To what extent does it appear from Figure 13-1 that the Allegheny Ludlum Steel Corporation had adopted the marketing concept at the time of this example?

(8)

Occasionally, the organization may restrict possible alternative strategies. For example, the company with an ability to produce a new line of products with which its marketing organization has had no experience, perhaps requiring totally new marketing methods, may find it necessary to restrict its development. As an alternative, it may have to contract for marketing services from more expert sources.

methods of achieving differentiation

Marketing efforts can be differentiated by functions, products, geography, or customer groups, as suggested in Figure 13-2. In a general sense, the ability to differentiate along any of these dimensions will be influenced by the over-all size of an organization and its activities. Given an organization of sufficient size to support differentiation, the factors listed in Figure 13-2 may determine the manner in which responsibilities are defined and specialization encouraged.

(9)
Few marketing organizations of any size fit neatly into the categories shown in Figure 13-2. Most employ two or more means of differentiation. For example,

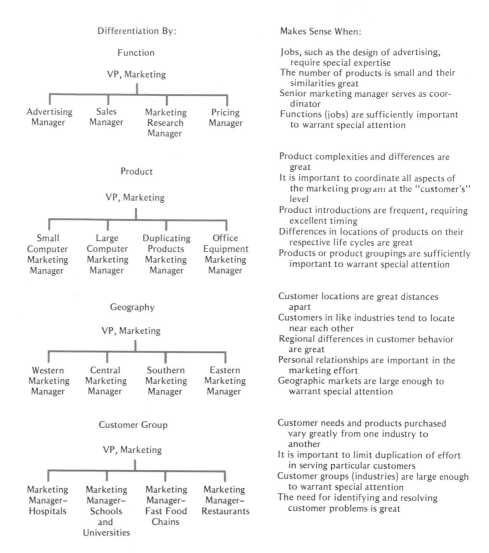

Figure 13-2. Factors influencing the way in which organizations are structured to perform marketing tasks.

Differentiation By:

Function

VP, Marketing

| Advertising Manager | Sales Manager | Marketing Research Manager | Pricing Manager |

Makes Sense When:

Jobs, such as the design of advertising, require special expertise
The number of products is small and their similarities great
Senior marketing manager serves as coordinator
Functions (jobs) are sufficiently important to warrant special attention

Product

VP, Marketing

| Small Computer Marketing Manager | Large Computer Marketing Manager | Duplicating Products Marketing Manager | Office Equipment Marketing Manager |

Product complexities and differences are great
It is important to coordinate all aspects of the marketing program at the "customer's" level
Product introductions are frequent, requiring excellent timing
Differences in locations of products on their respective life cycles are great
Products or product groupings are sufficiently important to warrant special attention

Geography

VP, Marketing

| Western Marketing Manager | Central Marketing Manager | Southern Marketing Manager | Eastern Marketing Manager |

Customer locations are great distances apart
Customers in like industries tend to locate near each other
Regional differences in customer behavior are great
Personal relationships are important in the marketing effort
Geographic markets are large enough to warrant special attention

Customer Group

VP, Marketing

| Marketing Manager– Hospitals | Marketing Manager– Schools and Universities | Marketing Manager– Fast Food Chains | Marketing Manager– Restaurants |

Customer needs and products purchased vary greatly from one industry to another
It is important to limit duplication of effort in serving particular customers
Customer groups (industries) are large enough to warrant special attention
The need for identifying and resolving customer problems is great

how would you characterize the way in which the marketing effort at Allegheny Ludlum is differentiated, based on information in Figure 13-1?

IBM long has been a leading proponent of differentiation in its efforts to market a line of computing hardware and software. According to professors E. Raymond Corey and Steven H. Star:

IBM began to specialize its field sales branches by user industry in the late 1950s. The need for specialization arose because computer applications varied greatly among such customer groups as the airlines, retailing establishments, and hospitals. "Software" programs tailored to applications in each user industry were being developed, and at headquarters the Data Processing Division marketing organization began to prepare industry marketing programs. . . . The sales volume base and the market potential were considered . . . to be sufficiently great (by 1971) to support specialization by user industry both at

445

headquarters and in the field. . . . Specialized branches each responsible for a particular customer group were established first in the major cities. . . . By early 1966 the [New England] District had ten branches which varied considerably in the degree to which they were specialized. A finance branch, for example, was responsible for sales to banks and other financial businesses throughout the entire District. An insurance group handled sales to insurance companies in Metropolitan Boston, Rhode Island, New Hampshire, and Maine, while a Hartford branch was responsible for insurance accounts in that area and in Western Massachusetts and Vermont as well as utilities in Western Massachusetts.[3]

(10)

Recently, IBM has established sales representatives who specialize in installation, equipment protection or maintenance, and the upgrading of systems already installed. In terms of Figure 13-2, how would you describe the way in whifh the IBM sales organization is structured?

methods of achieving coordination

We already have considered the type of coordination required within a marketing organization to achieve a marketing goal. In addition, other decisions made within an organization are cross-functional in nature, as suggested by Figure 13-3. The decision to drop an existing product can be just as significant to the plant manufacturing it and to financial planners as it is to marketing management. Similarly, a decision to improve customer service standards is of equal

Figure 13-3. Interests in marketing decisions among other parts of an organization, suggesting the need for coordination.

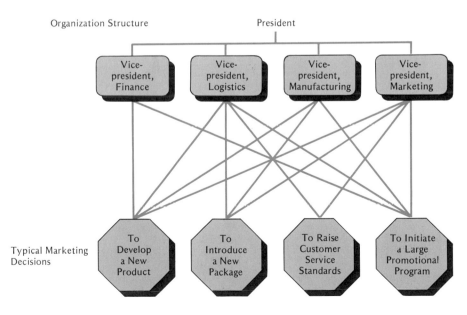

Organization Structure — President

Vice-president, Finance | Vice-president, Logistics | Vice-president, Manufacturing | Vice-president, Marketing

Typical Marketing Decisions

To Develop a New Product | To Introduce a New Package | To Raise Customer Service Standards | To Initiate a Large Promotional Program

[3] E. Raymond Corey and Steven H. Star, *Organization Strategy: A Marketing Approach* (Boston: Division of Research, Graduate School of Business Administration, Harvard University, 1971), p. 33.

446

significance to the logistics and marketing organizations. Other decisions, such as those to introduce a new package or initiate a large promotional program, have cross-functional implications as well. Finally, the process of developing a new product may involve nearly all the functions of an organization at one point or another.

Approaches to the achievement of coordination for various of these decisions include the designation of committees, venture teams, and product-or program integrators. The approach may depend on the task requiring coordination.

committees

Product-planning committees often are established to determine those products that should be added to, or deleted from, a company's line. In the retailing business, the equivalent of this may be a buying committee, which hears sales presentations from prospective vendors and selects those products that might best fit into a store's line of existing products. Equally common in many large organizations are packaging committees, which are given the task of reviewing either the structural or economic aspects of packaging and, in some cases, the graphic or creative aspects as well.

Committees are an excellent means of bringing a wide variety of talents to bear on a problem and establishing communication between related functions of an organization. But they often decide poorly, reflecting differences of opinion and compromises so typical of committees. Perhaps that explains why so many products are allowed to outlive their usefulness, either to customers or their manufacturers. Or why product lines in general are often managed so badly, as evidenced by their inexorable growth.

venture teams

Some firms have had particular success with the establishment of venture teams for the development and introduction of new products. As professors Richard M. Hill and James D. Hlavacek have pointed out:

> Tasks which are highly predictable can be best performed with hierarchical organizations characterized by formalized procedures. On the other hand, when tasks are uncertain and extensive problem solving is required, organizations that are less formalized and which emphasize self-control and member participation in decision making are more effective.[4]

The venture team, created by pulling together people with various talents who are then entrusted with all aspects of product development and possibly intro-

[4] Richard M. Hill and James D. Hlavacek, "The Venture Team: A New Concept in Marketing Organizations," *Journal of Marketing,* **36** (July 1972), pp. 44–50. Quote on p. 45.

duction to the market, is one informal device for dealing with uncertain tasks requiring extensive problem solving.

Venture teams have been found to operate most effectively when they are separated from the rest of the organization, composed of individuals with a variety of backgrounds and capabilities, relatively unstructured in their internal organization, characterized by a spirit of entrepreneurship that may be encouraged by special incentives linked to venture profits, linked directly to top management, given a relatively broad mission, and allowed a flexible life span without strict deadlines for the accomplishment of particular tasks. These very conditions, of course, may encourage delays and the lack of results among poorly selected team members. Perhaps of greatest importance is the improved likelihood that a venture team will consider a new product idea even though its eventual adoption might disturb the status quo. It is less likely to squelch new ideas than a formal organization composed of members with vested interests.

(11)   How would a venture team compare with a committee in terms of suitability for the task of developing new products?

integrators

Most often, integrators are appointed and charged with the task of coordinating demand and supply, packaging programs, and various inputs to customer service. Integrators typically have a great deal of responsibility but little authority. Professors Paul R. Lawrence and Jay W. Lorsch have identified the integrator as a growing force in large organizations and through their research have attempted to identify his or her characteristics:

1. Integrators need to be seen as contributing to important decisions on the basis of their competence and knowledge, rather than on their positional authority.
2. Integrators must have balanced orientations (as, for example, between production and sales, short-range and long-range thinking, etc.) and behavior patterns (as, for example, between people-oriented and task-oriented jobs).
3. Integrators need to feel they are being rewarded for their total product responsibility, not solely on the basis of their performance as individuals.
4. Integrators must have a capacity for resolving interdepartmental conflicts and disputes.[5]

(12)
(13)   How is this type of position similar to that held by Fred Holland in the Allegheny Ludlum marketing organization? What did a more senior member of the Allegheny Ludlum organization mean when he said what, "We often promote a good salesman into the job of product manager. It isn't until they get that job that they understand what selling really is."?

[5] Paul R. Lawrence and Jay W. Lorsch, "New Management Job: The Integrator," *Harvard Business Review*, **45** (Nov.–Dec. 1967), pp. 142–151. Quote on p. 146.

matrix organization

Efforts to provide coordination for large-scale marketing efforts, whether by product, geography, or customer groupings, often lead to the type of matrix organization pictured in Figure 13-4. In this type of organization, functional managers may be responsible for activities such as advertising for all products, with their results measured in terms of over-all sales compared with advertising expenditures. Product managers, on the other hand, typically are charged with making the proper use of advertising along with other types of marketing effort for their particular products. Their results often are measured in terms of sales for a particular product compared with the allocated costs of various marketing efforts devoted to that product.

Depending on the manner in which performances for functional managers and coordinators are measured, conflicts often can result at points where a product manager's plan disrupts that of an advertising manager, or vice versa. This helps explain the emphasis that Lawrence and Lorsch place on the ability of an integrator to resolve conflicts and disputes.

whither goest the product manager?

For some years, the position of brand or product manager has been considered an ideal way of providing bright, promising managers with an opportunity to assume program and, in many cases, profit responsibility at an early stage in their careers. It has been a major avenue of advancement in companies such as

Figure 13-4. Relationships, the measurement of results, and potential points of conflict (⊕) in a function-product matrix marketing organization.

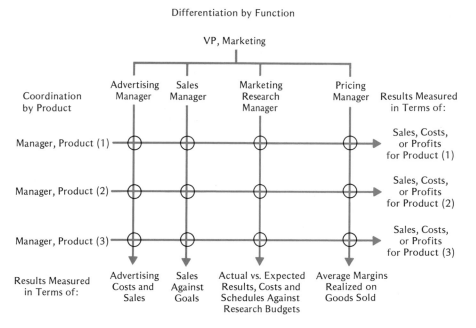

449

Procter & Gamble, which is said to have originated the concept in 1927. At Procter & Gamble, more than fifty brand groups are established in the manner shown in the simplified chart of the P&G organization in Figure 13-5. Here, the brand manager for Tide, for example, might work closely with a brand assistant and assistant brand manager on their brand's annual marketing plan development, ad copy, media planning and selection, sales promotion, package design, market research, and business analysis and forcasting. According to P&G's advertising vice-president, "This approach is . . . basic to our business philosophy."[6]

Pepsico, in contrast, is typical of several other large firms that have moved away from product or brand management in recent years. Mr. John Sculley, senior vice-president of the Pepsi-Cola Division of the company, proclaimed several years ago that the brand management concept was "certainly dead and buried at Pepsi."[7] Based on the organization chart for the Pepsi-Cola Division's marketing group, shown in Figure 13-6, where would you guess the coordination previously provided by brand managers now takes place? How would you analyze the organization of the Pepsi-Cola Division in terms of Figure 13-2?

According to Mr. Sculley:

> Traditional brand management was fine when you were dealing with a big, undifferentiated market. But today, consumer-goods companies are segmenting their market by age, income, geography, and even by "psychographics" or lifestyle. . . . [Brand managers] are usually younger guys who, if they are any good, quickly move to bigger and better assignments within their company. So they take a short-range view of building total volume and market share, and tend to neglect market segments, since this is more of a long-term proposition.[8]

Other arguments in favor of a functional or other organizational arrangement centralizing more authority at higher levels than the product manager's in the

(14)

(15)

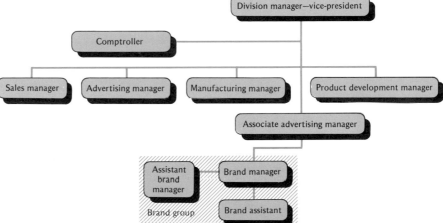

Figure 13-5. A simplified diagram of the organization for marketing effort at Procter & Gamble. Source: "The Brand Manager: No Longer King," *Business Week* (June 9, 1973), pp. 58–62 ff. See p. 58.

[6]"The Brand Manager: No Longer King," *Business Week* (June 9, 1973), pp. 58–66. Quote on p. 59.
[7]Ibid.
[8]Ibid.

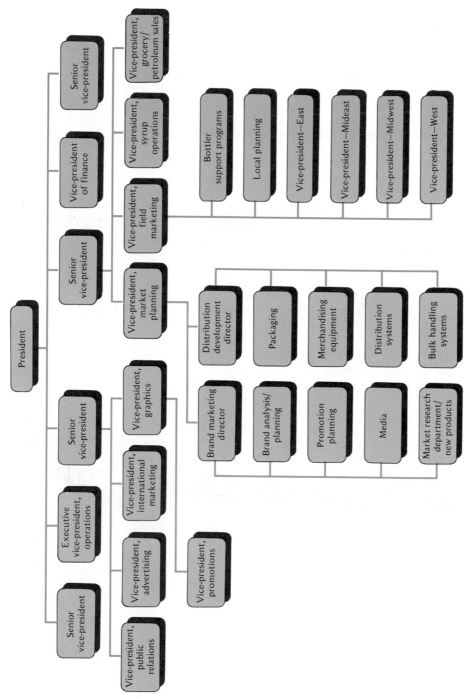

Figure 13-6. The marketing organization for the Pepsi-Cola Division of Pepsico following the discontinuance of the brand managers' positions. Source: "The Brand Manager: No Longer King," *Business Week* (June 9, 1973). pp. 58–62 ff. See p. 59.

organization are centered around the changing marketing environment. For example, decisions made by product or brand managers may involve issues of consumerism (pricing, package sizes, and labeling), the environment (packaging, product contents), and government regulation (advertising, channel policies, and pricing). These issues are becoming so important to some companies that decisions formerly made by product managers may be reserved for higher levels of management. Similarly, the brand or product management concept is thought by some to be strained to the breaking point by increasingly short product life cycles that preclude any longer-term 'association with a product or brand. What differences in qualifications would you look for in hiring product managers in companies with products of average life cycles of ten years and ten months, respectively?

(16)

At H. J. Heinz Co., product managers have been criticized for spending so much time trying to get "their fair share" of advertising, personal selling, and other available marketing resources that they have little time to keep track of what is going on outside their organization among customers. As a result, Heinz has reorganized its effort. It used to have a single product manager for bottled ketchup, for example, responsible for ketchup sold both to grocery retailers and institutions such as restaurants. But according to Heinz's general manager of foodservice marketing:

> There is quite a difference between selling ketchup to a retail grocery organization, which makes a profit on bottled ketchup, and to a restaurant chain, which gives the ketchup away.[9]

(17) (18)

To which types of differences do you think this manager is alluding? How might you reorganize the product managers for Heinz' soups, entrees, puddings, ketchup, bottled sauces, and mustard to meet the problem?

(19)

At Heinz, responsibilities of product managers were reassigned to give one manager, for example, responsibility for restaurant-pack soups, entrees, and puddings, all sold to restaurants. Another was assigned to manage all table condiments sold to grocery retailers. How would you analyze this new organization in terms of Figure 13-2?

(20)
(21)

What, in you opnion, are the implications of this debate for the future of the product-management concept? For marketing integrators, or coordinators, in general?

other factors influencing marketing organization

We have discussed the impact of the marketing concept and the use of integrators, or coordinators, on the form that marketing organizations assume. Among other factors influencing organization are the needs of a potential

[9]Ibid., p. 61.

market for a product or service, the extent to which a company makes or buys its marketing effort, competition, the relative emphasis on new-product development, and the limits on the capabilities of marketing managers.

market needs

Because of the nature of a product or the way in which it is used, customers may, as we saw in Chapter 10, require a great deal of transactional, logistical, or facilitating support. Transactional support, you'll recall, might involve the provision of detailed or complex information about a product and its use, perhaps to reduce the risk perceived as being associated with its purchase. Logistical support might involve the ready availability of inventory, a brief response time in filling market orders, or a close proximity of sales and inventory locations to the market place. Facilitating support includes the provision of credit, the supply of marketing information to channel members, and the postpurchase servicing of products. Transactional efforts are associated most closely with sales and advertising departments; logistical efforts with physical distribution, or traffic and transportation, departments; and facilitating functions with credit, marketing research, or service departments in a company's over-all organization. There often is a direct relationship in the extent to which these departments are found grouped under a common marketing executive and their importance for a successful marketing effort.

(22)
(23)
(24)
Based on this discussion, which types of functions would you expect to be grouped under a senior marketing manager in a firm producing standard grades of steel for sale to large customers and wholesalers in carload lots? A large regional baking company making daily deliveries direct to retail supermarket locations? A firm leasing cigarette vending machines to restaurants on the basis of a royalty payment to the lessor determined by the volume of sales realized by each machine?

the extent of make or buy

Marketers can fulfill all or some of the market needs for transactional, logistical, or facilitating functions by making or buying them. A firm may elect to employ its own sales force to sell directly to a large number of retailers, or choose to sell through one or more wholesalers, thus markedly reducing the size and complexity of its sales force and marketing organization. Compare, for example, the prominence of the sales organization in the Allegheny Ludlum Steel Corporation, shown in Figure 13-1, with that of the Pepsi-Cola Division of Pepsico, whose end product is produced and sold by numerous largely independent bottlers to retail outlets, shown in Figure 13-6. Similarly, firms may make or buy creative work for promotional programs, transportation, warehousing, and postpurchase service networks.

Make or buy decisions typically produce quantum changes in a marketing organization. For example, firms with relatively narrow product lines (in relation to market needs) or small dollar sales per customer may find that the economics of relying on a wholesaler for sales effort and the inventorying of its products are relatively favorable, as shown for a firm operating in the "buy range" of Figure 13-7. Buying marketing services results in costs that largely are variable and related to the margin (similar to a commission) paid the wholesaler for its services. To attempt to provide its own sales and inventory program would result in fixed costs for a firm far in excess of wholesale margins at relatively low sales levels. Fixed costs are those associated with the minimum sales force and warehouse network required to meet market needs, regardless of sales volume.

As a firm's product line is expanded, or its sales increase either in total or on a customer-by-customer basis, the relative economics of operating its own sales force and warehousing program often become more favorable. As shown in Figure 13-7, the variable costs associated with occasionally adding a new salesman or a new warehouse under the make alternative are lower than those represented by a wholesaler's margin. As a result, at the point where differences in these variable costs become great enough to defray the fixed costs associated with providing its own marketing effort, a company will find it more profitable to develop its own sales or warehousing capability, thus adding large numbers of people to the marketing organization at particular points in time.

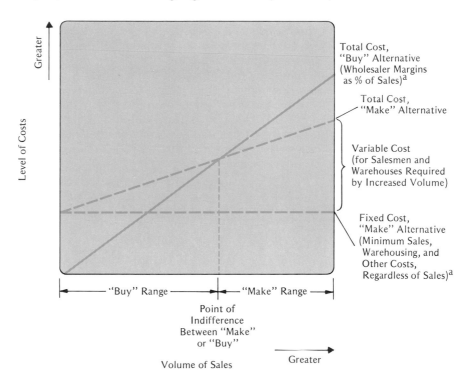

Figure 13-7. The relative economics of making or buying marketing effort.

Total Cost, "Buy" Alternative (Wholesaler Margins as % of Sales)[a]

Total Cost, "Make" Alternative

Variable Cost (for Salesmen and Warehouses Required by Increased Volume)

Fixed Cost, "Make" Alternative (Minimum Sales, Warehousing, and Other Costs, Regardless of Sales)[a]

Level of Costs

Greater

"Buy" Range   "Make" Range

Point of Indifference Between "Make" or "Buy"

Volume of Sales

Greater

[a]Note: In this simplified presentation, the fixed costs of central marketing administration are assumed to be the same under both alternatives, and are not shown.

454

Only the economics of make or buy are stressed here. Other factors, such as the relative desirability of maintaining control over the performance of various marketing functions, would represent major influences on the decision as well.

competition

A company's competitors might achieve superior marketing efforts, from the viewpoint of customers, thus requiring changes in its marketing organization. For example, recently NCR Corporation (NCR), formerly the National Cash Register Co., reassigned its 3,000-person domestic sales force to specific markets rather than products. Instead of selling only cash registers or the company's more recently developed line of computers, NCR salespeople began specializing in selling to four "vocational groups": retailing, financial, commercial-industrial, or medical-educational-government organizations. Subsequent to this change, a sales representative might sell both a cash register and computer to his or her department store account, for example. The company's founder, John H. Patterson, an early leader in industrial selling, used to exhort his salesmen: "Don't talk machines. Don't talk cash registers. Talk the customer's business."[10]

(25) Nevertheless, company sales representatives assigned to either cash register or accounting machine sales found it difficult to follow Patterson's advice. Based on what you have read elsewhere in this chapter, to what extent do you think NCR's entry into the computer business in the 1960s accounts for the company's eventual change from a product-oriented to a market-oriented sales organization?

relative emphasis on new-product development

A firm's marketing organization may reflect the relative emphasis that it places on new-product development. The establishment of separately identified responsibility for it recognizes the basic contrasts in the type of effort needed to maintain sales of an existing product as opposed to bringing a successful
(26) product to the market. Judging from the organization charts of Allegheny Ludlum, P&G, and the Pepsi-Cola Division of Pepsico, what would you guess is the relative emphasis placed on product development by these companies?
(27) What significance would you attach to the fact that, in some companies, product-development responsibilities are confined to either the manufacturing
(28) or research and development organizations? Would you expect to find this situation more frequently in companies producing industrial or consumer goods?

Producers of services may have an equally great need for organizational emphasis on new-product development. For example, the Bank of America now

[10] "NCR's Radical Shift in Marketing Tactics," *Business Week* (Dec. 8, 1973), pp. 102–104 ff. Quote on p. 102. Subsequent references to NCR are based on this article.

offers 130 different services, most of them developed and introduced in recent years. The First National Bank of Memphis, with research, product development, advertising, and promotional responsibilities grouped under a marketing director, has developed a number of services under its program to position itself as a bank for "doing things your way, not the bank's way." [11]

personal capabilities

The capabilities of individuals to meet customer and product needs, for example, sometimes limits the range of organizational alternatives. Returning to the NCR example, Mr. Patterson was an early advocate of the philosophy that great salespeople are made, not born. In part, this may have been a reflection of his difficulty in hiring competent salespeople for cash registers that were, early in the century, relatively complex pieces of machinery to unschooled retailers and NCR salespeople alike. By studying the sales techniques of his best salespeople, developing a canned approach on the basis of this observation, and spending a great deal of time coaching other sales representatives in this canned approach, Patterson found that he could help them increase sales. This effort led to the development of one of the first sales manuals and company-sponsored sales training schools, a school which graduated, among others, Mr. Thomas J. Watson, who later left NCR in 1913 to found IBM.

(29)
(30)
How would you interpret the recent changes in organization at NCR in terms of Figure 7-1, page 227? To what extent might it have been a result of the rising calibre of sales talent available to a company like NCR?

In order to facilitate the shift from a product- to a customer-oriented sales force, NCR increased its training budget 20 per cent to a figure of $3.6 million in 1974, requiring its sales force to spend 34,000 man-days at its $11 million educational facility in Dayton, Ohio.

span of control

The span of control—the number of people that one can supervise effectively—is a concept based on the limits of personal capabilities as well as the demands of various supervisory tasks. From the standpoint of an organization, the span of control is directly related to the number of levels, or positions, required in the organization's hierarchy. For example, how many organizational levels would be required to manage one hundred field sales representatives in a situation in which five sales representatives or managers represented the maximum number that could be supervised effectively? How many would be required if the span of control could be expanded to ten?

(31)

(32)
The span of control varies inversely with the difficulty of the supervisory task.

[11]"Tyros in the Marketing Game," *Business Week* (Sept. 15, 1973), pp. 129–130. Quote on p. 130.

Factors determining the difficulty of marketing management assignments include the geographic territory to be covered (the distances between typically dispersed field sales representatives, for example), the complexity of the selling task, the rate of turnover among marketing personnel (determining the amount of training for new people), and the intensity of sales effort and supervision desired.

For example, according to the vice-president of United States marketing for Del Monte Corp., a processor of grocery products: "As products multiply and the competition for shelf space increases, sale men have to be far more sophisticated in their approach."[12] As a result, D_l Monte recently restructured its entire field sales force, expanding from nine regional divisions to twenty-one. This change was intended to allow its sales representatives to "get as close to the customer as possible," made necessary by the growing size, complexity, and market power of Del Monte's chain store customers. Under Del Monte's new organization, actual selling to chain store buyers is the responsibility of an account representative. One level below him or her is a sales representative, who is responsible for visiting individual retail stores to help with restocking, display, and other merchandising chores.

organizing for multinational marketing effort

Given the relatively great increases in both international trade and direct foreign investments in recent years, questions regarding proper organizational approaches to multinational marketing have taken on increasing importance. Just as we concluded in the last chapter that marketing concepts, if not strategies, are "exportable" across national boundaries, organization principles discussed earlier largely vary only in degree in their domestic and multinational applications.

typical stages of development

The steps toward the development of full-scale multinational marketing efforts are illustrated by the experiences of the Rockwell Mfg. Co., now part of the Rockwell International Corporation, between 1957 and 1970. Early in the cycle, foreign activities represented a minor sideline for Rockwell. Later, an export department was formed to handle the documentation and transport arrangements for orders from non-United States markets. Still later, the growing importance of international business was recognized with the establishment of an international division with responsibilities for direct marketing efforts outside the United States. But the creation of both a separate export department and a separately identified international division created problems of communication

---

[12]"The New Supersalesman: Wired for Success," *Business Week* (Jan. 6, 1973), pp. 44–49. Quote on pp. 46–47.

between domestic United States and foreign marketing operations. According to the company's executive vice-president at the time:

> Our local marketing people abroad knew their customers, the local labor situation, and their own local market. But they lacked basic technical knowledge of our products and why we had designed them the way we had. At the same time, the United States product divisions had their domestic responsibilities, and thus lacked strong urgencies when it came to foreign markets.[13]

(33) What ways might you devise to deal with this problem?

(34) In response to its developing problems of communication between domestic and foreign marketing operations, Rockwell decided to return the responsibility for the marketing of groups of products abroad to its domestic product managers. What potential strengths and weaknesses would you associate with this action?

Like Rockwell, many firms operate with export departments, often with no direct sales representation in foreign countries, during early stages of their multinational marketing efforts. Later, with the establishment of an international division, company sales representatives may be assigned in foreign markets. At a point at which the volume of sales may justify it, a company may invest in manufacturing facilities in the foreign market in order to reduce the costs of assembly outside, and importation to, the market in question. This leads to somewhat self-supporting and independent international operations. It is at this point that a growing need for coordination may lead to the type of action taken by Rockwell.

An alternative is the creation of the "world corporation" organization for those firms in which multinational activities have become particularly important. This has been described as the means by which a company:

> looks at the entire world as its area of operations, and reaches out everywhere for markets, techniques, ideas, personnel, processes, and products. . . . It is organized so that no single national market or group of markets draws greater attention than its size dictates.[14]

Under the world corporation concept, for example, in a United States-based company, a United States division would be formed to operate alongside other divisions assigned non-United States territories. Each of the resulting divisions might have a greater degree of responsibility for marketing, production, procurement, and profits, drawing on a small central staff for financial and other types of support. This represents a decentralized approach to the management of multinational activities.

One study of several large firms concluded that there are four basic phases in international marketing activity.[15] They can be characterized as ethnocentrism

[13]"Why A Global Market Doesn't Exist," *Business Week* (Dec. 19, 1970), pp. 140–144. Quote on p. 140.

[14]*Organizing for Worldwide Operations,* Business International Research Report (New York: Business International Corp., 1965), p. 13.

[15]Yoram Wind, Susan P. Douglas, and Howard V. Perlmutter, "Guidelines for Developing International Marketing Strategies" *Journal of Marketing,* **31** (April 1973), pp. 14–23.

458

(35)

(36)

(home-country orientation), polycentrism (host-country orientation in one or more foreign markets), regiocentrism (a regional, multinational orientation), and geocentrism (a world orientation). How would you relate these stages to those described for companies utilizing export departments, international divisions, and world corporations as vehicles for implementing multinational marketing strategies? Does the experience of the Rockwell Mfg. Co. fit this pattern?

Under this framework, a company progresses from ethnocentrism to geocentrism (1) as it grows, (2) as it develops knowledge and experience in different national markets, (3) as the foreign market potential grows in size and heterogeniety in relation to domestic market potential, and (4) to the extent that its products are not embedded in the life-style or cultural patterns of consumers.

(37)

For example, to what extent would you expect companies marketing industrial machine tools as opposed to personal grooming products to be able to develop geocentric marketing strategies?

Furthermore, the authors of this study concluded that various types of effort may lend themselves better to different stages of organizational development. For example, a geocentric strategy might be more advantageous for production

(38)

and physical distribution than for promotional activities. How would you explain, for example, that executives interviewed in this study advanced the opinion that geocentric approaches would be much more appropriate for the development of product quality standards than for the conduct of marketing research?

centralization versus decentralization

Because of the geographic and cultural dispersion of markets around the world, questions regarding the degree of centralization, or central control, to be exercised in multinational marketing organizations are accentuated. Major arguments in favor of a high degree of centralization are that it (1) facilitates the coordination of marketing effort; (2) can offset the lack of management expertise in some parts of the world; (3) provides for better, closer control over far-flung activities; (4) offers better opportunities for the exchange of ideas between widely dispersed marketing groups; and (5) results in more travel but less duplication of administrative effort in relation to decentralized approaches. These benefits must be weighed against those generally attributed to decentralized organizations: (1) the encouragement of more effective local efforts through the assignment of profit responsibility to managers in local markets, (2) improved opportunities for management development, and (3) the development of marketing programs that are more sensitive to local needs.

Few companies operate at either extreme of the centralization-decentralization spectrum. Furthermore, the extent of centralized decision making may vary from one marketing function to another. For example, according to the vice-president of IBM World Trade Corp.: "While our final product specifications are determined at the headquarters of our Development Div. in the U. S., they

(39)

reflect inputs from at least 20 countries around the world."[16] How would you

16"Why a Global Market Doesn't Exist," loc. cit.

characterize the degree of centralization in product development that exists at IBM? In contrast, responsibilities for sales, promotion, and pricing are organized around national markets and customer groupings within those markets.

In one study of the operations of nine major United States-based companies in Western Europe, it was found that authority was delegated to local marketing organizations for 90 per cent of those firms' promotional decisions and 60 per cent of their pricing decisions.[17]

coordination without centralization

Alternatives to centralized responsibility and authority as a means of achieving coordination or integration include (1) the creation of multinational committees to carry out various phases of marketing planning, (2) periodic multinational marketing management meetings, and (3) rotating assignments for senior marketing managers among various national markets.

Although these approaches can lead to the cross-fertilization of ideas found useful in one market, of course, they provide no means for enforcing coordination, especially among national marketing groups with local profit responsibility. In a sense, the rotating of assignments at NCR led directly to the reorganization of the company's United States marketing effort into four vocational groups, described earlier in this chapter. The company's president was sold fully on the virtues of the reorganization, because six years earlier when he was head of NCR/Japan he had reorganized his group's marketing efforts on a vocational basis. That effort resulted in a 200 per cent sales increase with only an 11 per cent increase in the number of sales representatives.

standardization of the marketing effort

Centralized control can facilitate the standardization of marketing approaches across national markets. Professor Robert D. Buzzell has suggested that this can result in attendant cost savings, consistency in approaches to ever more mobile customers, improved planning and control, and the increased exploitation and exportation of all-too-rare good ideas.[18] Potential cost savings that he cites include those of product design, packaging, and the development of promotional materials. With increased travel and multinational readership of advertising media, particularly in Europe, the desirability of standardized brand names, packages, prices, and advertising themes is enhanced. As Buzzell points out:

> standardization can offer important economies to the multinational marketer. Even if these cost savings are attained at the expense of lower sales in some markets, the net effect on profits may be positive.[19]

[17] Richard J. Aylmer, "Marketing Decisions in the Multinational Firm," (Ph. D. diss., Harvard University, 1968), pp. 209–210.

[18] Robert D. Buzzell, "Can You Standardize Multinational Marketing?" *Harvard Business Review,* **46** (Nov.–Dec. 1968), pp. 102–113.

[19] Ibid., p. 105.

At the same time, standardization can lead to the development of products and marketing programs insensitive to the needs of local markets. For example, Yugoslavia is a nation with a population of about 20 million, but it is made up of six republics, with five nationalities whose three different languages are written in two different scripts. How many market segments are represented by these differences? How sensitive might a centralized marketing organization be to the needs of this "national" market?

Even where the language spoken is common, small differences can have a great impact. For example:

> A *cigarro* is a cigarette in Chile but a cigar in other Latin American countries. *Pico* means a pick or beak in most of Spanish America but you don't use it in polite circles in Chile. *Mantequilla* is butter, except in Argentina. *Manteca* is butter in Argentina but means grease or lard in other Spanish-American countries.[20]

nationalization in multinational marketing management

Leading multinational marketers have found it advisable for some time to staff their foreign operations with local nationals. For example, NCR rarely has had more than six Americans in multinational marketing positions outside the United States, even though the firm realizes a large share of its sales and earnings from non-United States markets. This practice has resulted in improved supervision, improved employee relations, and better results in many companies. What influence do you think it might have on the effectiveness of multinational marketing management, communication, and control?

the need for flexibility and multiple approaches

The experiences of leading multinational marketing companies suggest that a successful company must pursue a number of organizational policies and approaches simultaneously. A highly centralized approach to one market may not work in another where local management has developed to the point where it is ready to assume greater responsibility, or the demands of the market are hard to understand from afar. Standardization of product, price, or promotion may be possible in parts of Europe, but not in South America. And, because of local restrictions that prevent majority ownership of the local subsidiary of a multinational operation, it may be necessary to confine the role of the parent marketing organization to an advisory one, subject to profit-motivated interpretations of local managers. These factors, among others, suggest that flexibility is the name of the game in the organization of multinational marketing effort.

[20]Virgil D. Reed, "The International Consumer," in Eugene J. Kelley and William Lazer, eds., *Managerial Marketing: Perspectives and Viewpoints,* 3rd ed. (Homewood, Ill.: R. Irwin, 1967), pp. 586–600. Quote on p. 597.

(40)

organizational change

The diagram shown on page 438 suggests that a marketing organization should be a reflection of a firm's marketing strategy, which in turn results from marketing and organizational objectives. Thus, as corporate objectives and strategies change, so too should marketing strategies and organizations. This often necessitates a redefinition of jobs. And, because many managers subscribe to the organizational principle that advocates fitting individuals to jobs rather than vice versa, organizational change can result in substantial costs associated with the dislocation of individuals. Costs as well as the benefits of change must be assessed in considering changes in marketing strategies.

For example, there were sizeable costs involved in NCR's decision to shift from a product- to a customer-(vocational) orientation, described earlier in this chapter.[21] A New York securities house estimated that 10 to 12 per cent of NCR's salesmen quit as a result of the change, although NCR's management claimed that the figure was too high.

The change had variable effects on the morale of individuals, depending on how they were affected. Many salesmen were glad to have more products to sell. To others, this was a frightening prospect. In the change, the number of domestic vice-presidents of sales was reduced from eleven to eight and the number of regional vice-presidents from fifteen to eleven. As one of the vice-presidents reassigned the position of regional vocational director for retail at a 9 per cent pay reduction put it: "It has to be considered a demotion. My pride was hurt. I was under consideration for a Dayton financial vice-president spot."[22] Change does not occur without a cost.

summary

People organize their efforts to (1) differentiate between jobs and allow for specialization of effort, (2) to provide for coordination between tasks and people, (3) to define responsibilities and authority held by members of an organization, and (4) to reflect and support over-all strategies.

Given an organization of sufficient size to support specialization, marketing efforts and responsibilities may be differentiated by functional task, such as advertising or personal selling; by product; by geographic market territory; or by customer or industry group.

Other tasks or decisions may require a high degree of coordination. For example, committees may be formed to determine standards of customer service to be maintained. Venture teams, with responsibility for all aspects of the development and initial marketing of new products, may be formed. And integrators, with cross-functional responsibilities, may be given the responsibility for coordinating all aspects of the marketing program for a particular product. The need for coordination often leads to the creation of a matrix organization, with one set of managers responsible for various marketing functions and another responsible for coordinating marketing programs for products, geographic territories, or customer groupings.

[21] "NCR's Radical Shift in Marketing Tactics," op. cit., pp. 103–104.
[22] Ibid., p. 104.

Other factors influencing the shape of marketing organizations include (1) the needs of potential markets for transactional, logistical, or facilitating effort; (2) the extent to which an organization makes or buys its marketing effort; (3) competitive patterns; (4) the relative emphasis a firm places on new-product development and introduction; and (5) the limits on the capabilities of marketing managers to supervise the work of others effectively.

The form of a firm's marketing organization will be influenced as well by the extent to which it engages in mutinational marketing. Firms entering multinational markets often begin by exporting products under the direction of an export department. This may be followed by the establishment of foreign sales organizations, perhaps later supported by the importation of raw materials, local product design and manufacture, and management by one or more international divisions. A high degree of decentralization and local autonomy may characterize this stage of development. Finally, more mature firms may organize world corporations in which the responsibility for all international marketing and other activities is centralized at, and coordinated from, a world headquarters.

To the extent that it is possible, efficiencies obtained from the standardization of products and marketing activities may more than offset costs of lost sales in certain multinational markets. Furthermore, it may allow for the management of marketing activities by regions encompassing several nations. Nevertheless, the extent to which standardization is possible will vary with the nature of the products and particular marketing tasks under consideration.

Regardless of the extent to which authority is decentralized and vested in foreign marketing organizations, many American firms have minimized and even eliminated the use of American nationals as managers of their local multinational marketing units.

Whether concerned with domestic or multinational efforts, a marketing organization should be a reflection of a firm's marketing and corporate strategy. As strategies change, so do organizations. This may necessitate a redefinition of jobs and the refitting of available people to those jobs. Because the costs of such changes can be great, they should be weighed carefully against the benefits of reorganization.

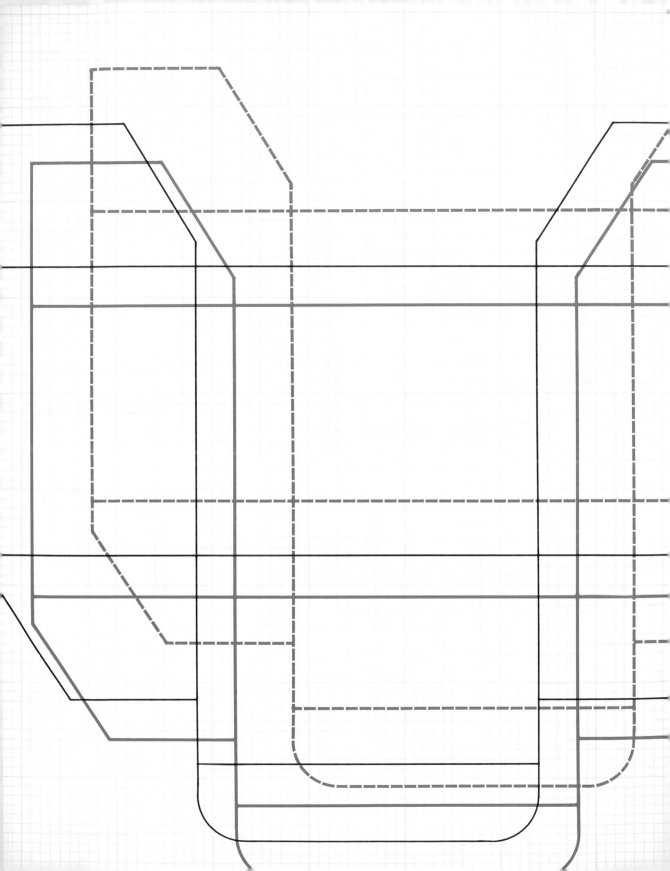

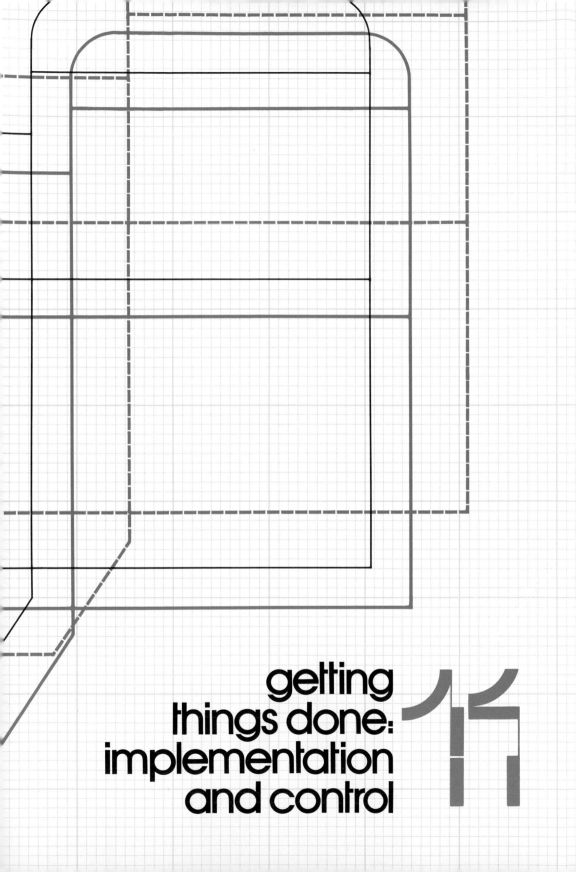

getting things done: implementation and control

11

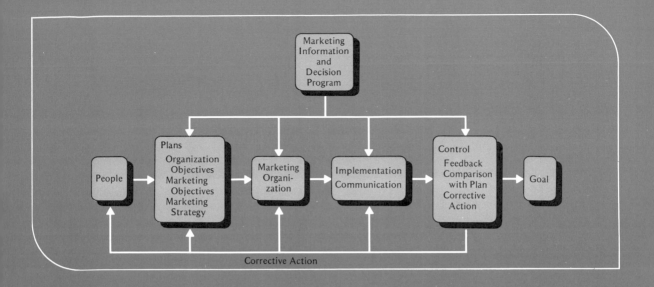

Corrective Action

Marketing thermostats are our main concern in this chapter. For if marketing management could develop methods for implementing plans and controlling activities that were as accurate and dependable as the thermostats found in most homes, it would find itself relieved of a good portion of the management task.

Think of it: you establish a plan and a goal by deciding how warm you want your house or room to be. The thermostat measures performance (temperature) on a continuing basis. It has a built-in thermometer both for monitoring data (room temperature) fed back to it and interpreting the data into decision-oriented information (stated in units of measurement called degrees). It has a device for turning on (implementing) the furnace when the temperature falls to a lower limit. Similarly, it shuts off the furnace (also an example of implementation) when the temperature exceeds an upper limit. Rarely does the temperature deviate from plan or goal by more than one or two degrees.

Compare this with what can happen in the real world of marketing control programs and implementation efforts. Assuming the existence of a plan, we may obtain little data with which to measure progress. Or our measuring device (thermometer) may be faulty, thus converting one kind of unuseable data into another kind of unuseable data, but not the kind of information we need for management purposes. We may have no definitely stated limits outside of which action is taken (equivalent to either turning the furnace on or off). And even if we do, the signal for action may get garbled or the recipient of that signal (equivalent to the furnace) may decide that the signal conflicts with the method of compensation or an already too heavy workload. In either event, the signal may not be followed so that implementation isn't achieved.

The example of the homely thermostat can serve as a worthy goal for current efforts to establish marketing control programs supported by well-designed marketing information programs to achieve the implementation and realization of plans.

This topic may well be the most critical one in this entire volume. Presumably, implementation with some chance of achievement can take place without a plan. But what good is a plan without implementation?

With this in mind, the objectives of our discussion are to (1) consider the nature of the control process and its relationship to the implementation of plans, (2) explore ways in which marketing information programs contribute to the control of marketing efforts, (3) introduce questions regarding the development of information programs for marketing management, and (4) discuss the manner in which performance measurement and control programs, along with organizational arrangements, can be integrated so that the implementation of policy takes place and marketing goals are achieved.

infoserv at Ansul

The Ansul Co., a Wisconsin-based company manufacturing and selling $120 million of specialty chemicals and fire-extinguishing equipment annually, set out to make the most effective use of its information sources several years ago.[1]

[1] This example is based on Richard L. Pinkerton, "How to Develop a Marketing Intelligence System," in Paul T. McElhiney and Henry S. Ang, eds., *How Marketing Works* (Dubuque, Iowa: Kendall-Hunt Publishing Company, 1971), pp. 25–34, and information supplied by company executives.

Its Fire Protection group established a marketing intelligence system by (1) creating a special marketing information group, (2) developing a form called an Infoserv report for the collection of important marketing information on an ongoing basis, (3) creating an intelligence library and data bank of information developed from various sources, and (4) designing a set of procedures for communicating information of importance for marketing management. Among the procedures included in the plan were requirements that

(1) the company's thirty-three salespeople and four regional managers seek out and report certain defined types of information on an Infoserv form in the manner shown in Figure 14-1;
(2) all Ansul executives initiate Infoserv forms where appropriate;
(3) the marketing information department acknowledge the receipt of all Infoserv reports and indicate any action taken on each;
(4) salesmen and others prepare special data forms profiling important competitors as well as customers;
(5) a filing and data-retrieval system be created;
(6) all incoming data be subjected to tests for their reliability and credibility (truth);
(7) information needs of operating managers be identified;
(8) dissemination procedures for each type of information be established;
(9) data recipients be reminded periodically to report back on any action taken on information received;
(10) data originators be informed of the use to which their information was put.

At an orientation seminar held at the home office the importance of the new marketing intelligence system was stressed by top management, including the company's former marketing vice-president who had become general manager of Ansul's Fire Protection Division. The quantity, but especially the quality, of Infoserv reports filed became one of the company's criteria in measuring the performance of field salespeople. Those filing few reports or incomplete reports were reminded periodically of the importance of this aspect of their work.

Within five months after the initiation of the program, 95 per cent of the field sales force was cooperating and filing an average of five Infoserv reports per month per person. About 20 per cent of the sales force was contributing 60 per cent of the total information, about as expected by management. In addition, with the help of follow-up meetings with regional managers and telegram reminders, comprehensive files were developed from information supplied by the field sales force concerning important customers, distributors, and competitors.

Today, several years later, Ansul's marketing intelligence system is still in place as an important function within the Fire Protection group. Although a number of refinements and procedural changes have occurred, it is still operated within the general scope of purposes and objectives that led to its initiation.

How would you appraise the success of this program? To what extent did its success depend on the extent to which its sales representatives were paid in salary or commissions? What other elements were instrumental in getting this program started? In keeping it going?

(1) (2)

(3)

(4)

Figure 14-1. An example of an Infoserv report filed by an Ansul Co. sales representative.

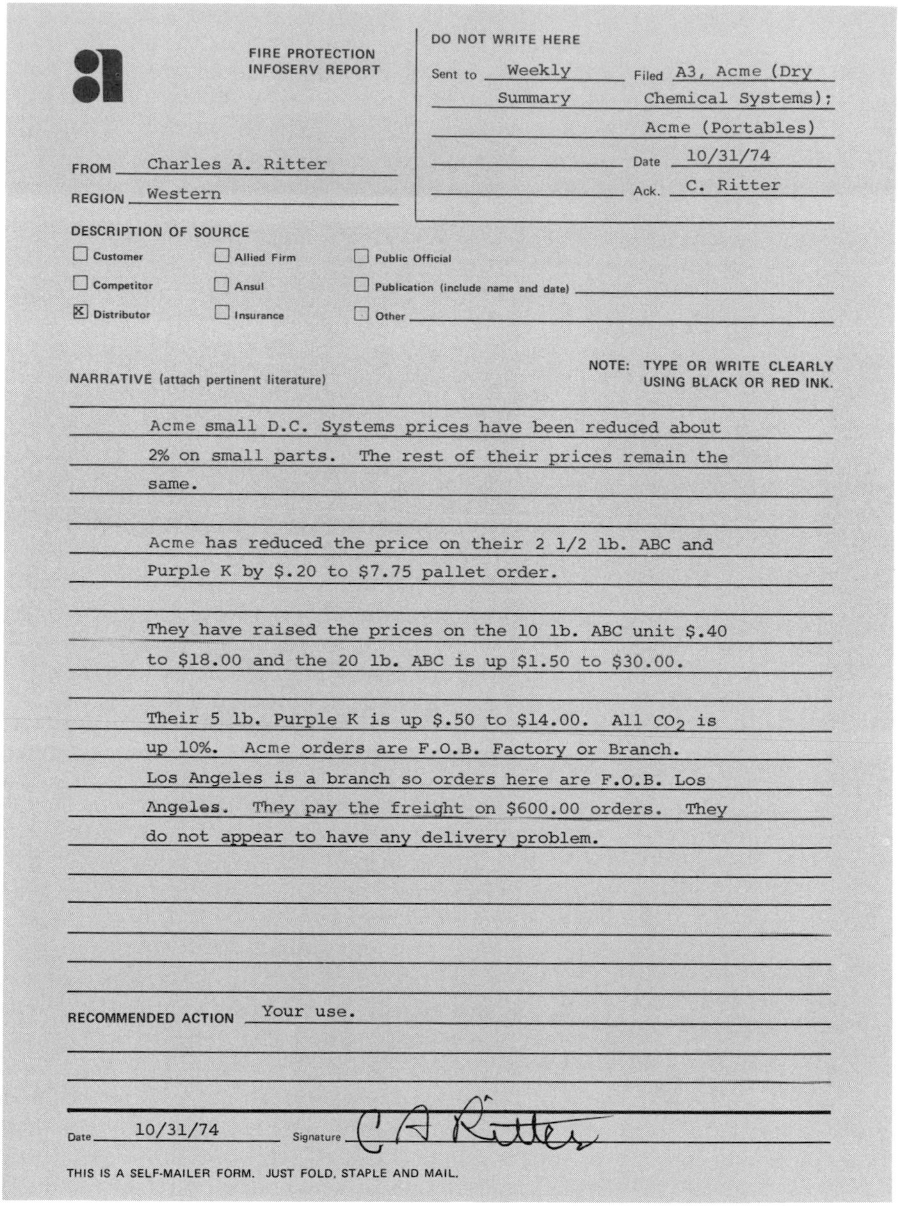

FIRE PROTECTION
INFOSERV REPORT

DO NOT WRITE HERE

Sent to Weekly Summary

Filed A3, Acme (Dry Chemical Systems); Acme (Portables)

Date 10/31/74

Ack. C. Ritter

FROM Charles A. Ritter

REGION Western

DESCRIPTION OF SOURCE

☐ Customer ☐ Allied Firm ☐ Public Official

☐ Competitor ☐ Ansul ☐ Publication (include name and date)

☒ Distributor ☐ Insurance ☐ Other

NARRATIVE (attach pertinent literature)

NOTE: TYPE OR WRITE CLEARLY USING BLACK OR RED INK.

Acme small D.C. Systems prices have been reduced about 2% on small parts. The rest of their prices remain the same.

Acme has reduced the price on their 2 1/2 lb. ABC and Purple K by \$.20 to \$7.75 pallet order.

They have raised the prices on the 10 lb. ABC unit \$.40 to \$18.00 and the 20 lb. ABC is up \$1.50 to \$30.00.

Their 5 lb. Purple K is up \$.50 to \$14.00. All CO_2 is up 10%. Acme orders are F.O.B. Factory or Branch. Los Angeles is a branch so orders here are F.O.B. Los Angeles. They pay the freight on \$600.00 orders. They do not appear to have any delivery problem.

RECOMMENDED ACTION Your use.

Date 10/31/74 Signature C A Ritter

THIS IS A SELF-MAILER FORM. JUST FOLD, STAPLE AND MAIL.

the nature of the implementation and control process

Marketing managers at the Ansul Co. set out to create a marketing information program, implemented their ideas, and instituted controls to insure continued adherence to the plan. It may sound easy, but implementation may well be the most difficult job a manager has—only a bit more difficult than controlling to insure follow-up.

Important steps in the implementation and control process are shown in Figure 14-2. They include the formulation and communication of plans; the measurement and appraisal of performance against plans; the determination of causes or deviations from plans; the actions to correct such deviation; and, if necessary, the reformulation of the plan. How would you categorize the actions taken at the Ansul Co. according to these steps?

As we'll see, it's impossible to define the points at which planning, implementation, and control begin and end in this process.

planning

For example, many marketing organizations utilize bottoms-up planning, in which the sales organization builds a forecast of future sales around the knowledge and expectations of individual sales representatives. This most important of all business planning statistics is developed on a bottoms-up basis to elicit commitment and support from the sales force of the plan that evolves from its

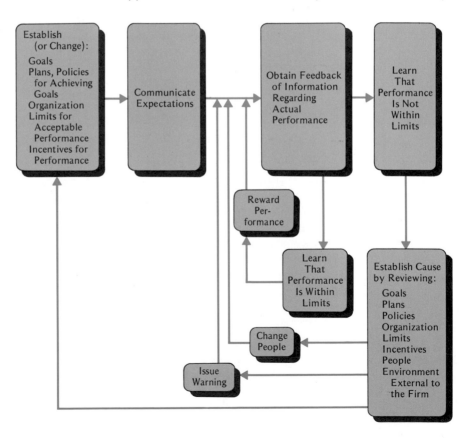

Figure 14-2. A framework for strategic planning and managerial control.

collective estimate. It is one way in which program implementation and control begins with the formulation of the sales plan.

Other organizations place major emphasis on top-down planning, in which the important inputs are provided by top marketing management on the basis of marketing research results, sales force inputs, a company's profit goals, and other information. Once formulated, plans are communicated to the lower ranks, including sales representatives.

(6)   Would bottoms-up or top-down marketing planning be likely to be more successful in a company in which sales representatives are paid a salary plus a significant bonus based on the extent to which their sales exceed individually set quotas?

Management by Objective. In recent years, MBO (management by objective) programs have become very popular in large and small organizations. Under this approach, each subordinate negotiates and signs a contract with his or her superior regarding financial and other objectives to be sought in a future period and the manner in which they will be achieved. In total, such contracts become the basis for an organization's operating plan. Progress toward these objectives is reviewed one or more times during the period in question, and final results are communicated by the subordinate to his or her superior along with explanations for deviations from the plan. The quality of both objectives and subsequent performance becomes the basis for performance appraisal and the negotiation of future MBO "contracts."

(7)
(8)   To what extent does MBO correspond to bottoms-up or top-down planning approaches? Assuming that MBO has been found to be very effective by many organizations, what does it suggest about the relative desirability of bottoms-up or top-down planning methods? To what extent were various of these approaches used by the Ansul Co. in planning its marketing intelligence program?
(9)

MBO has worked most successfully when the contract established between superior and subordinate truly represents the subordinate's as well as the superior's point of view.

Budgets. Budgets represent plans, ways of expressing the manner in which objectives will be achieved, and limits within which expenditures and other measures of effort are to be controlled. A budget for advertising expenditures in a marketing organization becomes an item in a corporate financial plan, an estimate of the advertising effort needed to achieve a sales goal, and a limit beyond which specific approval may be required for further expenditures. Typically, budgets are prepared in much the same way that other plans are formulated within a marketing organization.

communication

As we saw in our discussion of direct and indirect promotional efforts earlier in this book, effective communication requires not only the transmission of ideas and plans but also their reception and comprehension. And in the effective communication of plans and procedures, it may also be necessary to obtain

472

some evidence of acceptance and intended follow-through on the part of the recipient. To what extent does MBO satisfy these needs? To what extent did the methods used by the Ansul Co. conform with them?

measurement and appraisal of performance

What to measure is a frequent problem confronting many marketing managers. For example, should primary emphasis be placed on measures of sales efforts, such as the number and length of sales calls, or results, such as confirmed sales? Each approach may be more or less appropriate and effective under various conditions.

Would emphasis on the measurement and appraisal of sales efforts or results be more appropriate in a new firm introducing its first product, a complex

industrial cleaning device using new technology? In a firm compensating its sales force solely by means of salary? In firms emphasizing short-term or long-term sales performance?

Performance should be appraised on the basis of measures understood in advance by subordinates. There are often enough surprises in a performance appraisal without the rules of the game being changed as well. To rule out surprises and provide yet another basis for assessing managers, some organizations allow individuals to select measures of performance they feel are important to their jobs and their organization's success. These are then adjusted to conform with an over-all plan.

Too often, performance appraisals are based on measures either beyond the control of persons whose performances are being reviewed or on measures that are largely "automatic" in nature. For example, a new-product introduction may be impeded by the inability of a plant to supply enough of the product to marketing channels. Although it might be appropriate to use this event to appraise a product manager whose responsibility it may have been to coordinate new-product introduction efforts, it would be unfair to include a disappointing sales performance for the product in the review of a sales manager. In other cases, performance may be appraised on the basis of a manager's ability to adhere to a budget in a situation where budget items are predetermined by staffing limits and previously negotiated compensation limits.

Effective performance appraisals have been based on the simultaneous communication of results to subordinates and their supervisors. Under this approach, subordinates may be asked to evaluate and explain their own performance at the outset of an appraisal session. Such sessions may be held once or twice a year and often are timed to conform with the end of an operating period.

assessment of causes for deviant performance

Perhaps the first question facing us at this stage is "What constitutes deviant performance?" It is important, because only by sheer chance will actual performance reflect a plan or objective exactly. This requires that the limits around the objectives be established within which explanations of reasons for actual performance or corrective action will not be required. Such limits greatly reduce any largely wasted effort of tracing and explaining causes for small deviations from the plan in a marketing organization. They are the basis around which "exception reporting" programs are formulated. A feature of such programs is that they highlight only those dimensions of actual performance that are out of control or fall outside acceptable, preset limits. The latitude of performances that such limits allow may be related to the degree to which on-target performance is critical to a plan. For example, what relative degrees of latitude in setting limits around a target would you attach to a salesperson's sales performance as opposed to the quantity and quality of his or her Infoserv reports at the Ansul Co. in the situation described earlier in the chapter?

Before rewarding or penalizing individuals for performance that might deviate from a marketing plan, it is necessary to determine the extent to which such performance was within the control of the respective managers under review. For example, the recent energy shortages produced basic shifts in market patterns totally beyond the control of individual salespeople and even entire marketing organizations.

Similarly, many budget items may be sales related. At times when sales are greater than expected, salespeople may have to engage in more travel than originally planned in order to keep pace with customer inquiries. To restrict their travel to a predetermined budget figure would be foolish. As a result, many firms have adopted flexible budgets in which certain sales-sensitive budget cost items are adjusted to reflect sales results and actual expenditures compared with adjusted budget items.

It may be necessary for a manager to spend time observing a subordinate to assess reasons for subpar performance. Thus, a Doris Berendt at Philip Morris periodically travels with, observes, and attempts to correct ineffective behavior of members of her sales organization. To what extent would this be necessary, given the availability of information such as that presented in Figure 7-3, page 233?

corrective action

The nature of action required to correct a situation that is out of control will vary with the assessment of the cause. A general failure of sales representatives to file call reports or achieve sales quotas will be treated differently from behavior that is confined to one or two individuals. Generally disappointing results for a marketing plan may be related directly to depressed conditions in an important customer's business or in the economy in general. Or it may result from a defective product, ineffective advertising, insufficient distribution, or an inappropriately high price. Where this is the case, the strategy may have to be reformulated or a plan redrawn with lower goals. What did she mean when one marketing executive commented that "Failure to take corrective action and communicate it effectively constitutes an action of sorts"? What effect would this type of action have on a program of implementation and control?

Various means can be employed to reinforce desired behavior patterns so

474

that corrective action is made less necessary. Among the most important of these are the creation of incentives and the administration of rewards and penalties.

When we think of rewards and penalties, our thoughts often turn first to monetary compensation and promotions or demotions. But even though they won't buy much at the grocery store, other forms of reward such as attention, praise, or the opportunity to take part in personal development activities may be quite important for some marketing personnel.

Certain forms of compensation may not be thought of as involving a personal reward or penalty. For example, sales representatives compensated on a straight percentage commission of everything they sell know in advance what their compensation may be. Their reward is automatic and impersonal. Other forms, such as the popular quota-bonus approach in which compensation is paid in the form of a salary plus a bonus based on the extent to which a predetermined sales quota is met or exceeded, have a peculiar twist to them: while a salesperson's excellent performance may win a handsome bonus, it may lead to the raising of his or her sales quota for the following period.

(19) What do organizations relying heavily on automatic incentives such as straight commissions or semiautomatic quota-bonus approaches assume about the extent to which control over performance rests with the person being compensated? For this reason, many organizations have created pools of money for use in awarding discretionary bonuses based not only on a person's actual performance but also other factors thought to influence the performance. This type of reward, to the extent that it remains nonautomatic, often can be tied more effectively to sales or other marketing jobs with which two or more performance objectives may be sought simultaneously.

revision of plans

Where the causes for deviant performances are identified as the failure to anticipate a market shift or change in the environment of an inherently optimistic bias on the part of the planner, the plan may have to be revised in preference to a more localized corrective action. Where this is necessary, the cycle of planning, implementation, and control shown in Figure 14-2 begins anew.

Like any cycle, this one turns. And the fuel that keeps it turning is information provided by marketing information and decision programs.

marketing information and decision programs (MIDP)

In a sense, MIDP can be viewed as a refinery that converts data, corresponding to crude oil, into information, equivalent to refined fuel. As shown in Figure 14-3, this requires the creation of data files and the development of data-

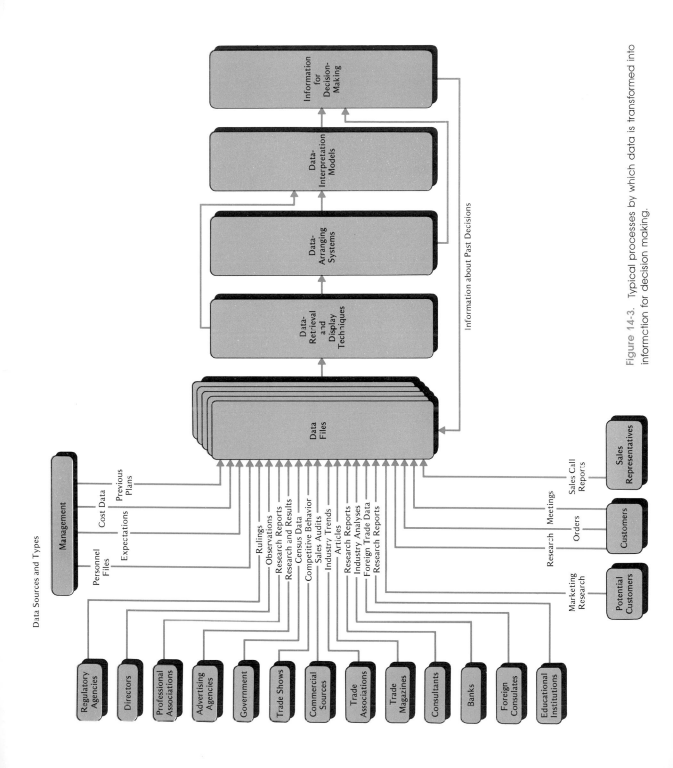

Data Sources and Types

Management		
Personnel Files	Expectations	Cost Data	Previous Plans

Regulatory Agencies — Rulings
Directors — Observations
Professional Associations — Research Reports
Advertising Agencies — Research and Results
Government — Census Data
Trade Shows — Competitive Behavior
Commercial Sources — Sales Audits
Trade Associations — Industry Trends
Trade Magazines — Articles
Consultants — Research Reports
Banks — Industry Analyses
Foreign Consulates — Foreign Trade Data
Educational Institutions — Research Reports

Data Files

Data-Retrieval and Display Techniques

Data-Arranging Systems

Data-Interpretation Models

Information for Decision-Making

Information about Past Decisions

Sales Representatives — Sales Call Reports
Customers — Meetings, Orders, Research
Potential Customers — Marketing Research

Figure 14-3. Typical processes by which data is transformed into information for decision making.

476

retrieval and display techniques, data-arranging systems, and perhaps data-interpretation models. Although formal marketing information systems date back at least to the late 1940s in organizations such as DuPont, only in recent years have a number of such programs been organized. This trend has been supported by the development of improved data-collection, retrieval, display, arranging, and analyzing techniques and devices.

creation of data files

In initiating a formal marketing information and decision program, the type of information to be collected and the manner in which it is to be organized and stored must be determined. This is especially important because of the wide variety and great volume of potentially useful information available from a number of sources, some of which are arrayed in Figure 14-3. No data is free. Sales call reports are generated at a cost. And even information that appears to be costless will no longer be free after it is processed for, and committed to, storage in the MIDP.

Marketing organizations with relative success in constructing MIDPs have based their selection of data for commitment to data files on the basis of the types of decisions frequently faced by management. Decisions give rise to questions, and more than one such question may relate to a particular decision, as suggested in Figure 14-4. The nature of such questions will suggest the manner in which data should be arrayed or arranged for decision-making purposes as well as the manner in which it should be stored in master data files. This in turn determines the nature of data to be collected in support of decisions of this type. For example, which items in the master data files listed in Figure 14-4 would have to be called on in a decision about whether to introduce a special deal for product X? Which possible arrangements of data (by now information) shown in Figure 14-4 should be produced for use in reaching this decision?

The extent to which data held on file can be used to deal with various questions posed by management depends on the degree to which the data are disaggregated, or broken into components. Disaggregation also may refer to the maintenance of data in a detailed time sequence as they are generated, so that new data are not combined with existing data. In recent years, improved data-retrieval and arranging techniques, with the capability of producing desired reports from detailed bits of information, have hastened the trend toward disaggregated, and hence more flexible files. To what extent could the data files listed in Figure 14-4 be disaggregated further?

data-retrieval and display techniques

Data-retrieval and display techniques range from manual to machine efforts in their orientation. The experience at General Mills describes the full range:

(20)

(21)

(22)

477

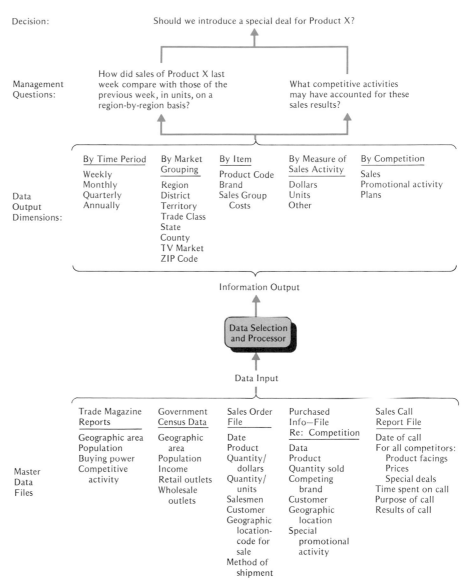

Figure 14-4. Influences on the design and maintenance of programs for translating internal sales data into management information.

Decision: Should we introduce a special deal for Product X?

Management Questions:

How did sales of Product X last week compare with those of the previous week, in units, on a region-by-region basis?

What competitive activities may have accounted for these sales results?

Data Output Dimensions:

By Time Period	By Market Grouping	By Item	By Measure of Sales Activity	By Competition
Weekly	Region	Product Code	Dollars	Sales
Monthly	District	Brand	Units	Promotional activity
Quarterly	Territory	Sales Group	Other	Plans
Annually	Trade Class	Costs		
	State			
	County			
	TV Market			
	ZIP Code			

Information Output

Data Selection and Processor

Data Input

Master Data Files

Trade Magazine Reports	Government Census Data	Sales Order File	Purchased Info—File Re: Competition	Sales Call Report File
Geographic area	Geographic area	Date	Data	Date of call
Population	Population	Product	Product	For all competitors:
Buying power	Income	Quantity/ dollars	Quantity sold	Product facings
Competitive activity	Retail outlets	Quantity/ units	Competing brand	Prices
	Wholesale outlets	Salesmen	Customer	Special deals
		Customer	Geographic location	Time spent on call
		Geographic location-code for sale	Special promotional activity	Purpose of call
		Method of shipment		Results of call

General Mills, like many packaged-goods marketers, purchases a large volume of market-tracking data such as store audit, warehouse withdrawal, and consumer panel data. The incompatibility of these "standard" reports with the specific desires of General Mills' marketing managers required the expenditure of a large amount of time and money in subsequent data analyses. Typical analyses included the comparison of actual sales to planned sales, actual sales to potential sales, sales to competitive sales, and increases in sales in response to marketing programs.

In the case of warehouse withdrawals, for example, such analyses were complicated because the data supplied by Selling Areas–Marketing, Inc. (SAMI)

. . . were fully itemized in four-week intervals with minimal analysis. The disaggregated mode of presentation, however, necessitated the use of many clerks to search through the computer print-out. This process itself actively discouraged . . . the formulation and testing of hypotheses.

An additional problem at General Mills was organizational conflict. Salespeople were using warehouse withdrawal data, and marketing managers were ignoring them for the reasons cited above. The additional cost of such data relative to their marginal benefits caused higher-level management to seriously question the continuation of the service.[2]

At about this time a marketing information and decision system called INF*ACT was devised to enable managers to gain access to data files by means of computer. Furthermore, they could obtain displays of accessed data by means of computer print-out or cathode ray tube (TV-like) display devices. This all required that large data bases be stored, updated, and made accessible at reasonable costs. Random-access disk storage greatly reduced costs, made retrieval time independent of file size, and significantly reduced search time, thereby improving the response time for typically impatient managers.

Even the ability to gain access to displayed file data won't encourage management use if the data can't be arranged in a form that becomes information for decision-making purposes. So INF*ACT was designed to allow managers to produce their own reports by requesting directly from the computer the items they wanted selected from data files, aggregated, and arranged prior to display. This required the use of a simple user-oriented computer language. But it allowed managers with different interests to make use of the same data files. Several years after the introduction of INF*ACT, the utilization of the system by General Mills' management averaged 150 hours per month, representing perhaps two thousand separate requests for information.

(23)

The designers of INF*ACT argue that even though marketing managers can identify the types of decisions they must make, few are able or willing to take the time to describe the process by which they make such decisions, thus making it impossible to anticipate specific questions they might ask. How, for example, is the nature of the decision-making process represented in Figure 14-4? As a result, they designed a system that

is not a complete MIS (management information system)—nor will it ever be. It is an evolving storage, retrieval, and analysis capability in a user-oriented environment. The way the user behaves in this environment will determine whether the data he can now retrieve will ever become information.[3]

data-interpretation models

Data-interpretation models go a step beyond data-arranging systems. They seek to provide analyses of information on which decisions can be based. Such analyses may involve the simulation of events, in which future costs or sales

[2]Reported in Lawrence D. Gibson, Charles S. Mayer, Christopher E. Nugent, and Thomas E. Vollmann, "An Evolutionary Approach to Marketing Information Systems," *Journal of Marketing*, **31** (April 1973), pp. 2–6.
[3]Ibid., p. 6.

under various assumptions and alternatives are calculated; or they may make use of optimization routines, in which the alternative producing the best outcome in relation to a specified objective is calculated and presented.

At the time the first data-interpretation models, involving techniques for assigning advertising expenditures to media in an optimum manner, were devised in the early 1950s, it was thought that they would be adopted widely by marketing management in the following decade. Such acceptance failed to materialize.

Restrictive assumptions had to be adhered to in optimizing models, removing them from the realm of reality for most managers. For example, early optimizing techniques developed for allocating advertising expenditures to media required that a manager assume that each additional increment of expenditure in a given medium would produce endlessly constant increases in market responses. Even though simulation techniques were less restrictive in their description of reality, they only represented the equivalent of large, complex calculators indicating results under various alternatives designated by management, with no assurance that the best alternative might be included among those studied.

Nevertheless, in recent years a growing number of data-interpretation models have been introduced in situations where criteria can be defined in advance for deciding which of a number of possible actions is the most appropriate under given circumstances. These range from relatively simple guidelines for day-to-day inventory control to models that provide direction for more strategic decisions.

Stock Control at L'eggs. In introducing its new hosiery product, packaged in egg-shaped containers and displayed on oval-shaped racks in supermarkets and other high-traffic outlets, L'eggs (Hanes Corp.) had a system developed to help it overcome chronic problems of out-of-stock and service problems in the hosiery business. This system tracked sales performance on a rack-by-rack basis, where two or more racks might be displayed in the same store. Resupply guidelines thus were provided to Hanes' route drivers for individual display units, relieving them of the job of deciding how much of each item to replace on a display.

Sales Control. In controlling day-to-day sales effort, a national food products manufacturer has established criteria regarding the length of time normally allowed between placement of orders by its major customers:

> These criteria are applied on a brand-by-brand basis. Failure of orders from specific customers to appear within the specified period results in an automatic signal for special sales action—a telephone call or an advancement in date of the next personal sales call, with special attention to the lagging brand. Wholesale slippage in the appearance of brand orders among a group of customers produces a "red alert" signal requiring closer examination and a consideration of special promotional action.[4]

---

[4] Kurt N. Schaffir and N. George Trentin, *Marketing Information Systems* (New York: Amacom, 1973), p. 33.

New-Product Introductions at Levi Strauss. In the sale of a new line of high-fashion garments for men and women called Fresh Produce, Levi Strauss several years ago chose to place the product only in retail outlets selected for their fashion-oriented clientele and their willingness to provide daily sale information on the items. Such information was monitored carefully, evaluated in terms of preestablished sales criteria, and used as the basis for a decision just six weeks after product introduction to (1) drop the item or (2) put the Levi name on it and expand its distribution to other of Levi's outlets.

A Competitive Bidding Model. In an example of greater strategic importance, a competitive bidding model was developed by the Operations Research group at RCA several years ago.[5] It relied entirely on information about five factors or judgments by marketing managers in preparing a bid. These factors included (1) the nature of the potential customer's bias for or against the bidder, (2) the sensitivity of the potential customer to a nominal price differential between competitors, (3) the probability that competitors would submit bids at various levels in relation to the prevailing market price, (4) the basic objectives of the bidder (for example, to maximize short- or long-term company profits, and (5) manufacturing and other costs for the product in question.

As a result, the model made use only of data supplied by knowledgeable managers. All it did was to reorganize management judgments in a way that made more systematic use of such judgments. It represented a simple, inelegant, and almost crude representation of the decision-making process.

Once developed, bids prepared by the model were compared with bids actually prepared and submitted by managers in seven cases. The results of this test are shown in Table 14-1. What do these results suggest, assuming that the lowest bid always wins in such situations? How would you account for them? What does this example suggest about the future possibilities for replacing marketing managers with computer-oriented models for data analysis?

(24)
(25)
(26)

Table 14-1 Seven Tests of the RCA Bidding Model

(1) Test	(2) Manager's Price Bid (in dollars)	(3) Model's Price Bid (in dollars)	(4) Lowest Competitive Bid (in dollars)	(5) Manager's Bid: % under (over) Lowest Competitive Bid	(6) Model Bid: % under Lowest Competitive Bid
1	44.53	46.00	46.49	4.2	1.1
2	47.36	42.68	42.93	(10.3)	0.6
3	62.73	59.04	60.76	(3.2)	2.8
4	47.72	51.05	53.38	10.6	4.4
5	50.18	42.80	44.16	(13.7)	3.1
6	60.39	54.61	55.10	(9.6)	0.9
7	39.73	39.73	40.47	1.8	1.8

* Source: Franz Edelman, "Art and Science of Competitive Bidding." *Harvard Business Review,* **43** (July–Aug. 1965), pp. 53–66. Quote on p. 56.

[5] Reported in Franz Edelman, "Art and Science of Competitive Bidding," *Harvard Business Review,* **43** (July–Aug. 1965), pp. 53–66.

A Forecasting Model.   Data-interpretation models have come into use at General Mills with the development of the INF*ACT system. For example, statistical models have been developed that allow managers to call for sales forecasts based on past sales trends and other factors. Similarly, sales results that might be expected from various levels of advertising expenditures can be produced on the basis of past relationships between sales and advertising expenditures under different sets of operating conditions for which data is retrieved from data files.

the information system as the basis for experimentation and modeling

A smoothly functioning information system producing dependable data can support experimentation and the development of decision aids. Professor David B. Montgomery describes two such examples:

> Anheuser-Busch . . . ran a series of market experiments over several years to assess sales response to advertising budgets and media. On the basis of these experiments they were able to cut their advertising budget from 14.8 million down to 10 million dollars. . . . It is something that management probably would not have had the nerve to do without having had it verified by the experiments. While reducing advertising, sales continued to grow faster than the industry and the per barrel cost of advertising [for the company's beer products] was dropped to one-half its previous level.[6]

The absence of a marketing information and decision system at Anheuser Busch would have delayed such experimentation by several years while a data base was being built to allow proper measurement and analysis.

The second example is that of a consumer-product manufacturer with a sales-call reporting system not unlike that of Ansul's Infoserv reports described earlier. The existence of this data base allowed the company to perform experiments to measure the response of sales-producing indicators to the frequency of sales calls very inexpensively. For example, one study examined the effect of call strategy on measures of product availability such as distribution (the proportion of total possible retail outlets in which the product had gained some shelf space), row count (the quantity of product on the shelf), shelf position (top shelf, eye level, bottom shelf, and so on), and out-of-stock conditions. Among the findings of this study were that both retail distribution and row count were influenced favorably by the frequency of sales calls on stores. Similarly, losses in distribution and row count could be recovered by restoring the original frequency of sales calls. Few of the gains achieved by doubling the frequency of sales calls from their original level were lost when the frequency was cut back to its original level. What types of decisions might be made on the basis of these findings?

(27)

(28)

What other types of experimentation could be conducted with the existence of data files such as those shown in Figure 14-4?

[6]David B. Montgomery, "Marketing Information and Decision Systems: Coming of Age in the 70s," Working Paper No. P-63 (Cambridge, Mass.: Marketing Science Institute, August, 1973), pp. 29–30.

the marketing manager's role in the implementation-and-control process

We have seen how marketing management helps to set organization goals and devise ways of achieving them. The nature of this planning activity determines in large measure the success of subsequent implementation and control. Middle marketing managers, including sales, advertising, marketing research, and product managers, are entrusted with much of the task of implementation and control. In this role, managers must serve as message centers or communication "filters." They must act as buffers between top management and the marketing operatives (salespeople, researchers, and others) who report to them. To a large degree it is their job to manage organizational conflict in such a way that it is a positive rather than a negative force in getting things done according to plan.

planning to foster congruence

The way in which organization strategies, organization policies, communications, performance measurements, and incentives are structured will determine the extent to which the actions of marketing operatives, such as salesmen, will at the same time (1) fulfill company strategies and policies, (2) constitute appropriate responses to "signals" from above, (3) represent "good" performance, and (4) result in rewards for the individual.

This simultaneous satisfaction of the needs of the organization, its managers, and marketing operatives can be termed *congruence*. It is illustrated in Figure 14-5. As suggested there, the various elements of a plan constitute forces that either push the circles, representing achievements, together or pull them apart. The bullseye in Figure 14-5 represents that part of an individual's "decision map" in which actions simultaneously achieve the greatest variety of purposes. What happens to the size of the bullseye, for example, if communications from top management to sales representatives do not reflect organization strategies and policies accurately?

(29)

Many firms, for example, measure the performance of advertising management in terms of the extent to which it works within a budget for advertising expenditures calculated on the basis of a sales forecast and a desired advertising-to-sales ratio. Thus, when sales fail to meet expectations, advertising expenditures that conform to the original budget may produce higher-than-desired advertising-to-sales ratios. Where efforts are made to conform to advertising-to-sales ratios and sales results fall below plan, advertising expenditures may be

(30)

reduced accordingly. How would you explain the effects of these performance measures in terms of congruence of results and the size of the bullseye shown in Figure 14-5? In which of these situations is less congruence achieved, assuming the organization's goal is to maximize profits through increased sales? What would you do to resolve this problem, common to many marketing organizations?

(31)

(32)

Similarly, performance measures and rewards for sales representatives often are based on the volume of products or services they are able to sell. To achieve

Figure 14-5. The decision map and the forces affecting the extent to which an operating action or decision creates mutual benefits for the individual sales representative, marketing management, and the organization. (Arrows pointing toward the center suggest forces increasing congruence and the size of the bullseye; arrows pointing from the center represent forces reducing congruence.)

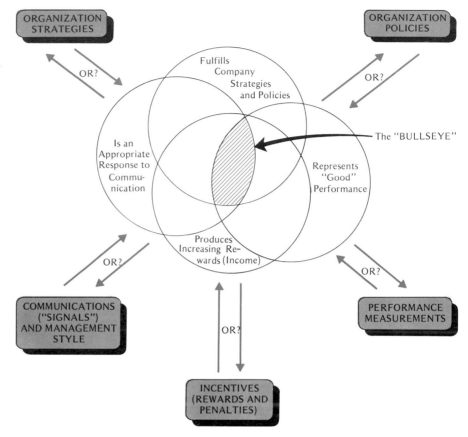

(33)

a large volume, products with both high and low profits to the organization may be sold indiscriminately. What can be done in a situation such as this to produce greater congruence between the organization's desire for greater profits and the individual's desire for greater rewards?

the marketing manager as filter and buffer

Marketing managers are central to an effective program of information and communication. In particular, they filter and interpret communications regarding strategies, policies, goals, performance measures, and incentives from top management downward. Similarly, they transmit signals about goals, results, and suggestions for change from marketing operatives upward, as suggested in Figure 14-6. They may have to make sure that the signals that are communicated through them don't get distorted, in the manner you perhaps have observed in playing the game, "pass it on," in which someone starts a message circulating in whispers around a group and the degree of distortion by the time it gets back to its originator provides the enjoyable climax. On the other hand, they may have

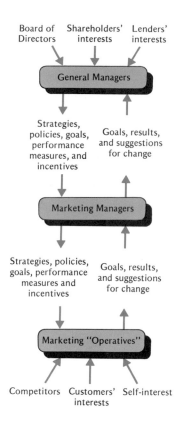

Figure 14-6. Marketing managers as communications links and buffers between general managers and marketing operatives.

to modulate the intensity of signals to insure that important messages are not ignored or unimportant ones exaggerated. This requires a feel for an organization, its goals, and the type of behavior most supportive of desired long-run performance. While some communications may be heavily interpreted, others directed either upward or downward may not be allowed to pass through the filter at all. As a top manager, would you prefer to see this filtering process at work on downward or upward communication? Would your view be different if you were a sales representative in the same organization?

(34)
(35)

managers of conflict

A major task of marketing managers is the management of conflict. Sources of conflict are suggested in Figure 14-6. Pressures exerted by boards of directors, shareholders, and lenders, for example, on top management produce one set of needs. Competitors, customers, and self-interest contribute to a totally different set of needs held by sales representatives and other marketing operatives.

We have discussed ways of reducing differences in these "sets of needs," and thereby reducing organizational conflict, through the structuring of organizational objectives and policies, communications, performance measure-

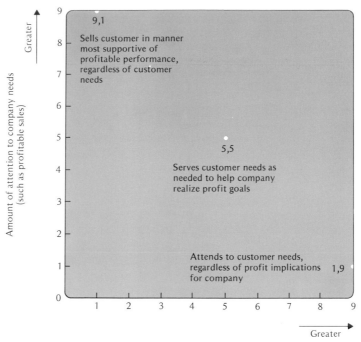

Figure 14-7. The sales grid, suggesting alternative ways in which sales representatives deal with conflicting loyalties to their customers and their companies. For a more complete discussion of this concept, see Theodore Levitt, *Marketing for Business Growth*, 2d. ed. (New York: McGraw-Hill, 1974), pp. 189–199.

ments, incentives, and even the organization itself. But it is idealistic to think that conflict can be eliminated and perhaps counterproductive to think that it should be. In fact, there may be types of conflict, such as that arising out of personal competition, that produce desirable results.

A common example of conflict in a sales organization is illustrated in Figure 14-7. How would you describe sales representatives falling at the two remaining empty corners in Figure 14-7? Good salespeople must identify with both their company and their customers, which at times creates difficult choices in order to serve the conflicting needs of each. A sales manager often must counsel sales representatives to avoid overemphasis on either company or customer needs to the detriment of the other. In terms of Figure 14-7, and recalling our discussion of Honeywell and Philip Morris in Chapter 7, what type of profile would be most desirable in the sale of computer systems? Cigarettes? How would you position Kim Kelley on this diagram, based on what you know about him from Chapter 7? As his sales manager, would you offer him any advice in his dealings with his company or his customers?

If conflict cannot or should not be eliminated, at least it should be managed. Do you know of anyone holding a job with the title of conflict manager? Probably not, and yet it may be the most critical of all marketing tasks and an important element in the implementation and control of marketing plans.

summary

The implementation-and-control process begins with the formulation of plans and policies and continues through the communication of expectations and the measurement and evaluation of performance against expectations. Finally, where necessary, it may require corrective action, including the possible reformulation of plans and policies. The degree of success achieved in implementing plans may depend on the extent to which those responsible for implementation are involved in the planning process, perhaps through a combination of top-down and bottoms-up planning.

Effective communication may require not only the transmission of ideas and plans, but also some assurance that they are received and comprehended.

Measurements of performance should be devised to encourage behavior that contributes to organization goals. For example, measures of sales effort may place less emphasis on immediate sales performance than measures of sales results and might be used most appropriately in organizations with goals of a similar nature.

Exception reporting, in which only performance that violates preset limits is highlighted for action, may greatly reduce the control task. It triggers investigations of causes of deviant performance and determinations of the appropriate corrective action to take in individual cases. It also may require alterations in the system of rewards to encourage desired behavior in the future.

The planning, implementation, and control of marketing programs requires a steady diet of marketing information and is assisted by marketing decision programs utilizing preset guidelines or analytic models. A marketing information and decision program comprises data files, in which data may be held in a disaggregated mode, much the way in which it is collected from sales invoices, sales call reports, shipping documents, and marketing research results. It requires some means for data retrieval and display. In the process, such a program may employ data-arranging systems that format desired data in a manner useful to management. In more modern programs, managers are given the opportunity, through interactive computer-related terminals, to specify the format in which they might want disaggregated data collected from the files and displayed before them on TV-like cathode ray tube display screens. In addition, combinations of items from data files may be analyzed by means of data-interpretation models ranging from those based on simple criteria that provide guidelines for day-to-day decision making to others utilizing simulation or optimizing techniques on which decisions of long-run strategic importance might be based.

Middle marketing managers, including sales, advertising, marketing research, and product managers, are entrusted with much of the task of implementation and control. In this role, managers must serve as message centers or communication filters. They must act as buffers between top management and the marketing operatives who report to them. To a large degree it is their job to manage organizational conflict in such a way that it is a positive rather than a negative force in getting things done according to plan. The circular nature of the process is emphasized by the importance of formulating plans that will include organization strategies, organization policies, communications, performance measurements, and incentives to encourage behavior that at the same time will fulfill company strategy and policies, provide a proper response to communications, represent good performance, and produce individual rewards.

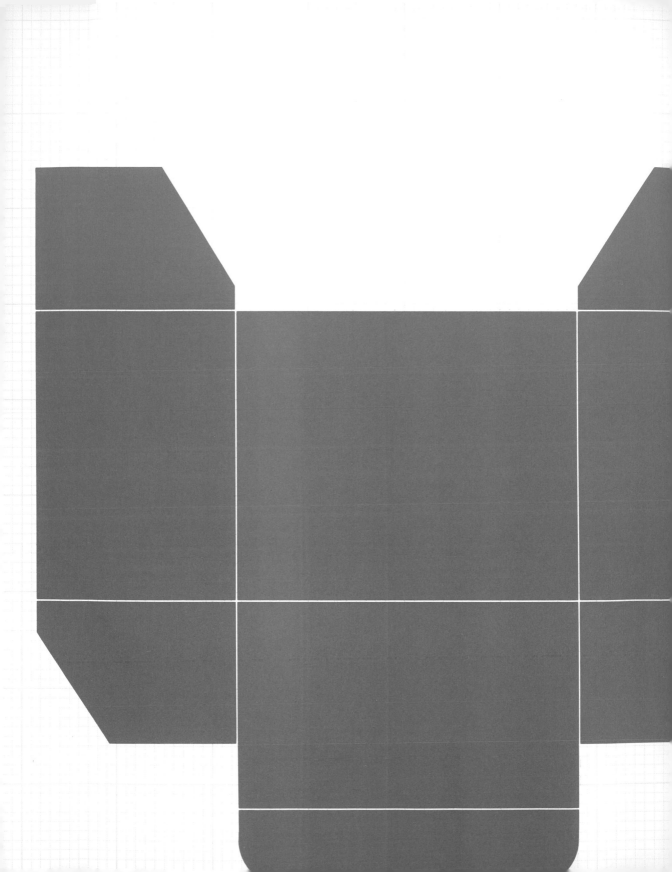

the output of
marketing
effort

15

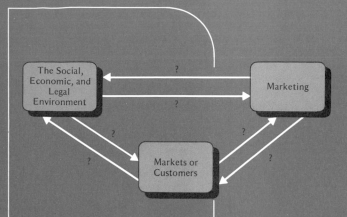

The Social, Economic, and Legal Environment

Marketing

?

?

?

?

?

?

Markets or Customers

More than half of the costs for the tangible goods (not including services) we buy goes for marketing effort. Putting it another way, more than half of the value of the tangible goods we buy is added by marketing effort. It depends on how you look at it.

What does our marketing effort produce? Of what economic value is it to a small firm introducing a new product? To a large firm attempting to maintain or increase an already large share of its market? Of what economic value is it to market segments (groups of consumers) that are increasing, constant, or declining in size? To customers who possess extensive product knowledge as opposed to those who do not?

What is the effect of marketing effort on society? Does it reflect or influence social values? Whatever the case, are these effects desirable? Are these effects primarily produced by advertising and selling activities? Or do we concentrate on these while overlooking the effects of distribution, pricing, and product development?

Is marketing effort a necessary ingredient for economic growth or does it represent a luxury indulged in by an affluent society?

To deal with these questions, we need to compare the inputs, in the form of time, money, and effort expended for marketing effort, with the results we gain from it as individuals, members of organizations, and members of society. To the extent that they are possible, international comparisons may help us gain further perspective on inputs to, and outputs from, marketing effort.

Up to now, we have concentrated on learning the craft of marketing. In these last two chapters we'll attempt to associate values with this craft.

Throughout this discussion, you'll be urged to answer the question: "Where do I stand?" If I've reached conclusions on this question, my intent is not to convey them to you. They are for you to determine.

the nature of the debate

According to a newspaper report several years ago, Harold Levine, president of the then Levine, Huntley, Schmidt advertising agency, was watching television one evening when he saw a film clip on a news program that aroused his ire.[1] The clip showed Betty Furness, New York City's commissioner of consumer affairs, in a supermarket comparing the prices of national and store (private) brands. The store brands were cheaper, and the commissioner went on to encourage consumers to try them.

"There's something wrong when statements like these aren't immediately answered by the advertising industry," Mr. Levine commented. "When a store brand is cheaper frequently it is inferior to a national brand. And in many instances where the quality is the same, the price is very often the same."[2]

When made aware of Mr. Levine's comment, Ms. Furness elaborated on her argument. "In many cases, store brands will either be as good as national brands or there won't be a . . . chance of telling the difference." Noting that her department's weighted weekly market basket of food for a family of four would be 9 per cent cheaper—$47.93 instead of $52.64—if only store brands were used, she added that such useage "is an excellent way to save some money."[3]

Additional facts that might or might not shed light on the validity of arguments made by Mr. Levine and Ms. Furness are (1) many store brands are packaged on the same machinery as national brands by national brand manufacturers and often contain the same ingredients, (2) some store brands at times may represent a national brand manufacturer's excess or "second-quality" product, (3) store brands often are sold at lower prices to consumers and higher margins to retailers, (4) that this seeming contradiction is made possible by the elimination of advertising and manufacturer selling costs for store brands, and (5) that less than 10 per cent of the value of all food items bought by consumers are store brands.

(1)
(2)

(3)

What does the exchange between Mr. Levine and Ms. Furness suggest regarding the output (or results) of marketing effort? How do consumers apparently perceive the relative values represented by manufacturers' and store brands of food products? How do you explain this?

This example is typical of many debates between marketers, consumers, advocates, economists, and others. Unfortunately, its distinguishing feature is that this particular debate was based on at least one fact. As we will see, most such debates reflect only opinion and perception, flimsy stuff on which to establish a basis for conclusion and action. Difficulties in establishing relevant facts suggest that the nature of the debate may change little in the future.

Perhaps it is useful to ask ourselves just how significant these debates are. One approach to this matter is a determination of the significance of marketing efforts in the United States and in other economies.

---

[1] This vignette is both quoted from and based on Leonard Sloane, "Advertising: On Store Brands," *New York Times* (Aug. 9, 1973), p. 57.

[2] Ibid.

[3] Ibid.

the level of marketing effort

Various imperfect measures of marketing effort in the United States economy can be cited. They include estimates of relative costs of marketing activities and the proportion of the work force engaged in marketing activities. These can be termed inputs to marketing at the national, or macroeconomic, level.

costs

Estimates of the proportion of consumers' expenditures (purchases at retail) absorbed by marketing activities at different points in time vary from 41.7 per cent to 58.9 per cent of the total. There are as many different methods and results as there are estimators. One set of rough estimates of trends in selected marketing costs for retailing, wholesaling, and manufacturers' (and producers') transportation, inventory carrying, selling, and other marketing, advertising, and packaging between 1950 and 1973 are presented in Figure 15-1. Because of the approximations used in arriving at these estimates, they are of use to us only in obtaining a general idea of the relative magnitude of various expense categories and the way in which they have behaved in relation to personal consumption expenditures.

(4)   What do the trends shown in Figure 15-1 suggest to you?

employment

One major study of historical trends in employment engaged in distribution concluded that in 1950 there were 407 persons engaged in commodity distribution for every 1,000 involved in commodity production in the United States.[4] This represented a nearly fivefold increase in the ratio since 1870, when only 88 persons were engaged in distribution for every 1,000 in production.

The Department of Labor has estimated that there were 9.2 million people engaged in selling alone in 1973, or about one person out of every eight employed in all jobs. Of these, nearly 60 per cent were retail sales clerks.[5] In earlier pages of this book, we have come into contact with retailers, wholesalers, advertising account executives, salespersons, sales managers, product managers, and other more general marketing managers. They have commanded salaries ranging from several thousand to several hundred thousand dollars per year.

[4] Harold Barger, *Distribution's Place in the American Economy Since 1869* (Princeton: Princeton University Press, 1955), pp. 7–8.
[5] *Statistical Abstract of the United States* (Washington, D. C.: Bureau of the Census, Department of Commerce, 1974), p. 351.

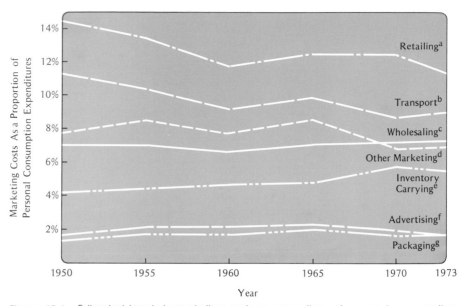

Figure 15-1. Estimated trends in marketing costs as proportions of personal consumption expenditures, 1950–1973. (a) National Income originating in retailing. (b) A portion of intercity transport of the types most likely engaged in by nonretailing and nonwholesaling enterprises, adjusted to reflect both private (manufacturers') and for-hire transport. (c) National income originating in wholesaling. (d) Calculated on the basis of 50 percent of all persons employed in nonretail selling (to adjust for wholesale salespeople) multiplied by a multiple of the average wage for nonretail salespeople. (e) Based on annual inventory carrying-cost factors for both manufacturers' and farmers' inventories depending in part on average short-term interest rates; annual cost factors for manufacturers' inventories ranged from 16.7 percent (in 1950) to 27.7 percent (in 1970) of the average value of inventory on hand, and annual cost factors for farmers' inventories ranged from 9.2 percent (in 1950) to 20.2 percent (in 1970) of the average value of their inventory on hand. (f) National advertising billings, based on the assumption that the volume of national advertising by retailers and wholesalers is balanced by the volume of local advertising by manufacturers; Sources: Compiled by McCann-Erickson Advertising Agency, Inc. for publication in *Printer's Ink*, 1940–1966, *Marketing/Communications*, 1967–1969, and *Advertising Age*, 1970 to present. (g) Calculated as 50 percent (the assumed national income factor rate) of packaging materials consumed, under the assumption that this approximates their labor and capital costs and provides as well for the design of graphics; Source: "Encyclopedia and Planning Guide," *Modern Packaging*, 12 (Dec. 1974). The source for information not otherwise documented is *Statistical Abstract of the United States* (Washington, D. C.: Department of Commerce, Bureau of the Census, 1974).

what does marketing effort produce?

Is the fruit of marketing effort sweet or bitter? Of the many dimensions on which we could explore this question, we'll concentrate on perhaps the two most important, economic and social. Throughout the discussion, every attempt will be made to distinguish fact from interpretation.

494

economic issues

Economic arguments in support of marketing effort identify it as a major contributor to a product's value, an essential ingredient in a nation's economic development, the means of delivering a higher standard of living at a lower average price for goods, an important means of competition, a means of achieving more efficient use of the world's resources, and a relatively efficient means of educating customers to evaluate alternative offerings rationally. Opponents of marketing practices cite it as a frequent cause of excessive costs that must be defrayed by higher-than-necessary prices, a parasitic by-product of economic development, an area of duplicated effort and great waste in a highly developed economy, a deterrent to existing or potential competitors, detrimental to the use of resources by encouraging customers to overspend and overconsume, and a means of manipulating customers to make uneconomic choices in their purchases.

Marketing Cost and Value Added. The most generally accepted measure of value is that price a customer is willing to pay for a product or service. When defined in this manner, value is a reflection of customer need, available alternatives, purchasing power, and perceived product qualities.

For years we have measured the value added by manufacturing processes as the difference between the value of finished products at the plant and the sum of costs for raw materials, components, energy, and purchased services. Few people question the "productive" nature of these activities; they often go by the very name *production,* an inherently honorable activity. The possibly misleading implication of this is that marketing activities are nonproductive. To counter this conclusion, efforts have been made in recent years to calculate the value added to goods and services by marketing activities.

Few question the contention that certain marketing activities add value to goods and services. For example, marketing research, often including inputs from sales personnel, contributes to greater form utility in goods by encouraging the design of products and services to meet customers' needs. Transportation, wholesaling, and retailing efforts create place utility or value, making goods available where they are wanted. Storage, either by manufacturers, wholesalers, retailers, or customers, enhances the time utility and value of goods, and promotional efforts provide information to customers leading to purchase decisions that are said to produce greater ownership utility or value.

It is perhaps the definition and determinants of value added by marketing that raise the greatest questions. Value added by marketing usually is measured in terms of the difference between the sale price for a product and the sum of the cost of goods sold (including value added by manufacturing activities), purchased services and utilities, and financing costs. This method of measuring value added is illustrated in Figure 15-2. Here, tea bags labeled with retailers' private brands move from a manufacturer to consumers through large retail grocery chains. Marketing value added can be measured at the manufacturer's, transport carriers', and retailers' levels in the channel of distribution. When accumulated, it amounts to 94 cents per pound, or about 41 per cent of the ultimate sale price of the product.

In this example, what happens to marketing value added, according to the accepted definition, if our tea bag manufacturer decides to raise its prices to

Figure 15-2. Marketing value added in a channel of distribution for a retailer's (private label) brand of tea bags.

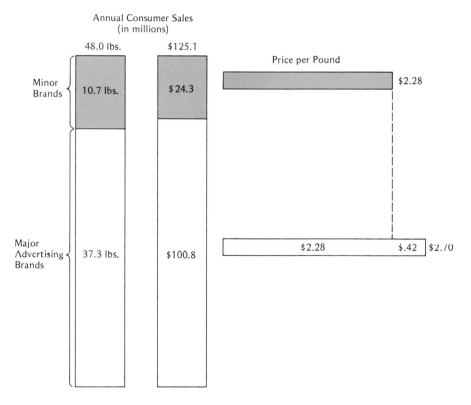

	Manufacturer	Transport Carrier	Retailer	Consumer =	Entire Channel
Sales (or delivered) price per pound	$1.65	$1.83	$2.28		$2.28
Less cost of goods sold	1.15	1.65	1.83		1.15
Less cost of purchased services	.15	.02	.02		.19
Value added by marketing activities	$ .35	$ .16	$ .43		$ .94

(6)

retailers by 20 cents per pound (to $2.03), inducing a retail price increase of 25 cents per pound to $2.53, and assuming no changes in manufacturing or marketing costs? Has marketing value been added?

Or consider the situation shown in Figure 15-3, based on actual data collected by the A. C. Nielsen Co. For a recent year, retailers sold 10.7 million pounds of private label (largely unadvertised) tea bags at an average price per pound of —you guessed it—$2.28. At the same time they sold 37.3 million pounds of major advertised manufacturers' brands at an average price of $2.70 per pound. How much value was added by advertising in this example? To what

(7) (8)

Figure 15-3. Relative sales and prices of major advertised and minor brands of tea bags in a recent year. Source: A.C. Nielsen Co.

Annual Consumer Sales (in millions)

48.0 lbs. $125.1

Minor Brands   10.7 lbs. $24.3

Price per Pound $2.28

Major Advertising Brands   37.3 lbs. $100.8 $2.28 $.42 $2.70

extent does your conclusion depend on whether tea bag manufacturers spent $10 million or $20 million to advertise their brands?

This phenomenon has led some to conclude that yet a fifth form of utility or value, psychic value, is added to many products by marketing effort. As the president of the Seven-Up Co., Ben Wells, put it recently, in describing the objectives of his company's marketing efforts:

> All this is directed toward the consumer. It is to convince the consumer that she is getting a better value in 7-Up than she will in some other drink, known brand or no-brand. The known brand might cost as much as 7-Up. The no-brand would be cheaper. . . . She would get more for the money in the no-brand.
>
> She knows that as far as the product is concerned, its quality is unimpeachable. That's what advertising does for a quality product. . . . She also feels that this product fits her personality—it has an affinity for her.
>
> Now she might get that kind of identity feeling with another known brand, but she would never get it from a no-brand: that's just a commodity; to buy it only because it is cheaper may give her satisfaction as a shrewd manager of the household budget, but none whatever as a provider of the best in food and drink for her family and herself.[6]

(9)

(10)

In an age when a smaller and smaller proportion of income is spent to meet the basic needs for a modest standard of living, is it possible that the importance of psychic utilities or values will continue to grow? What does this suggest for the relative importance of advertising in the marketing strategy of a manufacturer of consumer products?

Marketing and Economic Development.   Comparative data for various countries can be used to assess the relationship of marketing effort and economic development. Several measures of marketing activity for selected countries are presented in Table 12-3, page 430. They suggest that the United States has and uses more marketing resources for retailing, wholesaling, commercial transportation, and commercial communication than any other country in the world. Furthermore, it has the highest per capita GNP. The relationship of gross domestic product per capita and percentage of commercial (wholesaling and retailing) employment in the total labor force is shown for selected non-Communist countries in Figure 15-4.

(11)

These are facts. Do you conclude from them that marketing effort contributes to economic development or is an activity that firms in developed countries turn to, knowing that customers are able and willing to pay for it? A well-known management philosopher, Peter Drucker, does not hesitate to draw a conclusion:

> marketing is the most important "multiplier" of [less developed countries]. . . . It is in itself in every one of these areas, the least developed, the most backward part of the economic system. Its development, above all others, makes possible economic integration and the fullest utilization of whatever assets and productive capacity an economy already possesses. It mobilizes latent economic energy. It contributes to the greatest needs: that for the rapid development of entrepreneurs and managers.[7]

[6]"Marketer of the Year Wells Tells Uncola Story, Blasts Consumerists," *Marketing News* (April 1, 1974), p. 8.

[7] Peter F. Drucker, "Marketing and Economic Development," *Journal of Marketing,* **22** (Jan. 1958), pp. 252–259. Quote on p. 253.

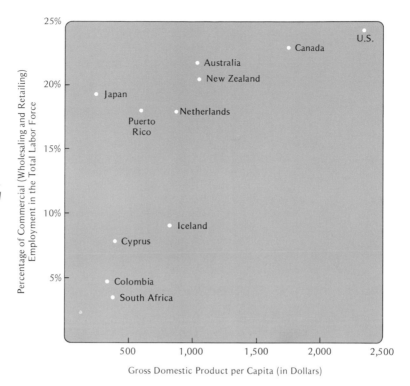

Figure 15-4.
Relationships between gross domestic product per capita and the percentage of commercial (wholesaling and retailing) employment in the total labor force, selected countries. *Source:* Lee E. Preston, "The Commercial Sector and Economic Development," In Reed Moyer and Stanley C. Hollander, eds., *Markets and Marketing in Developing Economies,* (Homewood, Ill.: Irwin, 1968), pp. 9–23, especially p. 16.

There are times, of course, when there is little doubt about the basic importance of an efficient marketing system for economic development. For example, the inability to distribute adequate food supplies before they spoil to a starving Indian or African population is testimony to the part that marketing efforts can play in supporting economic development at the most basic level.

Marketing and the "Standard of Living." In a general sense, the standard of living is equated to measures of economic development such as gross domestic product per capita. More specifically, we may tend to equate the standard of living with costs of products and services in relation to their value, the ease with which they can be acquired, and the extent to which varieties and quantities of product and service offerings are designed to meet customer needs.

Marketing efforts can be employed to stimulate demand for a particular product, create greater economies of scale in its manufacture and physical distribution, and thereby reduce the end unit cost and, hopefully, price to customers. Such efforts may include price reductions, the extension of credit, the use of a greater number of sales outlets more convenient to customers, new product modifications based on sales feedback, and increasing expenditures for direct sales or advertising. These efforts may produce greatly different results for entire industries as opposed to competing firms in those industries.

A useful marketing strategy for an individual firm in an industry may not achieve lower costs (or higher profits) for an industry, particularly in situations where it is not possible to enlarge the total market by stimulating primary

498

demand. This is illustrated by the decisions that might be made by firms A and B (which might be just as well be envisioned as the manufacturers of Clorox and Purex, major competing brands of household bleach, respectively) to advertise their competing products in a region of the United States under prior expectations shown in Table 15-1. As a product manager for Clorox with this view of the market, would you advocate that your firm spend $5 million or $7 million for advertising? As product manager for Purex, what would your answer be to your counterpart's decision on behalf of Clorox? What would the net effect of these two decisions be on profits (and long-term prices)? What actions would you suggest to avoid this situation?

At a more aggregate, or industry level, are marketing efforts more likely to lead to reduced costs in industries with products in an early or late stage in the product life cycle? Or with products with high or low fixed manufacturing costs?

Marketing efforts are thought by some to stimulate latent desires for "the better things of life" and make it possible, by means of readily available consumer credit, for individuals to enjoy a higher standard of living sooner than they might without such credit. The relationship between personal financial assets (other than equity in homes and other tangible goods) and various types of personal debt is shown in Figure 15-5. What does it suggest about the trend in the extent to which Americans have availed themselves of opportunities to purchase durables on credit?

The opposing view is that marketing efforts, and advertising in particular, create desire and demand, and in fact encourage consumers to buy products they may not need, at least in the eyes of the critics. Once created, such desires often can be fulfilled only through the incursion of debt. Economist John Kenneth Galbraith offers a summary of this view with an interesting twist:

> Advertising and salesmanship—the management of consumer demand—are vital for planning in the industrial system. At the same time, the wants so created insure the services of the worker. Ideally, his wants are kept slightly in excess of his income. Compelling inducements are then provided for him to go into debt. The pressure of the resulting debt adds to his reliability as a worker.[8]

To which of these sets of views do you subscribe? Is there a middle view?

The marketing concept stresses the basic purpose of marketing effort as that of detecting and satisfying customer needs. How then could there be an

Table 15-1   Dilemma for Marketing Executives in a Hypothetical Two-Firm Oligopoly

		Expected Profits under Various Levels of Advertising for Purex Bleach	
		$5 Million in Advertising	$7 Million in Advertising
Expected Profits under Various Levels of Advertising for Clorox Bleach	$5 million in Advertising	Clorox's profits = $11.0 million Purex's profits = $11.0 million	Clorox's profits = $ 7.0 million Purex's profits = $13.0 million
	$7 million in Advertising	Clorox's profits = $13.0 million Purex's profits = $ 7.0 million	Clorox's profits = $ 9.7 million Purex's profits = $ 9.7 million

[8] John Kenneth Galbraith, *The New Industrial State* (Boston: Houghton, 1967), p. 273.

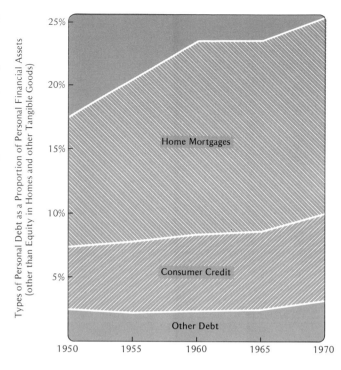

Figure 15-5. Trends in the relationship of personal debt to financial assets (other than equity in homes and other tangible goods) in the United States, 1950–1970. *Source: Statistical Abstract of the United States* (Washington, D.C.: Bureau of the Census, Department of Commerce, 1973), pp. 456 and 459.

Types of Personal Debt as a Proportion of Personal Financial Assets (other than Equity in Homes and other Tangible Goods)

Home Mortgages

Consumer Credit

Other Debt

argument about the extent to which marketing effort encourages the development of products and services of the type and quantity that do so? Much of the debate centers on the extent to which marketing emphasizes primary product functions (such as the economy of basic transportation offered by an automobile) as opposed to secondary product functions (such as automobile styling) in differentiating and promoting competing products.

As more and more competing products perform primary functions in a manner that meets the expectations of customers, it is possible that marketers are encouraged to turn to secondary functions as a means of appealing to prospective buyers. How do prospective buyers view this change in emphasis? Most marketing research studies suggest that for many product categories, including automobiles, substantial numbers of buyers use so-called secondary product functions as the means of deciding among competing products that all appear to perform primary functions equally well.

There is a tendency for critics of marketing's emphasis on secondary product functions to equate "important" with primary product functions and nonpsychic values and to equate "unimportant" with secondary product functions and psychic values. Defenders argue that what is important must be decided by each customer.

Critics, however, complain that it is precisely the emphasis on secondary product functions, appealing to status-seeking customers, that produces the type of consumption patterns that are not in the best interests of consumers, particularly those with limited means.

Economists rely primarily on the presence of competition rather than the marketing concept as assurance that short- and long-term market needs will be met. This suggests that we should consider the relationships between marketing effort and competition.

Marketing and Competition. To the extent that marketing efforts provide opportunities for the entry of new companies or new products, as some claim, they may encourage competition, innovation, efficiency, and lower prices. Others argue that marketing efforts, to the extent that they create customer or market franchises or loyalties, restrict opportunities for the entry of new firms or products, thus discouraging competition and all the good things it represents.

Explorations of the relationship between marketing and competition have branched in several directions. In Figure 15-6 the nature of this work is summarized. At various times it has attempted to measure relationships between marketing efforts and profits, the ease of entry into an industry, the concentration of firms within an industry, the number of competitors within an industry, competition, innovation, efficiency, and prices. A brief consideration of the results of several of the better-known studies of this nature may help us draw some conclusions of our own.

Figure 15-6.
Relationships of arguments explored by researchers that attempt to relate marketing effort to competition.

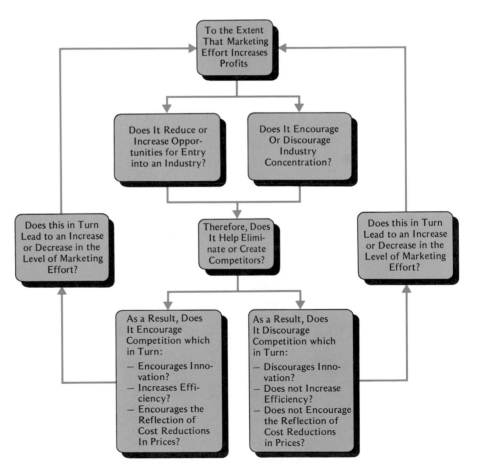

In one of the most extensive studies of the relationship between advertising expenditures, profits, and opportunities for entry, economists William Comanor and Thomas Wilson prepared the data shown in Figure 15-7. From it and related data, they concluded that (1) high industry outlays for advertising lead directly to high long-run profits, (2) the presence of restricted entry conditions can be inferred when high profits are maintained through time, and (3) therefore, high advertising levels serve to restrict entry.[9] Would you draw the same conclusions from data such as that presented in Figure 15-7?

(21)

In his study of twenty American industries, economist Joe S. Bain concluded that product differentiation was "of at least the same general order of importance . . . as economies of large-scale production and distribution"[10] in giving established market leaders a price or cost advantage over rivals. He estimated that through their product differentiation advantages, established industry leaders could sustain prices relative to potential new entrants on the order of 5 per cent higher for ten years or 10 per cent higher for five years in six of his twenty industries: cigarettes, automobiles, typewriters, "quality" fountain pens, liquor, and tractors. He concluded that advertising was the single most important basis for maintaining these differentials, and that only larger firms could achieve the saturation level required for certain advertising, obtain quantity discounts for advertising expenditures, and maintain an advertising budget over a long enough period of time to achieve the full cumulative effects of the effort.

(22)

Whether price or cost advantages gained in part through large advertising expenditures by market leaders have discouraged entry, contributed to concentration, and reduced the number of competitors is a matter for debate. What conclusions would you reach based on information in Figure 15-7 and in Table 3-7, pages 88–89?

In a study of 352 firms on *Fortune's* 1955 list of the 500 largest industrial corporations, economist F. M. Scherer found that the very largest firms realizing 19.9 per cent of the total sales for the entire sample of firms employed only 9.7 per cent of the total research and development personnel and registered only 10.4 per cent of the total patents granted for inventions in 1959, four years later, to the sample of firms. As a result of this and other explorations, he concluded that

> a little bit of bigness—up to sales levels of roughly $75 million to $200 million in most industries—is good for invention and innovation. But beyond the threshold further bigness adds little or nothing, and it carries the danger of diminishing the effectiveness of inventive and innovative performance.[11]

Although this work may shed light on certain of the relationships diagrammed in Figure 15-6, it says nothing about others. For example, what is the relationship between the number of competitors and the intensity of competition? Here we run into problems of measuring the intensity of competition. Identical prices for competing products, for example, may represent a highly competitive situation

[9]William Comanor and Thomas Wilson, *Advertising and Market Power* (Cambridge, Mass.: Harvard U.P., 1974), pp. 130–132.

[10]Joe S. Bain, *Barriers to New Competition* (Cambridge, Mass.: Harvard U.P., 1956), pp. 142–143 and 216.

[11]F. M. Scherer, *Industrial Market Structure and Economic Performance* (Chicago: Rand McNally, 1970), pp. 360–361.

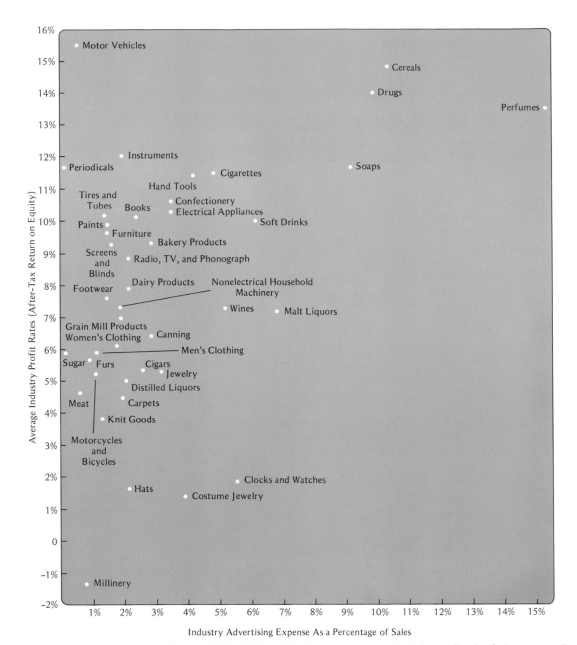

Figure 15-7. Relationships between average industry profit rates (return on equity after tax) and advertising-to-sales ratios for selected consumer goods industries in the United States, 1954–1957. *Source:* William Comanor and Thomas Wilson, *Advertising and Market Power* (Cambridge, Mass.: Harvard U. P., 1974), pp. 134–135.

to competing managements but an almost complete lack of competition achieved through "conscious parallelism" in decision making in the eyes of critics.

(23)
(24)

(25)

Most analyses of the relationships between marketing and competition use advertising expenditures as the measure of marketing effort, mainly because they are the most readily available measure. How valid do you think this measure is? Do you think the same relationships might be found between the ease of entry and concentration, for example, and other types of marketing effort such as price reductions, increases in the number of outlets through which an existing product is sold, or improvements in the design of an existing product? Because all of these efforts represent methods of competition, what does this say about the effect of current competition on future competition?

The diagram in Figure 15-6 suggests a two-way relationship between marketing effort and competition: that the level of marketing effort also may be a direct result of the level of competition and a measure of its intensity.

Marketing and the Use of Resources.   Marketing critics cite its preoccupation with promoting consumption. The degree to which it has succeeded can be measured in the large volume of unnecessary expenditures for products that largely go unused, often leading to a subsequent problem of disposal. Not only is such conspicuous and otherwise excessive consumption wasteful of increasingly scarce energy and other resources, but at times it can be harmful to the consumer as well.

In defense of marketing and the deployment of resources, it is argued that marketing can't bear all the blame for satisfying customer desires. If in fact potential customers become better educated, in part through marketing efforts, they will become more intelligent buyers. At such time as conservation of resources becomes sufficiently important, they will be able to apply their knowledge in buying and consuming accordingly. Finally, by means of the direct application of marketing effort, consumers can be instructed in ways of reducing their consumption and conserving resources. Thus, at times when energy has been in particularly short supply, petroleum refiners and marketers in their advertising have urged motorists to drive at efficient speeds, and utilities have instructed customers how to reduce the use of electrical power. We'll have more to say about this in the next chapter.

Marketing As an Efficient or Wasteful Device.   While much of marketing effort is labor-intensive, involving the transmittal of information from one person to another, advertising is to marketing what automation is to production. It provides a vehicle for the low-cost communication of information, impressions, and persuasive messages. Its effectiveness in communicating messages, often leading to increased sales, has been established time and again. How else do we explain the preoccupation with advertising as opposed to other types of marketing efforts in the research of various economists, given the relationship of advertising expenditures to all value added by marketing, as shown in Figure 15-1?

Poorly targeted marketing effort is properly attacked as being wasteful. However, the charge is often extended to marketing effort that is effectively targeted, but that makes use of advertising that inevitably reaches a certain percentage of irrelevant recipients. In fact, many of the complaints regarding television advertising originate from segments of the market other than those for which the advertising was targeted. Thus, the great strength of advertising, gained through the use of mass media, at once becomes its greatest weakness. It is perhaps the most difficult of all elements of the marketing mix to control.

The preoccupation with advertising as opposed to other types of marketing effort extends into the second major topic of this chapter, the social impact of marketing effort.

social issues

Marketing activities have given rise to a number of questions of social significance. Among them are questions of whether marketing influences or reflects social values, employs socially desirable methods, usefully stimulates customer aspirations, influences the availability and quality of communication media in a desirable manner, is suitable for all customer segments (particularly children), and encourages the efficient use of limited resources.

But before turning to these issues, it is necessary to raise several even more basic questions: In attempting to persuade, does marketing effort deceive? If so, does such practice establish a kind of ethical standard for those who are exposed to deceptive marketing practices? Are there cases in which the worthy nature of the objective may justify even questionable marketing methods?

Marketing Means. There is little question that perhaps the most basic objective of marketing effort is to persuade: to influence a potential "customer" favorably toward a person, product, service, or idea. This objective gives natural rise to a temptation on the part of marketers to engage in questionable practices, particularly those that may in fact be deceptive. And most often, we are not talking about practices that are grossly deceptive, because there is a strong belief that in order to be effective, marketing effort in general and promotional effort in particular must be believable. Thus, we are often confronted with borderline cases involving subjective judgments about whether reasonable members of the audience for which a particular effort is intended would be deceived.

For example, toy demonstrations on television may show additional equipment or accessories not included in the advertised price. Or an advertisement for an LTD Ford may correctly claim that the LTD is quieter than a glider when, in fact, the noise level inside a glider is a relatively high 85 decibels. What criteria would you establish for determining whether or not a marketing practice is deceptive? By your criteria, how would you judge either of these situations?

Studies have shown that most recipients of advertising messages, for example, are generally quite cynical about their contents. The believability of most such messages is very low. If this is true, it may raise serious questions about the effectiveness of much marketing effort. It leads critics to conclude that this constant exposure to messages with low credibility teaches recipients socially unacceptable values. Defenders of marketing, however, maintain that credibility is a highly subjective matter and may be confused with the level of interest in marketing messages themselves.

(26)

(27)

Concerns about the social effects of marketing methods have, of course, produced a great number of federal and state regulations designed to protect recipients of marketing messages. Thus, the FTC requires that the precise contents of a product, whether a toy or not, offered for sale for a stated price be displayed in the message promoting it or a disclaimer be included in cases in which reasonable recipients might be misled. As was the case with the Ford LTD ad, the FTC can, by mutual consent or a restraining order, require that a message regarded as deceptive be discontinued. At the state level, laws allowing consumers to retract without penalty agreements made with door-to-door salesmen up to three days after entering into such agreements are becoming quite common.

Marketing Ends. This brings us to an interesting question. Are there times when the marketing ends, in the form of the person, product, service, or idea being marketed, justify the means? Or conversely, should marketing effort, regardless of its credibility and quality, be denied to products thought to be undesirable or controversial?

These questions are brought into focus by matrix cells 2 and 3 in the diagram in Figure 15-8.

(28) For example, would you support the use of techniques designed to persuade by any means short of physical force to promote (1) a political candidate whom you oppose, (2) a political candidate whom you strongly endorse, (3) a brand of frozen peaches, (4) a new pain remedy, or (5) contributions to the Heart Fund?

Lest we become too moralistic about marketing methods, Daniel J. Boorstin, the historian, reminds us that

> Never was there a more outrageous or more unscrupulous or more ill-informed advertising campaign than that by which the promoters for the American colonies brought settlers here. Brochures published in England in the seventeenth century, some even earlier, were full of hopeful overstatements, half-truths, and downright lies, along with some facts which nowadays surely would be the basis for a restraining order from the Federal Trade Commission. Gold and silver, fountains of youth, plenty of fish, venison without limit, all these were promised, and of course some of them were found. It would be interesting to speculate on how long it might have taken to settle this continent if there had not been such promotion by enterprising advertisers.[12]

Figure 15-8. Relationships among perceptions of products and marketing methods, marketing ends and means.

		Nature of Products or Services (Ends)	
		Desirable	Undesirable
Nature of Marketing Effort (Means)	Above Reproach	(1)	(3)
	Questionable	(2)	(4)

[12] Daniel J. Boorstin, *Democracy and Its Discontents: Reflections on Everyday America* (New York: Random, 1974), pp. 26–27.

In January 1971 the FTC began its enforcement of a law prohibiting cigarette advertising on television. This was the first explicit regulation denying a marketing medium to a product thought to be harmful to health, or otherwise undesirable. Other industries, such as distillers of hard liquor products, long had voluntarily refrained from making use of television and radio media for advertising. But the regulation of cigarette advertising raised questions about whether there were other products that similarly should be restricted, regardless of the accuracy and lack of deception employed by marketers on their behalf. Among others, the use of television for advertising potentially unsafe toys has been criticized. Would you support the extension of specific regulations prohibiting the use of certain marketing methods for other products? Should this type of regulation be extended to include controversial ideas, such as birth control?

(29)
(30)

Up to now, we have considered some questions concerning the use of marketing methods at times to mislead or deceive potential customers. In discussing the remaining issues concerning marketing and society, we will assume that the marketing methods employed are above question.

Marketing As Influencer or Reflector of Social Values. A largely unsubstantiated debate has raged for decades over whether marketing effort influences or reflects social values. Those who see it as an influencing force generally take an unfavorable view of the process. For them, it includes a heavy emphasis on the promotion and distribution of things as opposed to nontangibles, contributing to a strong materialistic orientation among consumers. Their argument often is countered by one maintaining that material wealth often makes possible the pursuit of less materialistic activities or goals.

Critics maintain that marketing efforts can create demand for products or services—demand that in its satisfaction can lead to altered social values. A case in point that often is used is the program of planned obsolescence in an automobile industry supported in part by customers who trade in their autos every year or two. Defenders of marketing point to the very marketing concept as evidence that the major goal of marketing is to determine and satisfy customer needs, perhaps in the process bringing to the fore previously latent needs but not creating totally new ones. As economist George J. Stigler has put it:

> The market place responds to the tastes of consumers with the goods and services that are salable, whether the tastes are elevated or depraved. It is unfair to criticize the market place for fulfilling these desires, when clearly the defects lie in the popular tastes themselves. . . . It is like blaming the waiters in restaurants for obesity.[13]

Thus, the debate is reduced to one of whether marketing influences social values, whether consumers realize that their values are being influenced, whether in fact they mind it, and whether the entire process works for better or worse. Using the example of planned obsolescence in the automobile industry, what conclusions would you reach? Can you recall a recent purchase in which marketing created a desire on your part that did not previously exist? How capable do you feel you are to answer the question?

(31)
(32)
(33)

[13]"Intellectuals Should Re-Examine the Market Place; It Supports Them, Helps Keep Them Free: Prof. Stigler," *Advertising Age* (Jan. 28, 1963), pp. 73–78. Quote on p. 74.

Social Effects of Marketing Methods. Recently, I observed the following notice on the bulletin board of a local music school:

!!! SEX !!!

Now that I have your attention, if you would be interested in buying a three-year-old Selmer saxophone, in good condition, for just $350, please call Jeff, 757–6340.

This student, who probably had never taken a course in marketing, was employing a time-honored belief that sex is among those basic appeals that always get attention and sell products. Products from sauna massage parlors to industrial products have been sold by means of this appeal.

In another advertising campaign, the Volvo of America Corporation used the theme, "A Civilized Car Built for an Uncivilized World." In its ads it showed a vulnerable woman (preferably) safe and snug in her Volvo 164 as she drove through a violent storm passing fallen trees and leather-jacketed motorcyclists. To some, this theme stressed a method of avoiding a threatening environment. To others, it was another attempt to play on customers' fears, yet another sure-fire method to sell products. It typifies the promotional efforts for products as diverse as life insurance and home protection devices.

Still other marketing efforts have appealed to consumers' desires to be distinctly masculine or feminine. Characteristic of companies making heavy use of this appeal are manufacturers of health and beauty aids. In an age in which we are highly sensitive to chauvinistic views, this approach has been labeled sexist by some.

There is little doubt that these efforts reflect the basic interests of potential customers. The question is whether, by using such appeals to sell products, marketers contribute to society's preoccupation with sex, fear of fellow man and other forces, and sexism. What are your general views regarding this issue? Applying this view to the examples in this section, how would you evaluate them regarding their impact on social values?

(34)
(35)

Marketing and Customer Aspirations. To some, marketing efforts point the way to a better standard of living by (1) not only presenting products or services to people of lower incomes but doing so in settings that show how people live who are more affluent than they, (2) making product displays readily available to all, and (3) offering credit for the early acquisition of products that might not otherwise be available to persons with low incomes. To advocates of the view, marketing efforts make for a more highly motivated and responsible disadvantaged social group.

To others, marketing efforts raise the levels of aspirations of low-income people to levels that are impossible to reach. This leads only to frustration and bitterness, causes of subsequent violence.

(36)

To what extent do you believe that marketing, as opposed to other influences in our lives, is responsible for the undesirable effects of frustrated aspirations?

Marketing and Communication Media. The average cost of the newsprint, composition, and printing for a newspaper in the United States is more than its newstand price. Revenues from advertising often represent three-fourths of total revenues and help pay for distribution as well as return a profit to the publisher. Without advertising, the newstand price of a newspaper would have to be tripled or quadrupled, assuming no loss of sales because of the higher price. Other publications are given away and exist solely on advertising revenues for this support. This is true as well for radio and television.

There are those who maintain that most of the commercial communication media in this country could not survive without advertising. Not only does advertising itself educate people by providing information about products and services, it also makes it possible for us to receive noncommercial information at little or no cost, and with little or no influence from advertisers.

Critics of this system charge that communication media, vital to an informed and objective electorate, either have sold out to or been bought out by marketers. Regardless of who is responsible, they claim that the process has developed through several stages: (1) rising production costs for media; (2) the discovery that revenue could be generated through both subscriptions and advertising; (3) the desire on the part of media owners to maintain low prices to consumers to encourage circulation; (4) greater and greater reliance on advertising revenues tied to circulation figures; (5) the inability of media with little success in attracting advertising to survive; (6) a declining number of communication media in a given market, making it easier for advertisers to gain coverage by advertising in a smaller number of media; and (7) ultimately a large degree of control over the media by advertisers. This subjects consumers to a form of control of which they are not even aware. For example, a network may find it impossible to obtain sponsors for a controversial documentary. Thus, freedom of the press is inhibited.

As the late Howard Gossage, a controversial, but highly successful, advertising executive, put it: "What good is freedom of the press if there isn't one?"[14]

(37) (38)
(39)

How could this situation be remedied? Should such a course of action be followed? In view of this discussion, how would you interpret the advertisement shown in Figure 15-9?

Marketing and Children. There has been a growing interest in the use of marketing techniques directed at children, as well as the nature of the products being promoted. Few debate the need to minimize the exposure of children to the less desirable aspects of society. Much of the debate concerns whether or not marketing efforts should be directed toward children at all, and the nature of such efforts.

In defense of marketing for children's products directed to children, there is something to be said for exposing children at an early age to the techniques to which they will be subjected for the rest of their lives. Judgmental ability can be sharpened through practice in evaluating advertising at an early age. Furthermore, like it or not, children are consumers with the same types of needs and desires as adults. As children mature more rapidly through access to a wider range of communication media and educational methods, they participate in purchase decisions formerly made for them by a parent. Product information can be useful to them in participating in such decisions. Such arguments nevertheless assume that marketers should exercise great care in the methods employed to persuade children.

[14]Warren Hinkle, "The Adman Who Hated Advertising," *Atlantic Monthly,* **233** (March 1974), pp. 67–72. Quote on p. 68.

Why do two networks refuse to run this commercial?

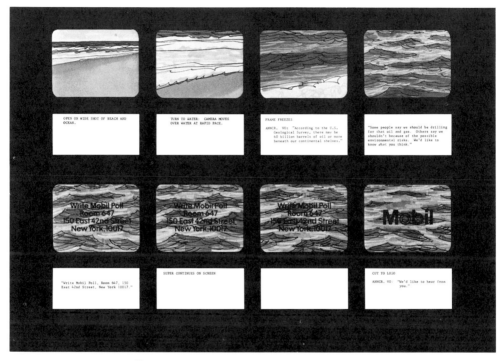

CBS:

"We regret that the subject matter of this commercial...deals with a controversial issue of public importance and does not fall within our 'goods and services' limitation for commercial acceptance."

ABC:

"This will advise that we have reviewed the above-captioned commercial and are unable to grant an approval for use over our facilities."

NBC:

"Approved as submitted."

As you can see from the storyboard reproduced above, we want to ask the public how it feels about offshore drilling.

But the policies of two national television networks prevent us from asking this question.

This is dangerous, it seems to us. Any restraint on free discussion is dangerous. Any policy that restricts the flow of information or ideas is potentially harmful.

The networks say that the public's need for information is best served in news programs prepared by broadcast journalists.

Behind the networks' rejection of idea advertising may be the fear that demands for equal time will be made. We have a reasonable answer to that. We offer to pay for equal time, when the request is legitimate.

We think *more* discussion, not less, is needed of vital issues such as the issue of America's energy needs. We're willing to buy the time to say what we should be saying. We're willing to buy time so you can hear opposing views.

But two big networks aren't willing to make time available, in this case.

You know the principle at stake here. You've seen it in writing, more than once:

"Congress shall make no law... abridging the freedom of speech."

You've seen it in the First Amendment to the Constitution of the United States. So have we.

We'd like to know what you think about either of these issues. Write Room 647, 150 East 42nd Street, New York, N.Y. 10017.

Mobil®

Figure 15-9 opposite. A copy of an advertisement that appeared in *The Wall Street Journal*, (June 17, 1974), p. 9.

Opposing views largely are based on the assumption that children are easily manipulated. They are unable to defend themselves against the clever approaches used by marketers. Their desires are easily stimulated. Parents then are put in the position of having to deny the child something shown in advertising, an unhealthy social and psychological phenomenon.

The most extensive research on the effects of television advertising on children has produced, among others, the following conclusions:

1. Between second and fourth grades children not only begin to discriminate between programs and commercials but also begin to understand the intent of the commercials.
2. By the sixth grade, children have relatively well-developed attitudes toward commercials.
3. Children do not "tune in" to commercials (that is, increase attention to them relative to program fare).
4. Children do form positive and negative attitudes toward advertisements (for example, adolescents are generally quite cynical toward advertising).
5. Television advertising is neither the sole nor necessarily the most influential determinant of children's wants and purchasing behavior.
6. Adolescents acquire consumer attitudes and skills from television advertising.[15]

(40)

What do these findings suggest to you about the need for restrictions on advertising directed to children?

Several steps have been taken in recent years to protect children from undesirable products or marketing techniques. This was one of the motivations for the ban on cigarette advertising from television. Similarly, manufacturers have been cautioned not to place primary stress on "deals," such as trinkets or other premiums, as opposed to the basic product being promoted in their advertising. Of perhaps greater importance up to now is the voluntary restraint practiced by manufacturers concerned about parent backlash from the use of marketing appeals directed to children.

the dialogue that never happens

The issues presented here have been debated for years, largely from a base of emotion rather than fact. During this time, little progress has been made in resolving them. Both as a means of explaining why little progress has been made in the past and why future progress may be difficult, professors Raymond A. Bauer and Stephen A. Greyser have pointed out that critics and defenders of marketing activities work from entirely different sets of assumptions and definitions. This has produced the setting for what they have termed "the dialogue that never happens."[16]

[15] Scott Ward, *Effects of Television Advertising on Children* (Boston: Marketing Science Institute, 1971), pp. 16–19; and *Children and Promotion: New Consumer Battleground?* (Boston: Marketing Science Institute, 1972), pp. 9–13.

[16] Raymond A. Bauer and Stephen A. Greyser, "The Dialogue That Never Happens," *Harvard Business Review*, **45** (Nov.–Dec. 1967), pp. 2–4 ff.

Table 15-2 Contrasting Assumptions and Definitions Used by Critics and Defenders of Marketing*

Terms Used by Both	Meaning to Critics	Meaning to Defenders
Competition	Price competition (as evidenced by price differences and price fluctuations)	Product differentiation (with identical prices for many competing products)
Product	Defined and differentiated in terms only of primary functions	Defined and differentiated in terms of secondary functions (assuming all competing products perform primary functions in a fashion acceptable to most consumers)
Consumer needs	Corresponds point to point to primary functions	Any customer desire on which the product can be differentiated
Rationality	Efficient matching of product to customer needs (by customer)	Any customer decision that serves the customer's perceived self-interest
Information	Any data that facilitates the fit of a product's proper function with the customer's needs (by the customer)	Any data that will (truthfully) put forth the attractiveness of the product in the eyes of the customer

* Source: Raymond A. Bauer and Stephen A. Greyser, "The Dialogue That Never Happens," *Harvard Business Review,* **45** (Nov.–Dec. 1967), pp. 2–4 ff. See p. 4.

For example, critics of marketing effort often assume that consumers, in general, are rather ill-informed and potentially easy for marketers to manipulate. Marketers and their defenders, in contrast, assume that consumers are relatively well educated in most of the world's commercial areas and use their purchasing power effectively to influence what is made and sold, where, and at what prices.

Implicit in much of what critics say is the belief that they know how consumers should behave. Marketers, on the other hand, base many of their decisions and views on information about how consumers do behave. The information is more likely to provide the basis for a valueless starting point.

What evidence can you find of these assumptions in the exchange between Ms. Betty Furness and Mr. Levine at the outset of this chapter? Or in other quotations presented here?

Table 15-2 contains additional contrasts in assumptions and definitions used by critics and defenders of marketing. Assuming this analysis has some validity, how could critics and marketers use this knowledge in resolving their differences? Do you see much hope of this happening?

summary

Roughly half of our expenditures for consumer goods pay for marketing activities of retailing, wholesaling, transportation, and the marketing efforts of manufacturing firms. However, when you consider the value created through such expenditures, represented by a larger variety of competing products designed to meet customer needs and made available at the time, place, quantity, and price desired by the customer, this well may be a bargain. As our economy has developed, the proportion of people engaged in distribution as opposed to manufacturing has steadily increased. This has given rise to a number of questions regarding the economic and social productivity of marketing efforts.

Economic arguments in support of marketing effort identify it as a major contributor to a product's value; an essential ingredient in a nation's economic development; the means of delivering a higher standard of living at a lower average price for goods and services; an important means of fostering competition; a means of achieving more efficient use of the world's resources; and a relatively efficient means of educating customers to evaluate alternative offerings rationally.

Opposing economists cite marketing as a frequent cause of excessive costs that must be defrayed by higher-than-necessary prices; a parasitic by-product of economic development; an area of duplicated effort and waste in a highly developed economy; a deterrent to existing or potential competitors; detrimental to the use of resources by encouraging customers to overspend and overconsume; and a means of manipulating customers to make uneconomic choices in their purchases.

If there is limited data to support any of these arguments, there is almost none to support views regarding marketing effort and social questions.

In the debate over social issues, marketing methods are sometimes confused with the perceived value of the products or services that they support. Few are the cases in which a product and the marketing methods used to help design and promote it are perceived by all as being above reproach. Even where this is the case, the debate continues along other dimensions.

Critics of marketing effort maintain that it represents an unfavorable influence on social values; relies too heavily on basic appeals such as sex, fear, and sexism; raises aspirations of low-income people to levels that are impossible to reach; has gained control of communication media to too great an extent; and manipulates groups of consumers less able to defend themselves against it, such as children.

Its defenders argue, on the other hand, that marketing reflects rather than influences social values; probably does not contribute to the already high preoccupation of the public with sex, fear, sexism, and other matters; provides incentives for low-income people by displaying and making readily available the means for a better standard of living; makes many communication media available to us at a reasonable price; and provides an education for all consumers, including children, who often are more perceptive than we give them credit for being.

Where do you stand on these economic and social issues?

Defenders and critics of marketing effort start from totally different sets of assumptions. This raises serious questions about the likelihood that the issues raised in this chapter ever will be resolved. At the same time, it suggests attitudes that marketers may have to adopt in the future to prove and demonstrate the worth of their activities to those served by our marketing system.

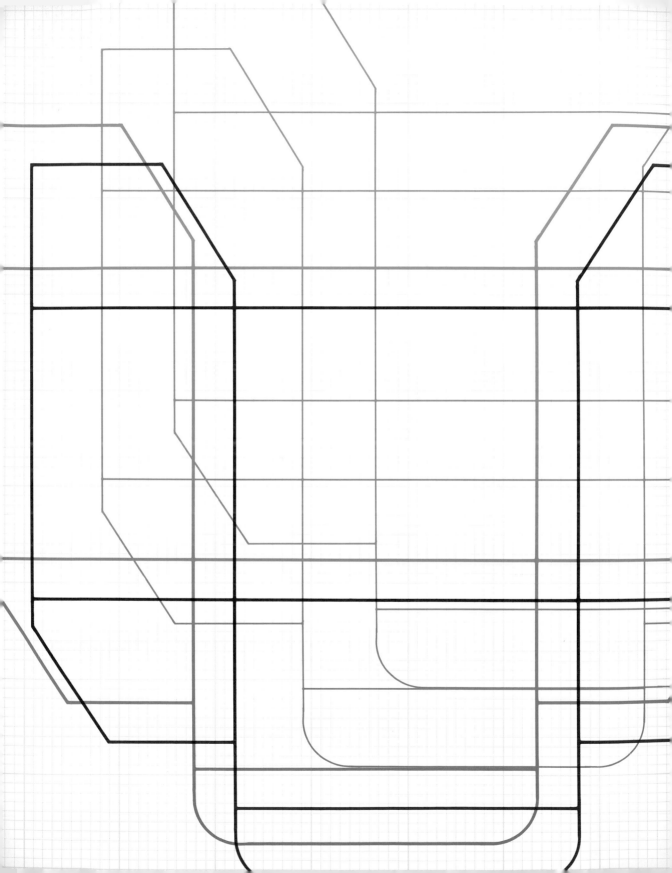

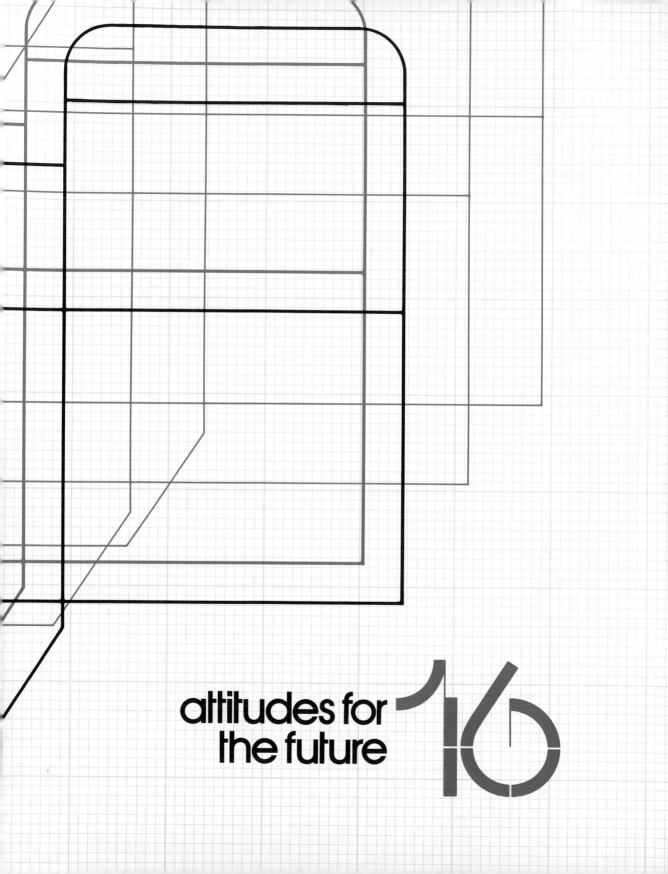

attitudes for
the future **16**

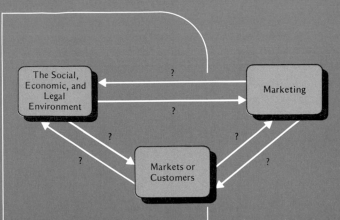

According to an old saying, "The future is important because we will be living so much of the rest of our lives in it." It's doubly appropriate to drag the saying out at this point, because chances are you're reading this book at an important juncture in your life, one at which you are choosing or changing careers, getting ready to market yourself.

With this in mind, this final chapter is laid out to allow you to (1) explore trends of importance to marketers and marketing institutions, (2) assess possible responses by various parties to these trends, and (3) consider the types of attitudes that will allow marketers to cope effectively in the future.

Several of your acquaintances from the book, including Sheldon Dietz, Kim Kelley, Doris Berendt, John Marttila, Fred Holland, and others may help you put marketing in perspective in planning your future careers. As you recall them in terms of the nature of their lives, backgrounds, capabilities, and beliefs, ask yourself whether they are artists or scientists. Or whether they may not be the practitioners of the craft suggested in the preface.

Perhaps they will suggest to you that marketing can be both fun and financially rewarding. But that should not be all that they suggest to you about the nature of this craft.

supermarket roulette[1]

Several years ago, California's consumer council decided to conduct a test to see how a shopper might fare in a typical unarmed encounter with a supermarket. According to a then current survey by Du Pont, the average shopper on an average visit bought 13.7 items in an average time of 27 minutes. Accordingly, a list of 14 items was drawn up. These were all packaged products—common staple foods and household necessities. Then a typical supermarket in the Sacramento area was selected. In the case of the 14 items, the store offered a total of 246 possible choices.

Five housewives were selected to participate in the test. Although picked at random, they were not average shoppers; each had had some college training as well as considerable family-marketing experience. Their instructions were simple: to make their selections solely on the basis of quantity and cost—for example, get the most possible for their money.

Each of the five women was given $10 and sent into the supermarket to buy the 14 items. They were clocked from the time they entered the store until they reached the check-out counter.

Only one of the women finished in less time than the average found in the Du Pont survey; she completed her shopping in 25 minutes. The other four women took, respectively, 35, 40, 55, and 60 minutes.

How did they fare? All five succeeded in picking the lowest-priced package of one item, cheddar cheese. But that was their only triumph. In the case of two of the 14 products, all five were baffled by the maze of prices and package sizes. For instance, there were fourteen different packages of white rice; not

[1]This example is quoted from E. B. Weiss, "Marketers Fiddle While Consumers Burn," *Harvard Business Review,* **46** (July–Aug. 1968), pp. 45–53. See p. 48.

one was in a one-pound package. The same was true of the six packages of salt, which ran a confusing range from four-tenths of an ounce to five pounds. Toilet tissue was packed in rolls of 650, 800 and 1,000 sheets—some single-ply, some double-ply. Of the ten cans of tuna, none was one pound or one-half pound; seven were fractional ounces.

In summary, possessing better-than-average educations, and spending more than the average amount of time, the five housewives as a group succeeded thirty-six times and failed thirty-four times to pick the most economical items.

(1) What would the results of this test suggest to you as a low-income con-
(2) sumer, a high-income consumer, a member of the staff of the FTC, or a market-ing (product line) manager in a grocery products manufacturing company? What action, if any, would you be stirred to take in any of these roles?

alternative scenarios for the future

The following alternative scenarios, suggesting possible ways to deal with this situation in the future, are based on known technology, consumerist objectives, and potential actions being debated by business regulators. They represent change based largely on technology, consumer education, regulation, and a responsive business community acting in the mutual interests of consumers and business.

Technology. The technological view sees a consumer of the future dialing a central grocery product distribution center on the phone. Upon hearing a coded tone, he or she dials the consumer number, which allows the center's computer to make its file of product information and prices available. Upon dialing the first ten letters of each product category desired, the consumer can obtain a file of brand, size, price, and deal information about all of the alternative competing products in that category available at the center. This information is displayed on a screen beside the telephone. If he or she wishes, more detailed information or pictures of any item can be requested. Or if he or she wishes to shop on some other basis, such as that of obtaining the lowest cost per ounce of a product purchased, a computer routine can be called on the telephone that will report the three products and packages with the lowest costs per ounce. Having completed the order, he or she once again dials the consumer number. The center's computer totals the order, compares the amount with that in the individual's bank account, and notifies the consumer of the delivery time for the order, assuming that there are sufficient funds in the consumer's electronic purchasing account at the bank.

Upon receiving and approving the order, the grocery distribution center's account at the bank is credited with the appropriate amount of money from the customer's account. Orders are picked and packed automatically from gravity-fed, computer-controlled order-picking machines and are placed according to the sequence of their delivery in waiting trucks. It is only at this point that the system reverts to old-fashioned methods of direct delivery to homes, with manual handling of individual orders. However, such orders are combined with similar small orders for drug and other products destined from

518

other suppliers to a particular neighborhood to reduce the costs of the individual delivery by increasing the density and average size of such deliveries.

The reduction in total cost made possible by the elimination of the traditional retail supermarket, handling of funds, and warehouse personnel more than defrays the costs of home delivery and the maintenance and operation of the central computer. Savings in shopping time and the prices paid for desired items exceed the modest equipment rental charge paid by the consumer to the telephone company or other equipment supplier.

Consumer Education. In this view the potential solution to the problem of confusion in the market place is seen in the education of the consumer by information-oriented advertising; various educational programs sponsored by retailers, manufacturers, Consumer's Union, and federal, state, and urban consumers' councils; and the growing use of pocket-sized computers for use in making in-store product-package-price calculations. Advocates of this view maintain that consumers are becoming more and more knowledgeable and will continue to be so given the information and resources available to them now.

Government Regulation. Regulation is seen by some as a solution to the problem of consumer purchasing. Milder forms of such regulation would have manufacturers or retailers adopt "unit pricing" in which the equivalent price per standard unit of measure (such as a pound) would have to be affixed to packages.

Under more stringent forms of regulation, the number and dimensions of package sizes might be regulated as well as pricing practices. Carrying it one step further, such package dimensions might be selected in such a manner that they have the same modular compatibility as a typical set of children's blocks. This would facilitate the handling and shipment of orders combining several sizes and types of packages.

The most severe form of regulatory solution might, in addition, include the requirement that products be registered on the basis of their uniqueness and the amount of competition desired within a particular product category. A basic objective would be to limit the number of me-too brands and confusing package sizes found on the supermarket shelves. It would resemble the form of regulation used to control the number of airlines competing on a particular route by the Civil Aeronautics Board (CAB).

The extent of regulation under this view would depend largely on the strength and nature of consumer complaints. It might be preceded by store picketing and boycotts of manufacturers' products by consumer groups.

Self-regulation by Manufacturers and Retailers. This view of the future emphasizes the anticipation and satisfaction of long-run consumer welfare as opposed to short-term consumer needs by individual manufacturers and retailers. It would suggest that enlightened manufacturers, for example, would be willing to (1) emphasize product information in their advertising and other promotional efforts; (2) limit the number of me-too brands that they might introduce; and (3) print nutritional contents, open dating information (stating the last day on which products should be sold), and unit prices on product packages, even if such practices required foregoing short-term profits. Similarly, retailers might refuse to stock products of manufacturers not taking such steps.

(3) Which of these views of the future do you think is most likely to materialize? Based on trends that are now discernable, it is quite possible that we may see elements of all of these views in the marketing future.

basic trends affecting marketing effort

It's appropriate at this point to review the various trends affecting marketing effort that we have discussed from time to time throughout this book. To avoid unnecessary repetition, the intent here is to concentrate on those trends exhibiting the greatest amount of change at the present time and those to which we've not devoted enough attention previously in the book. The trends are cataloged as environmental, institutional, and technological in nature.

environmental trends

All other environmental trends of importance for marketing in the United States have been overshadowed by the growth of consumerism. At the same time, however, we are witnessing potentially significant changes in the nature of markets. Both of these developments are the product of a number of basic environmental changes, which we discussed in Chapter 3. Among these are continuing increases in the sizes of markets, but at a declining rate due to the declining birth rate; the regionalization of population as family units continue to cluster in regional markets now able to support their own production and marketing systems; continued urbanization, or rather suburbanization of the population; a continuing high level of population mobility in the United States; increasing levels of education, income and, more important, proportions of incomes available for discretionary spending; a growing proportion of expenditures for services rather than tangible goods; the growing proportion of women in the nonhome work force; increasing government regulation of marketing activities and, more importantly, its failure in certain well-publicized cases. All of this is occurring at a point in time when limits on the world's resources are becoming painfully apparent and concerns are growing about pollution of all types.

Consumerism. In this century, the United States has witnessed three consumer movements. The first resulted just after the turn of the century from muckraker Upton Sinclair's exposure of meat packers, scandals in the ethical drug industry, and rising prices. By the time it had run its course in 1914, it had led to the enactment of the Meat Inspection Act, the Pure Food and Drug Act, and the act creating the FTC.

Once again, consumers in the 1930s, hard-pressed by the combination of a depression, rising prices, and further scandals in the drug industry, were moved to action. Boycotts were implemented, and housewives went on strike. By the time concerns had been quieted several years later, the Pure Food and Drug Act had been strengthened and the powers of the FTC to discourage deceptive or unfair business practices made broader.

The third and current age of consumerism generally is considered to have begun with President Kennedy's declaration of a "consumer's bill of rights" in 1962. It provided both a landmark and a definition, in that it asserted the rights of consumers to safety, to be informed, to choose, and to be heard. Implicit in consumerism is that these rights are to be asserted against the rights of others to create or market goods, services, people, or ideas.

Any movement requires an event or rallying point. Ralph Nader's publication of the book, *Unsafe at Any Speed,* and his subsequent David-and-Goliath battle in public with General Motors provided it. And at about the same time, Rachel Carson's publication of the best-selling book, *The Silent Spring,* helped broaden the scope of consumerism to include concerns about the rapidly deteriorating environment and the role of products and their use in the deterioration process. Similar studies of the plight of the poor helped extend these concerns to include responsibilities of business in general in dealing with the problem of poverty in the midst of plenty.

(4)   But why 1962? Why General Motors? Experience suggests that events such as these are merely the product and expression of already present concerns. What caused the consumer movement? Can you, for example, detect possible causes of consumerism in the supermarket shopping study that was discussed earlier in this chapter?

The statement of the consumer bill of rights implies a concern with the lack of product safety, poor information provided to consumers on which to base purchase decisions, a lack of choice in products or services, and the inability of consumers to register complaints and obtain redress of their complaints. Had these problems suddenly become acute, or were other factors at work as well?

In the face of a lack of evidence that these problems had suddenly become acute in other than isolated cases, we must seek other possible explanations. Among those that have been advanced are that (1) consumers feel that they require more information than ever before about the bewildering array of products and services and the methods and costs of financing their purchases, (2) they have a rising level of expectation about the dependability and safety with which products should perform, (3) they have been confronted with a deteriorating level of service at precisely the time when products have become more complex, (4) they have reached a level of affluence at which they can afford to pay for environmental improvement and equity among social classes as well as devote time to making these things happen, and (5) lawmakers have concluded that legislation to protect consumers is relatively popular and does not require vast appropriations of money.

Whatever the causes, consumerism is an ever-present force of great importance for current day marketers. It has produced laws such as the National Traffic and Motor Vehicle Safety Act of 1966, from which we still can feel the effects of higher vehicle costs, lower gas mileage, and fewer deaths from highway accidents. It was a law directed at a product associated with the deaths of more people than all other products combined. More recently, we have seen the establishment by Congress in 1972 of the Consumer Product Safety Commission to provide protection to the 20 million Americans injured, 110,000 permanently disabled, and 30,000 killed each year in product-related accidents other than those involving automobiles. The threat of publicity of product defects by this commission has induced a number of manufacturers to engage in the voluntary recall, repair, or replacement of defective products.

On other fronts, advertisers have been encouraged to present more factual information and are required by the FTC to retract misleading claims. We have seen the passage of truth-in-lending legislation specifying the manner in which prospective borrowers must be informed of the costs and other consequences of their decisions. The Fair Packaging and Labeling, or so-called truth-in-packaging, Act of 1966 required that consumer goods be clearly labeled in terms understandable to consumers and encouraged industry and government agencies alike to reduce the number of package sizes offered to consumers. More recently, in 1972, the Food and Drug Administration established a set of nutritional-labeling standards for packaged foods.

(5)

(6)

Recent studies suggest that so-called consumer-activists are not confined to any one group of people. One of the most extensive of these studies produced profiles for a representative demographic cross section of 912 couples in a Midwest industrial community and categorized them as pro-business and antibusiness, as shown in Table 16-1.[2] In total, the sample produced positive and negative responses to a list of statements as shown in Table 16-2. What signs of encouragement or potential problems for the business community in general, and marketers in particular, do you see in the data in Table 16-2? Based on information in Table 16-1, what would you conclude about the potential strength of the consumer movement and its continued impact on marketing practice?

Changes in the Nature of Markets. An increasing number of market segments can be identified for a wider range of goods and services than ever before, in the opinion of many. This probably is not only a function of the growing size of the United States and world population, which in itself would increase the number of different, identifiable, and viable market segments for any particular class of goods or services.

In addition, it is thought that United States consumers are beginning to reflect many of the values held by their counterparts in the postindustrial societies of Western Europe. Among these are (1) an increasing attempt to express themselves and help fashion their identities by means of their purchases; (2) a growing emphasis either on expenditures for nonmaterial items such as education and travel or material items that will facilitate expenditures for nonmaterial items, such as motor homes, books, and travel clothing; and (3) a growing tendency to identify themselves with leisure-time activities rather than their jobs. In addition, we have seen in the United States an increase in the tendency of consumers to rent rather than buy products, particularly housing—a possible reflection of their desire to remain mobile.

(7)

(8)

All of these trends are seen as a manifestation of a need for identity in a world that increasingly forces people to become numbers and to deal with computer-controlled systems rather than people. To what extent do recent major expenditures by your family, other than for your own education, reflect these trends? To what extent do you think they are true for the 50 per cent of all American families with incomes of less than $10,000 per year?

[2] Thomas P. Hustad and Edgar A. Pessemier, "Will the Real Consumer-Activist Please Stand Up: An Examination of Consumers' Opinions about Marketing Practices," Working Paper No. P-57-E, (Cambridge, Mass.: Marketing Science Institute, June, 1972).

Table 16-1 Dimensions on Which Profiles of 912 Pro-Business and Antibusiness Wives Could Be Differentiated*

Dimension	384 Pro-Business Wives	162 Antibusiness Wives[a]
Demographic (age, etc.)	No difference between the two groups	
Highly regarded values	Obedience, helpfulness, dependability, religiosity, capability, loyalty, education	Courage, cleanliness, equality, political influence
Latent occupation abilities[b]	Mechanical, numerical, low-level service-oriented jobs	High-status, influential jobs
Activities engaged in[c]	Personal, home, and family-oriented jobs	Social or neighborly activities, activities with high leadership or intellectual content, speaking to groups, saving money
Media listening and reading habits	Lower exposure to radio and print media; more likely to read *True Story* and *Modern Romances*	Greater exposure to radio and print media; more likely to read *Time* and *U. S. News and World Report*
Product usage rates	Higher for candy bars, soft drinks, TV dinners, hair spray, pain relievers, butter, and vacuum cleaners	Higher for feminine hygiene spray, wine, and savings accounts
Socioeconomic measures	Lowest occupational status for husband, lowest education level for wife	Highest occupational status for husband, highest education level for wife
Product ownership	Few significant differences	
Ownership of innovative products	No significant differences	
Recognition of brand names and advertising slogans	No significant differences	

* Source: Based on a survey of 912 wives selected as a representative demographic cross section of a Midwest industrial community, as reported in Thomas P. Hustad and Edgar A. Pessemier, "Will the Real Consumer-Activist Please Stand Up: An Examination of Consumers' Opinions about Marketing Practices," Working Paper No. P-57-E (Cambridge, Mass.: Marketing Science Institute, June, 1972). *Note:* Only items on which the measures for the two groups produced significant differences are listed.

[a] 366 wives were found to be neither pro-business nor antibusiness.

[b] Defined as the respondents' perceived abilities to perform, if trained, a variety of 50 occupations and professions.

[c] Defined as the relative frequency with which respondents participated in each of 77 domestic, social, cultural, and political activities.

Table 16-2 **Relative Attitudes of a Representative Cross Section of Residents of a Midwest Industrial Community Toward a Series of Business-Related Statements***

Statement	Reaction Score on a Scale of −1 (negative) to +1 (positive)	
Pollution is a serious problem	.55	
Consumers need more government control of business practices	.46	
Businesses are concerned about the public they serve	.28	
Business is responsive to the consumer (consumer sovereignty)	.28	Agree[a]
There are too many products and brands available today	.21	
"Other people" do not care about pollution	.16	
Magazine industry does a good job	.12	
Newspaper industry does a good job	.04	
Advertising is a good source of consumer information	−.02	
Retailing-selling practices are in the consumer's best interests	−.02	Neutral[a]
Television industry does a good job	−.03	
American businesses are honest	−.09	
Advertising is a valuable institution	−.17	
Business pricing practices are fair and honest	−.18	
Advertising and promotions are truthful	−.19	
Automobile industry does a good job	−.20	
Products and services are of high quality	−.21	Disagree[a]
Advertising and promotional practices are not objectionable	−.22	
Breakfast cereal industry does a good job	−.25	
Drug industry does a good job	−.26	
Detergent industry does a good job	−.31	

* Source: Based on a survey of 912 wives selected as a representative demographic cross section of a Midwest industrial community, as reported in Thomas P. Hustad and Edgar A. Pessemier, "Will the Real Consumer-Activist Please Stand Up: An Examination of Consumers' Opinions about Marketing Practices," Working Paper No. P-57-E (Cambridge, Mass.: Marketing Science Institute, June, 1972).

[a] As interpreted by the researchers themselves.

The Allocation Era. Recent visible shortages of energy in the United States and other parts of the world have made citizens in the more highly developed regions more conscious of potential shortages of food, fertilizer, paper, chemicals, and other basic products. For many products, the primary marketing task will no longer be that of encouraging use and building sales, but rather one of allocating available supplies to markets with more than adequate demands. This has raised questions about the continued importance of the role of marketing management in industries beset by too much demand, a situation for which past marketing effort ironically has been variously credited or blamed. For example, in the past the job of a marketing manager for a typical electric utility has ranged from that of supervising the development of advertising campaigns intended to stimulate new uses of electricity to that of managing retail stores selling a wide range of electrical appliances. How may this change in the allocation era?

(9)

institutional trends

Institutional trends concern changes occuring in the distribution channels for products and services. Among those of current interest are the polarization of retailers, increases in non-store retailing, shortened life cycles for retail institutions, changing roles for wholesalers, the growing use of shared services, and the increasing use of marketing by non-profit organizations.

Polarization in the Retailing Structure. The spread of the supermarket philosophy of low prices, low margin, limited services, high volume, and hopefully respectable profits to nongrocery products is rapidly taking place. It has become an accepted mode of operation for the retailing of products as diverse as popular cameras, drugs, insurance, and small appliances. Eventually, it may become epitomized by the superstore, offering in a store somewhat larger than that of the typical supermarket a limited assortment of many product categories, all characterized by relatively frequent purchase, the need for little sales assistance, and frequent price comparisons by shoppers.

At the same time, specialty stores offering a wide assortment of a limited number of product categories have grown rapidly. Witness, for example, the popularity of stores offering only furniture, film and processing services, home electronics of all types, or floor coverings. Most of these are organized as chains to obtain economies of quantity buying and standardized operation.

Each of these types of retailing establishments fulfills a different set of consumer needs. Both, however, emphasize economies of scale in their operation. As professor and consultant William R. Davidson points out:

> Between the poles are conventional and often nonprogrammed single-line stores of the family apparel, hardware, drug and jewelry types. For these stores and their supply systems, the polarization is suggestive of increased obsolescence and profit difficulties in the 1970s.[3]

Increases in Nonstore Retailing. At one time, executives of a company now called the Jewel Companies, Inc. were contemplating the time when they would discontinue the sale of coffees, teas, spices, and related grocery items direct to consumers' homes by driver-salesmen in the Midwest. Today they have second thoughts, as the business has reversed its previous decline and the company's Direct Marketing Division operates more than 1,500 "home shopping service" routes.

Several years ago, it was thought that Sears, Roebuck and Co. would eventually discontinue its mail-order business in urban areas, making it available only in smaller rural markets. Today, it is a rapidly growing aspect of Sears' business, especially in urban markets. A related form of retailing, the catalog store offering display merchandise for which orders can be placed, has recently enjoyed great popularity.

One of the fastest growing retailers in recent years was Avon Products, Inc., now selling more than a billion dollars per year of a wide line of household,

[3] William R. Davidson, "Changes in Distributive Institutions," *Journal of Marketing,* **34** (Jan. 1970), pp. 7–10. Quote on p. 8.

health and beauty aids, and related products by means of in-home sales representatives.

Organizations from airlines to petroleum refiners and marketers have instituted direct-mail selling efforts for travel and recreational products directed to their passengers and credit card holders, respectively.

Trends toward nonstore retailing probably reflect the increasing value placed on their time by consumers as well as the declining attractiveness of the social aspects of shopping by females as a growing proportion of them fulfill needs for socialization at a work place outside the home. Which of these nonstore retailing methods do you think are the forerunners of the method of nonstore retailing described at the outset of this chapter? What differences would you expect to see in the types of products handled by nonstore and in-store retailing methods? How is this reflected in your own purchasing patterns?

Shortened Life Cycles for Retail Institutions. As suggested in Table 8-5, page 276, the time required for a new type of retailing institution to achieve maturity has been shortened over the years. This has required retailing entrepreneurs who rely heavily on growth continually to seek new retailing forms and opportunities for diversification into related existing forms. Thus, we have seen the creation of large organizations claiming expertise in retailing management, whether of traditional department or discount stores. These companies rely on their abilities to finance, train managers and employees, and physically distribute goods efficiently in becoming literally retail distribution companies. For those not willing or able to adapt and maintain flexibility in a world of change, the future is bleak.

Changing Roles for Wholesalers. The role of the wholesaler in the distribution of consumer goods has changed markedly in recent years. We have discussed the polarization of retailing operations toward companies operating either large single stores oriented to the sale of high-volume merchandise or chains of speciality stores offering large assortments of a particular type of goods but enjoying the benefits of central buying and merchandising. This has enabled retailers to achieve volumes of sales sufficient to allow them to deal directly with manufacturer-suppliers for a growing volume of merchandise.

The growth of the supermarket in the grocery products industry illustrates one of these poles. The growth of discount drug chains illustrates the other. Grocery products wholesalers have had to replace their loss of supermarket chain business by forming voluntary or cooperative relationships with groups of independent supermarket operators who require the economies of scale that centralized buying, warehousing, transportation, and private-label programs provide. Drug wholesalers, losing profitable high-volume items to direct distribution methods, have had to rethink the margins required to produce sufficient profit returns on low-volume items that they are expected to continue to handle for all types of drug retailing organizations.

In the distribution of industrial goods, we have witnessed the rise of the specialty wholesaler as opposed to the stagnation of the general-line wholesaler. This reflects the growing complexity of products demanded by industrial buyers as well as the increasing difficulty with which an industrial customer and his wholesaler can maintain familiarity with new technologies in a wide line of products. Here again, change is the rule rather than the exception.

526

Growing Use of Shared Services. In seeking the more efficient use of limited resources, it is inevitable that more firms will turn to the increased use of shared services, both in physically distributing and promoting their products. Thus, the use of privately owned trucks for the transportation of goods appears to have peaked out in favor of the use of common carrier truckers that hold themselves out to carry any products anywhere for any customers for which they have legal authority to do so. Similarly, public warehousing volume has grown in relation to that of private warehousing.

Organizations operating "captive" distribution and promotional organizations are seeking means of serving others. Thus, a New York-based manufacturer of pasta products making daily deliveries to retail outlets and restaurants by means of its own crew of driver-salesmen seeks to contract to deliver products for other firms with the same needs. A large manufacturer of household detergents seeks to enter into a joint venture with one or two other large manufacturers to operate a system of distribution warehouses that can serve the needs of the several firms.

In promoting products, we have seen the use of "tie-in" advertising, such as a national advertising campaign sponsored by manufacturers of several products that are consumed for breakfast. These campaigns provide all cooperating firms with national exposure for their products at lower-than-usual costs, as well as allow each to tie individual promotional efforts to some feature of the shared program. We are now beginning to see the emergence of "marketing" companies, those who offer to make available to other firms marketing expertise formerly restricted to products of their own manufacture. For example, the Colgate-Palmolive Co. markets products for England's Wilkinson Sword Ltd. (razor blades), United Biscuit (cookies), and Weetabix (breakfast cereal) in the United States . This has allowed Colgate-Palmolive to expand its product line to match that of its competitors while restricting its budget for new-product development to its own products. It has provided effective representation in a highly competitive market for its English associates.

(13) What other opportunities for new marketing enterprises based on the concept of shared services occur to you? They may form the basis for a future-oriented new-business venture.

Marketing for Nonprofit Purposes. Challenges of marketing on behalf of nonprofit endeavors are illustrated by the frustrations of the new team selected to design advertising for the Kidney Foundation several years ago. As Herb Fried, of the Davis Fried Krieger advertising agency put it:

> kidney disease is not glamorous. It's not like heart disease, you know, beautiful, THE HEART. . . . And it's not even like cancer which is—*you* know . . . Kidney disease is—you know, you think of *urinating*.[4]

At least one major television network indicated great reluctance to broadcast his solution, a sweaty, simulated boxing match, featuring a fighter in dark trunks delivering a crippling "kidney punch" to a game young heavyweight who spends most of the remaining fifty seconds collapsing in agony, writhing on the canvas, lunging desperately for the ropes and—with the last of his strength

---

[4] Ron Rosenbaum, "Tales of the Heartbreak Biz," *Esquire,* **82** (July 1974), pp. 67–73 ff. Quote on p. 67.

—trying to pull himself up again. With March, kidney month, rapidly approaching, Herb Fried wondered whether his firm would have the Kidney Foundation account any longer than the advertising agency that had handled it previously.

This example calls attention to the growing importance of marketing for nonprofit purposes in a highly developed, postindustrial society. One estimate by Philip Kotler has placed the size of the nonprofit sector at more than 20 per cent of the United States economy, and its advertising level at something close to 15 per cent of the total costs for advertising in the United States. This includes expenditures (1) by the Advertising Council to promote twenty or so programs such as Smokey Bear and Religion in American Life, (2) on behalf of political candidates, (3) by federal and state governments, and (4) by institutional advertisers.[5] This effort deals largely with the marketing of ideas or concepts rather than tangible products. Given this characteristic, is it likely to be more or less controversial than marketing on behalf of profit-oriented organizations?

(14)

The growth of marketing effort on behalf of nonprofit enterprises has raised questions about standards to be followed in carrying it out and methods to be employed in measuring its effectiveness. For example, need an ad promoting safety be as truthful as one selling soap? In at least one case, the U. S. Army found the promotional efforts that represented an essentially unchanged Army as the "New Army" backfired as word-of-mouth impressions from new recruits reached home-town buddies.

(15)

Other questions are posed by this trend. Is it, for example, more difficult to measure the effectiveness of marketing effort on behalf of the Kidney Foundation or Pop-Tarts? Is it as important to be able to do so?

(16)

(17)

Herb Fried and his colleagues finally decided to scrap the boxing match as a symbolic method of appealing for support for the Kidney Foundation. Instead, they designed an ad acceptable to the media, the foundation, and the offended boxing organizations that you may have seen. Under the caption, "Being attached to a kidney machine is no way to spend a childhood," it showed a little girl attached to a kidney machine holding a teddy bear. The girl's face had to be hidden, however, to circumvent agency strictures against using the healthy to portray the afflicted. This practice had grown out of problems resulting from showing real patients in ads who died subsequent to the publication of the advertising. How would you assess the ethical implications of this solution?

(18)

technological trends

Institutional changes are supportive of, and effected by, technological trends. How does the development of automated retail check-out equipment and data collection based on the adoption of the Universal Product Code for grocery products illustrate this statement?

(19)

Among major technological trends of importance for marketing are the introduction and use of the computer in all phases of marketing effort, improvements in the collection and analysis of data for marketing decision making, the

[5] Bernice Finkelman, "Kotler Says: 'Growing Nonprofit Sector, Now 20% of Economy, Becoming Marketing-Conscious,'" *Marketing News* (Jan. 15, 1974), pp. 1 and 3. Quote on p. 1.

development of increasingly complex products and marketing effort required in a postindustrial society, and our entry into an era of visibly scarce resources in which technological alternatives will have to be found for commonly used products.

The Computer. We have discussed a number of ways in which the computer will be employed more heavily in marketing effort. Manufacturers will use it to process data collected from actual or potential customers regarding their geographical dispersion, actual purchasing habits, and needs. Thus, they will obtain greater insight into the nature of their actual or potential markets than might otherwise have been available through the data generated by marketing research efforts. By such means, for example, Philip Morris maintains a data file on each of the roughly 500,000 retail outlets for cigarettes, using it to allocate salespeople and track actual as opposed to potential sales through each account.

Similarly, computers are being used to maintain inventory files that are updated as transactions are made, thus insuring up-to-date knowledge of product availability and the accomplishment of better customer service with a smaller amount of total inventory. At warehouses, inventories are controlled, and in some cases, orders picked, by means of computer-controlled automatic picking machines. Deliveries may be planned and truck routes formulated as part of this process. And promotional effort may be carried out, and complaint letters answered, by means of personalized letters addressed to individuals but prepared by means of computer-driven printers.

At the retail level, we have reviewed earlier in this book similar uses of the computer and, in addition, its use in improving stock control and store layout of merchandise, eliminating the need for manual store pricing and drastically reducing the time required to transact sales. Ultimately, we have contemplated its use in transacting sales and transferring funds for various nonstore retailing ventures.

What does all of this mean for marketers? It should help them improve the productivity of marketing personnel, inventories, and new-product introductions. Improved productivity should get translated into lower prices per given level of convenience.

On the other hand, one of the distinguishing features of marketing activities in the world has been their heavy reliance on people and human interaction. What effects will fewer people in the warehouse, fewer people in the retail store, and computer-printed letters in reply to complaints have on marketing management? For example, what effect do you think it will have on retail store and brand loyalty among consumers and the level of satisfaction with products and promotional efforts on their behalf? How will these effects vary by types of products or services?

Improved Data Collection and Analysis. In a sense, the enormously increased capacity to analyze existing data by means of computers has placed a greater responsibility on management both to understand the meaning of the results of the application of analytic techniques and to insure that the quality of data being analyzed is above reproach. The data "horn of plenty" provided by the computer is imposing a discipline on marketing managers akin to the rich kid in the candy store with unlimited funds but a limited stomach. There is an implicit cost of some magnitude associated with each additional massaging of data even if the explicit, out-of-pocket costs are declining.

All of this is occurring at a point in time at which a flood of data regarding retail sales of consumer goods may be released with hitherto unknown speed by the introduction of new methods of capturing such data by means of electronic point-of-sale registers.

From all of this we should learn better ways of collecting data, still the most expensive of research stages, to serve multiple purposes. Along with improved methods of analyzing small samples and assessing their confidence limits in terms of the cost, as opposed to the value of information that they provide, more efficient research efforts and better decisions for the marketing research money spent should result.

Increasing Product-System Complexity. Many individual products have been simplified, either in design or use. We can think, for example, of such products as the Wankel engine, life insurance, the frozen dinner, printed circuit boards and replaceable electronic modules, and the fast-food restaurant meal. However, in the desire to meet customer needs more completely, many firms now market products that, in combination, form systems requiring a knowledge of components and their interactions on the part of both the marketer and the customer.

This is particularly true in the marketing of industrial products. Firms have developed or acquired the capability of designing, building, and even operating entire facilities ranging from nuclear power generating stations to football stadiums. This has become known as the turn key product, requiring only that the new owner unlock the door and operate the machinery. As we've said, even that might be done for the new owner. Systems marketing requires skills in detecting needs and communicating product features of a higher level than required in the past. It involves marketing to a much greater degree in the entire product design process. It is leading to a higher proportion of leasing as opposed to outright sales, particularly of units involving very large expense, and it may require a much more extensive postpurchase service capability than previously thought necessary.

Consider, for example, the task of marketing and servicing the line of dry-copy copying machines produced by the Xerox Corporation. The majority of its revenues are realized from royalties computed on the basis of the number of copies produced by each machine leased (rather than sold) to a customer. Through the years, Xerox has developed an extensive line of machines, ranging from small portable, relatively slow machines to a machine capable of producing 7,200 copies per hour and to other machines capable of printing in color or on both sides of a sheet of paper. What implications do the nature of this product line and Xerox's leasing policy have for the sales representative responsible for locating and recommending the appropriate model of machine to new accounts? What implications do they have for the company's service organization? Perhaps it would not surprise you to know that under Xerox's service program in 1975 customers in the United States, on the average, had to wait about three hours for service from one of the company's more than 10,000 service representatives when a machine "went down."

(22)

(23)

Effects of Limited Resources. As the demand for an increasing number of products exceeds available supplies in the future, higher prices will serve as major mechanisms for allocating limited supplies. Perhaps even more important for marketing effort, they will foster the development of substitute materials and technologies through research. It will be the task of marketers to sell substitute materials and technologies at prices that will be a little lower or not at all lower than their long-accepted counterparts and to help divert demand by means other than price.

We will see repeated many times over the experience of E. I. Du Pont de Nemours & Co. (Du Pont) in marketing its newly developed synthetic fiber, nylon, some years ago. Until Du Pont had earmarked a substantial promotional effort directed to ultimate consumers of hosiery and other products in which nylon could be used as a raw material, it found it difficult to sell nylon to fabricators of those products.

applicability of current marketing concepts for the future

How well do commonly accepted marketing concepts hold up against the environmental, institutional, and technological changes taking place in our society? Will we be forced to discard most of them, or can they be adapted to accommodate these trends? A discussion of three of these, the marketing concept, the marketing mix, and marketing as a device for stimulating demand, may give us some answers to these questions.

The Marketing Concept. In our earlier discussion of the marketing concept, we suggested that it deals with the detection and satisfaction of customer needs at a profit. And yet, you say, we've just talked of the growth of marketing efforts on behalf of nonprofit endeavors. Does this mean that the marketing concept cannot be applied in these cases? Furthermore, profit is a concept found by some to be at odds with social and environmental development, in some cases with the very quality of life that we experience. Should we delete the reference to profit in the concept?

Rather than delete references to profit, it may be more appropriate to broaden the meaning of the word when used in the context of the marketing concept. Instead of using profit (return in excess of expenditures) in reference to a marketer only or a marketer in combination with a customer, it may be more sensible to use it to refer to the marketer and customer in combination with all "third-party" individuals and organizations that can be summed up by the word *society*. In "calculating" profit, we can measure returns in terms of nonmonetary units, such as satisfaction, as well as monetary units. Expenditures may include nonmonetary inputs such as time or discomfort as well as money.

Using these ideas, we broaden the meaning of the term *transaction* to include monetary and nonmonetary exchanges between a marketer, its customer, and all relevant third parties. For example, we might picture the nature of the transaction involved in the marketing of automobiles with pollution-

(24)

control devices, as shown in Figure 16-1. How many of the items exchanged in the transaction pictured there represent products and money in the traditional sense of the terms?

Our broadening of the marketing concept allows us to apply it to a number of situations involving nontraditional products, customer needs, and nonmonetary exchanges that we have considered earlier. Some of the products include grass seed (or green lawns), political candidates (or better government), and home loans (or comfortable housing in advance of the ability to pay for it).

(25)

How would you, for example, diagram the nature of the exchanges between a political candidate (marketer), potential supporters (customers), and third parties?

Similarly, organizations and individuals may market their products and themselves to a number of customer groups. For example, a manufacturing organization may design portions of its promotional effort to sell its products and to sell itself to potential investors, employees, and regulatory bodies.

This sounds good. But what problems does it present to the practicing marketer? First, in a commercial endeavor, his or her results are measured in terms of sales and monetary profits. As we have seen, many of the returns resulting from transactions such as the one diagrammed in Figure 16-1 are nonmonetary in nature. Although managements often proclaim their long-term interests in nonmonetary benefits, they don't factor them into short-run performance measures. This may suggest that some ways need to be found to translate nonmonetary returns into monetary returns to commercial marketers of products and services.

A second major problem is that customers may or may not take note of nonmonetary expenditures and returns in making a decision to buy a product, service, person, or idea. If they properly assess nonmonetary expenditures but not returns, they may refuse to buy.

Figure 16-1. The true nature of the transaction, assessed in monetary and nonmonetary terms, involved in the marketing of automobiles with pollution-control devices.

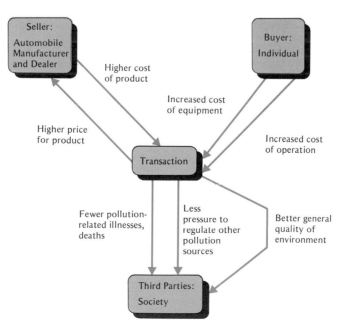

Such was the case with the installation of pollution-control equipment on automobiles. The customer could see the immediate incremental expenditure for new cars equipped with such devices as well as the added expenditure for gasoline as the result of poorer mileage performance caused by the devices. Customers were either unwilling or unable to assess the long-term returns in the form of cleaner air for themselves and their children, even though they would endorse the abstract idea of a better environment. Manufacturers of new automobiles, applying the broadened marketing concept, may well have concluded that the returns to their companies, their customers, and society (third parties) represented a need sufficiently great to offer automobiles with pollution devices. But no one company could afford to do so until the social values of auto-pollution control were made explicit by federal regulation requiring such devices on new models and penalties for failure to comply.

(26)
(27)
You'll recall that after the introduction of new automobiles equipped with pollution control devices with incremental costs of several hundred dollars and several miles less per gallon of gas, the demand and prices for used cars without such equipment increased rapidly. Also, a black market in services to remove such devices from new cars sprang up. What does this customer behavior indicate about the accuracy with which automobile marketers assessed their customers' perceptions of need prior to the passage of federal regulation? Assessing returns and expenditures as in Figure 16-1, what could an automobile manufacturer prior to regulation do to apply the marketing concept in the broader sense we have developed here?

(28)
(29)
Even where expenditures and returns can be translated into monetary terms, customers may be unwilling or unable to compare the relative value of future returns in exchange for current expenditures. For example, a study conducted in 1974 concluded that over the typical fourteen-year life of a refrigerator (1) power to operate a refrigerator purchased in 1972 for $300 would cost $700 and (2) in exchange for a $65 increase in purchase price for better insulation and a more efficient motor, a customer could reduce his or her expenditures for power by 50 per cent with no significant change in maintenance costs. As a marketing manager for a manufacturer of refrigerators, would you recommend that your firm put some or all of its efforts into the design and marketing of a model with the features suggested above for $365? What would you do?

The Marketing Mix. Increasingly rapid product life cycles, with their implications for shifting market segments, adjustments in the relative emphasis on direct and indirect methods of promotion, and channels of distribution and pricing, suggest the need for greater flexibility in the management of marketing effort in the future. Without the introduction of more effective and efficient means of tracking and adjusting marketing effort to life-cycle changes, how long can the trend toward shorter product life cycles continue before excessive marketing costs make product costs prohibitive? Probably not for very long.

This suggests that even though the concept of marketing as an interrelated mix of efforts will continue to have meaning, marketing management will have to devote more effort to understanding the nature of the interrelationships in order to calibrate efforts under changing conditions.

The marketing environment of the future also may require changes in the emphasis devoted to elements of the mix by various companies. In particular, manufacturers of certain consumer products will be required to devote more attention to postpurchase distribution as the Consumer Product Safety Act begins to take effect on a more widespread basis. This will necessitate more and more frequent product recalls, a form of reverse distribution unknown and somewhat distasteful to many marketing managers. As one stated to me recently, "Recalling a previously sold product is much harder than selling it in the first place." It involves products that are no longer owned or controlled by the selling firm. It requires more sophisticated product and customer tracking systems than all but a few firms have at present. In at least one case, the manufacturer of Bon Vivant soups, faced several years ago with the need to recall a large amount of a potentially lethal product, literally was forced into bankruptcy by the magnitude and cost of the effort.

(30)
(31)
What do problems of solid waste disposal or getting voters to the polls in an election have in common with product recall? How can the marketing mix concept be employed in their solution?

(32)
Scarce resources will shift emphasis to product-line planning with the object of relating product profits to demands in such a way that the greatest profit (or customer value) can be derived from a limited resource. What effect will this have on firms maintaining a full line of products in order to serve their customers' perceived needs, even though such a policy may neither make the best use of available resources or produce the highest short-term profits?

Marketing Only As a Device for Stimulating Demand? It is becoming clear that marketing can no longer simply be regarded as a means for stimulating demand for a product, service, person, or idea. As we have seen, marketing has shared the blame for problems of energy shortages, pollution, and planned obsolescence because it has presumably overstimulated the demand for certain products and resources.

This has led to some rethinking of the role of marketing and the suggestion by Kotler that "demarketing," or efforts to bring about a planned reduction in demand, may be more appropriate in certain cases.[6] The philosophy that encompasses demarketing as a legitimate part of the marketing effort sees marketing as a device of organizational control for the regulation of demand as a part of a long-range plan. The design and execution of demarketing programs may be every bit as challenging as for marketing programs if the end objective of reduced demand is to be achieved with a minimum of customer alienation, badwill, and foreclosure of future marketing opportunities.

For example, several years ago many of the citizens of the state of Oregon concluded that it was important that the state discourage further immigration of residents of other states to Oregon, immigration thought to be putting serious pressures on the state's resources. In his speeches to visiting groups, its governor, Tom McCall, often began with comments such as:

I appreciate very much the opportunity to have been invited to address you. There was a slight delay in my acceptance of your invitation, but I can explain that. Rain fell here all last weekend, and I was busy putting sandbags in front of the capital.[7]

[6]Philip Kotler and Sidney J. Levy, "Demarketing, Yes, Demarketing," *Harvard Business Review*, **49** (Nov.–Dec. 1971) pp. 74–80.
[7]This quote, and information in the following paragraphs, was obtained from James Worsham, "If You Plan a Move to Oregon, You'll Love Pahrump, Nev.," *Boston Globe* (July 14, 1973), pp. 1 and 4. Quote on p. 1.

Similarly, he often ended his speeches with invitations to visitors to enjoy themselves but not to tell their friends about Oregon.

Oregon state officials joked about issuing twenty-four-hour visas. There was a humorous move to designate the mosquito as the state bird. But in a more serious vein, the state's Department of Tourism's out-of-state advertising budget was cut to 25 per cent of its former level, with mass-media ads limited to two issues of *National Geographic* magazine, but only the Midwest editions. And a new Eugene-based enterprise, called the Oregon Ungreeting Card Co., immediately found a brisk demand for ungreeting cards such as the ones shown in Figure 16-2. The cards usually contained an invitation of this sort: "Treat yourself to a fun-filled, sun-soaked vacation this year in Pahrump, Nevada."

This example humorously illustrates the type of promotional effort that might be employed in a demarketing program. In addition, of course, prices

Figure 16-2. Products of the Oregon Ungreeting Card Co.

People in Oregon don't take showers...

.... they just dry off!

Summers in Oregon only last two or three weeks...

.... if it doesn't rain!

Oregonians never water their lawns...

.... they simply drain them.

Last year in Oregon 677 people fell off their bikes........

.... and drowned.

(33)
(34)
(35)
might be raised, the outlets through which a product is made available restricted, and the product itself redesigned to appeal to a smaller market segment. Which of these efforts would be most appropriate in supporting a program to reduce demand temporarily? Which would be more effective in bringing about a more permanent reduction in demand? What equivalents to these actions could the state of Oregon employ in its demarketing efforts?

It is important that demarketing actions be fitted to the demarketing objective, whether it be a temporary or more permanent reduction in demand. Similarly, elements of the demarketing mix require the same careful organization and coordination as in a well-designed and executed marketing program.

(36)
Based on the information in our example, what degree of success do you think Governor McCall and the state of Oregon achieved in their demarketing efforts?

□□□

One measure of success might be the sales of the Oregon Ungreeting Card Co. The company, started with an initial capital of $120, sold a half-million ungreeting cards in its first year of operation. Its product line, expanded to include T shirts, bumper stickers, and posters as well as cards, was grossing $30,000 a month. The company also had begun producing ungreeting cards for California, Washington, Colorado, Texas, Arizona, Nevada, and Idaho. Another measure, however, was the fact that the rate of immigration to Oregon increased dramatically, making Oregon the eleventh-fastest growing state in the United States. In the words of Governor McCall: "[It] was the most disappointing boomerang I ever invented."[8] What do you think happened?

(37)

the marketing task and you

The task of detecting and satisfying customer needs at a profit requires a series of efforts ranging from planning to actually carrying out a marketing program. Our entire discussion, in fact, has been organized around this series of efforts, as shown in Figure 16-3.

the marketing task

More than half of this book has been devoted to the planning of a marketing strategy. Beginning with a definition of the product, we have assessed external elements such as potential target markets or customer groups, alternative sources of supply, competitors, and environmental trends. Of equal importance,

[8] Information in this paragraph was based on A. Richard Immel, "Try As They Might, Folks in Oregon Can't Deter New Residents," *Wall Street Journal* (May 22, 1974), pp. 1 and 29. Quote on p. 1.

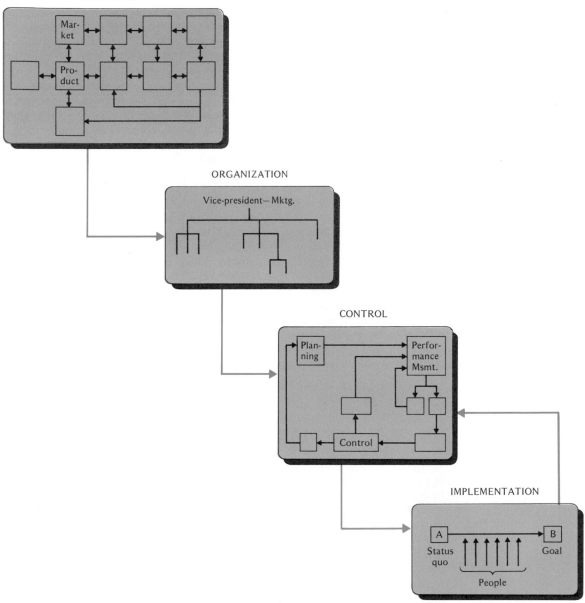

Figure 16-3. The nature of the marketing task.

we have appraised and developed internal elements, sometimes called the marketing mix, of a program in a manner consistent with the needs of the product and the market. These have included internally compatible combinations of product, price, promotional effort, and channels of distribution. The development of a marketing strategy has required the collection and interpretation of data on which estimates of the short- and long-run profitability and risk associated with a particular program could be based. Finally, we have had to adjust initially designed marketing programs in response to forecasts of insufficient profits, high projected marketing costs, or excessive risks in relation to prospective returns. Although portions of the marketing program planning effort lend themselves to highly creative inputs, the economics of the over-all plan must hold up under close scrutiny, whether the nature of the product is a consumer good or a person seeking a job or selling an idea.

As strategies begin to take shape, the organization of effort to accomplish a strategy can be carried out. As we have seen, this leads directly from estimates of the number of salespeople and supporting staff necessary to accomplish the task. It involves the definition and assignment of tasks (differentiation) and the establishment of lines of communication to facilitate coordination (integration) of the effort.

Controls such as sales plans and budgets serve not only to spell out operating goals but also allow an early assessment of the feasibility of plans as they are implemented. We have observed and discussed the types of actions that can be taken when a marketing program is "out of control."

Planning, organizing, and controlling are empty academic words without implementation—the effort required to move an organization, product, or person from the status quo to a goal, whether the goal is a certain number of units of sales or a political office.

Although the primary means of implementing a production plan is machines and the primary means of implementing a financial plan money, people are still central to the implementation of marketing programs. In fact, the word *people* in the box representing implementation in Figure 16-3 may be the only caption that identifies the process depicted as marketing.

people in marketing

The people in marketing include both sellers and buyers of products, services, ideas, and people themselves. Inevitably, they include you. Thus, you have no choice in whether you will be a part of the marketing process, or even whether you will play an active or passive role. Your only choice is what active role you will assume in it. The role may be restricted to that of a customer, which all of us assume at one time or another. Or it may be extended to those of salesperson, marketing manager, advocate of consumers' rights, or civil servant involved in administering laws concerning marketing efforts. Whether you choose to extend your current role in the marketing process probably depends on how you view the rewards and risks of such involvement and how you assess yourself, your interests, and your motives in life against those more actively engaged in marketing. To refresh your memory of some of the people we have considered in our discussion, pertinent facts about several are arrayed in Table 16-3.

Rewards. The rewards of successful marketing efforts may include money, power, prestige, and satisfaction. Financial rewards may range from Sheldon Dietz' modest income from perhaps one month per year of marketing effort to

Table 16-3 Some of the People in *Marketing* (in Order of Appearance)

Person	Task	Described on Pages	Selected (Not Necessarily Representative) Quote
Sheldon Dietz	Owner of The Six-Footer consumer goods manufacturing company	2–28	It's a good feeling to be part of the commerce of man in at least a small way.
John "Jock" Frane	President of United Blockhead, Inc.	142–152	I'm interested in profits, not sales results.
Leo Martin	Manager and part-owner of Dubrow's Cafeteria	153–154	During the higher-price era, the customer would buy a cup of coffee to go with his hamburger. Now he also buys dessert to go with his special, but at the regular price.
Helmut Schmitz	Assistant to advertising manager, Volkswagen of America, Inc.	199–201	How can anybody just make up ads before they know enough about the product?
Bob Levenson	Copywriter; Doyle Dane Bernbach (advertising agency)	199–201	In other agencies more often than not a rather rigid strategy is laid down and the "creative" people are instructed to implement it. In our place, if that happens, the first thing you do is question the strategy.
Kim Kelley	Sales representative, Honeywell, Inc.	219–221	A successful sale and success in selling depends on the development of a mutual trust between the salesman and the customer.
Roberta Wells	Salesperson, Philip Morris Inc.	221–224	I control what I do. If I screw up or exceed quota, it's because of something I do.
Doris Berendt	District manager, Philip Morris Inc.	229–235	Morton Levy (salesman reporting to Ms. Berendt)—lacks self-confidence; . . . has been a sales trainee for several months more than most; should we go along with him any longer?
Kenneth Kolker	Chairman, merchandising committee, Korvette, Inc. (discount department store)	284	We want to make Korvettes trendy and chic too, by having some real high-fashion items from time to time at low prices.
Dale Johnson	Owner and president, Johnson Mill Supply (industrial goods wholesaler)	296, 299–306	. . . unless a wholesaler . . . [can] meet customers' and suppliers' needs more efficiently than such organizations . . . [can] do so by dealing with each other directly the very existence of wholesaling companies . . . [will] be threatened.
Vincent P. Barabba	Director, Bureau of the Census (United States)	400	We've got to find out what information is most needed, cull that out, and then make it more graphic.
Fred Holland	Product manager, Allegheny Ludlum Industries, Inc.	442–444	My objective is to sell the sheet department to each salesman. . . . What I'm after is an improved performance on sheet and not a worse job for other important company products.
John H. Patterson	Founder, NCR Corporation	455–456	Don't talk machines. Don't talk cash registers. Talk the customer's business.

Table 16-3 **(Continued)**

Person	Task	Described on Pages	Selected (Not Necessarily Representative) Quote
Betty Furness	Commission of Consumer Affairs, New York City	492	[Usage of store brands] is an excellent way to save money.
Ben Wells	President, Seven-Up Co.	497	All this [advertising] is directed toward the consumer. It is to convince the consumer that she is getting a better value in 7-Up than she will in some other drink, known brand or no-brand.
John Kenneth Galbraith	Economist	499	. . . Wants so created [by advertising and salesmanship] insure the services of the worker. . . . The pressure of the resulting debt adds to his reliability as a worker.
Tom McCall	Governor, state of Oregon	534–536	Rain fell here all last weekend, and I was busy putting sandbags in front of the capitol.

Kim Kelley's handsome commission income. Over all, marketing jobs provide greater average incomes than others, mainly because the earnings of the lowest marketing operative, the salesperson, in many firms are limited only by his or her ability.

Jobs in marketing provide not only money, but power and prestige as well. Results of a continuing survey of the backgrounds of the chief executive officers of the one-hundred largest United States industrial corporations between 1948 and 1972, as shown in Figure 16-4, bears this out. They are consistent with results of other studies suggesting an even more marked increase in the proportion of chief executive officers with primary backgrounds in marketing in recent years. How could you possibly account for this?

(38)

John Marttila's power stems from the fact that political candidates generally believe that he knows how to get people elected to office, and Herb Fried must get a sense of satisfaction from a successful Kidney Foundation advertising appeal.

Risks. Rewards are not attained without risks. Perceived risks again may range from loss of money to loss of prestige or self-respect. Marketing is perhaps the field in which it is the most difficult to cover up shortcomings. Poor performance and resulting income penalties show up rapidly. This can be especially true for those selling or otherwise working on a straight commission basis.

Similarly, some may perceive certain marketing jobs as requiring a false front, catering to customers' whims, or making social demands that sap a person's self-respect over time. Stage characters such as Willy Loman in *Death of a Salesman* have reinforced this view.

Interests and Motives. It is safe to say that no one of our acquaintances listed in Table 16-3 views marketing as an end in itself. it is a means for achieving other things. Perhaps the most basic of these is financial rewards. To Kim Kelley, who

Figure 16-4. The chief executive's route to the top. Trends in the proportion of chief executives of the 100 largest industrial firms in the United States with various backgrounds. *Source:* Golightly & Co., International, as quoted in "More Room at the Top for Marketing Men," *Business Week,* (Aug. 12, 1972) p. 27.

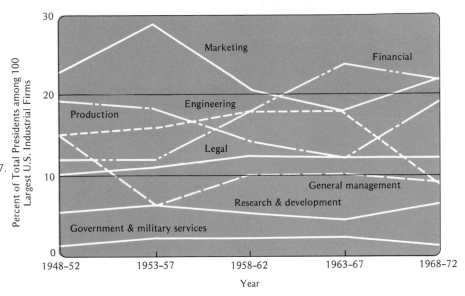

planned to deposit over $200,000 after taxes in the bank at the age of thirty-one by the time you read this book, financial rewards are direct. But even to Herb Fried, a successful Kidney Foundation campaign will attract more profitable advertising accounts. And John Marttila's fees go up with each successful political campaign.

But to what extent do the quotes listed in Table 16-3 suggest other interests or motives explaining why people hold marketing related jobs? To what extent do these interests and motives coincide with yours?

To some, marketing represents a way of having fun and getting paid for it. Advertising executive Jerry Della Famina has described his job, for example, as "the most fun you can have with your clothes on."[9] Undoubtedly, the pay adds to the fun.

Attributes of Success. What possible explanations can we give for at least the modest degree of success that all of the individuals listed in Table 16-3 have achieved? Woven through their descriptions and comments are suggestions of various factors. Among these are an interest in people and their needs; the ability to provide a relatively large amount of self-control and work without direct supervision; and a basic belief in the value of the product, service, person, or idea being marketed. What specific examples of each of these can you recall from among the people listed in Table 16-3? Does your acquaintance with these marketing people suggest additional attributes of success?

[9] Jerry Della Famina, *From Those Wonderful Folks Who Gave You Pearl Harbor* (New York: Simon & Schuster, 1970), p. 244.

marketing as something to be used

Marketing is a means to achieve personal, organizational, or other goals. As such, it is comparable to a tool. Early in the book the remark, "People do not rush out and buy new, faster quarter-inch drills. They buy faster quarter-inch-holes," was inserted to illustrate the fact that people don't buy products per se but rather the results that the products promise to deliver. Similarly, we're not interested in marketing as a self-fulfilling activity, but rather because of the goals it can help us achieve.

The goals may be worthy or not. Marketing can be used to serve all masters. And there is nothing inherent in marketing concepts or philosophy that provides much guidance in their use. Once again, people decide this. And that puts it squarely up to you.

summary

Marketing effort in the future will be affected by environmental, institutional, and technological trends, among others. Among the most important of the environmental trends are those having to do with the rebirth of consumerism and a concern for the rights of buyers rather than sellers. These have resulted from a number of contributing factors, which are considered in Chapter 3. In addition, basic changes in the nature of markets have reflected consumers' growing desires to express their individuality, channel their expenditures into nonmaterial items, identify themselves with leisure activities rather than jobs, and preserve their mobility through the lease as opposed to the purchase of goods. Finally, restricted supplies and an inability to meet existing demands have raised questions about the future value of marketing effort in resource-starved industries.

Environmental trends have fostered institutional changes. Among the more important institutional trends are the polarization of the retailing structure toward both mass merchandising and large specialty stores, increases in the volume of business done by nonstore retailing methods, reductions in the lengths of life cycles of retailing institutions, a continually changing but not diminishing role for whole-saling, an increase in the use of shared services, and the increasing practice of marketing for nonprofit purposes.

Institutional trends are supportive of, and effected by, technological trends. Among major technological trends of importance for marketing are the introduction and use of the computer in all phases of marketing effort, improvements in the collection and analysis of data for marketing decision making, the development of increasingly complex products and the accompanying marketing effort that they require in a postindustrial society, and the marketing of new products and technologies to serve as substitutes for those for which raw material shortages have developed.

All of this has raised questions about the applicability of current marketing philosophies for the future. An appraisal of three of these suggests that, with some adjustments, they will continue to have applicability. The marketing concept, stressing the detection and satisfaction of customer needs at a profit, will be applicable if the meaning of the term *profit* is expanded to accommodate transactions involving monetary and nonmonetary gains and losses to sellers, buyers, and society. The practice of marketing under this expanded concept will present greater challenges than under the traditional marketing concept. The marketing mix will be employed in the future as in the past, but with shifts in emphasis in its components in various industries. The implicit belief that marketing is a device for stimulating demand will have to be expanded to accommodate the idea that marketing effort will in the future be a device for controlling or regulating demand both upward and downward to meet corporate objectives.

In its expanded role, the marketing task of planning, organizing, controlling, and implementing marketing programs will require the best available people. For it is the relatively great importance of the quality of personal relationships and people that distinguishes marketing from other functional tasks such as finance or production in business.

All of us must play an active role in the marketing process as buyers. Our only choice is whether to expand the role as salespersons, marketing managers, advocates of consumers' rights, or government regulatory officials. In doing so, we will weigh possible risks ranging from loss of income, prestige, or self-respect against the potentials for substantial income, power, prestige, and satisfaction. We will assess ourselves in the light of what we perceive to be attributes of success in many marketing jobs: an interest in people and their needs; the ability to provide a relatively large amount of self-control and work without direct supervision; and a basic belief in the product, service, person, or idea being marketed.

appendix

sources of marketing information

Marketing information comes in packages of varied shapes and sizes, ranging from bound books to computer tapes. The purposes of this appendix are to (1) expose a novice to many sources of marketing information and to the ways of locating them and (2) assemble in one place a reference to such sources for practicing marketing managers. These objectives have influenced the organization of the appendix.

The indexes, bibliographies, directories, and dictionaries that are found in the first section are guideposts to other sources, invaluable in making a shortcut in the information-gathering process from sources of secondary data, including articles and other documents. The second section contains a list of selected books, keyed roughly to the chapters of this book. In the third section is an annotated list of important marketing periodicals. Next you'll find descriptions of selected marketing-oriented associations with wide influence, relatively large memberships, and active information programs. The remaining sections may be of greater practical value for someone seeking statistics for use in the decision-making process. Included here are listings of major government and nongovernment sources of statistics as well as descriptions of some of the more widely known panel and audit services.

indexes, bibliographies, directories, and dictionaries

Items in this section provide guideposts to the location of other sources of information. They are important in reducing the task of performing a search of available information about a topic, an organization, individuals, or their activities. As a first step in researching a topic, a bibliography on a particular subject might save you the trouble of searching out many references. Even if you are fortunate enough to find a bibliography on the topic of interest to you, you probably will want to update it by referring to one or more indexes under the topic of your choice. Directories of marketing organizations and individuals can prove invaluable in assembling a list of contacts for primary research efforts or in marketing or purchasing goods and services. Finally, several marketing-oriented dictionaries can supplement terms and definitions found in this book, and perhaps provide related terms for research "around" a topic.

indexes

Business Periodicals Index (monthly and cumulated annually). New York: The H. W. Wilson Company. A subject index to articles appearing in more than one hundred English language business periodicals, including the following of particular interest for marketing: Advertising Age, American Druggist Merchandising, Broadcasting, Chain Store Age, Distribution Worldwide, Industrial Distribution, Industrial Marketing, Journal of Advertising Research, Journal of Marketing, Journal of Marketing Research, Journal of Purchasing and Materials Management, Journal of Retailing,

Merchandising Week, Modern Packaging, Progressive Grocer, Sales Management, Transportation Journal, Vend, and Vending Times.

Guide to Special Issues and Indexes of Periodicals, 2nd ed., Charlotte M. Devers, Doris B. Katz, and Mary M. Regan. New York: Special Libraries Association, 1975.

Guide to Special Issues of Business Publications (continuing). Presented periodically in *Industrial Marketing* (see the listing for periodicals), this guide describes the contents of special issues of business magazines with present statistics, directory listings, and other information for some thirty industries.

Marketing + Distribution Abstracts (eight times per year). Wembley, England: Anbar Publications, Ltd., published in association with The Institute of Marketing. Abstracts of articles appearing in international periodicals that concern marketing and physical distribution. Its coverage of English periodicals supplements that of other bibliographies and indexes listed in this section.

The Marketing Information Guide (monthly, with indexes cumulated quarterly). Garden City, N. Y.: Trade Marketing Information Guide, Inc. An annotated index of current books, articles, and pamplets from private or public sources, with emphasis on statistics useful in marketing and economic research, published in the United States and other countries.

The New York Times Index (twenty-four times per year and cumulated annually). New York: The New York Times Company. Indexed articles that have appeared in *The New York Times,* including many of interest to marketers.

Public Affairs Information Service Bulletin (weekly and cumulated quarterly and annually). New York: Public Affairs Information Service, Inc. The most complete index to government documents, this index also lists by subject current books, pamphlets, periodical articles, and any other useful library material in the field of economics and public affairs. Among the periodicals indexed that are of particular interest for marketing are Journal of the Academy of Marketing Science, Canadian Vending (Canada), Commerce (Philippines), Consumer Legislative Monthly Report, Consumer Review, Consumer Reports, Discount Merchandiser, European Business (France), Industrial Marketing Management (The Netherlands), Journal of Advertising, Journal of Commerce, Journal of Consumer Affairs, Journal of Marketing, Journal of Purchasing, Journal of Retailing, Logistics and Transportation Review (Canada), Journal of the Market Research Society (England), Stores, Journal of Transportation, and What's New in Advertising & Marketing?

Published Data on European Industrial Markets. London: Industrial Aids Limited. An index of reports of commercial market research concerning European industrial markets available for sale.

Reader's Guide to Periodical Literature (twenty-four times per year, cumulated quarterly and annually). New York: The H. W. Wilson Company. Indexed articles that have appeared in the most popular general interest periodicals, including some of interest for marketing.

Social Sciences & Humanities Index (quarterly, cumulated annually). New York: The H. W. Wilson Company. Indexed articles that have appeared in periodicals in such fields as economics and sociology, of relevance for marketing.

The Wall Street Journal Index (monthly, cumulated annually). New Jersey: Dow Jones Books. Indexed articles that have appeared in *The Wall Street Journal,* including many of interest to marketers.

bibliographies

American Bibliography of Agricultural Economics (quarterly). Washington, D. C.: Department of Agriculture, The American Agricultural Economics Documentation Center. An index to papers and research notes, including a separate section on agricultural marketing, appearing in United States and Canadian journals of agriculture.

A Basic Bibliography on Marketing Research. Ferber, Robert, Alain Cousineau, Millard Crask, and Hugh G. Wales. 3rd ed. Chicago: American Marketing Association, 1974. The third edition of a comprehensive bibliography of periodical literature on marketing research to the end of 1973.

Brands: A Selected and Annotated Bibliography. Uhr, Ernest B., and William A. Wallace, ed. Chicago: American Marketing Association, 1972.

Intercollegiate Bibliography, Cases in Business Administration. Lindfors, Grace V., and Jean Burleson, ed. Boston: Intercollegiate Case Clearing House. Updated periodically, this is a bibliography of case problems, based on field experience with various organizations and prepared by faculty and students from a number of colleges and universities, indexed by functional orientation. For example, the edition listing cases filed in 1972 and 1973, published in 1973, lists, in annotated form, more than two-hundred cases on various aspects of marketing, providing a synopsis of each case as well as information about its length, authorship, and key topics. In addition, the Intercollegiate Case Clearing House publishes, from time to time, additional bibliographies of cases dealing with specific topics or areas of the world.

International Marketing. Goldstucker, Jac L., and José de la Torre, Jr., ed. Chicago: American Marketing Association, 1972.

Journal of Marketing. "Marketing Abstracts" section. Chicago: American Marketing Association, quarterly. Each issue of this widely read journal contains an annotated bibliography arranged by broad marketing topics.

Measuring Payout: An Annotated Bibliography on the Dollar Effectiveness of Advertising. New York: Advertising Research Foundation, 1973. Sources of information regarding advertising and its effectiveness in stimulating sales, arranged by year of publication, 1965–1972.

U. S. Small Business Administration Bibliography Series (occasional). Washington, D. C.: Small Business Administration. Bibliographies prepared for each of a number of types of small businesses to aid their owners and employees in carrying out various business activities, including marketing, more effectively.

directories

Ayer Directory of Publications (annual). Philadelphia: Ayer Press. A directory containing information about newspapers and magazines published in the contiguous states of the United States, Puerto Rico, Virgin Islands, Canada, Bahamas, Bermuda, Panama, and the Philippines. Information about each publication includes its circulation, basic advertising rates, page size, frequency of publication, and the name and address of its publisher.

Bradford's Directory of Marketing Research Agencies and Management Consultants (biennial). Fairfax, Va.: Bradford's Directory of Marketing Research Agencies. Names and addresses for, and descriptions of services provided by, marketing research agencies in the United States and other countries.

Directory of Department Stores (annual). New York: Department Store Guide, Inc., a subsidiary of *Chain Store Age*. A directory of department stores and chains, their executives and buyers, buyers' phone numbers, and information about resident (central) buying offices of importance to individuals selling to department stores.

Directory of Marketing Services and Membership Roster (of the American Marketing Association). Chicago: R. F. Clancy Co., 1973. Names and addresses of members of the American Marketing Association and a directory of firms providing marketing services in the United States.

Directory of Super Markets (annual). New York: Business Guides, Inc., a subsidiary of *Chain Store Age*. A directory of supermarkets, their executives and buyers, buyers' phone numbers, and other information of importance to individuals selling to supermarkets.

International Directory of Marketing Research Houses and Services (annual). New York: New York Chapter, American Marketing Association. Officers and a description of the scope of services provided by each firm.

Marketing Research in Europe (annual). Amsterdam: European Society for Opinion and Marketing Research. A comprehensive directory listing names, addresses, and principals of European marketing research organizations, as well as services provided by each.

National Franchise Directory (periodical). Denver, Colo.: Continental Reports, Inc. Names, addresses, types of businesses franchised, franchising costs, and other information for organizations engaged in franchising activities.

Newspaper Press Directory. Benn's Guide to Newspapers and Periodicals of the World (annual). London, England: Benn Brothers Ltd. Information regarding circulation, basic advertising rates, page sizes, the frequency of publication, and the names and addresses of publishers of periodicals in all countries of the world, with particular emphasis on British Commonwealth countries.

Standard Directory of Advertisers (annual). Skokie, Ill.: National Register Publishing Co., Inc. Information about 17,000 United States corporations, their trade names, sales, lines of business, executives, advertising agencies employed, and media used.

Standard Directory of Advertising Agencies (annual). Skokie, Ill.: National Register Publishing Co., Inc. Current information about United States advertising agencies, including their names, addresses, specializations, annual billings, breakdown of billings by media, executives, and major advertiser accounts.

Statistics Sources, 4th ed. Wasserman, Paul, and Joanne Paskar, ed. Detroit: Gale Research Company, 1974. A massive compilation of sources of statistics for all countries of the world, arranged alphabetically by key-word subject. Included in the types of sources referenced are dictionaries of terms, bibliographies and guides, almanacs, United States government monographs and annuals, United States government periodicals, publications of major censuses, annuals and yearbooks, and international sources. In the words of the editors, this is a basic "finding guide to statistical intelligence."

Trade Names Dictionary (periodical). Detroit: Gale Research Company. A list of thousands of trade and brand names, listed alphabetically with the type of product or service and its producer's name and address.

dictionaries

Encyclopedia of Advertising, 2nd ed. Graham, Irvin. New York: Fairchild Publications, 1969.

Marketing Terms: Definitions, Explanations, and/or Aspects, 3rd ed. Shapiro, Irving J. West Long Beach, N. J.: S-M-C Publishing Co., 1973. An extensive volume of concise definitions.

A Dictionary for Marketing Research. New York: Audits & Surveys, Inc., 1974. Terms concerning marketing research methods that are referenced to sources providing more extensive descriptions.

books

The following books are arranged in terms of their general marketing orientation or emphasis on some facet of the subject, with the latter listed by topics taken up in each chapter of this book. With very few exceptions, for "classic" treatments of certain topics, the list is limited to those books published no earlier than 1968.

general marketing (all chapters)

source textbooks

Alderson, Wroe. *Dynamic Marketing Behavior.* Homewood, Ill.: Richard D. Irwin, Inc., 1965.
Beckman, Theodore N., William R. Davidson, and W. W. Talarzyk. *Marketing,* 9th ed. New York: The Ronald Press Company, 1973.

Boone, Louis E., and David L. Kurtz. *Contemporary Marketing*. New York: Holt, Rinehart & Winston, Inc., 1974.

Buzzell, Robert D., Robert E. M. Nourse, John B. Matthews, Jr., and Theodore Levitt. *Marketing: A Contemporary Analysis,* 2nd ed. New York: McGraw-Hill Book Company, 1972.

Carman, James M., and Kenneth P. Uhl. *Phillips and Duncan's Marketing: Principles and Methods,* 7th ed. Homewood, Ill.: Richard D. Irwin, Inc., 1973.

Davis, Kenneth R. *Marketing Management,* 3rd ed. New York: The Ronald Press Company, 1972.

Dodge, H. R. *Industrial Marketing*. New York: McGraw-Hill Book Company, 1970.

Fisher, Lawrence. *Industrial Marketing: An Analytical Approach to Planning and Execution.* Princeton, N. J.: Brandon/Systems Press, 1970.

Hill, Richard M., Ralph S. Alexander, and James S. Cross. *Industrial Marketing,* 4th ed. Homewood, Ill.: Richard D. Irwin, Inc., 1975.

Howard, John A. *Marketing Management: Operating, Strategic, and Administrative,* 3rd ed. Homewood, Ill.: Richard D. Irwin, Inc., 1973.

Kelley, Eugene J. *Marketing Planning and Competitive Strategy*. Englewood Cliffs, N. J.: Prentice-Hall, Inc., 1972.

Kerr, John R., and James E. Littlefield. *Marketing: An Environmental Approach*. New York: Prentice-Hall, Inc., 1975.

Kotler, Philip. *Marketing Management: Analysis, Planning and Control,* 2nd ed. Englewood Cliffs, N. J.: Prentice-Hall, Inc., 1972.

Lipson, Harry A., and John R. Darling, *Marketing Fundamentals: Text and Cases*. New York: John Wiley & Sons, Inc., 1974.

McCarthy, E. Jerome. *Basic Marketing: A Managerial Approach,* 5th ed. Homewood, Ill.: Richard D. Irwin, Inc., 1975.

Marcus, Burton H., et al. *Modern Marketing*. New York: Random House, Inc., 1975.

Rachman, David J. *Marketing Strategy and Structure*. Englewood Cliffs, N. J.: Prentice-Hall, Inc., 1974.

Risley, George. *Modern Industrial Marketing*. New York: McGraw-Hill Book Company, 1972.

Rodger, Leslie W. *Marketing in a Competitive Economy,* 3rd ed. New York: John Wiley & Sons, Inc., 1973.

Stanton, William J. *Fundamentals of Marketing,* 4th ed. New York: McGraw-Hill Book Company, 1975.

Still, Richard R., and Edward W. Cundiff. *Essentials of Marketing,* 2nd ed. Englewood Cliffs, N. J.: Prentice-Hall, Inc., 1972.

Taylor, Weldon J., and Roy T. Shaw. *Marketing—An Integrated Analytical Approach,* 3rd ed. Cincinnati: South-Western Publishing Co., 1975.

Webster, Frederick E., Jr. *Marketing for Managers*. New York: Harper and Row, Publishers, 1974.

Wills, Gordon. *Strategic Issues in Marketing*. New York: John Wiley & Sons, Inc., 1974.

Zober, Martin. *Principles of Marketing*. Boston: Allyn & Bacon, Inc., 1971.

books of readings

Britt, Steuart H., and Harper W. Boyd, Jr. *Marketing Management and Administrative Action,* 3rd ed. New York: McGraw-Hill Book Company, 1973.

Engel, James F., Henry F. Fiorillo, and Murray A. Cayley, ed. *Market Segmentation*. New York: Holt, Rinehart & Winston, Inc., 1972.

Enis, Ben M., and Keith K. Cox. *Marketing Classics,* 2nd ed. Boston: Allyn & Bacon, Inc., 1974.

Kelley, Eugene J., and William Lazer. *Managerial Marketing: Policies, Strategies, and Decisions.* Homewood, Ill.: Richard D. Irwin, Inc., 1973.

Kotler, Philip, and Keith J. Cox. *Readings in Marketing Management.* Englewood Cliffs, N. J.: Prentice-Hall, Inc., 1972.

McCarthy, E. Jerome, John F. Grashof, and Andrew A. Brogowicz. *Readings in Basic Marketing.* Homewood, Ill.: Richard D. Irwin, Inc., 1975.

handbooks

Britt, Steuart H., ed. *The Dartnell Marketing Manager's Handbook.* Chicago: Dartnell Corporation, 1973.

Buell, Victor P., ed. *Handbook of Modern Marketing.* New York: McGraw-Hill Book Company, 1970.

European Advertising & Marketing Handbook (periodical). London: European Data Index Limited.

Riso, Ovid, ed. *The Dartnell Sales Promotion Handbook,* 6th ed. Chicago: The Dartnell Corporation, 1973.

product-consumer fit (chapter 2)

Day, Ralph L., and Thomas E. Ness, ed. *Marketing Models: Behavioral Science Applications.* Scranton, Pa.: Intext Educational Publishers, 1971.

Engel, James F., David T. Kollat, and Roger D. Blackwell. *Consumer Behavior,* 2nd ed. New York: Holt, Rinehart & Winston, Inc., 1973.

Farley, John U., John A. Howard, and L. Winston Ring. *Consumer Behavior: Theory and Application.* Boston, Mass: Marketing Science Institute and Allyn & Bacon, Inc., 1974.

Howard, John A., and Lyman E. Ostland. *Buyer Behavior: Theoretical and Empirical Foundation.* New York: Alfred A. Knopf, Inc., 1973.

Howard, John A., and Jagdish N. Sheth. *The Theory of Buyer Behavior.* New York: John Wiley & Sons, Inc., 1969.

Jenkins, John R. G. *Marketing and Consumer Behavior.* New York: Pergamon Press, Inc., 1972.

Kassarjian, Harold H., and Thomas S. Robertson. *Perspectives in Consumer Behavior,* rev. ed. Glenview, Ill.: Scott, Foresman and Company, 1973.

Robertson, Thomas S. *Innovation and the Consumer.* New York: Holt, Rinehart & Winston, Inc., 1971.

Walters, C. Glenn. *Consumer Behavior: Theory and Practice,* rev. ed. Homewood, Ill.: Richard D. Irwin, Inc., 1974.

Ward, Scott, and Thomas S. Robertson, ed. *Consumer Behavior: Theoretical Sources.* Englewood Cliffs, N. J.: Prentice-Hall, Inc., 1973.

product-environment fit (chapter 3)

Holloway, Robert J., and Robert S. Hancock, ed. *The Environment of Marketing Management: Selections from the Literature,* 3rd ed. New York: John Wiley & Sons, Inc., 1974.

Howard, Marshall. *Legal Aspects of Marketing.* New York: McGraw-Hill Book Company, 1964.

Katona, George. *The Mass Consumption Society.* New York: McGraw-Hill Book Company, 1964.

Wilcox, Clair. *Public Policies Toward Business.* Homewood, Ill.: Richard D. Irwin, Inc., 1966.

product-company fit (chapter 4)

Butrick, Frank M. *How to Develop New Products for Sale to Industry.* Englewood Cliffs, N. J.: Prentice-Hall, Inc., 1971.

Foster, Douglas W., *Planning for Products and Markets.* London: Longman, 1972.

Gisser, Philip. *Launching the New Industrial Product.* New York: American Management Association, Inc., 1972.

Karger, Delmar W., and Robert G. Murdick. *New Product Venture Management.* New York: Gordon and Breach, Science Publishers, Inc., 1972.

Luck, David J. *Product Policy and Strategy.* Englewood Cliffs, N. J.: Prentice-Hall, Inc., 1972.

Marvin, Philip. *Product Planning Simplified.* New York: American Management Association, Inc., 1972.

McGuire, E. Patrick. *Evaluating New-Product Proposals.* Conference Board Report no. 604. New York: National Industrial Conference Board, 1973.

Wasson, Chester R. *Dynamic Competitive Strategy and Product Life Cycles.* St. Charles, Ill.: Challenge Books, 1974.

pricing (chapter 5)

Lynn, Robert A. *Price Policies and Marketing Management.* Homewood, Ill.: Richard D. Irwin, Inc., 1967.

Oxenfeldt, Alfred R. *Pricing Strategies.* New York: American Management Association, Inc., 1975.

Palda, Kristian S. *Pricing Decisions and Marketing Policy.* Englewood Cliffs, N. J.: Prentice-Hall, Inc., 1971.

Taylor, Bernard, and Gordon Wills, ed. *Pricing Strategy: Reconciling Customer Needs and Company Objectives.* London: Staples, 1969.

indirect promotion (chapter 6)

Aaker, David A., and John G. Myers. *Advertising Management.* Englewood Cliffs, N. J.: Prentice-Hall, Inc., 1975.

Aaker, David A. *Advertising Management: Practical Perspectives.* Englewood Cliffs, N. J.: Prentice-Hall, Inc., 1975.

Barton, Roger, ed. *Handbook of Advertising Management.* New York: McGraw-Hill Book Company, 1970.

Borden, Neil H. *The Economic Effects of Advertising.* Homewood, Ill.: Richard D. Irwin, Inc., 1942.

Caples, John. *Tested Advertising Methods,* 4th ed. Englewood Cliffs, N. J.: Prentice-Hall, Inc., 1974.

Dirksen, Charles, Jr., and Arthur Kroeger. *Advertising Principles and Problems,* 4th ed. Homewood, Ill.: Richard D. Irwin, Inc., 1973.

Dunn, S. Watson, and Arnold M. Barban. *Advertising: Its Role In Modern Marketing,* 3rd ed. New York: Holt, Rinehart & Winston, Inc., 1974.

Engel, James F., Hugh G. Wales, and Martin R. Warshaw. *Promotional Strategy,* 3rd ed. Homewood, Ill.: Richard D. Irwin, Inc., 1975.

Hodgson, Richard S. *The Dartnell Direct Mail and Mail Order Handbook,* 2nd ed. Chicago: The Dartnell Corporation, 1974.

Kleppner, Otto. *Advertising Procedure,* 6th ed. Englewood Cliffs, N. J.: Prentice-Hall, Inc., 1973.

Nicosia, Francesco M. *Advertising, Management, and Society: A Business Point of View.* New York: McGraw-Hill Book Company, 1974.

Quera, Leon. *Advertising Campaigns: Formulation and Tactics.* Columbus: Grid, Inc., 1973.

Riso, Ovid. *Advertising Cost Control Handbook.* New York: Van Nostrand Reinhold Company, 1973.

Sandage, C. H., and Vernon Frybarger. *Advertising Theory and Practice,* 9th ed. Homewood, Ill.: Richard D. Irwin, Inc., 1975.

Simon, Julian L. *Issues in the Economics of Advertising.* Chicago: University of Illinois Press, 1970.

Stansfield, Richard H. *The Dartnell Advertising Managers' Handbook,* 2nd ed. Chicago: The Dartnell Corporation, 1975.

Tillman, Rollie, and C. A. Kirkpatrick. *Promotion: Persuasive Communication in Marketing,* rev. ed. Homewood, Ill.: Richard D. Irwin, Inc., 1972.

Wright, John S., Daniel S. Warner, and Willis L. Winter, Jr. *Advertising,* 3rd ed. New York: McGraw-Hill Book Company, 1971.

Wright, John S., and John E. Mertes. *Advertising's Role in Society.* St. Paul: West Publishing Co., 1974.

direct promotion (chapter 7)

Baer, Earl E. *Salesmanship.* New York: McGraw-Hill Book Company, 1972.

Engel, James F., Hugh G. Wales, and Martin R. Warshaw. *Promotional Strategy,* rev. ed. Homewood, Ill.: Richard D. Irwin, Inc., 1971.

Haas, Kenneth B., and John W. Ernest. *Creative Salesmanship: Understanding Essentials,* 2nd ed. Beverly Hills, Calif.: Glencoe Press, 1974.

Pederson, Carlton A., and Milburn D. Wright. *Salesmanship: Principles and Methods,* 5th ed. Homewood, Ill: Richard D. Irwin, Inc., 1971.

Riso, Ovid, ed. *The Dartnell Sales Manager's Handbook,* 12th ed. Chicago, Ill.: The Dartnell Corporation, 1975.

Russell, Frederick A., Frank H. Beach, and Richard H. Buskirk. *Textbook of Salesmanship,* 9th ed. New York: McGraw-Hill Book Company, 1974.

Stanton, William J., and Richard H. Buskirk. *Management of the Sales Force,* 4th ed. Homewood, Ill.: Richard D. Irwin, Inc., 1974.

Still, Richard R., Edward W. Cundiff, and N. A. P. Govoni. *Sales Management: Decisions, Policies, and Cases,* 3rd ed. Englewood Cliffs, N. J.: Prentice-Hall, Inc., 1976.

Stroh, Thomas F. *Training and Developing the Professional Salesman.* New York: AMACOM, American Management Association, 1973.

Tillman, Rollie, and C. A. Kirkpatrick. *Promotion: Persuasive Communication in Marketing,* rev. ed. Homewood, Ill.: Richard D. Irwin, Inc., 1972.

Wotruba, Thomas R. *Sales Management: Planning, Accomplishment and Evaluation.* New York: Holt, Rinehart & Winston, Inc., 1971.

distribution: the retailer's view (chapter 8)

Corbman, Bernard P., and Murray Krieger. *Mathematics for Retail Merchandising,* 2nd ed. New York: The Ronald Press Company, 1972.

Duncan, Delbert, Jr., Charles F. Phillips, and Stanley C. Hollander. *Modern Retailing Management: Basic Concepts and Practices,* 8th ed. Homewood: Ill.: Richard D. Irwin, Inc., 1972.

Gist, Ronald R. *Basic Retailing: Text and Cases.* New York: John Wiley & Sons, Inc., 1971.

——. *Management Perspectives in Retailing,* 2nd ed. New York: John Wiley & Sons, Inc., 1971.

James, Don L., Bruce J. Walker, and Michael J. Etzel. *Retailing Today.* New York: Harcourt Brace Jovanovich, Inc., 1975.

Marquardt, Ray A., James C. Makens, and Robert Roe. *Retail Management: Satisfaction of Consumer Needs.* New York: Holt, Rinehart & Winston, Inc., 1975.

Ozanne, U. B., and S. D. Hunt. *The Economic Effects of Franchising.* Madison: Graduate School of Business, University of Wisconsin, 1971.

Rachman, David J. *Retail Strategy and Structure: A Management Approach,* 2nd ed. Englewood Cliffs, N. J.: Prentice-Hall, Inc., 1975.

Wingate, John W., Elmer O. Schaller, and F. Leonard Miller. *Retail Merchandise Management.* Englewood Cliffs, N. J.: Prentice-Hall, Inc., 1972.

distribution: the wholesaler's view (chapter 9)

Beckman, Theodore N., Nathanael H. Engle, and Robert D. Buzzell. *Wholesaling,* 3rd ed. New York: The Ronald Press Company, 1959.

Bucklin, Louis P. *Competition and Evolution in the Distribution Trades.* Englewood Cliffs, N. J.: Prentice-Hall, Inc., 1972.

Hill, Richard M. *Wholesaling Management: Text and Cases.* Homewood, Ill.: Richard D. Irwin, Inc., 1963.

Vance, J. E., Jr. *The Merchant's World: The Geography of Wholesaling.* Englewood Cliffs, N. J.: Prentice-Hall, Inc., 1970.

distribution: the manufacturers' view (chapter 10)

Certain books in the following list contain readings on numerous issues of importance for retail and wholesale distribution as well.

Ballou, Ronald H. *Business Logistics Management.* Englewood Cliffs, N. J.: Prentice-Hall, Inc., 1973.

Boone, Louis E., and James C. Johnson. *Marketing Channels.* Morristown, N. J.: General Learning Press, 1973.

Bowersox, Donald J. *Logistical Management.* New York: The Macmillan Company, 1974.

Bucklin, Louis P. *A Theory of Distribution Channel Structure* Berkeley: Institute of Business and Economic Research, University of California, 1966.

Clewett, Richard M., ed. *Marketing Channels for Manufactured Products.* Homewood, Ill.: Richard D. Irwin, Inc., 1954.

Heskett, James L., Nicholas A. Glaskowsky, Jr., and Robert M. Ivie, *Business Logistics,* 2nd ed. New York: The Ronald Press Company, 1973.

Lee, Lamar, Jr., and Donald W. Dober. *Purchasing and Materials Management.* New York: McGraw-Hill Book Company, 1971.

Lewis, Edwin H. *Marketing Channels: Structure and Strategy.* New York: McGraw-Hill Book Company, 1968.

Machman, Ronald. *Marketing Channels.* Columbus: Grid, Inc., 1974.

Mallen, Bruce E. *The Marketing Channel: A Conceptual Viewpoint.* New York: John Wiley & Sons, Inc., 1967.

Moller, William G., Jr., and D. L. Wilemon. *Marketing Channels: A Systems Viewpoint.* Homewood, Ill.: Richard D. Irwin, Inc., 1971.

Smykay, Edward W. *Physical Distribution Management,* 3rd ed. New York: The Macmillan Company, 1973.

Stern, Louis, ed. *Distribution Channels: Behavioral Dimensions.* Boston: Houghton Mifflin Company, 1969.

Walker, Bruce J., and Joel B. Haynes, ed. *Marketing Channels and Institutions: Readings in Distribution Concepts and Practices.* Columbus: Grid, Inc., 1973.

Walters, C. Glenn. *Marketing Channels.* New York: The Ronald Press Company, 1974.

Westing, J. H., I. V. Fine, and G. J. Zenz. *Purchasing Management: Materials in Motion.* New York: John Wiley & Sons, Inc., 1969.

marketing research (chapter 11)

Boyd, Harper W., Jr. and Ralph Westfall. *Marketing Research: Text and Cases,* 3rd ed. Homewood, Ill.: Richard D. Irwin, Inc., 1972.

Day, Ralph L., and Leonard J. Parsons, ed. *Marketing Models: Quantitative Applications,* 2nd ed. Scranton, Pa.: Intext Educational Publishers, 1971.

Ferber, Robert, ed. *Handbook of Marketing Research.* New York: McGraw-Hill Book Company, 1974.

Frank, Ronald E., William F. Massy, and Yoram Wind. *Market Segmentation.* Englewood Cliffs, N. J.: Prentice-Hall, Inc., 1972.

Govoni, Norman A. P. *Contemporary Marketing Research: Perspectives and Applications.* Morristown, N. J.: General Learning Corporation, 1972.

Green, Paul E., and Donald S. Tull. *Research for Marketing Decisions,* 3rd ed. Englewood Cliffs, N. J.: Prentice-Hall, Inc., 1975.

Jolson, Marvin A., and Richard T. Hise. *Quantitative Techniques for Marketing Decisions.* New York: The Macmillan Company, 1973.

Kotler, Philip. *Marketing Decision Making: A Model Building Approach.* New York: Holt, Rinehart & Winston, Inc., 1971.

Luck, David J., Hugh G. Wales, and Donald A. Taylor. *Marketing Research,* 4th ed. Englewood Cliffs, N. J.: Prentice-Hall, Inc., 1974.

Montgomery, David B., and Glen L. Urban, ed. *Applications of Management Sciences in Marketing.* Englewood Cliffs, N. J.: Prentice-Hall, Inc., 1970.

Montgomery, David B., and Glen L. Urban. *Management Science in Marketing.* Englewood Cliffs, N. J.: Prentice-Hall, Inc., 1969.

Payne, Stanley L. *The Art of Asking Questions.* Princeton: Princeton University Press, 1951.

Ramond, Charles. *The Art of Using Science in Marketing.* New York: Harper and Row, Publishers, 1974.

Schoner, Bertram, and Kenneth P. Uhl. *Marketing Research,* 2nd. ed. New York: John Wiley & Sons, Inc., 1975.

Siegel, Sidney. *Nonparametric Statistics for the Behavioral Sciences.* New York: McGraw-Hill Book Company, 1956.

Stasch, Stanley F. *Systems Analysis for Market Planning and Control.* Glenview, Ill.: Scott, Foresman and Company, 1972.

Wentz, Walter B. *Marketing Research: Management and Methods.* New York: Harper and Row, Publishers, 1972.

Worcester, Robert M., ed. *Consumer Market Research Handbook.* New York: McGraw-Hill Book Company, 1972.

Zaltman, Gerald, and Philip C. Burger. *Marketing Research: Fundamentals and Dynamics.* New York: Holt, Rinehart & Winston, 1975.

Zeisel, Hans. *Say It with Figures.* New York: Harper and Row, Publishers, 1968.

formulating marketing strategy (chapter 12)

Berg, Thomas L. *Mismarketing: Case Histories of Marketing Misfires.* New York: Doubleday & Company, Inc., 1970.

Cateora, Philip R., and John M. Hess. *International Marketing,* 3rd ed. Homewood, Ill.: Richard D. Irwin, Inc., 1975.

Fayerweather, John. *International Marketing.* Englewood Cliffs, N. J.: Prentice-Hall, Inc., 1970.

Hill, Roy W. *Marketing Technological Products to Industry.* New York: Pergamon Press, Inc., 1973.

Levitt, Theodore. *Marketing for Business Growth.* New York: McGraw-Hill Book Company, 1973.

Miracle, Gordon E., and Gerald S. Albaum. *International Marketing Management.* Homewood, Ill.: Richard D. Irwin, Inc., 1970.

Patty, C. R., and H. L. Vredenburg, ed. *Readings in Global Marketing Management.* New York: Appleton-Century-Crofts Educational Division, 1969.

Ryans, John K., and James C. Baker. *World Marketing: A Multinational Approach.* New York: John Wiley & Sons, Inc., 1967.

Thorelli, Hans B., ed. *International Marketing Strategy.* Baltimore: Penguin Books, 1973.

getting things done: organization (chapter 13)

Corey, E. Raymond, and Steven H. Star. *Organization Strategy: A Marketing Approach.* Boston: Division of Research, Graduate School of Business Administration, Harvard University, 1971.

getting things done: control (chapter 14)

Shapiro, Stanley J., and Jean-Charles Chebat. *Marketing Management: Readings in Operational Effectiveness.* New York: Harper and Row, Publishers, 1974.

Spitz, A. Edward. *Marketing Resources: Allocation and Optimization.* New York: Petrocelli Books, 1974.

Trentin, H. George, and Kurt H. Schaffir. *Marketing Information Systems.* New York: American Management Association, Inc., 1973.

the output of marketing effort (chapter 15)

Aaker, David A., and George S. Day, ed. *Consumerism: Search for the Consumer Interest,* 2nd ed. New York: The Free Press, 1974.

Backman, Jules. *Advertising and Competition.* New York: New York University Press, 1967.

Barger, Harold. *Distribution's Place in the American Economy Since 1869.* Princeton, N. J.: Princeton University Press, 1955.

Caves, Richard E. *American Industry: Structure, Conduct, Performance.* Englewood Cliffs, N. J.: Prentice-Hall, Inc., 1967.

Clewett, Robert L., and Jerry C. Olson, ed. *Social Indicators and Marketing.* Chicago: American Marketing Association, Inc., 1974.

Comanor, William, and Thomas Wilson. *Advertising and Market Power.* Cambridge, Mass.: Harvard University Press, 1974.

Cox, Reavis, Charles S. Goodman, and Thomas C. Fichandler. *Distribution in a High-Level Economy.* Englewood Cliffs, N. J.: Prentice-Hall, Inc., 1965.

Goble, Ross, and Roy T. Shaw. *Controversy and Dialogue in Marketing.* Englewood Cliffs, N. J.: Prentice-Hall, Inc., 1975.

Lavidge, Robert J., and Robert J. Holloway, ed. *Marketing and Society: The Challenge.* Homewood, Ill.: Richard D. Irwin, Inc., 1969.

Levy, Sidney J., and Gerald Zaltman. *Marketing, Society, and Conflict.* Englewood Cliffs, N. J.: Prentice-Hall, Inc., 1975.

Preston, Lee. E. *Markets and Marketing: An Orientation.* Glenview, Ill.: Scott, Foresman and Company, 1970.

Scherer, F. M. *Industrial Market Structure and Economic Performance.* Chicago: Rand McNally & Co., 1970.

Schumpeter, Joseph A. *Capitalism, Socialism, and Democracy.* New York: Harper and Row, Publishers, 1942.

Vernon, J. M. *Market Structure and Industrial Performance: A Review of Statistical Findings.* Boston: Allyn & Bacon, Inc., 1972.

attitudes for the future (chapter 16)

Kelley, Eugene J., and William Lazer. *Social Marketing: Perspectives and Viewpoints.* Homewood, Ill.: Richard D. Irwin, Inc., 1973.

Kotler, Philip. *Marketing for Non-Profit Organizations.* Englewood Cliffs, N. J.: Prentice-Hall, Inc., 1975.

Rathmell, John M. *Marketing in the Service Sector.* Cambridge, Mass.: Winthrop Publishers, Inc., 1974.

Weiss, Edward B. *Marketing to the New Society.* Chicago: Crain Communications, 1973.

Wish, John R., and Stephen H. Gamble. *Marketing and Social Issues: An Action Reader.* New York: John Wiley & Sons, Inc., 1971.

Zaltman, Gerald, Philip Kotler, and Ira Kaufman, ed. *Creating Social Change.* New York: Holt, Rinehart & Winston, Inc., 1972.

periodicals

The following periodicals of importance for marketing are selected from a larger available number on the basis of (1) the frequency with which they present material dealing with marketing issues of general or specific interest; (2) their presentation, from time to time, of survey data on a particular marketing topic; and (3) their readership among students and practitioners of marketing.

Advertising Age (weekly). Chicago: Advertising Age. Weekly news of advertising campaigns, trends, and issues as well as results of surveys (cited elsewhere) of advertising agency costs and profits, United States and international advertising agency billings, and leading advertisers' expenditures for advertising in general and by specific media.

Advertising Quarterly. London: Advertising Association. Reports of research regarding advertising as well as an annual compilation of advertising expenditures in England.

Chain Store Age, Supermarket, Headquarters Edition (monthly). New York: Lebhar-Friedman, Inc. A magazine aimed at supermarket chain managers, this publication contains articles about important trends, new-product lines, and an annual outlook for supermarket operations in the January issue.

Distribution-Warehouse Cost Digest (biweekly). Washington: Marketing Publications Incorporated. A practical guide to warehouse operations, with various issues focusing on work measurement, productivity standards, layout, and supervision.

Distribution Worldwide (monthly). Philadelphia: Chilton Company. Articles about current concepts and practical applications in physical supply and distribution, with some emphasis on international developments.

Drug Topics (biweekly). Oradell, N. J.: Medical Economics Company. A magazine containing articles of interest for drug retailing, including reviews of new products, management techniques, and public policy issues.

Electrical Wholesaling (monthly). New York: McGraw-Hill Publications Co. Articles of interest to wholesalers of electrical supplies, including an annual industry forecast and review in its December issue.

European Journal of Marketing (three times per year). Bradford, Yorkshire, England: MCB, Ltd. Reports (in English) of research in marketing authored by contributors from many countries, with abstracts of each article in English, French, and German.

Handling & Shipping (monthly). Cleveland: Industrial Publishing Company. Articles on the management of physical distribution as well as transport companies, including a presidential issue each September that concentrates on topics of interest to senior management.

Industrial Distribution (monthly). New York: Buttenheim Publishing Corporation. A magazine for wholesalers of industrial products, this periodical presents an "Annual Survey of Distributors' Operations," containing statistics regarding sales, costs, and productivity measures in each March issue.

Industrial Marketing (monthly). Chicago: Crain Communications, Inc. Concentrating on matters of importance for advertising agencies and advertisers of industrial products, this publication presents a quarterly survey of "Ad Volume in Business Publications," an annual survey of "Agency Billings in Business-to-Business and Corporate Advertising," and an annual (April) compilation of a "Guide to Special Issues of Business Publications" that, in turn, contain statistics for various industries.

Industrial Marketing Management (semimonthly). Amsterdam: Elsevier Scientific Publishing Co. Published in cooperation with the European Association for Industrial Marketing Research, this journal presents reports of research results and discussions of marketing research techniques.

Journal (quarterly). London: The Market Research Society. Articles concerning marketing research techniques and reviews of recently published books.

Journal of Advertising (quarterly). DeKalb, Ill.: American Academy of Advertising. Articles and book reviews regarding advertising practices, theory, and trends.

Journal of Advertising Research (bimonthly). New York: Advertising Research Foundation. Articles and research reports on advertising and broader marketing issues of importance for advertising.

Journal of Consumer Research (quarterly). Chicago: American Marketing Association. Articles specializing in describing research efforts in consumer behavior, especially those with strong sociological or psychological orientations.

Journal of Marketing (quarterly). Chicago: American Marketing Association. The academic journal with the largest circulation, the *JM* contains articles of relatively broad interest, short summaries of current legal cases of relevance for marketing, biographies of marketing leaders, book reviews, and bibliographies of articles and other items on marketing topics.

Journal of Marketing Research (quarterly). Chicago: American Marketing Association. Reports of research of a more technical nature than those presented in its sister publication, *JM,* as well as articles discussing methods for carrying out marketing research. From time to time, less technical "survey" articles are included on topics of interest to marketing researchers. A book review section also is included.

Journal of Purchasing and Material Management (quarterly). Tempe, Arizona: National Association of Purchasing Management. Reports of research and other contributions dealing with topics of interest for procurement and materials management as well as reviews of recent books on these subjects.

Journal of Retailing (quarterly). New York: New York University Institute of Retail Management. Research papers and book reviews on various retailing topics.

Marketing in Europe (monthly). London: The Economist Intelligence Unit Limited. Statistics regarding market trends and potentials for various product-line and national market combinations.

Marketing Times (six times per year). New York: Sales and Marketing Executives International, Inc. Short articles by practitioners about selling and sales management.

Mass Retailing Merchandise (monthly). Chicago: Merchandise Publishing Co., Inc. Practically based articles on merchandising practices and trends among discount department store chains, quarterly sales and earnings statistics for such companies, and estimates of retail market size for various types of consumer merchandise.

Media Decisions (monthly). New York: Decisions Publications. Short articles, based largely on the practical experiences of advertisers and advertising agencies, as well as annual data for advertising cost trends.

Modern Materials Handling (monthly). Boston: Cahners Publishing Co., Inc. A trade magazine describing equipment and techniques for materials handling as well as approaches to broader management issues of material control.

Modern Packaging (monthly). New York: McGraw-Hill Publications Company. Articles presented in this magazine concentrate on packaging engineering and technology, as well as statistics regarding packaging activity levels and material price changes and an annual estimate of the total value of various materials used for packaging purposes.

NARD Journal (semimonthly). Chicago: National Association of Retail Druggists. Legislative as well as management matters of interest to pharmacists, managers, and owners of retail drug stores.

Progressive Grocer (monthly). New York: The Butterick Division, American Can Co. Articles dealing with merchandising trends in supermarkets, management problems, and an annual report, based on an extensive survey, of the grocery industry, including retailing and wholesaling, in its April issue each year.

Purchasing (biweekly). Boston: Cahners Publishing Co., Inc. Articles concerning purchasing and purchasing management techniques (of importance to marketers) as well as trends and expectations, mostly with an industrial product focus.

Purchasing World (monthly). Barrington, Ill.: Technical Publishing Co. Articles on purchasing management by practitioners as well as continuing data regarding price trends and purchasing plans for industrial goods.

Retail Control (monthly). New York: Financial Executives Division, National Retail Merchants Association. Articles by accountants and retailers on matters of credit, store security, inventory management, and other areas of control.

Sales Management (semimonthly). New York: Sales Management. Concentrating on issues of importance for sales managers, this magazine has become very well known for four annual statistical issues, including (1) the "Survey of Buying Power" in a July issue, presenting indices based on differences in income, population, and retail activity for United States and Canadian markets; (2) the "Survey of Buying Power, Part II" in an October issue that, among other things, includes projections of data presented in the first part; (3) a "Survey of Industrial Purchasing Power" in an April issue; and (4) a "Survey of Selling Costs" the first issue in January.

Stores (monthly). New York: National Retail Merchants Association. Short articles on retail merchandising and store management as well as activities of the NRMA.

Supermarketing (monthly). New York: Gralla Publications. A newspaper of supermarket management, stressing current news and trends for new product lines as well as management practices.

Traffic Management (monthly). Chicago: Cahners Publishing Co., Inc. Articles emphasizing new management techniques; corporate case studies; and new equipment for transport, warehousing, inventory control, and physical supply and distribution in general.

Traffic World (weekly). Washington, D. C.: The Traffic Service Corporation. A popular news magazine in transportation, concentrating on transport regulatory and legislative developments.

Transportation & Distribution Management (six times per year). Washington, D. C.: The Traffic Service Corporation. Subtitled, "the magazine of physical distribution plans and strategy," this publication presents articles about physical distribution services, issues, and techniques.

Transportation Journal (quarterly). Chicago: American Society of Traffic and Transportation. Papers largely by scholars on topics of transportation and logistics economics and management as well as reviews of books on these topics.

Women's Wear Daily. New York: Women's Wear Daily, Inc. The newspaper of the fashion industry, but including articles of broader appeal to marketers.

associations

The following is an annotated list of associations, selected both for their general orientation to marketing and marketing related matters and their publication programs, which provide sources of information about marketing. In addition, many other industry-oriented trade associations may have divisions or groups devoting attention to marketing matters. Also, wholesalers and retailers have organized into many product-oriented interest groups that are not included on the following list. The source for the information presented in this section is Margaret Fisk, ed., *Encyclopedia of Associations,* Vol. I, 9th ed. (Detroit: Gale Research Co., 1975).

American Advertising Federation (AAF). 1225 Connecticut Ave., N.W., Washington, D. C. 20036. Among the largest of organizations in its field, membership is comprised of managers of advertising clubs, advertisers, advertising agencies, advertising trade associations, media, and allied forms interested in furthering "a better understanding of advertising through government relations, public relations, and advertising education, and to further an effective program of advertising self-regulation." It publishes an *Exchange and Washington Report* ten times per year.

American Association of Advertising Agencies (AAAA). 200 Park Avenue, New York, N. Y. 10017. Membership includes advertising agencies interested in fostering, strengthening, and improving the advertising agency business; advancing the cause of advertising as a whole; and aiding its member agencies to operate more efficiently and profitably. Sponsors research on issues related to advertising.

American Marketing Association (AMA). 222 S. Riverside Plaza, Suite 606, Chicago, Ill. 60606. A professional society of marketing and marketing research executives, sales and promotion managers, advertising specialists, teachers, and others interested in marketing. Its primary objectives are to foster research and the exchange of knowledge about marketing. Publications include (1) *The Marketing News,* semimonthly; (2) *Journal of Marketing,* quarterly; (3) *Journal of Marketing Research,* quarterly; (4) *Proceedings,* annually; and (5) occasional marketing bibliographies, books, monographs, and pamphlets on marketing.

Association of Industrial Advertisers (AIA). 41 East 42nd. St., New York, N. Y. 10017. Membership comprises business communications professionals associated with advertiser and advertising agency companies, students, and educators interested in the support of research and the exchange of information regarding industrial advertising. Publications include, among others (1) *AIA Newsletter,* monthly; and (2) *Industrial Marketing Digest,* monthly.

Consumer Federation of America (CFA). 1012 14th St., N.W., Suite 901, Washington, D. C. 20005. Comprised of national, regional, state, and local consumer groups interested, among other things, in promoting the rights of all consumers in harmony with the general welfare; stimulating and coordinating consumer programs; acting as a clearing house for the exchange of information; and engaging in fact finding, analysis, publication, and dissemination of information on consumer issues. Publications include (1) *News and Comment,* monthly; (2) *Directory of State and Local Government and Non-Government Consumer Organizations,* semi-annually; and (3) testimony on consumer issues.

Consumers' Research (CR). Bowerstown Road, Washington, N. J. 07882. A nonprofit service, supported by subscriptions to its publications, reporting laboratory tests on a wide range of goods for consumers; providing technical and related information to schools, colleges, adult education groups, and governmental and quasi-governmental agencies; and cooperating with government agencies in the development of test methods for consumer products. Publications include (1) *Consumers' Research Magazine,* monthly; (2) *October Handbook of Buying Issue,* annually; and (3) reprints and educational leaflets.

Consumers Union of the U. S. (CU). 256 Washington St., Mount Vernon, N. Y., 10550. Supported by the sale of its publications, this organization tests, rates, and reports information on competing brands of durable goods, foods, and other products. Publications include (1) *Consumer Reports,* monthly, including an *Annual Buying Guide* issue each December; and (2) special reports on particular areas of consumer interest, such as automobiles, health, and family planning.

Direct Mail Marketing Association (DMMA). 230 Park Ave., New York, N. Y. 10017. Members include users, creators, and producers of direct mail interested in studying consumer and business attitudes toward direct mail and fostering legislation to facilitate direct mail advertising. Publications include a *Direct Mail-Marketing Manual.*

Distributive Education Clubs of America (DECA). 200 Park Ave., Falls Church, Va. 22046. Its membership includes high school and college students interested in retailing or wholesaling as a profession. Its publications include (1) *Newsletter,* monthly during the academic year; and (2) *DECA Distributor,* quarterly.

International Advertising Association (IAA). 475 Fifth Ave., New York, N. Y. 10017. Membership includes individuals in eighty countries engaged in the advertising or marketing of products and services abroad and/or interested in the support of research and the exchange of information on these matters. Publications include, among others: (1) *IAA* Airletter, bimonthly; (2) *International Advertising Expenditures,* biennially; (3) *Concise Guide to International Markets,* occasionally; and (4) *IAA World Directory of Marketing Communications,* as needed.

International Materials Management Society (IMMS). 114-A Huron Towers, 2200 Fuller Rd., Ann Arbor, Mich. 48105. A professional society of engineers, educators, and executives, including those responsible for purchasing management, interested in advancing the theory and practice of material management and material handling systems in manufacturing distribution, purchasing, warehousing, transportation, and military operations. Publications include (1) *Journal,* monthly as part of *Modern Materials Handling* magazine; and a (2) *Review,* quarterly.

International Organization of Consumers Unions (IOCU). 9 Emmastraat, The Hague, Netherlands. Comprised of national consumer organizations, its objectives are, among others, to assist and actively promote genuine efforts throughout the world in consumer self-organization as well as governmental efforts to further the interests of the consumer. Publications include (1) *Newsletter,* monthly; (2) *Consumer Review,* bimonthly; (3) *International Consumer,* quarterly; and (4) *Consumers Directory,* biennially.

Marketing Communications Executives International (MCEI). 2130 Delancey Place, Philadelphia, Pa. 19103. Membership includes executives engaged in the supervision, planning, execution or direction of marketing communications as well as educators teaching marketing communications. Its primary objectives are the encouragement of research and the exchange of information about marketing communications. Publications include a monthly newsletter.

Marketing Science Institute (*MSI*). 14 Story St., Cambridge, Mass. 02138. A corporate membership (sponsored) organization formed "to contribute to improved marketing performance by developing objective, factual information about marketing practices and their efforts; by devising and testing new methods for analyzing these facts; and by appraising social and economic issues related to marketing." It conducts seminars and institutes and carries out an extensive program of publication of working papers and technical reports resulting from sponsored research.

Mass Retailing Institute (*MRI*). 570 7th Ave., New York, N. Y. 10018. Members include managers of retailing chains, with manufacturers and other suppliers of mass retailers enrolled as associate members interested in conducting research and educational programs on all phases of self-service general merchandise retailing. Publications include, among others (1) *Quarterly Merchandising Performance Record;* (2) *Mass Retailers' Merchandising Report,* annual; and (3) *Operating Results of Self-Service Department Stores,* annual.

National Association of Purchasing Management (*NAPM*). 11 Park Place, New York, N. Y. 10017. Membership includes purchasing agents and buyers for industrial, commercial, and utility firms, educational institutions, and government agencies interested in the dissemination of information on procurement and the development of more efficient purchasing methods. Its publications include (1) *Bulletin of NAPM,* monthly; and (2) *Journal of Purchasing and Materials Management,* quarterly.

National Association of Wholesale-Distributors (*NAW*). 1725 K St., N.W., Washington, D. C. 20006. A federation of national, state, and local associations as well as individual wholesaler-distributors interested in fostering the exchange of information about wholesaling management. Publications include a monthly *Newsletter.*

National Council of Physical Distribution Management (*NCPDM*). 222 W. Adams St., Chicago, Ill. 60606. Membership includes business executives, educators, and consultants interested in advancing and promoting the management science of integrating transportation, warehousing, material handling, protective packaging, inventory size and location, and other areas of customer service. Publications include (1) *NCPDM Comment,* monthly; and (2) occasional research reports.

National Retail Merchants Association (*NRMA*). 100 West 31st St., New York, N. Y. 10001. Composed of department, chain, and specialty store managers interested in the exchange of information concerning retailing management. Its publications include, among others (1) *Stores Magazine,* monthly; and (2) *Retail Control,* ten times per year.

Sales & Marketing Executives International (*SMEI*). 380 Lexington Ave., New York, N. Y. 10017. The largest of marketing-oriented organizations, its membership includes executives concerned with sales and marketing management, research, training, and other managerial aspects of distribution. It promotes the exchange of knowledge and information through research, workshops, rallies, clinics, and seminars. Publications include (1) *Marketing Times,* bimonthly; and (2) materials on selling, marketing, and sales management.

statistical sources

This section includes governmental and nongovernmental reports that include statistics useful to marketers.

government reports

Business Conditions Digest (monthly). Washington, D. C.: Bureau of Economic Analysis, Department of Commerce. Brings together many of the economic time series found most useful by business analysts and forecasters, including estimates of recent months' activities for indicators for which actual data are not yet available.

Business Statistics (biennial). Washington, D.C.: Department of Commerce. A historical record of the statistics presented monthly in the *Survey of Current Business*.

Survey of Current Business (monthly). Washington, D.C.: Department of Commerce. The most current monthly and quarterly statistics on a number of general business indicators for national income; industrial production; farm income and marketing; inventories; commodity prices; advertising; wholesale and retail trade, by product category; and other statistics on an industry-by-industry basis.

U. S. Economic Census Program, Department of Commerce. The largest single source of statistical data regarding the United States commercial market is contained in reports of the U. S. Bureau of the Census' economic census program. Such reports, based on data collected from business establishments in years ending in numbers 2 and 7, include information from the censuses of retail trade, wholesale trade, selected service industries, construction industries, manufacturers, mineral industries, and transportation. This information can be used to gauge potential markets, to analyze sales performance, to allocate promotional effort, to determine appropriate sales territories, to decide on locations for new facilities, and to study trends in the development and location of business activity. Information from the economic census program is available in published volumes, to be described subsequently, and in more detailed form on computer tapes that can be purchased from the Bureau of the Census. It can be obtained from the Publications Distribution Section, Social and Economic Statistics Administration, Bureau of the Census, Washington, D. C. 20233.

   1972 Census of Construction Industries. In two volumes, this census enumerates information about construction establishments in the United States grouped by twenty-seven industry codes referring to general contractors and builders, special trade contractors, or land subdividers and developers. Information about these establishments includes the number of employees; payrolls; selected payments for materials, components, and supplies work subcontracted to others; payments for renting or leasing machinery and equipment; capital expenditures (excluding land); total 1972 receipts; receipts during 1972 from construction, sale of land, and other sources; fixed assets; and depreciation. This information is organized by type of construction (building, nonbuilding, other), location of the construction work (home state or in other states), ownership of construction projects (public or private), class of construction (new or maintenance and repair work), work done for other construction contractors or builders, and geographic areas, including census geographic (multistate) regions, census geographic divisions, and states.

1972 Census of Manufacturers. In five volumes, this report contains information about 420 manufacturing industries. Information presented about each includes employment, payroll, man-hours, inventory, capital expenditures, and the cost of materials, resales, fuels, electricity, and contract work. A subsample of firms also provides information about the type of fuel consumed, supplemental labor costs, the quantity of electricity consumed, gross value of fixed assets, and rental payments. This information is organized by census (multistate) regions and states. In addition, the locations of manufacturing plants are tabulated for industries by state and county and for counties by industry.

1972 Census of Mineral Industries. In two volumes, this presents information about establishments primarily engaged in the extraction of minerals, defined in terms of forty-two industries and five industry groups, including metal mining, anthracite (coal) mining, bituminous coal and lignite mining, oil and gas extraction, and mining and quarrying nonmetallic minerals other than fuels. Basic information about each of these establishments includes employment; payroll; man-hours; cost of supplies, resales, fuels, electric energy, and contract work; capital expenditures; quantity of electric energy consumed; supplemental labor costs; gross book value of fixed assets; mineral rights and geological expenditures; and mineral development and exploration expenditures. Detailed statistics are organized by geographic region and state as well as type of operation. Selected statistics are presented by size of establishment.

1972 Census of Retail Trade. In four volumes this contains tabulations—for retailers engaged in about one-hundred different kinds of businesses—of information about the number of establishments, sales, the size of the payroll, legal form of organization, and number of people employed. This basic information is tabulated by line of business, size of establishment (single operating facility), size of firm, size of city, and various geographic classifications, including state, SMSA, areas outside SMSAs, counties with five-hundred retail establishments or more, cities with five-hundred retail establishments or more, and counties and cities with 2,500 inhabitants or more. The form in which this information is presented is shown in Figure A-1.

1972 Census of Selected Service Industries. In two volumes, this presents data for more than 150 kinds of service industries, including hotels, garages, legal services, and the like. The information includes the number of establishments, receipts (sales), payroll, employment, and the legal form of organization. It is organized by size of establishment (individual operating location), size of firm, and various geographical areas including state, SMSA, counties with three-hundred selected service establishments or more, cities with three-hundred selected service establishments or more, and all counties and cities with 2,500 inhabitants or more.

1972 Census of Transportation. In three volumes, devoted to (1) the National Travel Survey, (2) The Truck Inventory and Use Survey, and (3) the Commodity Transportation Survey.

The National Travel Survey provides profiles of the volume and characteristics of nonlocal travel (at least 100 miles away from home) from a sample of 24,000 civilian households in the United States. Information presented includes the number of households taking trips, persons taking trips, number of trips taken, person-trips, person-miles, person-nights, and overnight accommodations used; characteristics of the traveler, household, and trip; purpose of the trip; means of transport; travel to and through selected states and by region. It is organized by travel for the

Sic code	Geographic area and kind of business	All establishments				Establishments with payroll				
		Number	Sales	Operated by unincorporated businesses		Number	Sales	Payroll, entire year	Payroll, first quarter 1972	Paid employees for week including March 12
				Sole proprietorships	Partnerships					
			($1,000)	(number)	(number)		($1,000)	($1,000)	($1,000)	(number)

	Retail Trade, Total . . . .
	Building Materials, Hardware, and Farm Equipment Dealers
52	Total . . . .
52 Ex. 525	Building materials and supply stores . . . .
521	Lumber and other building materials dealers . . .
522	Plumbing and heating equipment dealers . . . . . .
523	Paint, glass, and wallpaper stores . . . .
524	Electrical supply stores . . . .
5251	Hardware stores . . . .
5252	Farm equipment dealers . . . .
	General Merchandise Group Stores
53 Part	Total . . . .
531	Department stores . . . .
533	Variety stores . . . .
539	Miscellaneous general merchandise stores . . . .
539 Pt.	General merchandise stores . . . .
539 Pt.	Dry goods stores . . . .
539 Pt.	Sewing and needlework stores . . . .

Geographic areas:

State
SMSA's
Areas outside SMSA's
Counties with 500 retail establishments or more
Cities with 500 retail establishments or more

(Similar but less detailed data are shown for counties and cities with 2,500 inhabitants or more.)

Figure A-1. Example material and the format for presentation of the 1972 Census of Retail Trade.

United States as a whole, nine multistate travel regions, selected states, and (as travel destinations) Europe, Mexico, and Canada.

The Truck Inventory and Use Survey contains information collected from a sample of 114,000 of the nearly twenty million trucks registered in the United States in 1972. These include trucks operated in private and for-hire commercial use, but not by public agencies. It includes basic information about number of vehicles, number of truck-miles, major use of vehicle, annual and lifetime vehicle miles, year model, body type, vehicle size class, single unit of combination and axle arrangement, type of fuel, range of operation, acquisition, cab type, truck fleet size, and maintenance. The data is organized by state and the District of Columbia.

The Commodity Transportation Survey includes data regarding the volume and nature of shipments made during 1972 based on a probability sample of 13,000 plants representing manufacturing establishments with twenty or more employees as well as a sample of smaller establishments. Data are presented for each of eighty-six shipper (commodity) classes as well as products classified in more detailed fashion, including tons, ton-miles, means of transport, length of haul, and weight of shipment. Data for commodities are organized by origin and destination areas, including twenty-seven production areas (each consisting of one or a cluster of SMSAs) and selected states. The form in which this information is presented is shown in Figure A-2.

1972 Census of Wholesale Trade. In two volumes this contains tabulations—for wholesalers engaged in 118 kinds of business—of information about the number of establishments, sales, payroll, employment, operating expenses, and end-of-year inventories. This basic information is organized by line of business, size of establishment (individual operating location), size of firm, city size, legal form of

TCC code	Commodity	Number	Percent distribution by means of transport							
			All means of transport	Rail	Motor carrier	Private truck	Air	Water	Other	Unknown
	Tons of Shipments									
	U.S. total									
20	Food and kindred products									
201	Meat, poultry, and small game; fresh, chilled or frozen.									
2011	Meat, fresh or chilled, not salted									
20111	Carcasses, primal or fabricated cuts and boneless meat									
20119	Meat, fresh or chilled, n.e.c.									
2012	Meat, fresh frozen									
20121	Carcasses (whole or part), primal and fabricated cuts, boneless meat									
20129	Meat, fresh frozen, n.e.c.									
2013	Meat products									
20131	Lard.									
20132	Meats and sausage, cooked, cured, dried, smoked, or salted									
20134	Canned meat									
20139	Meat products, n.e.c.									
2014	Animal byproducts, inedible									
20143	Grease, inedible tallow, and other inedible animal oil mill products, including foots.									
20144	Animal refuse: tankage, meat meal, dried blood, and related products.									
2015	Dressed poultry and small game, fresh, chilled or canned									
20151	Dressed chickens									
20156	Liquid, dried, or frozen eggs									
2016	Dressed poultry and small game, fresh frozen									
20161	Dressed poultry and small game, fresh frozen									

Geographic areas:

Census geographic regions
Census geographic divisions
Selected States

Figure A-2. Example material and the format for presentation of the 1972 Commodity Transportation Survey.

organization, and type of wholesaling operation. In regard to the latter item, it presents sales of merchant wholesalers and agents and brokers by 555 different commodity lines and sales of manufacturers and sales branches and sales offices by 610 different product lines. Geographic areas for which this information is presented include states, counties with two hundred wholesale establishments or more, cities with 5,000 inhabitants or more, and SMSAs. The form in which this information is presented is shown in Figure A-3.

1970 Census of Population. The largest source of demographic, economic, and social data regarding the individuals making up consumer markets in the United States is contained in reports of the U. S. Bureau of the Census' population census, taken every ten years in years ending in 0. The 1970 Census of Population, for example, collected information on the location of people by such dimensions as age, race, education, income, ownership or rental of houses and apartments, and the number of rooms in such dwellings. The information can be used to aid in

Sic code	Geographic area and kind of business	Total						Merchant wholesalers		Other operating types[1]	
		Estab-lish-ments	Sales	Inventories, end of year 1972	Payroll, entire year	Payroll, first quarter 1972	Paid employees for week including March 12	Estab-lish-ments	Sales	Estab-lish-ments	Sales
		(number	($1,000)	($1,000)	($1,000)	($1,000)	(number)	(number)	($1,000)	(number)	($1,000)
50	Wholesale Trade, Total										
501	Motor vehicles and automotive equipment										
5012	Automobiles and other motor vehicles										
5013	Automotive equipment										
5014	Tires and tubes										
502	Drugs, chemicals, and allied products										
5022	Drugs, proprietaries, and sundries										
5028	Paints and varnishes										
5029	Chemicals and allied products, n.e.c.										
503	Piece goods, notions, and apparel										
5033	Piece goods (woven fabrics)										
5034	Notions and other dry goods										
5036	Men's and boys' clothing and furnishings										
5037	Women's, children's, and infants' clothing										
5039	Footwear										
504	Groceries and related products										
5041	Groceries, general line										
5042	Frozen foods										
5043	Dairy products										
5044	Poultry and poultry products										
5045	Confectionery										
5046	Fish and seafoods										
5047	Meats and meat products										
5048	Fresh fruits and vegetables										
5049	Groceries and related products, n.e.c.										

Geographic areas:
State
Counties; cities with 5,000 inhabitants or more (data by area only)
SMSA's
Counties with 200 wholesale establishments or more

Figure A-3. Example material and the format for presentation of the 1972 Census of Wholesale Trade.

retail store location decisions, the allocation of advertising effort, the assignment of door-to-door salespeople, or the selection of sample sizes for market research. Information from the Census of Population is available in published volumes, to be described subsequently, and in more detailed form (down to single and groups of city blocks) on computer tape. It can be obtained from the Publications Distribution Section, Social and Economic Statistics Administration, Bureau of the Census, Washington, D. C. 20233. The Bureau of the Census has established over 170 private, governmental, and academic organizations, at their request, as Summary Tape Processing Centers that can furnish data from the tapes for a fee.

The Census of Population is really two censuses in one, comprising both a collection and tabulation of items about population and housing, as follows:

Census of Population. This census presents the results of questions asked of from 5 to 100 per cent of the population of the United States, including questions about relationship to head of household; color or race; age; sex; marital status; state or country of birth; years of school completed; number of children ever born; employment status; hours worked last week; weeks worked last year; last year in which worked; occupation, industry, and class of worker; activity five years ago; income last year; country of birth of parents; mother tongue; year moved into this house; place of residence five years ago; school or college enrollment; veteran status; place of work; means of transportation to work; Mexican or Spanish origin or descent; citizenship; year of immigration; when married; vocational training completed; presence and duration of disability; and occupation-industry five years ago. This information is organized for presentation in the following reports:

Volume 1, 58 Parts (one per state plus other areas). Characteristics of the population are organized by area and statistics are presented for states, counties (by urban-rural residence), SMSAs, urbanized areas, minor civil divisions, census county divisions, all incorporated places, and unincorporated places of 1,000 inhabitants or more regarding some or all of the information described here.

Volume II, Subject Reports. Each report in this volume concentrates on a particular subject. Among the characteristics covered are national origin and race, fertility, families, marital status, migration, education, employment, occupation, industry, and income. Detailed information and cross relationships are provided on a national and regional level; in some reports, data for states or SMSAs are shown.

Census of Housing. This census presents the results of questions asked of from 5 to 100 per cent of the population of the United States, including questions about the number of housing units at an address; telephone; access to unit; kitchen or cooking facilities; condition of housing unit; rooms; water supply; flush toilet; bathtub or shower; basement; length of residence; commercial establishment on property; value; vacancy status; months vacant; components of gross rent; heating equipment; year structure was built; land used for farming; source of water; sewage disposal; bathrooms; air conditioning; automobiles; clothes washing machine; clothes dryer; dishwasher; home food freezer; television; radio; and second home. This information is organized for presentation in seven volumes of which the following are of greatest use for marketing:

Volume 1, 58 Parts (one per state plus other areas). Characteristics for states, cities, and counties are organized by area and statistics are presented for states, counties, SMSAs (by urban-rural parts), urbanized areas, places of 2,500 inhabitants or more, and places of 1,000 inhabitants or more regarding some or all of the information described here.

Volume II, Metropolitan Housing Characteristics. In one report for each SMSA, this series presents census housing data in detail.

Volume III, Block Statistics. In one report for each urbanized area, this series presents information regarding many items described here for each urban block.

Volume V, Residential Finance. A national report on the financing of privately owned nonfarm residential properties, such as mortgage characteristics and homeowner expenses.

ADMATCH. A computerized address-matching program offered by the Data Users Service Office of the Bureau of the Census to allow marketing researchers to match data collected by the residential address of the information source to data contained in block and census tract tabulations of the Census of Population and Housing. This can facilitate the process of calculating market penetration statistics based on a customers' address list.

Economic Indicators (monthly). Washington, D. C.: U. S. Council of Economic Advisers. The most up-to-date compilation of statistics regarding national (United States) economic activity, including sources and disposition of personal income, farm income, expenditures for plant and equipment, employment, business sales and inventories, trade balances, prices, and financial indicators.

Federal Reserve Bulletin (monthly). Washington, D. C.: Division of Administrative Services, Board of Governors of the Federal Reserve System. Analyses of recent financial developments as well as up-to-date economic indicators, including activities of financial institutions, industrial production, construction, consumer and wholesale prices, and international trade volumes.

The U. S. Industrial Outlook (annual). Washington, D. C.: Bureau of Domestic Commerce, Department of Commerce. This volume projects (currently to 1980) sales trends and influencing factors in sectors of United States economic activity including building and forest products, basic materials, transportation, distribution and marketing, consumer goods, communications, machinery, instrumentation, power and electrical equipment, and business and consumer services. In addition, various editions highlight important environmental influences.

Statistical Abstract of the United States (annual). Washington, D. C.: Bureau of the Census, Department of Commerce. An excellent starting point for United States data, this is a general review of statistics collected by the United States government and other public and private organizations, organized around the following topics, among others: population; vital statics; geography and environment; labor force, employment, and earnings; prices; business enterprise; communications; energy; transportation; manufacturers; distribution and services; foreign commerce and aid; and metropolitan area statistics.

Statistical Yearbook (annual). New York: United Nations. The most comprehensive source of information about world economic development. Data presented in this volume for most countries of the world include, among others, GNP, population, manpower, agriculture, forestry, fishing, industrial production, mining and quarrying, manufacturing, construction, energy, internal wholesale and retail trade, international trade, transport, communications, consumption, balance of payments, wages and prices, national accounts, finance, health, housing, education, science and technology, and culture.

Survey of Consumer Expenditures, 1972–1973. Washington, D. C.: Bureau of Labor Statistics, Department of Labor. To be published in complete form in 1977. It updates the survey last taken in 1960–1961 and presents comprehensive data regarding consumer expenditures, savings, and income arranged by United States city and by income, size of family, and age and occupation of family head.

nongovernment reports

Advertising Age Surveys. Published in *Advertising Age* magazine (see *Advertising Age* on list of periodicals). Included in the annual survey of results published in this magazine are the following:

International Agency Section (published each year in an early March issue). Presents a list of agencies ranked by billings and listed by country, with profiles for individual agencies.

U. S. Agency Section (published each year in an early March issue). Presents profiles of several hundred United States advertising agencies, including major accounts and billings during the previous year.

Top 100 National Advertisers (published each year in a late April issue). Presents profiles of the advertisers and brands providing the largest billings during the previous year for national magazine, newspaper supplement, network TV, spot TV, network radio, and outdoor advertising media.

National Expenditures in Newspapers (published each year in a June issue). Tabulates brands of United States companies that bought $10,000 or more in national newspaper advertising space during the preceding year.

Four A's Agencies Cost, Profits (published each year in an early August issue). Presents ten-year trends for important items in advertising agencies' operating statements.

Marketing Reports (published each year in a late August issue). Profiles the one-hundred top United States national advertisers in the preceding year, including information about their marketing personnel, their advertising agency account executives, and their advertising-to-sales ratios.

Percentage of Sales Invested in Advertising (published each year in a late September issue). Presents advertising-to-sales ratios for various industries.

Annual Consumer Expenditure Study (annual). New York: Gralla Publications. This appears in the September issue of *Supermarketing* magazine and presents statistics by product line for purchases in grocery stores.

Commercial Atlas & Marketing Guide (annual). Chicago: Rand McNally & Co. Of particular use in allocating sales effort, this volume, in addition to presenting detailed maps of the United States, includes information about population, households, retail sales, and auto registration.

Dartnell Survey of Compensation of Salesmen (semiannual, with the 18th survey published in 1976). Chicago: The Dartnell Corporation. Presents survey information regarding compensation practices for salespeople in the United States and Canada.

European Marketing Data and Statistics (annual). London: Euromonitor Publications, Ltd. Presents basic economic indicators by European country, largely obtained from UN statistical sources, but presented in a handy format.

The Growth of World Industry (annual). New York: United Nations Department of Economic and Social Affairs. In two volumes, this report contains data regarding trends in the number of mining, quarrying, and manufacturing establishments; employment in them; and volumes of commodities produced by them over a ten-year period for most countries of the world, of use in assessing export or import opportunities.

A Guide to Consumer Markets, Helen Axel, ed. (semiannual). New York: The Conference Board, Inc. Contains statistics, largely edited from Bureau of the Census and other reports, concerning United States population, employment, income, expenditures, production and distribution, and prices.

Handbook of Basic Economic Statistics (monthly). Washington, D. C.: Bureau of Economic Statistics, Inc., Economic Statistics Bureau of Washington, D. C. An up-to-date sourcebook of statistical and economic data collected by the United States government. Included in the data presented are sections devoted to production, labor productivity, prices, and general business indicators.

Market Guide (annual). New York: Editor & Publisher Co., Inc. Presents current detailed information about United States cities, counties, and SMSAs, including population, households, transportation facilities, banking services, principal industries, climate, tap water, retail outlets, and newspapers.

Marketing Economics Guide (annual). New York: Marketing Economics Institute. In three volumes, this service presents annual estimates of population and retail sales estimates (for nine product types) for a large number of cities and counties and all SMSAs.

Profile of U. S. Consumer Market Segments (annual). New York: Daniel Starch & Staff. Presents information obtained from a sample of United States households regarding purchases of goods and services such as autos, household furnishings, travel, life insurance, and others.

Standard Rate & Data Service (frequencies to be noted subsequently). Skokie, Ill.: Standard Rate & Data Service, Inc. The most complete source of information about advertising rates and requirements, this service presents such information for business publications (monthly); consumer magazines and farm publications (monthly); direct-mail lists (semiannually); medical and pharmaceutical publications (bimonthly); network, television and radio (bimonthly); newspapers (monthly); print production (quarterly); spot radio (monthly); spot television (monthly); transit advertising (quarterly); and weekly newspapers (semiannually). The volumes for newspapers, spot radio, and spot television contain market data by state, county, city, and metropolitan area. In addition, the Standard Rate & Data Service publishes similar services for Britain, Canada, France, Italy, Mexico, and West Germany.

Survey of Buying Power (annual). Presented in a July issue of *Sales Management* magazine. Contains information for all United States SMSAs, including population, households, effective buying income, retail sales, and Buying Power Index computed by giving a weight of five to the market's share of total United States effective buying income; three to its share of total United States retail sales; and two to its share of total United States population and then dividing the sum of the weighted percents by ten. This produces an index useful in allocating promotional effort. A second volume, published in an October issue of *Sales Management* magazine each year, projects Buying Power Indexes for the same markets for five years into the future.

Survey of Distributor Operations (annual). Conducted by *Industrial Distribution* magazine (see list of periodicals), this survey, presented in the March issue of the magazine, offers operating data for general-line and specialist industrial distributors (wholesalers of industrial products and suppliers) on a region-by-region basis.

Survey of Industrial Purchasing Power (annual). Presented in an April issue of *Sales Management* magazine. Contains data on a United States county-by-county basis—broken down by Standard Industrial Code (product) for larger counties—regarding the number of manufacturing plants, the number of large manufacturing plants, total value of shipments, the percentage of total United States shipments, and the proportion of total shipments from large plants. This information may be helpful in allocating sales effort for industrial products.

Survey of Selling Costs (annual). Presented in a January issue of *Sales Management* magazine. Contains data for United States markets concerning the cost per sales call by type of salesperson and territory, basic field selling expenses for seventy-seven metropolitan markets, selling expenses as a share of sales in major industries, and transportation costs. In addition, it presents information concerning costs of living and traveling outside the United States.

World Advertising Expenditures (biennial). New York: Starch INA Hooper. Sponsored jointly by the publisher and the International Advertising Association, this survey yields estimates of advertising expenditures, by media, for sixty-three countries.

World Trade Annual. New York: Walker and Company. Each year, this five-volume publication documents the volume and value of trade between countries of the world of some ten major classifications and nearly a thousand subcategories of products, listed by Standard International Trade Classification (SITC).

commercial auditing, survey, and directory services

F. W. Dodge Corporation. New York. Presents results of surveys of actual and planned construction activity.

Dun & Bradstreet Companies, Inc. New York. Offers, for nearly all firms of any size, information about the nature of their business, financial statements, and credit ratings. In addition, Dun & Bradstreet prepares lists of firms, addresses, and officers by line of business, sales volume, and geographic location.

Market Research Corp. of America (MRCA). New York. Provides information about consumers' buying patterns based on diary data obtained from a panel of cooperating consumers thought to be representative of a cross section of consumers in the United States. Among the types of information available from MRCA are the volume of purchases, prices paid, and retail outlets from which purchases were made for a wide variety of consumer goods.

National Purchase Diary Panel, Inc. Floral Park, New York. Offers information about consumer buying patterns obtained from diaries maintained by a national (United States) panel representative of consumers in general.

A. C. Nielsen Co. Northbrook, Illinois. Offers several services, including a periodic audit of radio listening and television viewing patterns. Of perhaps greatest interest for marketers is its periodic audit of retail stocks, orders, and sales volumes for competing products in a number of lines of grocery, drug, and related products.

R. L. Polk Company. Publishes a variety of information, including many city directories (listing household addresses and residents by street), auto registration holders, and a variety of mailing lists.

Selling Areas—Marketing, Inc. (SAMI). New York. Offers information about consumer product movements out of wholesaler or chain warehouses on a geographic, product-by-product basis.

SPEEData, Inc. New York. Offers data about consumer product movements from wholesaler or retail chain warehouses for a variety of products on a geographic basis.

Daniel Starch and Staff. New York. Based on a detailed testing procedure, this organization prepares readership data for newspapers and magazines as well as for individual advertisements appearing in such publications.

Small Business Management Series (occasional). Washington, D. C.: Small Business Administration. A series of booklets providing discussions of special management problems in small companies. Included in this series are the following booklets of particular relevance for marketing:

New Product Introduction for Small Business Owners (69 pages, SBA Catalog No. 1.12:17). Provides basic information to help owners of small businesses to understand better what is involved in placing a new or improved product on the market.

Management Audit for Small Retailers (50 pages, SBA Catalog No. 1.12:31). Includes 149 questions to guide an owner-manager in examining himself or herself as well as the nature of the business operation.

Small Store Planning for Growth (99 pages, SBA Catalog No. 1.12:33). Discusses the nature of growth, the management skills needed, and some techniques for use in promoting growth. Included is a consideration of merchandising, advertising and display, and checklists to aid in increasing transactions and gross margins.

Selecting Advertising Media—A Guide for Small Business (120 pages, SBA Catalog No. SBA 1.12:34). An aid to the small businessperson in deciding which medium to select in promoting a product, service, or store to potential customers and how to make the most of advertising expenditures.

Small Business Marketing Aids (occasional). Washington, D. C.: Small Business Association. A series of leaflets prepared by various authorities to provide suggestions and management guidelines for small retail, wholesale, and service firms. Included among the more recent publications in this series are:

No. 156, "Marketing Checklist for Small Retailers," by George Kress and R. Ted Will.

No. 154, "Using Census Data to Select a Store Site," by Louis H. Vorzimer.

No. 152, "Using a Traffic Study to Select a Retail Site," by James R. Lowry.

No. 143, "Factors in Considering a Shopping Center Location," by J. Ross McKeever.

No. 140, "Profit by Your Wholesalers' Services," by Richard M. Hill.

glossary of terms used in this book

The Definitions Committee of the American Marketing Association has an impossible task in attempting to define to everyone's satisfaction and for general use words used in marketing. At times in its recent deliberations, that group has had to consider as many as ten reasonably acceptable definitions for a single term. This should emphasize the subjective nature of developing definitions.

Nevertheless, you need to know what I had in mind in using a particular term. Also, you need to know how my usage and meaning might differ from more general or common usage. Thus, the terms in this glossary are defined as I've intended them to be used in this book. Alternative definitions reflecting popular usage, where appropriate, also will be cited.

Basic terms are listed alphabetically, but subheadings for several of the terms are not. Where subheadings are used, as in the second entry ("advertising"), definitions for all items to which the subheading relates are to be read with the definition for the subheading itself. For example, the complete definition for "mass consumer advertising" is found under "advertising" (the basic or root term), "mass," and "consumer." Thus, mass consumer advertising is "paid, non-personal communication designed to inform or persuade members of a particular audience (advertising) directed to a large, heterogeneous audience (mass) of individuals who personally consume advertised products or services (consumer)." The purpose of this format is to give you an organized picture of activities with a complex terminology, such as advertising or wholesaling, in such a way that the relationship of terms becomes evident.

Page numbers on which each term is used in the book are shown alongside each entry. It may be useful, if using the glossary while not reading the book, to turn to the reference to see how a particular term is used in context.

Account executive: Typically a person with responsibilities for (1) providing liason between an advertiser and its advertising agency and (2) coordinating all aspects of the agency's effort on behalf of its client advertiser, including planning, research, copy writing, the preparation of art work, media selection, ad production, sales promotion, public relations, and accounting.   (197–200)

Advertising: Paid, nonpersonal communication designed to inform or persuade members of a particular audience.   (191–197)

By audience:

    Consumer: Directed to individuals who personally consume advertised products or services.

    Mass: Directed to a large, heterogeneous audience.

    Class: Directed to a select group of consumers, especially of higher income.

    Trade: Directed to wholesalers and retailers as a means of obtaining product distribution.

    Industrial: Directed to users of products, raw materials, or components for business purposes.

By type of advertiser:

    Local (retail): Designed to feature both the product or service and the specific places where they can be obtained.

    National (general): Designed to feature primarily the product or its manufacturer for use in several geographic markets, regional or national.

By function:

    Product:

        Brand: Designed to feature a specific product or service, by brand or company name, sometimes referred to as selective demand stimulation.

        Generic product: Designed to feature a product type (such as milk) but not a brand or company (dairy) name, sometimes referred to as primary demand stimulation.

    Cooperative: Designed to feature both a product and the retail or wholesale establishment from which it can be purchased, this type of advertising is placed by the retailer (or wholesaler) but is paid for by both the retailer and its suppliers (hence the term cooperative).

    Institutional: Designed to feature a company or organization, but not a specific product or service.

By type of media:

    Print:

        Newspapers:

            By type of advertising:

                Display: Featuring illustrations, the use of color, and other visual devices as well as words.

                Classified: Featuring short announcements that most often do not make use of display devices.

            By type of advertiser:

                Local (retail): Purchased by local establishments, often retailers, at rates substantially below those quoted for national (general) advertisers.

                National (general): Purchased by nonlocal, nonretail organizations.

        Magazines:

            By audience:

                Consumer: Directed to those who purchase products or services for their personal consumption.

                Trade: Directed to wholesalers and retailers.

                Industrial: Directed to manufacturing firms.

                Professional: Directed to professional groups such as lawyers, doctors, or teachers.

            By type of coverage:

                Regional: Restricted to initial distribution to a specific region.

                National: Offering national distribution, sometimes by means of regional editions carrying advertising intended for communication only to each region.

Direct mail: Any direct advertising, including catalogs, that is sent through the mail to definite, specific potential buyers.

Broadcast:

Television:

Local: Placed by local sponsors, often retailers, and including cooperative advertising placed by a retailer but paid for by both the retailer and its supplier.

National spot: Placed by general (national) sponsors, but broadcast on a nonnetwork basis, originating in the station from which it is telecast.

Network: Placed by general (national) sponsors and broadcast simultaneously by a network of stations drawing on one originating studio.

Radio:

Local, national spot, and network: Definitions similar to those for comparable terms used in television advertising.

Outdoor:

Posters: Printed panels mounted on standard poster structures (often called billboards), measuring 12 by 25 feet.

Painted bulletins: Printed panels, often more custom-made than printed panels.

Spectaculars: Large illuminated, often animated, signs.

Transportation (or transit):

Outside: Printed panels placed at transportation terminals and on the outside of transport vehicles, such as taxis.

Inside: Printed panels placed inside passenger-carrying vehicles operated by mass transit companies.

Point of purchase: Encompassing a wide range of printed panels, racks, or other devices placed at points where featured products or services are purchased.

Specialty: A variety of tangible, often useable, items carrying a company or brand name and often a short sales message, typically distributed by mail.

Directories: Compilations of information directed to individuals (as the telephone Yellow Pages) or industrial firms on a local, regional, or national basis.

Word of mouth: Endorsements for products or services passed directly among actual or potential users or buyers.

Assembly (as a marketing function): The act of bringing products of the same or a different nature together in one location for subsequent shipment or sale in larger units or quantities, a function most commonly performed for agricultural products by operators of businesses such as stockyards or grain elevators.

(264, 268)

Assorting (as a marketing function): The act of bringing products of a different nature (or information about them) together in one location for subsequent shipment or sale to customers desiring to purchase some or all of the resulting assortment, a function performed most commonly for types of products, such as hardware or drug items, involving broad assortments of merchandise.

(264, 268)

Authority (in organizations): Limits describing actions that an individual in an organization may take in the performance of a job. (443–444)

Bait-and-switch tactic: The practice of quoting a low price or offering a good value on one or a limited number of units of an item for the purpose of attracting prospective customers, typically to a retail store, in order to sell them something similar to, but more expensive than, the advertised item. (153)

Blind testing: Typically the testing of two or more unidentified, competing products for the purpose of establishing preferences in use among a sample of prospective buyers; product appearance is eliminated further as a variable when conducted with blindfolded respondents.

Brand: A name, often presented in a certain style (or logotype) by which a product is identified to prospective cutomers.

Manufacturer's brand: Owned by, and affixed to, its products by a manufacturer; sometimes referred to as a national brand. (492)

Private (retailer's) brand: Owned by, and affixed to, a retailer's products by its suppliers. (288, 492)

Break-even analysis: The process of determining the volume of sales needed to defray all fixed and variable costs of operation. More formally, a break-even point is the quantity of sales at which the contribution (sales revenue less variable costs) per unit multiplied by the number of units sold just equals the total of fixed costs incurred in making and selling a product or service. For example, a firm incurs the following fixed costs each year in manufacturing and selling its products:

Depreciation on plant	$100,000
Fixed manufacturing labor and administration	450,000
Marketing administration	100,000
Sales force salaries	350,000
Advertising	200,000
Total	$1,200,000

Its products sell for $20 per unit, for which the variable costs of production (for materials and direct labor) are $6 and transport costs $2 per unit, leaving a contribution of $12 per unit. Thus, the volume of sales needed to reach a break-even position is $1,200,000 divided by $12, or 100,000 units.

(149, 412–414)

Buying process: The steps a prospective purchaser may go through in arriving at a purchase decision, including the realization of a need; becoming aware of alternatives; collecting information; narrowing a selection in terms of type, size, price, and brand; product or service trial; postpurchase reinforcement or dissonance; and repurchase. (35, 37–40, 421–423)

Cannibalization: The process by which a new product gains a portion of its sales by diverting them from an existing product (the reverse of enhancement).

(115, 116–118, 150–151)

Captive sales force: A group of salespeople employed and paid by an organization to sell only its products or services. (24)

Cash cow: A product in a mature or declining stage of its product life cycle requiring little investment and produced at low cost, to be "milked" for as much profit as it may be able to produce. (128)

Catalog showroom: A retail outlet displaying samples and catalogs from which products can be ordered at discounted prices for subsequent delivery direct from a supplier's factory or warehouse. (285–286)

Centralization (in organizations): The concentration of authority (freedom to take action) and responsibilities (jobs or tasks) in a relatively small number of individuals occupying top-ranking positions in an organization. (459–460)

Channel captain: An organization in a channel of distribution that assumes leadership for firms from which it buys and to which it sells by absorbing risk on their behalf and generally engaging in actions designed to benefit its suppliers and customers as well as itself. (357)

Channel control: The ability of a manufacturer or other channel entity to influence the behavior of those with which it deals in a channel of distribution. (355–357)

Channel leadership: The willingness of a firm in a channel of distribution with the potential for doing so to take action on behalf of the well-being of those firms with which it deals as well as itself. (357–358)

Channel of distribution: See distribution channel.

Channel vision: A policy under which a firm attempts to determine where, and to what extent, in a channel of distribution, marketing functions should be performed. (339–341, 358)

Clayton Act: An act of Congress, passed in 1914, that supplemented the Sherman Act by prohibiting, "where the effect will be substantially to lessen competition or tend to create a monopoly," the following practices: (1) discrimination in price between purchasers of a like grade, quality, or quantity of a commodity sold (later to provide the basis for the Robinson-Patman Act); (2) leasing or selling goods on the condition or agreement that the lessee or purchaser shall not use or deal in goods provided by a competitor of the lessor or seller; (3) interlocking directorates (comprising board memberships held in common) in directly competing corporations, except banks or transport companies, of more than $1 million capital; and (4) acquisition of one corporation by another engaged in interstate commerce where the effect might be substantially to lessen competition. (83)

Clutter (in advertising): The incidence of numerous, short commercials, particularly on television, increasing the potential level of confusion on the part of the intended recipients of the advertising messages. (193)

Commercial (as in advertising): A paid, nonpersonal communication by broadcast media (radio or television) designed to inform or persuade members of a particular audience. (109)

Commission (on sales): Remuneration for sales effort based directly on the amount of sales realized, paid subsequent to the achievement of the sale.

Commodity: (1) A generic product category, or (2) a product that cannot be distinguished, in the minds of potential customers, from like products produced by competitors. Many agricultural products provide examples of this meaning of the term. (180–181)

Concept testing: An effort to assess reactions of potential customers to descriptions of products or services before such products or services are fully developed. (389–390)

Consignment sales: Sales not completed until products, usually placed with a retailer by a supplier, are resold. Payment for goods placed on consignment is not due until such goods are resold. (9)

Conspiracy in restraint of trade: An explicit agreement by two or more competitors to restrict competition in any manner, including actions taken to drive a third competitor out of business. (84, 166)

Consumer: The end user of a product or service. In popular usage, this word often is used interchangeably with the term *customer*. However, in this book, the latter term is used to refer to all buyers, whether or not such buyers become end users (consumers) of purchased products or services.

Consumer Product Safety Act: An act passed by Congress in 1972 creating a Consumer Product Safety Commission with authority to (1) set mandatory safety standards for consumer products except those such as foods, drugs, autos, and other products covered by separate laws; (2) name brands and companies when publishing information regarding potentially injurious products; (3) ban the distribution of such products without a court hearing; and (4) charge the top managements of offending companies with criminal as well as civil violations. (521–522)

Consumerism: A philosophy advocating the rights of consumers to safety, to be informed, to choose, to be heard, and to assert such rights against those of others to create and market goods, services, people, or ideas. (291, 520–522)

Containerization: The shipment of goods packed in metal boxes capable of being moved by, and transferred between, two or more modes of transportation. Such boxes typically possess standard fittings for handling and standard sizes of 10-, 20-, 30-, and 40-foot lengths, 8-foot heights, and 8-foot widths. (350–351)

Contribution: The monetary difference between revenues realized and the variable costs incurred in the production and sales of one or more units of a product. For example, the contribution of a product sold for $1.50 per unit for which variable costs (those varying with the volume of product made or sold) are $.40 for manufacture and $.25 for marketing is $.85 per unit, or $850 for every 1,000 units sold. (105, 107, 149)

Control: Assuring that desired results are obtained.[1] (471–475)

    Management control: The process by which managers assure that resources are obtained and used effectively and efficiently in the accomplishment of the organization's objectives.[2]

    Operational control: The process of assuring that specific tasks are carried out effectively and efficiently.[3]

Convenience (consumer) goods: Those for which a consumer is willing to purchase any of several known substitutes rather than make the additional effort required to buy a particular item or brand. (270–271, 336)

Copyright: A grant of protection to authors, song writers, and other creators of publishable material from copying by would-be competitors for a specified period of time. (82)

Cost of goods sold: The purchase price (often including costs of transport and handling incurred in acquiring goods) of goods subsequently resold. Typically used by "resellers" (wholesalers or retailers), this item often is calculated by subtracting an end-of-period inventory valuation from the sum of a beginning-of-period inventory valuation and the value of goods placed in stock during the period of time in question. (276)

Cost-plus pricing: A determination of a price for a product by adding to its direct, variable costs of production (in manufacturing) or acquisition (in wholesaling or retailing) an amount to cover marketing, administrative, and other overhead costs and contribute to a targeted profit figure. (156–157)

Credit: A loan extended, often for the purpose of facilitating the acquisition of goods and services in advance of the payment for them. (76, 499–500)

Culture: The complex whole that includes knowledge, belief, art, morals, law, custom, and any other capabilities and habits acquired by man as a member of society. (40–42)

Deal (pricing): The practice of offering short-term price discounts, typically through the device of offering more merchandise for the existing price or a lower price for the same quantity of merchandise, thus producing a reduced per unit price for a specified period of time. (154)

---

[1] Robert N. Anthony, *Planning and Control Systems: A Framework for Analysis* (Boston: Division of Research, Graduate School of Business Administration, Harvard University, 1965), p. 10.
[2] Ibid., p. 17.
[3] Ibid., p. 18.

Dealer: A generic term often used to refer to retailers of various types.

Decay rate: The rate at which sales decline after the conclusion of a promotional effort, typically used in connection with measuring the long-term effectiveness of advertising. (193)

Decentralization (in organizations): The delegation of authority (permission to take action) and responsibilities (jobs or tasks) to the greatest possible number of an organization's members assigned to the lowest possible levels in an organization's hierarchy. (459–460)

Deceptive pricing: Any practice that leads a potential customer to think incorrectly that he or she is getting a bargain. (167)

Decoder (in communication): One who receives a transmitted "signal," processes it, and decides whether or not to make use of it in some manner. In promotional strategy, it commonly refers to those who receive messages intended to create awareness of, persuade someone to try, or induce action to buy a particular product or service. (181–183)

Demarketing: Efforts to bring about a planned reduction in demand or the rate of increase in the level of demand for a product or service. (534–536)

Demography: The science of vital statistics (demographic data) concerning such matters as birth rates, deaths, diseases, ages, and the location of populations. (65–70)

Department store: A retail establishment containing several separately identifiable, separately managed departments organized around lines or types of goods. The Bureau of the Census further defines such establishments for its purposes as those having 25 or more employees.

    Conventional department store: A full-service, full-margin store, typically offering credit, delivery, and other services.

    Discount department store: A limited-service store offering goods at lower-than conventional department store margins (price levels), sometimes providing services in exchange for additional charges.

Detailing: The provision, in retailing establishments, of merchandising assistance by suppliers' representatives, often including the preparation of displays and the stocking of shelves on a regular basis. (282)

Differentiation (in organizations): The process of identifying, and assigning people to, distinctly different tasks to foster greater efficiency in each job by making it possible for individuals to specialize their efforts. (440–442, 444–446)

Discretionary expenditures: Purchases of items other than food, shelter, and basic clothing essential to survival. Typically, they are expenditures that are postponable. (74–76)

Disposable personal income: Personal income after income and other taxes. (73–74)

Dissonance (postpurchase): Uncertainties about the "rightness" of a purchase decision after the purchase, particularly for a buyer associating a high level of risk with his or her purchase. (38–39)

Distribution center: A facility to which goods are shipped for short-term storage, sorting, consolidation, repacking, or even repackaging, for subsequent shipment to customers. Often, orders are received, inventory records maintained, and local sales offices located at such a facility. (353)

Distribution channel: The path followed by title to, and the physical exchange of, a good or service and information attendant to its sale and transmission from original sources to end users, described by organizations participating in the exchange of title to, and physical possession of, such a good or service. (262–263)

Distribution company: A firm offering all physical distribution services, including transportation, warehousing, inventory control, and order processing, relieving potential manufacturer-customers of the need to devote attention to these tasks and allowing them to concentrate on promotional aspects of marketing effort. (315, 317)

Distributor: A generic term often used to refer to wholesalers of various types.

Elasticity (price-demand): The extent to which the demand for a good or service varies inversely to price. Products experiencing percentage declines in unit demand greater and smaller than accompanying percentage increases in prices are said to have price-demand elasticity and price-demand inelasticity, respectively. (139–140)

Encoder (in communication): One who translates a message for transmission in such a way that it will be received in the intended manner. (181–183)

End-use product: A product not purchased for resale or other business purposes. (73–74)

Engel's laws: Developed in 1857 by a German statistician, Ernst Engel, these "laws" maintain that families with higher incomes tend to spend for current consumption (1) more money in absolute terms, (2) a smaller proportion of their total expenditures for food, (3) roughly the same proportion of their total expenditures for housing and household expenditures, and (4) a higher proportion of total expenditures for such items as clothing, transportation, recreation, health, and education, in comparison to families with lower incomes. (73)

Enhancement: The process by which a new product contributes to increased sales of existing products (the reverse of cannibalization). (116)

Ethnocentrism (in organizations): Home country orientation in the organization of multinational marketing efforts, typically involving the centralization of authority and responsibility for major marketing decisions at a headquarters located in the home country (rather than the foreign markets) of the organization. (458–459)

Exclusive dealing: The practice of requiring the exclusive purchase of all of a customer's goods from a single source, prohibited in interstate commerce by the Sherman Act. (83)

Exclusive distribution: The sale of a product or service through only one wholesale or retail outlet in a defined market area. (335–336)

Experiment: An effort to measure cause-and-effect relationships under controlled conditions. (385, 387)

Factor: An organization that buys at a discount uncollected accounts receivable or sales invoices accumulated by sellers for the purpose of collecting such invoices to produce a profit for the factor and free its customers' funds for other uses. (315, 317)

Fair Packaging and Labeling Act: More popularly referred to as the "truth-in-packaging" legislation, it was passed by the Congress in 1967 to require that consumer products sold in interstate commerce be required to bear labels specifying the (1) identity of the product, (2) name and place of business of the manufacturer, (3) net quantity of contents, and (4) net quantity of a serving when the number of servings is represented. In addition, it authorizes the administering agencies (the FTC for all products except foods, drugs, and cosmetics, for which the Department of Health, Education, and Welfare is responsible) to impose additional regulation on a product-by-product basis where needed. (522)

Fair trade laws: Laws at one time on the statute books of states (36 in 1973) permitting resale price maintenance, which, prior to their passage, would have been held to be conspiracy in restraint of trade. Legislation exempting fair trade practices from national laws prohibiting conspiracy in restraint of trade was repealed by the United States government in 1975. Resale price maintenance refers to the practice of requiring adherence to a prescribed price in the reselling of goods, usually established by a manufacturer in selling to a wholesaler or retailer. It provided protection to all sellers from deep price cutting and a means for maintaining minimum margins for resellers. Although resale price maintenance in some states could be imposed on all resellers by the establishment of an agreement between a manufacturer and only one customer in the state (the so-called nonsigners' clause) and in others by merely notifying actual and potential customers, the policing and enforcement of resale price maintenance agreements was left to those firms implementing the policy.   (167–168)

Family life cycle: The stages of development through which a family passes from family birth to death. These stages have been labeled, in order: single bread-winner, newly married couples, full nest (couples with children at home), empty nest (couples without children at home), and solitary survivors.   (70–72)

Federal Communications Commission (FCC): An agency established by the Communications Act of 1934 to administer the act in licensing and controlling practices of radio and television broadcasters in the "public interest, convenience and necessity." This, on occasion, has included indirect control over advertising and advertising practices, primarily through the consideration of complaints at the time of the periodic license renewal process.   (109)

Federal Trade Commission (FTC): One of the most powerful of the regulatory agencies, the FTC was established by the Federal Trade Commission Act of 1914 to police unfair competition prohibited by the Sherman Act. The Wheeler-Lea amendment to the Act in 1938 broadened the scope of jurisdiction of the FTC to include practices injurious to the public as well as competitors. Through this and other legislation, the commission's scope of authority has come to include pricing practices (under the Robinson-Patman Act), advertising practices, and even the effects of these practices on industry concentration.

(84, 506–507, 520–522)

Fixed costs: Costs that essentially do not vary with modest changes in the volume of output or sale of products or services. Such costs typically are associated with such items as interest on investment, depreciation, and administration (in manufacturing) and implicit intermediate-term commitments to an advertising budget or sales force (in marketing).   (105–106)

Food and Drug Administration (FDA): Created by the Pure Food and Drug Act of 1906, this federal agency is charged with the task of prohibiting the adulteration and misbranding of foods and drugs in interstate commerce, maintaining an extensive testing program in support of this effort.   (82, 84)

Forecasting: The process of making expectations of the future explicit.

(393–399)

Judgmental techniques: Primarily the use of opinion, based on knowledge of the past and beliefs about the future, for forecasting.   (394)

Consensus: Relying on the combined judgments of two or more people.

(394)

Delphi method: Relying on experts who make, compare, and remake predictions until such predictions converge.   (394)

Time series analysis: The examination of sales patterns in relation to, or over, periods of time.   (394–395)

Moving average: The basing of a prediction on an average of experiences over two or more of the most recent periods of time.   (394)

Exponential smoothing: The basing of a prediction on a weighted average of experiences, with the most recent experience given a higher weight than others. (394)

Trend projection: The basing of a prediction on the assumption that past patterns of activity over time can be extended into the future. (394–395)

Analysis of causal relationships: The examination of sales patterns in relation to factors other than time. (395–396)

Regression analysis: The process of examining levels of activity for two or more related activities in hopes of being able to project future levels of one on the basis of forecasts for the others. (395–396)

Econometric analysis: The process of projecting sales or other activities by means of modeling efforts making use of two or more regression and other statistical analyses designed to simulate future events on the basis of past relationships. (396)

Foreign direct investment: Investment by a firm headquartered in one country in facilities for the production or sale of products or services in other countries. (425)

Franchise: A contractual agreement allowing a customer to use a supplier's name and receive assistance in location, merchandising, or other matters in return for the purchase for resale of the supplier's product or a separately specified franchise fee.

Franchise (customer): The relative reputation and saleability that a company, its brands, and its products or services possess in the minds of customers. (356)

Franchising: The granting, in return for the sale of products or services or a specified fee, of supporting services by a supplier to a reseller, typically a retailer. Such supporting services have included the use of a trademark or brand, merchandising assistance, advice on location, financing, and limits on the number of directly competing outlets. More recently, the growth of firms relying primarily on franchising fees rather than the sale of product in businesses such as fast foods, motels, and other service industries has drawn new attention to the practice. (288–289)

Frequency (in promotion): The number of times during an advertising campaign that a member of the targeted audience is exposed to a particular message. (212)

Functions (of marketing): Activities necessary for the distribution of all goods from original sources to end users. (263–268, 338–341)

Transactional functions: Tasks, such as buying, selling, and risk assumption, necessary for the transfer of title (ownership of) goods or services between two or more parties. (264, 268, 338–341, 349–350)

Logistical functions: Tasks, such as assembly, storage, assorting, and transportation, necessary for the transmission of goods and services in the desired form, quantities, and assortments to the proper place at the right time. (264–268, 338–341, 350–353)

Facilitating functions: Tasks such as postpurchase service and maintenance, financing, information dissemination, and channel coordination or leadership required for the sale and continued use of products or services. (267–268, 338–341, 353–355)

Gatekeeper phenomenon: The exercising of control by one person over the promotional messages reaching another. (187–188)

Geocentrism (in organization): A world orientation in organizing for multinational marketing effort, in which an organization views the entire world as its area of operation, giving no single national market or group of markets greater attention than its size dictates and opening many management jobs to nationals of countries other than those in which an organization is headquartered. (458–459)

Gross national product (GNP): The value of all goods and services produced by a nation.

Hierarchy of effects (in buying): A view that holds that buyers experience several stages in the purchase process, including (1) learning, the development of awareness, knowledge, and understanding; (2) attitude change, the development and selection of one of several buying alternatives; and (3) overt behavior, the establishment of an intent to buy and the buying action itself. (187)

Household: A unit of measure defined by the Bureau of the Census as a housing unit representing separate living quarters. (72)

Image: An impression, made up of associations, that a potential customer forms on the basis of a brand, picture, aroma, word, or other communication about a product or service. Subsequent purchase decisions depend as well on the customer's self-impressions and their "fit" with those of a product or service. (204–205)

Impulse purchase: A purchase decision made without prior explicit planning, often on the basis of direct contact with, or exposure to, a product. (344)

Incremental revenue, costs, and profit: The differences in amounts of revenues, costs, and profits resulting from two levels of sales or other activities. (146)

Institutional advertising: (See advertising; by function; institutional.) (206–207)

Instrumented store: A retail outlet in which layout, shelf-space allocation, inventory control, ordering, and other decisions would be made by computer on the basis of data captured at the point of sale, possibly through the use of product codes capable of being electronically scanned and translated into inputs for decision making. (358–361)

Integration (in organizations): Efforts to coordinate the work of specialists in an organization, particularly where timing or a consistent approach to customers (as in marketing effort) are important. (442–443, 446–452)

Intensive distribution: The sale of a product or service through all or the most available wholesale or retail outlets in a defined market area. (335–336)

Interdependent product (pricing): Products that depend on each other for their sales and use, raising questions of how to price each relative to its cost. Examples are razors and razor blades, cameras and film, and durable goods and their repair parts. (154–156)

Interorganization management: The exercise of influence over decisions made in one organization by members of another organization to encourage the achievement of benefits to both organizations, for example, in a channel of distribution. Such influence often is achieved by the careful structuring of incentives with the needs of each organization in mind as well as the willingness to forego short-term gains to realize long-term mutual benefits. (357–358)

Interstate Commerce Act: Passed in 1887 by Congress, this first act to regulate commerce in the United States established the ICC and authorized it to prohibit railroads from offering different prices to various customers for similar services provided under essentially similar conditions. Subsequent amendments to the act have brought carriers by other modes of surface transport, including water, pipe line, and highway, under its economic and safety regulation. (82, 84)

Intertype competition: The sale of merchandise associated with one type of retail outlet through a retail outlet of a different type; for example, the sale of drug items by supermarkets. This practice has also come to be known as scrambled merchandising. (337)

Inventory echeloning: The practice of determining the number of inventory locations for a product-line item on the basis of its volume of sales, with items selling in low volume stocked in one central inventory and more popular items stocked not only in a central inventory but also at outlying points in a marketing territory. (353)

Inventory turn(over) rate: The ratio of sales (at cost) to average inventories (at cost), usually over the period of a year. The same result can be obtained by comparing sales to average inventories if both are calculated on the basis of market values. Thus, a product with annual sales of $4 million at cost sold from an inventory averaging $1 million in value at cost is said to have a turnover rate of four. (276)

Logistics: The management of all activities that facilitate movement and the coordination of supply and demand in the creation of time and place utility in goods and services. (350–354)

Loss leader: A product or service sold at lower-than-normal margins for the purpose of attracting customers who might purchase other items at normal margins. As a result, loss-leader items should have well-established "normal" prices in the minds of potential customers. (153–154)

Management by objective (MBO): A philosophy of management that advocates the process of having managers at each level in an organization establish objectives for their future performance, as well as means for achieving them, and obtain the concurrence of their respective superiors for their plans. Both objectives and methods thus provide means for measuring and reporting subsequent progress and performance as well as identifying reasons for deviations from expected performance. (472)

Manufacturers' representative: See wholesaler. (14, 313–314)

Margin (gross): The difference between the sale and purchase prices of products, as used in retailing and wholesaling. In manufacturing, it is the difference between the sale price and the manufactured cost of a product before the deduction of costs such as those for marketing and administration. For example, the margin on an item sold for $10 for which the purchase price or manufactured cost was $7 would be $3 or 30 percent ($3 divided by $10). (346–348)

Markdown: A reduction in the originally established price of a product, typically in a retail establishment. The reduction in terms of a percentage is calculated by dividing the amount of the reduction by the original price. Thus, the percentage markdown for a product for which the price is reduced from $4 to $3 is ($4 − $3) divided by $4, or 25 per cent. (278)

Market matrix (or grid): A diagram in which customer needs or product uses are arrayed against groups of potential customers identified by demographic or other characteristics for the purpose of assessing market potentials by pinpointing needs or customer groups poorly served by competitors. (6–7, 45–46)

Market share: The proportion of total sales for a product category or total purchases by a market segment, or a combination of both, that is realized by a product or company. Because of negative connotations of this term for some, *sales penetration index* is used synonymously with market share in some industries. (87–90, 417)

Market testing: An attempt to assess the saleability of a product or service or effectiveness of a marketing strategy by actually introducing it to a limited geographic area, if possible under typical market conditions. (391–393)

Market value: The amount potential buyers are willing to pay for a product, service, or idea, regardless of the price asked for it. (137–138)

Marketing: The process in a society by which the demand structure for products, services, or ideas is anticipated and controlled (either enlarged or contracted) through their conception, promotion, exchange, and physical distribution.

Marketing concept: The philosophy that the primary function of an organization is to detect and satisfy customer needs at a profit. It often represents a shift in emphasis from selling products or services that a plant is able to produce to the manufacture and sale of products or services customers need.

(55–58, 531–533)

Marketing information and decision program (MIDP): A coordinated series of processes for converting data into information of use for decision making through data-collection, retrieval, display, arranging, and analyzing techniques and devices. (475–482)

Marketing mix: Elements of marketing strategy, including (1) internal elements of product, price, channels of distribution, and direct and indirect promotion, and (2) external elements of markets, competition, other company products and programs, and environmental factors. (407–409, 418–424, 533–534)

Marketing research: A systematic study or investigation conducted to establish facts or to solve problems relating to the marketing of goods and services.[4]

Markon: For our purposes, the same as margin or markup. However, others sometimes use it in the same alternative manner described for markup. (See the discussion of markup.)

Markup: In monetary terms, the difference between the quoted sales price and the cost of goods to be sold. In percentage terms, it is calculated for our purposes as the above amount divided by the quoted sales price. For example, a product quoted for sale at $2 and costing $1.50 would have a markup of $2 − $1.50/$2, or 25 per cent. It is used here in the same way as the term *margin*. Others sometimes use it to denote the percentage relationship between the difference of quoted sales price and the cost of goods sold divided by cost of goods sold. When stated in percentages for our example, this would produce a result of $2 − $1.50/$1.50, or $33\frac{1}{3}$ per cent.

Matrix organization: In marketing, the assignment of responsibilities in such a way that one group of managers (including those for sales, marketing research, advertising, etc.) is responsible for insuring the contribution of specialized, differentiated, functionally oriented expertise to the marketing effort while another group (composed of so-called product or brand managers) is responsible for integrating the functional inputs to provide effective marketing programs for products, brands, or product lines. (449)

"Me-too" product: A product designed to emulate a successful competitor in order to gain a share of the existing market (selective demand). (103–104)

Middleman: Generally refers to any intermediary between manufacturers and end users in a channel of distribution, typically a retailer or wholesaler. (41)

Motivation research: An investigation into the basic psychological and sociological reasons why customers act the way they do in purchasing goods and services. Such research often employs in-depth interviewing and psychological testing. (385–386)

Multinational marketing: Planned effort to sell and distribute goods or services across national borders. (426–434)

[4]David J. Luck, Hugh G. Wales, and Donald A. Taylor, *Marketing Research,* 4th ed. (Englewood Cliffs, N. J.: Prentice-Hall, 1974), p. 10.

National income: GNP less capital consumption (depreciation), indirect business taxes, and other relatively insignificant items. (74)

Needs (customer): Basic factors underlying customer motivations for acquiring goods and services, categorized into physiological needs for food, drink, shelter, and safety; sociological needs for belonging, love, and esteem and status relative to others; and psychological needs of self-understanding, self-satisfaction, and self-realization. (33–34)

Net profit: Gross profit (sales less cost of goods sold) less operating and administrative costs from which dividends are paid and return on investment is realized. (276)

Net sales: Gross (total) sales less returns of, or allowances (discounts) on, merchandise sold, typically in retailing or wholesaling. (276)

Net worth: The difference between an organization's assets and liabilities. (276)

Nutritional labeling: The practice of stating on the package for a food product (1) the proportion of individual daily nutritional requirements contained in various quantities and (2) the specific contents of the product. (291)

Oligopoly: An industry made up of a relatively small number of sellers. (162–163)

Open dating: The practice of placing dates on the packages of perishable products sold at retail for purposes of alerting potential customers to the freshness of such products. (291)

Packaging: The placement of products in containers for purposes of promotion or protection. (204–205, 210–211)

Palletization: The placement of products on square platforms, usually made of wood and several feet on a side, for purposes of gaining efficiencies in moving them as a unit by means of motorized lift trucks. A common size of pallet, 40 by 48 inches, is capable of accomodating up to 2,000 pounds of cased (boxed) goods. (351)

Patent: A grant of protection from would-be copiers to an inventor of a product for a definite period of time. Such a grant, made to persons obtaining certification from the Patent Office of the originality of their product or process, currently is extended for seventeen years in the United States. (82)

Penetration (pricing strategy): A pricing strategy based on a low price relative to actual or potential alternatives, designed to (1) stimulate purchase by several customer groups (market segments), (2) gain a large share of the market, (3) facilitate production economies, and (4) preempt potential competitors from entering a market. (159)

Perfect competition: A market situation in which supply and demand relationships, rather than any one competitor, determine price levels. This phenomenon is most likely to arise where there are many relatively small sellers of goods, such as agricultural products, that are impossible to differentiate from those produced by competitors. (162)

Personal income: The amount of money available to individuals before income and other taxes. (72–73)

Physical distribution: The movement of, coordination of supply and demand for, and creation of time and place utility in, finished products moving from suppliers to their customers. (350–354)

Piggybacking: The transportation of truck trailers on railroad flatcars, also known as trailer on flatcar (TOFC). (351)

Planned purchase: A purchase decision made in advance of the final direct contact with, or exposure to, a product, usually used in describing customer buying behavior in retail establishments. (344)

Planning: Any effort to make the future more orderly through the anticipation of possible events and the development of policies and methods for use in dealing with them. (471–472)

    Bottoms up: Based on a synthesis of plans made by individuals, beginning at the lowest, and continuing up through successively higher levels of management in an organization. (471–472)

    Top down: Based on the preparation of plans at the highest level of management in an organization for communication to successively lower levels. (471–472)

    Strategic: Planning concerning matters (1) of longer-term significance to an organization's performance, (2) committing an organization to a certain mode of operation, or (3) central to an organization's basic business objectives.

    Tactical: Planning concerning matters (1) of short-term significance to an organization's performance, and (2) dealing with the way in which longer-term strategies will be carried out and already established objectives achieved.

Polycentrism (in organization): An approach to organization for multinational marketing effort in which such efforts outside a home country are carried out on a somewhat decentralized basis by marketing groups oriented to, and headquartered in, each foreign market. (458–459)

Population (in sampling): The total group from which a sample is drawn for data-gathering and estimating purposes.

Postponement (principle of): A philosophy of management that holds that an organization should postpone changes in the form and identity of its products to the latest point in the marketing flow and postpone changes in the location of its inventories to the latest possible points in time prior to their sale, primarily to reduce the risks associated with having the wrong products at the wrong place at the wrong time and in the wrong form. (339–341)

Postponement and speculation (principle of): A theory that a speculative inventory will appear at each point in a distribution channel whenever its costs are less than the net savings to both buyer and seller from postponement (of commitment of a product to a particular form or specific market). (339–341)

Preemptive marketing strategy: A strategy that seeks to discourage another from introducing a new product or marketing campaign, possibly by means of a more rapid product introduction or promotional program or a large price reduction. (104)

Price: The amount for which a product, service, or idea is offered for sale, regardless of its worth or value to potential buyers.

Price controls: Regulations that restrict the magnitude of changes that can be made in prices—changes typically measured from prices during a base period of time. Such controls often are instituted by governments at times when demand so exceeds available supplies that there is a great potential for price inflation (166)

Price discrimination: The quoting of different prices to two customers purchasing products or services under substantially the same circumstances at roughly comparable costs to the seller for promotion, physical distribution, and other activities. (166–167)

Price leadership: A phenomenon in which one firm traditionally is the first in its industry to make price changes to which competitors conform. The phenomenon may result from a conscious policy on the part of the traditional price leader or its competitors. (163–164)

Price lining: The offering of products in a product line for sale at specific price levels, often maintained by seeking products to fill out a product line that can be manufactured and marketed to sell at a predesignated price. (150)

Price-minus pricing: The philosophy in which a product is designed to be sold at a predesignated price, with resulting profits determined by the level of cost associated with its manufacture and distribution. (157)

Primary data: Data collected directly by the user or specifically for the user in such a manner that the conditions and assumptions under which the data are collected are well known to the user. (381)

Primary demand: The total demand for a type of product or service, rather than an individual brand of product, or for products or services of an industry rather than a particular company in the industry. (42–43, 206–208)

Product: As used in this book, a tangible object, service, idea, or person. A suit of clothes, suit-cleaning services, an idea for developing a new suit-cleaning process, or a person applying for a job at a cleaning establishment all meet this definition of product.

Product life cycle. The progression of a product from birth to death, typically thought to encompass four stages: (1) introduction, (2) rapid growth, (3) maturity, and (4) decline. (124–129, 421)

Product line: All of the products or services offered by an organization, or in one or more groupings of related items. (109–118, 149–156)

Product manager: Typically a person with responsibility for coordinating all aspects of marketing for a product or product group, from design and development through market introduction to continuing marketing programs.
(107, 442–443, 449–452)

Product positioning: (1) The process of identifying the needs of market segments (groups of customers with common characteristics), product strengths and weaknesses, and the extent to which competing products are perceived to meet customer needs; determining the market segment(s) toward which major marketing effort will be directed on behalf of a product; and deciding on the appeals to be used in promoting the product to one or more segments; and (2) as used in advertising, the means by which products, often of essentially the same composition and capabilities, can be given a character through advertising that is intended to differentiate them from competing products, perhaps by using such products themselves as the basis for comparison. (51–53, 209–210)

Product recall: The retrieval by a manufacturer of products that it has placed in the hands of wholesalers, retailers, or end users. Such retrieval typically is prompted by a discovery of a defect in the product. (534)

Product testing: The solicitation of reactions to products by encouraging their actual use among a sample of typical potential customers, if possible in a manner that allows comparison with competing products along critical dimensions.
(390)

Profit target analysis: The process of determining the volume of sales needed to defray all fixed and variable costs of operation and return a predetermined level of profit on investment. It involves the same procedures as those for performing a break-even analysis (see the definition for, and illustration of, break-even analysis on page 581), except that fixed costs are calculated to include a predetermined level of dollar profit that represents a targeted return on investment, often that required as a minimum by a company's management. In the example shown for break-even analysis, fixed costs were $1,200,000, the contribution per unit was $12, and the break-even volume of sales was $1,200,000/$12, or 100,000 units. If annual dollar profits needed to return a targeted percentage of investment were $600,000 in this case, the total of fixed costs and the required profit would be $1,800,000 ($1,200,000 plus $600,000), producing a profit target of $1,800,000/$12, or 150,000 units in sales.

Promotion: The use of communications to persuade or convince prospective customers.

   Direct: More personal forms of promotion such as face-to-face selling.

   Indirect: Less personal forms of promotion such as advertising, branding, and packaging.

Pruning (product line): The deletion of items from a line of products, or a line of products from an organization's total offerings. (122–124)

Public warehouse: A facility operated by a firm holding itself out to provide storage, materials handling, inventory control, and other services to customers on an as-needed basis. (315, 317)

Pull (marketing strategy): A marketing strategy in which the manufacturer rather than the channel of distribution assumes a great share of the burden for promotional effort, often through the use of advertising directed at potential end users or buyers. Such a strategy often may accompany a relatively intensive distribution program offering low percentage margins to channel intermediaries, and most often accompanies the sale of noncomplex products at low per unit prices. (423–424)

Pulsing (in advertising): A promotional strategy in which advertising expenditures and efforts are put forth in periodic waves under the assumption (for which conflicting evidence exists) that such a strategy is the most economic way of building a desired level of customer awareness. (212)

Push (marketing strategy): A marketing strategy in which the channel of distribution rather than the manufacturer assumes a great share of the burden for promotional effort, often through the use of personal selling efforts directed to customers. Such a strategy often may accompany a selective distribution program offering high percentage margins to channel intermediaries and most often accompanies the sale of relatively complex products at high per unit prices. (423–424)

Quantity price discounts: Lower prices offered with the sale of larger quantities of a product, made possible by lower promotional and physical distribution costs per unit and occasionally lower product costs per unit. The Robinson-Patman Act requires that (1) the same discounts be made available to all customers making purchases under comparable conditions and (2) quantity discounts for products sold in interstate commerce be justified by cost economies. (148)

Rack jobber: See wholesaler, merchant, full-function. (282, 313)

Random sampling: The selection of a subset of a total population in such a way that all members of the population, however it is defined, have an approximately equal chance of being selected, for purposes of describing various aspects of the total population at a reduced cost for data collection. The selection of a subset in this manner typically permits more to be known about the reliability or representativeness of the information obtained from the subset of the total population. (386)

Reach (in promotion): The breadth of coverage of an advertising program, expressed in terms of the number of different potential customers exposed to a promotional message. (212)

Regiocentrism (in organization): An approach to organization for a multinational marketing effort that emphasizes decentralization and organization of effort by regions, perhaps comprised of two or more contiguous countries speaking the same language, at comparable levels of development, or belonging to the same economic community. (458–459)

Reliability (in marketing research): The accuracy with which data portrays reality, of particular importance when information collected from a subset of a total population is used to obtain estimates for the entire population.

(384, 386–387)

Responsibility (in organization): Limits describing the nature of a job to be performed by an individual, including the manner in which the performance of the job is to be measured. (440–442, 443–444)

Retailing: A commercial activity in which the majority of product sales are made to end users. (257–292)

Retailing cycles: A theory that holds that forms of retailing pass through life cycles of introduction, rapid growth, maturity, and decline just as products or services do. (283–286)

Return on investment (ROI): Total contribution less fixed costs as a percentage of investment during a period of time. Consider the following example: a product yielding $10 per unit in contribution (the excess of sales revenue over variable cost per unit) and selling at a rate of 100,000 units per year yields a total contribution of $1 million. If fixed costs for marketing commitments (for the year) and manufacturing operations (depreciation on plant and equipment) approximate $500,000, the resulting contribution in excess of fixed charges would be $500,000. If an investment of $2 million were required for the operation, the annual return on investment would be $500,000 divided by $2,000,000, or twenty-five per cent (before taxes and dividends). (116–118, 149)

Risk reduction (in buying and selling): A problem-solving process engaged in by buyers designed to reduce uncertainties associated with the purchase of products or services about which they have little knowledge, that are of complex design, that are offered at high per unit prices, or for which there is social importance attached to the right purchase decisions. Sellers, recognizing the nature and importance of this problem-solving process, may take steps to assist buyers in carrying it out. (184–187)

Robinson-Patman Act: Legislation passed by the Congress in 1936 that essentially extended coverage of the Sherman Act to include channel intermediaries as well as manufacturers by prohibiting discriminatory pricing practices and promotional allowances (not offered to all customers buying under substantially the same circumstances) in interstate commerce under circumstances where the effect might be "to substantially lessen competition or tend to create a monopoly." This act, of primary importance for marketing, is administered by the FTC.

(83, 85, 166–167)

Roll out: The process by which a firm with a product offered for sale in a regional market, perhaps as part of a test, extends the physical distribution and promotion of the product to a much wider geographical area. (119–120)

Sampling (in marketing research): The selection of a subset of a total population for purposes of obtaining data useful for drawing conclusions about either the subset or the total population.

Sampling (in promotion): The placement of product samples either with channel intermediaries (through personal sales contact) or with end users (often by direct mail) for the purpose of encouraging product trial. (190)

Scrambled merchandising: The tendency for retail establishments to offer a growing number of product types, leading to an increasing duplication of assortments among various types of retail establishments. This has led to an increase in what has been termed intertype competition among, for example, supermarkets offering drug products and discount drugstores offering a growing number of items previously sold in supermarkets. (287–288, 337)

Secondary data: Data neither collected directly by the user nor specifically for the user, often under conditions that are not well known to the user.   (381–383)

Segmentation (market): The process by which groups of potential customers are identified by geographic area, buying behavior patterns they hold in common, common perceptions they may hold for a product or service, or common uses to which they might put a product or service, for the purpose of (1) designing more efficient marketing programs that can be directed (targeted) primarily to one or more selected segments or (2) "positioning" a product in relation to competition in a particular market segment.   (45–47)

Selective demand: The demand for one competing product or service as opposed to another.   (43–44, 206–208)

Selective distribution: The sale of a product or service through a carefully selected subset of all available wholesale or retail outlets in a given market area.   (335–336)

Sellers' market: A situation in which demand exceeds available supplies, a situation more favorable to sellers than buyers. The term *buyers' market* is used to describe the opposite of this situation.   (345)

Shared services: The utilization of services concurrently by two or more firms, whether such services are provided by one of the two cooperating firms or a third party. Examples of such services are common carrier transportation, a combined captive sales force, or public warehousing.   (527)

Sherman Antitrust Act: Passed by Congress in 1890 to prohibit (1) monopolies or attempts to monopolize and (2) various acts, including contracts, combinations, or conspiracies intended to restrain trade. The act was aimed primarily at firms operating at one particular level in a channel of distribution, particularly manufacturers. Its coverage was explicitly extended to include contractual relationships between buyers and sellers at two or more levels in a channel of distribution by the Robinson Patman Act of 1936.   (83–84)

Shopping (consumer) goods: Those for which the consumer has limited information, no strong preferences, and sufficient perceived risk to warrant an initiation of a search to obtain information and develop preferences.   (270–271, 336)

Signal (in communication): The strength of a message sent from an encoder to a decoder in the process of communication. Its strength may depend on the extent to which the encoder and decoder share the same field of experience, the frequency with which the signal is transmitted, the expertise with which it is designed, and the methods (media) by which it is transmitted.   (182–183)

Simulation: The process of modeling things, problems, or concepts.   (385, 387–388, 481)

Skimming (pricing strategy): A pricing strategy based on a high initial price and successively lower prices designed to (1) appeal in sequence to customer groups (market segments) placing successively greater emphasis on price while (2) earning high per unit profits necessary to defray development costs on the first units sold.   (158–159)

Source effect (in communication): The extent to which the nature of a source influences the manner in which the communication transmitted by it is received. For example, salespeople in general may have greater credibility than advertising; but those perceived to be inexpert may have less. Other source effects may eminate from the seller's or brand's name recommendations by friends, as well as the medium used for communication.   (182)

Span of control: The number of people that one person can supervise effectively.   (456–457)

Specialty (consumer) goods: Those for which a consumer is willing to expend the effort required to purchase a most preferred item rather than to buy a more readily accessible substitute. (270-271, 336)

Speculation (principle of): A philosophy of management that holds that changes in form, and the movement of goods to forward (market-oriented) inventories, should be made at the earliest possible time in the marketing flow in order to reduce the costs of production and the marketing system, respectively.

(339-341)

Stake (in distribution channel relationships): The extent to which one organization in a channel of distribution relies on another for its success or even survival. For example, a firm selling 80 per cent of its output to a single customer is said to have a high stake in its relationship with that customer. (356-357)

Standard Metropolitan Statistical Area (SMSA): Defined by the Bureau of the Census as one or more cities with at least 50,000 in population and the counties contiguous to them that make up an economically integrated unit. (67)

Supermarket: Any retail establishment through which grocery products are sold realizing more than $500,000 in sales per year.[5] (108-109, 525)

Superstore: (1) Any retail establishment with more than about 30,000 square feet of selling space through which primarily convenience consumer goods are sold. (2) Any retail establishment through which grocery products are sold realizing more than $5 million in sales per year.[6] (288, 525)

Survey: The organized solicitation of information or opinions from a sample or population of respondents for the purpose of drawing conclusions about the population. Typical survey techniques include mail or telephone questionnaires or in-person inverviews. (385-387)

Target market: The group of customers to which a marketing program is directed because, among other reasons, of (1) the potential strength of the need for a product, service, or idea it is thought to possess, (2) the ease of communicating with it, and (3) the need to extend sales to new groups of customers.

(46)

Terms of sale: Specifications by a seller of the price, trade discount, payment period, point of transfer of title, responsibilities for defraying costs of transportation, and other provisions accompanying the sale of a product or service.

(283)

Test marketing: (See market testing) (119, 391-393)

Total cost concept (in logistics): An approach to the appraisal of logistics alternatives that takes into account: (1) inventory carrying costs as well as those of transportation; (2) attempts to measure trade-offs between these two major types of logistics costs; and (3) a final decision based on the total of these costs produced by one or more logistics system configurations, including facility locations, transportation methods, and inventory-control procedures.

(352-353)

Trade show: A gathering of sellers and buyers for the purpose of displaying and surveying, respectively, new products, processes, or services.

Trademark: Any word, name, symbol, or device or any combination thereof adopted and used by a manufacturer or merchant to identify its goods to distinguish them from those manufactured or sold by others that may be registered for protection from would-be competitors for goods or services sold in interstate commerce. Under the present law, based on the Lanham Trade-Mark Act passed by Congress in 1947, names, symbols, titles, designations, slogans,

---

[5]"41st Annual Report of the Grocery Industry." *Progressive Grocer* (April, 1974), p. 130.
[6]Op. Cit., "41st Annual Report of the Grocery Industry," p. 179.

character names, and distinctive features of radio or other advertising also are protected.

Trading up: An attempt to induce a current owner of a product to purchase a more expensive model or version of the same product. (151–153)

Unfair trade laws: Laws that prevent the sale of merchandise at retail for less than the amount paid for it or less than such an amount plus a minimum specified margin. Such laws are enforced in varying degrees by perhaps half the states of the United States. (167)

Uniform Commercial Code: A set of rules adopted by forty-nine states describing legal guidelines and limits for a wide range of commercial activity, including sales contracts, title to property, warranties, various practices for financing exchange, physical transfer, and bills of lading provided by transport carriers to shippers. (83–86)

Unit pricing: The quotation of prices in a retail establishment not only on the basis of the quantity contained in a package, but also on the basis of a standard quantity held in common for many products. Standard quantities used for this purpose include quarts, pounds, and dozens. (168, 519)

Universal Product Code (UPC): A ten-digit number affixed to a wide variety of grocery and other items in a way that facilitates their identification by an electronic scanner over which such goods might be passed at a retail check-out stand. (291, 358–362, 528)

Utilities (in products or services): Features that add value to products or services, including form, time, place, and ownership utility. Form utility is said to be created when products are designed and made in forms in which they are desired, time utility when they are made availalble at the time they are desired, place utility when they are made available where they are desired, and ownership utility when they are owned by the individuals who desire them.

Validity (in marketing research): The extent to which research measures what it purports to measure. (386)

Value: The sum of benefits or utilities associated with the ownership, possession, or acquisition of a product or service. These may be rational (often economic) benefits, or benefits appealing to the senses, the need for variety, or the psychic need for style or social acceptability. (137–138)

Value added: The extent that an organization enhances the price customers are willing to pay for its goods or services through the creation of form, place, time, or ownership utilities. In marketing, this term has come to be used most often in connection with retailing and wholesaling enterprises. It is calculated by subtracting from sales receipts the value of merchandise, supplies, fuel, purchased energy, and contract work purchased from other business organizations. (346–347, 495–497)

Variable costs: Costs that vary directly with the volume of goods or services produced, sold, or distributed. Such costs typically can be stated on a per unit basis, and often include costs of manufacturing labor, materials, and transportation. (105)

Variety store: A retail establishment offering many kinds of merchandise at low per unit prices and with few attendant services.

Venture team: A group, created by bringing together people with various capabilities, that is then entrusted with all aspects of product development and possibly the market introduction of the product. (447–448)

Wheel of retailing: A theory that holds that low margin, low price, volume-oriented forms of retailing offering few services are introduced periodically, only to evolve into institutions offering goods at higher margins and higher prices and with a wider range of accompanying services to be replaced by retailers once again offering low margin, low price, volume-oriented, limited-service policies with each "turn of the wheel." (283–286)

Wholesaler: An organization selling products principally for industrial use or resale. (295–327)

Merchant wholesaler: A channel intermediary, or middleman, that not only buys and sells goods for its own account, but also takes physical possession of such goods.

Full-function wholesaler: A merchant-wholesaler performing all transactional, logistical, and facilitating functions. (313)

General-line wholesaler: A merchant-wholesaler offering a wide (broad) assortment of related types of goods. (313)

Special-line wholesaler: A merchant-wholesaler specializing in offering a deep assortment (for example, many competing items) of one category of product. (313–314, 323, 526)

Voluntary wholesaler: A wholesaler establishing contractual relationships with a number of retailers to undertake transactional, logistical, and facilitating functions on their behalf. (323–324, 526)

Rack jobber or service merchandiser: A merchant-wholesaler performing all types of marketing functions, in addition to undertaking to stock and otherwise service its products on retailers' shelves. (282, 313–314)

Limited-function wholesaler: A merchant-wholesaler concentrating its efforts on providing some, but not all, transactional, logistical, and facilitating functions. (313–314)

Cash-and-carry wholesaler: A merchant-wholesaler providing no transportation or financing for the goods it sells, requiring customers to pick up and pay cash upon purchase for all goods purchased. (313–314)

Drop shipper: A merchant-wholesaler buying goods, on occasion, for delivery directly to a customer's place of business, but not taking physical possession of such goods. (313–314)

Agent or broker: A channel intermediary, or middleman, who performs primarily transactional functions, buying and selling goods for the account of others, rarely taking physical possession of such goods and rarely providing financing for such transactions. (313–316)

Manufacturer's agent: An individual who undertakes to represent several manufacturers in selling often complementary lines of products to prospective customers on a commission basis. (313–314)

Broker: A wholesaler who seeks out buyers on behalf of sellers, or sellers on behalf of buyers, for one or more manufacturers, typically for compensation on a commission basis. (313, 315–316)

Commission merchant: A wholesaler who, in addition to providing brokerage functions, may store and control inventories for products bought and sold for the account of others. (315–316)

Selling agent: A wholesaler who contracts, on a commission basis, to assume responsibility for all sales of a manufacturer's product, often devoting exclusive effort to one manufacturer's product line. (315–316)

Export and import agency: An agent who performs transactional functions in international trade as well as a number of specialized logistical functions involving the preparation and processing of documentation needed to transport products across international borders. (315–316)

Auction company: An agent who displays and sells at auction, on a commission basis, goods owned by others. (315)

Purchasing agent or resident buyer: An agent who purchases goods, on a commission basis, for one or more accounts, often retailing organizations. (315)

Wholesaling: The business of selling products principally for industrial use or resale.

World corporation (as a form or organization): A philosophy in which an organization regards the entire world as its area of operation, organizing so that no single national market or group of markets draws greater attention than its size or potential might warrant. (458–459)

index